The Treasury of Good Sayings

A Tibetan History of Bon

Dran-pa Nam-mkha', highly venerated image in silver (photographed by Per Kvaerne)
(see p. xxxii)

The Treasury of Good Sayings
A Tibetan History of Bon

Edited and Translated by
SAMTEN G. KARMAY

MOTILAL BANARSIDASS PUBLISHERS
PRIVATE LIMITED • DELHI

Reprint : Delhi, 2005
First Indian Edition : Delhi, 2001
First Published : U.K., 1972

ISBN: 81-208-1779-6 (Cloth)
ISBN: 81-208-2943-3 (Paper)

MOTILAL BANARSIDASS
41 U.A. Bungalow Road, Jawahar Nagar, Delhi 110 007
8 Mahalaxmi Chamber, 22 Bhulabhai Desai Road, Mumbai 400 026
236, 9th Main III Block, Jayanagar, Bangalore 560 011
203 Royapettah High Road, Mylapore, Chennai 600 004
Sanas Plaza, 1302 Baji Rao Road, Pune 411 002
8 Camac Street, Kolkata 700 017
Ashok Rajpath, Patna 800 004
Chowk, Varanasi 221 001

Printed in India
BY JAINENDRA PRAKASH JAIN AT SHRI JAINENDRA PRESS,
A-45 NARAINA, PHASE-I, NEW DELHI 110 028
AND PUBLISHED BY NARENDRA PRAKASH JAIN FOR
MOTILAL BANARSIDASS PUBLISHERS PRIVATE LIMITED,
BUNGALOW ROAD, DELHI 110 007

TO

MY MOTHER

CONTENTS

ILLUSTRATIONS

PREFACE

THIS volume is a partial translation of the Tibetan text, *Legs-bshad-mdzod*, a history of the Bon religion which its adherents claim to be a pre-Buddhist system of beliefs in Tibet and which has survived many persecutions and still covered large parts of the country up to the occupation by Communist China in 1959.

Its characteristic outlook, probably indigenous to Tibet, and somewhat dissimilar to the atheism of Buddhism, aroused interest in European scholars as early as 1880 when A. Schiefner published *Das weisse Nāga-Hunderttausend.* He was later followed by A. H. Francke who translated parts of the *gZer-mig*, *A Book of the Tibetan Bonpos*, a text of considerable importance. Further, in 1950 H. Hoffmann produced *Quellen zur Geschichte der tibetischen Bon-Religion* whose sources are, however, mainly accounts made by Tibetan Buddhists from their point of view.

Personal contacts between Bonpos, the followers of Bon, and European scholars were made only after the flow of Tibetan refugees into India in 1959. This has made large quantities of new material available to scholars who have the means and time to embark on thorough investigation. In 1961 Dr. D. L. Snellgrove took a special interest by inviting a couple of Bonpos from India, with whose assistance he surveyed the whole range of the religion at first-hand, allowing the Bonpos to express what they knew about their own religion. The result was the publication of *The Nine Ways of Bon* in 1967. This remarkable work is invaluable for students of Bon in so far as doctrinal studies are concerned, but it does not deal with the historical development of Bon as conceived by the Bonpos themselves. It would, therefore, now be desirable to prepare a full account of this, but such a work would require a vast amount of material which at present is beyond access. Nevertheless, it was with this in mind that I felt it would be useful to students of the subject if—as a start—one single account of the developments of Bon from the beginning up to the present, as prepared by the Bonpos themselves, were translated into English.

I acknowledge my great debt of gratitude to Professor R. A. Stein through whose help I was able to obtain a microfilm of the

Tibetan text belonging to the École Française d'Extrême-Orient, Paris, and to Dr. D. L. Snellgrove who generously placed his private library at my disposal. The advice and encouragement they both gave me during my work was invaluable.

I am also much indebted to Mr. H. E. Richardson who lent me several Tibetan texts, allowing me to keep them for a considerable time.

I would like to express my warmest thanks to Professor D. C. Twitchett and Professor W. Simon who both gave me advice and made suggestions.

My thanks are also due to Dr. J. D. Moores without whose kindness and generous help the English of the book would have been much less smooth.

My acknowledgements would not be complete without mention of my Tibetan colleagues: Abbot Sangye Tenzin Jongdong who supplied me with a number of Tibetan texts and Lopon Tenzin Namdak who helped me to identify many of the place-names which I have put on the map, the preparation of which I owe to Mr. P. Denwood, who also checked the proofs of the English translation. I must also express my thanks to Mr. E. D. Grinstead, then librarian at the British Museum, and to the Central Research Fund of London University.

Finally, I would like to record my gratitude to the School of Oriental and African Studies in the University of London where this work has been done and through whose support, including the kind co-operation of Mr. J. R. Bracken, the Secretary, its publication has been made possible.

SAMTEN G. KARMAY

London
June 1970

ABBREVIATIONS

DN	*Deb-ther sngon-po* by 'Gos gZhon-nu-dpal.
GRB	*rGyal-rabs bon-gyi 'byung-gnas* by Khyung-po Blo-gros rGyal-mtshan.
KhG	*mKhas-pa'i dga'-ston*, Section JA, by dPa'-bo gTsug-lag Phreng-ba.
KTDG	*bKa'-'gyur brten-'gyur-gyi sde-tshan sgrig-tshul bstan-pa'i me-ro spar-ba'i rlung-g.yab bon-gyi pad-mo rgyas-byed nyi-'od* by the Abbot Nyi-ma bsTan-'dzin.
LShDz	*Legs-bshad-mdzod* by Shar-rdza bKra-shis rGyal-mtshan.
Mvy	*Mahāvyutpatti.*
SG	*Srid-rgyud* rediscovered by Gyer Thogs-med.
STNN	*Sangs-rgyas-kyi bstan-rtsis ngo-mtshar nor-bu'i phreng-ba* by the Abbot Nyi-ma bsTan-'dzin.
TBK	*bsTan-pa bon-gyi klad-don-gyi rang-'grel* by sGa-ston Tshul-khrims rGyal-mtshan.
THD	*Documents de Touen-houang relatifs à l'histoire du Tibet.*
TNT	*bsTan-rtsis-kyi rnam-bshad mthong-ba'i dga-'ston-nam dogs-bsal pan-tsa li-ka'i chuṇ-po* by the Abbot Nyi-ma bsTan-'dzin.
TPS	*Tibetan Painted Scrolls* by G. Tucci.
TTGL	*Zab-mo'i gter-dang gter-ston grub-thob ji-ltar byon-pa'i lo-rgyus mdor-bsdus bkod-pa rin-chen vaiḍūrya'i phreng-ba* by Kong-sprul Yon-tan rGya-mtsho.
ZhNyL	*rDzogs-pa chen-po zhang-zhung snyan-rgyud-kyi lo-rgyus bla-ma brgyud-pa'i rnam-thar chen-mo* by sPa bsTan-rgyal bZang-po.

INTRODUCTION

The Legs-bshad rin-po-che'i mdzod dpyod-ldan dga'-ba'i-char (the Precious Treasury of Good sayings, pleasant rain for the wise) presents what is known among Bon-po histories as *bsTan-'byung*, a class of works which in their most comprehensive forms cover the history of all Tibetan religion. The author, Grub-dbang bKra-shis rGyal-mtshan Dri-med sNying-po, composed, among many others, five books entitled *mDzod-lnga* (the Five Treasuries), one of which is this work, and he defines it as *Bon-gyi byung-khungs ston-pa gtso-bo legs-bshad-mdzod* (the Treasury of Good sayings that fully reveals the origin of Bon).[1]

bKra-shis rGyal-mtshan tells us that the work was begun in the year Water-Male-Dog (chu-pho-khyi, 1922) whilst he was expounding his work *sDe-snod-mdzod* (the Treasury of Scriptures) to a group of his disciples,[2] and there are some parts where the material is rather carelessly arranged as if he left it to his pupils to read the sources and collect the information for him. He was born in Shar-rdza, a district in Khams, in 1859[3] and died in 1935.[4] He is believed to have left no body behind when he died, as a result of having practised the teaching of rDzogs-pa chen-po (Great Perfection) and thus he is referred to as 'Ja'-lus-pa.[5] Indeed he was an ardent follower of the rDzogs-pa chen-po and

[1] The others are *Lung-rig-mdzod*, *sDe-snod-mdzod*, *dByings-rig-mdzod*, and *Nam-mkha'-mdzod*, see bKra-shis rGyal-mtshan, *Bon-'chad mkhas pa'i mgul-rgyan*, f. 34b3.

[2] This is stated in the colophon of the text which ends as follows: *LShDz* f. 272b4: *sa ral zhes pa chu pho khyi lo'i 'brug zla'i dkar phyogs kyi dus tshes bzang por dbu brtsams te rang gnas dben khrod kun bzang bde ba chen po'i bsti gnas thar gling byang chub ljon pa'i skyes mos tshal zla 'od bdud rtsi 'tsher ba'i khang bzang dam par / phyogs kyi 'dus sde'i tshogs la sde snod rin po che'i mdzod 'chad pa'i thun gseng gi cha rnams su mdo sngags kyi bstan pa'i 'byung khungs spyi dang lo rgyus rnams phyogs gcig tu tshig nyung don 'dus su tshad ma gsum gyi sgo nas bsdebs te bsgrigs pa 'dis kyang mnyam med* (273a) *rgyal ba'i bstan pa rin po che phyogs dus kun tu dar zhing rgyas te 'gro kun phan bde'i legs tshogs ma lus yid bzhin 'jo ba'i rgyu ru gyur cig /*

[3] The date is given among the later additions to *STNN*, see *infra*, p. xvii n. 1.

[4] This date is obtained from a one-folio prayer belonging to the Abbot of sMan-ri, Sangs-rgyas bsTan-'dzin, composed by our author just before his death in which he mentions his age as seventy-six.

[5] See *infra*, p. 53 n. 1.

is admired for his work, the *dByings-rig-mdzod* (the Treasury of Knowledge of the Celestial Sphere) which is an intensive study of the rDzogs-pa chen-po. Thus he became very widely known not only among Bon-pos but also in some Buddhist circles. He is the only Bon-po scholar who ever had pupils from the Yellow Hat sect. His *Legs-bshad-mdzod*, on the other hand, has not attracted so much interest among Tibetans owing to their customary lack of concern about historical problems. It is, however, an invaluable work since no other writer has surveyed so thoroughly the various records of the origins and early development of Bon. Moreover, bKra-shis rGyal-mtshan attempts to cover the whole range of Bon-po history from the earliest times to his own day. I know of no other work equal to this in scope among Bon-po histories.

Although the author does not attempt to establish a firm chronology of events, he has arranged his material in roughly historical sequence. Many pages of the work contain long lists of religious teachers, and their birth-places, monasteries, and hermitages are sometimes mentioned. From this it is clear that bKra-shis rGyal-mtshan consulted a large number of Bon-po works. However, although he usually indicates the sources of his information, in some places he simply incorporates passages into his work without mentioning their origin. Sometimes there is obscurity due probably to imperfect understanding of his sources, and many of the names in his lists are otherwise unidentifiable and their authenticity may be open to question. His main sources were general historical works and individual biographies, a small number of which are available in printed editions, but many existed only in manuscript form in Tibet, and outside they are completely inaccessible. This explains why I have been unable to identify many of the passages quoted in the work. The style of writing often differs from one page to another since the unacknowledged quotations are extensive, and the resulting obscurity scarcely permits a sure translation in some places. But, of course, the more inaccessible the sources, the greater the value of the work to European historians. Defects in our author's method are less important than the presentation of new material.

The first edition was taken from printing blocks made by the author's disciple Khod-po sKal-bzang rGyal-mtshan in Shar-rdza in Khams. It contains 274 folios and the printing is very distinct. A copy is preserved in the École Française d'Extrême-Orient (T. 0545), Paris. The present work is entirely based on that copy.

THE SCOPE OF THE WORK AND ITS SOURCES

The work is in seven chapters or sections, and each of them deals with different stages in the development of the Bon-po religion.

The first section gives an account of how the universe and living beings came into existence. It relates in detail the different views of the origin of existence, and there is an extensive description of the land of 'Ol-mo lung-ring and its importance as the centre of civilization, in contrast to Kailāsa which is the centre of the earth.

Already this section shows our author assembling material from a variety of sources. A few passages are quoted from the *bDen-gnyis*, a philosophical treatise by Me-ston Shes-rab 'Od-zer (*STNN* 1058–1132).[1] Much more is based on the *lHa-'grel*, known as *lHa-sras don-'grel* from its author's name, and rediscovered in (*STNN*) 1067 by gNyan-ston Shes-rab Seng-ge.[2] It is a commentary on the *mDzod*[3] by lHa-gshen Yongs-su Dag-pa (*KTDG*, p. 14). It is from these works that the different views of the origin of the world are drawn. They also supply material

[1] All dates which I preface with the letters *STNN* come from the cycle of Rab-byung given in the *Sangs-rgyas-kyi bstan-rtsis nor-bu'i phreng-ba* (Delhi, 1965) composed in 1842 (p. 38) by the Abbot Nyi-ma bsTan-'dzin (b. 1813, ibid., p. 37) who became the twenty-second abbot (usually given the title sKu-mdun = His Presence) of the monastery of sMan-ri (see *infra*, pp. xxxix, 142) in 1836 (*STNN*, p. 37). His sources for working out his dates are mostly biographies of religious teachers, histories and genealogies of different clans (*TNT*, p. 56), and he had also consulted many religious texts which were available to him. Indeed, the monastery sMan-ri is well known for its rich collection of old Bon-po texts.

The value of his dates before Srong-btsan sGam-po may be doubted and even in later datings he may occasionally be proved wrong. For instance, he puts Karma Pakśi in Wood-Mouse year of the 2nd Rab-byung (*STNN*, p. 32), i.e. in 1144, whereas *DN* (p. 485) and *Re'u-mig* (p. 21) give Wood-Mouse 1204. But it may be a recommendation that he rarely dates the discovery of a prophetical text earlier than he dates a name which occurs in the text. In fact I have noted only one doubtful instance (see *infra*, p. xxxvii). The work has been added to and brought more up to date by later writers. A translation in English and conversion of the dates into European chronology of the *STNN* is in preparation by the Abbot Sangs-rgyas bsTan-'dzin and Mr. Per Kvaerne.

[2] See *infra*, p. 153. [3] See *infra*, p. 8 n. 4.

relating to 'Ol-mo lung-ring, but the main source for this is the *mDo-'dus*, the short version of sTon-pa gShen-rab's life and probably the earliest of his biographies, a 'rediscovered text' of about the eleventh century.[1] The author also quotes from an unspecified *mDzod-'grel* (commentary on the *mDzod*). Since there are many of these and they are not available for consultation, I cannot identify it. The author quotes in a similar way from an unidentified *mDo*. This is the *gZer-mig*, rediscovered in about the eleventh century,[2] which figures as a more important source in later sections, as do five other sources used in this section: the *rTsa-'grel*, known in full as the *Zhi-khro rtsa-'grel*, an analytical treatise on the tranquil and wrathful divinities, rediscovered in the twelfth century;[3] the *Dri-med*, passed on orally to Blo-ldan sNying-po (b. 1360),[4] the long version of sTon-pa gShen-rab's life; the *Zhing-mdo* which I cannot identify; the *sGra-'grel*, a commentary on the *mDzod*, rediscovered in the twelfth century;[5] and the *bsGrags-byang*,[6] a history.

The second section into which the work is divided, is primarily concerned with the life of the Teacher, gShen-rab Mi-bo who is the protector of the present age. Before becoming gShen-rab, he went through a series of lives and eventually became gSal-ba, the younger brother of Dag-pa who is the direct predecessor of gShen-rab and the last of seven Teachers. gSal-ba, together with his younger brother, Shes-pa, hears in Heaven the exposition of Everlasting Bon by the Teacher 'Bum-khri Glog-gi lCe-can, while his elder brother, Dag-pa preaches Bon to men in the world under the name of gTo-rgyal Ye-mkhyen. Before coming into the world, gSal-ba orders Shes-pa to preach Bon to the gods in his place and explains that he is going to propagate Bon in the world in the place of Dag-pa who is now to retire from his work. gSal-ba predicts that when he finishes his work in the world, Shes-pa will be the future Teacher. Then gSal-ba comes down from Heaven with two attendants, rMa-lo and gYu-lo. He chooses the country and kind of family where he intends to be born. Leaving his two attendants on Mount gYung-drung dgu-brtsegs in 'Ol-mo lung-ring, he transforms himself into a white syllable A which enters the head of his father, dMu-rgyal rGyal-bon Thod-dkar, whilst a red syllable MA enters the body of the

[1] See *infra*, p. 4 n. 1.
[2] See *infra*, p. 4 n. 1.
[3] See *infra*, p. 166 n. 4.
[4] See *infra*, p. 4 n. 1.
[5] See *infra*, p. 8 n. 4.
[6] See *infra*, p. 17 n. 2.

mother, rGyal-bzhad-ma. After nine months and ten days the mother gives birth to a son. He is given the name of sTon-pa gShen-rab Mi-bo kun-las rnam-par rgyal-ba (the Teacher gShen-rab, the Lord of Man, the Conqueror). gShen-rab, at the age of about ten, begins to preach his doctrine in the realms of the earth-gods (sa-bdag), of the serpents (i.e. the underworld), and of the airborne divinities. When twelve years old, he transforms himself into many teachers who propagate his doctrine in different countries. This doctrine consists of the four Portals and the Treasury (sgo-bzhi mdzod-lnga).[1] Then he marries ten women and they bear eight sons[2] and two daughters. All the sons become his disciples and take charge of the different establishments he has founded. Now gShen-rab finds himself confronted with a rival, the demon Khyab-pa Lag-ring who dwells in Kong-po in Tibet. Khyab-pa, after failing to deceive gShen-rab, manages to entice and carry off one of gShen-rab's daughters, gShen-za Ne'u-chung who later bears him two sons. However, gShen-rab takes back his daughter and his grandsons to 'Ol-mo lung-ring. Because of this, Khyab-pa now sends his followers to steal gShen-rab's seven horses and they bring them and hide them in Kong-po. With four of his attendants gShen-rab sets out after the horses. Khyab-pa unsuccessfully tries to block his way with snow at the frontier of Za-hor. Here gShen-rab teaches the Bon-pos of Za-hor, Kashmir, and Gilgit the Bon of Spells. Then he goes to Zhang-zhung, but Khyab-pa again tries to block his way with fire at the frontier of sTag-gzig and Zhang-zhung. Here he imparts the Bon of Bombs and Spells. Then he goes to the source of the four rivers of Tibet, but Khyab-pa once more blocks his way with sand. However, he overcomes all this and gives to the Bon-pos of Tibet a Bon[3] about prayers to the gods, another about the expelling of demons, and also shows them various ritual objects. Finally, gShen-rab reaches Kong-po where further skirmishes occur between gShen-rab and Khyab-pa, but gShen-rab as usual wins in the end. Then gShen-rab goes back with Khyab-pa who outwardly agrees to be his pupil, but gShen-rab realizes that Khyab-pa intends no good. One day in the absence of gShen-rab, Khyab-pa burns

[1] On these, see D. L. Snellgrove, *Nine Ways of Bon*, London, 1967, pp. 16–19.

[2] See *infra*, p. 3 n. 2.

[3] Bon is here used in the sense of precept or set of precepts.

gShen-rab's dPe-sgrom, a box containing all gShen-rab's books, and escapes to Kong-po highly pleased with his revenge. However, gShen-rab pays no attention to Khyab-pa. At the age of thirty-one he becomes a monk, leaving his houses, his family, and all his comforts behind. He assumes the name of Khri-gtsug rGyal-ba. Now when gShen-rab is in solitude practising meditation, Khyab-pa comes to see what he is doing. On seeing the hardship gShen-rab endures in the course of religious practices, Khyab-pa breaks down and confesses all his misdeeds to him. Then gShen-rab returns from his solitude with Khyab-pa, who now becomes a leading disciple, and starts to make arrangements for the ordination of the rest of the disciples who are not yet ordained. After this gShen-rab spends most of his time in solitude till he dies at the age of eighty-two. Mu-cho lDem-drug, one of gShen-rab's sons, acts as an apostle of gShen-rab after his death. He expounds the teaching of gShen-rab to many pupils from different countries.

The material for this section is mostly drawn from the following sources: the *Nyi-sgron*, known in full as *rTsa-rgyud nyi-zer sgron-ma* (*KTDG*, p. 16), a treatise on cosmogony and the history of Bon by Dran-pa Nam-mkha' (eighth century),[1] and the already-mentioned *mDo-'dus*, both of which provide extensive material for gShen-rab's earthly life. Other sources such as the *Drang-don mun-sel sgron-ma* (*KTDG*, p. 27), a treatise on rDzogs-pa chen-po by Dran-pa Nam-mkha', and the *Nam-mkha' sems-mdzod* (an unidentified text on rDzogs-pa chen-po) are quoted mostly in connection with the previous existences of gShen-rab, especially the one immediately before his descent to earth where, as 'Chi-med gTsug-phud (later gSal-ba), he expounded the rDzogs-pa chen-po. But several other works have also been used for gShen-rab's life. They are the *Sha-'bal*, known in full as *Sha-'bal nag-po glog-gsas-kyi rgyud*, one of the nine rGyud of Phur-pa (*KTDG*, p. 10), rediscovered probably in 1038;[2] the *rNam-rgyal*,[3] a ritual concerning the worship of gShen-rab in a different manifestation; the *Zhi-ba yongs-rdzogs*, known in full as *Zhi-ba g·yung-drung yongs-rdzogs*, a treatise on tranquil divinities, rediscovered in 1017;[4] and the *mChod-gtor*

[1] See *infra*, p. 16 n. 3.
[2] See *infra*, p. 45 n. 2.
[3] See *infra*, p. 174.
[4] See *infra*, p. 129 n. 1.

rgya-che-'grel (*KTDG*, p. 13), a commentary on the *mChod-gtor rtsis-mgo bdun-pa*, rediscovered in 1017.[1]

The third section is exclusively devoted to the history of the gSang-sngags (Secret Spells) and rDzogs-pa chen-po taught by 'Chi-med gTsug-phud. He is one and the same person as gSal-ba who became gShen-rab.

Before becoming gShen-rab, 'Chi-med gTsug-phud was born in Heaven as the child of the heavenly beings 'Phrul-gshen sNang-ldan and bZang-za Ring-btsun. 'Phrul-gshen flew down in the form of a cuckoo and landed on the right shoulder of bZang-za Ring-btsun as she was resting beside a lake. Later she gave birth to a son, to whom she spoke thus:

> O son born of a virgin woman,
> You are a shoot grown without a seed being sown,
> Stay here in this precious cool place.

She dug in the golden sand and built a little shelter, leaving him in it. After nine days she went back to see him. To her surprise he recognized her and smiled at her. She was greatly impressed by his beauty and especially the large knot of hair on top of his head. So she gave him the name 'Chi-med gTsug-phud (the Deathless one who has a hair-knot). Later he listened to the teaching of gShen-lha 'Od-dkar in Heaven. bKra-shis rGyal-mtshan, our author, when tracing the history of the later transmission of this teaching distinguishes seven parts: the Five gSas-mkhar,[2] Ma-rgyud, and rDzogs-pa chen-po.

First the Five gSas-mkhar.

sPyi-spungs skor-gsum (the Three Cycles of sPyi-spungs).[3] gSang-ba 'Dus-pa is born to the king Zhi-ba-ldan and queen lHa-sbyin-mdzes in sTag-gzig. When he grows up he listens to the doctrines of *sPyi-spungs skor-gsum* in the presence of 'Chi-med gTsug-phud. He then practises them in nine different places and in each place he subdues Dregs-pa pho-rgyud ('the male arrogant ones') and builds a temple. At the same time sTag-la Me-'bar, who is dealt with in the following section, subdues Dregs-pa mo-rgyud ('the female arrogant ones'), particularly one called Srid-pa rGyal-mo, by giving her his semen, and in consequence she now occupies an important place among Bon-po religious protectors.

[1] See *infra*, p. 129 n. 1.
[2] See *infra*, p. 45 n. 2.
[3] See *infra*, pp. 15 n. 3, 45 n. 2.

The author points out that this is how the practice of sByor-ba (sexual union) and sGrol-ba (deliverance) in tantric teachings arose.

Phur-pa.[1] sTag-la Me-'bar is born to the king Yang-rgyal lHa'i rGyal-po and queen sTag-za He-ting in sTag-gzig. They have a servant whom the king beats and the queen scolds. At his death he says he will be born to them as a son. Later the queen gives birth to twin brothers. One is called sTag-la Me-'bar and the other Dhar-sha Ghri-ba. sTag-la becomes religious whilst his brother becomes evil-minded. They quarrel with each other. Dhar-sha beats his mother when she says his behaviour is improper. He later cuts off his father's head with a sword and leaves home. He goes to the south of sTag-gzig where he even eats human beings, and thus the country is threatened with destruction. In order to save the country and sentient beings, sTag-la now in desperation practises the cycle of Phur-pa in Brag-phug rong-can, having obtained it from 'Chi-med gTsug-phud. However, although his magical practices in Phur-pa are directed against his twin brother, they do not affect him, and sTag-la does not get any response from the divinities whom he invokes. Seeing his helplessness, the goddess of compassion, Thugs-rje Byams-ma, shows her face to him and predicts that he will not be able to bring the divinities to his assistance to subdue his brother, if he shows compassion towards him. She instructs him to be vigorous and arrogant. Following the instructions, he kills his twin brother by magical means and so manages to save sentient beings and the country.

Now bKra-shis rGyal-mtshan relates how these teachings were transmitted to lHa-gshen Yongs-su Dag-pa, Klu-grub Ye-shes sNying-po, and rGyal-gshen Mi-lus bSam-legs who promulgated them in the realms of gods, serpents, and men. lHa-gshen Yongs-su Dag-pa was born in Heaven and was a pupil of gSang-ba 'Dus-pa from whom he learnt about the doctrines of *sPyi-spungs skor-gsum*.

Klu-grub Ye-shes sNying-po is born to mDzes-ldan and gNyan-lcam brJid-ma in sTag-gzig. First they have no children and go for help to a 'serpent-priest' who tells them that they should make offerings to serpents, and then gives them his

[1] See *infra*, p. 45 n. 2.

spittle which they eat. Later the wife gives birth to a son whom they accordingly call Klu-grub ('obtained from serpents'). He meets Mi-lus bSam-legs and asks for the doctrines of *sPyi-spungs skor-gsum*. Mi-lus sends him to Yongs-su Dag-pa saying that Yongs-su Dag-pa has better knowledge concerning the real truth (nges-pa'i don) than he has. Yongs-su Dag-pa in turn sends him to gSang-ba 'Dus-pa saying that the latter has still better knowledge about the truth. Then Klu-grub begins to practise what he has learnt from gSang-ba 'Dus-pa. However, he is still unable to understand the truth, so he goes back to his original teacher, Mi-lus bSam-legs, and asks if he can tell him what kind of gShen can really reveal the truth. So he tells him that gShen-lha 'Od-dkar, who dwells in a palace made of precious crimson stones in the sky, is the only one who can really teach the truth. So Klu-grub transforms himself into a garuḍa and searches for gShen-lha, but fails to find him. In his despair he meets a goddess and asks her if she knows gShen-lha's whereabouts in the sky, but she replies that she has not seen him anywhere in the sky and suggests he should look for him in the sea. Then Klu-grub transforms himself into a fish and begins to search for gShen-lha in the ocean, but he cannot find him there either. Then he meets a white man who tells him that he will find gShen-lha neither in the sky, nor in the sea, nor on the earth, but only in meditation. So Klu-grub returns home and begins to meditate. Now gShen-lha suddenly appears in front of him and Klu-grub asks why he has been unable to find gShen-lha till then. gShen-lha explains to him that since he was originally conceived from serpents his insight is inferior to that of man, that the goddess and the white man were gShen-lha himself, and that he was always with him though he could not be seen. Now Klu-grub realizes the truth and gShen-lha instructs him to go to bZang-za Ring-btsun to learn more about the doctrines of *sPyi-spungs skor-gsum*. He later stays in Chu-mig brgya-rtsa continuing his meditational practices.

Ge-khod.[1] Although it is traditionally grouped among the Five gSas-mkhar the cycle of Ge-khod is quite different in origin. The author relates that it was first taught by the sage A-ti Mu-ver.

[1] See *infra*, pp. xxix n. 2, 45 n. 2.

Ma-rgyud.[1] Mi-lus bSam-legs is born in rGyal-mkhar ba-chod. When the king of the country is about to die, the small neighbouring kingdoms declare that they are going to annex the country. So the people gather together and pray to the goddess Byams-ma. After a year the queen gives birth to a son who is highly intelligent and learns many doctrines from gSang-ba 'Dus-pa and sTag-la Me-'bar, and particularly Ma-rgyud from Yongs-su Dag-pa. Whilst he is practising the cycle of Ma-rgyud, the six Mother Guardians come and ask him if he knows thoroughly the precepts of Ma-rgyud, and he replies that he understands them very profoundly as he has met the six great scholars. They bring a skull full of water taken from the ocean, dip a reed into it, and giving him the reed, say that the Bon of Ma-rgyud is like the ocean, the teacher's knowledge of it is equivalent to the water in the skull, and his knowledge of Ma-rgyud is like the water on the reed. Now Mi-lus gets very despondent and asks them how and from whom he can learn it fully. They tell him that he must go and learn it from bZang-za Ring-btsun who is the source of Ma-rgyud. So Mi-lus begins to learn the three rGyud from her and later comes back and practises them.

rDzogs-pa chen-po.[2] bKra-shis rGyal-mtshan now considers the rDzogs-pa chen-po, the source of which is much the same as the others. However, here he distinguishes two separate transmissions. One reaches Tibet through India from sTag-gzig and is called the Bon of India, and the other through Zhang-zhung called the Bon of Zhang-zhung. In conclusion the author notes that the gSang-sngags, by which he means the Five gSas-mkhar, appeared in 'Ol-mo lung-ring after the death of gShen-rab.

The material in this section has been gathered from a very wide variety of sources as might be expected, since it is concerned with very important Bon-po doctrines. The accounts of the teachings of 'Chi-med gTsug-phud and his life are mainly based on the following works: the *Phun-sum tshogs-pa'i rgyud* (*KTDG*, p. 13), a treatise on rDzogs-pa chen-po, rediscovered in 1088;[3] the *Nyi-sgron* and the *Khu-byug rang-'grel*, a commentary on the *Khu-byug* (*KTDG*, p. 12), which is a rDzogs-pa chen-po

[1] See *infra*, p. 45 n. 2.

[2] See *infra*, p. 51.

[3] See *infra*, p. 154.

text, rediscovered in 1017;[1] the *Khyung-chen*, known in full as the *lTa-ba khyung-chen g·yung-drung gsang-ba'i rgyud*, one of the six rGyud of Khro-bo and concerned with the tantric teachings, rediscovered in 1038;[2] and the *Thig-le dbyings-mchad*, a tantric text, rediscovered in 1017.[3] These also figure as most important sources for later sections. In connection with 'Chi-med gTsug-phud's teaching he uses an unidentified *'Grel-bzhi*. There are two of these, one by Dran-pa Nam-mkha' and the other by the Four Scholars (*KTDG*, p. 26). The latter was rediscovered in 1017.[4] Both are commentaries on the *Gab-pa*. The stories of gSang-ba 'Dus-pa, lHa-gshen Yongs-su Dag-pa, and Klu-grub Ye-shes sNying-po are probably based on the *sPyi-spungs don-rgyud* (*KTDG*, p. 8) and the *Rig-'dzin 'dus-pa* (*KTDG*, p. 10) both of which are concerned with tantric teachings and are said to have been passed on orally to Blo-ldan sNying-po (b. 1360).[5] However, the author does not actually refer to them and they are quoted only when there is a need to explain the origin of the teaching. The material for the stories of sTag-la Me-'bar is mainly supplied by the *Don-bsdus rtsa-ba'i 'grel-chen*, a commentary on the *Phur-pa* (*KTDG*, p. 18), rediscovered in 1038.[6] The story of rGyal-gshen Mi-lus bSam-legs is mainly based on the *Ma-rgyud thugs-rje nyi-ma*, the rite of Ma-rgyud, rediscovered by Gu-ru rNon-rtse (b. 1136),[7] and other works such as the *gZhi ye-sangs rgyas-pa'i rgyud* (*KTDG*, p. 10), which is one of the three rGyud of Ma-rgyud, also rediscovered by Gu-ru rNon-rtse, and the *bSen-thub*, rediscovered in (*STNN*) 1017.[8] For the material on rDzogs-pa chen-po the author has drawn mainly on the *Ye-khri mtha'-sel* (*KTDG*, p. 13), a treatise on rDzogs-pa chen-po, the date of the rediscovery of which is unknown, and the *lTa-ba spyi-gcod-kyi bshad-byang* (*KTDG*, p. 12), a part of the *Zhang-zhung snyan-bgyud*[9] which a rDzogs-pa chen-po text claims to be a work belonging to the eighth century. In connection with the transmission of these teachings the author also uses some other works such as the *Gab-pa* and the *rNam-thar chen-mo*; the latter is a text concerned with the

[1] See *infra*, pp. 51 n. 8, 129 n. 1.
[2] See *infra*, p. 45 n. 2.
[3] See *infra*, p. 129 n. 1.
[4] See *infra*, p. 129 n. 1.
[5] See *infra*, p. 182.
[6] See *infra*, pp. 45 n. 2, 145 n. 1.
[7] See *infra*, p. 166
[8] See *infra*, p. 129 n. 1.
[9] See p. xxxviii, *infra*, pp. 52, 111.

life stories of the transmitters of the *Zhang-zhung snyan-brgyud* which is also used in later sections.

The fourth section deals briefly with the genealogy of the Shākya clan, the Tibetan kings, the ancestry of Confucius, the rulers of Me-nyag and Mongolia, and the genealogies of dMu-gshen, Bru, Zhu, sPa, rMe'u, and Khyung in Tibet. The author cites many accounts of the genealogy of gShen-rab; for example, the fathers of Gautama and gShen-rab were brothers, and gShen-rab and the demon Khyab-pa Lag-ring were also brothers. Then he carefully points out that such suggestions are contradictory to the traditional view, but nevertheless, since the sources are of considerable importance, they deserve careful consideration.

The fifth section gives an account of how the Bon doctrines spread from their land 'Ol-mo lung-ring to other countries and especially to Tibet. It deals in great detail with the propagation of Bon and the persecution by the king Gri-gum in gTsang, in consequence of which the teaching of some Bon doctrines was forbidden and the texts relating to them concealed to prevent their destruction.

The sixth section dwells upon the restoration of the Bon-po priest-authority by the son of the king Gri-gum, sPu-lde Gung-rgyal, its ascendancy lasting till the mid eighth century, and the second persecution by the king Khri-srong lDe-btsan (b. 742) leading to the renewed concealment of texts.

The seventh section is the longest and most informative. It deals in great detail with the rediscoveries of the hidden texts at the beginning of the tenth century in gTsang. In this section the author takes great pains to narrate the renewal of the Bon-po doctrines and the firm footing gained by them in gTsang and some other parts of Tibet with their various monastic establishments. The author concludes this section with the traditional Bon-po chronology of the future duration of gShen-rab's teaching.

Constant sources throughout these last four sections are the *Nyi-sgron*, the *Byams-ma*, which is a text concerning worship of the goddess Byams-ma rediscovered by Khro-tshang 'Brug-lha (*STNN* 956–1077);[1] the *bsGrags-byang*, which is a historical work, and the *Srid-rgyud*, another history. Much material has been drawn from these first three sources in Section V where

[1] See *infra*, p. 124.

the arrival of Bon in Tibet and its decline are related. The *Nyi-sgron* is no longer used in Section VI, and it is the *bsGrags-byang* and the *Srid-rgyud* that provide material for the second persecution and the hiding of texts. In Section VII the *Srid-rgyud* is used, especially the prophetical chapter concerning the discoverers of texts.

THE MAIN HISTORICAL ISSUES

The *Legs-bshad-mdzod* claims to be a history of Bon. My aim has been to provide a translation of those parts of the work which seem most likely to be of interest to historians. The opening sections of the work dealing with the coming of gShen-rab and his earthly life may contain much that is of interest to students of Bon as a religion, but it is not the kind of evidence from which the historian will derive much satisfaction. It is partly for this reason and partly because they cover the same ground as the *gZer-mig*, some chapters of which have already been translated by H. A. Francke, that I have not translated them here.[1] My translation, in fact, begins with what are perhaps the first statements in which the historian may have a chance of coming nearer to the kind of certainty he is looking for. They occur in the middle of Section IV where the author, after dealing with the genealogies of gShen, Bru, Zhu, sPa, rMe'u, and Khyung, proceeds to recount the arrival of Bon in Tibet. My translation continues through all the remaining sections of the work with the exception of the closing part of Section VII where history gives place to prophecy in the future chronology of gShen-rab's teaching. The work then closes with some verses of prayers and the colophon.[2]

Place of Origin

Concerning the arrival of Bon in Tibet and its provenance, our text states that Bon first reached Tibet in gShen-rab's lifetime when he paid a visit to Tibet travelling from 'Ol-mo lung-ring

[1] For details see *infra*, p. 4 n. 1. [2] See *supra*, p. xv n. 2.

in sTag-gzig, passing through Zhang-zhung. Bon-pos claim then that their religion came ultimately from the country 'Ol-mo lung-ring, gShen-rab's birthplace. It was located in sTag-gzig according to Bon-po tradition. However, sTag-gzig itself cannot be clearly located.[1] Since the Tibetan epic and biographical literature persistently puts it in the west, Western scholars have vaguely suggested Persia.[2]

However, by the thirteenth–fourteenth centuries 'Ol-mo lung-ring had come to be viewed in a very special light, indeed in much the same way as the Buddhist Sukhāvatī (bde-ba-can), a land in which no ordinary human being lives, beyond the reach of neighbouring countries, imperishable and therefore unlike the rest of this world. Moreover, it affords a comfort superior to that normally experienced in the world of sensual impressions. Consequently many prayers[3] were composed and repeated by men of religion hoping to be born there in the next life. Pictures of it were painted showing it as a completely fabulous place.[4] But it is nevertheless reported as forming a part of this world, indeed as being the centre of civilization, and geographical fact and myth are inextricably entangled whenever it is described. It is dominated by Mount gYung-drung dgu-brtsegs which is situated in the centre, with four rivers flowing from its base into the four different directions. In front of the mountain we find the lake Ma-phang and around it mountains such as sPos-ri ngad-ldan and places like Brag-phug rong-can. Such is the description of 'Ol-mo lung-ring found in *GRB* (pp. 4–7) and *LShDz* (ff. 9a4–14b4). We cannot but recognize the area of Kailāsa in front of which lies the lake Ma-phang, the source of the Brahmaputra, Indus, Sutlej, and Karnali. Moreover, the following verses quoted from *mDo-'dus* in *LShDz* (f. 9a5) and

[1] H. Hoffmann, *Quellen zur Geschichte der tibetischen Bon-Religion*, Verlag der Akademie der Wissenschaften und der Literatur in Mainz, 1950 pp. 212–13; R. A. Stein, *Les tribus anciennes des marches sino-tibétaines*, Paris, 1961, p. 29.

[2] H. Hoffmann, loc. cit. (see previous note) and also *The Religions of Tibet*, London, 1961, pp. 95, 99, 109; R. A. Stein, *Recherches sur l'épopée et le barde au Tibet*, Paris, 1959, p. 4 *passim*; D. L. Snellgrove and H. Richardson, *A Cultural History of Tibet*, London, 1968, p. 99.

[3] For some examples of this kind of prayer one may see *sKye-sgo gcod-pa'i mdo* (Delhi, 1965) rediscovered by lHun-grub Thogs-med (see *infra*, p. 179) in a Wood-Tiger year (f. 32b3). Another example is the *bDe-chen zhing-gi smon-lam rnam-mkhyen grong-'jug* composed by our author.

[4] For an instance see Snellgrove, *Nine Ways*, Illustrations XXII.

Kun-las btus-pa'i 'grel-ba (f. 39b2) are most explicit in their description of 'Ol-mo lung-ring:[1]

As for the land of gShen, 'Ol-mo lung-ring,
Its size is 50 square dpag-tshad (4,000 fathoms),
It is made in the likeness of Mount Sumeru (Ri-rab) with its four continents,
Situated in the North-East of Jambdivipa ('Dzam-bu-gling),
To the South of the mountain Nimindhara (mu-khyud-'dzin),
At the base of the tree of 'Dzam-bu,
In front of the snow mount Ti-tse[2] (Kailāsa),
Beside the turquoise lake Ma-phang (Manasarovara),
At the source of the great four streams,
Near the mountain sPos-ri ngad-ldan.

In spite of this seeming identification of 'Ol-mo lung-ring with the area of Kailāsa, biographers of gShen-rab in general regularly maintain that Mount Kailāsa, lake Manasarovara, and the mountain sPos-ri ngad-ldan merely represent those situated in

[1] *gshen yul 'ol mo lung ring ni / dpag tshad lnga bcu chu zhing mnyam / gling bzhi ri rab tshul du grub / 'dzam bu smrig shad shing gi rtsa / ri bo gangs can ti tse'i drung / mtsho ni ma phang g·yu mtsho 'gram / chu bo chen po bzhi 'dus mgo / spos ri ngad ldan nye ba'i sa /*

[2] According to *mDzod-phug* (p. 23) and *sGra-'grel* (p. 104), Ti-tse (usually Ti-se) is a Zhang-zhung term meaning water, but we have another word for water: 'ting' (see *mDzod-phug*, p. 24; *sGra-'grel*, pp. 106, 110 [cf. mNyam-med Shes-rab rGyal-mtshan, *mDzod-'grel 'phrul-gyi sgron-me*, f. 29a6]); also 'ting-nam' (see Zhu Nyi-ma Grags-pa, *sGra-yi don-sdeb snang-gsal sgron-me*, p. 18). However, *mDzod-phug* (p. 24, on p. 28—spelling: 'Ting-tse') and *sGra-'grel* (p. 106) use it as an alternative for Ri-rab (Sumeru).

Ti-tse, also according to Bon-po tradition, is the god of Mount Kailāsa, just as Thang-lha or Pom-ra are the names of the mountains and their gods. The divinities of the Ge-khod cycle (see *infra*, p. 331 l. 28, *KTDG*, p. 10) are believed to reside on Ti-tse, and they are Ku-pyi Mang-ke, A-ti Mu-ver, and dBal-chen Ge-khod gsang-ba drag-chen, and are known as the Three Protectors (mGon-po rNam-gsum). They are usually referred to as the gods of Zhang-zhung (see *infra*, pp. 45 n. 2; cf. *TPS* ii, p. 724 n. 30).

Ti-tse is a very much disputed mountain. It is on this mountain that the well-known story of Mi-la Ras-pa's victory in taking it over from a Bon-po priest, sNa-ro Bon-chung, is located. After Mi-la Ras-pa's stay, this mountain became an exclusive hermitage (sgrub-gnas) of the bKa'-brgyud-pas, and when they identified it with the snow mountain mentioned in the *Abhidharmakoṣakārika* (Otani vol. 115, no. 5590, p. 119 [9gong8]): *'di nas byang du ri nag po/ dgu 'das gangs ri'o . . . /*, the Sa-skya-pas disapproved and thus a geographical disputation followed between the two sects. For details see dKon-mchog bsTan-'dzin, *Gangs-ri chen-po ti-se dang mtsho-chen ma-dros bcas-kyi sngon byung-gi lo-rgyus mdor-bsdus-su brjod-pa'i rab-byed shel-dkar me-long*, ff. 12b1–16b3.

'Ol-mo lung-ring in sTag-gzig. It may be worth noting that similar notions are also quite normal among Tibetan Buddhists. Although Uḍḍiyāna (Swat) is a real place, the rNying-ma-pas have been very successful in making it mythical, and Shambhala, too, comes into this category. In order to outdo the Buddhists, some Bon-po writers have attempted to identify 'Ol-mo lung-ring with the latter. Places known as sBas-yul (Hiding place) and possessing a similar semi-mythical character are prevalent in the religious literature of the Bon-pos and rNying-ma-pas.

'Ol-mo lung-ring must probably therefore be identified as an area around Kailāsa which was once the central part of Zhang-zhung.[1] Zhang-zhung then probably covered what is now the West of Tibet extending from Khyung-lung dngul-mkhar to Dang-ra khyung-rdzong in the East, to gTsang in the South, and to Kashmir in the West.[2] As the central Tibetan kingdom grew in military power and expanded towards the West, Zhang-zhung was crushed and annexed, and the whole area which is now Western Tibet became virtually tibetanized in the seventh–eighth centuries A.D.

One of the places offered to Bon-pos at a feast of reconciliation by the king Khri-srong lDe-btsan is called 'Ol-mo-lung. Our author lists it among the places that were in the Upper Land while *bsGrags-byang* (f. 79b) and *GRB* (p. 41)[3] put it in the Lower Land. Thus there is further confusion concerning its location. However, it is also said in the *bsGrags-byang* (f. 24a6) that gShen-rab preached most of his doctrines in the area of Kailāsa, whilst the *Srid-rgyud* (f. 17a4) states that Zhang-zhung is the source of Bon and from there it spread to sTag-gzig and other countries (ibid., f. 7a6). A probable explanation of all this confusion seems to be this: After the persecutions of Bon and Buddhism and the collapse of the central Tibetan kingdom, the location of 'Ol-mo lung-ring was completely forgotten. Around the tenth century fresh Buddhist teachings began to flow into Tibet from India causing the Bon-pos to reorganize themselves, and consolidate their position. Among other things they felt the need to identify the location of 'Ol-mo lung-ring which they

[1] See R. A. Stein, *Les Tribus anciennes des marches sino-tibétaines*, Paris, 1961, p. 28 *et passim*.

[2] Cf. *infra*, p. 27.

[3] Giving the forms: 'or-mo lung-ring; and bon-mo lung-ring respectively.

knew only as the source of Bon. Confident that there could be nothing ordinary about the origins of Bon, they placed 'Ol-mo lung-ring in sTag-gzig, conceived of as being somewhere outside Tibet in the West. Our author, perhaps trying to make sense out of texts like the *gZer-mig* and *gZi-brjid*,[1] imagines the far side of Zhang-zhung as bordering on sTag-gzig, for gShen-rab, according to him, after travelling from sTag-gzig to Za-hor, and through Zhang-zhung, finds himself back at a point where sTag-gzig and Zhang-zhung meet and from there he proceeds towards Tibet.

Persecution

It is possible that the tradition of Bon coming to Tibet from 'Ol-mo lung-ring in sTag-gzig may give us a clue to its geographical origins, but owing to the inconsistency among Bon-po authorities themselves, we can only talk of probabilities.

The kind of agreement between independent historical sources, which provides the critical historian with firm fact, is not available in the case of Tibet before the seventh century. The first date that can be fixed with such certainty seems to be A.D. 649, the death of Srong-btsan sGam-po. Not only the dates but also the existence of most of the kings[2] listed by Tibetan historians as having preceded Srong-btsan sGam-po are questioned by Western historians in view of the complete lack of convincing evidence.[3]

[1] *gZer-mig*, vol. kha, f. 49b4: gShen-rab first reaches the frontier of sTag-gzig and Tibet (bod-dang stag-gzig-gi so-mtshams), then he proceeds to the source of the four rivers of Tibet (bod-gyi chu-bo bzhi-'dus-kyi mgo—clearly referring to Manasarovara, see *supra*, p. xxix). From here (f. 50a5) he travels to Mu-phya dum-pa-tshal in Zhang-zhung (Zhang-zhung mu-phya dum-pa-tshal), and lastly (51a1) he reaches gTsang lu-ma dgu-dgyes from which he goes to Kong-po (f. 51b1).

gZi-brjid, vol. nya, section 39, *sTon-pas bdud-khams thar-bar bkod-pa'i mdo*, f. 96a5: gShen-rab first reaches the frontier of sTag-gzig and Tibet at a place called Dag-sha-dung where he meets people from Za-hor, Yu-gur, Kha-che, and Bru-sha. Then after travelling further (f. 97a1) he reaches the frontier of sTag-gzig and Zhang-zhung, and still further on (f. 97b4) the frontier of Tibet and Zhang-zhung. Thence he goes to the source of the four rivers of Tibet, and (f. 98a3) at last sets out for Kong-po.

[2] The number varies. Bon-po sources give thirty-two, but Buddhist sources mostly give fewer.

[3] J. Bacot, *L'Histoire du Tibet*, Paris, 1962; Snellgrove, Richardson, op. cit., pp. 21–6.

The king Gri-gum, during whose reign Bon first suffered persecution in Tibet, figures as the eighth king in the traditional Bon-po list. He is said to have been the first king to leave his body behind on earth, this having come about as a result of the peculiar circumstances in which he was killed. It seems at least probable that he was a chieftain ruling over some tribes in central Tibet at some period prior to the reign of gNam-ri Srong-btsan, father of Srong-btsan sGam-po. The strange story of his death is to be found in the very early Tun-Huang documents.[1] These, however, contain no reference to his persecution of Bon. This is only to be found in texts probably of much later date, and it is on such material that our author has relied.[2] According to them the issue was the political power of the priests which threatened the future of Gri-gum's lordship. His violent death is seen as 'retribution' for his treatment of Bon. Reinstated by his son, sPu-lde Gung-rgyal, the religion flourished until the second persecution. This occurred under the king Khri-srong lDe-btsan, a descendant of Srong-btsan sGam-po, in consequence of the royal favour which was bestowed upon the rival doctrines of Indian Buddhism. It occurred, therefore, at a time and under circumstances which make comparison with independent historical sources possible, and there can be little doubt that Bon underwent persecution at this time. Khri-srong lDe-btsan was born in 742 and died around 797. The persecution almost certainly occurred somewhere between 780 and 790, and according to Bon-po tradition was the outcome of a disputation and contest of miraculous powers between the two religions.[3] Key figures in the conflict between Bon and Buddhism were Khod-spungs Dran-pa Nam-mkha'[4] and Gyer-spungs sNang-

[1] See *THD*, pp. 96–100, trans. p. 123.

[2] *Nyi-sgron*, for example; see *infra*, p. 16 n. 3.

[3] See *infra*, p. 94 n. 2.

[4] He is an interesting character and very important in the later development of Bon. He is regarded as the 'Saviour of the Degenerate Age' (snyigs-ma'i mgon-po). Accordingly his cult is widely practised and there are many texts concerning it (see *infra*, p. 331, l. 25, p. 338, l. 27, p. 342, l. 16). We know little about his historical existence and can consult only isolated fragments in the West. The *Tshe-dbang snyan-rgyud-kyi lo-rgyus* (section 3 of the *Tshe-dbang bod-yul-ma*, see pp. xxxviii, 176 n. 6) contains a short account of him, and it states (f. 14b3) that he had twin sons who were Tshe-dbang Rig-'dzin (whose life is in four volumes, see *infra*, p. 346, l. 26) a Bon-po teacher (eighth century) and Pad-ma 'Byung-gnas (Padmasambhava). See also sKal-bzang rGyal-mtshan, *bsTan-grags brgal-lan drang-po bshad-pa lha-mi dgyes-pa'i 'bel-gtam*, f. 35a. The rNying-mapas also recognize this story as the Bon-po account of Padmasambhava (mKhyen-

gzher Lod-po.[1] The former in due course abjured Bon and became Buddhist, a fact also confirmed by Buddhist sources,[2] but the second—at least in the view of some Bon-po authorities—was the instrument of a second piece of 'retribution' which nearly brought about the death of Khri-srong lDe-btsan. Thus there are some parallel elements in the stories of the two persecutions. Moreover, according to the traditions followed by our author, the Four Scholars and a number of other Bon-po teachers were involved in both persecutions, during lives of preternatural length. This—together with the fact that the earliest documents contain no reference to Gri-gum's persecution of Bon—may seem to suggest the possibility that later Bon-po historians have made two persecutions out of what was in fact only one.

Textual Antiquity

It is the belief of the Bon-pos that sTon-pa gShen-rab during his lifetime in this world expounded the philosophy of Bon in all its fullness as contained in the *bKa'-'gyur*. However, there is some debate as to whether the Teachings of gSang-sngags as found in the *bKa'-'gyur* were included by sTon-pa gShen-rab in his teaching. It is claimed by many Bon-po authorities that they were withheld by sTon-pa gShen-rab as being too difficult to be disclosed on earth until a later stage. How this is said to have come about has been explained above.[3] However, in either case the teachings were complete within two decades or so after gShen-rab's death.[4]

This is, of course, totally incompatible with the certainty expressed by all European students of Bon that a large part of the

brtse, *rGyal-sras gu-ru pad-ma 'byung-gnas-kyi rnam-thar mdor dril-ba bsgrags pa bon-lugs-ltar bstan-pa, Rin-chen gter-mdzod* TI). Following the *Tshe-dbang snyan-rgyud-kyi lo-rgyus*, *TNT* (p. 54) states that Dran-pa Nam-mkha' had two sons and they were born when he was twenty-seven, but *SG* (f. 51a5) mentions only one son: Tshe-dbang Rig-'dzin (see also *infra*, p. 94 n. 2). Dran-pa Nam-mkha' 's 'abjuration' (nan-ban) is also mentioned in *TTGL* (f. 28a3) and *SG* (f. 51a5) and his name occurs in *rGyal-po bka'-yi thang-yig* (f. 30b6). *TPS* (ii, p. 727) says he was exiled during the persecution. A biography of him in eight volumes is said to have been discovered by gSang-sngags Gling-pa (see *infra*, p. 346, l. 27).

[1] A passage from his life story has been translated into English by D. L. Snellgrove and H. Richardson, op. cit., pp. 103–4.

[2] *TTGL*, f. 28a4.

[3] See *supra*, pp. xxi–vi.

[4] See *infra*, p. 15 n. 3.

doctrines as they survive in the *bKa'-'gyur* represent a stage in the development of Bon which was only reached after contact with Buddhism had led the Bon-pos to rebuild their doctrinal system along Buddhist lines, that is to say when Bon rose again after the second persecution. It is also the view of Tibetan Buddhists that many Bon-po texts are plagiaries. The Bon-po himself recognizes that Bon and Buddhist teachings are identical. This is clearly stated by Dran-pa Nam-mkha'[1] and our author.[2] sTon-pa gShen-rab, the founder of Bon, is believed to have manifested himself as four distinct masters (gTsug-lag srid-pa'i bu-bzhi), (i) as dPyad-bu Khri-shes who teaches medicine, (ii) as gTo-bu 'Bum-sangs who teaches ritual, (iii) as Kong-tse who teaches astrology, and (iv) as Shākya Muni who teaches Dharma. However, our text gives only two of the above, and with different names: 'Phrul-bu-chung for astrology and Yid-las sPrul-ba for medicine. However, the four including Shākya Muni are mentioned in *GRB* (pp. 19–20) and *bsGrags-byang* (f. 17a6). In view of this Bon-pos have never seen any reason to contest the fundamental theories of Buddhism such as the ideal of Enlightenment, the doctrines of rebirth, impermanence, and vacuity (stong-pa-nyid). In Tibet it is the Buddhists who call Bon-pos heretics (Phyi-pa, outsider) since they do not consider Shākya Muni as the founder of their religion. On the other hand, Bon-pos do not consider the Buddhists as heretics, because in following Shākya Muni they are simply following another aspect of sTon-pa gShen-rab. However, although—in the Bon-po view—Bon existed in complete form before any word of Buddhism ever came to be heard in Tibet, as a result of the persecutions almost the entire body of Bon-po literature was believed to have been abandoned or concealed. The later development of Bon therefore took the form of a gradual rediscovery of those hidden texts, and this our text displays with particular amplitude. The first masters who came upon the Bon-po texts in (*STNN*) A.D. 913 are said to have been some Nepalese wanderers, and this was followed by similar events in various places till gShen-chen Klu-dga' 's time (*STNN*) 996–1035.[3] His findings took place in (*STNN*) 1017. Although

[1] See *infra*, pp. 90–1.
[2] See *infra*, pp. 185–7.
[3] See *infra*, pp. 126–31.

he was not the first master who found Bon-po texts he is considered the most renowned teacher and the chief of the many 'text discoverers' (gter-ston) who followed him in later centuries. From his discoveries Bon-pos began to build up the materials which were later grouped into two parts known as *bKa'-'gyur* and *brTen-'gyur*. Because of his fame many disciples sought his spiritual instructions, and it was through his influence that Bon-pos later scarcely made any attempt to draw converts or to earn support from powerful men, whilst the Buddhist hierarchies invariably sought favours from the rulers of Tibet as well as those of foreign countries, a practice which led ultimately to the weakening of Tibet as a nation. This attitude may have been due to distant memories of the times when political participation had resulted in Bon-pos being obliged to save their ancient national and religious culture by desperate means. gShen-chen Klu-dga' was an ordinary householder working among his village people. Most of his life was spent in a hermitage called Brag-dkar which was near his village in the district of 'Bri-mtshams mtha'-dkar in gTsang. It is said that it was in this place that he had first received signs that he would discover Bon-po texts. His findings involved such a wide variety of texts that in later centuries he was charged with plagiarism by Buddhists, especially by the 'Bri-gung bka'-brgyud-pas and dGe-lugs-pas.[1] Among his followers the masters of Bru, Zhu, sPa, and rMe'u were the most influential. These clans were all resident in areas close to large Buddhist centres and they were the main centres of later developments. The functions of these clans are very similar to that of Sa-skya and other well-known Buddhist families. In each place a monastery was founded by a religious master belonging to that particular clan whilst his brother took charge of the affairs of the family. The spiritual succession usually passed from uncle to nephew (khu-dbon) so that a religious tradition would grow up which traced its source back to a religious master also coming from that particular family. Among the clans Bru and rMe'u were particularly active in establishing religious centres. The monastery known as gYas-ru dben-sa-kha was founded in (*STNN*) 1072 in gTsang by Bru gYung-drung

[1] 'Jam-dbyangs bZhed-pa, *Grub-mtha'i rnam-bshad rang-gzhan grub-mtha' kun-dang zab-don mchog-tu gsal-ba kun-bzang zhing-gi nyi-ma lung-rigs rgya-mtsho skye-dgu'i re-ba kun-skongs*, section ka, ff. 67a8–68a. Also see *infra*, p. 130.

Bla-ma and there were many writers in these monasteries. The scholar of rMe'u, Tshul-khrims dPal-chen (b. *STNN* 1052), founded the monastery known as dPal-ldan bzang-ri in the eleventh century in sNye-mo in gTsang, and later many well-known monk-scholars belonged to this tradition.

Not all the discoverers of the Bon-po texts were learned men. Many of them were simply shepherds, hunters, pilgrims, traders, and travellers who just happened to come across texts which were either abandoned or just left as objects of worship or purposely hidden in ancient temples, stūpas, caves, the archives of old families and even in all kinds of wooden, metal, and clay images. However, a friendly relationship existed between Bon-pos and the rNying-ma-pas. When a Bon-po found a Buddhist text he simply handed it over to a rNying-ma-pa, and the same in reverse. Even Textual Initiation (lung) is transmitted from one to the other, and considered highly important in both traditions when a new text comes to light. Since this was a time of resurgence of religious activities, whilst Bon-pos and rNying-ma-pas were busy building up their new collections which were precious to them since they believed that the texts had been hidden by the ancient masters whose spirits were now in themselves, other Buddhist monks made journeys to India seeking new authentic Buddhist texts and religious masters from whom they could obtain personal spiritual instructions impossible with gTer-ma,[1] though, of course, even Bon-pos praise a text if it is believed to have enjoyed continuous transmission and not been buried in the ground. Consider, for instance, the text called *'Dul-ba kun-'byung dbyings-dag rgyud* which the abbot Nyi-ma bsTan-'dzin describes as gter-du ma-song-ba'i bon gser-gyi zhun-ma dang mtshungs-pa (an unburied text is like molten gold, *KTDG*, p. 3). The emphasis on rediscovered texts created a chance for gain by means of forgeries. This has led to concern with authenticity.

If an important part of Bon doctrine is considered as derived from Buddhism, then of course many of the texts said to have been found cannot in fact have lain hidden since the time of the persecutions, and the assumption is therefore made by European historians that the texts were in fact composed by those who claim to have rediscovered them, and the stories concerning their

[1] i.e. rediscovered texts.

discovery invented to give them authority. No such texts would then be authentic in the way Bon-pos believe—hence the term 'apocryphal' applied by Western scholars to gTer-ma.[1] Even so this does not seem to exclude the possibility that some texts were actually hidden or mislaid and then refound especially when the discoverers were unlettered men. Moreover, not all gTer-ma relate to matters in which Bon and Buddhism coincide. The possibility of texts of this kind dating back to pre-persecution times would then be limited only by the antiquity of the Tibetan written language, and it is now admitted by some Western scholars that written Tibetan may go back beyond the formal introduction of Buddhism in the seventh century.[2] These texts would be those relating to the matters covered by the first four of the Nine Ways, often grouped under the collective name of Bon of Cause (rgyu'i bon).[3] In this area Western scholars agree that we have Bon uninfluenced by Buddhism. Actually, however, in the first persecution it is specifically stated by our author that half of the Bon of Cause was permitted to remain by Gri-gum and therefore not concealed. No limitations, however, are suggested concerning what texts were hidden in the second persecution.

The prophetical texts may also cast some light on the problem of antiquity of origin in Bon-po texts. For example, the *Srid-rgyud*, reported to be the work of Dran-pa Nam-mkha' (eighth century), also contains prophetical passages attributed to other teachers of his time such as sTong-rgyung mThu-chen. It was rediscovered in 1310 by Gyer Thogs-med (b. *STNN* 1280), but in the prophecies, though many names are given of men who lived after the eighth century and before 1310, none lived later than 1310. gShen-chen Klu-dga' (*STNN* 996–1035, lHa-ri gNyen-po (*STNN* 1024–91), Gu-ru rNon-rtse (b. *STNN* 1136), and dPon-gsas Khyung-rgod-rtsal (b. *STNN* 1175) are examples. The *Kha-byang gsal-byed nyi-ma'i dkyil-'khor* is said to have been passed on orally to Blo-ldan sNying-po (b. *STNN* 1360) by sTang-chen dMu-tsha Gyer-med (eighth century) and contains names like mNyam-med Shes-rab rGyal-mtshan (*STNN* 1356–1415). The only case in which a prophecy in a text relates to an

[1] *TPS* i, p. 109.

[2] B. Laufer, 'Origin of Tibetan Writing', *JAOS*, vol. 38 (1918), pp. 34–7.

[3] See *infra*, p. 31 n. 2.

individual who was born considerably later than its alleged discoverer is the *Tshe-dbang bod-yul-ma'i lung-bstan.*[1] It concerns Tshe-dbang Rig-'dzin whose father is said to have been Dran-pa Nam-mkha'. The text is reputed to have been discovered in *(STNN)* 1269 by Bon-zhig gYung-drung Gling-pa (b. 1346-1405) , although Bru mTshungs-med bSod-nams Blo-gros (*STNN* 1337-1401) is mentioned in one of the prophecies. But the date of its discovery is surrounded by some confusion, for the chronologist (*STNN,* p. 23) calls the year an Iron-Hare year, when in fact 1269 is Earth-Snake. Iron-Hare does not come until 1291. Another possibility is that he confused it with Earth-Hare year which is 1279.

The accusation that textual discovery is in large measure a fiction employed by the Bon-pos to invest texts with an antiquity they do not possess is one which the rNying-ma-pas have had to face as much as the Bon-pos. However, the most important texts of the rNying-ma-pas, such as the *rGyud-'bum* are not believed to have originated in finds of this kind, but to have been the revelations of mKha'-'gro-ma. This constitutes a method of transmission unknown to Bon. But something not unlike it is to be found in a certain type of oral tradition. It is true that the main text of the Oral Tradition, known as the *Zhang-zhung snyan-brgyud,* is a text which enjoyed continuous transmission from Gyer-spungs sNang-bzher Lod-po (eighth century) to our author's day, and is said always to have been passed from one master to not more than two pupils, for which reason it is sometimes called *Chig-brgyud* ('Single transmission'). However, there is also another kind which is believed to have been passed on orally in a vision by a master, who had lived at a time of persecution, to a teacher living at a very much later date who in some cases claims to be a reincarnation of the original master. For example, Gyer-mi Nyi-'od (b. *STNN* 1108), who seems to be the first recipient of this kind of tradition, received precepts orally in a vision from Dran-pa Nam-mkha' (eighth century). But in proportion to the gTer-ma, even this second kind of Oral Tradition is much less in quantity, as will be seen in Section VII. The longest work of this kind is the *gZi-brjid* (also known as *Dri-*

[1] See MS. in Snellgrove Collection bearing the title *Shog-dril bcu-ba lung-bstan ngos-bzung.* It is the seventeenth section of the *Tshe-dbang bod-yul-ma* or *sNyan-(b)rgyud rin-chen sgron-gsal.*

med). It is reputed to have been passed on orally to Blo-ldan sNying-po (*b. STNN* 1360) by sTang-chen dMu-tsha Gyer-med (eighth century). Extracts from this work concerning essential parts of Bon-po doctrine have been worked on by Dr. D. L. Snellgrove and translated into English[1]—the first time any such attempt has been made to understand the full depth of this complex religion. However, a text belonging to the class of the Oral Tradition need not necessarily have come down to us in either of the ways so far discussed. For instance, the *Tshe-dbang bod-yul-ma*, although it bears the title *sNyan-(b)rgyud rin-chen sgron-gsal*, is thought of as having been discovered in the same way as the textual treasure. This might explain why our author has not grouped the gTer-ma and Oral Tradition separately in Section VII, although the degree to which miraculous—hence historically unserviceable—factors are involved is obviously much greater in the one than in the other.

Extent of Survival

Cases of oral revelation seem to begin some two hundred years later than the textual finds, but our author records continuing instances of both right up to the time of his own teachers, bDe-chen Gling-pa (*b. STNN* 1833) and gSang-sngags Gling-pa (b. *STNN* 1864). The full body of pre-persecution teachings is, in fact, regarded by the Bon-pos as not yet having been fully recovered. However, our author's explicit restriction of his allusions to texts reputedly of ancient origin obscures the extent to which the Bon-pos have never ceased adding to the early material by continually producing commentaries and observations.

It is not, moreover, only in this way that our author is selective concerning the later history of Bon. He mentions the foundation of the monastery of sMan-ri in (*STNN*) 1405 in Thob-rgyal in gTsang by mNyam-med Shes-rab rGyal-mtshan (*STNN* 1356–1415) who had been an abbot in gYas-ru dben-sa-kha which was destroyed by flood. He does not relate how, as the dGe-lugs-pas gradually gained a firm footing in the fifteenth century in gTsang, Bon-pos like other minor Buddhist sects became weak and once more suffered minor persecutions, for

[1] The above-mentioned *Nine Ways of Bon*.

example in Khams under the rule of the fifth Dalai Lama.[1] sMan-ri in fact received no direct persecution, but in any case Bon-pos remained active in preserving their tradition, for in (*STNN*) 1834 another monastery, gYung-drung-gling was founded by sNang-ston Zla-ba rGyal-mtshan (b. *STNN* 1796), and a disciple of his, Shes-rab gYung-drung (b. *STNN* 1838) founded the monastery of mKhar-sna not far from sMan-ri. These monasteries remained the main Bon-po centres in central Tibet right up to the Communist Chinese occupation of Tibet in 1959. But there were many other monasteries in central and other parts of Tibet, and rGya-rong is one example. It is here that the printing blocks of nearly the whole *bKa'-'gyur* as contained in *KTDG* were made. For lists and histories of the monasteries I refer the reader to the *gYung-drung bon-gyi bstan-pa byung-ba brjod-pa*, a most comprehensive recent work of dPal-ldan Tshul-khrims—a rare example of this kind of writer among the Tibetan refugees in India. If—as it seems—our author bKra-shis rGyal-mtshan, was reluctant to acknowledge any decline in Bon in recent times, the tragic events of 1959 would have troubled him particularly acutely. He would nevertheless have been pleased to see that they have not succeeded in effacing the tradition of Bon and that monks of high standing in its hierarchy are working together for the restoration of religious life in India. The process of rehabilitation began under the leadership of Slob-dpon bsTan-'dzin rNam-dag at the Bon-po settlement near Simla established in 1966 under the name of Thob-rgyal gsar-pa (New Thob-rgyal). The sixth abbot, Shes-rab bsTan-pa'i rGyal-mtshan, of gYung-drung-gling is also living in the settlement together with the newly appointed abbot, Sangs-rgyas bsTan-'dzin, of sMan-ri who thus figures as the thirty-second in a line of succession extending over more than five and a half centuries.

[1] This persecution occurred in 1649 (*Re'u-mig*). See also Sangs-rgyas rGya-mtsho, *Vaiḍūrya ser-po* (New Delhi, 1960), Part 2, pp. 375, 307; Th'u-bkvan Chos-kyi Nyi-ma, *Grub-mtha' thams-cad-kyi khungs-dang 'dod-tshul ston-pa legs-bshad shel-gyi me-long*, Varanasi, 1963, TA, p. 312; Sum-pa mKhan-po Ye-shes dPal-'byor, *mTsho-sngon-gyi lo-rgyus-sogs bkod-pa'i tshangs-glu gsar-snyan* (*Vaiḍūrya ser-po*, Part 2, and the *Annals of Kokonor*, edited by L. Chandra, New Delhi, 1960), pp. 432–5.

I. Sangs-rgyas bsTan-'dzin lJong-ldong, the present abbot of the new monastery at Dolanji in Himachal Pradesh, India (see p. xl)

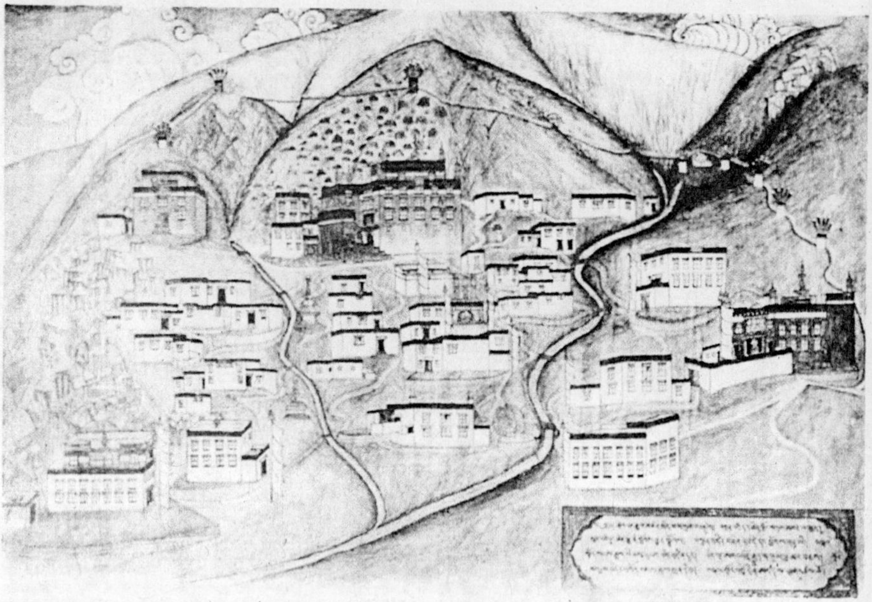

II. sMan-ri, the original monastery in Tibet (painted by A-mchod, photograph from the collection of Per Kvaerne) (see pp. xxxix, 142)

III. gYung-drung-gling (painted by A-mchod, photograph from the collection of Per Kvaerne) (see p. xl)

IV. 'Chi-med gTsug-phud, highly venerated image in bronze (see p. xxi)

V. gTso-mchog, statue in gilt bronze (see p. 135)

VI. sTag-la Me-'bar, statue in gilt bronze (see p. 45, n. 2)

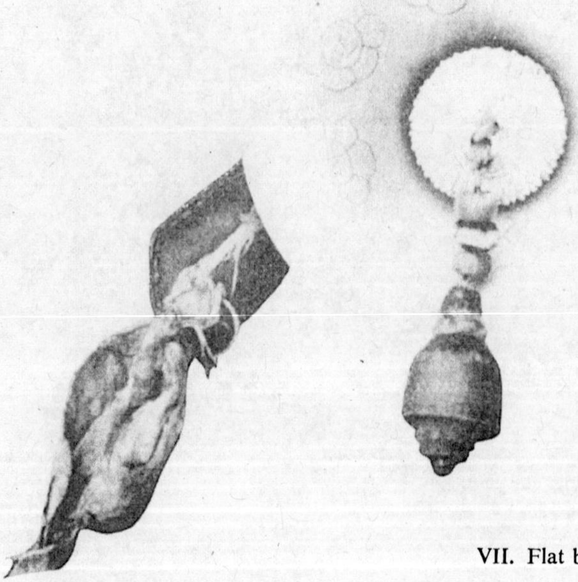

VII. Flat bell (see p. 146)

THE TREASURY OF GOOD SAYINGS

English Translation

SECTION IV

[PART 2]

(115b3) The genealogies of gShen, the master of the Doctrine (and of Bru, Zhu, sPa, rMe'u, and Khyung-po)

A. The main facts
B. General summary

A. I. The lineage of dMu-gshen
II. The lineage of royal Bru
III. The lineage of powerful Zhu
IV. The lineage of holy sPa
V. The lineage of scholarly rMe'u
VI. The lineage of excellent Khyung

I. The lineage of dMu-gshen

a. In 'Ol-mo'i-gling of sTag-gzig[1]
b. In gTsang of Tibet

a. Kong-tsha gYung-drung dBang-ldan,[2] son of the Conqueror, was one of sTon-pa gShen-rab's eight sons; his mother was Kong-za Khri-lcam.[3] sTon-pa gShen-rab was the son of the above-mentioned dMu-rgyal rGyal-bon Thod-dkar.[4] (116a)

[1] On 'Ol-mo'i-gling see Introduction, pp. xxvii–xxxi.

[2] *LShDz* (f. 36a4): *hos bza' rgyal med la sras gto bu 'bum sangs dang / dpyad bu khri shes gnyis 'khrungs / dpo bza' thang mo la sras lung 'dren gsal ba dang / rgyud 'dren sgron ma 'khrungs / gsas bza' ngang ring la sras 'od drug thang po 'khrungs / phya bza' gung drug la rgyal ba'i gdung sob mu cho ldem drug 'khrungs / kong bza' khri lcam la dmu rgyal gyi gdung rgyud 'dzin pa'i rgyal sras g·yung drung dbang ldan 'khrungs / rgya bza' 'phrul bsgyur la sras 'phrul bu chung 'khrungs /*

[3] She was given in marriage to sTon-pa gShen-rab by her father Kong-rje dKar-po in Kong-po. See *gZer-mig*, vol. kha, f. 58a1.

[4] See *LShDz*, f. 31a6.

According to the prophecy in the *bsTan-pa gnyer-gtad-kyi mdo*[1] this lineage will continue till the next Enlightened One appears:

> O you son of a conqueror, Kong-tsha dBang-ldan, . . .
> Until the next Enlightened One comes,
> Spread the lineage of Mi-rje Srid-pa,[2]
> Preserve the lineage of royal dMu.

[1] This is the 61st and last chapter of *gZi-brjid*. sTon-pa gShen-rab's life-story is available in three versions: *'Dus-pa rin-po-che dri-ma med-pa gzi-brjid rab-tu 'bar-ba'i mdo* (often referred to simply as *gZi-brjid* or more often as *mDo dri-med* or just *Dri-med*) is the long version (mdzad-mdo rgyas-pa) and is in twelve volumes with sixty-one chapters (see D. L. Snellgrove, *Nine Ways*, pp. 5–8). It is said to have been passed on orally to sPrul-sku Blo-ldan sNying-po (b. *STNN* 1360*) by sTang-chen dMu-tsha Gyer-med (eighth century A.D.). *KTDG* p. 3: . . . *mdzad mdo rgyas pa sprul sku blo ldan snying po la / stang chen dmu tsha gyer med kyis snyan du brgyud pa mdo bzhi* (see *infra* p. 340, l. 10) *yod pa'i nang tshan dri med gzi brjid bstan pa'i mdo la / dum pa nyi ma'i grangs ldan la le'u drug cu re gcig bzhugs pa'o /* See also *infra*, p. 182. Some extracts known as the Nine Ways (theg-pa dgu (cf. *infra*, p. 31 n. 2)) and taken from chapters 7, 8, 9, 10, 12, 13, 14, 15, and 16 have been edited and translated by Snellgrove, op. cit.

'Dus-pa rin-po-che'i rgyud gzer-mig (often referred to simply as *mDo gzer-mig* or *gZer-mig*) is the medium-length version (mdzad-mdo 'bring-po) in two volumes with eighteen chapters. It is said to have been translated by Vairocana (see *infra* p. 163 n. 1). Later it was rediscovered by Drang-rje bTsun-pa in bSam-yas khri-thang dur-khrod. *KTDG*, p. 3: *mdzad mdo 'bring po gter ston drang rje btsun pas bsam yas khri thang dur khrod nas rnyed pa'i gzer mig ces pa'i mdo dum pa gnyis la le'u bco brgyad yod pa dang /* Drang-rje bTsun-pa was a close contemporary of rMe'u lHa-ri gNyen-po (*STNN* 1024–91). For the full history of this text see *infra*, p. 163. A commentary on this text by Zhang-ston Tshul-khrims Blo-ldan (fourteenth century), and a commentary on *mDo g·yung-drung klong-rgyas*, the ritual part of *gZer-mig*, by 'Gro-mgon bDud-rtsi rGyal-mtshan (a contemporary of 'Gro-mgon Blo-gros rGyal-mtshan (*STNN* 1198–1263) see *infra*, p. 140) are mentioned in *KTDG*, p. 15. The first seven chapters have been edited and translated by A. H. Francke (published in *Asia Major*, *A book of the Tibetan Bon-pos*, i (1924), iii (1926), iv (1927), v (1928), vi (1930), N.S. i, Pt. ii (1949). A brief summary of this work is also given by H. Hoffmann, *The Religions of Tibet*, pp. 85–97.

Dus-gsum sangs-rgyas byung-khungs-kyi mdo (often known as *mDo-'dus*) is the short version (mdzad-mdo bsdus-pa) in one volume with twenty-two chapters. It is said to have been translated by sNya-chen Li-shu sTag-ring (eighth century, see *infra*, p. 56) from sTag-gzig. *TNT*, p. 46: *snya chen li shus rtag gzigs nas bsgyur ba'i mdo 'dus . . . /* It was hidden in bSam-yas mchod-rten dmar-po by sNya-chen Li-shu sTag-ring and later rediscovered by Sad-gu Rin-chen Grags-pa and Dre'u-rgya Ra-dza (also contemporaries of rMe'u lHa-ri gNyen-po). *KTDG*, p. 3: *mdzad-mdo bsdus pa bsam yas mchod rten dmar po nas a tsa ra* (ācārya) *mi gnyis kyis rnyed pa'i mdo bzhi* (see *infra*, p. 320, ll. 35–8) *nang tshan / dus gsum sangs rgyas byung khungs kyi mdo'am mdo 'dus su grags pa le'u nyer bzhi pa dang /* For details of this discovery see *infra*, pp. 160–2.

[2] A name for the lineage of dMu.

---

* All dates in these notes preceded by the abbreviation *STNN* are conversions into European chronology of dates given in that work.

We know that its descendants still exist from innumerable reports in the biographies of ascetics who went to that land[1] by means of magic or who had seen them in their visions.

b. The Son of the Conqueror, gYung-drung dBang-ldan, had four sons: 'Od-kyi rGyal-po, Thog-gi rGyal-po, 'Brug-gi rGyal-po, and 'Gar-bu-chung. The eldest, 'Od-kyi rGyal-po, had three sons: dMu-bon A-pa Ru-ring, dMu-rje Thum-thum rNal-med, and dMu-rje rGyal. From these descended dMu-gshen sNang-ba'i mDog-can[2] and others. From the middle one, Thog-gi rGyal-po, a line of descendants leads down to dMu-gshen Dran-pa Nam-mkha'[3] and his descendants. From the first of the two youngest ones, 'Brug-gi rGyal-po, came all the descendants of the family of dMu-gshen of gTsang in Tibet.[4] (116b) 'Brug-gi rGyal-po had a son dMu-bon Yo'u-brtan; his son was dMu-bon Thong-ltol; his son was dMu-bon sKyes-lo-tshal; his sons were: gShen Grol-ba, dMu-kha sPo-mi-spo, dMu-kha Ye-mi-ye, dMu-le Yol-ba, and dMu-long or 'Brum-bu. At that time the Tibetan king gNya'-khri had a son named Mu-khri bTsan-po who had faith in Bon and, having practised the secret doctrine of sPyi-spungs,[5] he achieved the supreme and the ordinary attainments. In particular, he invited a hundred and eight scholars of Zhang-zhung led by dMu-kha sPo-mi-spo and dMu-rje Yang-rgyal, and paid homage to them. Thenceforward, up to Khri-srong lDe-btsan, during the reigns of thirty-seven kings all Bon-priests were the object of their homage. But when in the course of these reigns an evil-minded king and his ministers wickedly caused the doctrines to decline, all the gShen-po, having hidden the Bon texts, departed, some to the 'Celestial Sphere', some to solitary places for meditation and others to Sog-po sprel-slag-can (Mongolia).[6] (117a) The two dMu-gshen[7] had resided in Tibet during all those reigns, being like gCo-btsun and Mu-zi[8] and having gained power over death. Now they went to the country of

[1] i.e. 'Ol-mo lung-ring.

[2] For more detail see *infra*, p. 44.

[3] See the Introduction, p. xxxii n. 4; *infra*, p. 94 n. 2.

[4] Later this family came to be known as gShen-tshang and the place where they lived is called gShen Dar-lding (see *infra*, p. 132 n. 2).

[5] Concerning Mu-khri bTsan-po and the doctrine of sPyi-spungs see *infra*, p. 44.

[6] A detailed account of this is to be found *infra*, pp. 105 et seq.

[7] dMu-kha sPo-mi-spo and dMu-rje Yang-rgyal.

[8] See *infra*, p. 38 n. 3.

Tsong-ka. A descendant of theirs, called dMu bKra-gsal Klu'i rgyal-po went to 'Dam (in gTsang) and settled down in 'Bri-mtshams. He ruled over all the districts. He married lHa-rgyan and they had three sons: Mi-g·yo mGon-po, rDo-rje mGon-po, and dBang-phyug mGon-po. Mi-g·yo mGon-po had three sons: dPal-mgon-gsas, 'Brug-gsas, and rGod-gsas. As 'Brug-gsas had no son he performed the rites of 'child-procuring' so three sons were born to him. The elder ones were called Klu-dga'[1] and Klu-brtsegs, for they were born after performing the rite of Klu-'bum. The youngest was named Ge-khod as he was born after invoking the Ge-khod Gods. dPal-mgon-gsas is also known as Bon-gyi Srid-g·yang-babs.[2] The lineage of Klu-dga' is described later.[3]

II. The lineage of royal Bru

The lineage of royal Bru has two main branches: (117b) Sa-bru and gNam-bru. Sa-bru is known as dPal-ldan Sa-skya-pa in other chronicles. As for the gNam-bru, the essence of all Enlightened Ones in the person of an individual divine son named 'Od-zer mDangs-ldan, descended to the place of Bar-lha 'od-gsal[4] from the sphere of 'Og-min stug-po bkod-pa,[5] for the sake of sentient beings. Then he decided to go to the human world and so descended at the place of rTsa-gsum-lha[6] where he turned the wheel of Bon for the gods. As he looked at the world from the summit of Mount Meru, he perceived that a demon called Ngam-len Nag-po together with his phantoms was inflicting suffering on humans and animals in the form of various harmful illnesses, and damaging the crops with frost in the countries of Uḍḍiyāna,[7] Gilgit,[8] and Tho-gar.[9] In order to convert them he rode on a drum with magical skill; the gshen of Ya-ngal guided him, and the gshen of mTsho-cog supported his body and together with musical sounds he went to the countries

[1] A brief life-story of him (*STNN* 996–1035) is to be found *infra*, pp. 126–9.

[2] Cf. this genealogy *bsTan-'byung*, f. 103a4.

[3] See *infra*, p. 132.

[4] A name for the regions similar to those known in Buddhism as Avṛha, Atapa, Sudṛśa, and Sudarśana (*Mvy* 3102, 3103, 3104, 3105).

[5] Similar to Buddhist Akaniṣṭa (*Mvy* 3106).

[6] Similar to Buddhist Trāyastriṃśa (*Mvy* 3079).

[7] Tib. O-rgyan.

[8] Tib. Bru-sha.

[9] On Tho-gar see Das, *Tibetan–English Dictionary*, p. 589.

of Uḍḍiyāna, Gilgit, and Tho-gar. The king of Tho-gar, Sad-ver gSal-'bar, in whom a strong faith arose, invited him to his palace. The king asked a Bram-ze called gSal-'bar to examine the marks on the body of this son of a god and to give him a meaningful name (118a). The Bram-ze said:

> These things being due to the external and internal harmony of the Law of Interdependence,
> He (is called) Bru since he came down from heaven.
> He (is called) Sha since he was truly of divine birth,
> (And) as his cranium had a hole in it he was called Bru-sha gNam-gsas sPyi-brtol.

In that country Bru-sha gNam-gsas sPyi-brtol subdued the demon Ngam-len Nag-po and converted all his attendants. He made humans and animals happy. As he expounded the high ways of Bon to the people of the country many of them attained supernatural powers. Moreover, having been offered the kingdom by the king of Tho-gar, Sad-ve gSal-'bar, he ruled the whole country. He had a son, lHa-bu gSas-chung, and lHa-bu gSas-chung had a son mTsho-btsan-skyes who was a great translator. mTsho-btsan-skyes had nine sons. The five elder brothers lived in Gilgit. And the four younger ones quarrelled at first with bTsad-po rTsod-sde of mNga'-ris, but afterwards bTsad-po rTsod-sde invited them and paid them homage. (Consequently) all the lands from the three regions of mNga'-ris[1] down to the four quarters of Tibet[2] came under the domination of Gilgit.[3]

[1] They are sPu-rangs gangs-kyis bskor, Gu-ge g·ya'-yis bskor and Mang-yul chab-kyis bskor, see R. A. Stein, *L'épopée tibétaine de Gesar dans sa version lamaique de Ling*, Paris, 1956, p. 31.

[2] They are gYas-ru, gYon-ru, dBus-ru, and Ru-lag, see *infra*, p. 40 (for some variant spellings see Stein, op. cit., p. 31). I translate ru-bzhi the 'Four Quarters', but the implication is the 'Four Regimental Territories'. The word ru-ba was originally applied to nomads and is still so used in Amdo, for when a nomadic tribe moves from one place to another—as they do all the year round—they say ru spor-ba = 'move the settlement'. When the Tibetans took up arms and moved about in armed bands ru simply came to mean 'army'. I can cite many instances of this usage: ru-dpon = 'commander', ru-mtshon = 'spear', ru-dar = 'flag', ru-'dren sde-bzhi = the 'four leading armies'. 'Horn' or 'brigade' (F. W. Thomas, *Tibetan Literary Texts and Documents Concerning Chinese Turkestan*, pt. ii, p. 418), 'Banner' or 'Wing' (*TPS* ii, p. 738) have been suggested to explain the use of ru-bzhi to indicate the area of dBus-gTsang, which was divided into four regimental territories each governed by two or three nobles who led the army of his particular area into battle. 'Brigade' comes closest to my interpretation.

[3] No other history records any domination by Gilgit over Tibet. However, according to *bsTan-'byung* (f. 106a7) a Tibetan king (btsad-po) did invade Gilgit

(118b) One of these four younger sons (of mTsho-btsan-skyes) was named gYung-drung rGyal-mtshan. He proceeded to gTsang and had two sons. The elder son was Khyung-nag-'dzin; he had a son gYung-drung Seng-ge. gYung-drung Seng-ge had three sons. The eldest was Nam-mkha' gYung-drung;[1] two of his four sons were: Rin-chen rGyal-mtshan and Shes-rab rGyal-mtshan.[2] They were contemporary with the Great Incarnation gShen (Klu-dga') 'the Deathless Second Enlightened One'. The great Bru father (Nam-mkha' gYung-drung) and son (Khyung-gi rGyal-mtshan) met the lama Klu-dga', the Great gShen, and (later) at the great monastery of gYas-ru dben-sa-kha[3] the study of metaphysics including works like the *mTshan-nyid srid-pa'i mdzod-phug*[4] was established. They laboured extensively to teach the doctrine by means of exposition, disputation, and composition. I shall give their genealogy later.[5]

III. The lineage of powerful Zhu

The lineage, which descended from sMug-po-ldang, has two branches in the Upper Land (Western Tibet): Ba-tshab and 'Bri-g·yas. A descendant of 'Bri-g·yas was the first who per-

and this seems to be in agreement with the *THD* (p. 25) in which it is stated that a Tibetan minister, sKyes-bzang, invaded Gilgit in A.D. 737.

[1] *STNN* 994–1054.

[2] Concerning this genealogy, cf. *bsTan-'byung*, ff. 104b7 et seq.

[3] See *infra*, p. 139 n. 1.

[4] *Lung-mtshan-nyid srid-pa'i mdzod-phug* (often referred to as *Srid-pa'i mdzod-phug* or *mDzod-phug* or simply *mDzod*) is considered to belong to the class of bKa'. It is said to have been translated from the Zhang-zhung language by sTong-rgyung mThu-chen of Zhang-zhung and Se-bon Sha-ri dBu-chen of Tibet (eighth century). It was rediscovered by gShen-chen Klu-dga' (see *infra*, p. 126), by gNyan-ston Shes-rab Seng-ge (see *infra*, p. 153 n. 4) and again by rMa-ston Srol-'dzin (see *infra*, p. 168 n. 3). See also *KTDG*, p. 2.

The work is mainly concerned with cosmogony. Many commentaries were composed on this work (see *KTDG*, p. 14). *mDzod sgra-'grel 'phrul-gyi lde-mig* of Dran-pa Nam-mkha' (eighth century) known in short as *mDzod sgra-'grel* or *sGra-'grel* is regarded as of special importance among the commentaries. According to the colophon it appears to have been rediscovered by rMa Jo-lcam who was also known as rMa lCam-me and was a son of rMa-ston Srol-'dzin (b. *STNN* 1092). However, our author makes no mention of it either in the list of rMa lCam-me's discoveries (see *infra*, p. 169) or anywhere else. *KTDG*, p. 14 says simply that it belongs to the Northern Textual Treasure. Thus since rMa lCam-me's discoveries took place in Byang gsang-brag rgya-bo we may safely say that the text was rediscovered by rMa lCam-me, a fact which escaped our author's eye though he used it as one of his principal sources.

[5] See *infra*, p. 139.

formed the 'posthumous evocation ritual' and also the founder of the (119a) spiritual lineage of Zhu-g·yas. He was named gShen lCags-kyi Bya-ru-can, the Bon-po of gYas and was an authority on the three hundred and sixty kinds of 'evocation ritual of the spirits of the dead'.[1] He was the chief of the Bon-pos who performed the 'posthumous evocation ritual of the killed' and the 'ritual of guidance' when the prince sPu-lde Gung-rgyal invited many Bon-priests at the time of his father's death. The prince's father the king Gri-gum was murdered by Lo-ngam rTa-rdzi as a punishment for his opposition to Bon during his reign.[2] He was one of the 'Intervening Pair'. Then from Srid-gshen sKal-pa bZang-po, the son of dBal-bon Dri-rgod, came a string of descendants like a crystal-rosary ending with Thar-ba Byang-chub. As they settled in Zhu-yi Ba-mo of gTsang they became known as Zhu-tshang. Thar-ba Byang-chub had three sons: lHa-legs, lHa-rung, and Legs-po. Legs-po[3] heard that the Great gShen had rediscovered the textual treasure in 'Bri-mtshams and so he went to meet that lama. The lama thought that he was a suitable disciple and imparted to him many kinds of Bon. In particular, he made him master of the secret doctrine of the Mental Teachings. And so he became known as Zhu-g·yas Legs-po, the Great gShen Meditator.[4] His descendants up to the present I shall briefly review later.[5]

IV. The lineage of holy sPa

A gracious and beautiful descendant of Sangs-po 'Bum-khri and Chu-lcam rGyal-mo[6] came down (119b) from

[1] For more texts of this kind see *infra*, p. 283, ll. 36–7, p. 313, ll. 6–12.

[2] A detailed account of his persecution of Bon is to be found *infra*, pp. 58 et seq.

[3] Born *STNN* 1002.

[4] Concerning this genealogy cf. *bsTan-'byung*, f. 107b6.

[5] See *infra*, p. 137.

[6] Sangs-po 'Bum-khri and Chu-lcam rGyal-mo represent very important figures in Bon-po tradition. They came from eggs and are said to be the original parents of man and animals. Sangs-po is called the king of Phenomenal Existence (yod-khams srid pa'i rgyal-po) and stands in opposition to the king of Nothingness (med-khams stong-pa'i rgyal-po). These two kings represent white and black, right and wrong, and thus god and demon who are born together with every human being. See *mDzod-phug*, p. 6; *sGra-'grel*, p. 52; *SG*, f. 22a1; mNyam-med Shes-rab rGyal-mtshan (*STNN* 1356–1415, for his life see *infra*, p. 140), *mDzod-'grel 'phrul-gyi sgron-me*, f. 10b1, 12a7; sGa-ston Tshul-khrims rGyal-mtshan (fourteenth century), *mDzod kun-las btus-pa'i 'grel-ba rnam-par 'byed-pa'i lde-*

the place of the Gods of Clear Light to the place of rTsa-gsum-lha.[1] He turned the wheel of Bon for the gods. Having decided to propagate Bon in the country of Zhang-zhung in the Southern Island (jambu-dvīpa), he proceeded to rNam-rgyal lha-rtse in Zhang-zhung. He exhibited various supernatural powers. Then he went to a crystal cave on Mount Kailāsa and, having performed ascetic practices for three years, achieved union with his three tutelary deities. Whereupon he assumed the name of Khri-mon lCags-kyi Bya-ru-can. In the country the people used to say: 'On the earth (only) the king of Zhang-zhung is great, in the heaven (only) the god's son sPa-ba is beautiful', so since then he has been called holy sPa. The kings of Tibet paid homage to his descendants whose line was like a rosary of gems. They spread the doctrine of Bon in all directions. One of his descendants, sPa-ston sPa-mchog,[2] was contemporary with Klu-dga', the Great gShen. Hearing that the Great gShen had discovered the textual treasure in 'Bri-mtshams, sPa-ston went to meet him and so the Great gShen declared sPa-ston a master of Tantric Teachings and taught him the *Khro-bo dbang-chen* and other tantric doctrines. The history and genealogy of sPa-ston sPa-mchog will be given later.[3]

(120a) V. The lineage of scholarly rMe'u

A descendant of the father and mother[4] of phenomenal existence came down from the (realm of) the Gods of Clear

mig, f. 18b2 (see *infra*, p. 22 n. 5). Cf. *gZi-brjid*, vol. kha, book 3, f. 22a1 (trans. D. L. Snellgrove, *Nine Ways*, p. 67); *gZer-mig*, vol. ka, f. 21b5 (trans. A. H. Francke, *A Book of Tibetan Bonpos*, *Asia Major*, i (1924), p. 329, and H. Hoffmann, *The Religions of Tibet*, pp. 104–5).

Sangs-po also plays many roles in gShen-rab's life. In the trinity lHa gShen Srid-pa (i.e. gShen-lha 'Od-dkar, sTon-pa gShen-rab and Srid-pa Sangs-po 'Bum-khri), see *gZer-mig*, vol. ka, f. 19b2 (trans. Francke, op. cit., p. 326)) he represents the third, the God of Phenomenal Existence. Chu-lcam represents in esoterical texts the Great Mother (yum-chen) Sa-trig Er-sangs (i.e. Shes-rab Byams-ma) and in tantric texts and in the Great Perfection she represents lHa-mo bZang-za Ring-btsun (*sGra-'grel*, p. 54, cf. *LShDz*, f. 62a4 and *ZhNyl*, f. 11a1) as well as the religious protector known as Srid-pa rGyal-mo (the queen of Phenomenal Existence, *LShDz*, f. 72a1) who is one of the Ma, bDud, and bTsan gsum (see *infra*, p. 48 n. 4). For her iconography as a religious protector see *infra*, p. 135.

[1] Trāyastriṃśa (*Mvy* 3079).

[2] He was born in *STNN* 1014. Concerning him see *infra*, p. 135.

[3] See *infra*, p. 135. Concerning this genealogy cf. *bsTan-'byung*, f. 110a2.

[4] See *supra*, p. 9 n. 6.

Light and, having been born in the family of Yig-tshang-can he had two sons: rMa and rMe'u. The latter had a son named Ngam-len sKyol-po and, having performed the rite of dBal-phur,[1] he beheld the countenance of his tutelary divinity and so attained supernatural powers. He rode a turquoise dragon and, using his rosary of rag-sha (a nut) as a whip, he travelled from the snowy mountain Kailāsa to the peak of Mount lHa-ri gyang-tho. The king gNya'-khri bTsan-po paid him homage. Later, having transformed himself into the bodies of two conch-like vultures which flew to the place of gYas-ru-shangs (in gTsang) and after flying round and round landed on the top of Shun-gyi sman-mo g·yu-mkhar. There they became two bright crystal eggs from which rMe'u 'Dul-ba-brtson and gYu-gshen Tho-dkar were born. In Zhog they parted, one going up, the other down. The one that went up did much to promote higher meditation. The one that went down had a son named gYu-gshen; his son was rMe'u rGyal-gyi lHun-po; his son was sKyid-gsum-'dzom; he had two sons: sTong-chab and Pad-stong. sTong-chab had three sons. The middle one was called rMe'u-rog dBal-bon; he had a son lHa-ri gNyen-po[2] who was known as the second 'Lion of Speech';[3] (120b) his son was gSas-mkhar Bla-ma; he had four sons and the third one was named Shākya-brtan; he had four sons, the eldest of whom was dGongs-mdzod, the Great Hermit of rMe'u.[4] lHa-ri gNyen-po and Dam-pa, the Hermit are known as the 'Two rMe'u sTon-sgom' (scholar and meditator).[5] The stories of their contact with the teachers of Bru, Zhu, and sPa, and their genealogy are related below.[6]

VI. The lineage of excellent Khyung

Rig-snang 'Od-gyi rGyal-po, the manifestation of Kun-tu bZang-po,[7] decided to help sentient beings. Three garuḍa birds emanated from his body, speech, and mind who flew and landed in the grove of beautiful flowers of Kha-yug in Zhang-zhung. The people of the country were astonished to see them and said that they had never seen such birds, but an old man remarked

[1] On dBal-phur see *infra*, p. 45 n. 2.
[2] *STNN* 1024–91.
[3] Tib. sMra-ba'i Seng-ge.
[4] *STNN* 1030–96.
[5] Concerning this genealogy cf. *bsTan-'byung*, f. 108b6.
[6] See *infra*, pp. 137 et seq.
[7] Similar to Buddhist Samantabhadra (*Mvy* 648).

that the birds were male garuḍa birds, for they had horns. When the three birds flew away the people looked in the place where they had been and found four eggs rolling about, one white, one black, one yellow, and one variegated which had been produced by the warmth of the touch of the birds' claws on the ground. From each egg appeared a handsome boy and they were given the names: Khyung-dkar Thog-la-'bar, Khyung-ser lHa-khyung, (121a) Khyung-'phags Khra-mo, and Mu-khyung-rgyan. So it is said. Each of them owned a precious 'life-stone',[1] a self-produced precious castle, and a miraculously created turquoise lake. The eldest brother Khyung-thog-'bar built a hundred and eight shining temples. The second brother lHa-khyung-rgyan erected the temple of gZo-bo khyung-lag. The third brother Khyung-'phags Khra-mo built the temple of lHa-rtse gung-nam. The youngest brother Mu-khyung-rgyan built eight temples. As they gained power over death they laboured extensively for the welfare of sentient beings. They were worshipped by the early kings of Zhang-zhung. The Tibetan kings from gNya'-khri bTsan-po down to Seng-khri bTsan-po also highly revered them. After a period of opposition to Bon by Gri-gum, the prince sPu-lde Gung-rgyal invited many Bon-priests including Mu-khyung-rgyan, lHa-khyung-rgyan, and others.[2] He venerated them highly. Their doctrines were spread again extensively. Mu-khyung-rgyan had two sons: sTag-sgra Don-gtsug and dPal-gyi Gir-ti. sTag-sgra Don-gtsug went to the country of sTag-gzig and brought back many texts (121b) of Bon to Zhang-zhung and Tibet. He made translations of them and spread the doctrines. When Khri-srong lDe-btsan assassinated the king of Zhang-zhung (Lig-mi-rgya),[3] Khyung-po sTag-sgra Don-gtsug ascended the throne and upheld both the laws of the king (his predecessor) and the religious rules of Bon.

dPal-gyi Gir-ti had a son mChog-gi sGron-ma dPung-sgra-zur; his son was bKra-rgyal; his son was Legs-mgon; his son was Gyer-chen Zla-med; he had two sons: Ra-sangs Khri-ne and Ra-sangs Khod-ram; the latter's son was Ra-sangs Klu-rgyal. sTag-sgra Don-gtsug had a son bTsan-sgra Don-gtsug; his son was Gyer-nam Zur-rtse; his sons were sTong-rgyung Ring-mo and Khyung-rgyal sTag-la-skyes.

[1] Tib. bla-rdo.

[2] Cf. *supra*, p. 9.

[3] For details see *infra*, pp. 86–7.

sTong-rgyung Ring-mo ascended the throne to which sTag-sgra Don-gtsug had succeeded when the king Lig-mi-rgya was assassinated. sDong-rgyal from the upper part of Zhang-zhung and sDong-dmigs from the lower part said that it was wrong for the throne to be held by an uncle and a nephew[1] and came with an army. sTong-rgyung Ring-mo lost his throne and escaped. On the way—an indication of his supernatural powers—wherever his feet and walking stick (122a) touched three flowers appeared. The soldiers of Zhang-zhung chased him by following the footprints which he left on the way. But he, realizing this, transformed himself into water when he reached the lake of rMa'i bKra-ring-lha in mDo-khams and so, leaving no trace, got away. Thus arose the saying: 'The yogin is not attached to his supernatural powers, but his supernatural powers are attached to him.' Khyung-po rNal-'byor was the son of (Khyung-rgyal) sTag-la-skyes and was the father of Khyung-po Mi-la Grub-pa. Mi-la Grub-pa was also called Shes-rab rGyal-mtshan. His son was Mi-la Thos-pa dGa'-ba and later he was known as Mi-la Ras-pa.[2]

Khyung-'phags Khra-mo[3] was held in great reverence by the line of the kings of Zhang-zhung and Tibet. Eventually he rode a blue dragon and went to rGya-mo-rong of mDo-smad. He married lHa-mo mDangs-ldan. He had four sons who were known as 'the Four Eternal Sons' and several others. The doctrines of Bon flourished, and his authority increased. In my opinion this was the time when Vai-ro[4] went to rGya-mo-rong.

B. General summary

In the Upper Land there were (the teachers who belonged to) Bru, Zhu, sPa, rMe'u, (122b) the lineage of dMu-gshen; and the Eighteen Teachers of gYas-ru,[5] etc. In the Middle Land there were the teachers of white, black, and yellow Khyung-po; and the Eighteen Ascetics of mDo-khams, etc. In the Lower Land there were the Four Swastika Sons, etc. There are still innumerable descendants of these ascetics in gTsang, dBus, and

[1] sTong-rgyung Ring-mo the uncle, sTag-sgra Don-gtsug the nephew.

[2] For this genealogy, cf. *bsTan-'byung*, ff. 110b7 et seq.

[3] See *supra*, p. 12.

[4] On Vairocana see *infra*, p. 23 n. 2.

[5] For the list of these teachers see *infra*, p. 140.

mDo-khams. They are of noble birth since although human they are descended from gods; they are of good origin since they are descended from knowledge-holders; they are efficient in promoting the welfare of sentient beings since they are blessed by the Enlightened Ones of ten quarters. The *Bla-ma rig-'dzin-gyi skong-ba*[1] says:

Holy persons, descendants (of ascetics), blessed (by Enlightened Ones),
I, not knowing their efficiency in promoting the welfare of sentient beings,
Have blasphemed, reviled, despised them with untrue words,
As I now confess to the lamas who are their descendants.

The facts are these. Therefore, as long as there are such descendants in the world the line of distinguished royal families will survive and all the Doctrines of the Enlightened One will accordingly continue to exist, flourish and spread, and the welfare of sentient beings be promoted. The king, the priest, and the doctrine came into existence together as of equal authority; they continue to exist together as priest and patron.

[1] A ritual text.

SECTION V

The first appearance of the precious doctrines of Everlasting Bon of the Enlightened One and the rise and decline of its exposition and performance in India, China, Zhang-zhung, and especially Tibet, Land of the Snows[1]

(123a) Having thus outlined the history of the lineages of the kings and the gShen, and the source of the doctrine, I shall expound how his doctrine was spread from 'Ol-mo'i-gling to other countries and, in particular, Tibet.

A. Outline
B. Detailed survey

A. The *mDo-'dus*[2] says:

> The 'Original Words' and later doctrines of Bon
> Were translated into various languages
> By each of the Six Translators in his own country
> From the language of the Eternal Gods.

According to this work, then, the 'Original Words' were delivered by the Teacher, and the three profound forms of Propagation of Bon Doctrine,[3] which developed in 'Ol-mo'i-gling after

[1] This title and all subsequent titles appear in the original text—according to the Tibetan custom—at the end not the beginning of the section.

[2] See *supra*, p. 4 n. 1.

[3] There are three kinds of *bsgrags-pa skor-gsum*: The Three Cycles of the Propagation of Sher-phyin (sher-phyin bsgrags-pa skor-gsum) for which see *KTDG*, p. 6; the Three Cycles of the Propagation of sPyi-spungs (spyi-spungs bsgrags-pa skor-gsum) and the Three Cycles of the Propagation of the Great Perfection (rdzogs-chen bsgrags-pa skor-gsum). For details of the latter see *LShDz*, ff. 98a1 et seq. and *infra*, pp. 56, 154–6.

The Three Cycles of Propagation of sPyi-spungs with which we are concerned are said to have been propagated in the land of Gods, of Serpents, and of Man by lHa'i gShen-po Yongs-su Dag-pa, Klu'i gShen-po Ye-shes sNying-po, and

the death of the Teacher, were taken by the Six Great Translators to their own countries as soon as they had become proficient in the three wisdoms[1] under Mu-cho[2] in 'Ol-mo'i-gling. They made translations of them and made them known. The *mDo-'dus* and *rTsa-rgyud nyi-sgron*[3] are in agreement over the Six Translators: (123b) The eminent translators are dMu-tsha Tra-he of sTag-gzig, Khri-thog sPa-tsha of Zhang-zhung, Hu-lu sPa-legs of Sum-pa, lHa-bdag sNgags-dro of India, Legs-tang rMang-po of China, and gSer-thog lCe-'byams of Phrom. They studied under Mu-cho and possessed miraculous powers.

How the translations were made

The language of the Eternal Gods derived from the speech of the 'God of dMu-gshen', and was the language of the people of

rGyal-rigs-kyi gShen-po Mi-lus bSam-legs (concerning the life-stories of these teachers see *LShDz*, ff. 74a3 et seq., and Introduction, *supra*, pp. xxii–iv). *GRB* quotes *mDo'dus*, p. 32:

mthar ni nga yi bstan pa 'di /
mang la rgyas pa'i bon sde dang /
nyung la 'dus pa'i bon sde dang /
gsang ba zab pa'i bon sde rnams /
lha yul klu yul mi yul du /
brgyud nas 'byung ste dar rgyas so / . . .
lha bon yongs su dag pa dang /
klu bon ye shes snying po dang /
rgyal ni mi lus bsam legs kyi /
bon rnams 'ol mo gling du 'byung /
ston pa mya ngan 'das rjes su /
'ol mo gling du bon rnams 'dus /

These are mostly tantric teachings: *man ngag mang la 'grel ba don rgyud rgyas pa'i skor . . . / man ngag nyung la 'dus pa ngo sprod kyi skor . . . / man ngag dmar la 'dril ba lung don 'bring po'i skor . . . /* See *LShDz*, ff. 67b3, 80b2 et seq., and 102a3 (cf. also *TNT*, pp. 50–1 and *TBK*, p. 3a7).

[1] thos pa bsam pa sgom pa (correspond to Skr. śravaṇa, cintā, bhāvanā). *LShDz*, f. 45a6.

[2] Mu-cho is one of the eight sons of sTon-pa gShen-rab. See *supra*, p. 3 n. 2. He was also gShen-rab's apostle. See *gZer-mig*, vol. kha, f. 279a3; *LShDz*, f. 53b1.

[3] *gSang-ba rtsa-rgyud nyi-zer sgron-ma* (often referred to as *rTsa-rgyud nyi-zer* or *rTsa-rgyud nyi-gron* or *rGyud nyi-sgron* or *rGyud nyi-zer* or simply *Nyi-sgron*) is attributed to Dran-pa Nam-mkha' (eighth century). Later it was rediscovered by lHa-bzher gYung-drung Bla-ma in Tsong-kha'i skabs-gnyen mtsho-nag. See *infra*, p. 173. Kun-grol Grags-pa speaks (*bsTan-'byung*, f. 62a6) of the existence of long and short versions of *Nyi-sgron*.

rGyal-sa pho-brang gling-brgyad.[1] From this three hundred and sixty languages emanated. A hundred and sixty-four of them were in 'Ol-mo'i-gling and a hundred and ninety-four were outside the ring of the snowy mountains of dBal-so that enclose 'Ol-mo'i-gling. The languages into which the Bon texts are translatable are enumerated in the *bsGrags-byang*:[2]

> In 'Dzam-bu-gling there are one thousand different languages, and the Bon reached the ears of three hundred and sixty of these.

The three translators of sTag-gzig, dMu-tsha Tra-he, Khri-thog sPa-tsha, and Hu-lu sPa-legs[3] expounded their translations to Sad sPungs-dun, Gyer-sangs gTsug-phud, dMu-tsha Ting-rim, dMu-bon brTan, dMu-mkha' lDing-nam, and dMu-rje sPal-pa dGu-'byung of sTag-gzig. (124a) They interpreted them to the Bon-po Mu-khod of Zhang-zhung, the gShen-po Li-sha of India, the gShen-po Bra-ba Me-ru-can of Kashmir, the gShen-po Pa-va Shang-shang of Tho-gar, and the gShen-po Ge lTe-ne Lo-rgya of Gilgit. Legs-tang rMang-po expounded them to the gShen-po gTsug-lag dPal-ge of China and Vairocana of Ba-gor and (the doctrines of Bon) reached China. gSer-thog lCe-'byams transmitted them to rNgam-pa lCe-ring of Ge-sar, Mu-spungs gSal-tang of Sum-pa, Sha-ri dBu-chen of Tibet, and lCe-tsha mKhar-bu of Me-nyag, and they translated them into

[1] The eight palaces of sTon-pa gShen-rab in 'Ol-mo lung-ring. See *LShDz*, ff. 11a5–12b1, and Snellgrove, *Nine Ways*, Illustration XXII.

[2] A manuscript in Oslo bearing on the title-page the name *Bon-chos dar-nub-g(y)i lo-rgyus (bs)grags-pa rin-chen gling-grag(s) ces bya-ba dmongs (rmongs)-pa blo'i gsal-byed* (ff. 1a, 95a2), is in fact the text usually known as *'Phrul-ngag bon-gyi bsgrags-byang* or *gYung-drung bon-gyi bsgrags-byang* (often referred to as *bsGrags-byang*) and most of the passages quoted in our text can be traced in this manuscript. Also the passages quoted by the abbot Nyi-ma bsTan-'dzin in his *TNT* (pp. 44, 48, 55, and 59) as being from the *bsGrags-byang* are to be found in it (ff. 14b1, 15a6, 74a5, and 16a1).

It is probably a commentary on the text known as *bsGrags-pa rin-chen gling-grags* and claims to have been composed by rGyung-ya Bla-chen Khod-spungs (f. 1a5) and was apparently rediscovered by mTha'-bzhi Ye-shes Blo-gros in bSam-yas under the combined titles of the commentary and the text as *bsGrags-byang rin-chen* (see *infra*, p. 123, and also *bsTan-'byung*, f. 52b5).

Unfortunately this first quotation in our text is among those I cannot trace in the Oslo MS., but the copy is a very carelessly made one and omissions have probably occurred.

[3] Here the translators appear to be men of sTag-gzig, but earlier they are said to have come from sTag-gzig, Zhang-zhung and Sum-pa. See *supra*, p. 16.

their own languages and promoted their diffusion. Furthermore, it is said in the biography of Gyer-mi:[1]

> At the time the Teacher Mu-cho was delivering the teachings
> In the shining temple of dKar-nag bkra-gsal,[2]
> Classifying (the scriptures of Bon) into a hundred parts as 'Exoteric and Esoteric Codes' and expounding them,
> Twenty-one knowledge-holders (rig-'dzin), including myself,
> Listened to the traditional expositions of Bon, and diffused them widely;
> We diffused the secret doctrines of Bon far and wide by means of miraculous powers.

B. I. When they were spread (124b)
II. Where they were spread
III. What kinds of Bon were spread
IV. How they were spread

I. When they were spread

At first the 'Bon of Cause' was spread. The *bsGrags-byang*[3] says:

> The 'Bon of Cause' first appeared at the time when people were living until the age of a hundred.

Then the 'Bon of Effect' was spread. The same authority says:

> The 'Bon of Effect' appeared at the time when people were living until the age of ninety.

It is said in the *Zhi-khro rtsa-'grel*[4] that the 'Bon of Cause and Effect' appeared at the time when people were living until the age of ninety and eighty respectively. But what is meant is that the (doctrines of Bon) were extensively spread after the translators diffused them in their own countries.

[1] See *infra*, p. 21 n. 6.

[2] A detailed account of the building of this temple is to be found in *gZer-mig*, vol. kha, ff. 81a3 et seq.

[3] *bsGrags-byang*, f. 24a5.

[4] *Zhi-khro rtsa-'grel* or *Zhi-khro rtsa-'grel chen-mo* was rediscovered by sPrul-sku Gu-ru rNon-rtse (b. *STNN* 1136). For details see *infra*, p. 166.

II. Where they were spread

The *Srid-pa rgyud-kyi kha-byang*[1] says:

The truth of Bon and its miraculous message were spread and the gShen flourished in the territory of sMyug-ma bu-khur (baby-carrying bamboo) in the East, 'Jag-ma glu-len (singing reeds) in the North, gNam-mtsho gling-dgu (nine heavenly lakes) in the West, and Dom-sgro nag-po (black bear-skin bag) in the South. They were also spread and the gShen flourished from up in Khyung-lung dngul-mkhar (the silver castle in the garuḍa valley)[2] down to Sum-pa glang-gi gyim-shod and Brag shel-le rgya-skar.

III. What kinds of Bon were spread

The *sGra-'grel* says: (125a)

The Divine Bon of 'Edible Tributes', the Bon of 'posthumous evocation' for secular use, and the Bon of 'Perfect Mind' were spread.[3]

By this is meant the offering of 'edible tributes' to gods, and the appeasing of demons with ransoms; the performance of 'posthumous evocation rituals' and the ritual of guidance for spirits; the instruction in the 'meaning of mind' and guidance towards salvation.

IV. How they were spread

a. General exposition
b. Detailed exposition

a. (The doctrines of Bon) spread from 'Ol-mo'i-gling of sTag-gzig to India, Zhang-zhung, and China. From these three they spread to Tibet. The *bDal-'bum*[4] says:

[1] *SG*, f. 14a3. *Srid-pa rgyud-kyi rnam-thar kha-byang chen-mo* is often referred to as *Srid-pa rgyud-kyi kha-byang* or simply *Srid-rgyud* or *Kha-byang*. It was rediscovered by Gyer Thogs-med in 1310 in rTa-gnyan pha-bong bon-mo (see *infra*, p. 181). It is described as the work of Dran-pa Nam-mkha'.

[2] This was an important Bon-po centre: as gShen-rab's birth-place, see H. Hoffmann, op. cit., p. 96; as the old capital of Western Tibet, see Snellgrove, *Four Lamas of Dolpo*, p. 14; as a fort, *THD*, p. 115. A Bon-po monastery called mDo-sngags grags-rgyas-gling was founded in this place in (*STNN*) 1936 by 'Jigs-med Nam-mkha'i rDo-rje (b. *STNN* 1897).

[3] Cf. *infra*, p. 60.

[4] The full title is *Bon-nyid snying-po bdal-ba'i 'bum*, but often known simply

> After the death of the Teacher the Scripture will appear in the South, then in the East, and then in the North.

By the North is meant the land of snows: Tibet. Furthermore, it is also said in the *Theg-rim gsal-sgron*:[1]

> It was transmitted to India, China, and Zhang-zhung. From these it was transmitted to Tibet; therefore, there was a 'Triple Transmission' (gsum-'gyur).

However, there was not only a 'Triple Transmission', there was also some direct transmission from sTag-gzig to Tibet during the reigns of the Seven Khri[2] as the *Nyi-sgron* says:

> During the reigns of the divinely-born Khri-btsan-lde,[3] Khyung-po sTag-sgra Don-gtsug[4] (125b), sNya Li-shu sTag-ring,[5] Bhe Shod-kram,[6] and gCo-bon Khri-gtsug, carrying precious gold dust, travelled through many countries the languages of which were strange to them and reached gYung-drung dgu-brtsegs and other places in sTag-gzig. They were admitted to the presence of the learned Sad sPungs-dun of sTag-gzig, the nine translators including Gyer-sangs,[7] the nine scholars, and many preachers. The priests of sTag-gzig were not poor, but in order to emphasize the greatness of Bon they offered them a gold maṇḍala and requested them to impart the secret doctrines of the 'Three Propagations of sPyi-spungs'.[8]

So they were given eighty-six great rGyud,[9] and three hundred

as *bDal-'bum*. This is classed as bKa' and was later rediscovered by gTsang-gi ban-dhe mi-gsum (the three Buddhists from gTsang), who were contemporaries of sPrul-sku Lung-bon lHa-gnyan (b. *STNN* 1088). It is considered to be a Bon-po plagiarism of Buddhist works, see Snellgrove, *Nine Ways*, p. 260 n. 42. For full history see *infra*, p. 152 (cf. also *KTDG*, p. 6).

[1] This work is probably identical with the *Theg-rim*. See *infra*, p. 23 n. 1.

[2] See *LShDz*, ff. 107a2 et seq.

[3] This name does not occur in the Seven Khri and so is difficult to identify.

[4] See *supra*, p. 12.

[5] A sketch of his life is to be found *infra*, p. 57.

[6] See *infra*, p. 80.

[7] See *supra*, p. 17.

[8] See *supra*, p. 15 n. 3.

[9] The word rGyud in Buddhist writing corresponds to the term Tantra but I am doubtful about using in a translation of a Bon-po work a term which by its nature prejudges the issue of the origin of the doctrines concerned in a manner inconsistent with the views of the Bon-po author, so I give the noun always in its Tibetan form. Moreover, the word rGyud does not always mean Tantra as it is used by the Tibetan Buddhists. For example, it means here simply

minor rGyud—a total of 16,000 chapters—and the rites of religious protectors consisting of five hundred chapters.[1] They put them into bags of tiger and leopard skin and then into leather boxes. They loaded them on to a wild ass, a Shang-shang, a crane, and a vulture. Three other vultures carried the *Phyi dbal-phur nag-po* and *Nang lta-ba sems-nyid gtan-la phab-pa*[2] containing three hundred and sixty chapters. Two other wild asses carried the rGyud of dBal-ram,[3] Rol-ba, 'Bum-pa, and Ge-khod[4] and their rites. (126a) In short, twenty-eight great secret doctrines reached the three regions of mNga'-ris in Tibet from Mount gYung-drung dgu-brtsegs, the centre of 'Ol-mo'i-gling, the country of Bon, sTag-gzig, without any delay in Khotan (Li), Nepal, or Zhang-zhung. From the three regions of mNga'-ris they spread throughout gTsang, and dBus, and mDo-khams. Hence the four scholars, one of whom was Li-shu sTag-ring, were known as the 'Four Great Translators of Tibet'.

b. i. Zhang-zhung
   ii. India
   iii. China
   iv. The history of the First Spread of the Doctrine in Tibet

i. How the doctrines of Bon spread to Zhang-zhung

The biography of Gyer-mi says:

We three—lDe-bon Gyim-tsha,[5] sNya-bon Li-shu sTag-ring, and myself sTang dMu-tsha[6]—having loaded a hundred and twenty-two birds including vultures and cranes with the tantric texts of 'Exoteric, Esoteric, and Secret doctrines of Bon', and many rites (of tantric divinities) came to Zhang-zhung from sTag-gzig. We diffused them widely with the help of innumerable knowledge-holders (rig-'dzin) and scholars.

'treatise', 'exposition'. On other usages of rGyud see Snellgrove, *Nine Ways*, Glossary, p. 294.

[1] Our author gives no specific titles. Limited sources make identification impossible at the present time.

[2] These texts were later rediscovered by Khu-tsha Zla-'od (b. *STNN* 1038), see *infra*, p. 145.

[3] i.e. dBal-chen Ram-pa, a tantric divinity, cf. *infra*, pp. 32, 115.

[4] Tantric divinities.

[5] See *infra*, p. 49.

[6] Gyer-mi or Gyer-mi Nyi-'od, a text-discoverer (gter-ston), lived in the twelfth century. He claims to have been sTang dMu-tsha or sTang-chen dMu-tsha Gyer-med (eighth century) in a previous life. For a short account concerning the life of Gyer-mi Nyi-'od see *infra*, p. 156.

> Then, having become proficient in the 'Exoteric and Esoteric doctrines of Bon', we established meditational centres in many places. Innumerable people obtained realization.

It is also said in the *Nyi-sgron* that the scriptures of Bon and (other) sacred books, temples, and shrines flourished in Zhang-zhung before they appeared in gTsang and dBus. (126b) The *'Dul-ba gling-grags*[1] says that the *'Dul-ba'i-lung*[2] and some other texts were translated into the language of Zhang-zhung from that of sTag-gzig by rDzu-'phrul Yes-shes. Further, whenever the doctrines of Bon spread to Tibet, India, or China, most of them reached those countries from Zhang-zhung, for many of the texts show their origin by giving some Zhang-zhung words at the beginning. Some other texts were translated from the languages of India, China, Sum-pa, and Me-nyag into Tibetan, as we know from the fact that they begin in these languages.

The *Sher-phyin 'bum-pa*,[3] which 'The Others'[4] claimed that they had received from the land of Nāga, was delivered by our Teacher, because Shākya Muni did not labour for the welfare of sentient beings in the land of Nāga.

ii. How the doctrines of Bon spread to India

The texts of 'Indian Bon' first spread from 'Ol-mo'i-gling of sTag-gzig to Zhang-zhung, then to India. The Commentary of *mDzod kun-las btus-pa*[5] says:

[1] The full title of this text runs: *'Dul-rgyud bsgrags-pa gling-grags*, but in short it is referred to as *bsGrags-pa gling-grags* or *'Dul-rgyud gling-grags* or *'Dul-ba gling-grags*. sPa bsTan-rgyal bZang-po attributes this work to Dran-pa Nam-mkha' (see *ZhNyL*, f. 74a8). It was rediscovered by Slob-dpon Gang-zhug Thog-rgyal in Mang-mkhar lcags-'phrang (see *infra*, p. 166). However, Abbot Nyi-ma bsTan-'dzin speaks (*KTDG*, p. 24) of the existence of three different texts bearing the title of *bsGrags-pa gling-grags* and so does Kun-grol Grags-pa in his *bsTan-'byung* (f. 60b4), but unconvincingly lists them under a different text-discoverer. Until we see them ourselves we cannot know.

[2] *'Dul-ba'i-lung* is the same as *'Dul-ba gsang-lung* which was rediscovered in Yar-lha sham-po by rMa-ston Shes-rab Seng-ge who was a grandson of rMa-ston Srol-'dzin (b. *STNN* 1092). See *infra*, p. 170.

[3] This corresponds to the Buddhist sūtra prajñāpāramitā and is in sixteen volumes. It is often referred to as *Khams-chen* or *Khams-chen stong-phrag brgya-ba* (for details see *KTDG*, p. 6). It was rediscovered by gShen-chen Klu-dga' (*STNN* 996–1035). See *infra*, pp. 130–1. Cf. *LShDz*, f. 34a4.

[4] Tibetan gzhan-sde, which in Bon-po texts refers to the Buddhists.

[5] *mDzod kun-las btus-pa* (often referred to as *mDzod kun-btus*) is a work of sGa-ston Tshul-khrims rGyal-mtshan (fourteenth century). It has been edited and published by S. T. Jongdong and S. G. Karmay (Kalimpong, 1961). The

The 'Indian Bon' was acquired by the gShen-po of Zhang-zhung, Ka-khyung sPungs-pa. Then during the (reign) of the Indian gSas-'od gYung-drung, it was transmitted to India.

Also the *Theg-rim*[1] and others were transmitted to India from Zhang-zhung, then to Gilgit, and then to Tibet, (127a) as the texts themselves record at the beginning in the languages of those countries. And it is my opinion that the transmission occurred as thus recorded. The *Theg-rim* was translated into Tibetan from the language of Gilgit by Vairocana.[2] The *Theg-rim*[3] says:

> I myself Vairocana made the translation of the great Everlasting Bon without sparing myself and then entrusted it to the king.

The accounts of 'The Others' said that many tantras, including Kālacakra, were translated (from the language of) Shambhala. In fact, they were transmitted from 'Ol-mo'i-gling, because we know from the mDo that the Indians call 'Ol-mo'i-gling by the name of Shambhala. The texts of 'Indian Bon' are very numerous. I shall deal briefly with them later.[4]

iii. How Everlasting Bon spread to China

In China first to appear was the science of the 'Astrological Calculation', etc. The Enlightened One, sTon-pa gShen-rab Mi-bo, taught the science of the hundred and sixty kinds of astrology to 'Phrul-bu-chung, the nephew of Kong-tse 'Phrul-rgyal.[5] He prophesied in the *Dri-med* that this science would appear in China in the future:

> O you the master of purification, sPang-la gNam-gshen,
> In the East of 'Dzam-bu-gling,
> In the capital of Ga-cu rGya,

commentary with which we are concerned here is by the same author and is a cosmogony entitled *rNam-par 'byed-pa'i lde-mig* (f. 2a3).

[1] *Theg-pa rim-pa mngon-du bshad-pa'i mdo-rgyud* (usually known as Theg-rim). It was rediscovered by the Three Buddhists of gTsang (gtsang-gi ban-dhe mi-gsum, contemporaries of Lung-bon lHa-gnyan (b. *STNN* 1088)) in Yer-ba (see *infra*, p. 152). It has been edited and published by S. T. Jongdong and S. G. Karmay (Kalimpong, 1961).

[2] According to Bon-po tradition this Buddhist eighth-century translator assisted also in the translation of Bon-po works.

[3] *Theg-rim*, f. 8b2.

[4] See *infra*, p. 113.

[5] Concerning his life see *gZer-mig*, vol. kha, ff. 78b4 et seq.

Will be born as the magic king of Cu-tse,
And will replace the erroneous calculations
Arrived at by the demon king, 'Khor-ba, (127b)
Through the magic science of astrology.

Furthermore, the four medical texts,[1] which make up one of four sections of one of the vehicles of the 'Bon of Cause', were also taught by our Teacher. When the demon Ram-pa Dug-'byed inflicted on sentient beings the age of disease, the Teacher taught dPyad-bu Khri-shes[2] the nine ambrosia mDo and the like, and he made sentient beings happy. He prophesied in the *Dri-med* that the sage Yid-las sPrul-ba would serve as an antidote to (the demon) in the future:

O you sage, Yid-las sPrul-ba,
When the demon spreads disease (again),
You will represent a person who will be called 'Tsho-mdzad Ye-shes,
In Pad-ma spungs-pa of Uḍḍiyāna,
And will replace the poison of demon Ram-pa
With healing ambrosia.
You will turn the wheel of the 2,000 kinds of 'Diagnosis'.

Later (the four medical texts) were translated into Tibetan from Chinese as texts of 'The Others'. They said that before the doctrine of Shākya Muni appeared in China nothing had been heard of a Buddha or his doctrines. Such a comment is just a selfish fabrication. Before the doctrines of Shākya Muni reached China the perfect Bon Doctrines of the Enlightened One, the Teacher of Bon, were known there. After the death of gShen-rab Mi-bo (128a) the 'six ornaments of the learned men of the world' acquired wisdom in the presence of the apostle, Mu-cho, and when they diffused the doctrines of Bon in their own countries, the great scholar of China, Legs-tang rMang-po made many translations of Bon texts in China. His diffusion of Bon in China is something I have already mentioned.[3] Some Bon texts of the Great Perfection were also transmitted to China from Zhang-zhung and Tibet. The *rNam-thar chen-mo*[4] says that the (spiritual

[1] On these see *KTDG*, p. 5.

[2] See *supra*, p. 3 n. 2.

[3] See *supra*, p. 17.

[4] *rDzogs-pa chen-po zhang-zhung snyan-*(b) *rgyud-kyi lo-rgyus bla-ma brgyud-pa'i rnam-thar chen-mo* (or just *rNam-thar chen-mo*) is a work of sPa bs Tan-rgyal

lineage of the Great Perfection) was passed on from Drod-skyes 'Chi-med gTsug-phud[1] to great dPon-chen Hor-ti. After the ten who followed came Ra-sangs Khri-ne-khod.[2] He passed it on to the others in Sum-pa and China. The *brGyud-pa'i gsol-'debs*[3] says:

> I pray to Sum-bon A-ba-ldong,[4]
> Who diffused the doctrine of the Great Perfection in Sum-pa.
> I pray to rGya-bon gSal-ba 'Od-chen,[5]
> Who holds the spiritual lineage of the Great Perfection in China.

From this work too we learn that the doctrines of Bon existed there (i.e. in China).

Also tantric Bon appeared in China, for the *gYung-drung skabs-'phrin*[6] says that rGya-bon Zing-ba mThu-chen,[7] having practised the secret doctrine of sPyi-spungs in Gong-bu dmar-ru in China, attained realization. The *Ma-rgyud phyag-mchod*[8] says:

> In the colourful cave of Mount Nyi-dbar mdangs-len of China,
> Brightly glowing ruddy-faced Zing-ba mThu-chen (dwells). (128b)

Further:

> In the water-garden of
> Excellent Mount Tse-mang of China,
> A Chinese yoginī named Dod-de (dwells).

Furthermore, some histories tell us that nine Mon-bon attained the Enlightenment simultaneously in Gong-bu dmar-ru in China. Among the texts of Bon are also many books which

bZang-po also known as rGyal-sras sPa.

[1] Concerning his life-story see *LShDz*, ff. 62a4–63a6, Introduction, p. xxi.

[2] Concerning dPon-chen Hor-ti and Ra-sangs Khri-ne see *infra*, pp. 52–4.

[3] A prayer book of the spiritual successors of the Great Perfection (rdzogs-pa chen-po).

[4] See *infra*, p. 54.

[5] See *infra*, p. 54.

[6] *gYung-drung skabs-'phrin* (often referred to as *sKabs-'phrin*) is a tantric text and was rediscovered by dPon-gsas Khyung-rgod-rtsal (b. *STNN* 1175). See *bsTan-'byung*, f. 63a7. However, our author does not list this text under the rediscoveries of dPon-gsas Khyung-rgod-rtsal (see *infra*, p. 173).

[7] See *infra*, p. 48.

[8] A prayer book of Ma-rgyud.

originated in Chinese, such as *rNam-rgyal rgya-nag-ma*,[1] etc. If the doctrines of Bon had not existed in China no one could have attained realization of the Enlightenment (i.e. before Buddhism reached China). It is difficult for ignorant people to understand this subject properly however much they try, just as it is almost impossible for even an intelligent person to understand the process of the origin, duration, and cessation of phenomenal existence though he may study it all his life. I have not narrated here in detail how people attained realization through practising the Exoteric, Esoteric, and Secret Bon which spread to India, China, and Zhang-zhung, etc., as they will be included in the narration of how the Doctrines of Bon spread to Tibet.

iv. The history of the First Spread of the Doctrine in Tibet

(A) Summary
(B) Elucidation

(A) sNya-chen Li-shu sTag-ring went to 'Ol-mo'i-gling where he made the acquaintance of many preachers, including the three scholars of sTag-gzig,[2] (129a) and translated many Bon texts. The *Yang-rtse klong-chen*[3] says:

> When sNya-chen Li-shu sTag-ring was 1,200 years old he loaded cranes and vultures with 11,000 texts of essential Bon, and travelled from sTag-gzig to Kailāsa in the space of a meal-time and then to bSam-yas in the space of another meal-time. He acted as preceptor at the royal court.

But a greater number of Bon texts were translated into Tibetan from the language of Zhang-zhung. The *Nyi-sgon* says:

> The Bon-pos of Tibet, the clear-minded Khyung-po sTag-sgra Don-gtsug, sNya Li-shu sTag-ring, Bhe Shod-kram, and gCo Khri-gtsug were sent to Zhang-zhung to search for texts of Bon together with a wild yak's hornful of gold dust. They

[1] On this text see *infra*, p. 174.

[2] They are dMu-tsha Tra-he, Khri-thog sPa-tsha, and Hu-lu sPa-legs. See *supra*, p. 17.

[3] The full-title of this work is *rDzogs-pa chen-po yang-rtse klong-chen* and it is attributed to Li-shu sTag-ring (eighth century) and was later rediscovered by bZhod-ston dNgos-grub Grags-pa in lHo-brag khom-mthing. For details see *infra*, p. 154 (also cf. *KTDG*, p. 26).

> made contact with the four Zhang-zhung scholars and, offering them the gold dust, they entreated them to impart to them the doctrines of Bon. The Zhang-zhung scholars imparted the texts of the Four Great Secret Doctrines of Bon, the Five Great 'Bum,[1] and many other exoteric and esoteric texts of Bon both in detailed and condensed form. Carrying the books they went back to dBus, Tibet, and presented the books to the king who was well pleased.[2]

The three, Se, lDe, and Me[3] of Tibet obtained most of the mDo and rGyud from sTong-rgyung mThu-chen[4] of Zhang-zhung, and many of them were translated from the Zhang-zhung language into Tibetan. (129b) The *bDal-'bum* says:

> In the place of Bye-ma g·yung-drung, sTong-rgyung mThu-chen expounded ten thousand texts of Bon to Sha-ri dBu-chen of Tibet and made translations of them.

And the *mDzod*[5] says:

> At the source of Chu-mig brgyad-cu rtsa-gnyis in Bye-ma g·yung-drung on the military frontier between Zhang-zhung and Tibet sTong-rgyung mThu-chen of Zhang-zhung and Sha-ri dBu-chen of Tibet co-operated in compiling translations of the 'Original Words' of gShen-rab Mi-bo from the language of Zhang-zhung into Tibetan.
>
> There were many languages in Zhang-zhung, but they can be reduced to four groups: the languages of Phug-pa (Inner), of Bar-ba (Central), of sGo-pa (Outer), and the colloquial idiom. Most (of the translations were made from) the language of Zhang-zhung sMar, that is, the language of Outer Zhang-zhung.[6]

[1] They are Khams-brgyad 'bum, dGe-rgyas 'bum, 'Dul-'bum, Lam-'bum, and Don-'bum, see *KTDG*, p. 6 (cf. Das, op. cit., under 'bum).

[2] Cf. *supra*, p. 20.

[3] Se-bon Sha-ri dBu-chen, lDe-bon Gyim-tsha rMa-chung, and Me-nyag lCe-tsha mKhar-bu (see *infra*, p. 49).

[4] See *infra*, p. 49.

[5] *mDzod*, p. 125. See *supra*, p. 8 n. 4.

[6] Concerning the language of Zhang-zhung sMar see Nyi-ma Grags-pa, *sGra-yi don-sdeb snang-gsal sgron-me*, p. 6 (ed. and published by Tenzin Namdak, Delhi, 1965).

(B). (AA) Outline
(BB) Detailed survey

(AA) The people of earlier times asserted that the term Bod-khams (the realm of Tibet) was a corruption of the word Bon-khams. Authoritative books also confirm it. The *gYung-drung las rnam-pa dag-pa'i rgyud*[1] says:

> During the period of the 'Four Scholars',[2] the 'Four Guardians', and the three Ge, Mi, and sPun, the land (of Tibet) was the land of Bon.

Since Everlasting Bon and its law came into existence before the emergence of the first king of Tibet and his laws, (130a) the country had been known as Bon-khams.

The original characters of Tibetan writing were first devised by the Enlightened One. The *mDo*[3] says:

> Thirty consonants form the basis of Bon texts,
> The introductory sign (mgo) leads the way, and the 'full-stop' (shad) creates divisions.
> The dot (tsheg) promotes clarity.
> The vowels i, e, o, u, and sub-joined letters
> Are added as circumstances require.

By this means the characters of sTag-gzig, sPung-yig, were made up from the pure letters of the gods. Then they developed into the Zhang-zhung Yig-rgan, then into sMar-sbrag, and then into the great and small sMar. From the great sMar derived dBu-can gnam-zab,[4] and the small sMar developed into 'Bru-mar. It is said that the Yig-sna was compiled from 'Bru-mar.

Some of 'The Others' say: the Tibetan characters were made up by the Lo-tsā-ba Thu-mi and, since the Indian characters did not include CA, CHA, JA, ZHA, ZA, and HA, he borrowed them from (the characters of) Za-hor (Jālandhara). Again some

[1] This work belongs to the class of bKa' and was translated by sTong-rgyung mThu-chen and Sha-ri dBu-chen at Bye-ma g·yung-drung in gTsang-stod. It was rediscovered by Gyer-mi Nyi-'od (*STNN*, twelfth century) in Byang Dang-ra khyung-rdzong (see *infra*, p. 160; cf. *KTDG*, pp. 2–3).

[2] They are sTong-rgyung mThu-chen, lDe-bon Gyim-tsha rMa-chung, Me-nyag lCe-tsha mKhar-bu, and Se-bon Sha-ri dBu-chen. See *infra*, p. 49.

[3] In his *dByings-rig-mdzod* (vol. ka, f. 47b2) our author gives this quotation as being from *gZer-mig*, but I cannot trace it in the new edition (1966) of *gZer-mig*, vol. Kha, Chapter 13, f.113b.

[4] *GRB* (p. 36): *smar chung dbu chen du bsgyur / smar chen 'bru mar bsgyur /* (From) the small sMar derived dBu-chen. (From) the great sMar derived 'Bru.

say: as the syllabary of Uḍḍiyāna had them the Tibetan ones came from there. But these are empty words, for if they had been taken from (the syllabary of Za-hor) it would have been unnecessary to look for them in another one. They were trying to suggest that in Tibet no letters existed during the series of thirty-two kings, that is up to gNam-ri Srong-btsan, (130b) and the system of writing was established in the time of Srong-btsan sGam-po. So it was just a way in which they could praise their doctrines, Dharma kings, and ministers, and abuse Bon. But they were not aware that in praising the Dharma kings they were in fact insulting their ancestors. The doctrines of the Enlightened One—i.e. the 'Bon of Cause and Effect'—existed before Srong-btsan sGam-po; this would have been impossible without a system of writing. Apart from that, the rulers of great kingdoms would be at a loss as to when to act positively and when to act negatively in practical matters (such as) taxation and the assignment of (administrative) offices and so on. They would be just like animals!

Further, the *Srong-btsan bka'-chems*[1] says:

> As the Tibetan word for Sanskrit EKA could not be written down the Tibetan letter CA was invented (to write the word GCIG). As the word for DHARMA could not be written down the letter CHA was invented (to write the word CHOS). As the word for LOKA could not be written down the letter JA was invented (to write the word 'JIG-RTEN). As the word for NAMA could not be written down the letter ZHA was invented (to write the word ZHES). As the word for RUPA could not be written down the letter ZA was invented (to write the word GZUGS). 'A was invented as there was no long sound in Tibetan for the Indian ones.

Apart from that, even if you think that the rest are all Indian characters, there is again an obvious contradiction, for we can see now that the Indian and Tibetan characters do not correspond in sound and form (131a). The *Ma-rgyud*[2] says:

> The Indian and Tibetan letters are certainly not similar to each other.

[1] This work is ascribed to Srong-btsan sGam-po and is also known as bKa'-chems ka-khol-ma.

[2] *Ma-rgyud thugs-rje nyi-ma*, rediscovered by sPrul-sku Gu-ru rNon-rtse (b. *STNN* 1136) in rTa-nag dung-phor. See *infra*, p. 166.

Therefore, you should believe what the Teacher Padma says:

When (the texts of) the dharma of India were being translated into Tibetan.
It was impossible to transliterate the Indian characters into Tibetan.
So the thirty characters were modelled on Tibetan.
The names of gods were taken from the sounds of the elements.
The spells were not translated but were left as they were originally.

(BB) (I) How the Bon spread to Tibet during the lifetime of the Teacher.
(II) How the Bon spread after his death.

(I) When the Teacher came to Tibet[1] he imparted authority to invoke the gods, to exorcize demons, to expel the Yug,[2] in the way I expounded above.[3] (As a result) nowadays the gods and demons of Tibet listen to orders and carry out whatever task is entrusted to them. Since they long ago made vows under the powerful orders of the Teacher, now if a Bon-po makes offerings to the gods they give protection, if he strikes the demons they are subdued, and if he exorcizes them they depart. This is also the reason why Bon-pos are said to be subduers of demons. At that time the Teacher taught only how to offer the gods ritual objects such as the incense of aromatic shrubs or libations made from roasted barley grains, and to appease demons with ransoms. He ordered them to pay attention to the orders of Bon-priests. But at that time he did not preach the ultimate truth (131b). Nevertheless, as I said before, he prayed that one day the Higher Ways of Bon would spread (to Tibet).

(II) (i) What kind of Bon spread in the time of gNya'-khri.
(ii) How it spread during the reigns of the Seven Khri.
(iii) How it was finally abolished.

[1] An account of gShen-rab's coming to Tibet and teaching Bon to the Tibetan Bon-pos is to be found in *gZer-mig*, vol. kha, ff. 52a1 et seq. See also the translation of the passage in Snellgrove, *Nine Ways*, p. 14. Cf. *TNT*, p. 51 and *LShDz*, ff. 39a1–43a2. Introduction, p. xix.

[2] A demon who brings misfortune.

[3] See *LShDz*, f. 39b5.

(i) The *Byams-ma*[1] says:

During the reign of gNya'-khri the twelve kinds of knowledge of the 'Bon of Cause' spread:

1. The divine Bon which is the knowledge of protection.
2. The Bon of Phyva which is the knowledge of prosperity.
3. The dispensation of ransoms which is the knowledge of ostracizing demons.
4. The gShen of the visual world which is the knowledge of 'evoking the spirits of the dead'.
5. The requirements of removal which are the knowledge of purification.
6. The Bon of attitude which is the knowledge of elimination.
7. Medical diagnosis which is the knowledge of beneficence.
8. Astrological calculation which is the knowledge of destiny.
9. The nine rituals which are the knowledge of incantation.
10. The deer which procures the knowledge of soaring.
11. The sortilege of Ju-thig which is the knowledge of foresight.
12. The Bon of magic which is the knowledge of travelling.[2]

These are called the twelve kinds of knowledge.

The meanings of these are as follows: the divinities give protection, if one invokes them. Wealth increases, if one calls for 'fortune' (g·yang). Demons are appeased, if one gives them ransoms. The spirits of the dead attain happiness, if one performs the 'evocation ritual'. The guardians are satisfied, if the distinctions of purity and impurity are observed. No anxiety arises, if animosity is eliminated. No obstruction stands in the way of life, if the alleviation of diseases is practised. The destinies of the past and of the future are grasped, if one consults astrologers.

[1] This was rediscovered by Khro-tshang 'Brug-lha (*STNN* 956–1077) in Byang gsang-brag rgya-bo. See *infra*, p. 124.

[2] The 'Bon of Cause' (rgyu'i bon) later came to be considered as having four parts. They are the first four of the Nine Ways of Bon (theg-pa rim-dgu'i bon) see Snellgrove, *Nine Ways*, pp. 9–11, for full details. The twelve kinds of knowledge (shes-pa bcu-gnyis) thus assume the following groupings: 2, 7, 8, 9, 10, and 11 are incorporated into the Way of the gShen of Prediction (phyva-gshen theg-pa), 1, 3, 5 into the Way of the gShen of Visual World (snang-gshen theg-pa), 6, 12 into the Way of the gShen of Illusion ('phrul-gshen theg-pa) and 4 into the Way of the gShen of Existence (srid-gshen theg-pa). The 'Bon of Cause' is also called the secular way ('jig-rten-pa'i theg-pa), *infra*, p. 34, and also known as the Four Ways of Divine Bon (lha-bon sgo-bzhi), see *infra*, p. 59.

One is able to argue with demons, if one appeases them with ransoms of clay. One is able to fly to the place of bTsan,[1] (132a) if one offers them deer of barley flour. One can have clairvoyance that distinguishes good and evil, if one prays to the god of sortilege. One is able to travel to the abodes of gods and demons, and eliminate their harmful intentions, if one offers them the incense of aromatic shrubs.

The bodyguards of king gNya'-khri, mTshe and gCo'u, practised the rite of dBal-chen Ram-pa[2] which they acquired without any effort. When the army of the 'Four Borderlands'[3] threatened the Tibetan king they prayed to the host of the divinities of Ram-pa, and as they beheld the countenance of the divinities they attained realization. It is prophesied by the Conqueror in the *Dri-med*:[4]

> O you Nam-mkha' sNang-ba'i mDog-can,
> When the time has come,
> In the snowy land of Tibet,
> At the place called lHa-ri gyang-tho,
> Together with the first of the Seven Khri,[5]
> Support the king, the priest, and the doctrine equally . . .
> Diffuse tantric doctrines.

[1] A kind of demon believed to be living in a given locality. However, a distinction must be made between this and the bTsan of the Ma bDud bTsan gsum which occur on p. 48. The latter is a religious protector.

[2] Concerning this deity see *infra*, p. 115.

[3] Tib. mtha'-bzhi, i.e. sTag-gzig (Iran), India, Hor, and China.

[4] This quotation is taken from the *bsTan-pa gnyad-gtad-kyi mdo* the sixty-first chapter of the *Dri-med* (see *supra*, p. 4 n. 1).

[5] Tib. *khri-bdun pa-la bdun-tshigs dang* / This phrase is very vague. We find a similar phrase in *THD* (p. 81): *khri'i bdun-tshigs dang bdun* / I have translated it simply as the first of the Seven Khri since the *Dri-med* here refers it to gNya'-khri bTsan-po who is the first of the seven traditional 'Divine Enthroned Ones' (gnam-gyi khri-bdun). However, the word bdun-tshigs, in the mythological genealogy of the kings of Tibet, refers to the fourth of the seven sons of Yab-bla bDal-drug. *SG* (f. 22b7): *phyva rje yab bla bdal drug dang / dmu btsan rgyal mo gnyis kyi sras / lhe'u rje mched bdun bya ba yin / lha sras de yi bdun tshigs ni / khri sad (sras) 'bar(bar) ba zhes kyang bya* /

> The sons of the Lord of Phyva, Yab-bla bDal-drug,
> And the queen of dMu, rGyal-mo,
> Are the seven lHe'u-rje,
> The middle one of the seven of those divine sons,
> Is called Khri-sras Bar-ba.

Moreover, *bsGrags-byang*, (f. 26a2) gives: *yar gyi gcen gsum . . . / mar gyi gcung gsum . . . / bar ba ni khri bar la bdun tshigs zhes kyang bya* / Thus the word 'tshigs'

dMu-gshen Nam-mkha' sNang-ba'i mDog-can, realising that the time of the prophecy had now come, went to Tibet to diffuse the doctrine. 'Four Miraculous Goddesses'[1] supporting his feet with the help of a dragon, a garuḍa, and a lion, he descended to earth from heaven. He acted as preceptor to king gNya'-khri bTsan-po. (132b) Thus the king, the priest, and the doctrine appeared side by side. The *bsGrags-byang*[2] says:

> (The king gNya'-khri) acquired the Bon of Spyi-spungs from gShen Nam-mkha' sNang-ba'i mDog-can and practised it.

The Lord travelled from lHa-ri gyang-tho to Yar-lung sog-kha. The people of the place carried him on their necks. Ever since there has been a saying:

> The Mount is lHa-ri gyang-tho.
> The Lord is gNya'-khri bTsan-po.
> The Priest is sNang-ba'i mDog-can.
> The Bon is the sPyi-spungs.
> The castle is Byi-ba stag-rtse.

clearly means 'middle'. Therefore, the tshigs of seven is obviously the fourth. So the fourth son of the seven sons is named as Khri-bdun-tshigs ('the middle one of the seven') and is the father of gNya'-khri bTsan-po. This is confirmed by the following passage. *THD* (p. 81):

> *lha gnam gyi steng nas gshegs pa* /
> *gnam lhab kyi bla na* /
> *yab lha(bla) bdag(bdal) drug bzhugs pa'i sras* /
> *gcen gsum gcung gsum na* /
> *khr'i bdun tshigs dang bdun* /
> *khri bdun tshigs kyi sras* /
> *khri nyag khri btsan po* /

> He (gNya'-khri btsan-po) descended from the height of the heavens.
> Above the mid-heaven,
> Dwells Yab-bla bDal-drug with his sons.
> In between the three elder brothers and the three younger,
> There was the 'Middle One of the Seven Enthroned Ones'.
> In all there were seven sons.
> The Mighty Enthroned One Nyag-khri,
> Was the son of the 'Middle One of the Seven Enthroned Ones'.

bsGrags-byang (f. 26a5) identifies Yab-bla bDal-drug as lHa dBang-po brGya-byin (Sakrodevendra). The *drug* is not to be understood as indicating that there were six Gods. It is interesting to note that *SG* spells Nyag-khri as it is spelt in *THD* and gives a curious reason for it (f. 23a1): *ltag pa'i bdud sgor sra (skra) nyag gcig dang 'khrel ('brel) nas gshegs pa'i sras / lde nyag ri (khri) brtsad (btsad) po lags so* / A similar story (maintaining the traditional spelling gNya'-khri) is recorded in *bsGrags-byang* (f. 27b5): *ma'i gnya' bar zla dgu ngo bcu bsdad pas gnya' khri* . . . / Our author follows the traditional account of this.

[1] See *infra*, p. 75.

[2] *bsGrags-byang*, ff. 28b6–29a1.

Thus this is one of the ways in which the king, the priest, and the doctrine came into existence side by side on the earth.

(ii) (aa) Refutation of the assertion of others
(bb) Affirmation of our correct statement

(aa) Some of 'The Others' say: During the reigns of thirty-one kings, that is up to gNam-ri Srong-btsan, the state was sustained by Bon, sGrung, and lDe'u, etc. The four secular vehicles of Prediction, Visual World, Illusion, and Existence spread to Tibet. This is how Bon came to be the first doctrine in Tibet.[1] (133a) Thus have I seen a history of Bon doctrine in Tibet falsely trying to disprove the spread of the 'Bon of Effect' in the time of those kings. In my opinion, these assertions were made up by those who were excessively attached to their doctrines and take pleasure in praising themselves and despising others. (Therefore), I cannot agree to hold them true. If one takes that line, (what about the following authoritative statements?) The *Dri-med* says:

> O you Nam-mkha' sNang-ba'i mDog-can,
> The first of the Seven Khri,[2]
> Support the king, the priest, and the doctrine with no discrimination.
> Diffuse tantric doctrines.

I quoted the same passage earlier.[3] The *dBal-ram* says:

> The king gNya'-khri and his ministers passed into heaven after practising the dBal-ram.

The *Nyi-sgron* says:

> Mu-khri bTsan-po entreated Nam-mkha' sNang-ba'i mDog-can to impart to him the full version of the basic text of *Khro-bo dbang-chen*.[4]

[1] This view of the Buddhists has been confirmed by Snellgrove, *Nine Ways*, pp. 10–11; H. Hoffmann, op. cit., p. 108. However, Bon-pos do not admit that the 'Bon of Cause' was the only kind that existed before Srong-btsan sGam-po, but believe that the 'Bon of Effect' was also practised.

[2] See *supra*, p. 32 n. 5.

[3] See *supra*, p. 32.

[4] Concerning this text see *infra*, p. 45 n. 2.

The *sKabs-'phrin*[1] says:

> Mu-khri bTsan-po practised the doctrine of sPyi-spungs at lHa-ri gyang-ma gyang-tho.

This is not all. I shall also expound later[2] how those kings practised the 'Bon of Cause and Effect' according to the exposition of the *Byams-ma*. No person, who has a reputation for rational thought, can contradict the authority of the Enlightened One. It would be very foolish to regard the opinion of (133b) ordinary people as rational unless it conforms to the authority of the Enlightened One.

(bb) 1. How the 'Rules of Discipline' were spread
2. How the Tantric Teachings were spread
3. How the Great Perfection was spread

1. Although the Teacher, being an Enlightened One, had been fully ordained as a monk from the earliest time, he, for the sake of others, made vows in the presence of the sage Legs-ldan rGyal-ba.[3] He ordained his followers as monks. He let them take charge of the establishment of his doctrines. The 'Six Ornaments of the World of Learning' diffused (the teachings) in translation. In furtherance of the 'Rules of Discipline' in particular, dMu-tsha Tra-he of sTag-gzig, one of the 'Six Ornaments of the World of Learning', met the 'Four Noble Youths'[4] and received full ordination at once.[5] He upheld the 'School of Solitary Asceticism'. He had a disciple Khri-lde 'Od-po who upheld the 'School of the Study of the Original Words'.[6] Khri-lde 'Od-po had a disciple lHang-lhang gTsug-phud who composed the commentary *rNam-'byed lde-mig* on the *'Dul-ba rgyud-drug*.[7] The latter had a disciple Dvangs-ba Yid-ring who composed the

[1] A tantric text rediscovered by dByil-ston dPon-gsas Khyung-rgod-rtsal (often known as dPon-gsas Khyung-thog in Buddhist works) in Mang-mkhar lcags-'phrang (see *supra*, p. 25 n. 6).

[2] See *infra*, p. 44.

[3] See *GRB*, p. 18, and *LShDz*, f. 44b3. He was a disciple of gTo-rgyal Ye-mkhyen (concerning whom see *gZer-mig*, vol. ka, f. 2 *passim* [trans. A. H. Francke, op. cit., *Asia Major*, i (1924), p. 305; and *LShDz*, f. 32a6]).

[4] They are Yid-kyi Khye'u-chung, gTo-bu 'Bum-sangs, rMa-lo, and gYu-lo, see *gZer-mig*, vol. kha, f. 48b6 and *LShDz*, f. 39a3.

[5] Usually 'ordination' is accomplished in four separate stages.

[6] See *infra*, p. 37 n. 3.

[7] *'Dul-ba rgyud-drug* has been considered as bKa' (i.e. the original words). *KTDG*, p. 3: . . . *phal cher sdom byed dam pa'i rgyud / dus chen dus btsan sdom*

long commentary *Dri-med gsal-ba'i lde-mig* on the *mNgon-pa sde-bzhi.*[1] Dvangs-ba Yid-ring had a disciple Thugs-dkar Ye-shes who composed the treatise *gSal-sgron* concerning the *Las-khrid bzhi-bcu-pa*. Thugs-dkar Ye-shes had a disciple Gung-rum Ye-shes who diffused the doctrine extensively. Gung-rum Ye-shes had a disciple 'Od-lha gSal-'bar who upheld the 'Order of the Great Occasion'[2] (134a) 'Od-lha gSal-'bar had a disciple rDzu-'phrul Ye-shes, who, realizing that the time had now come to diffuse the 'Rules of Discipline' in Zhang-zhung and Tibet, brought five hundred relics of the Teacher from the 'Four Self-evolved Shrines' and journeyed to Zhang-zhung and Tibet by means of magic. He diffused the doctrine far and wide. These teachers constitute the spiritual lineage of the ('Rules of Discipline') of sTag-gzig.

At that time Ge-khod-dpal of Zhang-zhung saw the figure of a monk again and again in his vision wearing six different kinds of shining clothes. A period of prayer followed, and then he met

byed rgyud / yongs rdzogs rnam dag sdom byed rgyud / so thar bye brag 'byed sdom rgyud / gcig nyams gcig len las sdom rgyud / spyi bsdoms 'gog pa phyogs sdom rgyud dang drug go / 'di dag bka' 'gyur gyi dbur gzhug na byin che zhing khyad par 'phags pas legs snyams / It concerns monastic discipline and is said to have been compiled by gYung-drung gTsug-gshen rGyal-ba otherwise known as Yid-kyi Khye'u-chung (see p. 35 n. 4; *LShDz*, f. 35a5). *GRB* quotes *mDo-'dus*, p. 19: *'dul ba rgyud drug gtsug gshen rgyal bas dsdus /* (cf. *GRB*, p. 22). It has been listed among three different discoveries. First it was rediscovered (*STNN* 913) by the three ācāryas in bSam-yas (for details see *infra*, p. 118). Then it was rediscovered (*STNN* 1067) by gNyan-ston Shes-rab Seng-ge (for details see *infra*, p. 153). Lastly, it is said to have been rediscovered again by *Gu-ru rNon-rtse* (b. *STNN* 1136). For details see *infra*, p. 166. However, *bsTan-'byung* makes mention of this text only under the discoveries of the three ācāryas, see f. 45b7. Abbot Nyi-ma bsTan-'dzin speaks (*TNT*, p. 54) of the existence of two kinds of the *'Dul-ba rgyud-drug*, one belonging to the Upper Tradition of 'Dul-ba (rules of discipline) and the other belonging to the Lower Tradition of 'Dul-ba.

[1] This is attributed to Mu-cho lDem-drug, the apostle of gShen-rab (see *supra*, p. 3 n. 2). See *KTDG*, p. 14, and *LShDz*, f. 53b6, cf. *GRB*, p. 22. This work is regarded as lost even in Tibet. However, according to *bsGrags-byang* (f. 22b2), it was transformed into Buddhism.

[2] The 'Order of the Great Occasion' is one of the four traditional groups of the 'Rules of Discipline' ('dul-ba). *TBK* (p. 6): *so sor thar pa'i sde dang / dus chen pa'i sde dang / phal chen pa'i sde dang / 'gog pa'i sde dang bzhi'o /* Explanations of them are given by our author in his *sDom-pa gsum rnam-par 'byad-pa'i gzhung-don gsal-bar byed-pa'i 'grel-ba legs-bshad 'phrul-gyi lde-mig*, f. 33b3: *dang po ni khrims phra rags kyi 'bras bu so so sgo thar du 'dod pa'o / gnyis pa ni ston pa snga ma bstan pa la tshogs bsags nas ston pa phyi ma'i zhal mthong ba dang dus mnyam du 'tshang rgya bar 'dod pa'o / gsum pa ni rtsa ba bzhi la gnang bkag gam tshe'i stod smad du gnang bkag yod pa'o / bzhi pa ni phyogs mthun thams cad spang ba'i sde'o /*

rDzu-'phrul Ye-shes in person who conferred on him full ordination at once and gave him the name of Ye-shes Tshul-khrims.[1] He had a disciple gYung-drung Tshul-khrims who built the temple of gYung-drung lha-rtse at Shel-gyi brag-dkar rtse-rdzong. The latter had a disciple gTsug-phud Tshul-khrims who built the temple of gYung-drung brtsegs-pa[2] on Mount dGra-bcom-pa-dpal. They sustained (the tradition of) the eight spiritual schools[3] founded by the Teacher, and spread the 'Rules of Discipline' in Zhang-zhung far and wide. The latter had a disciple Ga-cu gTsug-phud rGyal-ba[4] who built the temple of gYung-drung khri-'dus at 'Dam-shod snar-mo, and also that of Khri-'dul gsang-ba at Brag-nag rta-mgo gsum-pa. gTsug-phud rGyal-ba had two disciples, (134b) Ya-gong Ye-shes rGyal-ba and Pham-shi dPal-gyi dBang-phyug. These two were also known as 'the two men of Tibet'.[5] The *'Dul-rgyud bsgrags-pa gling-grags* says:

> gTsug-phud Tshul-khrims had four disciples: Ga-cu gTsug-phud rGyal-ba, Ya-gong Ye-shes rGyal-ba, Pham-shi dPal-gyi dBang-phyug, and lDe-btsun Rab-gsal. At that time the spiritual lineage of the 'Rules of Discipline' of gShen split up into two groups, Ga-cu and Pham-shi formed one group. Ya-gong and lDe-btsun formed another group.

That of Ya-gong belonged to the 'Order of Individual Liberation'. As to their meditation, they made patience its object. As

[1] Between Ye-shes Tshul-khrims and gYung-drung Tshul-khrims a name has been missed out: it is Khri-'bar gTsug-phud. See dPal-ldan Tshul-khrims, *gYung-drung bon-gyi bstan-pa byung-ba brjod-pa*, p. 5: *de bzhin spos ri ngad ldan gyi nub phyogs dpal phu'i ri sdebs g·yung drung steng gi dgon pa gnas brtan stong dang drug brgya ldan pa zhang zhung mkhan po khri 'bar gtsug phud kyis btsugs /*

[2] For the whereabouts of these temples see dPal-ldan Tshul-khrims, ibid., p. 5.

[3] These are given by our author in his *bDe-chen zhing-gi smon-lam-gyi don gsal-bar byed-pa'i 'grel-ba nyi-ma'i snying-po*, f. 28b2: *ston pa'i 'khor sde bzhi ni / thos pa'i sgro 'dogs bcad pa bka 'gzhung nyan bshad kyi sde dang / yang dag don la 'jug pa shing drung mi rtag pa bsgom pa'i sde dang / sgrub pa rtse gcig byed pa ri khrod cog pu'i sde dang / rang sems yeng med bsgoms pa brag dgon dka' thub kyi sde dang bzhi'o / . . . ya brgyad ni / bsrung khrims nyis brgya lnga bcu bsrung ba dag pa drang srong gi sde dang / gtsang khrims nyi shu rtsa lnga bsrung ba gtsang ma gtsug phud kyi sde dang / gtan khrims sna lnga bsrung ba tshul gnas dge bsnyen gyi sde dang / dus khrims yan lag brgyad bsrung ba bsnyen gnas yan lag gi sde dang bzhi la pho mo gnyis gnyis phye bas brgyad de . . . /* Cf. the last four *gZer-mig*, vol. ka, f. 219a6.

[4] The teachers named so far in this paragraph constitute the spiritual lineage of the 'Rules of Discipline' of Zhang-zhung, see *GRB*, p. 34.

[5] These last two constitute the spiritual lineage of the 'Rules of Discipline' of Tibet, see *GRB*, p. 35.

to their practices, they observed the customs and rules (of their order). They expected to gain the result (of their practices) individually. They built the temple of bDud-'dul g·yung-drung khrims-gnas in the valley of lHa-sa yer-ba. The demon Nag-po Ser-gdong was subdued. Twenty-nine 'religious centres' grew up including Zang-zang lha-rtse. Pham-shi followed the 'Order of the Great Occasion'. As to their meditation, they made the 'cessation of senses' its object. As to their practices, they observed the customs and rules (of their order). As to the result (of their practices), they expected to gain Enlightenment after a great 'kal-pa' when the doctrines came to an end. (135a) Thirty-eight 'religious centres' grew up, such as: Ra-za g·yung-drung rol-ba and so on.

(The teaching of) the 'Rules of Discipline' appeared in Tibet during the reigns of the Seven Khri. The *Nyi-sgron* says:

> During the period of the so-called Seven Khri each king had a priest bodyguard. So the priests had great influence. At that time Ga-cu, Ya-gong, Pham-shi, and lDe-btsun (founded) large 'religious centres', and (built) temples and shrines.

During the time of the twenty-five spiritual successors of Ya-gong and the thirty spiritual successors of Pham-shi, (the teaching of) the 'Rules of Discipline' was extensively spread. Ya-gong rGyal-ba had a disciple lDe-btsun Rab-gsal. He had a disciple Mu-zi gSal-bzang. Pham-shi had a disciple gCo-btsun Ye-shes (Tshul-khrims). It is also said in some authoritative books that Mu-zi took ordination in the presence of both lDe and gCo. As to gCo-btsun Ye-shes, he gained power over death, and fostered the doctrine during all those successors.[1] He passed joyfully into nirvaṇa as he listened to the prophecy of rDzu-'phrul Ye-shes[2] that in the future the 'Bon of Cause and Effect' would spread. Mu-zi, having decided to be as a seed of the doctrine in the future, (135b) went to Amdo, and dwelt in the cave of Brag-dkar rtse-'dus on Mount rMa-ri del-gsum. He meditated on the 'cessation of senses'.[3] These teachers constituted the spiritual

[1] i.e. during the thirty successors of Pham-shi.

[2] See *supra*, p. 36.

[3] The tradition tells us that Mu-zi gSal-gzang went into a kind of trance (Tib. 'gog-pa, lit. suppression) which lasted for centuries (*GRB*, p. 40, *TNT*,

successors of mNga'-ris, in upper Tibet. After that the teaching of the 'Rules of Discipline' spread throughout dBus and gTsang. The *Nyi-sgron* says:

> Monks gave their thoughts to Bon. Their conduct followed the customs and rules (of their orders). They copied, recited, and read the *rNam-dag-'bum*.[1] They removed obstacles by making offerings of Tsha-tsha and water. Their virtuous practices were the ten perfections.

2. (1) How (the teaching of) the 'Stage of Emanation' was spread.
(2) How (the teaching of) the 'Stage of Perfection' was spread.[2]

(1a) How the doctrine of sPyi-spungs was spread.
(1b) How the doctrine of the other 'Perfect Ones' spread.

(1a) α. Outline
β. How the people practised it

α. During the reigns of the six Khri[3] the Tantric Teachings, in particular the doctrine of sPyi-spungs, were spread. The *Nyi-sgron* says:

> Mu-khri entreated sNang-ba'i mDog-can to impart to him the full version of the basic text of *Khro-bo dbang-chen*. He practised them at lHa-ri gyang-tho and attained inconceivable supernatural powers.

The *Byams-ma* says:

> His (gNya'-khri) son Mu-khri bTsan-po achieved this understanding through (136a) studying, practising, and meditating.

p. 53). Eventually he was disturbed in (*STNN*) A.D. 888 by Sog-ston Khri-'bar Tshul-khrims (see *infra*, p. 105).

[1] The full title is *rNam-dag tshul-khrims 'dul-ba'i 'bum*. It is identical with the *'Dul-'bum* (see *supra*, p. 27 n. 1).

[2] Tib. bskyed-rim and rdzogs-rim (in Buddhism = Skr. utpattikrama, sampannakrama, on these see Snellgrove, *The Hevajra-Tantra*, vol. i, pp. 22 ff.). Here, however, these two terms apply specifically to two different stages of instruction, the first of which consists of five Pha-rgyud (for which see *infra*, p. 45 n. 2). These belong to either A-dkar theg-pa or Ye-gshen theg-pa for the details of which see Snellgrove, *Nine Ways*, pp. 10–11. The second term covers the Ma-rgyud and Great Perfection which belong to Bla-med theg-pa for which see ibid., p. 11.

[3] i.e. from Mu-khri bTsan-po to Srib-khri bTsan-po (see *LShDz*, f. 107b1).

> He became a translator in sTag-gzig and other countries. He invited a hundred and eight great scholars from Zhang-zhung. (During his reign) thirty-seven 'religious centres' were established in Tibet.

The thirty-seven 'religious centres' are, according to the *sGra-'grel*:[1]

> Thirteen 'religious centres' in dBu-ru, seven in gYon-ru, eight in gYas-ru, and nine in Ru-lag, thirty-seven in all. The thirteen in dBu-ru are: Ngan-lam ral-gsum, 'Dam-shod snar-mo, 'Phan-yul brag-dkar, Mal-dro ba-rab, mChims-gyi brag-dmar, Has-po ri-thang, lHa-sa yer-ba, gNam-gyi re-gong, gNam-mtsho do-ring, sTod-ros lung-gsum, sKyid-shod lung-nag, Re-rkyang sha-mtha', and mChog-gon rgyal-mo-khang. The seven in gYon-ru are: 'Ol-kha shug-gcig, Nyang-yul shing-nag, Kong-yul bre-sna, gYe-lung gangs-bar, Yar-lung sog-kha, Klum-shod thang-dmar, and Ma-dro mtsho-shod. The eight in gYas-ru are: 'U-yug sa-nag, Shangs-kyi zhong-zhong, Brud-kyi mkhar-gdong, rTa-nag rkyang-phu (136b) 'Jad-kyi rgyang mkhar, sTa-phu dros-lhas, gTsang-gi gyer-phug, and Zang-zang lha-brag. The nine in Ru-lag are: Nyang-stod stag-tshal, Chu-mgo rdo-ring, mKhar-chen brag-dkar, mTsho-rnga'i dril-chung, gNyan-rtse thang-shod, Gram-pa kha'u, Rag-za thang-zlum, Mang-mkhar mdo-phug, and lHa-yul gung-thang.[2] In these places the exposition, study, meditation, and performance (of Bon teachings) were extensively practised. The same authority[3] says:

> A congregation of Bon-pos was in Ngan-lam ral-gsum. A congregation of Bon-pos was in 'Dam-shod snar-mo, . . . A congregation of Bon-pos was in lHa-yul gung-thang.

Furthermore, the *bsGrags-byang*[4] gives:

> Khyung-lung dngul-mkhar, Gangs ti-se, sPos-ri ngad-ldan, mTsho ma-phang, Brag-phug rong-chen, mTshal-ri zur-gsum, rGyal-mkhar ba-chod, Gangs-kyi byi-ba-mkhar, Chu-mig brgyad-cu rtsa-gnyis, Gangs-gnyan rta-sgo, mTsho mu-le-khyud, Dang-ra'i mtsho, Khri-'od khyung-rtse, Khri-'od

[1] *sGra-'grel*, p. 21.

[2] For the identification of these places see dPal-ldan Tshul-khrims, op. cit., pp. 12 et seq.

[3] *sGra-'grel*, p. 21.

[4] I cannot trace this quotation in *bsGrags-byang* (Oslo MS.).

ri-thang, Mang-mkhar lcags-'phrang, Ra-za g·yung-drung rol-ba, lCim-lung brag-phug mtha'-ka-ru, Zar-gyi stag-sna, rTa-nag rkyang-phu, gTsang-brag zang-zang-mo, (137a) dGon-pa bya-rgod-tshang, Nyang-ro rta-shal (also ltag-zhal), Nyang-ro sham-po rtse-dgu, Nyang-ro srub-kyi stag-tshal, Yar-gyi thang-lha, Yar-lung-gi lha-ri gyang-tho, Yar-lung-gi mkhar btang-ka-med, bSam-yas brag-dmar, 'Gran-gyi ri-bo, 'Phan-yul 'gro-mar phug-mo, gNam-mtsho phyug-mo, Zlum-shod sgang-tshal, Kong-yul se-mo bon-thang, Kong-yul bre-sna, rGya'i gong-bu dmar-ru, Sum-pa glang-gi gyim-shod, and Shel-le rgya-skar, thirty-seven in all.[1]

As to the priests who maintained them, the *bsGrags-byang*[2] says:

> Sixty-seven priests resided in these 'religious centres'.

They were (as follows): Nine priests who possessed supernatural powers; nine scholars, nine magicians, and forty other preachers. The *Nyi-sgron* says:

> In the thirty-seven 'religious centres' there were forty-eight ascetics, twenty-four preachers, thirteen gYu-rnga-can (having turquoise drums),[3] nine scholars, and nine magicians.

'A-zha Blo-gros[4] specifies ten priests who possessed supernatural powers: Mu-khri bTsan-po, Ha-ra Ci-par, sTag-ver Li-ver, A-nu 'Phrag-thag, Sad-ne Ga'u, Zing-ba mThu-chen, Shad-bu Ra-khug, (137b) sPe-bon Thog-'phrul, sPe-bon Thog-rste, and Thad-mi Thad-ke.[5] The *Gleng-gzhi bstan-pa'i 'byung-khungs*[6]

[1] For the identification of most of these places see dPal-ldan Tshul-khrims, op. cit., pp. 14–15.

[2] *bsGrags-byang*, f. 33a6. The names and number of priests in these lists vary in the sources as we shall see. Our author himself does not conform to either the *bsGrags-byang* or *Nyi-sgron* (see *infra*, pp. 42 et seq).

[3] See *infra*, p. 58.

[4] An abbot and a very well-known scholar of gYas-ru dben-sa-kha (see *infra*, p. 140).

[5] Short references to the accomplishments of these priests are to be found *infra*, pp. 44 et seq.

[6] R. A. Stein identifies this work with the *rGyal-rabs bon-gyi 'byung-gnas* (see *L'épopée et le barde au Tibet*, p. 39, Paris, 1959). However, our author's reference to the *Gleng-gzhi bstan-pa'i 'byung-khungs* (Stein, op. cit., p. 39 reads *Gling-bzhi bstan-pa'i kun-byung*) does not correspond to the *rGyal-rabs bon-gyi 'byung gnas* (*GRB*, pp. 44–5). So they would seem to be separate works, but concerning the authorship of the *Gleng-gzhi bstan-pa'i 'byung-khungs* we cannot say more until the text is found.

gives nine of them excluding Shad-bu Ra-khug. As for the nine scholars they were: the scholar of Zhang-zhung, sTong-rgyung mThu-chen, Za-rang Me-'bar of sTag-gzig, lHa-bdag sNgas-dro of India, Legs-tang rMang-po of China, gSer-thog lCe-'byams of Phrom, rNgam-pa lCe-ring of Ge-sar, Sha-ri dBu-chen of Tibet, lCe-tsha mKhar-bu of Me-nyag, and Mu-spungs gSal-tang of Sum-pa. But according to the 'Southern Textual Treasures'[1] the nine scholars were: Se Sha-ri dBu-chen, proficient in traditional teachings, authoritative books and precepts; lDe Gyim-tsha, proficient in tantric hidden meanings; Me-nyag mKhar-bu, proficient in verse mDo; mTha'-bzhi Bum-chung, proficient in the 'parallel enumerations' of the 'Bum; sPe-bon gTo-rgyal, also proficient in the 'parallel enumerations'; rGya-bon 'Bri-thang sNa-ba, proficient in the exoteric, esoteric, and mystic cycles; dMu-gshen Ting-ver, proficient in languages; (138a) 'Gro-mgon lHa-dpal Klu-ring, proficient in the meaning of 'Spread and Receiving'; and Khyung-po Gyer-zla-med, proficient in philosophical theory, meditation, and conduct. They were all proficient in many fields of study, and were great masters of their own particular subjects.

The eight preachers were: rNgam-pa lCe-ring, dMu-tsha Gyer-med, Za-rang Me-'bar, Mu-spungs gSal-tang, Dran-pa Nam-mkha', rGyung-bon Mu-khod, rJe-rgyal lHa-sgom, and Blon-chen Mu-thur.

The twenty scholars were: gNub-bon Dran-pa Nam-mkha', Khyung-po sTag-sgra Don-gTsug, sNya-chen Li-shu sTag-ring, Gu-rub bTsan-dor Mi-sar, Phu-lu Gru-'dzin, Bhe-bon Shod-kram, Gyim-thang rMa-bo, Sum-pa Mu-phya, Has-po Dug-'dul, Phyva-bon sTag-ra Gyer-shag, Ba-gor Dod-de rGyal-ba, lJang-tsha 'Phel-snang, gNub Mar-gshen gZhi-btsan, Khyim Gi-ra Mon-par, mGar lHa-gshen 'Phyis-pa, sKu Gyim-thang rMa-bo, 'Gur dPon-blon gSas-chen, mChims Khri-zur sTong-lod, mKha'-'gro Co-za Bon-mo, and 'Gos Khri-stong rGyal-po.

The nine great magicians were: Li-bon Mu-cho who could raise a snowy mountain with his nails; (138b) gCo Gyim-bu Lan-tsha who made aromatic herbs gather themselves; rGya-bon Mu-cho who could turn the world upside down; Sum-pa Mu-phya who made an ocean float on the surface of a piece of wool; Khu-bon mThong-grags who ringed Mount Has-po with a noose

[1] See *infra*, p. 191.

of fire; Zhang-zhung Mu-cho who could conjure up monstrous demons; lJang-tsha 'Phel-snang who made waterfalls flow upwards; 'Jang-bon 'Phen-snang who could shake a mountain with the tip of his forefinger; rMa-bon Thugs-dkar who could measure the river of sKyi with his strides.

The forty-two preachers were: ten priests who attended on kings; ten priests who took part in discussion with the ministers; ten priests who guarded the borders of Tibet; and ten priests who guarded the lower part of Sum-pa stong-sde, and in addition to that the two priests of bKra-shis gYang-len Ngo-sprod making forty-two in all. They were called by these names in accordance with the activities assigned to them, but in fact they all attained the position of the 'Four Knowledge-holders'.[1]

At that time, the Tibetan kingdom was the land of Bon; the kings were great, the priests were dignified, laws were strict, and the subjects were happy. In Zhang-zhung and Tibet as kings were gods, human beings were well protected. (139a) As the priests looked after life, the kings were able to live long. As they lived mainly in virtue, they were happy in all their rebirths. As the 'cord of dMu' hung from the heaven, the 'ladder of dMu' was sound. As they invoked undefiled gods, they received protection from them. As the ministers were wise in politics, government was stable. The activities of the 'United System' (i.e. church and state) flourished.

At that time, the nine priests and others who attained supernatural powers guided sentient beings to salvation. The twenty scholars and others turned the wheel of exposition, disputation, and composition (of the doctrines). The nine magicians suppressed heretics. The forty-two preachers and others made sentient beings happy. The monks observed their rules. The meditators practised their meditations. The ascetics performed 'Veneration, Realisation, and Application' (of tantric rites). The exposition, practice, and application of the doctrines flourished extensively.

At that time, in India, Dharma flourished, in China 'astrological calculation' flourished, in Phrom diagnosis flourished, and in Tibet and Zhang-zhung only Everlasting Bon flourished, although other fields of study were also popular (139b).

[1] *dByings-rig-mdzod*, vol. ka, f. 135b6: *rnam par smin pa dang / tshe la dbang ba dang / phyag rgya chen po dang / lhun gyis grub pa /*

In general, the monks were revered by the kings, but in particular the kings were attracted by the signs of realization shown them by the priests, knowledge-holders who possessed supernatural powers. The king granted the priests three honours to mark the superiority of their nobility to his own. For the body: the honour of not having their hair cut at the ends, a turban of white silk on which a feather of the king-bird, the vulture, was fixed, a robe of white lynx-skin the collar of which was made of tiger, leopard, and caracal skin, a pair of shoes made of silk with silver chains as laces. In the matter of speech, they were accorded the honour of always speaking before the king gave any orders or the ministers put forward any propositions. As an honour for the mind their taxation was made equal to that of the king.[1]

The Bon of the Six Great Lamas[2] was undoubtedly spread during the Seven Khri. The *Byams-ma* says:

> The Bon of Supreme Universality, the Bon of the Supreme Way, the Bon of Supreme Conduct, the Bon of Supreme Achievement and (140a) the Bon of Supreme Emancipation[3] spread. (Similarly) the View, Contemplation, and the 'cessation of senses',[4] the latter being said to have begun from this time.

β. The popularity of the doctrine of sPyi-spungs was great during the reign of Mu-khri bTsan-po, the son of gNya'-khri (bTsan-po). dMu-gshen sNang-ba'i mDog-can entreated rGyal-gshen (Mi-lus bSam-legs), and Klu-grub[5] (Ye-shes sNying-po) to impart (the doctrine of sPyi-spungs) to him and, having found a partner in the goddess 'Od-ldan Zer-'phro-ma, he practised the teaching in the palace of Ri-rgyal lhun-po. He achieved union with his deity of wisdom as the supreme attainment and acquired infinite supernatural powers; he made gods serve him. He put insolent gods and demons under vows, the gods venerated him and offered him food, he produced a rain of flowers from the sky, etc. He transmitted the teaching to rGyal-gshen Mu-khri bTsan-po. The latter practised it with the help of the Four

[1] For the three honours cf. *sGra-'grel*, p. 23, and *GRB*, p. 39. The latter gives more detail and there are variations.

[2] See *infra*, p. 58.

[3] These probably correspond to the texts named *supra*, p. 27 n. 1.

[4] See *supra*, p. 38 n. 3.

[5] Cf. *supra*, p. 15 n. 3.

Miraculous Goddesses[1] on Mount Gyang-ma gyang-tho. As the ordinary attainment he exhibited many wonderful supernatural powers: he flew into the sky like a bird, sat on the surface of water, travelled through space by transforming himself into a dragon (or) an eagle (or) a lion, planted flowers in the desert, (140b) produced rivers in dry valleys, spat fire, subdued demons by lightning, arranged the sun and moon as a maṇḍala, made gods and demons serve him, made the Four Miraculous Goddesses his attendants, lived on a diet of meditation, etc. As the supreme attainment he achieved union with the body of (his deity) dBal-gsas rNgam-pa.[2] Then, the king (Mu-khri

[1] See *infra*, p. 75.

[2] dBal-gsas rNgam-pa is widely worshipped by the Bon-pos (see Snellgrove, *Nine Ways*, pp. 109, 111). The main (gzhung) ritual text of this divinity is entitled *dBal-gsas las-rim* and is said to have been composed by Dran-pa Nam-mkha' (see *KTDG*, p. 17) and was rediscovered by rMa-ston Srol-'dzin (b. *STNN* 1092) in Dang-ra Khyung-rdzong (see *infra*, p. 167). It belongs to the five kinds of rGyud which Bon recognizes. The deities concerned are known as the Five Perfect Ones of the gSas-Palace (gsas-mkhar mchog-lnga). The five kinds do not include Ma-rgyud since all of them are regarded as Pha-rgyud. However, a different version of the five including Ma-rgyud is to be found in the *gZhi-lam-gyi 'grel*, f. 58b4.

The first three of the Five are the sPyi-spungs rgyud (also known as the dBang-chen skor-gsum or sPyi-spungs bsgrags-pa skor-gsum, see *supra*, p. 15 n. 3). Since the five divisions are frequently referred to later it seems appropriate to add here some notes on all the deities involved:

(i) dBal-gsas rNgam-pa. Already dealt with.

(ii) lHa-rgod Thog-pa. Scarcely known and only mentioned when dBang-chen skor-gsum are enumerated.

(iii) Khro-bo gTso-mchog mkha'-'gying. Again very widely worshipped. The main ritual text entitled *Khro-gzhung mgo-mtshar rgyas-pa* (or simply Khro-bo dbang-chen) is said to have been compiled by the gShen of Gods, Serpents and Man (concerning whom see *supra*, p. 15 n. 3) from the *Khro-bo rgyud-drug* (see *KTDG*, pp. 9, 17). It was rediscovered by gShen-chen Klu-dga' (*STNN* 996–1035) in 'Bri-mtshams mtha'-dkar (see *infra*, p. 126). The *Khro-bo rgyud-drug* is also said to have been rediscovered by gShen-chen Klu-dga', but was destroyed. Another discovery was made in earth-tiger year (*STNN* 1038) by Khu-tsha Zla-'od in sPa-gro phug-bcal (see *infra*, p. 145). *KTDG*, p. 8: *gShen gter rgyud drug dmod pa'i rkyen gyis nub kyang / rgyud chen drug gter chen bon gyi rgyal po khu tsha zla 'od 'bar gyis sa mo stag gi lo la spa gro phug bcal nas dngos grub du brnyed pa . . . /* For the *Khro-bo rgyud-drug* see ibid., pp. 8–9.

(iv) Phur-pa. Also widely worshipped. The texts dealing with this divinity are in three groups (see *infra*, p. 305, ll. 13–23 *and KTDG*, pp. 18–20). However, the texts which are available at the present time are the nine rGyud of Phur-pa (phur-pa'i rgyud-dgu). For these see *KTDG*, p. 10. From these rGyud the ritual text entitled *dBal-phur nag-po drag-po gting-rdzogs spyi-don nyi-shu rtsa-lnga* was compiled by sTag-la Me-'bar, a disciple of sTon-pa gShen-rab (see Snellgrove, *Nine Ways*, p. 118, also for his life-story see *LShDz*, f. 66a3, Introduction, p. xxii). An extensive commentary on the ritual text entitled the *Don-bsdus rtsa-ba'i 'grel-chen* explaining the whole range of those rGyud is also attributed to him

bTsan-po), diffident about diffusing the teaching because of its profundity, did not teach it to others. Consequently for three generations the secret teaching of Bon completely disappeared, and the king's ordinary attainment was hampered. At about that time, thinking that the tantric Bon would decline, the Four Miraculous Goddesses of Earth, Air, Fire, and Water[1] took the leather box (of texts) out of the secret royal treasury and bestowed on the Bon-po of Mon, Ha-ra Ci-par who was able to understand them without instruction. He practised the teaching with the priestess sTag-ver Li-ver as his partner in the vicinity of lHa-ri, Mon-ri, and rGya-ri. As the supreme attainment his body became translucent. As the ordinary attainment he exhibited many wonderful supernatural powers: he pulled out a noose of rainbow from within a rocky cave and tied up wild men and demons, (141a) made devils serve him, made rivers flow backwards, rode on wild animals as if they were horses, hurled mountains as Zor,[2] rolled his antagonists on the ground by just casting his eyes at them, etc. The priestess sTag-ver Li-ver practised the teaching beside the lake Mu-le and attained realization. She possessed infinite supernatural powers: she made wild animals as tame as calves or sheep, overpowered water-spirits, mountain gods, and the lords of the earth, was able to transform

(*KTDG*, p. 18). This divinity corresponds to Buddhist Phur-pa = Skr. kīla (*Mvy* 4387). However, we cannot say anything concerning their origin until detailed comparative studies are carried out.

Concerning the name sTag-la Me-'bar, it applies to two different beings: one is a divinity and the other is a priest whom we have already met. See also *LShDz*, ff. 71b2, 84a1, 86a2. It is the divinity that is of most interest and importance to the Bon-po tradition. The divinity takes three forms: white, black, and red (stag-la spu-gri dkar-nag dmar-gsum = the white, black, and red razor of sTag-la, see *KTDG*, p. 23). The red razor of sTag-la Me-'bar (stag-la me-'bar spu-gri dmar-po) is set against Buddhists whenever the Bon-pos are under their pressure. Thus it is called the doctrinal weapon (bstan-pa'i mtshon-cha). Hoffmann's attempt (op. cit., p. 104) to connect this divinity with L. A. Waddell's Tiger Devil (*The Buddhism of Tibet*, p. 520) is pure conjecture. This divinity does not have the form of a tiger-headed human body at all.

(v) dBal-chen *Ge-khod*. Another tantric divinity. There are five rGyud dealing with this divinity (see *infra*, p. 329, l. 21, *KTDG*, pp. 10–11) from which the ritual text entitled *Ge-knod gsang-ba drag-chen* was compiled by rJe Rin-po-che (or known as mNyam-med Shes-rab rGyal-mtshan, *STNN* 1356–1415). Concerning other versions of the rite see *KTDG*, p. 22. The three Me-ri rGyud (see *KTDG*, p. 10) are also here said to belong to the last class of the Five Perfect Ones of the gSas-Palace.

[1] For the names of these goddesses see *infra*, p. 75.

[2] See Glossary.

herself into anything, etc. After living in the world of man for three hundred and sixty years she went to the 'Celestial Sphere' without leaving her body behind. Ha-ra Ci-par and sTag-ver Li-ver transmitted the teaching to A-nu 'Phrag-thag of Zhang-zhung. The latter, through practising it with his partner gYung-drung rGyal-mo on Mount Kailāsa, actually beheld the countenance of the Five Divinities.[1] He possessed infinite supernatural powers: he set fire to the land of demons by means of a 'gold bomb', liberated through death the enemies of the Doctrine with a 'bomb of lice',[2] destroyed the bodies of his antagonists with a 'bomb of poison'; he would eat poison as food; he made non-human beings serve him, etc. After living for two hundred and fifty-five years he attained enlightenment by making his body translucent. He transmitted the teaching to Sad-ne Ga'u of Zhang-zhung. (141b) The latter, through practising it with his partner Klu-lcam 'Bar-ma in Dang-ra g·yu-bun, was able to perform many miracles: he cured leprosy, turned back armies, floods, and rivers, made wild animals into beasts of burden, emitted flames from his body. He attained enlightenment by making his body become clear as the sky. He transmitted the teaching to Thad-mi Thad-ke. The latter, through practising it with his partner sMan-gcig gYu-lo-ma in Dang-ra khyung-rdzong, achieved the supreme attainment. When the armies of Se-lde, Tal, Ta-mi, Shud, Kye-mang, and Gu-ge in Zhang-zhung numbering sixteen thousand men came in a body to engage him, he made them faint and collapse instantaneously through his meditational power. Once he threw his hat into the sky and it became an eagle and pursued the enemies of the Doctrine. Transforming his shoes into a donkey, he liberated a devil through death. With his spittle he put out a fire that was spreading through a house. Thus his miraculous acts were beyond imagination. Having lived for two hundred and seventy-seven years he disappeared into the sky riding on a turquoise dragon. He transmitted the teaching to Shad-bu Ra-khug. (142a) The latter, through practising it with his partner Rang-gsal Don-ldan-ma, achieved the supreme attainment. As the ordinary attainment

[1] They are gSal-ba Rang-'byung, dGe-lha Gar-phyug, Bye-brag dNgos-med, dGa'-ba Don-grub, and Kun-snang Khyab-pa. For further details of these see Snellgrove, *Nine Ways*, p. 261 n. 59.

[2] Cf. *GRB*, p. 47; *infra*, p. 98.

he exhibited many wonderful supernatural powers: transforming himself into a tiger or a leopard he travelled through wild places full of savage beasts. Transforming himself into a vulture, he flew into the sky; he openly summoned the dBal-mo[1] to the flesh and blood of his antagonists, knew other people's thoughts, filled those who were miserable with happiness, etc. He passed away at the age of two hundred having become translucent. He taught the precept to the Chinese priest Zing-ba mThu-chen. The latter, through practising it with his partner rGya-lcam dKar-mo in Gong-bu dmar-ru, achieved the supreme attainment. As (the ordinary attainment) he (exhibited) supernatural powers: transforming himself into a wolf he openly summoned his antagonists; he made water gush from a wall, he prolonged the life of those at the point of death, he hung his cloak over the sun's rays, he made the 'substitute-body' of the Chinese king go away of its own accord. Having bestowed the teaching on sPe-bon (Thog-'phrul) he went to the 'Celestial Sphere'. The latter, through practising it with the help of dKar-mo sPyan-gcig-ma (142b) in Yar-lha Sham-po, gained the level of realization. There was a lake called gYu-ri in Kha-yug of Zhang-zhung so big that sMra zhi-hrangs[2] would take three days to go round it. sPe-bon made it into a turquoise and put it on the nape of his neck. He made demons and sea-goddesses serve him. Riding on a sunbeam he went round the world. He brought down a rain of flowers. He promoted the welfare of sentient beings by transforming himself into many bodies, etc. His was a wonderful life-story. He lived for two hundred and sixty-one years and, having transmitted (the teaching) to sPe-bon Thog-rtse, he attained enlightenment and left no body behind. After taking sPa-za Kun-dga' as his partner sPe-bon Thog-rtse practised (the teaching) in 'Phan-yul brag-dkar and achieved the levels of supreme and ordinary attainment. He rode on a wild yak or a crocodile and made Ma, bDud, and bTsan[3] serve him. He exhibited many marvels simultaneously, etc. His wonderful

[1] A class of goddesses, see *gZi-brjid*, vol. kha, chap. 9, f. 1864 (Snellgrove, *Nine Ways*, pp. 109–111) see also *infra*, p. 136.

[2] Name of a horse.

[3] Ma, bDud, and bTsan are the three principal religious protectors. Ma: Srid-pa rGyal-mo (see *supra*, p. 9 n. 6, and for liturgical texts see *KTDG*, p. 25). bDud: 'Byams-pa Khrag-'go (for liturgical text see *TPS*, p. 711) and bTsan: A-bse rGyal-ba. (For liturgical texts see *KTDG*, p. 25.)

life-story is beyond imagination. When he was one hundred and thirty-five years of age he passed away without leaving his body behind. He transmitted (the teaching) to sTong-rgyung mThu-chen of Zhang-zhung. The latter, with the help of mTsho-sman rGyal-mo, practised it in gNam-mtsho do-ring and achieved realization. (143a) He delivered enemies and evil spirits by scattering gold-(dust) and white mustard seeds. He carried the lake of gNam in the lap of his white silk robe. He threw rocky mountains as Zor. He lived on meditational food. He made the Five kinds of Divinities[1] emanate from inside his body, etc. His supernatural powers were beyond imagination. Having promoted the welfare of human and non-human beings he left for the 'Celestial Sphere'. He transmitted (the teaching) to Se dMu-tsha Sha-ri dBu-chen, lCe-tsha mKhar-bu-chung of Me-nyag, and lDe-bon Gyim-tsha rMa-chung. They, having taken lHa-lcam 'Od-'phro, Klu-za mThing-btsun, and rMa-btsun Phyug-mo as their partners, practised it in the cave of Mang-mkhar lcags-'phrang. As a sign of realization Sha-ri dBu-chen, riding on a blue water horse, travelled about on the lake of gYun-bun. Sea-goddesses offered him food. lCe-tsha, having transformed himself into a golden man on a horse, crossed the rivers sKyin and rMa. Gyim-tsha rode around on a rock. He made wild animals beasts of burden. Their signs and wonders were beyond imagination. The three of them, flying into the sky, passed away without leaving any remains (143b).

(1b) How the doctrines of the other 'Perfect Ones'[2] spread.

α. How the Phur-pa was spread
β. How the Ge-khod was spread

α. I have related earlier[3] how the Phur-pa was transmitted from sTag-la Me-'bar[4] up to dBal-bon Kha-yal Me-'bar. The latter taught it to dBal-bon gNod-sbyin-'dul in sTag-tshal rgod-kha'i-yul. The latter taught it to dBal-bon 'Od-spungs in dBal-'bar lha'i yul. The latter taught it to dBal-bon Khyung-lag-can in sTag-rtse lha'i mkhar. The latter taught it to dBal-bon sTag-slag-can in dBal-yul 'od-ma'i tshal. The latter taught it to the Bon-po

[1] See *supra*, p. 47 n. 1.
[2] See *supra*, p. 45 n. 2.
[3] See *LShDz*, f. 87a6.
[4] Concerning his life-story see ibid., f. 66a3 and cf. ff. 84a1 et seq.; also see Introduction, p. xxii.

of Gru-gu, Kha-yal Me-'bar in Grub-yul grug-stod. The latter taught it to 'Ol-bon Mig-gcig in 'Ol-yul 'ol-mkhar. The latter taught it to Ti-ti Me-slag-can in the country of Mu-stegs kha-'bar. The latter taught it to the Bon-po of Bram-ze, Kha-yal Me-lce-can in the country of Bram-ze 'thib-gnon. The latter taught it to the Bon-po of India, A-ga-ru Nag-po. The latter taught it to the Bon-po of Nepal, Tsan-tsan lCe-ring in Thang-shod in Nepal. The latter taught it to the Bon-po of Kashmir, Gyang Ti-gsas in Kashmir. (144a) The latter taught it to the Bon-po of Li, sPungs-rgyung mThu-chen in lJang-ra smug-po in Li. The latter taught it to Ge Ti-gsas rNga-chung-can in Zhang-zhung. The latter taught it to the Bon-po of sMra, Ko-long lHa-gsas in Tibet. The latter taught it to the Bon-po of 'Phan, Kha-'byams lCags-kyi Bya-ru-can in 'Phan-yul. The latter taught it to the Bon-po of China, dBal-'bar lHa-gsas, in 'Grim-thang in China. The latter taught it to gSas-mkhar Me-'bar in Yar-yul lha'i-thang. The latter taught it to Dran-pa Nam-mkha' in Tibet, who kept it for aggressive purposes.

β. I have related how the Me-ri was transmitted from sTon-pa gShen-rab up to Khri-lde lCags-kyi Bya-ru-can.[1] From him up to Tshe-spungs Zla-ba rGyal-mtshan the transmission is the same as that of the Mental Teachings which I shall relate later.[2]

The Ge-khod was transmitted from lCags-kyi Bya-ru-can to sTag-sna rGyal-po of Zhang-zhung. It then passed down through Khri 'Od-gsal, gSang-ba gTing-rum, Sad-ne Ga'u, rGyung-ne Khod-spungs, Hris-pa Gyer-med, Tso-mi Gyer-chen, and This-dmar sPungs-rgyung, (144b) to Dran-pa Nam-mkha'.

(2) How (the teaching of) the 'Stage of Perfection' was spread[3]

α. The spread of the Ma-rgyud[4]

β. The spread of the oral tradition of the Great Perfection

α. I have described the transmission up to sNang-ba'i mDog-can earlier.[5] The latter on request taught it to Paṇḍita A-nu 'Phrag-

[1] See *LShDz*, f. 88b6.

[2] See *infra*, p. 111.

[3] This is the section (2) announced on p. 39.

[4] See *supra*, p. 29 n. 2.

[5] i.e. from rGyal-gshen Mi-lus bSam-legs (for his life-story see *LShDz*, f. 74b2) to sNang-ba'i mDog-can, see *LShDz*, ff. 89a6–95b4.

thag of Central Zhang-zhung who studied it through three hundred and sixty-six kinds of great hardship and achieved the supreme and the ordinary attainments. On request A-nu 'Phrag-thag taught it to Paṇḍita Sad-ne Ga'u of Outer Zhang-zhung who studied and practised it through twenty-three great insights and gained the stage of realization.

In all, the Ma-rgyud has come down through six lines of transmission. They are as follows: the transmission of the supreme entity of Bon, the transmission of the mystic goddesses, the transmission of the oral teaching of ascetics, and the transmission of scholarly translators. (The texts of the teaching) were translated from the languages of Inner, Outer, and Central Zhang-zhung (into Tibetan) by sNang-ba'i mDog-can of Inner Zhang-zhung, A-nu 'Phrag-thag of Central Zhang-zhung, and Sad-ne Ga'u of Outer Zhang-zhung. At about that time there were eighty ascetics in Kha-yug of Zhang-zhung and Tibet. (145a) They were the Six Great Lamas of the Upper Land,[1] the Thirteen Lineage Transmitters,[2] the Four Scholars of the Lower Land,[2] the Nine Scholars,[3] the Nine Blessed Priests,[4] the Nine Magicians,[5] the Nine Miraculous Mothers,[6] the Nine Subduers of Border Troubles,[6] and Nine Holders of Scriptural Law,[6] and the Three Sages of the Transmission.[6] They all achieved both the supreme and ordinary attainments, and acquired power over death. I have not recorded the history of their great achievements in detail.

β. Although the texts of the Great Perfection are innumerable, they can all be reduced to the Four Cycles of Scriptural Tradition, the Three Cycles of Propagation,[7] and the Nine Cycles of Mind Abatement.[8]

[1] See *infra*, p. 58.

[2] See *infra*, p. 58.

[3] See *supra*, p. 42.

[4] See *gZhi-lam-gyi 'grel*, ff. 105b5–106b1. Our text pays little attention elsewhere to this last group of ascetics.

[5] See *supra*, p. 42.

[6] See n. 4 *supra*.

[7] See *supra*, p. 15 n. 3.

[8] Tib. sems-smad sde-dgu. They are the *Byang-sems gab-pa dgu-skor* (*Byang-sems gab-pa* or just *Gab-pa*) which is listed under three textual treasures (see *infra*, pp. 130, 150, 153, also p. 61, where one of the many commentaries composed on this work and listed in *KTDG*, p. 26, the *mKhas-bzhi gab-'grel* is quoted), then the *Khu-byug* (see *infra*, p. 57), and lastly the seven small texts called the *Sems-phran sde-bdun* making nine in all (*KTDG*, p. 12, cf. *dByings-rig-mdzod*, vol. ka, f. 25).

The Four Cycles of Scriptural Tradition are the *Phyi lta-ba spyi-gcod*, the *Nang man-ngag dmar-khrid*, the *gSang-ba rig-pa cer-mthong*, and the *Yang-gsang gnas-lugs phugs-chod.*[1] (145b) Three modes of transmission were involved: multiple transmission, direct transmission, and the two combined. Multiple transmission separated into two streams: a disordered stream and an orderly one. It is because one of these streams appears to be disordered in comparison with the other that it is referred to as the disordered one. So from 'Chi-med (gTsug-phud) and the Teacher and source of transmission, gSang-ba 'Dus-pa;[2] the transmission to Gyer-spungs involves three modes. As for the orderly (stream of transmission), gSang-ba 'Dus-pa, the last of the Nine Thought Transmitters,[3] transmitted the teaching to the gShen of the Gods, that of the Serpents and that of Man,[4] from whom it came down through (the rest of) the twenty-four gShen.[5] Direct transmission occurred through Ta-pi Hri-tsa to Gyer-spungs. Combined transmission occurred when the disordered and orderly streams (of multiple transmission) combined with direct transmission to meet—through (what thus resulted in) a fivefold process—in Gyer-spungs from whom the transmission descended to the present time. I have related earlier how the teaching was transmitted from the Nine Thought Transmitters to the gShen of the Gods, the Serpents and Man.[6] I shall describe shortly how the lamas who preceded Gyer-spungs in the line of the disordered stream attained realization. 'Chi-med gTsug-phud transmitted the teaching to dPon-chen Hor-ti. The latter transmitted it to Kun-mkhyen Don-grub. (146a) Having understood (the non-reality of) external objects, body and mind, dPon-chen Hor-ti and Kun-mkhyen Don-grub released themselves into (the

[1] These four texts and the *Nyam-brgyud* (see *infra*, p. 111) constitute the main body of the book known as *Zhang-zhung snyan-brgyud* said to have been passed on orally to Gyer-spungs sNang-bzher Lod-po (a contemporary of king Khri-srong lDe-btsan, see *infra*, p. 97 for his life, *ZhNyL*, ff. 25b5–29a8) by dPon-chen Ta-pi Hri-tsa, concerning whom see ibid., f. 25a2.

[2] For life-stories of 'Chi-med gTsug-phud and gSang-ba 'Dus-pa see ibid., ff. 11b5–12b7; *LShDz*, ff. 62b3, 65b5; and Introduction, pp. xxi–xxii.

[3] For these see *ZhNyL*, f. 5a4 and *LShDz*, ff. 87a1 et seq.

[4] Here the gShen of Man is different from the gShen-po Mi-lus bSam-legs I earlier referred to (see *supra*, p. 15 n. 3). *ZhNyL*, f. 20b2.

[5] *ZhNyL* (f. 20a3) gives sTon-pa gShen-rab instead of gSang-ba 'Dus-pa as the first of the twenty-four.

[6] *LShDz*, ff. 95b6 et seq.

sphere of) primordial origination.[1] Having meditated for nine years in Brag-dmar-shad, Tshe-spungs Zla-ba rGyal-mtshan, a

[1] Tib. *gdod-ma'i gzhi*, Lit. the 'primordial basis'. According to the Mental Teachings (sems-phyogs, Lit. Mental Class) of the Great Perfection (rdzogs-chen) in Bon-po tradition this 'primordial basis' is a state from which all notions of the cycle of existence ('khor-ba in Buddhism = Skr. saṃsāra) and escape from that sorrow (mya-ngan-las 'das-pa, Skr. nirvāṇa) come forth. A rDzogs-chen-pa might gain or rather return to this state from which he is said to have come into the cycle of existence. See *dByings-rig-mdzod*, vol. ka, f. 148a2; vol. kha, f. 73b1; cf. Snellgrove, *Nine Ways*, pp. 229 et seq. and note 79. Bon-pos consider it the beginning of the cycle of existence (*dByings-rig-mdzod*, vol. ka, f. 197b6), but, however, according to Buddhists, the cycle of existence has no beginning since it is produced by ignorance (see Tsong-kha-pa, *Byang-chub lam-rim*, ff. 195a7, 277b3).

To attain or rather to return to this origination which is known as *Ye-shes rDzogs-pa'i sku* or *Srog-med gYung-drung-gi sku* or *'Ja'-lus 'Pho-ba chen-po'i sku* or *gZhon-nu Bum-pa'i sku* (*dByings-rig-mdzod*, vol. kha, f. 152b3), a rDzogs-chen-pa has to go through a process of four stages known as the 'Four Appearances' (snang-ba bzhi). *dByings-rig-mdzod*, vol. kha, f. 111b3: *bon nyid mngon sum gyi snang ba / nyams snang gong 'phel gyi snang ba / rig pa tshad phebs kyi snang ba / bon nyid zad sa'i snang ba /* The first of these relates to the 'primordial basis' and is to be recognized by the rDzogs-chen-pa as the primary practice. The second is a mere method which strengthens the understanding of the first by certain further practices (*dByings-rig-mdzod*, vol. kha, f. 126b4). The third is a stage where the improvement reaches its peak (tshad-la phebs-pa). The fourth is the stage where the rDzogs-chen-pa attains the ultimate or returns to the primordial origination. *dByings-rig-mdzod*, vol. kha, f. 112a2: *dang po'i gzhi bon nyi mngon sum ma mthong na gzhan gsum gyi 'char gzhi med pas dang po bon nyid mngon sum gyi snang ba rten gzhi ltar 'char ba'o / de nyid shar nas bon nyid kyi nges pa rnyed pas rang byung gi ye shes rang las rnyed ces bya'o / mngon sum pa de nyid lta stangs gyis gcun pas snang ba de dag gi 'phel rgyas nas nyams gong 'phel du 'byung ngo / de nas nyams kyi 'phel zad nas tshad la phebs pa ste / 'phel pa ma zad na nyams thug pa med pas bon la zin pa med cing sangs la rgya dus med pa las / nyams kyi 'phel zad nas bstan pa'i tshad la phebs pas rig pa tshad phebs kyi snang ba 'byung ba'o / de nas tshad la phebs pa de nyid de las gzhan du mi 'gyur na sku gsum 'bras bur 'dod pa dang khyad med la / dngos snang mtshan ma'i bon la mthar thug tu byed pa thun mongs ba rnams dang mtshungs nyid las / snang nyams gzhi la thim ste / phra rags snang shes nub nas ka dag bon zad la sbyor bas bon nyid zad pa'i snang ba 'byung bas na go rim de ltar nges pa'o /*

On the last stage the so-called three Dengs-pa (dissolution) occur (*dByings-rig-mdzod*, vol. kha, f. 152a2): the dissolution of external objects (snang-ba), of the body ('lus), and of the mind (sems). In the words of the *Bon-sku'i smon-lam gti-mug gnyid-skrogs*, f. 2b8:

dngos kun 'od gsal ngang du dengs /
gzugs phung 'od kyi lus su dengs /
sems ni rig pa'i ngang du dengs /
dengs pa gsum du 'byung ba na /
blo zad bon zad chen po yis /
g·yung drung 'pho ba chen po'i sku /
lus 'di ma spangs ngang du bzhengs /

Thus it is that the rDzogs-chen-pa can be called 'Ja'-lus-pa ('translucent body') for having completed the three Dengs-pa, his body has become translucent like

disciple of Kun-mkhyen (Don-grub), disappeared like the light of a rainbow, having rendered the external and internal impurities of his body translucent. The latter's disciple Ra-sangs Klurgyal having meditated in sPo-dmar accomplished the Four (Stages of) Appearance. The latter's disciple dPon-chen Ta-pi Hri-tsa having meditated for nine years in sTag-thabs seng-ge'i brag attained the body of the perfection of wisdom.[1] After meditating for nine years in Ne-ring the latter's disciple Ra-sangs Ku-ma Ra-dza penetrated (the nature of) the three bodies.[2] Having meditated for thirteen years in solitude the latter's disciple Ra-sangs bSod-rtse brought himself to the stage of Voidness.[3] The latter's disciple was Sad-ne Ga'u of Zhang-zhung whose (bodily) elements vanished after he had meditated for sixteen years in a cave. The latter's disciple was Gu-rub lHasbyin who meditated for eleven years in Bya-tshang without ever visiting any secular community and his body became translucent. The latter's disciple was Gu-rub dPal-bzang, who, by practising (the teaching) as he dwelt in the mountains, transformed his material body into the body of bliss.[4] The latter's disciple was Ra-sangs Khri-ne, who, having practised (the teaching) in gCan-rong in the South, achieved the supreme and the ordinary attainments. (146b) The latter's disciple was the Bon-po of Sum-pa A-ba-ldong who diffused (the teaching) in Sum-pa, and whose disciple rGya-bon gSal-ba 'Od-chen transmitted it to China, and (in his turn) had a disciple 'Jag-rong gSas-mkhar. (Having practised the teaching) the three of them succeeded in extinguishing the apparent materiality (of their bodies) and attained transcendence. 'Jag-rong gSas-mkhar taught the precept to his second son Grub-pa rGyal-mtshan who, having practised it in Brag-dmar stag-tshang, transcended external and internal

a rainbow. The rdzogs-chen-pa can then live as long as he wishes and usually lives a very long time, e.g. Gyer-spungs (see *infra*, p. 55). Also *dByings-rig-mdzod*, vol. kha, f. 104b5: . . . *gzugs phung rang snang rang 'od du lhag nas phung gzhan rang sar dag ste / srog med g·yung drung gi sku grub pas / 'khor ba ma stong gi bar du bzhugs nas 'gro don mdzad pa ni / dper na gyer chen dran pa nam mkha' lta bu'i dgongs spyod bla na med pas rtogs par bya la /*

[1] Tib. ye-shes rdzogs-pa'i sku, see *supra*, p. 53 n. 1.

[2] The three bodies are Bon-sku, Longs-sku, and sPrul-sku (see Snellgrove, *Nine Ways*, p. 261 n. 59).

[3] This refers to the fourth stage of the 'Four Appearances', see *supra*, p. 53 n. 1.

[4] Equivalent to ye-shes rdzogs pa'i sku see *supra*, p. 53 n. 1.

materiality. The latter's disciple was Khyung-po bKra-shis rGyal-mtshan, who, having meditated for twenty-one years in the cave of Sa-ti in Zhang-zhung, achieved the body of bliss. The latter's son and disciple was Legs-mgon, who, having meditated for eight years on the isle of the lake of Ri-ti, dissolved his apparent materiality into light. The latter's disciple was Ma-hor sTag-gzig, who, although he meditated for twelve years on Mount Kailāsa, still was unable to find assurance and so returned to his lama and, offering ten measures of gold, asked: 'Although I have practised (the teaching) for so many years I have found no assurance. I entreat you to impart (further) instruction to me.' The lama said: 'I do not want your gold.' He gave him instruction. (147a) Having meditated for (another) six years, he attained realization.[1]

Incidentally, the twenty-four lamas in the line of the orderly transmission which started from the source of transmission, gSang-ba 'Dus-pa are all also 'Ja'-lus-pa. The teacher[2] of Gyer-spungs, Ta-pi Hri-tsa, was likewise 'Ja'-lus-pa. He meditated for nine years in sTag-thabs seng-ge'i brag. At the age of five hundred and seventy-three Gyer-spungs, having promoted extensively the welfare of sentient beings, grasped the 'Pho-chen-gyi sku after hearing the exposition of the *Le'u-brgyad-pa*[3] (from dPon-chen Ta-pi Hri-tsa) and entered the sphere of (primordial) origination with equanimity.[4] The latter's disciple was rGya Tig-gsas-chung, who, having meditated in Me-la-rgyung, attained the idea of the body of Bon. After living for three hundred and seventeen years he passed away. The latter's disciple was dMu Tso-ge, who, having practised (the teaching) for a long time, cleansed himself of the impurities of his body and, after living for one hundred and seventy-three years passed away like a bird flying into the sky. The latter's disciple was dMu Tso-stong, who, having meditated in a hermitage called Shang-shel-rong, made the elements (of his body) vanish (147b) and, after living a hundred and thirteen years, passed away like an eagle flying

[1] For these teachers cf. *ZhNyL*, ff. 13a5–19a2.

[2] Our text wrongly reads slob-ma = disciple.

[3] This text is a part of the *Zhang-zhung snyan-brgyud* subtitled *Man-ngag le-brgyad*, VA in the alphabetical order, and is said to have been passed on orally to Gyer-spungs just before he died by Ta-pi Hri-tsa. See *Man-ngag le-brgyad*, f. 22b4.

[4] See *supra*, p. 53 n. 1.

into the sky. The latter's disciple was dMu Shod-kram the Great, who having meditated in Gangs-gnyan rta-sgo, attained the body of the perfection of wisdom. After living for a hundred and seventeen years he passed away like a lion jumping into space. The latter's disciple was dMu rGyal-ba Blo-gros, who, by meditating in Zang-zang lha-brag, accomplished the 'Four (Stages of) Appearance'[1] and, having promoted extensively the welfare of sentient beings, at the age of two hundred and seventy passed away as wind is lost in space. The latter's disciple was dPon-rgyal bTsan-po, who, having meditated on Mount Shang-brag in gYas-ru, grasped the idea of the Conqueror. To promote the welfare of sentient beings he remained alive for one thousand six hundred years and then transforming himself into a turquoise cuckoo he went off towards the south-west to suppress demons.[2]

In short, there is no need to boast about the profundity of Bon as it is evident that (the many practisers of Bon) became 'Ja'-lus-pa. Since this is considered to be a remarkable fact by many (Buddhist) sects, it would be worth recording here at length, but I fear prolixity. The continuation of the line of the transmission of dPon-rgyal bTsan-po will be related later.[3]

(148a) The Three Cycles of Propagation. I have described the transmission from the Three Bodies to the gShen of the Gods, that of the Serpents and that of Man.[4] Klu-grub (the gShen of the Serpents) transmitted the teaching to the teacher 'Od-zer dPag-med of sTag-gzig. It then passed down through Mun-pa Kun-gsal, and 'Phrul-gshen sNang-ldan to gSang-ba 'Dus-pa. This is the Transmission of Changeless Sages. From gSang-ba 'Dus-pa it then passed down through sTong-rgyung mThu-chen, Se-bon Sha-ri dBu-chen, and lDe-bon Gyim-tsha rMa-chung to lCe-tsha mKhar-bu of Me-nyag. This is called the Transmission of the Scholarly Translators. sNya-chen Li-shu sTag-ring is the great master of the Three Cycles of Propagation. The king gNyan sTag-spungs and his wife found, as their share of off-spring, a beautiful girl in a grove. They gave her the name of sTag-za Li-ver. (Later), by performing the rite of the mChog-

[1] See *supra*, p. 53 n. 1.

[2] For short life-stories of these teachers from rGya Tig-gsas-chung to dPon-rgyal bTsan-po see *ZhNyL*, ff. 29b1 et seq.

[3] See *infra*, p. 111.

[4] *LShDz*, f. 98a6.

lnga, she became a man. As son and heir this man (was called) gNyan Li-shu sTag-ring. He held dominion and spread the Doctrine for eighty-two years. Then he went to sTag-gzig and sought (instruction in) many kinds of Bon. (148b) By practising them he achieved the supreme and the ordinary attainments. At the age of seven hundred he entreated dBal-bon Rum-po to impart magical spells to him. He made many translations of Bon texts from India and China. He overpowered mystic goddesses in the eight burial places.[1] When he was two thousand two hundred years old he went to sTag-gzig (again) and made many translations of essential Bon texts into Tibetan. His displays of supernatural powers are beyond comprehension. He consorted with the daughter of lDe Gyim-tsha rMa-chung as his secret partner. He achieved mastery of the vital channels, vital breath, and vital fluid. He beheld the countenances of every external, internal, and secret divinity. He diffused the doctrine throughout the six essential countries of the world by translating it into the languages of those countries. He promoted the welfare of sentient beings until he was two thousand five hundred years old. Having achieved the body of bliss he was free from birth and death. His supernatural powers and miraculous performances are beyond comprehension. They can be read about in detail in his biography.[2] So the teaching spread and was transmitted from Li-shu (sTag-ring) and his partner down through eighteen great ascetics. They all achieved the supreme and the ordinary attainments.

(149a) The Nine Cycles of the Abatement of Mind. The *Khu-byug*[3] says:

> The Master gShen-lha 'Od-dkar[4] transmitted the idea of the Original Teacher to the master 'Chi-med gTsug-phud by transforming his thought into a turquoise cuckoo.

In this turquoise cuckoo we have the Merciful Teacher

[1] These are said to be in sTag-gzig. For the names of the places see Snellgrove, *Nine Ways*, Illustration XXII. Also *gZhi-lam-gyi 'grel*, f. 27b5.

[2] The details given in the present text are the most exhaustive references I have seen. I do not know to what biography the author alludes.

[3] See *supra*, p. 51 n. 8.

[4] A sage who is the teacher of sTon-pa gShen-rab, see *gZer-mig*, vol. ka, ff. 19a4 et seq. (trans. A. H. Francke, op. cit., *Asia Major* i (1924), p. 274 *passim*), and *LShDz*, f. 25b6. Cf. *supra*, p. 9 n. 6. Also for details of gShen-lha 'Od-dkar see *LShDz*, ff. 57b5 et seq.

manifesting as the thought carrier Tshad-med 'Od-ldan.[1] 'Chi-med gTsug-phud transmitted the teaching to gShen gSang-ba 'Dus-pa and Yum bZang-za Ring-btsun in the manner described in detail in the *Mang-'grel* and *Nyung-'dus*.[2] These are called the Six Thought Transmitters. Further the *Khu-byug* says:

> The transmission passed from gSang-ba 'Dus-pa down through rMa-lo Dar-dpyangs, lHa-gshen Yongs-su Dag-pa, Mi-lus bSam-legs, and Ye-shes sNying-po to sNang-ba'i mDog-can.

They are called the Six Great Lamas. But in the Tantric Teachings we find sTag-la (Me-'bar) in place of rMa-lo (Dar-dpyangs). The teaching then passed from (sNang-ba'i mDog-can) down through Mu-khri bTsan-po, Ha-ra Ci-par, sTag-ver Li-ver, A-nu 'Phrag-thag, (149b) Sad-ne Ga'u, Thad-mi Thad-ke, Shad-bu Ra-khug, Zing-ba mThu-chen, and sPe-bon Thog-rtse, to sPe-bon Thog-'phrul. In addition to these the *Khu-byug* gives Hring-ni Mu-ting, Sum-pa dBu-dkar, and Glang-chen Mu-ver. These are called the Thirteen Lineage Transmitters. In the Tantric Teachings we have the Four Miraculous Goddesses instead of the last three since they unsealed the secret teaching which had been hidden by Mu-khri bTsan-po and transmitted it to Mon-bon Ha-ra Ci-par and his partner sTag-ver Li-ver. So in my opinion where the Mental Teaching is concerned it is not necessary to count them in. After that the transmission passes from sTong-rgyung mThu-chen down through Se and lDe to Me. These are called the Four Scholars.

(iii) How Bon was finally abolished[3]

1. Where it was abolished
2. What was abolished
3. At the time of which king and priest it was abolished
4. How it was abolished

1. Some have said that Bon was abolished in gTsang, but not in dBus, and others have said that it was abolished only in dBus.

[1] An imaginary sage, see *LShDz*, f. 60b2.

[2] These are two of the Three Cycles of Propagation of sPyi-spungs (see *supra*, p. 15 n. 3).

[3] This is the section (iii) announced *supra*, p. 30.

However, since the authoritative books are reliable we must look to them. (150a) The *bsGrags-byangs*[1] says:

> It was abolished only in gTsang, but not in dBus and beyond.

The *sGra-'grel*[2] says:

> In dBus Bon was not abolished but still practised.

The *dBang-chen* says:

> In parts of Tibet Bon was at one time abolished.

So the first two sources agree over the abolition of Bon in gTsang, but the third source in my opinion must be interpreted to mean that the 'Bon of Effect' was abolished in parts of Tibet, but the 'Bon of Cause' was not, for it says:

> The king said to the priests: 'Since in this country there is no room for both my authority and yours, I shall have only the "Four Ways of Divine Bon" and make its practitioners, Ge-khod This-'phen and gCo Gyim-bu Lan-tsha, my attendants. The rest of the priests must leave the four quarters of Tibet.' The text continues: Gyim-bu Lan-tsha said: 'If the "Four Ways of Divine Bon" are maintained the church will survive and therefore it will indeed be better if I remain. I shall be glad if the "Four Ways of Divine Bon" are not abolished.'
>
> Of the 'Four Ways of Divine Bon' he was allowed the one and a half ways which concern exclusively the 'Bon of Cause'.

So these authorities indicate that the 'Bon of Cause and Effect' was abolished in gTsang, but in dBus, although the 'Bon of Effect' was abolished, I think some of the 'Bon of Cause' remained. (150b) Otherwise what can the king's statement that the rest of the priests must leave the four quarters of Tibet mean if not that the other priests (apart from those who remained) must leave the country.[3]

2. The *dBang-chen* says:

> At the request of Gyim-bu Lan-tsha the king gave him one and a half ways of (the Four Ways of Divine Bon) which concern exclusively the 'Bon of Cause'.

This shows us that the whole 'Bon of the Visual World' and half

[1] *bsGrags-byang*, f. 35b2. [2] *sGra-'grel*, p. 27. [3] Cf. *GRB*, p. 40.

of the 'Bon of Existence' escaped destruction. The *rDzogs-pa gsas-mkhar*[1] says:

> The Divine Bon of 'Edible Tributes' was not abolished. A half of the Bon of 'posthumous evocation' for secular use was abolished. All the 'Bon of Perfect Mind' was abolished.

The *rNam-dag*[2] says:

> The great 'Bum and all the Bon of Mental Teachings were hidden.

That is what we learn from these works.

3. The *dBang-chen* says:

> In the time of the foolish king Gri-gum bTsan-po calumny began to circulate concerning the priests and the king.

The *Phyi-rgyud*[3] says:

> lDe Gyim-tsha rMa-chung practised the rituals of powerful religious protectors and became proud of his magical power. Calumny began to circulate concerning the priests and the king.

This happened in the time of Gri-gum bTsan-po. (151a) Concerning the priests, the *rTsa-rgyud nyi-zer sgron-ma* says:

> Bon was abolished in the early days of the 'Four Scholars'.

That is what it says.

The same authority says:

> The king (Gri-gum bTsan-po) practised Bon up till his twenty-seventh year.

As for the duration (of the period of abolition), the *Ju-thig rgyud-'bum*[4] says:

> The king Lo-ngam rTa-rdzi was killed after thirteen years of rule.
>
> Then sPu-lde Gung-rgyal ascended the throne.

Thus sPu-lde gained the throne after Lo-ngam's thirteen-year

[1] I cannot identify this text.

[2] To identify these texts is extremely difficult since they are not likely to be in libraries outside Tibet, and, moreover, the author uses only the marginal titles of the Tibetan texts in this case.

[3] See *supra*, n. 2.

[4] The long version of the *Ju-thig*, a book of sortilege, see *KTDG*, p. 25.

reign. It is said that seventeen years passed from the abolition up to the revival of Bon.

4. A. Reasons for the abolition
B. The manner in which the Bon was abolished
C. How the 'retribution'[1] occurred

A. The *mKhas-bzhi gab-'grel*[2] says:

> Some of the 84,000 ways of Bon and all its texts were destroyed some by time, some by karma, and some by cause.

According to this authority, then, they were destroyed by time, karma and cause. Firstly, time: as the conduct of sentient beings in general had become coarse and the duration of life had decreased, the degenerate age having been reached, the conservation of the essential doctrine on earth (151b) became difficult. The same authority says:

> As the merits of sentient beings decreased the profound Everlasting Bon was at one point abolished.

Secondly, karma: among Tibetans there was little merit and the five poisons were rife. Moreover, the merits of the king were exhausted. Since he was a prey to the five poisons and fully guilty of the ten sins, he became unfit to hear the Teaching. In this context the saying 'It is not sentient beings that count, but their karma' is applicable.
Thirdly, cause: the *bsGrags-byang*[3] says:

> Three major forces were aflame with power. Three small forces added the fuel of calumny to the flames.

As the king was the most important of all and proud of his great power, he was aflame with anger. The priests were proud of their knowledge and were aflame with pride. The ministers were proud of their intellect and were aflame with jealousy. The three small forces: calumny was on the lips of the ministers, evil spirits

[1] Tib. dbu-yog, for the meaning of which cf. E. Haarh, 'the identity of Tsu-chih-chien, the Tibetan "king" who died in 804 A.D.', *Acta Orientalia*, vol. xxv, 1–2, p. 124. It is not a straightforward term meaning retribution and is used by Bon-pos to describe the misfortunes suffered by Tibetan kings in consequence of having persecuted Bon.

[2] See *supra*, p. 51 n. 8.

[3] *bsGrags-byang*, f. 36a1.

entered the heart of the king, and the spread of evil rumour seemed to add fuel to the fire. So Everlasting Bon was abolished. This is how the calumny arose.[1] The minister Li bTsan-bzher said: (152a) 'O Lord, if the priests rose above you, they would seize your power', and so on. The minister Zing-pa Rad-na said: 'O Lord, I beg you to issue orders banishing the priests.' And an Indian beggar called Ratna Siddhi was wandering in the country and said: 'Now it seems that the king and the priests are on the same footing, but when his sons succeed him the kingdom might be taken over by the priests.' Calumny of this kind came between king and priests.

B. When the king was seriously thinking of abolishing the Swastika Bon—time, karma, and cause thus coinciding—Bru-sha gNam-gsas[2] said: 'O Lord, I request you to put off this discussion. But even if you take action I entreat you (not to abolish) the "Four Ways of Divine Bon" and to keep one priest to deal with them. If you do not, your own life will be in danger as the fearful divinities will be offended.' This was his request. The king summoned all the priests and said: 'Listen priests. It seems to me (152b) that in this country there is no room for both my authority and yours. I shall have the "Four Ways of Divine Bon" and Ge-khod This-'phen[3] and gCo Gyim-bu Lan-tsha as my attendants. The rest of you must all leave the four quarters of Tibet.'

The great minister Ra-sangs Khod-ram said:

'O Lord, since sin is inseparable from the one who commits it, one is bound to fall into hell.
Since virtue is common to everybody, one ascends the ladder of heaven.
If one perfects one's meditation, one attains enlightenment.
If one practises Everlasting Bon, one is happy here and in the next life.
I ask you not to issue this order.'

But the king said that there was no room for both authorities

[1] What now follows is a résumé of the event described in detail in the *sGra-'grel*, pp. 24–7. Cf. also *GRB*, pp. 41–2.

[2] See *supra*, p. 7.

[3] This priest and the others who figure in the rest of the story are not named in the genealogies.

and did not accede to the request. Then rGyung-ya Bla-chen said:

'O all you priests, the king's word once said is said.
The commoner's word is uttered to be repeated,
Just as a hornless cow keeps on butting.
All priests must make for the borders.
I call upon Gyim-bu Lan-tsha to leave with the rest of us.'

Gyim-bu Lan-tsha said: 'In spring if the clouds in the sky do not disperse, rain falls from them. (153a) In winter if the water on the ground does not dry up, steam rises in spring. If one practises virtue in this life, one will enjoy the result in the next life. If the "Four Ways of Divine Bon" are maintained, the church will survive. So I had better stay and I shall be happy if the "Four Ways of Divine Bon" are not abolished.' He did not wish to go. The other priests gave him one and a half of the 'Four Ways of Divine Bon' which concern exclusively the 'Bon of Cause'. Another one and a half (of the 'Four Ways of Divine Bon') were hidden in gSang-brag rgya'o in the North.[1] Ge-khod This-'phen said: 'If none of the other priests is allowed to remain, I am not going to stay either.' He did not wish to stay.

Then, loading wild asses and buffaloes, etc., with the texts of the six great ways of the 'Bon of Cause and Effect',[2] the priests made their journey to Byi-ba-mkhar in Kha-yug of Zhang-zhung. In Byi-ba-mkhar they gathered together and discussed (the situation). sKye-chen Mu-thur said: 'The king, courtiers, and women, have taken to beer and armed themselves with weapons. If we do not take care, we, the priests, are in danger of being murdered. It is possible that the doctrine also might be destroyed like fire swamped by water. Therefore, you, Khye'u Dran-pa and Khod-nan Yo-phya take the texts of two ways of Bon and go to Yar-lung sog-kha. You, the "Four Scholars", take the texts of two more ways of Bon (153b) and go to Dom-sgro nag-po in the South to establish the doctrines there. You,

[1] *GRB* p. 42: *der bon sgo phyed dang gnyis gyim bu lan tsha la bzhag / bon sgo phyed byang phyogs brag rgya bo la lus /* The accounts do not quite correspond, therefore.

[2] We have already seen that one and a half of the 'Four Ways of Divine Bon' were still to be permitted and another one and a half were hidden. Thus there were still six ways of the Nine Ways of Bon to be attended to.

dMu-tsha Gyer-med and Blon Ra-sangs Khod-ram, take the texts of the two remaining ways of Bon and go to gNam in the North. Just as the sun, moon, planets, and stars rise and set, rotated by the wind in space, once more a barbarian king will be born in Tibet and abolish the doctrines. But though the sun and moon set, they rise again and so will Bon doctrine gradually spread in the future.' Some of the remaining priests went up into the mountains of barren rock or snow. Some went off to islands in lakes or to forests. Others went to the northern plain and dwelt there practising nectar-procuring rituals. The *dBang-chen* says:

> Intending to establish the doctrine in lHo-bal mon,[1] priests set out from Byi-ba-mkhar in Upper gTsang. Omens warning that the doctrine would not be successfully established appeared (on the way), such as: unpleasant sounds in the sky, snow-storms. They returned from rNil-mtsho rde'u-mgul and hid all the texts in 'Bri-mtshams mtha'-dkar for the place possessed propitious qualities. (154a) Dran-pa and Yo-phya hid their texts in Mount Ram-po-dpal in Yar-lung. dMu-tsha and Ra-sangs Khod-ram went to the North and hid their texts in Zang-zang lha-brag, Dang-ra khyung-rdzung, and in the rock of rGyung-srub gsang-ba.

Thus having hidden the texts, like treasures, the priests travelled down from Sum-pa glang-gi gyim-shod. On setting out they prayed: may we reach Sog-po sprel'u-slag gon-pa, 'Jang-mi mig-dgu, Hor and rTsa-mi shing-mi, etc., without interference. May the doctrines of Everlasting Bon be exalted. May youths who have merit and are fortunate and noble in body in due time discover the hidden texts like flowers growing in the grass. May the doctrines be established through the discovery of concealed texts and be a blessing. The *rNam-dag* says:

> Priests of evil disposition, having handed the king over to a demoness,[2] left for Sum-pa glang-gi gyim-shod.

Concerning the 'Rules of Discipline'[3] some have said it was

[1] Nepal.
[2] Demoness refers to Srid-pa rGyal-mo, concerning whom see *supra*, p. 9 n. 6.
[3] These form a part of the 'Bon of Perfect Mind', cf. *supra*, p. 19.

destroyed in the time of Gri-gum, and others in the time of Khri-srong. (154b) Khyung-po Blo-gros rGyal-mtshan and Abbot Nyi-ma bsTan-'dzin said that it was destroyed by the king Mu-la Mu-sang who was not a member of the Zhang-zhung royal line, at the time when the two sects[1] who followed the 'Rules of Discipline' were involved in a dispute the cause of which had been attributed to an Indian called Dharma Ghri-ti.[2] Nevertheless, it is said in the *'Dul-ba gling-grags* that one thousand eight hundred years had passed since the abolition of the 'Rules of Discipline' up to the moment when Mu-zi was roused from his state of 'cessation of senses' by Sog-ston.[3] The Lord[4] also agrees with this authority. In my opinion the 'Rules of Discipline' still existed in the time of Khri-srong. The *Srid-rgyud* speaks of five hundred Bon-po monks who were forced to follow the Buddhist vinaya. At that time, 'Tsho-bon Don-grub, rNo-bon Khye'u-cho sNang-ldan, and gShen-bon lHa-gnyan took three volumes of manuscripts containing *gShen-gyi 'dul-ba* and *mDzad-khrims*, etc., to sTag-gzig. These texts are said not to have undergone concealment. Abbot Nyi-ma bsTan-'dzin maintained that those texts were to be known as the 'Upper Tradition' of the 'Rules of Discipline'.[5] sGa-ston[6] maintained that those three monks returned (from sTag-gzig) to La-stod (in gTsang) after thirty-five years and diffused the teaching of the 'Rules of Discipline'. The *Byams-ma* also speaks (155a) of priests who were proficient in the *'Dul-ba rgyud-drug* existing in the time of the Four Bon-po Kings.[7] During the reign of Gri-gum—apart from a few texts of the 'Bon of Cause'—almost all the 'Bon of Cause and Effect' was abolished, but teachers who were dwelling in some parts of the country, and carrying on the spiritual lineage of the 'Rules of Discipline', having gained power over death, were undoubtedly persecuted in the time of Khri-srong.

[1] For these two sects see *supra*, p. 37.

[2] Our author here refers to two works: one by Khyung-po Blo-gros rGyal-btshan who mentioned it in his *GRB* (p. 49) and the other is Abbot Nyi-ma bsTan-'dzin's *TNT* (p. 53).

[3] Sog-ston Khri-'bar Tshul-khrims, concerning whom see *infra*, p. 105.

[4] mNyam-med Shes-rab rGyal-mtshan (*STNN* 1356–1415). For his life-story see *infra*, p.140.

[5] *TNT*, p. 54.

[6] sGa-ston Tshul-khrims rGyal-mtshan (fourteenth century).

[7] They are lHa Tho-tho-ri sNyan-shal, Khri-gnyan gZung-btsan, sTag-gong sNyan-gzigs, and gNam-ru Srong-btsan. See *LShDz*, f. 109b1.

C. The *rTsa-rgyud nyi-sgron* says:

> Gri-gum bTsan-po[1] was born to become an enemy of Bon. He abolished it all. Not even an echo of it was left. Priests were banished beyond the borders. The 'retribution' for abolishing Bon fell upon the king. He was reborn as the demon Mang-snya U-ver. He was murdered by his subject Lo-ngam who wrung his neck.

According to this authority, as the king and ministers were dancing and singing, and having a leisurely time after the abolition of Bon, a fearful white man appeared in the sky and said: 'Your life, O king, and that of your ministers will suddenly be cut off.' Then he disappeared. An evil spirit entered the heart of the king who had brought the disfavour of Bon on himself. He sent a message to Lo-ngam: 'I have banished (155b) the priests who were equal to me in power. But now as I have no rival to fight with, you must prepare to be my opponent.' Lo-ngam of lHo-brag replied: 'You are a great and sublime king. I am a father of twelve small tribes. How can I agree to a war between a king and a subject? I am not fit to be the rival of a Lord. I beg you not to give me this order.' But the king did not listen and issued further orders: 'You are to come with your army. If you do not come, I shall soon bring my army and destroy you and all your people.' Now Lo-ngam was greatly perturbed. At night Lo-ngam had a dream in which a Bon religious protector disguised as a well-dressed young man said to him: 'You, Lo-ngam, do not need to be frightened. As for the king his heart is stirred by the Ma-bdud[2] (as a result of) the 'retribution' of the Bon. You cannot subdue him with your power, but if you prepare things which will separate him from his gods and then fight with him, you will be able to subdue him. Tell the king this: "Although

[1] *THD*, p. 97 and *SG*, f. 23b7 read this name as Dri-gum. This is possibly an earlier spelling. The story in our text of this king's order to his minister Lo-ngam to be his opponent is based on two works: *Nyi-sgron* (see *supra*, p. 16 n. 3) and *Gri-bshad*. They both attribute the violent death of the king to his Bon persecution. However, we do not find any indication of this motive in the *THD*. In the view of Bon-pos, who have seen them, these documents though historical are somewhat late works. On the other hand, it is quite possible that the Bon-pos adapted the story to suit their own convenience, and since we do not yet have any other materials with which to make comparisons except the Tun-Huang manuscripts, the version they give must be considered as the most reliable.

[2] Ma-bdud Srid-pa rGyal-mo, concerning whom see *supra*, p. 9 n. 6.

I am not fit to be the rival of a Lord, if it will make you happy, I will offer the combat to you as a game with musical accompaniments. So come next month at the time of the full moon, riding your royal horse Phum-dmar, carrying a (dead) monkey on the pommel of the saddle and a cat behind. (156a) Let your forehead be adorned with a silver-mirror. Flourish your sword above your head. Come with a hundred red cows and bulls loaded with sacks full of ashes. In each sack there should be a spear-head like a demoness's foot." These are the things you need to subdue your opponent. Then proceed: "If you do not prepare these, the gods and ghosts in this part of the country are easily offended and one never knows where danger to the life of the Lord may lurk. So I beg you to do as I say." This is what you should say to him.' Lo-ngam spoke according to his dream. The king was very pleased and said: 'Lo-ngam is good-hearted and very learned. I will do as he says.' Lo-ngam fixed the time of the battle when he would come with his army. Having prepared the army, weapons and musical instruments, he set out punctually. The king also went to much trouble to prepare the requirements listed by Lo-ngam and set out. Lo-ngam sent a messenger to the king in advance saying: 'Between us stands the difference that separates a king and his subject. Therefore, first I must offer you a ceremonial welcome and after that we shall enjoy ourselves as planned.' (156b) The king thought that what Lo-ngam said was true and replied: 'As we are not in any way equal, you should first meet me and then fight with me.' Then, as Lo-ngam gave him a ceremonial welcome with loud music, the red cows and bulls bolted. All the sacks of ashes with which they were laden were pierced by the spears. A wind caused a dust-storm to rise which lasted for a long time. A place called Nyang-ro thal-ba-tshal (dust-grove of Nyang-ro) is still said to exist. At the same time the 'cord of dMu' and 'ladder of dMu', by which the Lord could have ascended to the heaven, were cut by his sword (as he waved it above his head). The two guardians of his humanity had now left him because of his carrying a (dead) monkey and a cat. In the middle of the dust-storm, as the mirror on his forehead remained visible, Lo-ngam first aimed and shot an arrow at it, and then killed him (by wringing his neck).[1] The *Gri-bshad*[2] says:

Once upon a time,
A king of evil spirits entered the heart
Of the king Gri-gum bTsan-po.
No rival could be found to fight with him.
The embodiment of the murderous demon Ha-la
The king of murderers Lo-ngam rTa-rdzi
Was found as a rival for him.
Battles of words and real hand-to-hand fighting occurred.
Past action decreed the use of weapons.
The king Gri-gum rode the royal horse, Phum-dmar. (157a)
He tied a (dead) monkey and a cat to the back of the saddle.
He flourished his sword above his head.
He drove forward red cows and bulls carrying loads.
As a result of his tying on the (dead) monkey and cat,
The 'Royal Divinities' withdrew into heaven.
As he flourished his sword (above his head),
The 'cord of dMu' and the 'ladder of dMu' were cut off in the middle.
As he drove forward the red cows and bulls,
Day became night.
The king of murderers Lo-ngam rTa-rdzi
Shot at the forehead of the king and killed him.
With a lethal sword-arrow that had a black band around the middle.
From the king's mouth evil curses issued:
'By the signs of murder present on my body
May the practice of murder spread (even) to heaven.
By the mole of blood of my forehead
May the places and instruments of murder increase.
By the store of my weapons
May the lives of human beings be cut off.
May a practice of violent and false religion be spread from the borders.
May the kingdom and the world be filled with war and weapons.

[1] Cf. *SG*, f. 24a4; *GRB*, pp. 42–3 and *THD*, pp. 97 et seq. (trans. p. 123) where the same story is told with variations.

[2] See *supra*, p. 66 n. 1.

May the heads of evil spirits rise wildly as a result of the worship of Tshangs-pa.
May all evil spirits rise up on high.
These were the curses he uttered.
The king was murdered by a subject.
That is why he has since been known as Gri-gum (Murdered One).

(157b) Since Lo-ngam killed the king by making his mouth appear at the nape of his neck on a flat stone,[1] a stone called Nyang-ro ltag-zhal (nape-mouth of Nyang-ro) is said still to exist. As the 'red cord of dMu' and the 'nine-runged ladder of dMu' were cut off, the king's corpse remained on earth so Lo-ngam put it into a copper box and threw it into the river of Nyang at 'Da'-le zang-kha. He banished the princes, sPu-lde and Nya-khri, to Dvags-po and Kong-po.[2] He killed the important ministers and banished the lesser ones. He made the queen a shepherdess, and took the princess as his wife, and ruled the kingdom for thirteen years.

One day the queen, dBal-za Khri-btsun, went up the valley to look after her sheep, but fell asleep and dreamed of having intercourse with a handsome youth. When she woke up and looked around she found a white yak lying near the place where her head had been resting. Then one day she gave birth to a fatherless son whose size was like a mere fist of blood-meat. She was very ashamed and put the child into a horn. She brought him up close to her hearth-stone, and he grew more vigorous and

[1] i.e. he forced him down on to a flat stone and twisted his neck so that his mouth appeared where his nape should be.

[2] *Bu-ston chos-'byung* (f. 123b1): *de'i sras gsum gyi bya khri la spu khri* [sic] *gung rgyal zhes btags* /A note informs us: *che ba sha khri bar ba gri gum btsan po chung ba bya khri la spu de gung rgyal zhes grags* / Thus Bu-ston does not regard the king Gri-gum as the father of Sha-khri and Nya-khri, but as their brother. dPa'-bo gTsug-lag 'Phreng-ba states (*KhG*, JA, f. 7b4): *lha sras mched gsum yab kyi dkor mdzod nas* / He takes it that the king Gri-gum had three sons named Sha-khri, Bya-khri, and Nya-khri (ibid., f. 7b4). These sources do not conform to our text but the following do: *THD*, p. 98: *sras mched gnyis ni sha khyi dang nya khyir btagste* / *rkong yul du spyugste bkye'o* / Trans. p. 124: *Les deux fils, Sha-khyi et Nya-khyi, furent liés, bannis et déportés au Rkong-yul.* H. Richardson, 'A Ninth-century Inscription from Rkong-po', *JRAS*, 1954, facsimile facing p. 156: *dri gum btsan po'i sras gcen nya khyi dang* / *gcung sha khyi gnyis las* / *gcung sha khyi ni* / *lha btsan po* / *gcen nya khyi ni rkong yul du bzhugs ste* /

good-looking than any other child. He was given the name of Khrag-gi-bu Ru-las-skyes. When he grew up he asked his mother: (158a) 'Who is my father?' 'I found you in a yak's horn, so I have no idea who your father is', his mother replied. But he did not believe it and asked her again insistently: his mother said: 'Should we, mother and son, have been like this now if you had had a father?' She did not wish to tell him. Then one day when the boy was looking after horses up in the valley a white man riding a white horse came to him and said: 'I am the god of Yar, Sham-po. You are my son. There was a father named Gri-gum bTsan-po, but he was killed by Lo-ngam who took over the throne and kingdom.' The boy reported the event to his mother, who said: 'This is all true. All this royal place is your grandfather's palace. Your elder brother sPu-lde went to Kong-po and is still living there.' She told him the story in every detail.

Ru-las-skyes invited sPu-lde (from Kong-po) and made him ascend the throne at the palace Byi-ba stag-rtse. The people of dBus made Ru-las-skyes king and formed a small kingdom. They changed his name calling him king Khri-smon-bzung. Then, as he led an army to gTsang, the people of gTsang said: 'Our Lord has come' and invited the army in and pulled down the castle of Sham-po. (158b) They killed Lo-ngam, his son, and one thousand soldiers. In some books Ru-las-skyes is said to have smeared touch-poison on Lo-ngam's white dog and sent it home, whereupon Lo-ngam died from touching it.[1] At that time, in the country, all sorts of illnesses beset humans and animals. The crops were damaged by frost and hail. Misfortune of every kind occurred. So the diviners said: 'This is because of the king's corpse which was thrown into the river. Now we must search for it.' A search was carried out all along the gTsang-po, but nothing was discovered. One day at Nyang-stod stag-tshal someone asked a very skilful diviner to perform the rite, and he said: 'The king's corpse is held by Khod-de Ring-mo (a female water-spirit) in Kong-po. The method of getting it back is this: if we make many offerings to please the water-spirits, we shall get it.' The people made offerings to please the water-spirits and various sacrificial items and ransoms were put into the river. The water-spirits were satisfied and the corpse came to the surface.

[1] Cf. *THD*, pp. 98–9 (trans. pp. 124–5).

Then they built a tomb at Drang-mo drang-chung in Yar-lung. (159a) This was the first royal tomb and now there is a place called Bang-so-khrod. This explains the meaning of the saying: 'A tomb has been set up on earth in the world of phenomena.'

SECTION VI

The Second rise and decline of the precious doctrines of Everlasting Bon in the Land of Snows, Tibet

I have expounded how the Bon of 'Cause and Effect' of the gShen of dMu, the founder of our religion, spread to the six essential countries[1] from 'Ol-mo'i-gling, paying particular attention to their first rise and decline in Tibet. Now I shall relate the way in which Bon returned to give protection to the Tibetan kings and their subjects again. Some said that Lo-ngam was killed by poison and others said that he was murdered. Be this as it may, there are two (stages to the sequel):

A. The revival of the doctrines of Bon after the death of Lo-ngam and the enthronement of sPu-lde Gung-rgyal.

B. The second decline of Bon

A. (159b) The *Dran-pa'i lung-bstan chung-ba*[2] says:

When the Teacher sTong-rgyung mThu-chen was dwelling on the island of the lake of gNam, and practising the *Byin-rlabs bcu-gnyis*[3] bTsan-po sPu-lde Gung-rgyal invited him saying:

'O paṇḍita whose scholarly learning is profound,
I was originally the son of a divinely exalted one.
The bridge of the spiritual lineage of Everlasting Bon was not broken.
An evil spirit entered the heart of my father.
Bon was abolished and the priests were banished.
Punishment fell on all of us, the king and his ministers.
The king was murdered and the kingdom was taken over by the subjects.
The temples, erected by our ancestors, are in ruins.

[1] They are India, China, Zhang-zhung, Phrom, Bru-sha, and Tibet. See *LShDz*, p. 40a3.

[2] There are three versions of this prophetical text: one is long, one is medium length, and one is short. This last is the one with which we are concerned. They are said to have been passed on orally to Blo-ldan sNying-po (b. *STNN* 1360) by Dran-pa Nam-mkha' (see *KTDG*, p. 25).

[3] Possibly a tantric ritual text, but it is not known to me.

The palace of Nyang-ro sham-po was struck down by lightning.
Some (members of the royal family) were banished and others have become servants.
I beg you to have mercy on us and let us be under your orders!'

The teacher sTong-rgyung said: 'Invite a hundred knowledge-holders with the aim of reviving the doctrines of Bon. We shall get out the books which have been stored away and diffuse them!'

In conformity with these orders sPu-lde at once invited a hundred priests. They performed the 'posthumous evocation ritual of the killed' at Bre-sna in Kong-po. People were blessed and sPu-lde ascended the throne. (160a) The dead spirits were raised up and Gri-gum attained salvation. Up to this day the 'posthumous evocation ritual of the killed' of the king Gri-gum still exists; it is known as *Yog-bar-pa sum-rgya drug-cu*. The priests were accorded honour as before. sPu-lde said: 'My father hated Bon, but I will let it be revived. I must establish the "Great Universal Hammer" of the laws of Bon.' The *Gling-grags* and others tell us that when the priests decided to revive the doctrines there were a few texts left that had not been stored away and were not in the charge of custodian deities. They did not take out the hidden texts. The two brothers, Khyung-po Mu-khyung-rgyan and lHa-khyung-rgyan, were invited from Zhang-zhung to Tibet and brought with them the following texts: the five 'Bum,[1] the texts of the twelve Portals, the *mDzod*,[2] the ten *Phra-mo*, and many texts concerning different 'Vehicles'. They diffused them and so the doctrines revived.

This king is known by the name of Tho-legs bTsan-po since he did his best for sentient beings and the doctrines of Bon. sPu-lde's descendants constitute the six 'Good Ones of the Earth',[3] and the eight of Water.[4] The doctrines of Bon, which were practised during these thirteen reigns after sPu-lde, are as follows: the *Byams-ma* says:

(160b) The Bon of the thirteen 'Lineage-Transmitters' was spread: (1) Pha-rgyud lung-chen, (2) lTa-ba rdzogs-chen, (3) Byang-sems theg-chen, (4) gSas-mkhar rgyud-chen, (5)

[1] See *supra*, p. 27 n. 1.
[2] See *supra*, p. 8 n. 4.
[3] See *LShDz*, f. 108b2.
[4] See ibid., f. 109a1.

> Kun-gsal byams-chen, (6) 'Bum-khog dbang-chen, (7) rTse-'dus dbang-chen, (8) sDe-lnga mdo-chen, (9) gSang-lung dbang-chen, (10) rGyas-lnga 'bum-chen, (11) sDe-bzhi gzungs-chen, (12) Rig-pa'i gnas-chen, and (13) Bon theg-pa rim-pa-dgu.

(i.e. (1) The Father rGyud, (2) the Son rGyud, viz. the teachings of Great Perfection, and (3) those for 'Enlightened Beings', (4) the five kinds of rGyud of the 'Great gSas-Palaces', (5) the 'Fully Loving Mother', (6) the 'Everlasting Power of Perfection', (7) the 'Summit of the gSas-Palaces', (8) the five Precious mDo, (9) the five Great rGyud, (10) the 'Bum teachings including the *Bye-ma Nyi-khri*, (11) the 'spells', viz. the four 'Spells', (12) the five branches of knowledge, and (13) the 'Nine Ways of Bon'.[1]) Further the same authority says:

> Palaces, such as Byi-ba stag-rtse, 'citadels', and temples (161a) were built, and the laws of Bon, the 'Great Universal Hammer' were established.

Most of the Thirteen 'Lineage-Transmitters' lived as guide preachers. Here is a list of them: rGyal-gshen Mu-khri bTsan-po, Ha-ra Ci-par, sTag-ver Li-ver, A-nu 'Phrag-thag, Sad-ne Ga'u, Thad-mi Thad-ke, Shad-bu Ra-khug, Zing-ba mThu-chen, sPe-bon Thog-'phrul, and sPe-bon Thog-rtse. These were known as the ten 'Priest Masters', in addition to them according to the rGyud of sPyi-spungs (there were four others): the *sDong-po dgu-'dus-kyi blo-brdeg*[2] says:

> Mu-khri bTsan-po taught (the doctrine of sPyi-spungs) to

[1] (1) e.g. the *Khro-bo rgyud-drug* or *Phur-pa'i rgyud-dgu* (see *supra* p. 45 n. 2); (2) e.g. *rGyud-rgyal gser-gyi rus-sbal le'u sum-cu-pa*, rediscovered by bZhod-ston dNgos-grub Grags-pa in (*STNN*) 1088 in Khom-'thing temple (see *infra*, p. 154). See also *KTDG*, p. 12. (3), (6), and (10) are merely an enumeration of different kinds of 'Bum (= one hundred thousand). On 'Bum see also Snellgrove, *Nine Ways*, p. 260 n. 42. For the *Bye-ma nyi-khri* and further enumerations of 'Bum see *KTDG*, p. 6. (9) is the same as (4) for which see *supra*, p. 45 n. 2. (5) refers to Mother rGyud, e.g. *Ma-rgyud sangs-rgyas rgyud-gsum*, rediscovered by Gu-ru rNon-rtse (b. *STNN* 1136) in rTa-nag dung-phor (see *infra*, p. 166). (7) refers to gTsang-ma mtho-thog (the 'Pure Summit'). On this see Snellgrove, *Nine Ways*, p. 19. (11) The Four Spells (gzungs-mchog bzhi), were rediscovered (in *STNN* 1067) by Khye'u gNyan-'theng in gTsang-po nu-ma (see *infra*, p. 153). (12) is a general name which refers to no special texts and is common to Buddhism. (13) includes all the rest listed from (1) to (11).

[2] This text is a part of the *sDong-po dgu-'dus lta-ba'i rgyud-chen* (f. 4b1, 50a3) which has been published in Delhi by Tenzin Namdak (1967). It was rediscovered by rMa-ston Srol-'dzin in Dang-ra khyung-rdzong under the title of *Yang-gab dgu-skor* (see *infra*, p. 167).

> Khri-ma sTong-'phyo, 'Phyo-ma Ye-sangs, gNam-sman dKar-mo and gNam-phyi Gung-rgyal. After the secret teachings had ceased to exist, these four taught them to Mon-bon Ha-ra Ci-par.

So some would add the 'Four Miraculous Goddesses' to the ten. But the 'Mental Teachings' in the *Khu-byug* give Hring-ni Muting, Sum-pa dBu-dkar, and Glang-chen Mu-ver making thirteen in all. During the reigns of the five 'Middle bTsan-po',[1] that is up to the king Tho-ri Lung-btsan, the *Byams-ma* states:

> the sun of Everlasting Bon shone. (161b) The darkness of the mind of converts was removed as (the country) was flooded with the rays of learned teachers: the so-called 'Six Ornaments of the World of Learning': the scholar of sTag-gzig, dMu-tsha Tra-he, proficient in all the five branches of knowledge; the scholar of India, lHa-bdag sNgags-dro, proficient in Exoteric knowledge; the scholar of China, Legs-tang rMang-po, proficient in Esoteric knowledge; the scholar of Phrom, gSer-thog lCe-'byams, proficient in medical science; the scholar of Zhang-zhung, Tso-mi Gyer-rgyung, proficient in languages; the scholar of Tibet and Me-nyag, Nam-ra Tse-sku, proficient in cosmogony.[2]

These scholars were all learned in every branch of knowledge, comprehended all the 'Vehicles', understood three hundred and sixty languages, and possessed supernatural powers. It is not clear whether all these six scholars came to Tibet, but many scholars living in Tibet had met them. Up to the last of the 'Six bTsan-po', Tho-ri Lung-btsan-po or lHa Tho-tho-ri sNan-shal, there was not a sound of Buddhism.

The account of 'The Others' claiming that Buddhism was founded (in Tibet) during the reigns of lHaTho-tho-ri sNan-shal is given in the *bsGrags-byang*:[3]

> A 'Stūpa-carrier' (162a) came to Tibet from India and showed people a gold stūpa, saying: 'This is a Buddhist shrine.' The king did not stop him but said: 'There also exists (a religion) called Buddhism (chos).'

[1] See *LShDz*, ff. 109a4 et seq.

[2] Tib. srid-pa'i rgyud—Lit. the tradition of phenomenal existence.

[3] *bsGrags-byang*, f. 43a6.

The *Byams-ma* says:

> Up to Tho-tho-ri there was no sound of Buddhism in Tibet. A piece of teaching came down from heaven to the king Tho-tho-ri sNyan-shal: an image of cintamaṇi, and the *Pang-skong phyag-rgya-pa.*[1]

The *Srid-rgyud*[2] says:

> To the king Tho-tho-ri sNyan-shal . . .
> A sign appeared that Buddhism would come to Tibet,
> A gold stūpa a cubit in height,
> Sent from the assembly of the gods,
> By the Buddhist protectors of the three kinds,[3]
> It was thrown from heaven.
> And landed in the hands of the king,
> Together with the *sNying-po mudra*,[4]
> And the *Byang-chub ltung-bshags.*[5]
> Since the king did not believe in them,
> The dogma was not widely followed,
> But the *Thugs-rje chen-po*[6] did spread to some extent.

Thus although some Buddhist teaching occurred, neither the king nor ministers followed it but suppressed it. (When the last authority says that the *Thugs-rje chen-po* spread to some extent) it means that some people recited the 'Mantra' of *Thugs-rje chen-po*[7] as their daily prayers. (162b) The *Don-lgna*[8] of 'The Others' says:

> Up to the king Khri-thog-btsan there was no sound of the Three Precious Ones in the Land of Snows, but during the reign of his son, Tho-tho-ri sNyan-shal, a gold stūpa, the sūtra of *dGe-ba-bcu*, and the *Pang-skong Phyag-rgya-pa*

[1] Otani no. 933.

[2] *SG*, ff. 25a6, 25b1.

[3] They are Avalokiteśvara, Manjuśrī, and Vajrapāṇi.

[4] This is said to be a precious stone on which there were the syllables of the Yig-drug. *KhG*, f. 9b7: *mu dra'i phyag rgya zhes tshad khru gang tsam gyi nor bu'i rigs gyi rdo la yig drug rang byung can yod skad /*

[5] This text is not to be found in bKa'-'gyur, but two commentaries are in bsTan-'gyur. Otani nos. 5507 and 5506.

[6] This is another name of Avalokiteśvara and the texts dealing with Avalokiteśvara are known as the Thugs-rje chen-po'i skor. dPa'-bo gTsug-lag 'Phreng-ba gives twenty-one of them. See *KhG*, f. 17a2.

[7] These are the six syllables called the Yig-ge drug-pa.

[8] A history of Buddhism (chos-'byung) by gNam-lcags rDo-rje (see *infra*, p. 108).

descended upon the castle of Yum-bu bla-mkhar from heaven. This was how Buddhism was first discovered.

If this report that the sound of the Three Precious Ones did not exist up to that king meant that there the practice of taking refuge in Buddhism was unknown and that in this sense there was no sound of the Buddhist Three Precious Ones, then I would agree with it, but if you take it to mean in general that there was no sound of the Three Precious Ones, I would laugh. From the reigns of the Seven Khri up to this king refuge was taken in the 'Four Precious Ones' of Everlasting Bon and escape procured from fears and sufferings now and hereafter and ultimate enlightenment attained. Up to gNam-ri Srong-btsan, during the reigns of the 'Four Bon-po Kings'[1] (the following Bon doctrine was practised): the *Byams-ma* says:

> The Bon of 'Four Wonderful Orders' was spread: the *rGyas-pa 'bum*,[2] the *'Dul-ba rgyud-drug*,[3] the *mNgon-pa sde-bzhi*,[4] and the *mTshan-nyid sde-lnga*.[5] (163a) There came also innumerable priests who were proficient in those (teachings).

The twelve groups of teachings which I listed earlier,[6] and in particular the 'Four Wonderful Orders' were spread. There came innumerable scholars, translators, and ascetics who were proficient in those teachings. Details of the 'Four Wonderful Orders' will be given later.[7] It is said in the *Gling-grags* and elsewhere that during the reigns of those kings, Khyung-po sTag-sgra Don-gtsug, Li-shu sTag-ring, Bhe Shod-kram the Great, and Sum-pa Mu-phya[8] translated many texts from the languages of sTag-gzig and Zhang-zhung into Tibetan. They were contemporary with sTong-rgyung, Se, lDe, and Me whose fame as the 'Four Scholars' extended everywhere in Tibet.

The first of the five[9] kings who established Buddhism was Srong-btsan sGam-po who venerated the *Zhi-ba rgyas-pa*, *Khro-bo rgyas-pa*, *gSer-lung dri-med*, *Nyi-khri chig-'bum*, and *Dri-med*

[1] *LShDz*, ff. 109a6 et seq.

[2] For reference see *supra*, p. 74 n. 1.

[3] See *supra*, p. 35 n. 7.

[4] See *supra*, p. 36 n. 1.

[5] This is not a specific title, but five groups of texts. See *infra*, p. 313, ll. 17–31.

[6] This refers to the first twelve of the Bon of the Thirteen 'Lineage-Transmitters' (see *supra*, p. 73).

[7] This reference is not to be found in a particular place. Our author possibly meant us to find it under different textual discoveries.

[8] Cf. *supra*, p. 26.

[9] *LShDz*, ff. 110a5 et seq.

shel-mdog.[1] In his later years a spark of Buddhism came (to Tibet) from India. The *Srid-rgyud*[2] says:

> At the time of divinely born Srong-btsan sGam-po, . . .
> The Buddhist sūtra *Za-ma-tog*,[3]
> The sūtra of *dKon-mchog gsum*,[4]
> The sūtra of *rDo-rje gcod-pa*,[5] and *Padma dkar-po*,[6]
> Were venerated by the king.

(163b) Since the king also took a little interest in Buddhism whilst following Bon, 'The Others' have asserted that the king Srong-btsan sGam-po introduced Buddhism into Tibet. The *Byams-ma* says:

> (The king Srong-btsan sGam-po) took the princess Lig-tig-sman from Zhang-zhung as his wife and she brought with her a Zhang-zhung image of the Lord Teacher gShen-rab at the age of one which came from the temple of dKar-nag bkra-gsal in sTag-gzig 'Ol-mo'i-gling, and for it was built the temple of Them-chen.[7] From Nepal he took the Nepalese princess Khri-btsun as his wife and she brought with her a Nepalese silver image of Byams-pa 'Khor-lo[8] for which was built the temple of Ra-sa. From China he took the Chinese princess Kong-co and she brought with her a Chinese image of gShen-rab at the age of eight[9] for which was built the temple of Ra-mo-che. He invited a monk called Akārashilamati from India who brought with him an Indian sandal-wood self-created image,[10] and the noble bCu-gcig-zhal of lHa-sa[11] was erected (in consequence). The same authority continues:

[1] I have no means to identify these texts as *KTDG* does not record any except the *Nyi-khri chig-'bum* for which see *infra*, p. 283, l. 30.

[2] *SG*, ff. 30a7, 30b2.

[3] Otani no. 784.

[4] Otani no. 897.

[5] Otani no. 739.

[6] Otani no. 781.

[7] *KhG*, f. 44b4: *zhang zhung bza' li thig sman gyis them pu bkog pa'i lha khang bzhengs*. But this temple was probably destroyed earlier as it is hardly referred to in later histories.

[8] *KhG*, f. 25b6: *byams pa chos 'khor*, i.e. an image of Maitreya.

[9] This, of course, refers to the famous image known as Jo-bo in Jo-khang in lHa-sa. According to Bon-po tradition the identification of this image as Shākyamuni is erroneous!

[10] A mythical story concerning the sandal-wood image of Avalokiteśvara and Akārashilamati is given in *KhG* (ff. 23b4 et seq.)

[11] This is known as Thugs-rje chen-po 'phags-pa bcu-gcig-zhal, an image of Avalokiteśvara with eleven faces and according to Tibetan Buddhists it was the first image that was erected in Tibet. See *KhG*, f. 34a4.

> Because of the king's practice of Buddhism and of the jealousy of the 'Royal Divinities',[1] terrestrial gods, and water-spirits, the mKhar-chung of lHa-sa (164a) was struck down by lightning.[2] Many people were also killed by lightning. Plagues occurred and crops failed. The king also passed away at the age of thirty-six. At that time, a minister called Dar-ma said that the misfortune was due to Buddhism and so Buddhism was suppressed.

This is what we are told. The *Srid-rgyud*[3] says:

> As the king followed Buddhism,
> The thirteen 'Royal Divinities',
> And the gods of Tibet withdrew into heaven,
> The country was filled with confusion and unhappiness,
> It was thought to be due to the acceptance of Buddhism,
> And Buddhism was suppressed for a time.

It is said in the *bsGrags-byang* that although the five kings, up to Khri-rje gTsug-brtan, were the establishers of Buddhism, apart from just a few Buddhist practitioners, Bon was the only religion that was widely followed. The *Srid-rgyud*[4] says:

> Up to Khri-rje gTsug-brtan,
> The kingdom was under the protection of Everlasting Bon, . . .
> Under thirty-six predecessors of that king,
> The kingdom was under the protection of Everlasting Bon.
> The descendants of the Lord were powerful.

Now up to Khri-srong lDe-btsan there had been thirty-eight kings. Since Srong-btsan sGam-po and Khri-srong lDe-btsan followed Buddhism they are not included, but their thirty-six ancestors took refuge in Bon and (164b) attained salvation. One

[1] Tib. rje'i 'gul-lha, see *infra*, p. 99.

[2] mKhar-chung of lHa-sa possibly refers to lHa-sa mkhar-brag which some Tibetan traditions maintain was built by one of the wives of Srong-btsan sGam-po, but dPa'-bo gTsug-lag 'Phreng-ba (*KhG*, f. 44b6) rejects this following the *sBa-bzhed* version (*KhG*, f. 71a5; Stein, *sBa-bzhed*, p. 1) which attributes it to Khri-lde gTsug-brtan, the father of Khri-srong lDe-btsan. This is akin to the *bsGrags-byang's* account which simply reads 'father's temple' (yab-kyi gtsug-lag-khang, see *infra*, p. 84), and the lHa-sa mkhar-brag is said to have been destroyed when Khri-srong lDe-btsan was a minor (Stein, *sBa-bzhed*, p. 8).

[3] *SG*, f. 30b. Here the wording of the quotation in our text differs slightly from the manuscript.

[4] Ibid., ff. 26b4, 27a2.

may say that the king Gri-gum cannot be counted since he abolished Bon, but I would include him as he followed Bon in his early years. Up to the early years of Khri-srong lDe-btsan and during the five (Buddhist introductory) kings there were also the nine magicians as guide preachers. There was the priest Dran-pa Nam-mkha' and others. I have given the list of the nine magicians earlier.[1] Furthermore, the *Srid-rgyud*[2] says:

> sPe Ne-gu, Phrom-bon mThu-chen, Bhe Shod-kram, and rGya-bon Legs-tang rMang-po, etc. (assisted the king) in bringing 'Jang, Ga-gon, Phrom, China, Mon, and many other countries under Tibetan rule with their miraculous powers. All enemies were suppressed. The land of water-spirits, lHa-sa, was filled with people worshipping Enlightened Ones, performing tantric rituals, reciting and expounding the scriptural books, meditating on the meaning of mind, building temples, shrines, and so on. At that time there were also scholars and ascetics, such as: sNya Li-shu sTag-ring, Khyung-po sPu and gZu-tse, Gu-rub bTsan-po, Khyung-po Ra-sangs rJe-rgyal, Phu-lu Gru-'dzin, (165a) 'Gas-po He Dug-'dul, sTag-sgra Gyim-shad, gNub Mang-gnyer gZhu-btsan, 'Gar lHa-bzher Tshe-gsar, Bon-blon gSas-chen, and Vas Khri-zung sTong-slod. There were also many Bon priestesses who attained realization.

Honours and offices were distributed (to religious persons) as before. The official titles, which were given to the Bon-pos, are as follows: as the priests attended the king they were called sKu-gshen (body-priest). As they took part in discussion with the ministers they were called gShen-blon (priest-minister). As they were elevated by the Lords they were called Bla-bon (topmost-priest). As they were knowledgeable about the origin of the universe, they were called Kun-shes (all-knowing). As they diffused the doctrines of Bon of the Enlightened Ones, they were called Bon-gshen (Bon-priest). As they taught concerning virtue and vice, cause and effect, they were called sTon-pa (teacher). As they were given honours by the kings they were called Bon-chen (great priest). As they gave fatherly protection to inferiors they were called Pha-ba (father). As they observed strictly the

[1] See *supra*, p. 42.

[2] This is a summary of a passage in *SG* (ff. 26b5–28a3).

rules of the Lord (gShen-rab) they were called gShen-btsun (noble priest). As they saved the dead spirits by means of 'evocation rituals' they were called 'Dur-gshen (priests who perform the 'posthumous evocation ritual'). As they showed the path of salvation (to sentient beings) they were called 'Dren-pa'i dpon-gsas (guide master). Up to here I have outlined the Second Spread of the precious doctrines of Everlasting Bon in this Land of Snows.

B. (165b) I. Where it declined
II. At the time of which king and priest it declined
III. How it declined

I. It declined in Zhang-zhung and in dBus and gTsang in Tibet.
II. The *rNam-'byed*[1] says:

> It declined during the reign of Khri-srong lDe-btsan.

The *Zhang-zhung snyan-brgyud*[2] says:

> As far as the kings are concerned it declined during the reigns of the king Lig-mi-rgya of Zhang-zhung, the king Paṇṭa Likha of Mon, and the king Khri-srong lDe-btsan of Tibet.

As to the priests the *Yang-rtse klong-chen*[3] says:

> It declined during the lifetime of Bla-chen Dran-pa Nam-mkha', sNya Li-shu sTag-ring and in the later years of the Lord Khri-srong lDe-btsan.

The *Zhang-zhung snyan-brgyud*[4] says:

> The eminent scholars, who attained realization, preserved the doctrines. The ascetics, the representatives of the Conqueror, maintained them. The magicians, who possessed great power, guarded them. In Tibet and Zhang-zhung no Buddhism existed. Among the many ascetics living in Zhang-zhung at this time was the ascetic Tso-mi Gyer-chen. Among the many ascetics living in Tibet at this time were sPa Ji-phrom

[1] This is attributed to Dran-pa Nam-mkha' and is also known as *rNam-'byed 'phrul-lde* (see *infra*, p. 87.)

[2] The quotation comes from a part of *Zhang-zhung snyan-brgyud* known as *sNyan-(b)rgyud ma-nub-pa'i gtan-tshigs* (f. 2a6).

[3] I cannot trace this passage in Snellgrove's manuscript.

[4] *sNyan-(b)rgyud ma-nub-pa'i gtan-tshigs*, f. 1a3.

dKar-po, the 'Four Scholars', and (166a) Bla-chen Dran-pa Nam-mkha'.

III. a. The (major) causes and the minor causes.
b. How the actual decline of Bon (took place).
c. How 'Retribution' occurred.

a. The Major causes

i. How prayers were first said that Buddhism should appear in Tibet, the Land of Snows.
ii. The effect of the curses uttered previously by Gri-gum.[1]

i. The *Srid-rgyud*[2] says:

Long ago in the land of an Indian king three beggars stored up their alms. Later they became rich and their thoughts turned to good. They began to build a great stūpa called Bya-rung kha-shor, but all of them grew old and died before completing the work. At the time of their death each of them said prayers. They said to themselves: We are leaving this stūpa incomplete which we, with good intentions, built as a store of merit for the next life. Now we three beggars are no longer sustained by human life, but in the next life we shall obtain noble bodies and complete this virtuous work. One said: May I be born as an architect working on the building of this stūpa. One said: May I be born as a patron of the building of this stūpa. And one said: May I be born as a workman engaged on the building of this stūpa. (166b) Thereafter, the three beggars were born in India as a result of their prayers. They went on with the building and completed it. They said prayers when they died: the one who was a patron of the building of the stūpa said: May I be born some time as a powerful king in the kingdom of mNga'-ris (Tibet). The architect of the stūpa said: May I be born in Tibet as a Buddhist missionary. The builder of the stūpa said: May I be born in Tibet as a Bon-suppressing translator. Later they were born according to their prayers. The patron of the building of the stūpa was born as Khri-srong lDe-btsan, the architect of the stūpa as the Lotus-born, the builder as Bodhi Sattva.[3] Khri-srong lDe-

[1] See *supra*, p. 68. [2] *SG*, f. 31a1.
[3] This refers to the Indian teacher Shāntarakshita (mKhan-po Zhi-ba-'tsho.)

btsan was the son of a king. The Lotus-born was miracuously born. Bodhi Sattva was the son of a servant. He was born in an inferior family because of the prayers at his previous death in which he said that he wished to destroy Bon.[1]

ii. (167a) The decline was partially due to the curses of Gri-gum. The *Gri-shad* says:

> At this time and age.
> A wrong-minded king was born,
> Evil spirits are emerging everywhere,
> And confusion and wickedness are spreading.
> The outcome of the curses Gri-gum bTsan-po
> Uttered at a former time.

The minor causes

i. The others as a cause
ii. Ourselves as a cause

i. The *Srid-rgyud*[2] says:

Through the power of earlier prayers the king was more attracted by Buddhism than by Bon and in secret he followed it. This was not observed by human-beings but (only) by gods. The terrible divinities of the universe were displeased and misfortune fell on the Lord, the divinely born. Ghosts and demons engaged in soul-stealing. Plagues, wars, lightning, and hail occurred in lHa-sa. The human disease Long-dgu broke out and the animal disease Dal-rim. A search was carried out to find a diviner in the country and one called sPe Ne-gu was found. The king, ministers, and people gathered for the consultation. The king asked: 'What is wrong that in this country there are plagues, (167b) wars, lightning, hail, and animal disease is widespread?' sPe Ne-gu said: 'O Lord, all these plagues, confusion, and unhappiness are due to the impurity of a fatherless and incestuous child. This is the magic of Nal Mi-zan sNying-dmar. Through the impurity of this incestuous child, the undefiled gods and the thirteen "Royal Divinities"

[1] For this story cf. *mChod-rten chen-po bya-rung kha-shor-gyi lo-rgyus thos-pas grol-ba*, ff. 10a7–12a6.
[2] Here our author summarizes a passage from *SG* (ff. 31b7–33a5).

have become filled with hatred. So different forms of unhappiness have arisen in this country'. This left the king and ministers in doubt. The diviner was given gold and turquoise as a reward and was asked by the ministers: 'If the incestuous child is identified what ritual would be of benefit?' He said: 'If the incestuous child is identified from among a crowd of people and many priests belonging to different families do the ritual of exorcism, and send him away towards the south-west together with various "ritual objects", putting him on a brownish ox, that would be of benefit.' Many people gathered and, after a search, a fifteen-year-old boy was identified with the words: 'That is the child.' (168a) Thereupon, the boy was put on an ox together with ransoms and was sent towards the south-west. He reached India. A Buddhist said: 'Last night in my dream the sun shone on the Bodhi tree. This boy might be a fortunate one.' The boy studied Buddhism, and became a learned scholar possessing miraculous powers. He was called Aṇḍa Bodhi Sattva.[1] Through the power of the previous prayers in which he said he wished to destroy Bon, a vindictive thought now arose in his mind about the Bon-pos who had caused him to be sent away as a ransom. He sent the king and ministers a letter in which he wrote that it would be best if Bon were destroyed and Buddhism were followed. (His letter) and the king's faith in Buddhism coincided.

Similar accounts are also given in the *Gab-'grel* and other works. Furthermore, the *bsGrags-byang*[2] says:

A minister called gYu-sgra Ne-ra said to the king: 'O Lord, as it is necessary to be more vigorous in action than your ancestors, I am asking you to restore the temple of your father which has been struck down by lightning.[3] As for equipping it, in India there is said to exist (168b) the so-called Buddhism which is unlike Bon. It is easy to practice and light to bear. I beg you to have it here.' The minister mChims-bzher said: 'This Bon is heavy to carry. It is voluminous to learn. Its depth impedes accomplishment. Its protectors are easily offended. So I ask you to abolish it.' Through the power of

[1] See *supra*, p. 82 n. 3.
[2] I cannot trace this quotation in *bsGrags-byang* (Oslo MS.).
[3] Cf. *supra*, p. 79 n. 2.

previous prayers and the desire for superiority over his ancestors, the Lord began to consider (these suggestions).

The *commentary of Gab-ba*[1] says:

> At that time, even the sunlight appeared to be dim and the moon appeared to be dying. In a dream of the king Paṇṭa Likha of Mon a golden sun radiating heat into three thousand universes set behind the earth, and after that a shell-like moon rose. The king told his son Hang-yag his dream. Hang-yag reported it to the minister of Mon, Re-ba De-sho. It was transmitted from one person to another until it reached the ear of the king of Tibet.

ii. lDe-btsan Rab-gsal maintained the spiritual lineage of Ya-gong, and (169a) that of the Pham-shi was maintained by gCo-btsan Ye-shes. Mu-zi gSal-bzang had taken ordination from both lDe and gCo, and obtained the 'power over life' from Sad-ne Ga'u.[2] During the lifetime of sTong-rgyung mThu-chen, sPa Ji-phrom dKar-po, sNang-bzher Lod-po, Dran-pa Nam-mkha', and Li-shu sTag-ring, although the doctrines were extensively spread, there were many people whose conduct, owing to the law of decline, was perverse. It appeared that many monks, whose moral discipline had deteriorated, broke their rules. Priests, who were practising tantric rituals, became proud of their magical powers. Four great religious centres including gYung-drung rol-ba and twelve small ones were destroyed. The shrines of gShen disappeared into heaven in the form of light. Monks who observed their moral discipline became fewer.[3] The king considered what Bodhi Sattva had written to him and the way Bon-po monks were sinning, the way the light of the sun and moon had decreased, (169b) and the dream of the king of Mon. He said that the time had probably now come to abolish this Everlasting Bon.

[1] Cf. *supra*, p. 51 n. 8.

[2] And is mentioned here presumably because he was still surviving in a state of trance (cf. *supra*, p. 00 n. 8). This was a result of the quarrels among Bon-pos which are said to have taken place during the reign of Gri-gum.

[3] Here our text explains in a note that at this time though there was as yet no Lower Tradition of the Rules of Discipline ('dul-ba smad-lugs) for that begins with Mu-zi gSal-bzang (on whom see *infra*, pp. 105–6), the Upper Tradition (stod-lugs) did already exist (see *supra*, p. 64).

b. How the actual decline of Bon (took place)

i. The actual decline of Bon
ii. How Bon texts were hidden

i. (a) The decline of Bon in Zhang-zhung
(b) In Tibet

(a) The *Zhang-zhung snyan-brgyud*[1] says:

> During the reign of Khri-srong lDe-btsan there were ten ministers for external (affairs), ten for internal (affairs), and ten for the chancery, thirty in all. The king's power was great. He overpowered the wealthy king of sTag-gzig who made a promise to put long wooden bridges over the big rivers which cut the trade routes. He overpowered the king of Ge-sar Phrom who made a promise (to facilitate) navigation in the four borderlands. He overpowered the Buddhist king of India who agreed that they should be as patron and priest.

It was not through strength but through his past actions that he took over so many kingdoms and ruled them. Having done it, however, he became very conceited and he began to think about overpowering the king of Zhang-zhung. The same authority says:[2]

> At this time the king of Zhang-zhung was Lig-mi-rgya. Zhang-zhung had an army of nine hundred and ninety thousand soldiers. (170a) In addition Zhang-zhung exercised authority over the Sum-pa country in which it had a small regiment. Tibet had only forty-two thousand soldiers plus one small regiment, making forty-three (regiments) in all. Seeing that he could not subdue the king of Zhang-zhung by direct attack, he, being of an evil disposition, began to think about subduing him by means of treachery. At that time, the Tibetan king sent a clerical officer called sNam-nam Legs-grub who was hard-hearted and a deceitful talker with a wild yak's horn full of gold dust to the youngest queen of the king of Zhang-zhung, the eighteen-year-old sNang-bza' sGron-legs. He gave it to her and said: 'We, Tibetans, are discon-

[1] *sNyan-(b)rgyud ma-nub-pa'i gtan-tshigs*, f. 2b1. However, in some places the wording in our text differs from that of the Snellgrove MS.

[2] *sNyan-(b)rgyud ma-nub-pa'i gtan-tshigs*, f. 2b4.

solate that such a person as you, sNang-bza' sGron-legs, should be the lesser wife of the king of Zhang-zhung. The Tibetan king is also concerned about you. Is there any way in which we can put an end to this? If so, the Tibetan king will take you as his primary wife and you will be given two-thirds of the kingdom.' sGron-legs replied: 'Since the king of Zhang-zhung has an army which could cover the earth, and the Tibetan king has an army which could not even fill the middle part of a cow's skin, the (170b) Tibetan king could not subdue him by direct attack. But if you would use deceit and craft to subdue him, then next month with his attendants, he is travelling to an assembly in Sum-pa glang-gi gyim-shod from Zhang-zhung. So wait for him and kill him.' Although sNam-nam Legs-grub did not wish to rely on a woman he told her that he would make arrangements. They agreed that a sign should be placed on the top of the pass indicating what day the Zhang-zhung king would come. Then the Tibetan king and his ministers set out with many thousands of soldiers. The king and sNam-nam Legs-grub went first to the top of the pass and looked for the sign. They found a bowl full of water in which there were three things: a small piece of gold, a small piece of shell, and a poisoned arrow-head. The king said: 'The bowl full of water means that they are coming at the full moon of the next month. The piece of gold and shell indicate that gSer-phug (Gold cave) and Dung-phug (Shell cave) of Dang-ra should be garrisoned in readiness. The poisoned arrow-head means that (the Zhang-zhung king) is to be cruelly murdered. And so they waited. The two kings met and the Zhang-zhung king was killed by the Tibetan soldiers. (171a) Zhang-zhung which had a hundred thousand communities was defeated. Tibet which had ten thousand communities was victorious.

(b) The *rNam-'byed 'phrul-lde* says:

The king Khri-srong lDe-btsan summoned all his ministers and commanded that a Buddhist should be invited as his preceptor. 'Gos Khri-bzang Yab-lhag said: 'O Lord, divinely born, you are young. Your ancestor Gri-gum once suppressed Bon and his life was short and he was killed by Lo-ngam at the age of thirty-six. Your great grandfather Srong-btsan sGam-po nearly suppressed Bon and so his life was short and he died at the age of thirty-six.

'The temple was struck down by lightning,[1] the same fate as that of your great-grandfather will probably befall you.' The king said: 'The continuation of my past actions is Buddhism. So, whatever happens a Buddhist must be invited.' 'Gos Khri-bzang Yab-lhag said: 'So far during the thirty-eight reigns we have never had any experience of the grace of holy Buddhism. Now whether it is to be understood or not, whether it is to be taught or not, you, divinely born, have the power and may do whatever you please.'

The *Srid-rgyud*[2] says:

The king sent a translator to India to invite the teacher Padma Sambhava and (171b) Anḍa Bodhi to bring Buddhism (to Tibet). Thereupon, five hundred Bon-po monks were converted to Buddhism. Even in mTsho-rnga[3] Buddhism appeared. At that time, Ma-zhang Phrom-pa said: 'A highly degenerate time is approaching. Former Bon-priests are abandoned. The kingdom is in turmoil since wrong conduct is prevalent. The Lord and his subjects will be reduced to misery.' Khri-srong lDe-btsan said: 'A contest must be held between the Bon-pos and Buddhists (to find out) which is true and which is false; which has the greater magic and miraculous power.' In a place called Brag-dmar 'grin-bzang[4] a tent, which was made of cotton, was put up. Many Bon-pos and Buddhists were called to the meeting to take part in the contest. They followed the example set by the threefold world. Overseers from each party were appointed. Ngam sTag-ra Klu-gong[5] and sNam-nam Phrom-pa-skyes were nominated the Bon-po overseers. Bra-ba of Shākya-rung and sNyar sTag-btsan lDong-gzig were nominated the Buddhist overseers. 'Gos

[1] This closely agrees with the *Byams-ma*'s account, but the name of the temple is not mentioned (cf. *supra*, p. 79 n. 2).

[2] Here our author again summarizes a passage from *SG* (ff. 33a2–38b4).

[3] A sacred place where gShen-chen Klu-dga' rediscovered many texts (see *infra*, p. 126).

[4] The birth-place of Khri-srong lDe-btsan. See Tucci, *The Tombs of the Tibetan Kings*, p. 84. Stein, *sBa-bzhed* (p. 27) gives Pho-brang zur-phud skyang-bu-'tshal instead.

[5] Concerning whom see Richardson, *Ancient Historical Edicts at Lhasa*, pp. 1 et seq.

Khri-bzang Yab-lhag was appointed as a referee. Dran-pa Nam-mKha' was the advocate for Bon. Bodhi Sattva was the advocate for Buddhism. (172a) Each of them tackled his antagonist. Thereupon, Khri-srong lDe-btsan said: 'Observe, which is true and which is false, which has the greater magical powers. Once and for all Bon-pos and Buddhists must contest their skills.' Then the contest of skill began: sTong-rgyung mThu-chen rode his drum down the river and flew up into the air. The teacher Padma hung his cloak over the rays when the sun rose in the morning. Dran-pa Nam-mka' struck the sun and moon together like a pair of cymbals in the sky. Bodhi Sattva threw a thunderbolt into space which stayed there for a day. Se Sha-ri dBu-chen, having gone to the lake of Ma-phang, bestrode a water-horse and flew up into the sky. gNubs Nam-mka'i sNying-po left his rosary hanging in space. lCe-tsha mKhar-bu of Me-nyag made the river of Sog flow backwards. Rlang dPal-gyi sNying-po drew rainbow figures in space. lDe Gyim-tsha rMa-chung loaded wild beasts and drove them (like cattle). 'Bre dPal-gyi Blo-gros caught wild animals and milked them. sKu Gyim-thang rMa-bo made his drum and bell emit flame. Rlang gTsug-tor Rin-chen trained deer, wild asses, and antelopes as domestic animals. (172b) Khyung-po sTag-sgra Don-gtsug made tigers, leopards, bears, and brown bears as tame as dogs. rMa A-tsa-ra Rin-chen sat crosslegged in space. sNya Li-shu sTag-ring transformed himself into a vulture and flew through the sky. sKa-ba dPal-brtsegs cut off his head and put it back again. sPe Ne-gu invoked divinities who became visible. Ba-gor Vairocana's swift-footedness was equal to that of a bird. rMa-bon Thugs-dkar crossed the river of rMa in three steps. gNyan-pa dPal-sbyin stood a vase in space. Co-za Bon-mo tied three knots in a sword. Lang-gro dKon-mchog 'Byung-gnas sat in a big fire without being burned. The king and ministers were very pleased.

Bon-pos and Buddhists went on carrying out the king's order to compare their skills by bringing a murdered man to life, by restoring the spirits of the dead to their bodies by means of 'evocation rituals', and by debating. The Bon-pos are said in many books to have been superior, but I have not quoted them here owing to their length. Thus the king let Bon-pos and Buddhists contest so as to be able to condemn and suppress Bon, but since the Bon-pos, far from being defeated, had been highly successful, the king could not do anything. (173a) As the King, through the power of his previous prayers, wanted to practise Buddhism, and the Buddhists and ministers, who were interested in Buddhism, several times wickedly promoted calumny between the Bon-pos and the king, and as sentient beings in that degenerate age had so little merit and evil practice increased, whilst the Tibetans no longer submitted to the discipline of the precious Everlasting Bon, the essence of all doctrine, the time had arrived to suppress the doctrine once more. At that time, (the temple of) lHun-po-rtse at bSam-yas in dBus, the temples of mTha'-'dul and of Ru-non were built.[1] It is said that a hundred and eight temples were projected, but only thirty of them were completed. At that time, the king summoned all priests and said: 'You priests, since this holy Buddhism is good for both the here and the hereafter, I urge you to follow Buddhism and to abandon Bon. You, Bon-pos, can choose whichever you like, to follow Buddhism or drink the white water[2] (173b) or accept banishment from the four quarters of Tibet.' Thereupon, gShen Dran-pa Nam-mkha' spread his cotton dice-cloth and placed the dice of truth and falsehood on it. He flourished his precious sceptre over his head. He put his gold razor into his breast pocket and spoke thus:

> Listen, all of you, leaders and servants.
> You will probably seize our office.
> The human body is always difficult to obtain,
> But when one has obtained the perfect human body,
> One dare not drink water.[3]

Thus saying he cut off his own hair with the gold razor and putting the hair into his pocket, he went on:

> The king sPu-rgyal of Tibet,
> And ignorant living beings,

[1] According to Buddhist historians the temples in these last two places were built by Srong-btsan sGam-po (*KhG*, ff. 38a5–39a2).

[2] To drink water implies to commit suicide by drinking water excessively. This seems to have been a common method of committing suicide in the early days in Tibet. See *SG*, ff. 71b6, 72a2.

[3] i.e. commit suicide: see n. 2.

Buddhists and Bon-pos who are sitting here,
Believe in a religion which does not exist.
If you desire to make the kingdom white,
And wish to attain Enlightenment,
Why do you differentiate between me and you?
Why do you make a distinction between Bon and Buddhism?
The king of method and wisdom,
Radiates power and knowledge.
Alas, that the two should be (accounted) different,
And one subdued and the other not; (174a)
Alas, that spontaneous knowledge accomplished,
Should be accounted unaccomplished.
Alas, that you Buddhists should be deceived into introducing
Distinctions between virtue and vice into the shining knowledge of the mental sphere of sentient beings.
Alas, that those who do not understand in this way and are bound with the traditional teachings,
Should not, though they search after it, attain Enlightenment.
I am like the sun and moon in the sky.
I neither love nor hate sentient beings.
I am like precious gold of Ku-lang.
A person who had attained realization,
Would not have made a distinction between Bon and Buddhism.
He would make no distinction between his son and his enemy.
Firstly, the king is mighty,
Secondly, the Buddhists are jealous,
Thirdly, I have (no feeling of) partiality for anything.
Therefore, I shall be ordained.[1]

He cut his lock of hair with a pair of scissors and abjured his faith. At that time, all the priests realized that a time had come for Bon to be suppressed once more. Although they could easily have destroyed the king and his ministers in a moment by means of revenging magical violence, they decided not to use it but to make themselves calm and be indifferent. The king understood this. Dran-pa Nam-mkha' knew how the king and ministers were engaged in making arrangements to suppress Bon. (174b) One named mTha'-bzhi Khro-gsas 'Od-gzungs acted as a patron.

[1] These verses are taken from *SG*, ff. 43a4 et seq.

Priests (made copies) of Bon texts by writing on white cotton with red ink, some wrote on coloured Chinese and Tibetan paper with black ink. Most of the texts which there was no time to copy out were hidden without the king's knowledge. Some texts which had been copied out were given to the king and queen. The most important ones were hidden in the palace of bSe-sgo-can and sealed up with molten bronze. At that time, the Buddhists made many Bon texts into Buddhist texts. The 'Mental teachings' of Bon was transformed into the *Sems-lung-phyogs*[1] of Buddhism. The *gYung-drung khams-brgyad* was transformed into the *sTong-phrag brgya-ba* of Buddhism.[2] The *gYung-drung gser-gyi yang-zhun* was transformed into the so-called *lTa-ba gcer-mthong*.[3] The *Byang-sems gab-pa*[4] was transformed into the *Sems-smad-phyogs* of Buddhism. The *bsGrags-pa rin-po-che*[5] was transformed into the *Chos-mdzod gong-ma*. Thus many texts were made Buddhist and their titles changed. Some of the temples and shrines of Bon were destroyed. Some were repainted (175a) and their names changed to the temples of Buddhists.

At that time, Ma-bdud Srid-pa rGyal-mo was offended and appeared to the king in a dream in the form of a black woman with iron locks, three eyes, a grin of canine teeth, and a robe of peacock feathers. She said to him: 'Give me my texts and their commentaries of the Four Bon Portals and the Treasury, (making) Five. If you do not give them to me and either transform or destroy them, you will die and go to the bottom of hell, without time to practise the wrong religion, after sunset tomorrow.' Then she disappeared. So the king was frightened and neither dared transform nor destroy Bon after that. At that time, sPe Ne-gu, Bhe Shod-kram, lHa-ru gSer-yag, and Khu lHa-'dzin bore ill-feeling to the Lord. They put 'Dan-dkar and a drum and a flat-bell[6] into a boat and travelled along the gTsang-po. When they had travelled the distance of an arrow sPe Ne-gu held out his 'Dan-dkar to invoke the gods. The river

[1] This is not a specific title, but applies to the Great Perfection (rdzogs-chen) in general.

[2] See *infra*, p. 130.

[3] I cannot identify this work.

[4] This was rediscovered by gShen-chen Klu-dga' (see *infra*, p. 130).

[5] For this see *infra*, pp. 154–6.

[6] 'Dan-dkar is another name for sba-'khar (a cane) for which and also for the flat-bell, see Snellgrove, *Nine Ways*, p. 282, Illustration XIV (*a*), (*h*).

flowed backwards so the country was flooded. (175b) It is said that this is the reason why the regions between lHa-sa and bSam-yas are full of sand. The four priests flew into the sky with their drums and bells and landed at a place called gYa'-gang khyim-zhur. Many priests including Zhang-zhung Ver-stag, Khu-stod Bya-zhu-can, sTag-lo Bya-ru-can, and Sum-pa dBal-rgod loaded wolves, tigers, and leopards with texts of magic and prognostication and went to Mongolia, 'Jang, and China. Sum-pa kha-khyer and some others put many texts into copper boxes and, loading them on to wild asses, went to Sog-po sprel-slag-can. Zhang-zhung Ral-ba-can, mTha'-bzhi Bum-bu-chung, and several others, taking a number of texts with them, went to rGya-mo-rong in the East. Tshe-bon Don-grub, sNang-bon sTag-thur-can, Se-bon Khyab-tse, gShen Tshad-la Mi-gsum, and several others, each taking a volume of manuscripts, went to sTag-gzig. dBal lHa-khri, Me-nyag sTag-gsas, Khyung-po Ne-khrom, and several others went to the North and lived there on 'self-procuring rituals'. (176a) sTong Gyer-rgyung and Nyang dPal-mthong went to lHo-brag. sNyan Gyer-rgyung, Zhang-zhung sTag-thur and several others went to Bal-po bse-ris. The ones who possessed magic powers flew into the sky. Some, having transformed themselves into fire, water, and wind, departed. Some transformed themselves into vultures and geese and departed. Some turned daytime into the dark as they went. At that time, apart from the 'Four Scholars', the 'Nine Magicians', Li-shu and gShen Dran-pa Nam-mkha', all the priests went away in different directions, each taking a few texts with him. All this I have taken from the *Srid-pa rgyud-kyi kha-byang* and the *bsGrags-byang*.

ii. How Bon texts were hidden[1]

The *Srid-rgyud*[2] says:

> Dran-pa Nam-mkha' begged the king: 'Since I have taken Buddhist ordination I request you not to suppress this Ever-lasting Bon, the purity of phenomenal existence, but let it be concealed.' The king said: 'You have done well to be ordained. Copy out Bon texts on yellow paper and conceal them under-ground without damaging them. (176b) You should also say appropriate prayers.'

[1] This is the section ii announced *supra*, p. 86.

[2] *SG*, f. 46a6.

The *bsGrags-byang*[1] says:

> The 'Nine Magicians' and Dran-pa Nam-mkha' classified all the Bon texts in the spring of the ox year[2] and hid them in

[1] *bsGrags-byang*, f. 75a4.

[2] It is of great importance to try and fix this date with precision. After referring to this same passage in the *bsGrags-byang* the *GRB* continues (p. 59): 'Khri-srong (lDe-btsan) was born in Horse Year. At the age of twenty-one he established Buddhism. At forty-five he abolished Bon. He died at fifty-six.' Khri-srong was undoubtedly born in 742 (see *THD*, p. 51). This fits with the *GRB* as 742 was Water-Horse Year, but not with Bu-ston (Obermiller, *History of Buddhism by Bu-ston*, II Part, p. 186) or the Abbot Nyi-ma bsTan-'dzin (*STNN*, p. 29; *TNT*, p. 55), or our author (*LShDz*, f. 269a3) who all state that Khri-srong was born in Earth-Horse Year. The Abbot gives as his reason for favouring Earth-Horse the following facts: bSam-yas, he asserts, was founded in Earth-Tiger Year when Khri-srong was twenty-one; the concealment of Bon texts occurred after the building of bSam-yas, and the *SG* (f. 47b4) says the concealment occurred in Earth-Ox Year. Nyi-ma's dates in Western reckoning would thus be:

birth of Khri-srong 718
founding of bSam-yas 738
concealment of texts 749.

This, moreover, is manifestly out of line with *GRB* for by Nyi-ma's reckoning Khri-srong was only thirty when he abolished Bon. As to the founding of bSam-yas there is very little measure of agreement in Tibetan sources (see Tucci, *Minor Buddhist Texts*, Part II, pp. 28 et seq.). The Fifth Dalai Lama (*Bod-kyi deb-ther dpyid-kyi rgyal-mo'i glu-dbyangs*, p. 78) for example says Water-Tiger Year for the starting of building (i.e. 762), a year in which Khri-srong would have been twenty-one. This fits with *GRB*'s statement that at twenty-one he established Buddhism and also Khri-srong's second edict, which says that at the age of twenty he paid homage to the Three Jewels and abrogated the law which banned Buddhism (see Tucci, *The Tombs of the Tibetan Kings*, pp. 47–8; though Tucci himself in *Minor Buddhist Texts*, Part II, pp. 28 et seq., rejects 762–3 as the years of foundation; perhaps establishing Buddhism and founding bSam-yas were, in any case, not contemporaneous occurrences). However, there still seems to be a discrepancy between *GRB* and *bsGrags-byang* for Khri-srong did not reach the age of forty-five in an ox year, but in Fire-Tiger Year (786). However, the previous year (785) was Wood-Ox Year, and, in fact, the statement that he abolished Bon at forty-five is to be understood to mean that he completed the abolition at that age for earlier *GRB* (p. 59) states that he began to abolish Bon in Water-Pig Year (783) whilst concealment of texts began in Wood-Ox Year (785). Wood-Ox Year (785) seems, therefore, fairly certain to be the year referred to by *bsGrags-byang* as the year in which concealment began. It may be worth adding that the contest which preceded the abolition (see *supra*, pp. 88 et seq.) is said in *KhG* JA (f. 89b7) to have taken place in Pig-Year. This fits well with the *GRB* statement just noted, and the contest can be ascribed to Water-Pig Year (783). However, a further problem here arises. In our text (see *supra*, p. 90) the edict of abolition seems to follow immediately on the conclusion of the contest, and it is the edict of abolition that prompts Dran-pa Nam-mkha' 's conversion to Buddhism (see the Introduction, p. xxxii n. 4). Now *SG* (f. 51b1) says Dran-pa Nam-mkha' was thirty-one when the abolition of Bon led him to become a monk. Dran-pa Nam-mkha' 's birth is traditionally said to have

separate groups: the king of textual treasure, the four ministers of textual treasure and a further minister of textual treasure, making six in all. To be exact the five great secret textual treasures and one thousand seven hundred small textual treasures were hidden. In each temple of the Lord a Bon text was hidden and in the same way many textual treasures were hidden in mountains, rocks, and stūpas, etc.

In the light of these authorities (I will relate) which Bon texts were hidden and where. Altogether, the 'Original Words' of the Teacher contains the four 'Supreme 'Bum' and a hundred and eight minor 'Bum. The four 'Supreme 'Bum' are: (1) The 'Bum of Spells. This was hidden in Sum-pa glang-gi gyim-shod. It contains many kinds of spells known as rGyud-khri. (2) The 'Bum of mDo was hidden in sGro-rtsa in the North. The 'Bum of mDo consists of the Four Great mDo and a hundred thousand minor mDo. The four Great mDo are: the *Khams-gsum sems-can skye-'chi'i mdo*, the *sNod-bcud bskal-pa chags-jig-gi mdo*, (177a) the *Dus-gsum bde-gshegs byung-khungs-kyi mdo*, the *Bla-med go-'phang sgrub-thabs-kyi mdo.*[1] (3) The 'Bum of rGyud was hidden in Khyung-lung (dngul-mkhar) in Zhang-zhung. It has a hundred thousand rGyud: Exoteric rGyud; ten thousand; Esoteric rGyud: forty thousand; neither Exoteric nor Esoteric rGyud: ten thousand. Wrathful rGyud: ten thousand; the Stream of Compassionate rGyud: ten thousand; the rGyud of Zhang-zhung this-sngags: ten thousand; the Ambrosia rGyud: ten thousand making a hundred thousand in all. (4) The 'Bum of Wisdom has four mDo: the '*Bum of Srid-pa snang-ldan dkar-po* was hidden in lHo-brag khom-mthing. The '*Bum of Khams-brgyad* was hidden in Cog-ro mtha'-dkar.[2] The '*Bum of Thugs-rje nyi-ma stong-khyab* was hidden in the cave of sPa-gro stag-tshal seng-ge. The '*Bum of Bon-nyid snying-po bdal-ba* was hidden in the castle of lHa-sa'i yang-dben yer-ba.[3] The places where the textual treasures were hidden are: Zhang-zhung khyung-lung

been Horse-Year. Thirty-one years back from the year of the contest (783) brings us not to Horse-Year, but Snake-Year, the year preceding Horse-Year. Dran-pa Nam-mkha' could therefore have been thirty-one in 784 but not in 783. This I suggest must be the year of his conversion to Buddhism, a year which comes at the centre of the process of abolition.

[1] These were rediscovered by Sad-gu Rin-chen Grags-pa and Dre'u-rgya Ra-dza (see *infra*, p. 160).

[2] See *supra*, p. 22 n. 3.

[3] See *supra*, p. 19 n. 4.

which is between O-rgyan (Uḍḍiyāna) in the West and Tibet, Sum-pa glang-gi gyim-shod which is between China in the East and Tibet, (177b) Brag smyug-ma bu-khur-can which is between Nepal in the South and Tibet, Li-ving sgong-ring which is between Mongolia in the North and Tibet. In these four great places three hundred and sixty textual treasures were hidden. The four kings of textual treasure were hidden in bSam-yas mchod-rten nag-po, mChims-kyi gad-pa stag-'bring, Ra-sa'i 'phrul-snang, and gTsang-stod bye-ma g·yung-drung. The thirty-seven ministers of textual treasure were hidden in Glo-yul gang-'bar, Gangs ti-se'i-mgul, sPos-ri ngad-ldan-gyi-shar, Mang-nam brag-phug, Mang-yul byams-sprin, Khyung-lung dngul-mkhar, Za-dum dgu-rtse, sPa-gro stag-tshal seng-ge-phug, sKu-lha thang-lha'i-mgul, dBu-ru ka-tshal, sKu-lha skyog-khrom-gyi-rtse, sPa-sha gangs-kyi rtse-mo, Byang sgro-rtsa, Cog-ro mtha'-dkar, lHo-brag khom-mthing, gYas-ru gtsang-'phrang, gYas-ru khra-'brug, Brag rgya-bo, rTa-sgo gangs-mdun, Mang-mkhar lcags-'phrang, Zang-zang lha-brag, Yar-lha sham-po, rMa Pom-ra'i g·yas-zur, mTshal-gyi phug-mo-che, lHo-brag mkhar-chu, lHo-nub kha-byang, Gong-gi dbu-rtse, gSer-thang sha-ba-can, Tsha-ba rong-gi-snyog, (178a) lCum nag-po'i-brag, rTa-nag rkyang-phu, sKya-ra'i-phu, Brung-gi g·ya'-sil, Mang-yul byang-nam, sPa-gro skyer-chu, Brag-phu gsang-dmar, and Nyan-gyi se-bo-ri. The further minister of textual treasure was hidden in the castle of Yer-ba in dBus. Furthermore, many textual treasures were hidden on gNam-mtsho phyug-mo, in front of Pha-bong ru-rtse and Seng-ge kha-yel. After a discussion with the king a casket of texts was hidden in the central and four corner pillars (of the temple) of bSam-yas, another casket in the heart of (the image of) rNam-par sNang-mdzad (Vairocana), and one casket in each calf of rGyal-ba Byams-pa (Maitreya). Three hundred magical spells, which are like lightning, were hidden in the heart of gShin-rje-gshed (yamāntaka) and rTa-'grin (Hayagrīva). The rites of 'Dre-srin bu-dgu were hidden under the threshold beneath the images of the hawk and wolf on the outside of the door. Five textual treasures were hidden in each temple of Kha-non,[1] and Ru-non.[2] A hundred textual treasures were also hidden in lHa-dgu,

[1] There are nine of them for which see *KhG*, f. 40a2.

[2] See *supra*, p. 90 n. 1.

rGyung-dgu, various Bon Centres and rocky mountains. (The textual treasures were also hidden in other places, such as:) mChod-rten dmar-po, Pho-brang bse-sgo-can, Khrom-pa-gyang, Gas-kyi byi-ba-mkhar, Long-'gro rtag-rdzong, and Khri-'od stag-rtse. (178b) When Bon-pos hid the texts they prayed thus: 'May this solemn Everlasting Bon—as we have no power to practise it and have to hide it—be unchangeable as gold. May it be discovered by fortunate ones to guide sentient beings when the time arrives to convert them to Bon.' The 'Four Scholars', Khyung-po Gyer-zla-med, Dran-pa Nam-mkha' and other great priests who possessed miraculous powers; and lesser priests who possessed swift-footedness travelled to many places to conceal the texts—from Kailāsa down to Dar-rtse-mdo (Ta-chien-lu)—three hundred and sixty textual treasures and innumerable small textual treasures were concealed and white and black prayers were said. Some of the priests who possessed miraculous skills went away in various directions. Some went into the 'Celestial Sphere'. Some exchanged their former Bon-priest style of dress for that generally worn and put on a Dam-zhu dom-ra,[1] a warm woollen robe, carried a triple-topped walking-cane in their hands, and patterned bags of scripture on their backs. They set out to Sum-pa glang-gi gyim-shod.

(179a) c. How 'Retribution' occurred[2]

i. The account of the *Zhang-zhung snyan-brgyud*[3]
ii. The account of the *Byang-gter* (Northern Textual Treasures)

i. As Khri-srong lDe-btsan had killed the king of Zhang-zhung, the thousands of Zhang-zhung communities were separated from the thousands of Sum-pa communities. When Zhang-zhung[4] fell to pieces, the primary wife of the king of Zhang-zhung, whose name was Khyung-bza' mTsho-rgyal, thinking to get her revenge, invited Gyer-spungs sNang-bzher Lod-po and asked: 'Great body-priest, the Tibetan king Khri-srong

[1] A hat made of bear-skin similar to sTag-zhva for which see Snellgrove, *Nine Ways*, p. (277), Illustration IX (*a*).
[2] This section was announced *supra*, p. 82.
[3] The account which follows is a passage of the *sNyan-(b)rgyud ma-nub-pa'i gtan-tshigs*—a section of *Zhang-zhung snyan-brgyud*—and in some instances our historian introduces variants.
[4] Our text reads Bod.

lDe-btsan has murdered the Lord Lig-mi-rgya. The silken knot of the law of Bon is loosened. The golden yoke of the law of the king is broken. The doctrines of Everlasting Bon are suppressed. Such a time is the present. I ask you to be my avenger. Gyer-spungs replied: 'I have a rite called sPu; if I perform it with an ounce of gold for three years we can destroy the four quarters of Tibet. Another is called Khyung; if I perform it with half an ounce of gold for three months we can destroy Yar-lung together with Khri-srong and his attendants. (179b) Yet another is called rNgub; if I perform it with a quarter of an ounce of gold for a week and then throw the gold, we can kill the king alone. Which one is to be performed?' Khyung-bza' mTsho-rgyal being compassionate, said: 'It is not the fault of the Tibetan people but their king's. I ask you to perform the rNgub.' The Great Gyer-spungs went to the island of the lake of Da-rog where he put up a white tent patterned with deer, sat on a silk mat and performed the rNgub with a quarter of an ounce of gold for a week. Then he divided a drachm of the gold into three parts and at dusk threw one part which hit seven deer, who were lying on the mountain of Sog-kha'i spun-po killing two and causing five to become stiff. Now the mountain is called Yar-lung sha-ba-rengs (the stiff deer of Yar-lung). At midnight he threw the second part of the gold and hit the lake on the side of Mount Yar-lha sham-po. The lake dried up and the water-spirits ran away. Now the place is called Yar-lung mtsho-skam (the dry lake of Yar-lung). At dawn he hurled the third part of the gold and it struck the castle of Byi-ba stag-rtse. It caught fire and the king became ill. At that time, the intelligent king said: 'The killing of the Bon-protector king, the suppression of the doctrines of Everlasting Bon, (180a) the way in which the 'Bomb' came this morning—clearly Gyer-spungs is offended. We must elevate him again.' He ordered a hundred horsemen, giving them a large quantity of gold dust, to invite him. They, arriving in the valley of Dra-phye, gave some gold dust to a man of Zhang-zhung and asked him if he knew where Gu-rub sNang-bzher Lod-po was dwelling. The man said: 'The great Gyer-spungs is dwelling on the island of the lake of Da-rog. Since his body can appear in any form, you had better pray to him whatever you see and he will show you his face.' Then they crossed the lake in a boat and reached the island. They saw a crystal horn blazing on a silk mat. Knowing that it was Gyer-spungs they bowed, offered the gold dust, narrated the story, and made supplication. The crystal horn became Gyer-spungs and, showing his face, he said: 'The Bon-protector king was killed. Everlasting Bon is suppressed. If the Tibetan king had been killed the country would have fallen into misery. Considering this I acted only within limits although my mind was full of revenge.' The envoys said: 'The Tibetan king is ill. (180b) His subjects are in misery. Thus the punishment of Bon and its priests has fallen upon us. As we have been sent to invite you to be preceptor to our king we beg to come.' Gyer-spungs said: 'I want to make three conditions: we want a gold shrine large enough to enclose the body of the Zhang-zhung king. No taxation by the Tibetan king and ministers can be imposed on the people of Gu-rub when they come to Yar-lung sog-kha. None of the three hundred and sixty (kinds of) Zhang-zhung Bon, which I practise, are to be suppressed.' The three envoys agreed that they would keep the promises and he was invited. The Tibetan king, his ministers, and their subjects submitted to him and did all he ordered. As Gyer-spungs performed the rite of the *gSang-this-kyi-sngags*, many pieces of gold, which were like horse-tail hair, came out from the king's body. And so the king recovered from his illness. His subjects were relieved from their sufferings.

ii. Some time after the decline of Bon the Buddhist monks also broke their rules and polluted themselves with the wives or sisters or daughters of their people claiming them to be Phyag-rgya-ma (mudra). They tasted human flesh claiming it to be a 'mass of offering'. (181a) They indulged in various impurities claiming them to be 'sacred items'. So the 'Royal Divinities' were deeply perturbed: Yar-lha Sham-po looked away towards the West. Thang-lha Yar-bzhugs looked away towards the North. rMa Pom-ra looked away towards the East. lDong-lha dGung-grags looked away towards the South. The undefiled gods withdrew into heaven. The local gods and goddesses fled to other countries. It disgusted all the gods. The Indian demi-gods occupied their places. Around the same time, the spirits of the dead became ghosts since the Buddhists forbade the transmission of the 'posthumous evocation rituals'. The ghosts and Indian demi-gods combined to inflict plagues on mankind and disease on animals. Rain stopped. A Bon-po of sDong called gTer-bcug performed the rite of the *Thog-smad bco-brgyad* and so the temple of dKar-chung was struck down by lightning.[1] The king was also overtaken by illness. Although the Buddhists performed the 'Life-ritual' for him, no benefit was received from it. At that time, the diviners and soothsayers were consulted and they said that the misfortunes were due to the suppression of Bon and the banishment of its priests. If the priests were invited back and allowed to invoke the 'Royal Divinities' and if Dran-pa Nam-mkha' was permitted to return to his own faith, then benefit would be obtained. (181b) At that time, the priestess Co-za was under the privilege (of the king) at Brag mkhar-ba-can and was asked (if she knew where the Bon priests were). She said that she could bring them back, but others said that the priests had died in the northern desert. She replied: 'The priests are living in grass-huts in the North. They make ogres their servants and they milk wild and beautiful animals.' She was asked to go and invite the priests (to return) and was given Bya-bo full of gold and silver. She set out riding a mule called 'Phar-ma dgu-rkang and as she went she invoked the god of lDong. She came upon the priests and said: 'I have come here to invite you back as Tibet is afflicted by various forms of unhappiness. I beg you to come.' lCe-tsha mKhar-bu of Me-nyag said: 'Bon (has no other purpose) except to work for the welfare of sentient beings. As we feel compassion for sentient beings we must go.' All the priests returned. They arrived in bSam-yas. On looking around they saw four stūpas. gCo-gshen Phyag-dkar asked what those great stūpas were. (The Buddhists said): 'These are the four great stūpas of Me-tsa. If one circumambulates them one's impurity will be cleansed.' (182a) (gCo-gshen Phyag-dkar replied): 'I do not think that stūpas made from substances are wonderful.' As he said this and made gestures in space there appeared in the air a blazing stūpa of bDud-'dul sgra-sgrags g·yung-drung-brtsegs which was seen by all those who were near by. Then on entering the door (of the temple) they saw a large clay image, Khu-bon mThong-grags (one of the Bon-pos) asked: 'What is this?' (A Buddhist explained:) 'This is the great wrathful door-guard called Mahākala. If one reveres him he will remove obstructions.' Khu-bon mThong-grags replied: 'Since phenomenal

[1] Cf. *supra*, p. 79 n. 2.

existence is the (Buddha) body in its celestial environment what is there to be guarded by the wrathful door-guard?' Saying this and clicking his fingers (his thumb against his middle finger) the clay image turned into dust. This is the reason why nowadays there is no image of the door-guard. Then they went up to the top floor and looked at the clay images of Vairocana and his attendants. (The Bon priest) Sum-pa Mu-cho asked: 'What are these?' (He was answered:) 'The one in the centre is Vairocana and the others are the eight Bodhisattvas. If one makes offerings and supplications to these one will attain the ordinary and supreme accomplishments.' Sum-pa Mu-cho replied: 'I do not expect from material images to obtain the ordinary and supreme accomplishments.' (182b) He opened his chest and a blazing deity embracing his partner was seen in his heart. The Buddhist ministers were amazed. Then they went to the palace and jestingly exchanged greetings with the king. On the advice of the Bon-pos a Bon temple was built for suppressing demons.[1] A black stūpa was built in the Bon style.[2] In consequence the time of disease and sufferings was put to an end and sentient beings were made happy. That is why even now this stūpa subdues demons. Dran-pa Nam-mkha' was permitted to return to his own faith. As he gave 'Life-Consecration' to the Lord, the Lord's illness was cured. Then the Bon-pos were offered three countries: 'Ol-mo-lung, in the Upper Land, Kong-yul bre-sna in the Lower Land, and Yar-'brog thun-gsum in the centre. In the Upper Land they were offered (dominion over) three tribes: So, So-ngan, and Klo-bo. In dBus they were offered (dominion over) three tribes: Dre, Slong, and Kong. Thang-phu of lHa-sa was given to them as a place for worship and Yar-lung sog-kha as a place in which to dwell. At that time, the Lord said: 'Bon and Buddhism have each been suppressed in turn in the past. (183a) But now as I have called you back I ask you to bring out the textual treasures and to practise Bon and Buddhism together.'

[1] *bsTan-'byung* (f. 49a4): *bi har gling du gsas khang brtsigs*. Bi-har-gling is a temple in bSam-yas and its full name is dKor-mdzod bi-har-gling. (*KhG*, f. 96a6), but no Bon-po temple is recorded by *KhG*, anywhere in bSam-yas.

[2] According to *sBa-bzhed* followed by *KhG* (f. 97b6) and *rGyal-po bka'-thang* (f. 34b3) this black mchod-rten was built by Ngam rTa-ra Klu-gong (for reference to whom see *supra*, p. 88 n. 5). It became a very important place for many texts were hidden there (see *supra*, p. 96) as the Buddhists have also stated (Stein, *sBa-bzhed*, p. 28 followed by *KhG*, f. 90a4).

The vow to practise the two faiths together was kept for three years. Although the Buddhist ministers began circulating calumnies again and the king followed Buddhism he kept his promises and so the doctrines of Bon were not completely suppressed. This is also the reason why the doctrines of Bon have still survived in this Land of Snows, Tibet.

Khri-srong lDe-btsan had three wives: rGya-bza' Kong-cu, Tshe-spungs-bza' dMar-rgyan, and Chu-nam 'Bro-bza' dKar-mo. Although 'Bro-bza' and rGya-bza' had no offspring they had great influence since they favoured Buddhism. rGya-bza' is known by different names: Pho-yangs-bza' or Gyim-sham-bza', etc. Tshe-spungs-bza' was the mother of three sons, but since she was in favour of Bon she was amicably avoided by the king and had very little influence. It has been stated that the Buddhists frequently spoke ill of Tshe-spungs-bza'. The three sons in order of seniority are: Mu-tig bTsan-po, Mu-ne bTsan-po, Mu-thug bTsan-po.[1] Mu-ne succeeded to his father's throne. He laid the foundation of the Great Offerings in bSam-yas. (183b) He made his rich and poor subjects equal for three years. He ruled the country for a year and seven months. At the age of seventeen he was poisoned by his mother and died. The Buddhists tried the 'evocation ritual', but failed to summon the spirit (bla). It would enter someone and babble. Since the Buddhists had no 'evocation ritual of the spirits of the dead' they copied Bon, but people did not believe in it, for they knew that it was not theirs. Then Dran-pa Nam-mkha' summoned the spirit (of the dead boy) and pacified it. So the Lord Khri-srong, believing in Bon, said: 'Without the Bon of "posthumous evocation", the spirits of the dead cannot be guided.' The Bon of 'posthumous evocation' is one of the earliest (Bon rituals). There still exists a ritual called the *rGyal-po Mu-ne lhe-'dur*. The *bsGrags-byang*[2] says:

The divine prince who favoured Bon was banished to gTsang. Thus there was no descendant except Mu-thug, since Mu-tig, Mu-ne, and their father Khri-srong were all dead. So the prince Mu-thug was invited back from sPa-gro and he succeeded to the

[1] The order of seniority of the sons of Khri-srong lDe-btsan has always been a confused subject owing to the similarity of their names. In most Tibetan historical sources the following order is given: Mu-ne, Mu-thug or Mu-tsug, and Mu-tig. For a detailed study concerning their historical reality see E. Haarh, op. cit., pp. 146 et seq.

[2] *bsGrags-byang*, f. 90a5.

throne. The divinely born, (Mu-thug) grew tired of his subjects. He took away many Bon texts, medical texts, and special texts concerning various arts from his father's treasury and went to sPa-gro phug-gcal with Khyung-po Gyer-zla-med to conceal them. (184a) It is also said that the rGyud of dBal-phur and its supplementary texts were hidden by the Lord Mu-thug and Khyung-po Gyer-zla-med in sPa-gro phug-gcal. The 'Northern textual treasures' and the *rNam-'byed* agree that the king Khri-srong died at the age of fifty-nine. Some say that since the king Khri-srong favoured 'Bro-bza', queen Un-chung and queen dMar-rgyan were jealous. They poisoned him and he died at the age of thirty-six.[1] Mu-thug had three sons. Dar-ma Ral-ba-can[2] was highly meritorious and he became famous as the ruler of two-thirds of the world. At the age of eighteen the nine-storeyed palace was built at 'On-'jang-rdo. He invited Jinamitra from Kashmir and the language of the previous translations of Buddhist texts was revised. He imposed three forms of hardship: he forbade the translations of any tantras but the vinaya of gZhi thams-cad yod-par smra-ba (Mūla-sarvāstivāda) of sDe-ba bye-brag (Vaibhāṣika).[3] Even the measures—bushel, ounce, and so on—were altered according to the Indian manner. (184b) Each monk was given seven families from his subjects (over which he acted as patron). He would make his head-dress a seat (for monks) and then bow down to their feet. During his reign Buddhism spread far and wide. The Bon-po of Khyung-po, sTag-sgra Don-gtsug, and the Bon-po of Zhang-zhung, Dun-tang rGyal-ba acted as his bodyguards. As a sign of possessing magical powers they made the pool of 'Grang spout upwards. As they rolled their drum down the mountain of 'Grang a juniper tree grew in each place the drum touched. As they struck their flat-bells on rocks seven springs gushed forth. The divinely born decreed: 'Any person who is under my rule is forbidden to risk causing physical injury to the Bon-pos or to take advantage of the possessions of the Bon-pos, the "Drum-Carriers".' Taxes and honours were paid to them as under his ancestors. The

[1] See *supra*, p. 94 n. 2.

[2] Dar-ma Ral-ba-can was Mu-thug's second son. The eldest (not mentioned here) is known as gTsang-ma and is said to have been banished (see *LShDz*, f. 110b5).

[3] But *KhG*, f. 133a1: *sngags ma rgyud rnams ma bsgyur zhig zhes bka' bstsal*—an order was issued that the Mother Tantras should not be translated (into Tibetan).

bodyguards of the divinely born Dar-ma[1] were: the Bon-po of Me-nyag, rGyal-sum dPal-legs, and Se-bon Ye-shes-dpal. As a sign of having magical powers, they made earthen images talk, conjured up supernatural beings, and displayed other incredible magical signs. During the reigns of Khri Dar-ma 'Od-srung and Khri-lde Yum-brtan,[2] So Khri-thog rGyal-ba, Nyang-bon rDo-rje-mkhar, gYag-rgod Me-btsan, and Bhe Shod-kram were the bodyguards. (185a) So Khri-thog rGyal-ba was able to move mountains and dry up large lakes. Nyang-bon rDo-rje-mkhar flew into the sky. gYag-rgod Me-btsan, having transformed himself into tigers and wolves, fetched the 'Bomb-making spells' from Zhang-zhung. Bhe Shod-kram placed his bag in space and the black gNam-thel shrieked. Thus they possessed many extra-ordinary supernatural powers. During the reign of the divinely born dPal-'khor-btsan,[3] Pha-ba bTsan-legs acted as bodyguard and minister. During the reign of bKra-shis brTsegs-pa-dpal, Zas-dkar Chos-nyid acted as bodyguard. These accounts that I have been narrating are taken from the *bKa'-'bum* and other sources. After (this last king) the throne slipped into the hands of the subjects. The royal descendants wandered about in the borderlands. Tibet fell to pieces. It is said that from this time wherever a royal descendant went it was the custom for a Bon-po bodyguard to be with him. Many similar stories are told, but since they are unimportant I do not quote them. Nowadays in Kong-po and other places it is said that some Tibetan royal descendants went begging in villages.

[1] Another son of Mu-thug, generally known as Glang Dar-ma who reigned from 836 to 842.

[2] They are the sons of Glang Dar-ma (see *LShDz*, f. 111a1).

[3] The son of Dar-ma 'Od-srung.

SECTION VII

The Third Spread of the Doctrine: Textual Treasure and Oral Tradition

(185b) Having expounded the way in which the Second Spread and decline of the precious doctrines of Everlasting Bon took place and the textual treasures were concealed, I shall now deal with the Third Spread of the Doctrine which, through the powers of the prayers of the Enlightened One and of knowledge-holders, and with the arrival of the time to discipline the Tibetans, arose again with the discoveries of the textual treasures from various places in the upper and lower lands by many manifestations of knowledge-holders who diffused them all including the Oral Tradition teachings.

A. The history of the 'Original Words'
B. The history of the Textual Treasures

A I. The actual (sayings)
II. The (sayings) which have been classed with the actual ones

Ia. The 'Rules of Discipline'
Ib. The Tantric and Mental Teachings

Ia. The son of the king Lag-ngan called lHa-thu Khra-thang was punished (186a) by the Chinese sPun-mang and was banished to Mongolia. When he was looking after the horses of a governor in Mongolia called dPal-'bar, the king of Me-nyag named Rab-rtse-'dus bought him and let him look after his horses. As he came from Mongolia wearing a robe of monkey skin he was called Sog-po sPrel-slag-can (Mongolian monkey-skin robe). Whilst he was looking after the horses at rMa-ri del-gsum he went into a cave called Brag-dkar rtse-'dus which seemed dark at the entrance, but light inside. On entering he saw one who looked like a monk, but his hair grew down to the ground in coils. No sooner did he see the monk than he was filled with joy and was awakened from his past actions. Bowing down, he requested: 'O! Great one, emerge from your trance.' But the monk said nothing. The next morning he went there again and repeated his entreaty, but only an eyebrow moved. He returned again the following day and as he repeated his request the face moved a little. The next day at his request the monk arose from his trance and said: 'Alas! you impediment to continuity, are you human or non-human? What is the matter?' He replied: 'I am a human whose body is inferior and whose mind is in misery. I am owned by somebody else!' 'Well, then, can you receive the seed of my doctrine?' (186b). 'I shall follow you', he answered. The monk said: 'You may receive the seed of the doctrine. I shall not think of you as an impediment.' (Thereupon) he received full ordination at once and was given the monastic name, Khri-'bar Tshul-khrims. The teacher was Mu-zi gSal-bzang,[1] the manifestation of the apostle Mu-cho. The *Srid-rgyud*[2] says:

> There will be one called Mu-zi gSal-bzang,
> The manifestation of the mind of Mu-cho;
> Realizing (the earthly existence) as impermanent and illusory,
> He will enter the trance of the 'cessation of senses' at the rock of 'Dan-ma.

Khri-'bar Tshul-khrims (who looked after the horses) was the manifestation of gTsug-gshen rGyal-ba.[3] The same authority[4] says:

> There will be one called Khri-'bar Tshul-khrims of Mongolia,
> The manifestation of gTsug-gshen rGyal-ba,
> Who will abandon the earthly cycle of existence.

He had a disciple who was the son of 'Dan-ma Mu-'bar called 'Dan-ma Rin-bzang or gYag-slag-can. His monastic name was rGyal-ba gTsug-phud. The same authority[5] says:

> The manifestation of Drang-srong rGyal-ba,[6]
> Is 'Dan-ma rGyal-ba gTsug-phud.

He had a disciple who was the son of Grum-bon dBal-'bar called

[1] According to *STNN* the meeting occurred in A.D. 888.
[2] *SG*, f. 66b7.
[3] gTsug-gshen rGyal-ba is also known as Yid-kyi Khye'u-chung, see *supra*, p. 35 n. 4.
[4] *SG*, f. 61a1.
[5] *SG*, f. 61a2.
[6] This is the monastic name of gTo-bu 'Bum-sangs, see *supra*, p. 3 n. 2.

Grum-bu Shing-slag-can. His monastic name was Tshul-khrims gTsug-phud and he is said to have been the manifestation of gTsug-sras rMa-bo. He had a disciple who was the son of Zi Khrom-'bar called Ya-zi Bon-ston and his monastic name was (187a) Shres-rab Tshul-khrims. He was also called Bla Mu-thur dGongs-pa Rab-gsal.[1] The *Srid-rgyud*[2] says:

> A monk who has attained realization,
> The manifestation of dMu-tsha Tra-he,
> Later known as Mu-thur dGongs-pa Rab-gsal,
> His monastic name will be Shes-rab Tshul-khrims,
> He will be born in Sum-snang rma-yi-brag.

He had a disciple who was called gNyos A-rin who, overcoming all difficulties, went to Amdo. He met Mu-thur dGongs-pa Rab-gsal and took monastic ordination from him. His monastic name was Rin-chen rGyal-mtshan. He was the manifestation of Khri-lde 'Od-po. Bla-chen dGons-pa Rab-gsal had many Buddhist disciples. The king Glang Dar-ma suppressed Buddhism and some monks were killed. Some were forced to hunt, and others were banished. For eighty years no Buddhism was heard. Some say that it was for seventy-six years. At that time, at Brag-dkar phug-mo-che, lHa-lung dPal-ryi rDo-rje was practising tantrism. Disguised as Sa-thel Nag-po (a demon) he approached the king, shot him with a poisoned arrow, and the king was killed. Then, disguised (187b) as Bar-thel Khra-bo and gNam-thel dKar-po (two other demons), he ran away. Later when no Buddhist monk was there to restore Buddhism, gNyos-btsun A-rin was asked by lHa-lung dPal-rdo: 'Who is your abbot?' gNyos-btsun replied: 'My abbot is at rMa-ri del-gsum-gyi-brag and he is called Bla Mu-thur dGongs-pa Rab-gsal.' Thereupon, the Tibetans held a discussion and seven people, four from gTsang and three from dBus, set out. Six of them met the abbot (Bla-chen dGongs-pa Rab-gsal) and took monastic ordination. Bla-chen said: 'My spiritual lineage goes back to Bon and is the "Order of the Individual Liberation". Follow this. As for (religious) practices, you should observe the customs and

[1] According to Buddhist historians he belonged to a Bon-po family and later became a Buddhist monk. R. A. Stein. *sBa-bzhed*, pp. 83–4, However, Bon-pos, on the other hand, claim that he was a Bon-po monk and born in (*STNN*) A.D. 952. Also see *GRB*, p. 57.

[2] *SG*, f. 61a3.

rules (of this order). I want you to take four signs in memory of my being (the officiating) abbot. Your doctrine will be very extensive. Whichever doctrines of an Enlightened One are spread it is good.' So he gave them monastic ordination. The four signs the abbot gave were: the pillars of Sham-thab (cloth for lower part of body),[1] the end of thang-pa,[2] the top of Pad-zhu (lotus-hat),[3] and a mat[4]—all blue. If they cannot be entirely blue then they should have parallel seams in blue thread. (188a) In some old Buddhist monasteries ancient monastic robes thus marked are (still) to be seen. Of the seven Buddhists the four from gTsang were: Lo-ston rDo-rje dBang-phyug, Tshang-ge Shes-rab Seng-ge, 'A-zha rGyal-ba Blo-gros, and 'Bri Ye-shes sNying-po. The three from dBus were: Klu-mes Tshul-khrims Shes-rab, Rag-shi Tshul-khrims 'Byung-gnas, and rBa Ye-shes Blo-gros. And so the spiritual lineage of the lower Vinaya of 'The Others' is the same as ours. The *Srid-rgyud*[5] says:

> Since Dar-ma sPrel-mgo suppressed Buddhism,
> 'Retribution' (fell) upon him:
> He was killed by lHa-lung dPal-gyi rDo-rje,
> By means of disguised weapons.
> The Buddhist secular vows were broken,
> And the (spiritual) lineage of the vinaya was also interrupted.
> After that the transmission of Buddhist vows
> Was received from one called
> Mu-thur dGongs-pa Rab-gsal who had obtained it from Sog, 'Dan and Grum,[6]
> Just as gNyos-btsun A-rin took (monastic ordination) from him.

So it was transmitted to the Buddhists. The Buddhist history of 'The Others', the *Kun-gsal,* by gNam-lcags rDo-rje also conforms to the *Srid-rgyud*: (188b)

Klu-mes Tshul-khrims Shes-rab from dBus and others met

[1] See Snellgrove, *Nine Ways*, p. (271), Illustration III (*a*).

[2] Also known as rMad-g·yogs, see ibid., p. (270), Illustration II (*f*).

[3] Also known as Pad-zhva see ibid., p. (270), Illustration II (*b*), (*c*), and (*d*). *GRB* (p. 57) gives Pad-khug instead, for which see Snellgrove, *Nine Ways*, p. (273), Illustration V (*a*).

[4] Also known as Pad-gdan, see ibid., p. (272), Illustration IV (*c*), (*d*), and (*e*).

[5] *SG*, f. 72b6.

[6] They are Sog-po sPrel-slag-can, 'Dan-ma gYag-slag-can, and Grum-bu Shing-slag-can (see *supra*, pp. 105–7).

Bon-po dGongs-pa Rab-gsal and took monastic ordination from him. Klu-mes asked the Bon-abbot to give him a relic as he was returning to dBus. The Bon-abbot, giving him an 'Obs-zhu[1] put yellow earth on the top of it and then said: 'Wear this hat in memory of me.' (The custom of) wearing a yellow hat spread from that time. The Bon-abbot prophesied that there would be innumerable monasteries and monks in dBus and gTsang.

Our spiritual lineage of the 'Rules of Discipline' in gTsang is as follows: the disciple of gNyos-btsun Rin-chen rGyal-mtshan was the manifestation of lHang-lhang gTsug-phud, gNyos Kun-dGa' Tshul-khrims. His disciple was the manifestation of Dvangs-ba Yid-ring, mGar Rin-chen gTsug-phud. His disciple was the manifestation of Thugs-dkar Ye-shes, Pra-phud Tshul-khrims. His disciple was the manifestation of Gang-rum gTsug-phud, gNyos-lag Drug-pa Tshul-khrims Ye-shes. His disciples were the manifestation of Dran-pa Nam-mkha', Khro-tshang 'Brug-lha,[2] and the manifestation of 'Od-lha gSal-'bar, Sher-btsun gYung-drung Pra-phud. The disciple of the latter was the manifestation of Ye-shes Tshul-khrims, Gur-btsun gYung-drung rGyal-mtshan. His disciples were the manifestation of gYung-drung Tshul-khrims, (189a) 'Tsho-btsun Nam-mkha' rGyal-mtshan, and the manifestation of Pra-phud Tshul-khrims, gYung-btsun Jo-gdung. These two, one as officiating abbot and the other as teacher, ordained Dam-pa the Hermit[3] and Sum-ston Tshul-blo (Tshul-khrims Blo-gros). The *Srid-rgyud*[4] says:

The manifestation of gSer-thog lCe-'byams,
A monk named Dam-pa of rMe'u,
Whose understanding in trance is that of wisdom,
Will teach the doctrine and sustain it.
There will be one called Tshul-blo of the family Sum-pa.
The manifestation of Legs-tang rMang-po.

Those (teachers) came according to the prophecies both in the *Gling-grags* and *Srid-rgyud*. They all upheld the doctrine of the 'Rules of Discipline' in all parts of dBus and gTsang; and they laboured for the welfare of sentient beings. From here the

[1] A hat made of the skin of an animal known as 'obs, similar in shape to rTa-zhva (for which see Snellgrove, *Nine Ways*, Illustration VI (*b*).

[2] See *infra*, p. 124. [3] See *infra*, p. 138. [4] *SG*, f. 62b5.

spiritual lineage of the 'Rules of Discipline' divided into four different lineages: Bru, Zhu, sPa, and gShen. The history of the disciples of these four lineages who sustained the spiritual lineage of the 'Rules of Discipline' is explained in the *bsTan-pa'i rnam-bshad dar-rgyas gsal-sgron*[1] and others.

Here is the further history of the spiritual lineage of the 'Rules of Discipline' of the mNyam-med Chen-po, unrivalled in the threefold world: (189b) The disciple of Dam-pa was Me-ston Shes-rab 'Od-zer of Yar-'brog. The *Lung-bstan*[2] says:

> In Khar-bo gang-bzang shar-mgul,
> Shes-rab 'Od-zer will live,
> He is also among those I have blessed.

His disciple was the manifestation of Dran-pa Nam-mkha', gShen Nam-mkha' rGyal-mtshan.[3] His disciple was the manifestation of Dran-pa Nam-mkha', the representative of Bru, Me-ston Grags-pa'i-dpal of gYor.[4] His disciple was the manifestation of lHa-khri of Zhang-zhung, 'A-zha dDud-rtsi rGyal-mtshan.[4] His disciples were the manifestation of Hris-pa Gyer-med, 'A-zha Blo-gros rGyal-mtshan,[4] and the holy son of Bru, Dar-ma rGyal-mtshan.[5] Dam-pa's companion Sum-ston Tshul-blo (whom I mentioned) earlier[6] had two disciples: Bru rJe-btsun[7] and Mar-ston rGyal-legs, also known as sMan-gong-ba.[8] The latter's disciple was Zhang-ston bSod-nams-dpal of Ba-thang. His disciple was Sum-ston lHa-'Bum.[9] He and Bru-ston Dar-ma acting as abbot and teacher ordained gShen-ston Blo-gros rGyal-mtshan. His disciple was gShen-ston Ye-shes Blo-gros.[10] His disciple was sMan-gong-ba 'Dul-ba Blo-gros. His disciple was sMan-gong-ba Shes-rab Blo-gros. (190a) His disciple was rGya-rong-ba gYung-drung Ye-shes who lived in (the

[1] A history of Bon by bsTan-rgyal bZang-po.

[2] I cannot identify this prophetic text.

[3] See *infra*, p. 132.

[4] See *infra*, p. 140.

[5] Bru-ston Dar-ma rGyal-mtshan, also known as 'Dul-ba rGyal-mtshan an abbot of gYas-ru dben-sa-kha, see *infra*, p. 140.

[6] See *supra*, p. 109.

[7] Bru bDag-nyid rJe-btsun, an abbot of gYas-ru dBen-sa-kha (see *infra*, p. 140).

[8] b. *STNN* 1123.

[9] Also known as Bla-ma lHa, (b. *STNN* 1135).

[10] See *infra*, p. 132.

monastery of) mKhar-sna. His disciple was the Lord mNyam-med Chen-po[1] whose officiating abbot was Bru-ston Tshul-khrims Ye-shes. All these were the manifestations of former knowledge-holders and their coming had been foretold in prophecies, but owing to their length I have not recorded them. The successive abbots of the spiritual lineage of the mNyam-med Chen-po will be given later.[2]

Ib. The Tantric and Mental Teachings

i. The Bon texts of Zhang-zhung
ii. The Bon texts of India
iii. The Bon texts of Yong-lugs

i. The text known as *Zhang-zhung snyan-brgyud* is the most important among the three hundred and sixty Zhang-zhung Bon texts which the Tibetan king (Khri-srong lDe-btsan) promised not to suppress when he was subdued by the 'Bomb' of sNang-bzher Lod-po of Zhang-zhung. I have expounded earlier how both Tantric and Mental Teachings were transmitted from Gyer-spungs up to dPon-rgyal bTsan-po.[3] From dPon-rgyal bTsan-po (the transmission of the *Zhang-zhung snyan-brgyud*) separated into an upper and lower line. The Upper Transmission: dPon-rgyal bTsan-po taught the *bKa'-brgyud skor-bzhi*[4] to Gu-ge Blo-ldan. From the Six Enlightened Sages[5] it spread in the upper land and so is known as the Upper System of Oral Tradition. (190b) The Lower Transmission: dPon-rgyal bTsan-po taught Khyung-byid Mu-thur of Shang the detailed, medium-length, and condensed versions of the *Nyams-brgyud*,[6] and also the tantric oral precepts of Me-ri, including its long and short rites.[7] From the Five Incarnate Ascetics[8] it spread in the lower land and so is known as the Lower System of Oral Tradition. rTog-med Zhig-po of the Upper System, and 'Ol-sgom Kun-'dul of the Lower System imparted the full instruction (of the Oral Tradition) to Yang-ston Chen-po.[9] There were several

[1] See *infra*, pp. 140 et seq.
[2] See *infra*, p. 144.
[3] See *supra*, pp. 55–6.
[4] See *supra*, p. 52 n. 1.
[5] For brief life-stories of these see *ZhNyL*, ff. 50a5–54b8.
[6] See *supra*, p. 52 n. 1.
[7] See *supra*, p. 45 n. 2.
[8] For brief life-stories of these see *ZhNyL*, ff. 35a1–50b2.
[9] Yang-ston Chen-po Shes-rab rGyal-mtshan lived in the twelfth century. A brief life-story is to be found in *ZhNyL* (Yang-ston). Also see Snellgrove, *Nine Ways*, p. 4 n. 4.

transmissions from him, but they may be reduced to two: (*A*) Southern Transmission and (*B*) Northern Transmission. From Dam-pa 'Bum-rje up to Cig-chod Dad-shes.[1] (*B*) From Lung-sgom rTog-med up to rNam-grol Mu-lto-ba Chen-po.[2] The upper and lower, south and north are only so named from the difference in the places where the teachers lived.

Here is a list of the teachers of the lineage (of the Oral Tradition): the Six Enlightened Sages, the Five incarnate Ascetics, the Nine Teachers of Source-possessors, the Five Teachers of the Tantric and Mental Teachings, the Nine Knowledge-holders of the Scriptural Tradition, the Eight Lords of the Profound Path, the Two Protectors of Sentient Beings, (191a) the Three Teachers of Spiritual Lineage Holders, and the Eight Unrivalled Confidence-Possessors. Up to the present the oral and meditational traditions have both been transmitted from masters to pupils. Of these some attained 'Translucent Body' or 'No Residue' (during their lifetime)[3] and others attained enlightenment in the 'intermediate state' or in the sphere of 'Transcendental Reality'. The evidence for this: sounds were heard or lights seen or earth tremors felt (at their departures). Images and syllables issued (from their remains). All this is clear in their great biographies.

(The transmission of) Me-ri Bon[4] is generally the same (as that of the Oral Tradition) up to Tshe-spungs Zla-ba rGyal-mtshan.[5] The Bon-po of Zhang-zhung, Kha-yal Me-phung, entreated the latter to impart this teaching to him. He transmitted it to This-pa lHa-legs who was the second son of one called bTsan-sgra Byin-rlab-dpal. This-pa lHa-legs transmitted it to his son Ne-rog, he to his son gTsug-phud rNam-rgyal. He had four sons and transmitted it to the middle one, dBang-gi rGyal-mtshan. The transmission continued from father to son through Ring-ne, Khro-mo, Zang-nge, dPal-rtse, bTsan-rgyal, bTsang-grags, sMra-lo, and Drang-srong 'Od-rgyal. Hence it is called 'Father–son Transmission'. (191b) gCo-ston sMon-lam begged (to receive the teaching) from Drang-srong 'Od-rgyal and so the transmission proceeded to Dre-ston rGyal-mtshan, sPa Nyi-dpal bZang-po, sPa bsTan-rgyal bZang-po, and Ba-ye Ye-shes rGyal-mtshan. So (the teaching) flourished.

[1] These are known as the five sNgags-sems bla-ma (see *ZhNyL*, f. 86a9).

[2] See *ZhNyL*, ff. 55a1 et seq.

[3] See *supra*, p. 53 n. 1.

[4] See *supra*, p. 45 n. 2.

[5] See *supra*, p. 53; *ZhNyL*, f. 14a7.

ii. I have related earlier how the transmission of Zag-med thugs-rje occurred.[1] As previously stated Dran-pa Nam-mkha' transmitted this teaching to Tshe-dbang Rig-'dzin.[2] The way in which Tshe-dbang Rig-'dzin transmitted it to Lung-bon lHa-gnyan[3] is as follows: The *Srid-rgyud*[4] says:

> There will be one called Lung-bon lHa-gnyan,
> The manifestation of Tshe-dbang Rig-'dzin,
> Whose disposition is clear and pure,
> He will converse with the knowledge-holder (Tshe-dbang) as if he were human.

Thus Lung-bon lHa-gnyan is extolled in the prophecy. A feeling of sadness arose in him towards the cycle of existence. In his early life he practised 'Hail-provocation' and then, in expiation of this, abandoned all subsistence for three years and again all the worldly pleasure for another three years whilst he practised exploratory meditation. In consequence, when he was thirty-one he met Tshe-dbang the Hermit (without realizing it) and entreated him to impart instruction to him, but the teacher told him: 'We meet here, because the continuation of our acts is the same. Now do not stay here. Go home. On the way, ask the ḍakinī to give you a "life-consecration" so that it will benefit your life. (192a) In your country there is a patroness called Jo-rje whose practice in religion is neither Bon nor Buddhist, but who has attained realization in the External and Internal rites of Mañjuśri. She is (in fact) your own disciple, but pay homage to her as your teacher. If you meet Tshe-dbang the Hermit, you may receive instruction for the attainment of enlightenment in this life. So go to the mountains of Nyang-stod and search for him.' Having listened to what the ascetic said he began searching for the ḍakinī: 'I arrived in Ngam-ring and met a nun who was small, of negative disposition, and had torn lips. She was unfriendly to other people and had nothing to eat. Thinking that she must be the dakinī I bowed down and offered her what I had. I entreated her to give me a consecration and

[1] Zag-med thugs-rje is another term for the Great Perfection (see *LShDz*, ff. 98b4 et seq).

[2] He represents an important figure among the followers of the Great Perfection. He is said to have been a son of Dran-pa Nam-mkha' (see *TNT*, p. 54 and *supra*, Introduction, p. xxxii n. 4).

[3] b. *STNN* 1088.

[4] *SG*, f. 85a6.

blessing, but first: "Who said such things? What knowledge have I?" she retorted angrily. But as I begged her again and again she blessed me. We exchanged relics. Then I went home and the people at home were very pleased. Then, when I was thirty-two I wished to go to the mountains of Nyang-stod, but my family would not allow it and I was delayed for three years. At the age of thirty-five I was allowed to and so began searching (192b) for the Lord Tshe-dbang the Hermit in the upper and lower valleys of Mount Nyang-stod, but could not find him. Considering that he was not to be found by searching, I, without returning home, decided to go to some distant places like dBus or Khams. I set out from Nyang-stod towards the north of Pho-ma snying-ring but then I suddenly met the Lord, an ascetic wearing a red cotton robe and a loin-cloth made of tiger skin. He looked well-born, bright, high of eyebrows, yellow-haired, his flesh young like that of a youth. The Lord asked me: "What is your aim in looking for me?" No sooner had the Lord said this than I was overwhelmed by the faith that arose in me and since I had searched for him so hard and the truth was so great I wept. The Lord said: "Contemplate the misery of the cycle of existence, then weep! Contemplate the eight 'unpropitious states of existence', then weep! Contemplate the suffering of birth, old age, illness, and death, then weep! Contemplate the suffering of the 'ill-born', then weep!" So I stopped crying, and bowing down asked him to give me instruction. The Lord began telling me many ways by which I could make money, but I said to him: "I am not searching for money but asking you to give me instruction on investigation, meditation, practice, and achievement." The Lord said: "Nothing is to be investigated. (193a) Nothing is to be meditated on. Nothing is to be practised. Nor is anything to be attained. Go home." So I said to him: "Even though you do not give me any instruction I am going to remain with you wherever you go or stay." He said that since there was nothing to eat I should go away. But I replied that there was something to eat and I was not going. Then the Lord said: "Eat that flour down there and tomorrow morning I shall give you instruction." That night the Lord slept behind a rock and I slept on the other side below the rock. Next morning I wondered whether the Lord was still there and looked for him. He was, and I asked: "Now please give me instruction." Taking his previous word "Weep" as a basis he expounded the significance of the ordinary (drang-don). Taking his previous word "Nothing is to be investigated, etc." as a basis he expounded the significance of reality (nges-don). I stayed with him for twenty-one days receiving instruction.' Thus the teacher lHa-gnyan met the Lord Tshe-dbang at bKra-shis phyug-mo, Pho-ma snying-ring, Rin-chen spungs-pa and others and received instructions on the following treatises by Dran-pa Nam-mkha': the *Drang-don mun-sel sgron-ma* and the *Nges-don nam-mkha' 'phrul-mdzod*. (Instruction was also received on the treatises of Great Perfection:) the *Ye-khri mtha'-sel*, the *mChong-lung nyi-shu rtsa-lnga* the *rDzogs-chen nyi-ma'i snying-po*, and (193b) the *rGya-gar grub-chen bco-lnga'i zhal-gdams*, etc. Lung-bon lHa-gnyan transmitted them to Lung-bon 'Khor-lo rGyal-po and so (the teaching) flourished.

iii. The Bon texts of dBal-chen Ram-pa of Yong-lugs, loaded on blue wolves, were brought to Tibet by Khyung-gsas of Me-nyag from rGod in Zhang-zhung. They reached mDo-smad. There, in due course, appeared many ascetics who practised them, such as Mon-dri sTon-pa Shes-rab,[1] Shar-rtsa Drung-mu, and sKya-rtse Va-pa. A base was thus created from which the doctrine could spread from the borderlands.[2]

II. The sayings which have been classed with the actual ones

The history of the Oral Tradition, which gods, knowledge-holders, and mystic goddesses transmitted to their own manifestations as teachers, will be implicit in my account of the history of the textual treasures.

Here I shall expound in brief how the doctrines of Bon gradually rose (again). I have argued earlier that Bon was not completely suppressed during the reign of Khri-srong lDe-btsan.[3] At the time of the king Glang Dar-ma (194a) the kingdom of Me-nyag came into being between Tibet, China, and Mongolia. During (the reign of) the king of Me-nyag-gha Bon began to spread in mDo-smad owing to the rediscovery of the 'Rules of Discipline', and the spiritual lineage of the 'Individual Liberation' increased. Then, the 'Original Words' and the

[1] He is said to have lived in the ninth century, see *GRB*, p. 55.

[2] i.e. towards the centre of Tibet.

[3] See *supra*, p. 102.

textual treasures also began to spread more widely. Khyung-po Blo-gros rGyal-mtshan says:[1]

> dPon-rgyal bTsan-po maintained the spiritual lineage of the Bon of Zhang-zhung and lived in Tibet till the early times of gShen Klu-dga', and then, having given the precepts (of the *Zhang-zhung snyan-brgyud*) to Khyung-byid Mu-thur and Grom-pa lHa-rtse, transforming himself into a cuckoo, he went to the West for the purpose of suppressing demons there.

After the kings of Me-nyag came the thirteen royal descendants of Ji-'ghin (Genghiz Khan) of Mongolia. They ruled many countries such as: China, Tibet, 'Jang, Me-nyag, and the copper island of India. In Tibet there were twenty-one Bon-po official administrators. These, together with the Bon-pos of Bru, Zhu, sPa, and rMe'u, did much to promote the doctrine of Bon in mDo, dBus, and gTsang. Then, the Mongolian throne fell to the Chinese.[2] The emperor Tad-min Thas-slod ascended the throne (194b) in the year of the female water ox. After that, during (the reigns of) about five kings the doctrine of Bon remained moderately prominent in Tibet. More and more people wore yellow clothes and carried rosaries. The preceptor of This-tsang and his son, was the Bon-po of China, Cang-thang Thas-sri, which means in Chinese the Bon-po of Heaven (gnam-gyi Bon-po).[3]

B. The history of the Textual Treasures

I. When the discoveries of the textual treasures were made
II. How the text-discoverers found the textual treasures
III. Their classification into Southern, Northern, Central, Khams, and recent textual treasures

[1] *GRB*, p. 58.

[2] This sentence and the three sentences which conclude this paragraph are modelled on a passage in *GRB* (p. 58). The name Thi-tsang is probably the Tibetan version of T'ai Tzu 太祖 the first Ming emperor who came to the throne in 1368. However, *GRB* does not contain the sentence giving the name Tad-min Thas-slod with his accession date in the year of the female water ox. I do not know from what source our author can have drawn this. Presumably he thought the name equivalent to This-tsang, but the date does not fit, as female water ox year would have been 1373.

[3] Professor R. A. Stein has suggested to me that Chang-thang Thas-sri is a Tibetan transcription of the Chinese Chang t'ien-shih 張天師. Chang is the family name and t'ien-shih is a title meaning 'Master of Heaven'. He was a hereditary chief of the Chinese Taoists.

I. Dran-pa Nam-mkha' declared:

> This Bon has been hidden, but it will re-emerge naturally and will not be suppressed again.

And,

> The army of the borderlands will burst forth like autumn crops. The Tibetans will be regimented and made slaves. When the Tibetans are poor and weak Bon will be spread and practised.

Furthermore, it is said in many authoritative books that, when the royal descendants had been exterminated and ferocious subjects reigned in the kingdom and filled it with wickedness, Bon would spread from the borderlands like mushrooms bursting from the meadow.

(195a) Padmasambhava also prophesied:

> At the degenerate time men will live on other beings. Their clothes will be made of iron. Their actions will be sinful. Stirrups will be their roads. Horse-saddles will be their beds. Men with heads of iron will lead battles. At this time lowly people will have the seed of Bon. The knowledge of Bon-pos will be like an eagle in flight. I, Guru, myself will be there supporting the doctrine of Bon. Then from the East four great kings called Blon-po-can, Bong-bu'i rNa-mchog-can, Misha'i Za-ma-can, and rDzing-bu Pho-brang-can will come and spread Bon extensively.

II. a. General exposition
b. Detailed exposition

a. From the time of the suppression of Bon by the king Khri-srong lDe-btsan when he was thirty-two up to the discovery of the textual treasure by the Teacher Klu-dga', the great gShen, two hundred and sixty-eight years went by.[1] (195b) It is

[1] This calculation follows *STNN* which, relying on the account of *SG*, states that Khri-srong lDe-btsan was born in Earth-Horse A.D. 718 and when he was thirty-two in Earth-Ox A.D. 749 he suppressed Bon. gShen-chen Klu-dga' made the discovery in (*STNN*) Fire-Snake 1017 (see *infra*, p. 129). Thus, counting from A.D. 750 to 1017, two hundred and sixty-eight years elapsed. However, this calculation is based on incorrect dates. See *supra*, p. 94 n. 2.

said that three Nepalese ācāryas were the first of fifteen text-discoverers who preceded him.

Here the abbot Nyi-ma bsTan-'dzin comments:[1]

> Due to the ignorance (of the meaning of) the terms 'Second Rise' and 'Later Rise' some erroneously put the textual finds of the gShen, etc., as 'Second Rise' and the recent discoveries of the textual treasures as the 'Later Rise'. One calls the beginning of the doctrine 'First Rise'; and any restoration of it, after suppression and decline in consequence of the effects of wickedness, one calls 'Second' or 'Later Rise'. So if you have one suppression and two rises the former you call the 'First Rise' and the latter the 'Second or Later Rise'. This is the established tradition of former scholars and ascetics. Now, since no decline of the doctrine intervened between that[2] and the recent discoveries of the textual treasures, there is no point in using the terms rise and decline. So the 'Later Rise' of Bon must be accepted and held as beginning with the discovery of the three ācāryas.[3]

b. (196a) First, the history of how the three ācāryas rediscovered the textual treasure.[4]

i. The story
ii. Classification (of the texts)

i. Through the power of the prayers of Dran-pa Nam-mkha' and other knowledge-holders, and because of news reaching the ears of the three Nepalese ācāryas that one could get all the gold one wanted in Tibet, dKon-mchog Grags-pa, Nya-mo mGon-po, and Sadku Ratna went to Tibet. They reached La-stod, but no gold was to be obtained. On inquiring they were told that in bSam-yas there was a lot of gold. They went to bSam-yas. As they were performing circumambulations and the like, the custodian (of the temple) said to them: 'You, Nepalese, are very

[1] *TNT*, pp. 58–9.

[2] i.e. the discovery of the gShen-chen Klu-dga'.

[3] This final sentence is not in the text of *TNT* to which I refer. Our author may have seen a different version, but it seems more likely that he has added it himself, for it is not the discovery of the ācāryas that the author of *TNT* is talking about, but that of gShen-chen Klu-dga', and it is this which he considers as the effective beginning of the revival (see *TNT*, pp. 58–9).

[4] *STNN* A.D. 913. Also cf. *TPS* ii, p. 727.

reverent. (Continue your) prayers!' He led them into the temple and then went away closing the door. The Nepalese saw a box sealed with bronze. On lifting it they found it was very heavy. Thinking it must be gold, they took it. By day they hid in the forest and the night they spent in flight. They reached a place called Sri-ba in the valley of Ngan-lam. There they broke the seal and looked inside. A tiger-bag, a leopard-bag, and a bear-bag were revealed. On being opened they were found to be full of Bon texts. (196b) Then, they proceeded from sKyid-shod to sTod-lung. By the time they arrived there their victuals had run out. And so one stayed behind to look after the bags.

ii. (A) The Lower (Transmission)
(B) The Upper (Transmission)

(A) (I) The story
(II) The classification
(III) The transmission

(I) As the other two went searching for food they heard drum-beats in a village. They asked what was going on there and were told that (a Bon-po called) mTha'-bzhi 'Phrul-gsas was performing a Bon rite. Wishing to meet mTha'-bzhi they went to him. They told him that they had some Bon texts and were going to give them to him. In return they begged for food. So he gave them beer, a load of barley flour (rtsam-pa), and a carcass of meat. They returned (to their place) with him. They told him that they would not let him choose, but he could take one volume.

(II) mTha'-bzhi said: 'If I wanted a big one, then the tiger-bag is very big. If I wanted a beautiful one, then the leopard-bag is very beautiful, but I wish to receive a Bon text from the bear-bag.' He took out one volume and looked at it. It was the Bon rite of the *Nag-po rgyud-gsum*, the basic text together with its commentary and the short rite of the *Ma-mo nyi-shu khra-spyang sa-bdag*.[1] It is said that there was a small drawing of a mystic circle on the front of the wooden cover. (197a) Furthermore, there were also many magical Bon texts.

[1] These texts deal with Phur-pa, a tantric divinity. There are many versions of this rite, but for the one which is widely practised, see *supra*, p. 45 n. 2.

(III) The *Srid-rgyud*[1] says:

> There will be one called mTha'-bzhi 'Phrul-gsas,
> The manifestation of 'Phrul-gsas sGom-pa.
> He will open the secret door of a textual treasure.

On request mTha'-bzhi transmitted the texts to rGya-ston Khro-'phen of 'Ug. He transmitted them on request to Zug Ra-'phan of Yar-'brog and so they were transmitted from him to Ra-ston Klu-btsan of Shang, lHa-rje Bar-sgom, and Bru Nam-mkha' gYung-drung.[2] This is the transmission of mTha'-bzhi and is the Lower Transmission.

(B) (I) The story
(II) The classification
(III) The transmission

(I) Then, the three ācāryas went up from sTod-lung and reached a place called Nam-ra in the North. In Byang-'brog ru-thog they met 'Dar-ban Shākya Muni, mChims Shākya Bra-ba, and 'O-ma Byang-chub Seng-ge who had come from mDo-sras of La-stod together with a heavily laden horse. The ācāryas asked them where they were going and they told them that they were going to bSam-yas to look for Buddhist textual treasures. They told the ācāryas that the horse with the load was to be given to the key-holder (of the temple) as a fee. (197b) Thereupon, the ācāryas told them that they had rediscovered a Buddhist textual treasure and if they gave them the horse together with the load they would give them their bags of textual treasure. They (the Tibetans) being doubtful (tried) to remove the bags, but whichever they pulled at lights and sparks came forth. Thinking that they must be profound Buddhist texts, they gave the horse to the ācāryas and went away taking the bags with them. On the way they wanted to open the bags, but since many wonders occurred they could not open them. Then, reaching sMan-gong of mDo in La-stod, they stayed at the home of gZe-ban Shes-rab rGyal-mtshan who had a nephew called gZe-sgur and was a Bon-po. There, they made offerings of seven white grains of barley, and bowing down, said prayers. Then they opened the bags, but found the texts were all Bon texts. When two of the

[1] *SG*, f. 87b7.

[2] See *infra*, p. 139.

Buddhists said that the texts should be burned, more wonders occurred. 'Dar-ban took care of the bags. Shes-rab rGyal-mtshan said that it was certain that (the bags of texts) had powerful guardians and since they were themselves Buddhist it was inappropriate for them to keep the bags. He told the others that if they gave the bags to his nephew gZe-sgur he would pay for them. So the texts were given to gZe-sgur.[1]

(II) A full bowl of barley was found in the centre of the bear-bag. This is how the saying Sa-bon sha-smug-ma originated. It is said that three hundred and forty different Bon texts in all were found.

(III) gZe-bon had four great pillars of disciples and a confidential one making five. (199b) The four commissioned ones were: Sa-ston 'Brug-lha, sTong-'byams sGra-bla-skyab, dBang, and sNa-ro. gShen rNel-byid-gur was the confidential one. He requested gZe-bon in secret to impart to him many (teachings) including the *Phur-pa*, etc. After that rNel-byid thought that since his teacher was (in fact) Buddhist, it would be unlikely that he would want (to keep) the Bon texts (for himself). He invited gZe-sgur and offered him beer. gZe-sgur became intoxicated: whereupon rNel-byid took his walking stick and rosary and showed them to his wife saying that his box of the texts was to be sent to him. She handed (the box over to him). Then, he, offering gifts to his teacher, asked him to give the texts to him, but the teacher said: 'Copy them out and correct them properly. I cannot give you the master copies.' In spite of this, he did not return the master copies. It is said that the teacher was displeased. Whether or not it was retribution for this or for cutting off the heads of five kinds of snakes into which his sacrificial cakes were transformed while he was performing the rite of the *Sa-bdag-mo* of Phur-pa on the assumption that they were a bad sign, he became ill with leprosy. Before he became ill he transmitted the teachings to his disciple Zhang Blon-sgom Ring-mo. The latter transmitted them to rMe'u-rog dBal-po. He attained realization (by performing) the *Phur-nag*. He exhibited

[1] A list of texts follows for which I refer the reader to the original Tibetan (see *infra*, p. 283, l. 15–p. 284, l. 26). The texts are grouped according to the bags from which they came: the tiger-bag, p. 283, ll. 16–23; the leopard-bag, p. 283, ll. 24–33; the bear-bag, p. 283, l. 34–p. 284, l. 26.

many supernatural signs, such as thrusting his dagger into the rock of bKra in Gur-zhog. (200a) He transmitted the teaching to lHa-ri gNyen-po[1] and it spread. He transmitted it to the disciple of Sa-ston 'Brug-lha, Zhu Grang-ra Bon-po of Byang. He transmitted it to Zhu-g·yas Legs-po.[2] He transmitted it to sKyid-po[3] and sKye-se.[4] Zhu-g·yas Legs-po also transmitted it to Zug Ra-'phan. This was the Upper Transmission. The latter received both Upper and Lower Transmission and was known as Zug, proficient in the *Phur-pa*. Both Upper and Lower Transmissions are in harmony and even now many practise them. Since the *Phur-pa* had its own protectors of textual treasure it did not have any other earthly protectors. It is said that whoever practises this Northern Textual Treasure will be lucky and acquire great power. It is because the three ācāryas found the texts in bSam-yas skor-khang and travelled through northern areas disseminating them in La-stod that they are called the Northern Textual Treasures.

(*The discovery at Yar-lung brag-dmar*)

Texts[5] were rediscovered in Yar-lung brag-dmar by Sa-ston 'Brug-lha, the emanation of sTag-la Me-'bar.

(*The discovery of the bSam-yas ka-khol-ma*)

The history of bSam-yas ka-khol-ma is fourfold: (1) The concealment of the textual treasure. The gShen-po of India, Dran-pa Ye-shes, having consulted Khri-srong lDe-btsan, put the texts in a brown box which he hid in a pillar (called) Khra-mo. Then he covered it carefully. He foretold that when the time arrived a fortunate one with fully grown body, crooked form, and white complexion would discover it, and the texts would spread from Khams.

(2) The discovery of the textual treasure. One day in the Water-male dog year,[6] Yon-sgom Thar-mo of rKo-bo went to bSam-yas. (201a) He saw a big crack in a pillar and as he looked into it he saw a brown box without any cracks. He took it out and on looking inside he found it contained Bon texts. He left for Khams with them.

[1] See *infra*, p. 137. [2] See *infra*, p. 136. [3] See *infra*, p. 137.
[4] See *infra*, p. 137. [5] For list see *infra*, p. 285, ll. 25–36.
[6] *STNN* A.D. 962.

(3) The textual content.[1]

(4) The multiplying of the disciples. As rKo-bo (Yon-sgom Thar-mo) diffused the treasure in Shar Bu-'bor-sgong, later he was known as Shar-pa gTer-ston. On request he transmitted it to Bla-ma Ye-shes,[2] etc.

(*The discovery of bSam-yas dbu-rtse*)

The history of the discovery in bSam-yas dbu-rtse by mTha'-bzhi Ye-shes Blo-gros is threefold: (1) The discovery of the textual treasure. mTha'-bzhi Ye-shes Blo-gros went to bSam-yas from Khams as a beggar and one night in a dream a yellow man holding a club said to him: 'You, beggar, tomorrow morning should take the gift which is under the nest of a cuckoo, the king of birds, in the pinnacle of (the temple of) bSam-yas. (201b) You are blessed by Li-shu (sTag-ring).' He got up very early and went to look for the cuckoo's nest. He saw a cuckoo flying away from its nest and as he looked there he found a hole in which there was (a piece of) yellow silk one 'mda' ' in length and one ''dom' in width with letters on it. On looking further he found (another) piece of yellow silk with figures on it and a blue transparent stone like an egg. Taking them with him he left for home.

(2) The textual content. It is said that twelve different texts were found, among them the *bsGrags-byang rin-chen*, the *Zo-bo dbu-dgu'i phur-rgyud*, and the *dBal-gsas-kyi skong zlog bsad gsum-gyi mdos*, etc.

(3) The transmission. mTha'-bzhi Ye-shes Blo-gros went to 'Phan brag-dkar in dBus and met sTon-pa Ye-shes rGyal-mtshan[3] on the thirteenth of the dog month in the Earth-male mouse year. As he conversed with him and told him the history (of his texts) sTon-pa Ye-shes rGyal-mtshan, offering a roll of red woollen cloth, entreated him to impart his precepts to him. He then transcribed the texts correcting his work carefully.

(*The discovery on Gangs Ti-se*)

Texts were rediscovered on Gangs Ti-se by Nga-'phrang lHa'i dBang-phyug.[4]

[1] For this see *infra*, p. 286, ll. 10–14.

[2] mTha'-bzhi Ye-shes Blo-gros (for whom see below).

[3] He appears to have been an uncle of mTha'-bzhi Ye-shes Blo-gros (see *infra*, p. 126).

[4] For list see *infra*, p. 287, ll. 4–16. In this list is included a title *gSas-mkhar*

(*The discoveries of Shu-bon dGe-bsnyen*)

Once when three hunters, Mar-pa 'Phen-bzang, etc., were digging at the root of a tree to get stones beside a lake called Shel-mtsho mu-le-had in sPu-rangs, some charcoal emerged and on further digging three wooden boxes appeared. Having found many manuscripts in them they returned home and sold them to Shu-bon dGe-bsnyen. The manuscripts were the (202b) *Klu-'bum dkar nag khra gsum* in three volumes,[1] and the *Klu gnyan sa-bdag gtod-kyi 'bum* together with its ancillary texts.

(*The discovery in gSer-thang sha-ba-can*)

(Shu-bon dGe-bsnyen) is said to have found many texts of the 'Bon of Cause' such as the *Khrom-zlog*, etc., in gSer-thang sha-ba-can. He is also said to have rediscovered many texts such as the *gNyan-rje'i sgrub-thabs*, etc., in Shel-gyi pha-bong g·yu-ris-can.

(*The discoveries of Khro-tshang*)

The *Srid-rgyud*[2] says:

> There will be one called Khro-tshang 'Brug-lha,[3]
> The manifestation of Li-shu sTag-ring.

The discovery of the textual treasure made by Khro-tshang (must be dealt with in) three parts. (1) The discovery of the textual treasure. He was the son of Khro-tshang gSas-gnyan and Dar-za sGron. As a thunderstorm coincided with his birth, he was called 'Brug-lha. From an early age he began learning Bon and practising meditation. One day Phyva Keng-tse[4] prophesied to him that there was a textual treasure in the secret rock of rGya-bo in the North. Bearing this in mind he went (to the place) where he found the sign A on the front of the rock of Khyung-

sa-le sgron-ma which was already included among the treasure said to be found by the three ācāryas (see *supra*, pp. 119–21).

[1] These texts are also said to have been rediscovered by the three ācāryas (see *supra*, pp. 119–21).

[2] *SG*, f. 91a7. However, the quotation which follows should read Sa-ston 'Brug-lha. Our author has either misread or altered the name. The prophetic verses concerning Khro-tshang 'Brug-lha are found in *SG* (f. 62a3) and are as follows: *khri lde dgongs grags sprul ba ni / drang srong lus la rdzul 'phrul can / khro tshang 'brug lha bya ba 'byung /*

[3] *STNN* 956–1077.

[4] The Bon-po god of wisdom, see *gZer-mig*, vol. kha, f. 100a3 *passim*.

lding. He dug it up and found many texts of exoteric, esoteric, and secret Bon.

(2) The textual content.[1]

(3) The transmission. When the Lord was one hundred and twenty-two years of age and passing away in Shang he told his nephew A-da lHa-gsas that A-da's young daughter would be born (in her next life) as a god this being the continuation of her past action determined in the 'intermediate state'. After dying as a god she would be born (again in that place) with the name gZhon-nu and would follow Bon and be given the texts of Byams-ma. The Lord also said these verses:

> She will take on a (male) human body (after) dying as a god, (203b)
> And will be named gZhon-nu and possess the perfection of humanity.
> This gZhon-nu will bé blessed by a holy lama and,
> Will receive the share of the essence of Bon of Ma-rgyud.
> He will accomplish his life and attain the ultimate result.

Thus, prophesying, he went to rest. At that time, the Mongolian army surged (into Tibet) and the texts of A-da and Khro-tshang were hidden (again) in the rocky cave of Shang. Later the rocky cave collapsed, but though a search was made no texts were found. lHa-btsan (the son of A-da) had a son, lHa-rgyal who often heard his father say: 'When your grandfather was old he used to say that the Bon texts of the Lord and A-da had been hidden in the rock over there.' lHa-rgyal had a son called lHa-'gon who became an old man without having any children. He went to gather firewood near the rock. Thinking that this might be the rock in which his great-grandfather said that the Bon texts had been hidden, he looked round it. He found some pieces of manuscript here and there. He collected all of them. Some were in a bad condition and the ends were frayed. Some he could identify as the *Byams-ma rtsa-ba'i mdo*. He returned with all of them. From these the ritual texts of Byams-ma were compiled. (He remembered) his great-grandfather saying that (if those texts) were found they should be given to someone by the name of gZhon-nu. Thinking that the teacher gZhon-nu was very likely to be the one, (204a) he gave him the texts. The

[1] For this see *infra*, p. 288, ll. 3–14.

teacher is said to have given a horse and some cloth to lHa-'gon in return. The teacher travelled south to Kong-po where he transmitted the teaching to sGom-pa gYung-drung-skyab of Kong-po. It was transmitted from him to sGom-pa Rin-chen-dpal, Ka-gdams Ye-shes rGyal-mtshan of mTha'-bzhi and the latter's nephew, Ye-shes Blo-gros. Furthermore, some stories say that when Ka-gdams (Ye-shes rGyal-mtshan) came to dBus and gTsang, Zhang-ston bSod-rgyal requested him to transmit it to him, but Ka-gdams declined to transmit all the texts he had, (particularly) the ones which were profound. Later mKhan-chen Grags-rgyal[1] went to mTha'-bzhi in search of the master copies of the teacher gZhon-nu and found them all, but could not find anyone who was able to confer textual initiation on him. He said prayers to the texts. It is said that later he invited Zhang-ston to Dar-lding and asked him to give him textual initiation. Zhang-ston and mKhan-chen Grags-rgyal transmitted the teaching to bSod-nams Seng-ge. The latter transmitted it to sKyabs-ston Rin-chen 'Od-zer[2] and so it spread.

(*The discovery at 'Bri-mtshams mtha'-dkar*)

How gShen Klu-dga', the great eye of the Doctrine, made the discovery of Bon textual treasure which had been hidden in 'Bri-mtshams mtha'-dkar at the time of the suppression of Bon by the Tibetan king Gri-gum (204b). There are four sections:

(1) The life-story of the text-discoverer
(2) The discovery of the textual treasure
(3) The textual content
(4) The multiplying of disciples

(1) The *Srid-rgyud*[3] says:

There will be one called gShen-sgur Klu-dga',
Who is the manifestation of sTong-rgyung mThu-chen,
And is equal to 'Chi-med gTsug-phud.
He is of the lineage of dMu sGa-tsha gShen.
He will open the door of a textual treasure.

The lineage of this great text-discoverer is that of dMu sGa-tsha. His father had three sons. The first Klu-dga'; the second Klu-

[1] An abbot of Dar-lding of which see *infra*, p. 133 n. 1.
[2] A highly respected scholar of dPal-ldan ri-zhing for which see *infra*, p. 137.
[3] *SG*, f. 91b3.

brtsegs; and the third Ge-khod. I have related earlier the genealogy of their ancestors and how they came from the family of dMu-gshen.[1]

(2) There are various versions (of Klu-dga' 's story), but here is the one which he himself told:

When I was thirteen years of age my father said: 'You and Ge-khod go and collect some white sPang-rgyan[2] and sPra-ba.'[3] Ge-khod collected the sPang-rgyan. As I was going towards the rocks of mTha'-lung to look for sPra-ba I heard a sound without form from the sky saying: 'gShen Klu-dga', you will be given the gift of Bon.' As I looked round I saw a rock the top of which was filled with oil. (205a) I thought that it was the gift and kept it secret from my parents. I intended to go and dwell near that rocky place, but was unable to do so for a few years. At that time, dBus-gTsang and Zhu-g·yas were at war. While I was acting as mediator an arrow hit Klu-brtsegs and he was killed. It took a year to collect the fine which consisted of goats and sheep for the body and yaks for the head. The yaks for the fine were to be given by Ya-gyad-pa, but he was unwilling to give them. As I was able to run on foot as fast as Ya-gyad-pa riding on a horse, for my running I became known as Mighty Man. At about that time, I competed with sNe-nag Ye-mkhyen in skill and I sprained the joints of my spine. A cure was applied, but no benefit came of it. From the age of eighteen I became crooked and I have since been called gShen-sgur (Crooked gShen). I thought that perhaps it was retribution for not having been able to dwell near the rock when I had decided to (after) receiving the 'nectar'. At the age of nineteen I learned the *gYung-drung zhi-rgyan* and *khro-rgyan* and the *A-nu chab-gtor shog-gcig-ma* from dBon Ra-shag. I practised them at Brag-dkar,[4] auspicious signs occurred such as the 'flowing nectar', etc., from the very year I began to practise. Then, my father died and I had to come out of my retreat. As I stayed (at home) till the funeral was over it delayed me until the dragon year. (205b) That year I married Gar-za dPal-sgron and so the year passed. (After returning to my hermitage) at twilight in the snake year a woman appeared with a dark complexion, hair falling about

[1] See *supra*, p. 3.

[2] i.e. a medicinal herb.

[3] i.e. a vegetable tinder.

[4] i.e. the place near the rock.

her shoulders, grinning with canine teeth, and looking as if she was going to eat me. I remained in meditation without fear. But I found myself transported to the mountain of rDza skya-seng-nge during the night. In the morning I was returning to the hermitage and when I arrived at the foot of Brag-dkar, many boys with turquoise coronets, and girls wearing cotton robes, came to meet me bowing down and scattering flowers. By this too I remained unmoved to any joy, and they disappeared. Again, at twilight a large Chinese mask appeared to me, saying: 'I am going to eat you.' As I remained without fear, I was taken that night to the summit of the big mountain in front. When I was returning to the hermitage in the morning, many Bon-pos wearing tiger skin robes came to meet me playing drums and bells. (After a while) they disappeared. At twilight a big frog appeared to me in various phantom aspects and I was taken to the back of the North (mountain). On the way back in the morning (I came to) a rocky cave like a human face in which white water was dripping like a yellow fringe. (206a) As I put my copper bowl under it, it flowed into the bowl and filled it. I took up (a drop) with my ring-finger and tasted it, it had many kinds of excellent taste. Thinking that it was the 'nectar' I tasted it once more. During that day while I was making an offering of water the copper plate flew up into the air and landed on the ground. In the sky there were a lot of lights glistening like crystal which (all) dissolved in me. Then I heard a very big noise three times and four women with white complexion, wearing white cotton robes, and riding on a dragon, a garuḍa, a lion, and a tiger[1] appeared from the sky and landed in front of me. They said: 'Klu-dga', you will receive the gift of Bon! If you are taught will you be able to read? If you are instructed will you be able to meditate?' I replied: 'If I am taught I shall be able to read and if I am instructed I shall be able to meditate. I beg you to bestow the gift of Bon on me.' I brought some curds and made an offering for them. They said: 'Good. You are a manifestation, take this eight-inch dagger of crystal and keep it hidden for twelve years.' Having said that they disappeared in the sky. As I looked at the dagger, there—I saw—were the nine

[1] They are the rDzu-'phrul sman-bzhi—the Four Miraculous Goddesses (of whom see *supra*, p. 75).

ways of Bon; as one descends from the nine stairs of crystal one lands on a trunk like twisted sealing-wax; (206b) underneath that there is a square rock in the near edge of which is a red swastika and in front a white one. And so I searched for such a place until I found one. I looked at the rock to see whether it was movable. It seemed to me that it very likely was. I sent Jo-mo dPal-sgron to tell Ge-khod to come and bring a pick with him. He came and we tried to shift the rock, but failed. A snowstorm arose and we had to pause. That night in a dream someone said: 'Ge-khod is the incarnation of the planet Mars, therefore he is not a suitable person for the Doctrine to be entrusted to. Search by yourself!' The next morning I said to Ge-khod: 'I was only joking with you. How can a textual treasure be found in such a rocky place? Leave the pick, and go.' Ge-khod said: 'What you need is a treasure of food not a treasure of Bon texts!' Then, on the day of star Khra, the 24th of the second winter month, in the year of the female fire snake[1] I shifted the rock. Underneath it there appeared blue clay. After that there was the square rock on which red and white swastikas had been written. Underneath this square rock there was a big box and a small one. I looked inside the big one (207a) and there were many texts of the 'Bon of Cause and Effect'. Inside the small one there were many texts of the 'Bon of Effect'. While I was carrying the manuscripts back, they suddenly disappeared. I rushed back again to the place of the textual treasure and found the manuscripts there. As I took them and moved away, they flew off again. At night a man and woman with dark skin appeared in front of me and said: 'Do not take them. If you want them, bring a white sheep with red spots and a white yak as a pledge. Give us a sacrificial cake, and a 'Bṛang-rgyas[2] adorned with small red circles. Sit in front of us and copy out the manuscripts.' I copied the texts out accordingly.

[1] (Earth)-Snake 1089, but the Abbot Nyi-ma bsTan-'dzin (*TNT*, pp. 55-6) rejects this saying that gShen-chen Klu-dga' was poisoned by Lo-ston rDo-rje dBang-phyug (of whom see *supra*, p. 108) who was ordained (*STNN* 1009) by Bla-chen dGongs-pa Rab-gsal (b. *STNN* 952). Thus *STNN* gives that gShen-chen Klu-dga' was born in Fire-Monkey A.D. 996, rediscovered the textual treasure in Fire-Snake 1017, and died in Wood-Pig 1035.

[2] A kind of gTor-ma usually made of barley flour (rtsam-pa) and adorned with dyed butter.

(3) (i) The texts that were taken out at this time
(ii) The texts that still remain hidden
(iii) Digression demolishing false assertions

(i) 'I transcribed the texts from the big box on the slates. In the small box the *Khams-brgyad*, the *mDzod*, the texts of exoteric and esoteric and of the Mental Teachings were found.'[1]

(ii) Some say that there were altogether thirty-two boxes, two of which still remain hidden. This statement is misleading concerning the ones which remain hidden, and those which were taken out. Further, others say that there were only two boxes. This is not so, as we know from what the gShen himself said that there were thirty-seven boxes, but he did not take out more than two. (208a) So thirty-five are still buried with the textual treasure.[2]

(iii) Some of 'The Others' say:[3]

> A man called gShen-sgur Klu-dga' transformed Buddhism into Bon. He described the Yum-rgyas-pa as Khams-chen, the Nyi-shu rtsa-lnga-pa as Khams-chung, gave the word gtan-la dbab-pa as Bon-mdo,[4] (208b) described the gZungs-sde as Klu-'bum dkar-nag, making up a certain number of terms and items in order to be different from Buddhism, and hid them in the rock of mTsho-rnga 'dre-chung as a textual treasure. Later he pretended to have rediscovered them himself.

They tell such stories as these. My answer is: 'If the *Yum-rgyas-pa* had been transformed as Khams-chen, the edition of the *Khams-brgyad* could not be in sixteen volumes, one hundred and twenty-one chapters, three hundred and sixty sections, and one thousand and eight branches of Phyag-rgya. It has been composed (to explain) exhaustively all physical and metaphysical phenomena as being without substance in the realm of Bon (i.e. Truth). Your *Yum-rgyas-pa* consists of only twelve volumes

[1] For the list of texts see *infra*, p. 292, ll. 15–32. The titles in the list are grouped under the appropriate headings: Exoterical Texts (p. 292, ll. 15–21); Esoterical Texts (p. 292, ll. 22–8); Mental Teachings (p. 292, l. 29).

[2] For list see *infra*, p. 293, ll. 1–12.

[3] This refers to *Grub-mtha' thams-cad-kyi khungs-dang 'dod-tshul ston-pa legs-bshad shel-gyi me-long* (section TA, p. 62, Varanasi 1963) by Th'u-bkvan Chos-kyi Nyi-ma (1732–1802) composed in 1802. The TA section is rendered into English by S. C. Das (see *JASB*, 50 (1881), part i, pp. 195–205).

[4] Das has mistakenly taken it for the title of a text (ibid., p. 199), which it certainly is not.

Why does ours have four extra volumes (if it is yours transformed into Bon)? Does it not seem as if the *Yum-rgyas-pa* of Bon was transformed into Buddhism and the four (last) volumes were left over owing to an interruption in the work of transformation? Therefore, with any religious order the history of which one does not know, a foolish person may satisfy fools with his own creation, but to a wise man it would be a cause of shame. Moreover, the textual treasure of gShen Klu-dga' contains numberless profoundly exoteric and esoteric Bon which are endowed with tranquillity, richness, power, and ferocity. (209a) As they have all been transmitted to worthy disciples all of whom having practised them attained realization, exhibiting unthinkable supernatural signs, how could ascetics capable of such signs be produced by a Bon which is disguised Buddhism? Since the *Klu-'bum*,[1] etc., do not belong to the textual treasure of gShen-sgur, the assertion (regarding them) is merely nonsensical.

(4) The multiplying of the disciples

(AA) Outline
(BB) Detailed survey

(AA) Although (the gShen) was originally to keep (his discovery) secret for twelve years, he could not do so for more than eleven years. sBrag-sto Ku-ra built a stūpa of Enlightenment which was consecrated by lHa-rje Zhang, who, on being asked what kind of stūpa represented Dharmakāya, was unable to answer. Thereupon, (the gShen) gave a Bon exposition and so the secrecy was over. Then, the first person to ask for Bon was Me-nyag Na-gu. Offering a horse and a block of tea, he requested the Bon rite of the *gTor-ma dmar-po*. Considering that he was a worthy disciple (the gShen) imparted the *Khro-bo dbang-chen* to him. Then Zhu Legs-po[2] entreated the gShen to impart a large quantity of the Bon to him while serving him as an attendant. Then, lCog-la gYu-skyid came and entreated him to impart the scriptural books and others to him. Then, mTshe-mi Shag-'bar also requested Bon. (209b) These four were known as the Four Chiefs of Nyang-stod. Then, there were the Eight Pillars of Nyang-smad: Rong-khu A-tsa-ra, Rong-khu gYung-drung

[1] Cf. *supra*, p. 124.

[2] See *infra*, p. 134 n. 1.

gTsug-phud, Phug-pa rGod-gsas-skyob, sTag-sgom Tsang-po-'bar, Ra-shag 'Phan-pa-skyob, Ra-shag sKyid-dpal, and Bru-sha lHa-mgon-gsas.[1] After them, the Four Banners: Ja-sgom gYung-drung rGyal-mtshan, Bru-sha Khyung-gi rGyal-mtshan, Mar-pa Shes-rab rGyal-mtshan, and 'Dzi-ston dBang-gi rGyal-mtshan. Then, there were the Five Great Men of Cog-ro: Ra-shag Mu-mkhar, Dre-ston Ye-shes Zla-ba, 'Dzi-bon 'Phan-'bar, Con-pa'i-zi of lHa-rtse, and Shud sKyid-'brug. Then, there were three men from Nyang-stod who requested Bon: gZu Ye-shes Bla-ma, gZu mGon-chen, and Shu-bon dGe-bsnyen gTsug-phud. These were the disciples who actually met gShen-sgur.

(BB) (i) The descendants
(ii) The spiritual descendants

(i) Rin-chen rGyal-mtshan and Byang-chub rGyal-mtshan were the sons of gShen-sgur. Rin-chen rGyal-mtshan had two sons: Tha-ru and sMan-rgod. (210a) The former's son was Khyung-rgod. The latter's son was Jo-'khor. The latter's son was Jo-bo Bla-ma-'od. sMan-rgod's son was Dam-pa rGyal-tshab. The latter had four sons. The eldest one was Jo-bkra. The latter had four sons. The eldest one was Nam-mkha' rGyal-mtshan who became a monk. The second was Jo-rtse who had two sons; the first was gShen-ston Yon-rgyal and was a monk. The second was Jo-rgyal who had two sons, the elder was Shes-rab rGyal-mtshan who had two wives, and by his first wife, Bram-ze Me-tog-rgyan, had three sons: 'Od-'bum, 'Bum-dar, and Rin-chen-'bum. And by his second wife, Zhu-za, he had three sons: Khro-'bum, Khri-skyong Dar-po, and Khri-rje-'bum. Khri-skyong Dar-po abandoned the secular life and assumed the monastic name, gShen-ston Ye-shes Blo-gros.[2] He was the lama who designed and built the temple of Dar-lding and spread the Doctrine far and wide by means of the three activities of the scholar among many thousands of monks. Khro-'bum's son was Seng-ge-grags. The latter had two sons: bSod-rgyal-dpal and dPal-'od-dar. bSod-rgyal-dpal's sons were dPal-ldan bSod-

[1] There seem to be only seven names in the list.

[2] During his lifetime his family moved from 'Bri-mtshams (see *supra*, p. 6) to Dar-lding and he built the temple in (*STNN*) 1173, the full name of which is Dar-lding gser-sgo khra-mo'i gtsug-lag-khang.

nams and rNam-dag Dri-med both of whom became monks. dPal-'od-dar's sons were bDag-po dPal-ldan rNam-rgyal and Kun-dga' dPal-ldan. (210b) dPal-ldan rNam-rgyal went to China and received an official seal. He entirely rebuilt the palace of dGe-lding.[1] Kun-dga' dPal-ldan had a son A-skyid-dpal. The above mentioned gShen Dam-pa rGyal-tshab had four sons, the third of whom 'Bum-me Nag-po had a son Byang-chub Blo-gros. The latter's son was Legs-pa Byang-chub. The latter's son was mGon-po Rin-chen dPal-bzang. The latter's son was bZang-po-dpal. Again, the second son of gShen Dam-pa rGyal-tshab, lHa-rje Jo-'brug, had a son Don-'grub-'bum. The latter's son was 'Bum-dar. The latter's son was gYung-drung Khro-rgyal. The latter had two sons, rGyal-mtshan Grags-pa and gZi-brjid. The former's son was Grags-pa Seng-ge. The latter's son was dBang-grub rGyal-mtshan who lived in mNga'-ris, but later was invited back home. The latter's son was dMu-gshen mChog-legs rGyal-mtshan. The latter's son was gShen Nyi-ma rGyal-mtshan who built the great temple of Khri-bstan nor-bu'i-rtse. His son was Khri-'od rGyal-mtshan. From him up to gShen 'Dzam-gling dBang-'dus, who is the son of the present gShen Nyi-zla Tshe-dbang of sTod rta-zam and has been invited to the great throne, (211a) the line of descendants is like a crystal rosary. The *Srid-pa rgyud-kyi lung-bstan*[2] says:

> (In the family of) the gShen there will be one called Klu-dga', . . .
> His descendants will be innumerable.
> A great holy man will always be among them.
> The lineage will survive until the degenerate age.

Thus, since in each (generation) there will always be one blessed by knowledge-holders, this is the most noble lineage in this world. We are told in the authoritative books that even if one has only casual contact with them one will be saved from being born in the world of evil-beings. Their residence is Dar-lding ri-rgyal-dgon which is distinguished by the thirteen particular things.

[1] dGe-lding, where the family lived, is situated in a small town in gTsang. Dar-lding ri-rgyal-dgon, a monastery, is situated on a hill at the back of the town. The temple Khri-bstan nor-bu'i-rtse is in the monastery, which is said to have been founded by dMu-gshen Nyi-ma rGyal-mtshan (b. *STNN* 1360, see below).

[2] *SG*, f. 64a7.

(ii) The spiritual descendants were as follows: the Four Commissioned Ones, the Four Men from the Upper Land, the Eight Men from the Lower Land, the Five Men of Cog-ro, the Three Faithful Ones, the Twenty-five Devoted Ones and others. Concerning the Four Commissioned Ones:

1. The 'scriptural books' were commissioned to lCog-la.
2. The Tantric Teachings were commissioned to 'Dzi-ston and Me-nyag.
3. The Mental Teachings were commissioned to Zhu-sgom.[1]
4. Both the Scholar and Hermit of rMe'u[2] made contact with (the teachers of) Bru, Zhu, and sPa.
5. The Metaphysical Teaching, the *mDzod*, was commissioned to Bru.[3]

1. How the 'scriptural books' were commissioned to (211b) lCog-la gYu-skyid. Dran-pa (Nam-mkha') said:[4]

> There will be one called lCog-la gYu-skyid,
> The manifestation of 'Jag-rung gSas-mkhar.

He heard that gShen-sgur had rediscovered a textual treasure and went to him. He requested the teaching after realizing that the gShen was the Master of the Doctrine. lCog-la asked whether he could make a copy of the *Khams-brgyad*, but the gShen said: 'It will not do if I give it to you without copying it out myself first.' He replied: 'I will make one copy and offer it to you, my Teacher, and then, I shall copy it out for myself.' 'Will you accomplish them (both)?' He replied: 'I shall have no difficulty.' It is said that he made a good copy and offered it to the Teacher. Then he made another for himself. Nowadays in Amdo and other places there seems to be an edition with very detailed 'parallel enumerations' called the *Khams-brgyad* of lCog-la. He transmitted it to gYu-sgro Legs-pa. The latter transmitted it to rMe'u lHa-ri gNyen-po. The latter transmitted it to dPal-chen, the scholar of rMe'u.[5] And so it has been transmitted from him

[1] Zhu-g·yas Legs-po (b. *STNN* 1002).

[2] The Scholar is lHa-ri gNyen-po (*STNN* 1024–91) and the hermit is dGongs-mdzod Ri-khrod Chen-po, also known as Dam-pa Ri-khrod-pa or just Dam-pa (*STNN* 1038–96). For his life story see *A-khrid*, pp. 8–15).

[3] Bru-chen Nam-mkha' gYung-drung (*STNN* 994–1054).

[4] *SG*, f. 61a5.

[5] His full name is Tshul-khrims dPal-chen (b. *STNN* 1052).

up to my teacher, dBra-sprul bsTan-'dzin dBang-rgyal, who knew past, present, and future, and was equal to Dran-pa Nam-mkha'. The teachers in between are to be seen in the Book of Spiritual Successions.

(212a) 2. How the Tantric Teachings were commissioned. 'Dzi-bon 'Phan-rgyal entreated the Teacher to impart the *Khro-bo dbang-chen* to him. The Teacher gave even the (master) copy to him. He also gave him the cup containing the lees of the elixirs. He gave him the name of dBang-gi rGyal-mtshan. Some have said that since sPa-ston dPal-mchog[1] did not meet gShen-sgur, he got in touch with 'Dzi-bon and Me-nyag. But (in fact) when gShen-sgur was ill he bestowed the consecration of the *Khro-bo dbang-chen* on him. He proclaimed him a worthy master of Tantric Teachings and instructed him in detail to receive the sacred objects, the copy of the text and its supplementary texts; and the treatises on them from 'Dzi-bon. Then, dPal-mchog met 'Dzi-bon and requested the texts, the medicinal specimen of the 'pledge'[2] which had been used (by the teachers) from 'Chi-med gTsug-phud up to the 'Four Scholars'. 'Dzi-bon also gave dPal-mchog the 'Dance-spear'[3] and the cup[4] and appointed him to be in charge of the Tantric Teachings. Then he practised the *Khro-bo dbang-chen* in the solitude of Yang-dben and beheld the countenance of Srid-rgyal according (to the representation of) the basic liturgy.[5] Once he saw her face with lightning issuing from her eyes, whirlwinds from her nose, roaring thunder from her ears, her hair being like masses of clouds. (212b) She was adorned with ornaments of cemetery-bones; her eyes were up-turned, her nose was wrinkled up and her mouth was wide open. As she tore her chest with her hands he saw distinctly without any obstruction the body of gTso-mchog[6] in the centre of the wheel of her heart which is one of the six wheels of the three vital channels in the body. While he performed the medicinal

[1] He was born in (*STNN*) 1014.

[2] Tib. phud-gta'; it is the same as gta'-chen for which see Snellgrove, *Nine Ways*, p. (278), Illustration X.

[3] Tib. gar-mdung similar to mdung (spear) for which see ibid., p. (277), Illustration IX (*r*).

[4] Tib. ga'u which is supposed to be a cup containing the medicinal specimen of the 'pledge' (see above n. 2).

[5] This refers to *Khro-gzhung ngo-mtshar rgyas-pa* (of which see *supra*, p. 45 n. 2).

[6] For whom see *supra*, p. 45 n. 2.

rite of the *Phur-bu dgu* drops of nectar descended (into his mystic circle). The dBal-mo performed circumambulations around his mystic circle. They sang prophetic songs and danced. Be-dkar and the eight kinds of demons paid homage to him by singing Na-mo, dBang-chen gzhal-yas 'bar-ba-na (Praise to the great powerful one who is in the blazing palace), etc. Although he had fully achieved both ordinary and supreme attainments he held monastic practices in very high esteem. In later life he decided to abandon the secular life and went to the teacher Khro-tshang. When the Lord 'Brug (Khro-tshang) began to shave his hair, he saw a couple of wrathful deities embracing on each single hair. Wrapping the razor in a piece of white cotton he gave it to sPa-ston and said to him: 'If you abandon your secular life the goddesses are going to disdain you. (213a) (Therefore) practise meditation as a layman and expand the Doctrine.' His descendants: his nephew, sPa-ston Dar-ma was a disciple of dPon-gsas Khyung-rgod[1] and (was known by the name of) sPa rGyal-ba Shes-rab. The latter's son was sPa Don-grub-'bum. From him up to the present sPa Nyi-ma 'Bum-gsal,[2] who accomplished the 'Two Stages'[3]—whom I have met and from whom I was blessed to receive instruction—came descendants who were all the manifestations of knowledge-holders, whose coming had been prophesied. Their residence is the place called sPa la-bug. Concerning the spiritual descendants of sPa-ston dPal-mchog: he had many disciples, but the most distinguished ones are gShen Dam-pa rGyal-tshab, rMe'u-ston lHa-ri gNyen-po, rMe'u Dam-pa the Hermit and his nephew sPa-ston Dar-ma. The latter's disciple was sPa-ston Khyung-'bar. His disciples were Khro-chung-'bar and others. Then came a succession of ascetics. (One of them) was sPa dPal-ldan bZang-po who put the 'planet-demon' under an oath. So nowadays it is said that even the possession of some hair or a piece of the clothes of the teachers who belonged to the lineage of holy sPa can protect one from the epilepsy of the planet.

3. How the Mental Teachings were commissioned. (213b) Zhu-g·yas Legs-po heard of the fame of the textual discovery of

[1] He was born in (*STNN*) 1175. For more details about him see *infra*, pp. 173 et seq.

[2] He was born in (*STNN*) 1854.

[3] Tib. rim-gnyis. See *supra*, p. 39 n. 2.

the Teacher, the Great gShen, and went to meet him. The Teacher, in order to test the quality of his disciple, let him stay with him for eight years, cutting hay and firewood, transporting manure into the fields and carrying the thorny sticks (for the hedges of the fields), etc. Having seen that Legs-po's faith was as unchangeable as gold and his trust in him was neither too taut nor too loose like a bowstring in winter, the Teacher bestowed the textual initiation of the *Sems-smad sde-dgu* including the *Byang-sems gab-pa*[1] on Legs-po and imparted oral instruction on the texts and his own experience of them, just as one vaseful of water is poured (into another). Concerning his descendants: Legs-po's son was lHa-rje sKyid-po. From him a rustless golden rosary of descendants who were all great manifestations leads down to the present Rig-'dzin gYung-drung mThong-grol. The residence of Zhu-tshang is now known as dPal-ldan ri-zhing. Concerning his spiritual descendants: Legs-po transmitted the teaching to Zhu sKyid-po. The latter transmitted it to sKye-se. He transmitted it to both the Scholar and Hermit of rMe'u, etc. Their transmission can be seen in the Book of Spiritual Successions.

4. (214a) How the Scholar and the Hermit of rMe'u made contact with Bru, Zhu, and sPa. In general (the teachers of) Bru, Zhu, and sPa were the first (to establish) the doctrinal tradition. Bru-sha Khyung-gi rGyal-mtshan[2] composed the commentary of the *mDzod* and established the doctrinal tradition of the Metaphysical Teachings. The son of Zhu-g.yas Legs-po, sKyid-po, composed the commentary of the *Byang-sems gab-pa*[3] and established the doctrinal tradition of the Mental Teachings. sPa-ston dPal-mchog, composed the commentary on the *Thig-le dbyings-'chad*[4] and established the doctrinal tradition (of the Tantric Teachings). These three were met by rMe'u lHa-ri gNyen-po (the scholar) and rMe'u Dam-pa the Hermit. The

[1] On this text see *supra*, p. 51 n. 8.

[2] According to the abbot Nyi-ma bsTan-'dzin (*STNN* p. 31, *TNT* p. 58) Bru-chen Nam-mkha' gYung-drung (*STNN* 994–1054), the father of Bru-sha Khyung-gi rGyal-mtshan, was the person who commentated (*STNN* 1036) the *mDzod* for which see *supra*, p. 8 n. 4. However, the commentary has probably been lost as the abbot does not record it in *KTDG* (p. 14).

[3] This commentary is not recorded in *KTDG* (p. 26).

[4] A commentary on *Thig-le dbyings-'chad*, a tantric text (*KTDG*, p. 8), is said to have already been found, together with the text, by gShen-chen Klu-dga', but *KTDG* (pp. 16–17) does not mention any commentary on the text.

latter (also) having met Zhu sKye-se and Zhu sGrol-ba upheld their tradition of scholastic study, discipline, and meditative practices and diffused the Doctrine far and wide. Dran-pa (Nam-mkha') declared:[1]

> My spiritual son, lHa-ri, whom I have blessed,
> Will be born in the family of rMe'u.
> Proficient in the exoteric, esoteric, and secret Bon,
> He will spread the Doctrine far and wide.

And the *sKyang-'phags gnad-byang*[2] says:

> There will be one called rMe'u-sgom Dam-pa the Hermit,
> The manifestation of Tshad-med 'Od-ldan,
> Whose realization is equal to that of Kun-tu bZang-po.
> Hundreds of followers will attain Enlightenment. (214b)
> Ten of his spiritual descendants will labour for the welfare of sentient beings,
> And will deliver 5,000,000 to salvation.
> His spiritual lineage will remain until the degenerate age.

This is what is said. Concerning the descendants of rMe'u lHa-ri gNyen-po: he had three sons. gSas-mkhar Bla-ma was the eldest and he had four sons. The eldest was Dam-pa the Hermit. From him a line of descendants leads down to the present Precious One. Their residence is the place now known as dPal-ldan bzang-po-ri in Gur-zhog of Shang. Concerning the spiritual descendants: rMe'u lHa-ri gNyen-po had many disciples who upheld the doctrinal tradition of the Metaphysical, Tantric, and Mental Teachings, but the most eminent ones are: the Three Men from the Upper Land, the Three Men from the Lower Land, and the Four Men from dBus, etc. Thousands of scholar-ascetics, the kapāla-holders, followed him. The spiritual descendants of rMe'u Dam-pa the Hermit had been foretold in the *Kha-byang lung-bstan*:[3]

> There will be one called sGom-chen-'bar,[4]
> The manifestation of sTag-la Me-'bar.

And so, including him, there were the Four Commissioned

[1] *SG*, f. 87b6.

[2] This is a prophetic text by sKyang-'phags and is mentioned in *KTDG* (p. 24).

[3] *SG*, f. 87b7.

[4] For his life-story see *A-khrid*, pp. 14–19, and for the following list of disciples see ibid., pp. 12–13.

Spiritual Sons, the Two Sisters, the Eight Brothers, the Two Youngest Brothers, and the Fifty-eight Ascetics. There were more than one thousand hermits, (215a) and more than a hundred thousand persons who obtained spiritual instruction from him.

5. How the Metaphysical Teachings were commissioned to Bru. Both the father and son, Nam-mkha' gYung-drung and Khyung-gi rGyal-mtshan listened to gShen Klu-dga' expounding the Bon of Metaphysical Teachings such as the *sNang-srid mdzod-phug*, etc. (Later) in the great monastery, gYas-ru dben-sa,[1] the doctrinal tradition (of the Metaphysical Teachings) was established. Thousands of monks gathered there and it produced many eminent scholars. Concerning the descendants of Bru-sha Nam-mkha' gYung-drung: he had four sons, the youngest was Shes-rab rGyal-mtshan. The latter had four sons, the youngest was Ye-shes Grub-pa. Of the latter's four sons, the eldest was Nyi-ma rGyal-mtshan and the second was Zla-ba rGyal-mtshan. The latter's son was Ye-shes rGyal-mtshan. Nyi-ma rGyal-mtshan, the eldest, became the Master of the Northern and Southern Textual Treasures including that of rMa-ston Srol-'dzin.[2] He diffused (the Doctrine) far and wide by giving consecration, textual initiation, and instruction. His son was Nam-mkha' rGyal-mtshan. From him a line of descendants leads down to the present, Pan-chen Rin-po-che of bKra-shis lhun-po and his brother[3] in gTsang. (215b) The *Kha-byang*[4] says:

> The wheel of Bon will be turned for (the benefit of) the Thirty three Gods.

Thus, in conformity with the prophecy, when (the lineage of

[1] Also known as Bru-yi dgon-chen gYas-ru dben-sa-kha, it was founded (*STNN* 1072) by Bru-chen gYung-drung Bla-ma (b. *STNN* 1040). He is also known as Bru bDag-nyid rJe-btsun. The monastery certainly existed till 1386, for mNyam-med Shes-rab rGyal-mtshan (*STNN* 1356–1415) entered it when he was thirty-one and became an abbot there (see *infra*, p. 142). Not long after that the monastery was destroyed by flood.

[2] rMa-ston Srol-'dzin is a text-discoverer (b. *STNN* 1092), concerning whom see *infra*, p. 167.

[3] This was the fifth Pan-chen Bla-ma Blo-bzang dpal-ldan chos-kyi grags-pa bstan-pa'i dbang-phyug (1855–81). His Bon-po name was rNam-rgyal dBang-'dus rGyal-mtshan. See his biography the *Dad-ldan pad-tshal bzhad-pa'i nyin-byed snang-ba* (ff. 25a6–33b2) composed in 1889 by Blo-bzang bsTan-'dzin dBang-rgyal. No descendant of this family is known after the fifth Pan-chen Bla-ma.

[4] This title might refer to *SG*, but I cannot trace this passage in the manuscript at my disposal.

Bru) had completed its work of welfare for sentient beings in the human world the time had arrived to turn the wheel of Bon in the world of the Thirty-three Gods. Their residence was the great monastery, gYas-ru dben-sa, but now it has ceased to exist. Later through prayers the monastery, bKra-shis sman-ri,[1] came into existence for the welfare of sentient beings and now that has become a great gathering place for metaphysical studies and the spiritual practices of the Mental Teachings. As to the spiritual descendants, many different lineages developed after Bru-sha (Nam-mkha' gYung-drung) became the Master of the Bon of tranquillity, richness, power, and ferocity, and the Mental Teachings. But the Metaphysical Teachings, the *mDzod*, which was commissioned to Bru alone, were diffused and transmitted from him to Bru-sha Khyung-gi rGyal-mtshan, Bru bDag-nyid rJe-btsun, Bru-ston Nyi-ma rGyal-mtshan, both Me[2] and gNyos,[3] 'A-zha bDud-rtsi rGyal-mtshan,[4] 'A-zha Blo-gros rGyal-mtshan,[5] Bru 'Dul-ba rGyal-mtshan,[6] Bru rGyal-ba gYung-drung,[7] (Bru:) Nam-mkha' 'Od-zer,[8] bSod-nams rGyal-mtshan,[9] bSod-nams Blo-gros,[10] Nam-mkha' bSod-nams, Tshe-dbang rGyal-mtshan, Nam-mkha' Rin-chen, (216a) Bru rNam-rgyal Ka-ra,[11] and mKhas-grub Rin-chen Blo-gros.[12] The latter transmitted them to Shes-rab rGyal-mtshan, the Incomparable One.[13]

The *Kha-byang gsal-byed nyi-ma'i dkyil-'khor* by Blo-ldan[14] says:

> The teaching of the Triple Doctrine will be established in the centre of dBu-ru,

[1] Founded in 1405 by mNyam-med Shes-rab rGyal-mtshan (see *infra*, p. 142).

[2] 'Gro-mgon gYor-po Me-dpal (*STNN* 1134–68). For his life-story see *A-khrid*, pp. 24 et seq.

[3] gNyos Tshul-khrims rGyal-mtshan (b. *STNN* 1144). He is also called mKhas-pa dByar-mo Thang-ba.

[4] For his life-story see *A-khrid*, pp. 26 et seq.

[5] *STNN* 1198–1263. For his life-story see *A-khrid*, pp. 31 et seq.

[6] *STNN*: born 1239; *A-khrid* (p. 38): died aged fifty-five; i.e. in 1293. For his life-story see ibid., pp. 35 et seq.

[7] *STNN* 1242–90. For his life-story see *A-khrid*, pp. 39 et seq.

[8] He was the younger brother of rGyal-ba gYung-drung (see ibid., p. 41).

[9] *STNN*: born in 1268; *A-khrid* (p. 44): died aged fifty-four; i.e. in 1321.

[10] *STNN* 1277–1341.

[11] For his life-story see *A-khrid*, p. 47.

[12] For his life-story see ibid., pp. 48–50.

[13] *STNN* 1356–1415.

[14] sPrul-sku Blo-ldan sNying-po (*STNN*: born in 1360). It is said among the Bon-pos that he died at the age of twenty-five, i.e. in 1385. Concerning his work see *infra*, p. 182.

By Shes-rab rGyal-mtshan, the manifestation of sTong-rgyung (mThu-chen).

Thus, the prophetic books exalted this Lord and Precious One. His father was Klu-rgyal and his mother was Rin-chen-sman of the dBra family in sTegs-skyog in the vicinity of the Mount Gab-tog sha-ba in rGya-mo-rong in Eastern (Tibet). At his birth in the sky the sun, moon, and constellations were bright and some distinctly saw the gods and goddesses dancing. He knew the alphabet without learning it. Then, he learned the 'Bon of Cause' in the presence of his father and when ten years of age he took vows of preliminary ordination in the presence of Phyva-bla gYung-drung rGyal-mtshan and received the name of Shes-rab rGyal-mtshan. He obtained a number of consecrations and textual initiations of Bon from various teachers such as the one just mentioned. Then, Srid-rgyal,[1] the Exalted Mother, foretold (his entry into a monastery). When he left for the monastery he made a promise to his parents to see them once again. (216b) At the gold-filled river, 'Bri-chu in mDo-smad, he met the Venerable Blo-bzang Grags-pa (Tsong-kha-pa) and they exchanged four-line compliments. Then, at sGang-stod in Tsha-ba-(rong) he met mKhas-grub Rin-chen Blo-gros and entreated him to impart the consecrations and textual initiations of exoteric, esoteric, and secret Bon to him. After that he studied such subjects as Pāramitā, Pramāṇa, Vinaya, Abhidharma, and Mādhyamika at Nālanda in dBus under Rong-ston Shes-bya Kun-rig.[2] He took examinations in many Buddhist centres in dBus and gTsang where such studies were pursued. By means of the three activities of the scholar he overpowered numerous opponents and his fame as a Great Rab-'byams-pa (a profound scholar) penetrated far and wide. At the age of thirty-one he entered the monastery of gYas-ru dben-sa-kha. When he asked for the

[1] Srid-pa rGyal-mo (on whom see *supra*, p. 9 n. 6).

[2] *STNN*: born in 1345; *TNT* (p. 56): died aged eighty-five, i.e. in 1429, but no mention is made of when Nālanda was founded. However, according to *DN* (p. 1080): he lived from 1367 to 1449 and founded Nālanda in 1435. *Re'u-mig* also follows the latter version. Thus, according to *DN*, mNyam-med Shes-rab rGyal-mtshan (*STNN* 1356–1415) could not possibly have paid a visit to Nālanda. Moreover, Bon-po texts are not all in agreement on the subject for *A-khrid* (p. 51), asserts that he visited Nālanda after, not before, he entered gYas-ru dben-sa-kha. *de nas dgung lo sum cu rtsa gcig gi steng du / g·yas ru dben sa khar phebs te / grva sa'i rnam thar dang / bstan pa'i bya ba rgya chen po mdzad do / de nas dbus na len dra ru byon te /*

consecration and textual initiation of the *dBal-phur sde-skor don-gsum*[1] from Me-ston Kun-bzang rGyal-mtshan of Na-ring, he had a vision of Me-ston as sTag-la Me-'bar and his children as gods and goddesses. Me-ston bestowed on him the dagger and the whole text (of the *dBal-phur*) of Khu-tsha Zla-'od[2] prophesying that he would be the Master of the Doctrine. He possessed innumerable remarkable qualities which I should record. For example, he had a vision of the countenance of his tutelary deities, knowledge-holders, goddesses, and received consecrations and textual initiations from them, but they can be read in other books. (217a) After having been offered the abbotship of dKar-dmar dbu-rtse[3] by the two descendants of Bru, he effectively promoted the Doctrine by means of exposition, disputation, and composition, etc. At about that time, recalling his previous promise, he travelled to see his parents. On the return journey after seeing them, arriving in Dar-mdo[4] he perceived that the great monastery, dBen-sa-kha had been destroyed by flood owing to the jealousy of the Buddhists. While staying dejectedly in Dar-mdo, auspicious signs that he would become the Master of the Doctrine occurred such as a dream in which he swallowed the sun and moon, etc. On the strength of (further) prophecies of Srid-rgyal he thought that the Doctrine could be restored again and went to gTsang. When he arrived at the ruin of dBen-sa-kha he found many gifts such as the sacred *Khams-chen* of Bru and a gold butter-lamp, etc., as objects for worship. Then, he went to the hermitage of gYas-ru mkhar-sna where he engaged in spiritual exercises. Juniper grew in the places where his hair was scattered. He wrote the syllable KA on a stone with his hand. He left many permanent signs such as the imprints of his mendicant's staff and foot (in the rock). (217b) He composed a certain number of commentaries and treatises on the Bon text on metaphysics, the Tantric Teachings, and the Mental Teachings. Then, at the age of fifty he founded the monastery of bKra-shis sman-ri.[5] (When he visited) the site he came upon two ascetics who were about to leave. The Lord said to them: 'Stay, we shall make tea.' They replied: 'The water is too far away.'

[1] On the discovery of this text see *infra*, p. 145.

[2] On whom see *infra*, pp. 145 et seq.

[3] dBu-rtse dkar-po and dBu-rtse dmar-po were the names of the two colleges of gYas-ru dben-sa-kha.

[4] i.e. Dar-rtse-mdo (Ta-chien-lu).

[5] *STNN*: 1405.

But the Lord thrust his mendicant's staff into the ground and water sprang up. The two ascetics were filled with wonder. And so they made tea. Then, in the month of sa-ga, on an auspicious day he said to his disciple, Rin-chen rGyal-mtshan:[1] 'Take some white stones in a corner of your upper garment, close your eyes and then put down a stone after every ninth step.' He did accordingly, but he opened his eyes when he heard a roar. Sixty cells had appeared. Thereupon, the Lord said: 'If you had kept your eyes closed and had put all the white stones down it would have been bigger than the monastery of dBen-sa-kha, but it is not too bad. At any rate, though not very extensive, it will be durable.' Thus he prophesied. Having completed the building of the monastery he laid down monastic rules and promoted many of the studies and practices of exoteric, esoteric, and secret Doctrines. Furthermore, for the sake of revealing the greatness of the Doctrine he twice flew up into the sky (218a) with dMu-gshen Nyi-ma rGyal-mtshan,[2] and his hat, which was burned by the sun's rays during his flight, is still to be seen and is known as the 'Burned Hat'. The religious guardians Ma, bDud, and bTsan[3] served him as servants and accomplished all their tasks without delay. He had clear visions of sTong-rgyung (mThu-chen) and Dran-pa (Nam-mkha') and received the consecrations of exoteric, esoteric, and secret Bon, and prophetic instructions from them. They also passed on to him orally certain profound Bon texts. Moreover, he exhibited unbelievably miraculous and supernatural signs. Then, at the age of sixty, in wood sheep year, having appointed his disciple, Rin-chen rGyal-mtshan, as his representative, giving orders to tend the Doctrine and prophetic instructions concerning the future, he put up a tent at gTer-chu and turned the wheel of Bon for the disciples during the day and then by night for many non-human beings. And thus he passed away at dawn on the eighth of the third summer month. When three days had passed, his corpse rose up into the air a full cubit high above the seat. But when the two spiritual sons and other followers (218b) prayed to it to remain as an object of worship it came down and stayed down. At the time of cremation a rainbow canopy formed on all sides. A miraculous eagle appeared from the rainbow which rose in the West and

[1] Born *STNN* 1360.

[2] See *supra*, p. 133 n. 1.

[3] See *supra*, p. 48 n. 3.

having circled thrice (above the cremation) it disappeared towards the West again. At that time, his representative had a vision of his teacher who then made a promise to come on the fifth of the month of Cho-'phrul (every year). For the devoted followers of the future there appeared many objects of worship such as an image of Kun-tu bZang-po representing his body, an image of Shes-rab sMra-seng, the syllables, ĀḤ OṂ HŪṂ, representing his speech, and three sharīrams like lark's eggs, seven medium-sized ones like peas, many small ones like mustard seed representing his thought. One of the three large ones was taken to the world of gods and another to the world of water-spirits to the accompaniment of musical sounds, lights, and rays. One is still in the golden receptacle. As to his disciples there were two spiritual sons: Rin-chen rGyal-mtshan, the representative, and mNga'-ris bSod-nams rGyal-mtshan. Furthermore, there were ten Greatly Exalted Ones: Bru Shes-rab Seng-ge, Bru Nam-mkha' rGyal-po, Bru Kun-dga' dBang-ldan, and the rest. Hundreds of disciples who followed (his ways of teaching) the 'Rules of Discipline', Tantric and Mental Teachings became spiritually mature and emancipated. (219a) Thousands took some kind of vow, consecration, textual initiation, or instruction. In short, everyone in the Land of Snows who at the present time has entered the gates of the 'Rules of Discipline', Tantric and Mental Teachings is among the spiritual descendants of the Lord. Here are his successors: his representative, the Five Upholders of the Doctrine, the Three Incomparable Lotus, the Four Upholders of Doctrinal Life, the Three Great Unrivalled Ones, the Four Holy Teachers, the Nine Masters of the Triple Doctrine, and the present abbot, sKu-mdun Phun-tshogs Blo-gros dBang-gi rGyal-po.[1] They were all sages and (the manifestations of) knowledge-holders. The *Srid-rgyud*[2] says:

They will appear as manifestations.
Anyone in whom they cause the 'Enlightened Intention' and noble aspiration to arise,
Or who has any kind of contact with them,
Such as tasting the blessed water of a consecration,
Will, at their passing, be safely delivered from the three Evil Forms of Life,
And attain the 'Stage of Permanence'.

[1] Born *STNN* 1876. [2] *SG*, f. 90b5.

In brief, I have not just been listing a succession of abbots; we know from their individual biographies that they were certainly sages and the emanations of knowledge-holders and had been named in the prophecies; so we should esteem the decrees of the Great Incomparable One.

(*The Discovery of the sPa-gro-ma*)

(219b) The history of sPa-gro-ma is fivefold: (1) The concealment of the textual treasure. At the time of the suppression of Bon by Khri-srong lDe-btsan, Bla-chen Dran-pa Nam-mkha' arranged the cycles of the *dBal-phur nag-po* into three divisions. He placed the cycle of the *Lung-don rgyas-pa* with other treatises on medicine and astrology and the like in an iron box and concealed it in the palace of bSve-sgo-can. He placed the cycle of the *Las-thig* in a box of khadirā-wood and concealed it in the central tower of the palace. He placed the cycle of the *Man-ngag* in a precious box and concealed it in the heart of Khro-bo bDud-rtsi 'Khyil-ba in the chapel (of the palace). When the divinely born, Mu-thug bTsan-po, having ascended the throne of Tibet, became tired of it, he and Khyung-po Gyer-zla-med took out the boxes of the cycles of the *dBal-phur* (*nag-po*) from the palace of bSve-sgo-can and concealed them on the left side of sPa-gro phug-gcal, at the level of the waist, in a rock like a Mongolian engaging in battle, under a rock like a white lion opening its mouth wide, behind a rock like a black tortoise drinking water, at the foot of a rock with the large claws of a scorpion, in the centre of a brown rock like a burning flame, in a rocky cave that had the form of the sun. They entrusted them to the six Guardians of the Textual Treasure, Yar-lha Sham-po, etc.

(220a) (2) The life story of the text-discoverer. A chieftain of rTa-nag in 'Jad went to bSam-yas on a pilgrimage. On the way he stopped one night in Nyang-rong stag-tshal with a family called Khu-ye in which there was a daughter with whom he had intercourse. Then he went on to bSam-yas. While he was making offerings of butter-lamps he found a guide to textual treasure which he took home with him. Later a boy was born to the daughter of Khu-ye. He was given the name Khu-tsha Zla-'od[1] (the son of Khu, Moon-light), apparently because his mother

[1] Born *STNN* 1024. The abbot Nyi-ma bsTan-'dzin (*STNN* p. 31) states that Khu-tsha Zla-'od rediscovered the textual treasure in Earth-Tiger year 1038, but

was the daughter of Khu-ye and he was born on the fifteenth as the full moon rose. He is said to have been the emanation of Sad-ne Ga'u. When he grew up he asked his mother where his father was. On being told that the chieftain of rTa-nag was his father, he soon went to find him and told him that he was his son. His father said that he would investigate the matter. On his invoking gods in the third winter month it is said there occurred thunder, lightning, and hail. The chieftain said: 'Despite the fact that you are my son, you cannot be (treated) as my son. Take this share of my property and go.' He gave him the guide of the textual treasure in sPa-gro. He returned to his mother. When he was eighteen years old a Buddhist came and his mother offered him some beer. The Buddhist said to the boy: 'Let us go and find some textual treasures. If we find Bon texts (220b) you shall take them, if we find Buddhist texts I will take them, and if we find a treasure we will divide it.'

(3) The discovery of the textual treasure. Khu-tsha and the Buddhist travelled to sPa-gro and searched for the textual treasure, but nothing was found, though the search went on for two weeks. Thinking it was hopeless the Buddhist is said to have left. But while Khu-tsha was continuing the search his robe caught in the claws of the scorpion rock. Thinking that it might be there he began to dig according to the measurements in the guide. He found a rocky cave with four doors. Inside the first door there was a flat-bell,[1] in the second an upright bell,[2] in the third a horoscope chart, and in the fourth a razor.

(4) The textual content. With the flat-bell there appeared Bon texts, with the upright bell Buddhist texts, with the horoscope chart astrological texts, and with the razor medical texts.[3]

this makes Khu-tsha too young, for our text states (see below) that he made the discovery at the age of eighteen. On his discovery of Buddhist texts see *bsTan-'byung*, ff. 54b7, 75b2; *TTGL*, f. 42b6. Yon-tan rGya-mtsho (*TTGL*, f. 227b6) vaguely states that his text-discoverer came in the second Rab-byung (i.e. 1087–1146). Also cf. *TPS* ii, p. 727.

[1] Tib. gshang. For Illustrations see Snellgrove, *Nine Ways*, Illustration XII (*c*) and (*d*).

[2] Tib. dril-bu.

[3] For list see *infra*, p. 305, l. 10–p. 306, l. 9. The titles in the list are grouped under a series of special headings: Texts concerning the tranquil and wrathful divinities (p. 305, ll. 11–12) (under this heading is included the text *Khro-bo rgyud-drug* which was already included among the treasure said to have been rediscovered by gShen-chen Klu-dga', see *supra*, p. 130); Texts belonging to the three divisions of the cycles of Ferocious Phur-pa (p. 305, ll. 13–23); Texts concerning medicinal

(5) The transmission. The Buddhist, having returned to Khu-tsha said: 'You have discovered a textual treasure. I beg you to give me some texts.' So Khu-tsha gave him the Buddhist texts. Bar-sgom Ye-shes rGyal-mtshan of sBas-yul-rong requested Khu-tsha for the texts of the *Kun-bzang*. Then Khu-tsha said to mGar-nag 'Bum-chung of gNub-yul-rong: 'I have discovered a textual treasure, if you will copy the texts out I shall lend you all the master copies.' mGar replied: 'I have studied the Southern Textual Treasure for a year and so I know a little about them. Nevertheless, I would like to have your texts. Offering a robe and a horse to Khu-tsha he entreated him to impart the texts of the *gZer-phur* and made a copy of them. (222a) Then, having entrusted the boxes of the texts to mGar, Khu-tsha travelled to Nyang-stod. On the journey he, being an expert in medicine, was attacked by an ambush of five men organized by Brang-ti of dMu, another medical expert who was jealous of him. Khu-tsha, lashing his horse with his whip, escaped, but one of his medical pupils was struck by an arrow and his bowels burst. Khu-tsha having washed the bowels with milk pushed them back in and sewed up the cut with a white horse's tendon. The pupil recovered. Thereupon, Khu-tsha said to him: 'You, my boy, have saved my life.' He gave him all the precepts. Later Khu-tsha became known as Khu-tsha the doctor or the Learned gYu-thog, and mGar, offering him a copy of the *Khams-brgyad*, a roll of woollen cloth made of goat's hair and two bushels (of barley) for the field, asked for (permission) to copy out all the texts. But Khu-tsha said: 'Since Brang-ti the doctor is displeased with me I am not going to stay in this place. I do not want your possessions or scriptural books. I will let you copy out all the texts, but at the moment I am leaving for lHo-brag. Whilst I am away look for a copyist and get paper ready.' Having sealed up the boxes of the texts with sealing-wax, he said: 'Do not open the boxes until I come back. But you may use them if I die (before I return).' He set out for lHo-brag taking the medical texts. (222b) When mGar heard that Khu-tsha had died he went (to lHo-brag) taking his son, Khro-rgyal as a servant to see Khu-tsha, but the lama was really dead. Khro-rgyal having

ambrosia (p. 305, ll. 24–6); The cycles of Drag-sngags gzer-phur (p. 305, ll. 27–9); Texts concerning effective protection of the Doctrines (p. 305, ll. 30–8); Texts concerning meditative practices (p. 306, ll. 1–9).

returned home made offerings to the Guardians of the textual treasure and opened the six boxes. He made copies of the texts. Thus, the gift descended to mGar (Khro-rgyal). Both father and son had many disciples, but among them there were four Great Spiritual Sons: Jo-ston sKal-ldan Shes-rab of mDo-khams, Slan-ston Ti-se-ba of La-stod, Yang-la Thugs-rje of rNgod, and gNyan-ston Thugs-rje-'od of sTag-sde. The astrological texts were given to sPug-ston of Shang and now are known as the *gSas-mkhar-ma*. mGar-ston Khro-rgyal is also said to have rediscovered a text of the Great Perfection, the *lTa-ba klong-rdol* and the eighteen small rites of Phur-pa, etc., in sPa-gro skyer-chu.

(*The Zhang-zhung texts and their discoveries*)

The history of the discovery of the Bon texts of Zhang-zhung is fourfold: (1) The concealment of the textual treasure. The texts were first transmitted from the Bon-po of Zhang-zhung, Khyung-la dGra-'dul through a line of ninety-two descendants. At the time of the decadence of the Doctrine the texts were put into a copper box and hidden on the summit of the snowy Mount Ti-se. (223a) Later this was found by the Bon-po of Zhang-zhung, U-gu dGra-'dul. After having been transmitted to the Bon-po of Zhang-zhung, lHa-tho dKar-po who was able to make gods and demons serve him, the texts were hidden (again) in La-stod gtsang-po.

(2) The discovery of the textual treasure. In a dream a Buddhist, gZe-ston sPu-gu rGyal-mtshan, saw three persons dressed as Bon-po adherents who said to him: 'O Teacher, get up, we have a gift for you.' When he asked what they had, they said: 'To the East of this place there is a rock like a yak. From its base measuring four "'dom-pa" towards the East and South there are ritual texts of quelling, nurturing, summoning, and averting. You are to take them.' Thereupon gZe-ston, borrowing a pick from his benefactor, rNgog Byang-chub rDo-rje, began to excavate. But hail fell and lightning struck the rocks on the Western side. That night a woman whose body was of turquoise above the waist and copper below, a man with red locks, and a black man riding on a black horse wearing a turban of snakes, appeared (in his dream) and said to him: 'We are going to eat you!' He reflected: 'Since the practice of virtue is important to

me for my next life, I had better give up the whole thing.' Whereupon the same three Bon-pos appeared and said: 'Do not be diffident about the gift you are going to receive. As to the occurrence of the hail it is due to your failing to make supplications. Give a 'brang-rgyas[1] and a sacrificial cake, to the water-spirits, and a red sacrificial cake to the three owners of the textual treasure.' (223b) Having followed the instructions he began to excavate. First a skull appeared and on further excavation a copper box.

(3) The textual content. The following texts of Zhang-zhung *This* were found in the box: four texts of nurturing, the *This-dkar*; three texts of averting, the *This-dmar*; two texts of quelling, the *This-nag*, and one text (of summoning), the *'Dzab-this*—making ten in all.

(4) The transmission. rNgog Byang-chub rDo-rje said to gZe-ston: 'We have had hail (this year) and it is very likely that it will come again next year. I ask you, teacher, for a means of protection against hail.' He gave him the *'Dzab-this* and returned the pick. Then gZe-ston went to (the monastery of) dBen-sa-kha in Bar-go and handed over the texts to Bru-sha (bDag-nyid) rJe-btsun.[2] The latter imparted them to Dod-ci rGya-bon. gZe-ston also imparted them to Zhang-grags Bon-po and they became widely known.

(*The discovery of Ra-shag and Ra-ljags*)

The history of the discovery of textual treasure by (Ra-shag and) Ra-ljags is threefold: (1) The receipt of the textual treasure. When Ra-shag dNgos-grub-'bar and Ra-ljags gYu-bo were listening to the exposition of Bon in the presence of a Lama called Zug Ra-'phan in Yar-'brog, the wife of Zug said to the disciples: (224a) 'Two monks want you to come to the outside door.' When they went to the door, the two monks asked: 'We have a bag full of Bon texts. Would you like to have them?' They replied that they would. The two monks gave the bag to them, saying: 'In return you must give us a horse on the fifteenth of the month.' They went away. Thereupon, the two disciples were so pleased that they stopped hearing Bon (from their teacher) and went home. The teacher is said to have been displeased. The monks who brought the bag were probably

[1] On 'brang-rgyas see *supra*, p. 129 n. 2.

[2] An abbot of gYas-ru dben-sa-kha, see *supra*, p. 140.

in reality two miraculous ascetics, for later nobody came to fetch the horse and where they went was completely unknown.[1] But some say that the story which says that the texts originated from Drang-nga is (more) reliable.[2] The Bon-po of Ra-ljags was foreseen in the *Kha-byang lung-bstan*:[3]

> There will be one called Ra-ljags gYu-bo,
> The manifestation of Ra-sangs Khod-ram.

(2) The textual content. The bag was opened and ten texts of the Mental Teachings were found inside.[4]

Ra-ston (dNgos-grub-'bar) and Ra-sgom (gYu-bo) divided the manuscripts between them. Ra-ston received the following texts: the *Rig-pa dkar-po*, the *Sems-smad bco-brgyad*, and the *Gab-pa*. Ra-sgom received the following texts of the *gSang-ba yang-gter-gyi rgyud*, the mother and its sons, the *rGyud-smad bcu-bdun* (such as) the *gSer-gyi rus-sbal*, the *lTa-sgom spyod-pa'i lung*, and several of the *gSon-gshin* and the commentary of the *Phur-pa*. Ra-sgom withdrew into retreat and transcribed the manuscripts. As the wife of Ra-ston was very bad-tempered he went far away from home to do the transcribing. So his copies are said to have been very good. Later between the son of Ra-ston, Jo-gsas Kha-bo, and the son of Ra-sgom, sNying-po, animosity arose and so (the friendship between their fathers) is said to have been broken. Bru-ston Nyi-rgyal[5] expounded the *Gab-pa* of the Southern Textual Treasures with the help of the basic text and the commentary found by Ra-ston. Before Ra-ston's *Gab-pa* (appeared) the *Gab-pa* of the Southern Textual Treasures had been very difficult to understand. But the *Gab-pa* of Ra-ston was remarkable for its clarity. (225b) The manu-

[1] The two were Ra-shag 'Dre-chung and Dad-pa Tshul-khrims (see *infra*, p. 165).

[2] According to this version the texts would seem to have been given to Ra-ston and Ra-sgom by Drang-nga mDo-la (on whom see *infra*, p. 164) and this seems to be more likely since our author relates that the manuscripts of esoteric spells and the *gSon-gshin* were 'taken' by Drang-nga mDo-la apparently from Ra-ston and Ra-sgom (see *infra*, p. 151).

[3] *SG*, f. 94b6.

[4] But these were not the only ones. For the full list see *infra*, p. 308, l. 24–p. 309, l. 16. The titles are grouped under two headings: ten groups of texts belonging to the Mental Teachings (p. 308, l. 24–p. 309, l. 12) (under this heading is listed the title *Byang-sems gab-pa* which was already said to have been found by gShen-chen Klu-dga', see *supra*, p. 130); Texts of the Bon of Cause (p. 309, ll. 13–16).

[5] Bru-ston Nyi-ma rGyal-mtshan, a contemporary of Bru bDag-nyid rJe-btsun (b. *STNN* 1040). See *supra*, p. 140.

scripts of the esoteric spells and the *gSon-gshin* were taken by Drang-nga mDo-la. When he was travelling home from Nyang-stod he came upon gNyan-ston Khye'u Grags-pa. As Drang-nga was wearing a blue robe gNyan-ston asked him: 'Are you a Bon-po?' 'Yes, I am.' 'Have you got any Bon texts?' 'Yes, I do have some, if you want them I will let you have them.' Offering him a coat of mail, a turquoise, and a roll of woollen cloth, gNyan-ston requested the texts. He was the first to receive the Bon of esoteric spells and the *gSon-gshin*. Then he made Drang-nga who was about to return home further gifts of food for the journey. The son of Drang-nga, Seng-ge rGyal-ba, had no child by his first wife. So he took another wife called Dre-mo gYung-lcam, but his first wife did not let her stay with them. Dre-mo stole the (Drang-nga's) manuscripts and went away. She sold them to a person called dByil He-ru-ka[1] in a monastery called 'Brang-bu rtse-mthon.[2]

(3) The transmission. The texts were transmitted from He-ru-ka to his son, Shes-rab Seng-ge, rGya Bla-ma Khri-mkhar of Yar-'brog, Me gNyan-dga' of Yar-'brog, Zhang-ston Grags of sMan-thang, and mGar-ston Shes-rab Bla-ma.

(*The discovery in gNyan-gyi se-bo*)

The history of the discovery of the textual treasure in Mount gNyan-gyi se-bo is threefold: (1) The concealment of the textual treasure. When Ba-gor Vairocana was about to leave for Tsha-ba-rong, he concealed some profound texts of the Mental Teachings and (the atonement of) the religious defenders in Mount gNyan-gyi se-bo (in Nyang-stod) and entrusted them to gTer-bdag lHa-btsan.

(2) The discovery of the textual treasure. (226b) Ra-ston 'Bum-rje of gNyan came across a guide to a (textual treasure) which belonged to a lama. Following the guide which said that a textual treasure was to be found in Mount (gNyan-gyi) se-bo, he searched and found it.[3]

(3) The textual content.[4]

[1] Cf. *infra*, p. 173. dByil-ston He-ru-ka may be the same person.

[2] For the list of texts see *infra*, p. 310, ll. 3–17. In this list the titles are divided into two groups: Texts of the Bon of Cause (p. 310, ll. 3–5) and Esoterical Texts (p. 310, ll. 6–17).

[3] *STNN* 1137.

[4] For this see *infra*, p. 310, l. 30–p. 311, l. 2. The titles in this list are divided

(*The discovery of the Yer-rdzong-ma*)

The history of Yer-rdzong-ma is threefold: (1) The concealment of the textual treasure. In the time of Khri-srong (lDe-btsan), Dran-pa (Nam-mkha') and Vairocana concealed the Bon texts of India in lHa-sa yer-ba'i rdzong and (227a) entrusted them to the Textual Guardians Dur-bdud Nag-po of Mount Has-po, Brag-btsan dMar-po of bSam-yas and Klu-mo dKar-mo of lHa-sa.

(2) The discovery of the textual treasure. The *Lung-bstan*[1] says:

The Buddhists of gTsang, the chief and his retinue,
Manifestations of the monk Vairocana,
Will discover the textual treasure in Gling-gi chu-ba.

Accordingly, the three Buddhists of gTsang, Sum-pa Byang-tshul, 'Bre Tshul-seng, and gCer-bu dBang-phyug[2] went to bSam-yas in search of Buddhist textual treasures, but even after several years nothing was found. When they set out for home they said to themselves: 'We are supposed to be great men, it is shameful not to have found any texts.' So they went to Yer-ba and began to search. They discovered a textual treasure, but it was all Bon texts and (therefore) not what they wanted. They gave them away to Lung-ston 'Od-'bar, also known as gNyen-ston gZi-brjid.

(3) The textual content.[3]

(4) (228a) The transmission. gNyen-ston (gZi-brjid) transmitted the teachings to Gyer-ston Khro-gsas. The latter transmitted them to Lung-bon lHa-gnyan[4] and Mi-la Ras-pa[5]

into two groups: Texts of the Mental Teachings (p. 310, ll. 30–3); Texts concerning the protection of the Doctrines (p. 310, l. 33–p. 311, l. 2).

[1] *SG*, f. 95b5.

[2] *TTGL*, f. 106b3: *gter ston (g)sum tshogs ni / rkyang po grags pa dbang phyug / sum pa byang chub tshul khrims / 'bre shes rab byams pa /* and on f. 107b1: *gter ston (g)sum tshogs kyis 'bum dang tshad ma dang 'phrul gyi me long dgu skor sogs bon gter mang zhig bton . . . /* See also *bsTan-'byung*, f. 56a2. Yon-tan rGya-mtsho (*TTGL*, f. 227b6) vaguely states that these three Buddhists came in the 5th Rab-byung (i.e. 1267–1326).

[3] For this see *infra*, p. 311, l. 20–p. 312, l. 10. The titles are grouped under a series of special headings: Canonical Books (p. 311, ll. 20–8) (under this heading is included the title *mChod-gtor rgya-cher 'grel* which was already included among the treasure said to be found by gShen-chen Klu-dga', see *supra*, p. 130); Esoterical Texts (p. 311, l. 29–p. 312, l. 2); Mental Teachings (p. 312, ll. 3–7); Magical Spells (p. 312, ll. 8–10).

[4] Born *STNN* 1088.

[5] 1040–1123.

simultaneously. They both practised the rite of procuring hail-storms.[1] Mi-la having taken instruction in meditation from Mar-pa[2] became a Buddhist. gNyen-ston (gZi-brjid) transmitted the teachings to Gyer dBang-grub. The latter transmitted them to Gyer-ston Nam-mkha' gYung-drung. The latter transmitted them to Lung-bon lHa-gnyan.

(The discovery of the Shel-brag-ma)

The history of Shel-brag-ma is fourfold: (1) The concealment of the textual treasure. lDe Gyim-tsha rMa-chung concealed the texts in the rock of gTsang-po nu-ma and said prayers. He entrusted them to the Textual Guardian, lDong-btsan dKar-po.

(2) The discovery of the textual treasure. At gNya'-lung brag-ra in Nyang-stod there was a shepherd called gNyan-ston Shes-rab rDo-rje. He is said to have also been known as gNyan-'theng Re-ngan (lame gNyan) as he was lame. Whilst he was tending his sheep and goats one day a (ray of) white light appeared near him. He followed it, but it disappeared when he reached the base of a white rock. On looking around he discovered a crack in the rock. He opened it and came upon a cave full of volumes of books all round the walls.[3] (228b) And so he began to transcribe them, for which he later became known as gNyan-ston Shes-rab Seng-ge.

(3) The textual content. There are nine groups of texts.[4] gNya'-ston rDo-rje (a scribe) asked: 'How many books are there still

[1] This refers to the text *Thog-smad dgu-'grol*. See *infra*, p. 312, ll. 8–9.

[2] Mar-pa Chos-kyi Blo-gros (1012–97) of whom see *DN* ii, pp. 399 et seq.

[3] The discovery was made in (*STNN*) 1067.

[4] See *infra*, p. 312, l. 29–p. 314, l. 27. The headings of the nine groups are as follows: Texts which act like legs for the living and dead (p. 312, l. 30–p. 313, l. 16); Metaphysical Texts which are like the body (p. 313, ll. 17–31) (under this heading are included the title *'Dul-ba rgyud-drug* which was already included among the texts said to be found by the three ācāryas, see *supra*, pp. 120–2, and also *mDzod-gnas bcu-bdun* which is the same text as *Srid-pa'i mdzod-phug*, see *supra*, p. 8 n. 4); Texts which penetrate all other texts like hands (p. 313, ll. 32–7); Exoterical and esoterical texts which are like the vital organs (p. 313, l. 38–p. 314, l. 11); Meditative texts which are like organs of sense (p. 314, ll. 12–15) (under this heading is included the title *Byang-sems gab-pa* for which see *supra*, p. 51 n. 8, and also *Dug-lnga lam-khyer* which was already said to have been found by the three ācāryas, see *supra*, pp. 120–2); Texts concerning regular religious practices which are like daily food (p. 314, ll. 16–18); Texts concerning magical spells which are like weapons (p. 314, ll. 19–20); Texts concerning the protection of oneself and others which are like armour (p. 314, ll. 21–4); Texts which are like the head (p. 314, ll. 25–7).

left?' (gNyan-'theng) answered: 'The cave is still full of volumes!' 'Well, in that case, you had better bring out the ones you want as we have no time to transcribe them all.' Then when gNyan-'theng went to the cave (to fetch more books) he apparently found it shut and was unable to get any more books out. gNya'-ston rDo-rje died of leprosy for transforming some of the texts into Buddhism.

(4) The transmission. It is said that since the 'planet Mars' had hindered gNyan-'theng's discovery, his texts were not widely known and have been called the Dumb Bon. Nevertheless, since his manuscripts got scattered, later most of them became widely known and have been used by the fortunate ones in mDo, dBus, and gTsang.

(*The discovery of the lHo-brag-ma*)

The history of lHo-brag-ma is fivefold: (1) The concealment of the textual treasure. At the time of the decadence of the Doctrine the texts were hidden by Li-shu (sTag-ring) in the temple of Khom-mthing and entrusted to the Bya-ra ma-gsum (the three Guardian Mothers).

(2) The life-story of the text-discoverer. bZhod-ston dNgos-grub Grags-pa,[1] the emanation of Li-shu (sTag-ring), was born in sMan-thang of lHo-brag. His father was bZhod-ston lHa-tho (231a) and his mother was Shākya lCam. At an early age he became a monk at dPal-ldar ri-zhing. In the course of his studies there he became the best scholar among the monks. He founded a small monastery at mKhar-chu-brag, where he went to live expounding the *Byang-sems gab-pa*[2] and producing many scholars.

(3) The discovery of the textual treasure. One day[3] he was told by a Textual Guardian: 'If you are seeking the Great Perfection, it is in the central treasury of the temple of Khom-mthing. Take it out!' Thereupon, he went to Khom-mthing and opened the

[1] For more details of his life-story see *dGongs-brgyud drug-gi klad-don nyi-shu rtsa-bdun nyams-kyi man-ngag gnad-kyi yig-phyung*, ff. 24 et seq. According to the rNying-ma-pa tradition he is known as gTer-ston Grub-thob dNgos-grub and represents an important figure among the gTer-ston of the rNying-ma-pa as he rediscovered a number of Buddhist texts (*TTGL*, f. 41a4; *bsTan-'byung*, ff. 57a2, 80b3). He was a teacher of the rNying-ma-pa text-discoverer Nyang Nyi-ma 'Od-zer (*Re'u-mig*: born in 1136).

[2] See *supra*, p. 51 n. 8.

[3] *STNN* 1088.

door of the central treasury where there were many valuable things such as the saddle of khadirā-wood, the golden stirrups, the golden bridle, the turquoise rein, the silver belt and the whip of Khri-srong (lDe-btsan), etc. He put them aside. Then there was a bundle of manuscripts wrapped up in a Tantric cloak. He took it out and looked through it, but it was all Buddhist. (After putting it back) he came away and said prayers to mystic goddesses and made offerings to the Textual Guardians. Then he went to look for the texts again. There were fifteen treasuries. As he opened the door of the middle one in the first row of three he saw clearly the whole of the three worlds. (231b) Having made sure that the manuscripts were Bon texts he took them away with him. He went home and withdrew into retreat for three years and studied them while making offerings of sacrificial cakes. He grasped the meaning of the texts thoroughly.

(4) The textual content.[1]

(5) The multiplying of the disciples. There were (*a*) the Four Spiritual Sons and (*b*) the Four Eminent Scholars. (*a*) The two 'Or-ston brothers of Yar-'brog won the teacher's favour (232b) by making him many gifts. The lama of gTam-shul, Mye-ston won his favour by attending on him for eighteen years, and 'Bum Khri-'od of La-stod won his favour by coming from far away. (*b*) Concerning the Four Eminent Scholars: they were sNyi-ston of gTam-shul, bKra-shis-'od of La-stod, Zhang-ston Nam-mkha', and Bla-ma Jo-lde of dBu-ri. Since they grasped the lama's exposition they enjoyed high repute as scholars. In particular, rGya Jo-lde received a prophecy from the mystic goddess, Ye-shes dBal-mo, who said to him: 'You must ask bZhod-ston dNgos-grub Grags-pa for the Bon which enables one to attain Enlightenment in a single life. In continuation of his past acts he will impart it to you.' When he met bZhod-ston he duly reported the prophecy to him. bZhod-ston said: 'Yes, I have it and I have not imparted it to anyone yet. You are fortunate!' As soon as he had imparted the Bon to him which was contained in eleven manuscripts certainty of understanding arose in him. On his offering bZhod-ston two measures and a

[1] For this see *infra*, p. 315, l. 24–p. 316, l. 15. The titles in the list are divided into four groups under the following headings: Principal texts (of the Mental Teachings) (p. 315, ll. 25–38); Esoterical Texts (p. 316, ll. 1–2); Preceptive Texts (p. 316, ll. 3–8); and Precetive texts of the *Yang-rtse klong-chen* (p. 316, ll. 9–15).

half of gold, a horse, two loads of salt and a robe made of woollen cloth from dBus, he gave him the manuscripts to keep. But since it was too risky to do that (233a) he concealed them in the temple of bDud-'dul as soon as he had transcribed them. rGya Jo-lde transmitted the teaching to Bla-ma gNam-lcags. From him the line of transmission leads down to gYo-ston lHun-grub-dpal and so the teaching flourished. The Major Oral Tradition descends from Bla-ma Jo-lde to Zhig-po sNang-seng, sKyo-ston sNgags-pa, and gYo-ston (lHun-grub-dpal). The Minor Oral Tradition[1] descends from rGya-ston gNyag-chung to A-po sNgon-po, Chos-ston Zhig-po, lCe-ston gZung-grags, and Shākya 'Byung-gnas of Zur-bo-che. The latter transformed it into Buddhism giving it a Sanskrit title and altering the terms according to Buddhist terminology. He disguised his name as a text-discoverer rDo-rje bZhed-pa. The title he gave it was *sNyan-brgyud thugs-kyi me-long*. And so nowadays many Buddhists practise it.

(*Gyer-mi Nyi-'od and his discoveries*)

The way in which the textual treasure came to Gyer-mi Nyi-'od is threefold: (1) His life-story. When Se-ka sTon-pa was dwelling in the country of Phug-chung ra-mo a man wearing a robe of turquoise and a feathered hat came to him. He asked: 'Where have you come from?' The man answered: 'There is no certainty concerning where I have come from!' 'Where is your home?' (233b)

'As the whole world is the realm of Bon,
It is trivial to wish to have a particular place to yourself.
I was born in Zhang-zhung.'

'What is your ancestry?'

'Since everybody has Enlightenment as his basis,
It is trivial to think of ancestry and family.
My father's ancestors were called Gyer-mi.'

[1] Both the Major and Minor Oral Traditions are attributed to Li-shu sTag-ring (eighth century). The Major Oral Tradition refers to *Yang-rtse klong-chen* for which see *infra*, p. 316, ll. 9–15. The minor one is not recorded in the list of the texts since it is believed to have been transformed into Buddhism.

'What is your name?'

'Since in truth everything is uncertain,
There is no certainty about my name at all.
Some call me Nyi-ma 'Od-zer,
Some Bon-zhig Nag-po,
And others gYu-lus Bya-mgo.'

'How old are you?'

'Since time knows neither past nor future,
It is trivial to calculate seasons and years.
I am very old.'

'What are you doing with that bundle on your mendicant's staff?'

'Desired for its usefulness, the precious treasury,
Is unobtainable when you seek it desirously,
But unavoidable when you abandon it uncaringly.
Appearance holds nothing real to be attached to,
There is nothing here to be held on to yet it cannot be taken away.'

'Are you Bon-po or Buddhist?'

'When the sun shines on a golden mountain,
The mountain and the gold are identical.
If you take the dual view of things you may fall into extremism.'

'Where have you been up till now and where are you going?'

'I come from the Upper Land of Zhang-zhung. (234a)
I travelled by the Northern central way.
I am going to Slob-dpon-can.'[1]

'I entreat you to impart a precept to me.' 'Hear me then. Are you aware of the inescapability of death once you are born, the inescapability of rebirth after you are dead, the inescapability of roaming about in the cycle of existence after rebirth, and the impossibility of bliss in the world?' 'Will you stay here for some days?'

'The pure and lofty mountains afford blissful experiences.
And so I avoid urban places.'

[1] slob-dpon here stands for Dran-pa Nam-mkha', thus slob-dpon-can is the place where Dran-pa Nam-mkha' resides.

'Will you wear this blue robe?'

'My clothes are the clouds and the winds,
The warmth of my dress is inexhaustible.'

'Go and live up in those mountains, I will provide you with all the victuals you want.'

'I fear it may stimulate attachment.
My food will be provided by non-human beings.'

'Can I accompany you for a few days?'

'In the day I wander about on the summit of the Mount 'Thing-gin,
At night I fly round the celestial sphere.
You stay virtuous in the way you are,
But I, Nyi-'od, must withdraw into the sky.'

Having said that he went away. Then he went up to La-stod tshab-sde where he came upon a man who was riding on a horse and wearing fine clothes. The man said: 'Where are you going, beggar?' (234b) He replied: 'It is you who are the beggar!' The man said: 'I have all the food, money and clothes I want. How can a man be wealthier than I? People say that you crossed the river of mDog and gTsang-po without a boat. That is wonderful.' He answered:

'If you do not cross the ocean of the cycle of existence,
It is not much use being able to cross the gTsang-po.'

Once when he was in La-stod at the base of a stūpa a Buddhist ascetic came and said: 'Is there any ascetic who can exhibit supernatural signs in this region?' Lifting up the stūpa in his palm, he placed it on the heads of people. Everybody said that it was a great wonder. Then a boy seized one of the prayer-flags of his mendicant's staff and took it away. As he begged earnestly to have it back asking what the boy was going to do with it, local people asked him: 'Why do you entreat the boy so persistently for such a trivial thing?' He replied:

'I, Nyi-'od, am an ascetic free from all attachments.
The possession of a flag is of no advantage to me.
But it belongs to an owner who is elsewhere.
The boy himself will encounter an impediment.'

Thereupon, the boy is said to have died. Sometimes he would lie down on the ground and ask anybody who was passing: 'Has the dispute between demon Khyab-pa Lag-ring and gShen-rab (235a) been settled now?'[1] People would answer: 'I know nothing about it.' 'If you do not compose your own mind in peace it will never be settled.' On another occasion, going up to someone, he asked: 'Does the unborn lama understand (the meaning of) the "unborn"? It is difficult for an unborn lama to understand (the meaning of) the "unborn" if he has no keen interest in it.' Sometimes, having begged people for butter-rind, milk-cheese-rind, and rich bones, he burned them as smell-offerings. Then having eaten the singed objects he used to say: 'If one cannot eat it, it means one's attachment (to the world) has not been eradicated.' He used to say that he did not want the things which people gave him as alms, but the things which they did not give him. When they gave him what he wanted he is said to have given it to other people. This lama was the emanation of Gyer-spungs Dran-pa (Nam-mkha') and lived for three hundred years in the human world. In some stories he is said to have been the son of Khyung-po Gyer-zla-med.[2] Concerning his textual treasure his biography states:

> Unimpeded from revealing the secret textual treasures,
> At the age of twenty-two,
> He discovered the textual treasure of Bya-rgod gsang-ba.

There are many stories of this kind about him.

(2) (Concerning his works), there is (*a*) the inspired word, and (*b*) the textual treasure. (*a*) The *Nyams-len lnga-skor*, the *Man-ngag tshig-bzhi*, (235b) the *lDe-mig dgu-skor* and the liturgy of the *A-gsal* were passed on to him orally by Dran-pa Nam-mkha'. (*b*) He discovered the textual treasure in Dang-ra khyung-rdzong in the Earth mouse year.[3] It contains the *rTsa-rgyud gsang-ba bsen-thub*,[4] etc., many rGyud together with their

[1] Concerning the dispute between sTon-pa gShen-rab and Demon Khyab-pa Lag-ring see *gZer-mig*, vol. ka, ff. 256a4 et seq.; vol. kha, ff. 1a1–46a3.

[2] An eighth-century priest, see *supra*, p. 103.

[3] *STNN* 1108.

[4] This rGyud is the most important of all rGyud and it is referred to as rGyud-gyi rgyal-po (see *KTDG*, p. 8). Its discovery is also attributed to gShen-chen Klu-dga' (see *supra*, p. 130). A commentary on it was composed by 'Gro-mgon Blo-gros rGyal-mtshan (*STNN* 1198–1263), an abbot of gYas-ru dben-sa-kha (see *supra*, p. 140). The commentary is entitled *Yid-bzhin bkod-pa'i-rgyan* (see *KTDG*, p. 17).

ancillary texts of Tranquillity and Ferocity. Also the *gYung-drung-las rnam-par dag-pa'i mdo-rgyud.*[1]

(3) The transmission. When he met Se-ka Khri-thung, also known as Se-ka sTon-pa, Se-ka requested him to impart an 'essence' for the prevention of rebirth. Nyi-'od asked: 'What "essence" have you already learned?' He answered: 'I recite the A-dkar sa-le-'od (of the *sNyan-brgyud A-gsal sgron-me*) which I heard from Ba-sgom gYung-drung.' (Nyi-'od said): 'I have the *Man-ngag tshig-bzhi* which will help you to understand the *sNyan-brgyud A-gsal sgron-me.*' And he bestowed on him the precepts of the *A-gsal*. Then he said: 'This (teaching) has been transmitted orally from mouth to mouth from Kun-tu bZang-po up to the present time. Do not impart it to anyone (who is unfit).' Se-ka sTon-pa imparted it to Lama rMa-ston (Srol-'dzin)[2] who wrote it down. (236a) The *rTsa-rgyud gsang-ba bsen-thub* was bestowed on rMa-ston Srol-'dzin and he was instructed: 'If you want the companion text to this one, it is in the rock of Dang-ra khyung-rdzong. You can take it out.'

(*The discoveries of Sad-gu Rin-chen Grgags-pa and Dre'u-rgya Ra-dza*)

The history of bSam-yas ca-ti-ma is fourfold: (1) the concealment of the textual treasure. Li-shu (sTag-ring) and Vairocana concealed it in the red stūpa for the suppression of demons called Ca-ti[3] sgo-mang in the cemetery to the south-west of the throne in bSam-yas. They entrusted it to Pom-ra.

(2) The discovery of the textual treasure. Some bricks of the red stūpa began to fall down whereupon some manuscripts fell out. Discovered, upon examination, to be Bon texts, they were burned and apparently various unpleasant things occurred. Further, in iron female bird year the bricks fell down again. While the restoration was in progress a box was found containing many manuscripts of Bon texts. Thereupon, people said: 'Last year unpleasant things happened, it is risky to burn them.' So

[1] This is also considered to be very important and is put at the beginning of the Bon-po bKa'-'gyur (see *KTDG*, p. 3).

[2] On whom see *infra*, p. 167.

[3] ca-ti or sometimes tsa-ti is probably a Tibetan corruption of the Sanskrit word caitya meaning tomb, temple.

the box was hidden behind the clay images in the temple of bSam-yas. But Sad-gu Rin-chen Grags-pa and Dre'u-rgya Ra-dza,[1] two custodians of the temple, took it away by night loading it on a horse and set out (236b) by way of Kong-po to the South of Khams.

(3) The textual content. Eight groups of texts appeared.[2]

(4) The multiplying of the disciples. At that time, the first Khams-pa to study in dBus and gTsang was a disciple of Zhu-g·yas whose name was dBu-ston of Dir. The two (discoverers) went to him and said: 'We have manuscripts belonging to a Bon textual treasure, would you like to have them?' He replied: 'I went to dBus and gTsang in search of some manuscripts rediscovered by Lama gShen (Klu-dga'), but I found none. It is very improbable that among yours you have (some of the gShen's). Then they showed the texts to Sum-pa gTo-ston the first Khams-pa to study (in gTsang) under the Lord Gur-zhog-pa (lHa-ri gNyen-po) and rGya Khri-rje, and asked him if he would like them. He replied: 'Yes, I would; do not show them to other people, come to my country and propagate Bon there. I shall grant privileges to both of you.' Apparently they left

[1] These are two of the three ācāryas who found texts in bSam-yas in (*STNN*) A.D. 913 and travelled to La-stod in gTsang (see *supra*, p. 118). Forty-nine years later according to *bsTan-'byung*, these two returned to bSam-yas again and found some more texts (*STNN* gives the year as A.D. 961) *bsTan-'byung*, f. 51a4: . . . *mi lo zhe dgu nas / nya mgon rgya gar yul du gshegs / dkon grags sad rin bsam yas 'khor / sgo mang mchod rten dmar po nas / rin chen bse sgrom drug bton nas / dbu mchod phur ba 'bar la babs /* Our text replaces dKon-mchog Grags-pa by Dre'u-rgya Ra-dza.

However, from the narration of our author (see below) we note that the two text-discoverers met dBu-ston, who had searched for the manuscripts of gShen Klu-dga' (*STNN* 996–1035, see *supra*, p. 126), and also Sum-pa gTo-ston, a disciple of Gur-zhog-pa lHa-ri gNyen-po (*STNN* 1024–91). The two text-discoverers could not possibly have met anyone searching for manuscripts of gShen Klu-dga' in A.D. 961. Klu-dga''s discovery took place in *STNN* 1017. The meeting with Sum-pa is even more impossible chronologically.

[2] For list see *infra*, p. 320, l. 31–p. 321, l. 33. In the list the titles are grouped under eight headings: Canonical Books of 'Bum (p. 320, ll. 32–4) (here is included the title *Bye-ma* (or *rgyas-pa*) *nyi-khri chu-rgyun 'bum* which was already included among the texts said to be found by gNyan-ston Shes-rab Seng-ge, see *supra*, p. 153); Canonical Books of mDo (p. 320, l. 35–p. 321, l. 4); Esoterical Texts (p. 321, ll. 5–18) (under this heading is included the title *Phur-pa'i rgyud-dgu* which was already included among the texts said to be found by Khu-tsha Zla-'od, see *supra*, p. 146); Medical Texts (p. 321, ll. 19–21); Efficacious magic spells (p. 321, ll. 22–6); Texts concerning methods of causing harm (p. 321, ll. 27–8); Bon of the living (p. 321, ll. 29–30); Texts concerning the evocation of evil omens (p. 321, ll. 31–33).

the six boxes of manuscripts with Sum-pa gTo-ston. But after they had gone away to another place to perform sortilege, he entrusted them to his benefactress. Many traders arrived in the community. (238a) (Sum-pa) gTo-ston was involved in a fight between the traders and the people and his head was injured. When the two text-discoverers returned (Sum-pa) gTo-ston was dead from his head injury. They made inquiries about the manuscripts, but apparently failed to find them. One day the benefactress who had the boxes of the manuscripts in her keeping fell from some steps and her head was injured. A Bon-po named dBu-mchod Phur-pa-'bar who had some knowledge of medicine was called in and offered a coat of mail if he could do something about the injury. He noticed the boxes of manuscripts and said: 'I shall cure you, my benefactress. Keep this coat of mail for yourself. I would like the boxes of the manuscripts which the teacher entrusted to you.' She was very pleased and keeping her coat of mail, gave him all the boxes. Thus, eventually the gift came upon dBu-mchod Phur-pa-'bar. Then, not long after, sTon-btsun, the nephew of the great dBu-ston of Dir who was dead, gathered a number of people together and prepared tea for them. Offering a fine horse with a roll of silk to dBu-mchod (Phur-pa-'bar) he proclaimed: 'dBu-mchod Phur-pa-'bar is a text-discoverer, so every Bon-po must revere him as our teacher.' He is said to have requested him to impart Bon to him. dBu-mchod (Phur-pa-'bar) and Dir sTon-(btsun) are considered to be reliable sources. Since dBu-mchod possessed the 'wood-cover' of sNya Li-shu sTag-ring his books are said to have been invisible wherever they were. (238b) The teacher Sum-bham, etc., requested the venerable Dir sTon-(btsun) the Great, to impart the teaching to him and it flourished.

Dre'u-rgya (Ra-dza) and Sad-gu (Rin-chen Grags-pa) also rediscovered the cycle of Khrag-'thung Rol-ba together with its ancillary texts in Ca-ti dmar-po in bSam-yas. These texts had been hidden by Li-shu sTag-ring. They now transmitted them to 'Dru Yon-sgom Thar-mo. The latter transmitted them to the Teacher dBu-rol.

(*The discovery of the bKa' Drang-nga-ma*)

The history of bKa'Drang-nga-ma is threefold: (1) The concealment of the textual treasure.

(AA) In outline
(BB) In detail

(AA) From Kun-tu bZang-po to the king sPungs-pa there was a continuous line of transmission. Then on request the Bon-po of Zhang-zhung, Li-mur gTsug-phud, handed (the texts) over to Ba-gor Vairocana who made translations into Tibetan and gave them to the king Khri-srong lDe-btsan. So they were called 'the king's soul-nurturing Bon'. Then during the suppression of the Doctrine when Vairocana was about to be banished owing to the calumny started by the queen and Bon ministers the Bon texts were practised in secret. (239a) Just before his death the Lord (Khri-srong lDe-btsan) gave the texts to his son Mu-tig bTsan-po. The latter gave them to the Lord Ral-ba-can. The latter gave them to Dar-ma. When his son 'Od-srung and his son Yum-brtan by his second wife quarrelled the texts passed to the priest bodyguard, Drang-nga dPal-gyi Yon-tan. The latter gave them to (Drang-nga) dPal-gyi Grags-pa. The latter gave them to (Drang-nga) Rin-chen-dpal. The latter had no children and in later life he took a second wife, and a son named Drang-nga mDo-la was born to him. When this son was four years of age the father called upon his nephew, Drang-rje Dad-pa Tshul-khrims, a monk, and his brother, Ra-shag 'Dre-chung and instructed them saying: 'This is my testament. Conceal my texts until my son is thirteen. Before that you must never show them to anybody. (When he is thirteen) take out the texts and give them to him and practise them yourself as well.' (The father) died, and the texts were concealed in Nyang-smad, etc., according to the testament.

(BB) The history of the *mDo gzer-mig*.[1] It states:

> (This text) was found in (between) the cemetery and the throne in the South in bSam-yas.

[1] Our text inconsistently spells the title of this mDo as gZer-dmigs or gZer-mig. The latter form is the usual one. H. A. Francke translates (*Asia Major*, i (1924), p. 305): *Rays from the eyes of the Svastika*; Sarat Chandra Das's dictionary translates: *A key to memory*. However, this mDo is believed to have been rediscovered by Drang-rje bTsun-pa gSer-mig (see *infra*, p. 165). It is not improbable that the title *gZer-mig* might have been derived from the name of its discoverer Drang-rje bTsun-pa gSer-mig (the Golden eye monk, the Lord of Drang). It is quite possible that at first the text was called by the name of its composer or discoverer and a copyist's error changed SA to ZA. This would account for the

(239b) Concerning the meaning of this, gYung-drung Ye-shes's statement in his *bSam-yas gter-(')byung* that the text was rediscovered in Ca-ti is based on the following statement (from another text):

> The (mChod-rten) ca-ti dmar-po was built for the suppression of demons in the cemetery and (near) the throne in the south-west (of the temple).

Furthermore, some have said:

> When Drang-rje (mDo-la) was drawing a figure on the ground in the cemetery at the foot of Mount Has-po, some charcoal emerged and as he dug at it a slate box (containing the text) appeared, etc.

Thus, there are many different opinions concerning the story, but since no throne (near the cemetery) can be identified, they all seem unacceptable. The text, therefore, must have been rediscovered after eight years (of concealment) between the back of the throne of the red clay image and the base of the inside southern wall of the temple on which was depicted a cemetery, viz. birds, wild beasts, etc. This is the version which all (the best) scholars agree on.

(2) The life story of the text-discoverer. When Mar-pa sTag-la-dbang was living in 'O-yug a famine occurred. A mother with a child came to him begging. He took pity on the child and looked after them. On inquiring their lineage, he learned that it was Drang-nga. As they were suffering from under-nourishment their eyes had gone yellow and so the child was called gSer-mig (golden eye). (240a) Later, having wandered as far as bSam-yas, he became a monk and was known as Drang-nga bTsun-pa. He joined the custodians (of the temple). Then when he was thirteen (Dad-pa Tshul-khrims and Ra-shag 'Dre-chung)

meaningless title. There is no traditional explanation for this title. Our author, without specific reason, seems to put this text among a group of texts and attributes the translation of them all to Vairocana (see *supra*, p. 163), but Slob-dpon Tenzin Namdak (*mDo gzer-mig-gi dkar-chag*, f. 3a2) tentatively suggests, supporting his view with reasons, that the text was translated into Tibetan from the language of Zhang-zhung by Sad-ne Ga'u, a scholar of Zhang-zhung and a contemporary of the king Khri-srong lDe-btsan (742–97). For other references to this text see *supra*, p. 4 n. 1.

took out the texts from Nyang-smad, etc., and divided them between themselves and (Drang-nga bTsun-pa) beside the river of Nyang-po. Drang-nga bTsun-pa said: 'I know the history (of the texts) from the beginning.' He carried off the manuscript of the *mDo gzer-mig* which comprises eighteen chapters. As Mar-pa sTag-la had been very kind to him he decided to go and offer the text to him. On the way he came upon Mar-pa sTag-la who was coming from 'O-yug. Drang-rje said: 'I have a Bon text which has just been rediscovered in bSam-yas. As you, my Lord, have been very kind to me I am going to offer it to you.' When Mar-pa saw the text he revered it profoundly and began to transcribe it. But the master copy was apparently taken back to bSam-yas by Drang-rje himself. Ra-shag 'Dre-chung (and Dad-pa Tshul-khrims) took other texts belonging to the Mental Teachings such as the *rGyud-smad bcu-bdun* and travelled to Yar-'brog where they commissioned them to Ra-ston dNgos-grub-'bar and Ra-sgom gYu-bo of whose account I have made mention earlier.[1]

(3) The transmission. (240b) Mar-pa sTag-la sent for Bya-'ong Rin-chen saying that he had a Bon text which had just been rediscovered and that he should make a copy of it for himself. So Bya-'ong Rin-chen transcribed it. On request the latter transmitted it to rMe'u lHa-ri gNyen-po and so it spread simultaneously in all directions. Further, gYung-btsun Jo-gdung and Bru bDag-nyid rJe-btsun went together to Mar-pa and asked for the text. On request gYung-(btsun Jo-gdung) transmitted it to Dam-pa the Hermit. The latter transmitted it to Yar-me-ba.[2] The latter transmitted it to Sangs-rgyas Zhu-chen. From him up to me the rosary of transmission has not been broken.

(*The discovery in Kong-'phrang*)

Texts were rediscovered in the rock of Kong-'phrang by sPrul-sku Nyang-ston. They were the five texts concerning Ma-ge spungs-dkar, the five texts concerning Ma-ge nag-po, the five texts concerning Sel-gto yar-bon, etc., but I have not seen any detailed story of the discovery.

[1] See *supra*, p. 149.

[2] Me-ston Shes-rab 'Od-zer of Yar-'brog (*STNN* 1058–1132) is one of the Four Commissioned Spiritual Sons of Dam-pa Ri-khrod-pa (see *supra*, p. 138).

(*The discovery in Mang-mkhar lcags-'phrang*)

The *Lung-bstan*[1] by Khod-spungs[2] says:

The teacher Gang-zhug Thog-rgyal
The manifestation of Ba-gor Dod-de (rGyal-ba)
Will open the door of the textual treasure in Mang-mkhar lcags-'phrang.

The text-discoverer who had been thus extolled in the prophetic text found the following texts in Mang-mkhar lcags-'phrang: (241a) The *Bya-gdong thugs-dkar*, the *Rin-po-che gling-grags*, and the *Kun-snang-gi lha-ngo bstan-pa*, etc. Altogether fifty texts were found.

(*The discovery of the Dung-phor-ma*)

The history of the Dung-phor-ma is fourfold: (1) the concealment of the textual treasure. At the time of the decadence of the Doctrine some texts were concealed in Dung-phor bkra-shis and were entrusted to the Lam-gyi bya-ra ma-drug (the six mother-guardians of the Path).

(2) Concerning the text-discoverer: the authoritative book states:

A man possessing eighteen meaningful signs will rediscover and impart it to a fortunate one.

And, the *Srid-rgyud* says:[3]

There will be one called Gu-ru rNon-rtse,[4]
The manifestation of Thad-mi Thad-ke.
He will accept the gift of Dung-phor in rTa-nag.
He will bring benefit to sentient beings and guide them.

Thus, in accordance with the prophecies he who was known as sPrul-sku Gu-ru rNon-rtse was repeatedly told by mystic goddesses that he would find a textual treasure three years before

[1] *SG*, f. 94a5.

[2] This is the family name of Dran-pa Nam-mkha'.

[3] *SG*, f. 83a5.

[4] He was born in *STNN* 1136, and is known in Buddhist histories as A-ya Bon-po lHa-'bum. He rediscovered many rNying-ma-pa texts. See *bsTan-'byung*, ff. 58b4, 90b1, and *TTGL*, f. 43a5. Yon-tan rGya-mtsho (*TTGL*, f. 227b1) erroneously indicates that the text-discoverer appeared prior to the first Rab-byung (i.e. from 1027 to 1086). Also cf. *TPS* ii, p. 727.

(his discovery). As a result he discovered the textual treasure in Dung-phor of rTa-nag.

(3) The content.[1]

(4) The transmission, Lama gZhon said:[2]

> When I, the monk, gZhon-nu, was in Khams, I was told by mystic goddesses that I should receive my share of Bon from Gu-ru-can. Accordingly I went to meet the Gu-ru and entreated him to impart to me many consecrations and precepts, etc. One day when we were preparing an offering of a sacrificial cake, lama rNon-rtse holding a roll of white silk said: 'Since I have been working on the transcription of many copies of the *Ma-rgyud* I am now exhausted. I am giving you this roll of silk to enable you to share in transcribing the texts. As you were born of gods your thoughts are exceedingly clear and calm. Transcribe the texts without letting anybody see them.' He bestowed on me the whole cycle of the *Ma-rgyud.*

On request he imparted the teaching to the two sGom-pa.[3] (242a) They imparted it to Ka-gdams Ye-rgyal.[4] The latter imparted it to Zhang-ston Khu and Zhang-ston dBon,[5] and so the transmission proceeded up till now.

(*The discovery of rMa-ston Srol-'dzin*)

The history of how rMa-ston Srol-'dzin[6] rediscovered the textual treasure. (1) How he received the prophecy concerning the textual treasure. rMa-ston Srol-'dzin, the emanation of Sad-ne Ga'u, was dwelling in 'Jad-chu-'og. He was not very well off and when he was travelling to the North in search of his fortune he came upon an ascetic in a turquoise robe and a feathered hat lying in a cave. He asked: 'What are you doing here?' 'I am not very well,' the ascetic replied, 'You have a

[1] For this see *infra*, p. 325, ll. 17–28. In this list is included the title *'Dul-ba rgyud-drug* which was already included among the texts said to be found by the three ācāryas (see *supra*, pp. 120–1) and by gNyan-ston Shes-rab Seng-ge (see *supra*, p. 153).

[2] *gZhi-lam-gyi 'grel*, f. 104a6.

[3] For these see *supra*, p. 126.

[4] Ye-shes rGyal-mtshan.

[5] Zhang-ston bSod-nams dPal-ldan, the uncle and Zhang-ston bSod-nams rGyal-mtshan, the nephew. These two transmitted the teaching to dMu-rgyal Nyi-ma rGyal-mtshan (b. *STNN* 1360), see *Ma-rgyud rgyal-ba rgya-mtsho'i dal-gyi brgyud-rim*, f. 2.

[6] Born *STNN* 1092.

gTsag-cha (I expect). I want you to help me bleed myself.' So rMa-ston began to let blood from a vein in one of his arms. Apparently some milk emerged. Realizing that the ascetic was a saintly sage, rMa-ston bowing down asked: 'What is your name?' He replied: 'Some call me Bon-zhig Nag-po, some Lama bSam-chil and others gYu-lus Bya-mgo. In Zhang-zhung I am called Gyer-mi Nyi-'od.' Pretending it was a medical text, he gave rMa-ston the *rTsa-rgyud gsang-ba bsen-thub* and said: 'The companion text to this one is in the rock of Dang-ra khyung-rdzong and you should take it out. I am going to Slob-dpon-can.'[1] (242b) rMa-ston asked who the teacher was. He replied that the teacher was Dran-pa Nam-mkha' and then went away.

(2) The discovery of the textual treasure. rMa-ston began to search for (the texts) according to the Lama's prophecy. In the Earth-male mouse year[2] he opened the door of the textual treasure (in Dang-ra khyung-rdzong). For when the priests had originally gone to the North a small box of texts had been left in Dang-ra and (later) Gyer-mi Nyi-'od had concealed the box (in Dang-ra khyung-rdzong) and entrusted it to mTsho-sman (the goddess of the lake) and lHa-btsan of (Mount) rTa-sgo.

(3) The textual content.[3]

(4) The transmission. rMa-ston transmitted (the teaching) to Zhu-chen Ye-shes Rin-chen and Bru-ston Nyi-ma rGyal-mtshan. The latter transmitted it to gYor-po Me-dpal, etc.

(*The oral tradition of Bon-zhig Khyung-nag*)

Dran-pa Nam-mkha' prophesied in the *Srid-rgyud*:[4]
There will be one called Bon-zhig Khyung-nag,
The manifestation of myself.

Accordingly Bon-zhig Khyung-nag,[5] whose coming had been

[1] i.e. a place where one's teacher resides.

[2] *STNN* 1108.

[3] For this see *infra*, p. 326, l. 26–p. 327, l. 3. In this are included the following titles: *mDzod* (for which also see *supra*, p. 8 n. 4), *Kun-snang khyab-pa'i dkyil-'khor* and *rTsa-rgyud gsang-ba bsen-thub* which were already included among the texts said to be found by gShen-chen Klu-dga' (see *supra*, p. 130). The discovery of the last of these is also attributed to Gyer-mi Nyi-'od (see *supra*, p. 159). The text *Srog-gi seg-bdar che-chung* was also already included among the texts said to have been found by Khro-tshang 'Brug-lha (see *supra*, p. 124).

[4] *SG*, f. 80b2.

[5] Born *STNN* 1103.

foreseen, received the following texts orally from Srid-pa rGyal-mo: the cycle of the *Dri-med lhan-skyes* together with its ancillary texts and the rite of gTso-mchog. He transmitted them to 'Khrul-zhig lDong-bu.

(The discovery of rMa lCam-me)

The son of rMa-ston Srol-'dzin, rMa lCam-me, was a manifestation of Dran-pa (Nam-mkha'). The *Srid-rgyud*[1] says:

There will be one called rMa-ston lCam-me,
Whom I shall have blessed.

(243b) He discovered a textual treasure which was hidden in the secret rock of rGya-bo by sKu-gshen Pra-phud. The textual content: the *gTan-tshigs nges-pa'i gal-mdo*, the *rTsod-zlog rag-sha spyi-chings*, the *Zhi-gzungs khro-gzungs gsang-gzungs* together with its six ancillary texts, the *Kun-bzang A-dkar lha-sgrub*, the *rNam-dag sgron-ma* and the *rNam-dag rgyun-mchod*. The *Mu-tra'i las-rim* is said to have been his father rMa-ston (Srol-'dzin's) manuscript. They were transmitted to rMa-ston Drang-srong. The latter transmitted them to Khu-ston lHun-grub 'Od-zer.

(Concerning the life-story of the text-discoverer, sGom-chen gYung-drung-grags)

Ba-rong sTon-pa had a son whose father died before he grew up. His mother let him collect firewood in the mountains. One day his mother, giving him a rope and some food, sent him with some friends to collect firewood (to a distant place). On the way all his friends went on ahead, but he did not feel like going with them and went to sleep by the way. In his dream a man said to him: 'You and your mother need not feel sorrow. A gift will come to you in one or two years' time.' When he woke up he (still) could see the man clearly in front of him. (244a) As he went off to sleep again pure bliss arose in him. On another occasion, in a dream he saw a vast bird covering almost the whole sky, on the crown (of its head) there was a boy of crystal one inch tall who was reciting the A-dkar sa-le-'od. When he woke up he (could remember) the A-dkar sa-le-'od and as he recited it his understanding returned to the state of the 'primeval basis'.[2] As he recited

[1] *SG*, ff. 94b7–95a1.

[2] On 'primeval basis' see *supra*, p. 53 n. 1.

it continuously his insight became (vast) like the sky for which he was known as sGom-chen gYung-drung-grags of Ba-rong. He rediscovered the (following) texts in the snowy (Mount) rTa-sgo: the *Nang dmar-tshogs-kyi-bon* and the *Drang-mkhan lha-dkar-gyi-bon*, etc., many exoteric, esoteric, and secret rGyud. The *sNyan-brgyud kun-bzang A-skor*, etc., were orally passed on to him. He transmitted both the oral word and the rediscovered texts to Gur-sgom.

(*The discovery in Sham-po'i g·ya-ma dmar-po*)

Esoteric texts[1] were rediscovered in Sham-po'i g·ya'-ma dmar-po by Bal-zho sGom-chen.

(*The discovery in 'Gog-po seng-rdzong*)

Once when 'Jing-ston lHa-dga' was sleeping in a cave (called 'Gog-po seng-rdzong) which was in the monastery called Seng-grags in 'Bri-mtshams yen-rang he was told in a prophecy that he would find a textual treasure, and he found texts there.[2]

'Jing-ston transmitted the texts to sTag-lo Tshes-pa and the latter transmitted them to Zhang-grags of Glog-skya.

(*The discovery in rDo-rje gsang-phug*)

Medical texts were rediscovered in rDo-rje gsang-phug in gTsang-stod by Bu-mtsho Srid-pa'i rGyal-po. They were the *sMan-sgrub bdud-rtsi phum-phum dgu* and the *bDud-rtsi sman-gyi rgyud dgu*.

Bu-mtsho Srid-pa'i rGyal-po transmitted them to gShen Dam-pa rGyal-tshab.[3]

(*The discovery in Yar-lha sham-po*)

Texts[4] were rediscovered in Yar-lha sham-po by the son of rMa lCam-me,[5] rMa lHa-rgod Thog-pa or rMa-ston Shes-rab Seng-ge.

[1] For list see *infra*, p. 328, ll. 9–21. In the list is included the title *Thig-le-dbyings-'chad* which was already included among the treasure said to be found by gShen-chen Klu-dga' (see *supra*, p. 130).

[2] For list see *infra*, p. 328, ll. 25–32.

[3] He is a disciple of sPa-ston dPal-mchog (b. *STNN* 1014).

[4] For list see *infra*, p. 329, ll. 3–9.

[5] He was the son of rMa-ston Srol-'dzin who was born in *STNN* 1092 (see *supra*, p. 167).

rMa-ston Shes-rab Seng-ge transmitted the texts to rMa-ston Drang-srong and the latter transmitted them to Zhu lHun-grub 'Od-zer.

(*The discovery in rGyung-srub gsang-ba*)

(245b) Texts[1] were rediscovered in the rocky cave of rGyung-srub gsang-ba by 'Or-sgom Phug-pa of 'Jad-dol as had been prophesied to him by rMa-ston (Shes-rab Seng-ge).

'Or-sgom Phug-pa transmitted the texts to sPa-ston Rin-chen lHun-grub.

(*The discovery in Ge-khod gnyan-lung*)

Texts[2] were rediscovered in Ge-khod gnyan-lung by sKyo-ston of Chu-sa, the manifestation of Glang Mu-ne-ver of Zhang-zhung and Khyung-po Legs-blo.[3]

(*The oral tradition of Mar-ston rGyal-legs*)

Texts were passed on orally to Mar-ston rGyal-legs[4] by mKha'-'gro dKar-mo sPyan-gcig-ma. They were the *Du-tri-su'i zhi-gcod* together with the ancillary text. Also many other useful preceptive texts were passed on orally to him. He transmitted the texts to rNal-'byor rTogs-pa'i Seng-ge.

(*The discovery in sKyid-mkhar sngo-phug*)

(246a) Texts were rediscovered in sKyid-mkhar sngo-phug by mTsho-bon Khyung-gsas, the manifestation of Sum-pa Mu-cho. They were the cycle of the *gYu-'brang phyug-mo*, the *sMan A-ma-ra'i sgrub-skor*, the *bDud-rtsi ne'u-le'i rgyud bcu-gnyis*, four esoteric rGyud and two exoteric rGyud, etc. mTsho-bon

[1] For list see *infra*, p. 329, ll. 12–17.

[2] For list see *infra*, p. 329, ll. 21–6.

[3] sKyo-ston and Legs-blo (Legs-pa'i Blo-gros). *SG*, f. 93b5. A clue to the date of these text-discoverers (and of a number of others whose names occur later in our text and which I will note as they come) is provided by the fact that their names are mentioned in *SG* rediscovered by Gyer Thogs-med in 1310. Whether or not we are to assume that 'rediscovered' means 'composed' and unless we believe the author of the text genuinely to have possessed the gift of foresight all names mentioned in it must at least predate 1310. It may be worth adding that *SG* contains no names of persons definitely known to have lived later than 1310.

[4] Born *STNN* 1123.

Khyung-gsas transmitted the teaching to Zhu sGrol-ba gShen-rgyal.[1]

(*The discovery in Brag-dkar bya-rgod*)

Texts were rediscovered in Brag-dkar bya-rgod in Theb-chu by sKyang-'phags Mu-la Drung-mu,[2] the manifestation of Gyer-mi Nyi-'od. They were four 'Bum: the *gYung-drung chu-'bum*, the *gNyan-'bum*, the *lHa-'bum*, and the *Ba-ga yum-'bum* in thirty volumes. Today they are in Amdo.

(*The oral tradition of Dam-pa Rang-grol*)

The *Lung-bstan*[3] says:

There will be one called Dam-pa Rang-grol,
The manifestation of Tshe-dbang Rig-'dzin.

Texts[4] were passed on orally to Dam-pa Rang-grol[5] whose coming was foreseen by Tshe-dbang Rig-'dzin.

Dam-pa Rang-grol passed them on to Shar-chung Rin-chen rGyal-mtshan.

(*The oral tradition of Grub-thob Shar-ba rNal-'byor*)

Texts were passed on orally to Grub-thob Shar-ba rNal-'byor.[6] They were the *Shar-ba'i don-dril zab-mo*, the *Phyi-nang dge-spyod-kyi yan-lag*, etc.

(*The discovery in rMa-rgyal gyal-ga*)

Texts were rediscovered in rMa-rgyal gyal-ga by the text-discoverer gYu-lo dKar-po.[7] They were the *Rigs-drug thar-lam-gyi mdo*, etc., and some other preceptive texts.

[1] He was a teacher of rMe'u Dam-pa Ri-khrod-pa (1038-1096). See *supra*, p.138.

[2] Mentioned in *SG* (f. 96a7), hence presumably before 1310 (cf. *supra*, p. 171 n. 3).

[3] *SG*, f. 85b1.

[4] For list see *infra*, p. 330, ll. 8–14.

[5] Born *STNN* 1149.

[6] A disciple of Dam-pa Rang-grol (b. in 1149, see above); see *Shar-ba rnal-'byor-gyi 'gur-'bum*, section ka, f. 3a5 *passim*.

[7] The abbot Nyi-ma bsTan-'dzin (*KTDG*, p. 4) identifies this text-discoverer as Khye'u gNyan-'theng (of whom see *supra*, p. 153).

(*The discoveries in mTho-la rmog-mgo and sKabs-gnyen mtsho-nag*)

Texts were rediscovered in mTho-la rmog-mgo by lHa-bzher gYung-drung Bla-ma and Bra-bo rGyal-ba Grags-pa;[1] they were the eleven *sKor-tshom* (the *sPon-gsas rig-'dzin-gyi skor-tshom*, etc.) Texts were rediscovered in sKabs-gnyen mtsho-nag of Tsong-kha; they were: the *rDzogs-chen nyi-ma'i snying-po*, the *dBal-phur rag-sha bdud-'dul*, the *Khro-bo dbang-chen rol-ba*, the *Rigs-drug thar-lam-gyi mdo*, the *Dran-pa'i sgrub-skor*, the *rGyud nyi-zer sgron-ma*, the *Khro-bo gting-zlog*, etc.

Bra-bo sGom-nyag (or rGyal-ba Grags-pa) (247a) transmitted the teaching to Do-khong Phyogs-med, the latter to Nag-dpe Khro-rgyal Rin-chen and the latter to his son Shes-rab-'bum.

(*The discovery of the dPon-gsas-ma*)

The history of dPon-gsas-ma is fourfold: (1) The life-story of the text-discoverer. The *Lung-bstan*[2] by Dran-pa Nam-mkha' says:

> There will be one called dByil-ston He-ru-ka,[3]
> The manifestation of myself,
> Later he will be known as Khyung-rgod-rtsal.
> He will reveal secret textual treasures.

His father was dByil-ston rDo-rje Seng-ge. From his youth he was pious and intelligent. At the age of twenty-three he became ill and for seven days he saw the life of misery through which all beings in the six kinds of world were passing. He was frightened and went to practise meditation in Ti-se shel-phug where the nine knowledge-holders, including Dran-pa Nam-mkha', gave him outer, inner, and mystic consecrations and named him Khyung-rgod-rtsal.

(2) The discovery of the textual treasure. When Khyung-rgod-rtsal went to the rock of Zhal-bzang, he saw a shining crystal swastika on a square stone like a maṇḍala in the centre of the rock. He climbed it with a rope and as he began to dig with a

[1] Mentioned in *SG* (f. 95b6) hence presumably prior to 1310 (cf. *supra*, p. 171 n. 3)

[2] *SG*, f. 80b6.

[3] He was born in (*STNN*) 1175, and he is known as Khyung-thog-rtsal or Rig-'dzin rGod-ldem in the rNying-ma-pa tradition. He rediscovered a number of rNying-ma-pa texts. See *bsTan-'byung*, f. 63b1, 82b7; *TTGL*, f. 50b1. Yon-tan rGya-mtsho (*TTGL*, f. 227a6) seems to ascribe him to the period before the first Rab-byung (i.e. from 1027 to 1086), but it is not possible as we know from the dates of his contemporaries.

chisel a door appeared. Inside the door (247b) on a square, black stone like a mandala there were five zinc-coloured bluish-green earthen vases in the four directions and centre. On the top of each vase there was a Phur-pa (dagger) having its own 'family-sign'. He opened the vases and took out the manuscripts and refilled them with grain.[1] He replaced the door just as it was before. He kept secret (his discovery) for a year and then propagated it.

(3) The textual content.[2]

(4) The multiplying of the disciples. There were Four Commissioned Ones: 'A-zha Blo-gros rGyal-mtshan and Bru 'Dul-ba rGyal-mtshan who spread the teaching in the Lower Land; the great abbot of sPa, gYung-drung Seng-ge and sPa-ston rGyal-ba Shes-rab who spread the teaching in the Upper Land. They had numerous followers.

(*The oral tradition of mTshan-ldan Drung-mu Ha-ra*)

Texts[3] were passed on orally to mTshan-ldan Drung-mu Ha-ra by the knowledge-holder sTong-rgyung mThu-chen.

mTshan-ldan Drung-mu Ha-ra transmitted the teaching to rTsi-ra 'Od-zer rGyal-mtshan.

(*The discovery of the rNam-rgyal rgya-nag-ma and rNam-rgyal zhang-zhung-ma*)

The history of the *rNam-rgyal rgya-nag-ma* and *rNam-rgyal zhang-zhung-ma* is fourfold: (1) The concealment of the textual treasure. At the time of the suppression of Bon[4] Gyim-tsha rMa-chung concealed the *rNam-rgyal zhang-zhung-ma* in Rag-phrom and (249b) Legs-tang rMang-po of China concealed the *rNam-rgyal rgya-nag-ma* in rGya'i mchod-rten ka-ru.

(2) The discovery of the textual treasure. Dran-pa (Nam-mkha') said:[5]

There will be one called dBang-ldan gShen-gsas,
The manifestation of myself,
Whose conduct will display non-attachment.

[1] This was in (*STNN*) 1198.

[2] For this see *infra*, p. 331, l. 21–p. 332, l. 23.

[3] For list see *infra*, p. 332, ll. 31–5.

[4] By Khri-srong lDe-btsan.

[5] *SG*, f. 64b4 (of which he is the official author).

He will discover textual treasures and deliver sentient beings to salvation.

The text-discoverer Go-lde 'Phags-pa or dBang-ldan gShen-gsas lHa-rje or gNyos Nyi-ma Shes-rab[1] discovered the textual treasures in both places, and made translations of the manuscripts into Tibetan from the language of the pure gods in the mystic cave of rKe-bu na-ro. He also found the flat-bell called Khri-lo gnam-grags and many other things.[2]

(3) The textual content.[3]

(4) The transmission. Go-lde 'Phags-pa transmitted the texts to Khyung-po Nang-chen Grags-pa and his nephew dPon-dge and they transmitted them to Khyung-po bSod-rgyal.[4]

(*The discovery of the Pom-ra-ma*)

The history of Pom-ra-ma is threefold: (1) The discovery of the textual treasure. Texts were rediscovered in the marked rock on the right-hand corner of rMa Pom-ra by the text-discoverer sPrul-sku Kyu-ra (Blo-gros rGyal-mtshan).

(2) The textual content.[5]

(3) The transmission of the teaching to his disciples. There were the Four Commissioned Ones: sPrul-sku Kyu-ra commissioned the *Zhi-khro yongs-rdzogs* to Tsong-kha'i dGe-bshes, the *Thugs-sgrub* to 'Dan-ma Ri-ba, the *Go-cha che-chung* to rKo-ston gYung-drung and the *sGrol-byed spu-gri sum-cu* to Khrom A-dpal. On request the nephew of the text-discoverer (sPrul-sku Kyu-ra) Shes-rab 'Od-zer transmitted the whole teaching to rGya-ru Khro-bo rGyal-mtshan.

(*The discoveries of Bon-zhig gYung-drung Gling-pa*)

At the age of twenty-three Bon-zhig gYung-drung Gling-pa rediscovered the *rDzogs-chen gser-thur*, the *Dran-pa yab-sras-kyi sgrub-pa* together with the ancillary text and the *Pom-ra* cycle which had been concealed by Vairocana in sPa-gro stag-tshang.[6] On the mount of Phyug-mo-dpal in Nyang-stod he

[1] Mentioned in *SG* (f. 95b7), hence, presumably, before 1310 (cf. *supra*, p. 171 n. 3).

[2] Including Buddhist texts. See *bsTan-'byung*, ff. 65b7, 89b7.

[3] For this see *infra*, p. 333, ll. 22–34.

[4] bSod-nams rGyal-mtshan.

[5] For this see *infra*, p. 334, ll. 4–16

[6] *STNN* 1250; so Bon-zhig was born in 1228. He is known as rDo-rje Gling-pa

rediscovered the *Tshe-dbang bod-yul-ma*[1] comprising the basic text, the ancillary texts and the instructive texts.[2] On the Mount of Sha-ba in the North he rediscovered (251a) the following texts: the *Bon-sku kun-bzang-gi khrid-yig* together with the *Srung-ma srid-rgyal drel-dkar-ma*; the *Longs-sku rigs-lnga'i khrid-yig* together with the *Srung-ma (srid-rgyal) drel-nag-ma*, the *sPrul-sku gShen-rab-kyi khrid-yig* together with the *Srung-ma (srid-rgyal) drel-nag ma*, the *biography of Vairocana*, and the *Ma-'ong lung-bstan*. He also found a 'wishing jewel' of gods and water-spirits and the ear-turquoise of Ne'u-chung[3] together with its history and the *bTsan* cycle in Re-kyang shang-mtha'. Underneath the threshold of the temple in gTsang-'phrang he found a wonderful image of gShen-rab made of light-green turquoise which had been relegated there by Bodhi Sattva.[4] Now the image is kept in the hand of royal Bru.

Bon-zhig gYung-drung Gling-pa transmitted the *Tshe-dbang* cycle to mTha'-bzhi Ye-shes Rang-shar and then it descended to the nine foreknown spiritual sons. Bon-zhig gYung-drung Gling-pa transmitted the *Dran-pa* cycle, etc., to Bru mTshungs-med bSod-nams Blo-gros and the latter transmitted them to rDza-bo gYung-drung rGyal-mtshan.

(*The works of Bru mTshungs-med bSod-nams Blo-gros*)

The *Tshe-dbang bod-yul-ma'i lung-bstan*[5] says:

In the family of Bru there will be one whose name is bSod-
nams,

in the rNying-ma-pa tradition and he rediscovered a number of rNying-ma-pa texts. See *bsTan-'byung*, ff. 66a3, 94b7; *TTGL*, f. 81a3. This is confirmed by Yon-tan rGya-mtsho who vaguely indicates that this text-discoverer appeared in the fifth Rab-byung (1267 to 1326, *TTGL*, f.228a)

[1] A Tanka of this cycle is to be found in *TPS*, p. 554, no. 120 (Plate 155). However, Tucci, not knowing the subject of the Tanka, judges it to be based on Buddhist tantric theories.

[2] This was in (*STNN*) 1269. But see n. 5 *infra*.

[3] Ne'u-chung was a daughter of sTon-pa gShen-rab, see *gZer-mig*, vol. kha, f. 13b6.

[4] On whom see *supra*, p. 82.

[5] The 10th Shog-dril (f. 20a2), a section of the *Tshe-dbang bod-yul-ma* said to have been rediscovered by Bon-zhig gYung-drung Gling-pa in (*STNN*) 1269 (see *supra*, p. 175). Cf. *infra*, p. 177 n. 1. It is unusual for *STNN* to date the discovery of a text earlier than he dates a name which is the subject of a prophecy in the text. And this date may be incorrect, see Introduction, pp. xxxvii-xxxviii.

The manifestation of (Yid-kyi) Khye'u-chung,
He who makes contact with him will attain salvation.

Bru mTshungs-med bSod-nams Blo-gros,[1] whose coming had been predicted, wrote several books: (251b) They were the *mDzod-kyi gzhal-bya bsdus-pa*, the *gSang-sngags ngag-don*, the *sPyi-spungs sdom-tshig nang-bskyed-kyi rtsa-'khor gnas-lugs*, etc. He also composed many rites: the *dPon-gsas bla-ma'i sgrub-thabs*, the *Pom-ra* cycle, the *Shel-khrab* cycle, the *rNam-sras zhal-gzigs-kyi bstod-bskul*, etc.

(The discovery in Yang-dben yer-ba'i brag-rdzong)

Texts were rediscovered in Yang-dben yer-ba'i brag-rdzong by Gang-ston and Klu-ston. They were the *sNang-ba 'od-ldan-gyi rgyud*, the *gNam-phyi'i bdud-rtsi bum-sgrub*, and the *Zhang-zhung-bon lha-rgod drag-bdar*, etc.

(The discovery of sGom-pa Rin-chen)

Texts are said to have been rediscovered in the right-hand corner of rMa-rgyal Pom-ra by the monk sGom-pa Rin-chen of Khams. They were the *rDzogs-chen nyi-ma'i snying-po*,[2] the *dBal-phur nag-po bdud-'dul* cycle, and the *Khro-bo dbang-chen rol-ba*,[2] etc.

(The discovery in sKu-bla gangs-brag)

Texts were rediscovered in sKu-bla gangs-brag by the text-discoverer Gung-grags of Kong-po. They were the *mDo-sde bskal-pa bzang-po* in two volumes, the *Bon-spyod*, etc.

(The discovery in the temple of Khom-mthing)

Many texts of the 'Bon of Cause' were concealed by (252a) Khyung-po lHa-bzher, Nyang dPal-mthong and lHa-sgra of Zhang-zhung in the first treasury of the temple of Khom-mthing. Later the texts were rediscovered by sPa-bon Khyung-thog and rGyud-ston Ra-dza of La-stod. They were the *sNang-gshen-rgyud g·yung-drung gsal-byed*, the *rTsa-ba rin-chen rgya-mdud*,

[1] *STNN* 1277–1341. He was an abbot of gYas-ru dben-sa-kha (see *supra*, p. 140).

[2] These were also rediscovered in sKabs-gnyen mtsho-nag. See *supra*, p. 173.

the *Bon-khog srid-pa rnam-grol*, the *Lag-len rin-chen sgron-ma*, etc. sPa-bon Khyung-thog and rGyud-ston Ra-dza transmitted the texts to lHa 'Od-dkar and the latter to gNyer-ston of gYor-po.

(*The discovery in bSam-yas ca-ti dmar-po*)

sPrul-sku Bu-kyi Bu-nam rediscovered a manuscript in bSam-yas ca-ti dmar-po and handed it over to Glang-'od La-thung who, after deciphering the symbolic letters of the manuscript, produced the following texts: the *A-bsve brag-btsan sgrub-skor*, and the *Than-srog dril-sgrub*, etc., Glang-'od La-thung transmitted the texts to Khyung-po Nang-chen Grags-pa and the latter to bSod-rgyal.

(*The discovery in Rin-chen brag-rdzong*)

Texts were apparently rediscovered in Rin-chen brag-rdzong in gTsang by Bla-ma dBu-rnal of rDzong-brag. They were the *dMag-dpon gsang-sgrub*, etc.

(*The discovery in the East of lHa-sa'i phur-sgo*)

Texts were rediscovered in the East of lHa-sa'i phur-sgo by sBas Dang-la 'Byams-pa and Khyung-po Klu-mgon. They were (252b) the *mGon-lha dkar-po sgrub-tshogs*, the *dBal dang ma-tshogs-kyi sgrub-pa*, the *gSang-sgrub che-chung rgyud-sde*, the *gSang-ba 'phrul-gyi lde-mig*, the *Drang-don-gyi rgyud-sde*, and some texts of the *mTho-thog spyi-rgyug-gi bon.*

(*The discovery in lHo-ri nag-po*)

Texts were rediscovered in lHo-ri nag-po by the text-discoverer Khu-'dzin 'Jing-nag, the manifestation of gNam-gshen mThong-grags. They were the *bDud-kyi bzhung-sgrub*, the *bTsan-sgrub che-chung*, the *Klu'i mnan-gtad snying-gzer*, the *gSas-mkhar dbang-gi ti-ka*, the *gSas-mkhar rgyud-mo-che*, and the *lHa-bran bon-sde.*

(*The discovery of sPrul-sku La-byi rDa-rma*)

sPrul-sku La-byi rDa-rma, as foretold to him in prophecy by Brag-btsan, rediscovered the following texts: the *A-bsve thugs-sgrub las-tshogs drug-pa*, etc. He transmitted the texts to Do-skya bSod-nams rGyal-mtshan of A-khol.

(*The discovery in Brag-dmar rtse-gsum*)

Texts were rediscovered in Brag-dmar rtse-gsum by the hunter, Lo-pa Ma-ngor, the manifestation of Ma-hor sTag-gzig. He is said to have rediscovered nine different rGyud such as the *gShen-rab lha-mdzod chen-po'i rgyud*, the *'Khor-lo rgyud-sbyang-gi rgyud*, the *gShin-'dur phra-mo'i rgyud*, the *'Dus-byas bon-gyi rgyud*, etc.

(*The discovery of Se-gnyan Zhig-po*)

(253a) Se-gnyan Zhig-po of rGya-rong rediscovered three boxes of texts in the right-hand corner of dMu-rdo g·yung-drung spungs-rtse in rGya-rong.

The content of the boxes.[1]

(*The oral tradition of Gling-gshen Mu-la Thogs-med*)

Texts were passed on orally to Gling-gshen Mu-la Thogs-med by sTong-rgyung (mThu-chen). They were the *gSer-'od nor-bu 'od-'bar*, the cycle of the *Char-'bebs klu-sgrub*, the *sGra-bla rgyal-mo* cycle, etc.

(*The discoveries of Gu-ru Ban-chung*)

In Zangs-'brug 'khyil-ba the text-discoverer Gu-ru Ban-chung found the *Ku-vai-ra* cycle, and the cycle of the *Char-'beb yang-dag-ma*. In 'Brug-ri khung-mgo in rGya-rong he found the *Yongs-su Dag-pa* cycle, and the (254a) *gSas-mkhar me-ri 'khyil-ba*. In gNyan-tshungs in Khams he found four mDo; the *Dung-lo ljon-pa*, the *gYu-lo ljon-pa*, the *gSer-lo ljon-pa*, and the *Zangs-lo ljon-pa*. In rMa Pom-ra he found the *Rab-gnas spur-chog*, etc.

(*The discovery in rDo-di gangs-dkar*)

The text-discoverer lHun-grub Thogs-med came upon profound texts such as the *sKye-sgo gcod-pa'i mdo*, etc., which had been concealed in rDo-di gangs-dkar by the nine priests: Dran-pa (Nam-mkha'), etc.

(*The oral tradition of rDza-bo Rig-pa Rang-shar*)

Texts were passed on orally to rDza-bo Rig-pa Rang-shar by Tshe-dbang Rig-'dzin in the West of dMu-rdo in rGya-rong.

[1] For this see *infra*, p. 336, l. 28–p. 337, l. 13.

They were the *rDzogs-chen lta-ba thog-'bebs* together with its commentary. Also the cycle of the *gSang-'dus khyung-sprul sad-srung*, the *Drang-mkhan*, etc.

(*The discoveries of Gyer Thogs-med*)

A. (1) The concealment of the textual treasure. At the time of the suppression of Bon Legs-tang rMang-po concealed many texts at the top of a rock like a lion opening its mouth wide, and in the right-hand shoulder of sBar-zhabs brag-dkar in *mDo-smad* together with the guide and sealed them up. He said prayers.

(2) (254b) Concerning the text-discoverer, the *Srid-pa rgyud-kyi kha-byang*[1] says:

> A man called Gyer Thogs-med of the family of dBra, the manifestation of Zla-ba rGyal-mtshan, will open the door of the textual treasure in sBar-zhabs brag-dkar.

(3) The discovery of the textual treasure. When Gyer Thogs-med[2] was twenty-two in a vision he saw many ascetics, one of whom, having the appearance of an ācārya, said to him: 'We have come here from India and Zhang-zhung. In sBar-zhabs brag-dkar in mDo-smad there is a secret textual treasure and you are to take it out.' When he went to the place and was staying there the Textual Guardian displayed various miracles to him. Then Srid-pa rGyal-mo letting him see her face said to him: 'In the centre of the cairn of sBar-zhabs brag-dkar there is a guide to the textual treasure written on a long stone.' Accordingly after searching he found the long stone on which (the following instruction) was written: 'At a cubit's length beneath this point is the textual treasure. He who takes it out should make an offering of a black sheep with a white head to the Textual Guardian and place a vase containing five jewels in the place of the textual treasure. He should keep his discovery secret for nine months.' Then as he began to dig manuscripts appeared.[3]

Two arrows' lengths away from here there were two caves

[1] *SG*, f. 96b1.

[2] He is also known as Khod-po Blo-gros Thogs-med and rediscovered texts in (*STNN*) 1301 when he was twenty-two. Thus he was born in 1280.

[3] For the list of texts see *infra*, p. 338, ll. 20–38.

with a black pool like a copper bowl between them, in which there was a black snake the size of a spear. Beside the pool was the cycle of the *Yas-stag rang-'gros*, but he did not take it out. Since in the inner cave there were various cups made of precious stones, he wished to go into it, but as the snake began to look ferocious, he did not dare. In the outer cave there were ten relics of gShen-rab and the skull of Bram-ze sKye-bdun. He took these.

B. (1) The concealment of the textual treasure in rTa-gnyan pha-bong bon-mo. The great lo-tsā-ba Vairocana concealed a textual treasure in rTa-gnyan pha-bong bon-mo and said prayers.

(2) The discovery of the textual treasure. One day in a vision Gyer Thogs-med saw an ascetic carrying a trident who said to him: 'If you take care to venerate sKal-pa bZang-mo you will receive a gift.' (256a) The following year in a vision he saw a boy wearing white silk who said to him: 'In consequence of your previous acts you are to take the textual treasure of rTa-gnyan pha-bong bon-mo in the Iron-male dog year and propagate it in the Iron-female pig year.'[1] In the early morning on the twelfth of the first autumn month (of the Iron-dog year) a red man wearing a red silk robe and a tanned leather helmet, riding on a red horse and carrying a noose of snake in his hand said to him: 'I am bTsan-rgod dMar-po. Follow me and I will give you the gift which is in (rTa-gnyan) pha-bong bon-mo.' Having said that he disappeared by transforming himself into a hurricane. In the evening Gyer was told in a prophecy by Srid-pa rGyal-mo: 'Seven spans away from here there is a guide to the textual treasure.' In the morning he went to the place where after searching for a while he found the guide. It said: 'Three fathoms down from here there is a self-made door in the rock. Inside there are thirty-four rGyud, the relics of Enlightened Ones, golden images, and the 'Bum written in gold.' He opened the self-made door in the rock which was closed with a flat stone. He took out the golden images, the 'Bum written in gold and all the manuscripts (of thirty-four rGyud).

(3) The textual content.[2]

(4) The multiplying of the disciples. Gyer Thogs-med had

[1] These years are 1310 and 1311.

[2] For this see *infra*, p. 339, l. 31–p. 340, l. 2. Some texts were passed on orally to Gyer Thogs-med (see *infra*, p. 340, ll. 3–4).

many followers such as the Seven Dung-dkar Thogs-pa, etc., and in particular there were the Four Commissioned Ones who spread the teaching far and wide.

(*The oral tradition of sPrul-sku Blo-ldan sNying-po*)

Texts were passed on orally to sPrul-sku Blo-ldan sNying-po[1] by the knowledge-holders and mystic goddesses such as sTang-chen dMu-tsha Gyer-med, etc. (257a). They were in four groups.[2]

sPrul-sku Blo-ldan sNying-po transmitted the texts to Bhe-tsha Grags-pa rGyal-mtshan, etc., and so they flourished.

(*The mental textual treasure of dMu-gshen Nyi-ma rGyal-mtshan*)

As dMu-gshen Nyi-ma rGyal-mtshan[3] was blessed by gSang-mchog mThar-thug he obtained power over a vast treasury of mental textual treasure and his enlightened understanding of the one thousand six hundred maṇḍala was immense. His mental textual treasure consists of twelve volumes, including the (257b) *dKyil-'khor bcu-drug*, etc.

(*The oral tradition of sPrul-sku Khro-gnyen rGyal-mtshan*)

Texts were passed on orally to sPrul-sku Khro-gnyen.[4] They were the *bsKal-bzang mdo* in two volumes, the cycle of the *gSang-gcod yid-bzhin nor-bu*,[5] etc.

(*The discovery in Ra-sa rdzong-mgo*)

The text-discoverer called 'Tsho-sprul found a pair of silver vases which had been used at consecrations by Dran-pa (Nam-mkha'), the father, and (Tshe-dbang Rig-'dzin) his son, in Ra-sa rdzong-mgo in lCi. 'Tsho-sprul also found the text of the *Kun-bzang thugs-sgrub rin-chen sgron-me* and the *Ge-khod me-ri gyad-phur-gyi gzhung-mchod*. The former has become widely known but the latter has never been transcribed. The original manuscripts and one of the silver vases have remained in the

[1] Born *STNN* 1360.

[2] See *infra*, p. 340, ll. 10–22. Exoterical Texts (p. 340, ll. 10–14); Esoterical Texts (p. 340, ll. 15–17); Secret Texts (p. 340, ll. 18–20); Ultimate Secret Texts (p. 340, ll. 21–2).

[3] Born *STNN* 1360.

[4] He received the Oral Tradition in (*STNN*) 1386.

[5] This rite was published in India by the abbot of Phyug-so, gYung-drung rGyal-mtshan in 1966.

hands of his descendants till this day. The other silver vase is in the hands of the powerful Zhu.

(*The discovery in Kha-shu ra-'dra*)

Texts were rediscovered in Kha-shu ra-'dra by U-go gYung-drung-'bum. They were the *Khro-bo dbang-drag*, the *gSang-gcod*, the *gSang-ba 'bum-chen*, etc.

(*The discovery in Pha-bong gru-bzhi*)

Texts were rediscovered in Pha-bong gru-bzhi of 'Jing by Pho-chen Nam-mkha' 'Od-zer and Gar-tsha bSod-nams rGyal-mtshan. They were the *Khro-klong rnam-gsum* and the *Pom-ra'i sgrub-skor*. They also found four sharīrām made from the spittle of gShen-rab. (258a) The sharīrām, the guide, and the manuscripts have remained in the hands of their descendants till this day.

(*The discovery in Brag-dmar ke-ru*)

The *Srid-rgyud*[1] says:

There will be one called mTha'-bzhi Mi-nub gYung-drung rGyal-po,
The manifestation of Tshe-dbang Rig-'dzin.

Texts were rediscovered in Brag-dmar ke-ru by mTha'-bzhi Mi-nub gYung-drung rGyal-po[2] whose coming had been foreseen in the prophetic book. There were eighteen different texts, the *Bya-ra ma-dgu*, etc.

(*The discovery in Brag-dkar yang-dben*)

The *Srid-rgyud*[3] says:

There will be one called Ngu-za Nyi-ma,
Who is blessed by Gyer-mi Nyi-'od.

Texts were rediscovered in Brag-dkar yang-dben by Ngu-za Nyi-ma.[4] They were the *bsKal-pa bzang-po mdo-sde* and the *lDe-mig skor-tshom*.

[1] *SG*, f. 96a3.
[2] His presence in *SG* seems to place him before 1310 (cf. *supra*, p. 171 n. 3).
[3] *SG*, f. 96a4.
[4] See n. 2. *supra*.

(*The discovery in 'Dzing kha-rag ldong-phrom*)

Dran-pa Nam-mkha' states in the *Srid-rgyud*:[1]

A man called A-thang Yon-rin whom I have blessed will receive the gift in 'Dzing kha-rag ldom-phrom.

A-thang yon-rin[2] found the three cycles of *Zhang-zhung sgra-bla-ma* in 'Dzing kha-rag ldong-phrom.

(*The visual letters of Rong-bon gYung-drung 'Od-zer*)

Letters of light appeared before Rong-bon gYung-drung 'Od-zer.[3] (They spelt out) the *sTag-la spu-gri dkar-nag dmar-gsum*, the cycle of the *dBal-chen gsang-ba thugs-rgyud* and the cycle of *bTsan bDud Keng gsum.*

(*The oral tradition of sTag-za Rin-chen mTsho-mo*)

(258b) Texts were passed on orally to sTag-za Rin-chen mTsho-mo. They were the three rGyud of Ma-rgyud,[4] the cycle of the *Bla-ma yi-dam mkha'-'gro*, the *Ma-rgyud las-tshogs gter-phreng*, the *Tshe-dbang* cycle, the *bKa'-srung yum-sras sde-lnga*, the *'Pho-ba'i man-ngag*, the *Dug-bsal*, etc.

(*The oral tradition of dBu-za Rin-chen-gsal*)

Texts were passed on orally to dBu-za Rin-chen-gsal. They were the *gCod-gyi gdams-pa*, etc.

(*The discovery in Gab-tog Brag-ri*)

Texts were rediscovered in Gab-tog brag-ri in rGya-rong by Gu-ru Yon-tan Seng-ge. They were the cycles of the *Char-'beb g·yu-mtsho mer-ba*, the cycle of the *Tso-mi char-'beb dngul-g·yu-ma*, the *Ma-'ong lung-bstan sde-drug*, and the *gTer-srung Srid-rgyal* cycle.

(*The oral tradition of Gling-gshen bSod-nams Blo-gros*)

Texts were passed on orally to Gling-gshen bSod-nams Blo-gros. They were the *Ma-gsum-gcod* and some other small rites.

[1] *SG*, f. 96a6.

[2] See *supra*, p. 183 n. 2.

[3] Mentioned in *Tshe-dbang bod-yul-ma'i lung-bstan* (f. 20a5), hence before 1269 (cf. *supra*, p. 176 n. 5).

[4] This was also rediscovered by Gu-ru rNon-rtse. See *supra*, p. 166.

(The discovery in Kha-ba dkar-po)

Texts were rediscovered in Kha-ba dkar-po in Tsha-ba-rong by Khyung-po bKra-shis rGyal-mtshan.[1] They were the *Dran-pa A-dkar dgongs-'dus*, etc., by Vairocana.

(The discovery in Tshe-spungs gsang-ba)

Texts were rediscovered in Tshe-spungs gsang-ba by gYung-drung Tshe-dbang rGyal-po: the cycle of the *rDzogs-chen gser-gyi yang-zhun*, the *Srid-rgyal* cycle, etc.

(The oral tradition of Shel-zhig gYung-drung rGyal-po)

(259a) Texts[2] were passed on orally to Shel-zhig gYung-drung rGyal-po.[3]

(The oral tradition and discovery of sPrul-sku Sangs-rgyas Gling-pa)

sPrul-sku Sangs-rgyas Gling-pa[4] was responsible for the oral tradition and discoveries of texts and other items.[5]

(The discovery of Rig-'dzin Kun-grol Grags-pa)

The textual discovery of Rig-'dzin Kun-grol Grags-pa[6] consisted of the *Ma-mo rbod-gtong snang-srid zil-gnon-gyi sgrub-skor*, the *rTsa-ṙlung mkha'-'gro gsang-mdzod*, etc. His mental textual treasure consisted of the *Zhi-khro dgongs-'dus*, the *mKha'-'gro dgongs-'dus*, the *Bla-ma dgongs-'dus*, the *dMar-khrid dgongs-'dus*, etc. Furthermore, he composed many preceptive books and guides, etc.[7]

Now some of 'The Others' accept the teachings of the Four Recent Manifestations, viz. Blo-ldan sNying-po, Mi-shig rDo-rje, Sangs-rgyas Gling-pa, and Kun-grol Grags-pa as Late

[1] Mentioned in *SG* (f. 59b3), hence presumably before 1310 (cf. *supra*, p. 171 n. 3).

[2] For list see *infra*, p. 342, ll. 14–21.

[3] He is also known as Mi-shig rDo-rje and some Buddhist texts also were passed on orally to him, see *bsTan-'byung*, ff. 73a1, 92a1.

[4] Born *STNN* 1705.

[5] For list see *infra*, p. 342 ll. 23–33.

[6] Born *STNN* 1700. For a brief life-story of him see bKra-shis rGyal-mtshan, *Man-ngag rin-po-che a-khrid-kyi bla-ma brgyud-pa'i rnam-thar pad-ma dkar-po'i 'phreng-ba*, ff. 33b3–35b3.

[7] Kun-grol Grags-pa also wrote a general religious history of Tibet entitled *bsTan-pa spyi-yi 'byung-khungs* which is not listed here.

Textual Treasures claiming that the name of Bon has been given to unimaginable Buddhist teachings intended for the training of sentient beings by manifestations of the great O-rgyan and his disciples, since not being contrary to the 'Four Perceptive Seals' of View and Conduct,[1] they appear to constitute a sure path to enlightenment. These assertions are unacceptable since they are ill-considered. (260a) The nature of phenomena is the formless Void. The *mDzod*[2] says:

> As all phenomena
> Are ultimately the Void;
> Full attainment
> From its origin is immune to birth or rebirth;
> All phenomena have the character of Voidness.

When Bon is understood as Voidness there is nothing to choose between Bon and Chos. The definition Bon or Chos is only a matter of names.[3] In reality they are without substance. They are just an everyday form of words and letters the purpose of which is to protect all sentient beings from anxiety both ephemeral and perpetual. The *mDo*[4] says:

By definition Bon means unfailing protection. Therefore, Chos is not given the name of Bon. Chos and Bon each concern different subjects and have different words to express them. Bon itself is a word which defines. The *mDzod*[5] says:

> The notion of name in the three worlds,
> Implies self-definition. (260b)
> The notion of word in the three worlds,
> Implies discrimination.

Thus name and word are expressive speech forms. The subjects expressed in our system of Bon are the Triple Doctrine,[6] the

[1] They are: *'dus-byas thams-cad mi-rtag-pa'o / zag-pa dang bcas-pa thams-cad sdug-bsngal-ba'o / bon thams-cad ni stong-zhing bdag-med-pa'o / mya-ngan las 'das-pa thams-cad ni zhi-zhing bde-ba'o /* See *Bon-'chad mkhas-pa'i 'gul-rgyan*, f. 6b6. For a full discussion on these see Khod-po sKal-bzang rGyal-mtshan, *bsTan-grags-kyi brgal-lan drang-por bshad-pa lha-mi dgyes-pa'i 'bel-gtam*, f. 30a4.

[2] *mDzod*, p. 102.

[3] Concerning the way Tibetans normally use the words Bon and Chos see Snellgrove, *Nine Ways*, p. 1.

[4] I cannot identify this text.

[5] *mDzod*, p. 90.

[6] This consists of dka'-spyad-kyi sde, sla-'gyur-gyi sde, and gnyis-ka ma-yin-pa'i sde. For details of these see *gZer-mig*, vol. ka, f. 125a3.

Two Truths,[1] etc., i.e. not those of the Chos of which Bon is alleged to be the false name. If Chos had merely been called Bon then it would only be (a mass of) words devoid of real significance. For instance, if a man is called lHa-sbyin, it does not mean that lHa-sbyin is necessarily in him. If, according to the assertion of 'The Others', the teachings of the Four Manifestations, not being contrary to the 'Four Preceptive Seals', appear to constitute a sure path of enlightenment, then the earlier Bon textual treasures and earlier Bon doctrine would not teach anything of the path of enlightenment. It is as if someone were expounding the history of Bon without ever having seen any Bon texts. It is just tendentious talk.

It would be contradictory to suppose that the late Bon of the Four Manifestations was nothing but the teaching of O-rgyan and his followers, for it has been transmitted from the Enlightened One perfected in the three Bodies of Bon.[2] (261a) There is no difference in profundity between the earlier and late Bon. Bon or Chos are just appellations, in reality they are changeless. To put it concisely, Enlightened Ones in their unceasing efforts and compassion as they labour for the welfare of sentient beings have made manifest temporary revelations of both Bon and Chos. Therefore, the words and letters that for everyday purposes come down from the Three Bodies of Bon are called Bon, the words and letters that come down from the Three Bodies of Chos are called Chos. We follow different doctrines to achieve different purposes. Therefore, since the late Bon was transmitted from the Three Bodies of Bon it is called Bon, not Chos. If there are other teachings which come down from the Three Bodies of Chos (even if they are mingled with Bon), they may rightly be called Chos and I do not object to their being called Chos.

(*The discovery in Dang-ra khyung-rdzong*)

(261b) Dran-pa (Nam-mkha') concealed the *Khro-bo lha-rgod thod-pa snang-srid zil-gnon-gyi sgrub-pa* and its ancillary text in Dang-ra khyung-rdzong during the suppression of the Doctrine and entrusted them to a Textual Guardian. Later sKu-mdun

[1] These are kun-rdzob-kyi bden-pa and don-dam-gyi bden-pa corresponding to the Buddhist Savritisatyam, Paramārthasatyam (*Mvy* 6544, 6545).

[2] For the reference concerning these see *supra*, p. 53 n. 1.

bSod-nams Blo-gros[1] rediscovered them after receiving prophetic instructions from a mystic goddess. In the first month of the Iron-female hare year[2] when the period of secrecy imposed by the mystic goddess was over he wrote down on Tibetan paper the manuscript of the texts which was thirty lines long. Then he transmitted them to his spiritual son sKam-rigs gYung-drung Nyi-rgyal. Texts were also passed on orally to him. They were the *Du-tri-su mun-sel sgron-ma'i gzhung*, etc., and he transmitted them to sNang-ston Zla-ba rGyal-mtshan.[3]

(*The discovery of dBal-'bar sTag-slag-can*)

Texts were apparently rediscovered by dBal-'bar sTag-slag-can.[4] They were the rGyud of dBal-phur and its rites, the *bKa'-skyong drel-nag* cycle, etc.

(*The discovery of bDe-chen Gling-pa*)

The coming of my lama, bDe-chen Gling-pa,[5] the fame of whose outer, inner, and secret names pervaded the upper and lower lands of Amdo and Khams, (262a) was foreseen in a prophetic book as was also the receipt of the gift of textual treasure. The *gShin-rje gshed-nag-gi rgyud*[6] says:

Then when seven generations have passed,
A son blessed by the great teacher will arise,
In one of the four evil years with the name of Mi-'gyur.
In Uḍḍiyāna and the Celestial Sphere he will receive gifts.
He will be the Master of the thirteen secret Bon,
In particular, (of the teachings) which completely disappeared.
In the hermitage of Me-tog spungs-mdzes in Uḍḍiyāna,
He will meet the knowledge-holders and receive gifts from them.
By diffusing all the Bon which had disappeared,
He will spread the Doctrine far and wide.

The holy text-discoverer, whose coming was mentioned in the prophetic book, went to the cemetery of Uḍḍiyāna, the great

[1] *STNN*: 1784–1835. He became abbot in the monastery of sMan-ri in (*STNN*) 1810. On sMan-ri see *supra*, p. 142.

[2] This was in 1821.

[3] He was born in (*STNN*) 1796 and founded the monastery of gYung-drung-gling in (*STNN*) 1834.

[4] Born *STNN* 1832

[5] Born *STNN* 1833.

[6] This seems to be a work of gSang-sngags Gling-pa (see *infra*, p. 346, l. 17), but since it is not available I cannot trace the passage.

secret 'Celestial Sphere', at the age of thirteen and was commissioned to discover the thirteen great textual treasures belonging to the classes of exoteric, esoteric, secret, and ultimate secret Bon, a rGyud, a Lung, and a Man-ngag in each class making up twelve of the texts, the thirteenth belonging to none of these types.[1]

(263a) Many texts were also passed on orally to bDe-chen Gling-pa. He transmitted all his profound teachings to his four Commissioned Ones.

(The discovery of gSang-sngags Gling-pa)

The *Kha-byang*[2] says:

There will be one who, for the welfare of sentient beings, will open the door of textual treasure in four great places,
Twenty-five gifts of profound textual treasures will be bestowed on him.

Texts were rediscovered by the text-discoverer gSang-sngags Gling-pa[3] belonging to the classes of exoteric, esoteric, secret, and extraordinary texts.[4]

(The discovery of bDe-chen dBang-mo)

Texts were rediscovered by mKha'-'gro bDe-chen dBang-gi sGron-ma.[5] They were the *mKha'-'gro'i bka'-thang* in one volume and the *sNying-thig bcu-gsum*, etc.

Many textual treasures and oral traditions are not included here though they exist in the central and borderlands, but since no catalogue of them was available to me I have not been able to record them. Those of which I have made mention are taken from the histories written by holy persons whose discernment in the common and extraordinary fields is very extensive and

[1] For the list of texts see *infra*, p. 345, l. 26–p. 346, l. 5. The titles in the list are grouped under the following headings: Exoterical Texts (p. 345, ll. 26–9); Esoterical Texts (p. 345, ll. 30–3); Secret Texts (p. 345, l. 34–p. 346, l. 5).

[2] This passage I cannot trace in the manuscript of *SG* at my disposal.

[3] Born *STNN* 1864. For a brief biography see bKra-shis rGyal-mtshan, *Man-ngag rin-po-che A-khrid-kyi bla-ma brgyud-pa'i rnam-thar pad-ma dkar-po'i 'phreng-ba*, ff. 43a3–44b6.

[4] For list see *infra*, p. 346, ll. 13–28. In the list the titles are grouped under four headings: Exoterical Texts (p. 346, ll. 13–14); Esoterical Texts (p. 346, ll. 15–21); Secret Texts (p. 346, ll. 22–5); Extraordinary Texts (p. 346, ll. 26–8).

[5] Born *STNN* 1868.

who are known as infallible authorities. I have not just accepted whatever I (saw) or heard. So it is said:

> The country is full of false, lying, and specious textual treasures,
> And such as have no knowledge of doctrine and are fond of arguing and women.

Thus there are not only demons who pretend to be text-discoverers in order to undermine the Doctrine, (264a) but, because of the ineffable karmic forces which govern sentient beings, false textual treasures, which bring their ill-wishing to fruition, are numerous among ourselves and 'The Others'. They do great evil to the Doctrine.

Finally, the works by the scholar-ascetics of Bru, Zhu, sPa, and rMe'u; (as well as) the works of Me,[1] gNyos,[1] 'Gro-mgon,[2] sGa-ston,[3] sKyabs-ston,[4] mNyam-med Chen-po,[5] etc.—whose comings were foretold in prophetic books—are numerous and well deserve to be included in the category of bKa'-brten, but fearing to be prolix (I have not included them here).

III.[6] (*Their classification into Southern, Northern, Central, Khams, and recent textual treasures*)

a. The textual treasures classified into five (divisions), viz. Southern, Northern, Central, etc.
b. The textual treasures reduced to bKa' ('Original Words') and bKa'-brten (Dependent on the 'Original Words')
c. Digression concerning the duration of the Doctrine into the future[7]

a. i. The principal texts of the Northern Textual Treasures are those of the three ācāryas of Nepal. Other textual treasures which come into this category are those rediscovered by 'Phrang-lha'i dBang-phyug, Mar-pa 'Phen-bzang, Khro-'brug, gZe-ston

[1] These were abbots of gYas-ru dben-sa-kha (see *supra*, p. 140).
[2] 'Gro-mgon Blo-gros rGyal-mtshan, an abbot of gYas-ru dben-sa-kha (see *supra*, p. 140).
[3] sGa-ston Tshul-khrims rGyal-mtshan, not quoted—to my knowledge—in works earlier than the thirteenth century.
[4] sKyabs-ston Rin-chen 'Od-zer; see *supra*, p. 126 n. 2.
[5] On whom see *supra*, pp. 140 et seq.
[6] This is the Section III which was announced *supra*, p. 116.
[7] Not translated.

sPu-gu rGyal-mtshan, and that rediscovered in gYung-drung Seng-mchong-brag by Go-lde 'Phags-pa.

ii. The principal texts of the Southern Textual Treasures are those rediscovered by gShen Klu-dga'. (264b) Other textual treasures which come into this category are sPa-gro-ma, Shel-brag-ma, lHo-brag khom-mthing-ma, etc., also those rediscovered by Sa-ston 'Brug-lha, Ra-ljags, Bal-zho sGom-chen, 'Jing-ston Mu-lto-ba, Bu-mtsho Srid-pa'i rGyal-po, mTsho-bon Khyung-gsas, Khu-'dzin 'Jing-nag, etc.

iii. The Central Textual Treasures are Yer-rdzong-ma—bSam-yas skor-khang-ma rediscovered by the three ācāryas belonging to the Northern Textual Treasures which I mentioned earlier—bSam-yas ca-ti-ma, Drang-nga-ma, bSam-yas ka-khol-ma, and those rediscovered by Ra-ston 'Bum-rje.

iv. The Textual Treasures of Khams are those rediscovered by Gu-ru Ban-chung, Khod-po Blo-gros, sPrul-sku sKyang-'phags, dBang-ldan gShen-gsas, Bra-bo sGom-nyag, Kyu-ra rNal-'byor, rKo-bo gTer-ston, Se-gnyan Zhig-po, Tshil-po gTer-ston, 'Tshol-sprul, U-go gYung-drung-'bum, Pho-chen Nam-mkha' 'Od-zer, etc.

v. The Recent Textual Treasures are those rediscovered by rMa-ston Srol-'dzin, rMa lCam-me, rMa Sher-seng,[1] sPa-bon Khyung-thog, Gu-ru rNon-rtse, dPon-gsas Khyung-rgod-rtsal, (265a) gYung-drung Gling-pa, etc. Since those texts were called recent textual treasure by contemporary scholars, I put them into this section though they are no longer recent. Nowadays the texts rediscovered by Shel-zhig gYung-drung rGyal-po onwards are known as the Recent Textual Treasures.

b. The classification into bKa' and bKa'-brten.

i. There are as many as thirteen ways of classifying the bKa', but for the sake of simplification and conciseness, it will be convenient if we classify it into the perfect mDo, the pure and extensive 'Bum, the profound path of rGyud and the exalted Mental Teaching. The *mDo-'dus* also says:

After I die,
Attendants! into four divisions: mDo, 'Bum, rGyud, and mDzod;
Carry out the classification of bKa'.

[1] These two may be identical see *supra*, p. 170.

ii. There are, in short, two ways of classifying the bKa'-brten: the bKa'-brten which explains the import of individual canonical texts and the bKa'-brten which explains the import of canonical texts in general.

iii. (265b) Concerning the systematic classification of (both) bKa' and bKa'-brten there are two works by the great abbot Nyi-ma bsTan-'dzin: the *bKa'-dang bKa'-brten-gyi rnam-bshad nyi-'od rab-gsal* and the *sDe-tshan sgrigs-tshul-gyi dkar-chags gshen-bstan pad-mo'i nyi-'od.*[1] Since they are proof against authoritative criticism and logical objections and are the work of such (a great) scholar, they are fit to be trusted by us.

[1] See Bibliography.

BIBLIOGRAPHY

A. WESTERN WORKS

BACOT, J., *L'histoire du Tibet*, Paris, 1962.

—— THOMAS, F. W., and TOUSSAINT, CH., *Documents de Touen-houang relatifs à l'histoire du Tibet*, Paris, 1940.

DAS, S. C., 'Contributions on Tibet', *JASB* 50 (1881), Part I, pp. 189–205: trans. of the section 8 of *Grub-mtha' shel-gyi me-long* (q.v.).

—— *Tibetan–English Dictionary*, Calcutta, 1960.

HAARH, E., 'The Identity of Tsu-chi-chien, Tibetan "King" who Died in 804 A.D.', *Acta Orientalia*, XXV (1–2), pp. 121–70.

HOFFMANN, H., *Quellen zur Geschichte der tibetischen Bon-Religion*, Wiesbaden, 1950.

—— *The Religions of Tibet*, London, 1961.

LAUFER, B., 'Origin of Tibetan Writing', *Journal of the American Oriental Society*, vol. 38, New Haven, 1918.

OBERMILLER, E., *History of Buddhism by Bu-ston*, Heidelberg, 1931.

RICHARDSON, H. E., *Ancient Historical Edicts at Lhasa*, London, 1953.

—— 'A Ninth-Century Inscription from Rkong-po', *Journal of the Royal Asiatic Society*, 1954, pp. 57–73.

ROERICH, G. N., *The Blue Annals of gZhon-nu-dpal* (2 vols.), Calcutta, 1949 and 1953.

SNELLGROVE, D. L., *Four Lamas of Dolpo* (2 vols.), Oxford, 1967 and 1968.

—— *The Hevajra-Tantra* (2 vols.), London, 1959.

—— *The Nine Ways of Bon*, London, 1967.

—— RICHARDSON, H., *A Cultural History of Tibet*, London, 1968.

STEIN, R. A., *L'épopée tibétaine de Gesar dans sa version lamaïque de Ling*, Paris, 1956.

—— *Recherches sur l'épopée et le barde au Tibet*, Paris, 1959.

—— *Les tribus anciennes des marches sino-tibétaines*, Paris, 1959.

THOMAS, F. W., *Tibetan Literary Texts and Documents concerning Chinese Turkestan* (4 vols.), London, 1935, 1951, 1953, and 1963.

TUCCI, G., *Minor Buddhist Texts* (2 vols.), Rome, 1956 and 1958.

—— *Tibetan Painted Scrolls* (3 vols.), Rome, 1949.

—— *The Tombs of the Tibetan Kings*, Rome, 1950.

WADDELL, L. A., *The Buddhism of Tibet or Lamaism*, London, 1895.

B. BON-PO SOURCES

bKa'-'gyur brten-'gyur-gyi sde-tsan sgrigs-tsul bstan-pa'i me-ro spar-ba'i rlung-g·yab bon-gyi pad-mo rgyas-byed nyi-'od by the Abbot Nyi-ma bsTan-'dzin (b. *STNN*, 1813). Śatapiṭaka vol. 37, Part II (Delhi, 1965).

dGongs-brgyud drug-gi klad-don nyi-shu rtsa-bdun nyams-kyi man-ngag gnad-gyi yig-phyung, section 6 of the *rDzogs-pa chen-po yang-rtse klong-chen*, manuscript in Snellgrove Collection, 31 folios. Rediscovered by bZhod-ston dNgos-grub Grags-pa in 1088 (*STNN*).

rGyal-rabs bon-gyi 'byung-gnas by Khyung-po Blo-gros rGyal-mtshan. Edited by Sarat Chandra Das, Calcutta, 1915. Composed 1319 (?). (See p. 60 where date of composition is given as an Earth Female-Sheep Year related to date of foundation of Dar-lding which according to *STNN* was 1173.)

sGra-'grel, the *bDen-pa bon-gyi mdzod-sgo sgra-'grel 'phrul-gyi lde-mig*, attributed to Dran-pa Nam-mkha' (eighth century), rediscovered by rMa-ston Jo-lcam, a son of rMa-ston Srol-'dzin (b. *STNN* 1092). Published by Tenzin Namdak, Delhi, 1966.

sGra-yi don-sdeb snang-gsal sgron-me by Zhu Nyi-ma Grags-pa (Delhi, 1965).

bsGrags-byang, the *'Phrul-ngag bon-gyi bsgrags-byang*. Oslo MS. bears the title *Bon-chos dar-nub-g(y)i lo-rgyus (bs)grags-pa rin-chen gling-grag(s) ces bya-ba dmongs(rmongs)-pa blo'i gsal-byed*, 95 folios. Rediscovered by mTha'-bzhi Ye-shes Blo-gros, a disciple of rKo-bo Yon-sgom Thar-mo (*STNN* in 962 A.D.)

sNyan-(b)rgyud ma-nub-pa'i gtan-tshigs, section GA of the *Zhang-zhung snyan-brgyud*, manuscript in Snellgrove Collection, 9 folios.

bsTan-grags brgal-lan drang-por bshad-pa lha-mi dgyes-pa'i 'bel-gtam by Khod-po sKal-bzang rGyal-mtshan, a disciple of bKra-shis rGyal-mtshan of Shar-rdza (1859–1935). Xylograph, 53 folios, ed. Shar-rdza in Khams.

bsTan-'byung, the *bsTan-pa spyi'i 'byung-khungs yid-bzhin nor-bu 'dod-pa 'jo-ba'i gter-mdzod* of Kun-grol Grags-pa (b. *STNN* 1700), composed in 1766, B.M. Oriental MS. 13100, 176 folios.

bsTan-pa bon-gyi klad-don-gyi rang-'grel by sGa-ston Tshul-khrims rGyal-mtshan (*c.* fourteenth century), manuscript belonging to the Abbot Sangs-rgyas bsTan-'dzin, 16 folios.

bsTan-rtsis, the *Sangs-rgyas-kyi bstan-rtsis ngo-mtshar nor-bu'i phreng-ba* of the Abbot Nyi-ma bsTan-'dzin, composed in 1842 (Delhi, 1965).

Theg-rim, the *Theg-pa rim-pa mngon-du bshad-pa'i mdo-rgyud*, rediscovered by the Three Buddhists of gTsang, contemporaries of Lung-bon lHa-gnyan (b. *STNN* 1088), 8 folios (Delhi, 1961).

bDe-chen zhing-gi smon-lam-gyi don gsal-bar byed-pa'i 'grel-ba nyi-ma'i snying-po by bKra-shis rGyal-mtshan, Xyl. 34 folios, ed. Shar-rdza.

bDe-chen zhing-gi smon-lam rnam-mkhyen grong-'jug by bKra-shis rGyal-mtshan, Xyl. 6 folios, ed. Shar-rdza.

mDo gzer-mig-gi dkar-chags, composed *c.* 1965 by Tenzin Namdak (Delhi, 1967).

sDong-po dgu-'dus lta-ba'i rgyud-chen, rediscovered by rMa-ston Srol-'dzin in 1108 (*STNN*) under the title of *Yang-gab dgu-skor* (see infra, p. 326, l. 28), 50 folios (Delhi, 1967).

sDom-pa-gsum rnam-par 'byed-pa'i gzhung-don gsal-bar byed-pa'i 'grel-ba legs-bshad 'phrul-gyi lde-mig by bKra-shis rGyal-mtshan, Xyl. 286 folios, ed. Shar-rdza.

rNam-thar chen-mo, the *rDzogs-pa chen-po zhang-zhung snyan-(b)rgyud-kyi lo-rgyus bla-ma brgyud-pa'i rnam-thar chen-mo*, section KA of the *Zhang-zhung snyan-brgyud* by sPa bsTan-rgyal Seng-ge bZang-po, a contemporary of Bru rGyal-ba gYung-drung (*STNN* 1242–90), manuscript in Snellgrove Collection, 115 folios.

Bon-sku'i smon-lam gti-mug gnyid-skrogs by bKra-shis rGyal-mtshan, manuscript in my possession, 7 folios.

Bon-'chad mkhas-pa'i mgul-rgyan by bKra-shis rGyal-mtshan, Xyl. 38 folios, ed. Shar-rdza.

dByings-rig-mdzod, the *dByings-rig rin-po-che'i-mdzod gsang-ba nges-pa'i-rgyan* of bKra-shis rGyal-mtshan, composed 1907–9, vol. ka, 304 folios; vol. kha, 259 folios (Delhi, 1956).

Ma-rgyud rgyal-ba rgya-mtsho'i dal-gyi brgyud-rim, no author, manuscript in Snellgrove Collection, 2 folios.

Man-ngag rin-po-che A-khrid-kyi bla-ma brgyud-pa'i rnam-thar pad-ma dkar-po'i 'phreng-ba by bKra-shis rGyal-mtshan, Xyl. 45 folios, ed. Shar-rdza.

Man-ngag le-brgyad, section VA of the *Zhang-zhung snyan-brgyud*, manuscript in Snellgrove Collection, 23 folios.

Tshe-dbang snyan-rgyud-kyi lo-rgyus, section 3 of the *Tshe-dbang bod-yul-ma*, rediscovered by Bon-zhig gYung-drung Gling-pa (b. 1228), manuscript in Snellgrove Collection, 10 folios.

mDzod-phug, the *Srid-pa'i mdzod-phug* rediscovered by gShen-chen Klu-dga' (*STNN* 996–1035) in 1017 (*STNN*). Published by Tenzin Namdak, Delhi, 1966.

mDzod kun-las btus-pa'i 'grel-ba rnam-par 'byed-pa'i lde-mig by sGa-ston Tshul-khrims rGyal-mtshan, B.M. Oriental MS. 13099, 127 folios.

mDzod-'grel 'phrul-gyi sgron-me by mNyam-med Shes-rab rGyal-mtshan (*STNN* 1356–1415). Xyl. 128 folios, ed. gYung-drung-gling.

gZhi-lam-gyi 'grel, rediscovered by Gu-ru rNon-rtse (b. *STNN* 1136), manuscript in Snellgrove Collection, 303 folios.

gZi-brjid, the *Dri-ma med-pa gzi-brjid rab-tu 'bar-ba'i mdo*, transmitted orally to sPrul-sku Blo-ldan sNying-po (b. *STNN* 1360), 12 vols., ka to da with a final vol. a, altogether sixty-one chapters. (The first eight volumes were published by the Bon-po Foundation in 1967, Delhi.) Excerpts from chapters 7, 8, 9 of vol. kha; 10, 12, 13 of vol. ga; and 14, 15, 16 of vol. nga are ed. and trans. by D. L. Snellgrove, *The Nine Ways of Bon*, Oxford University Press, London, 1967.

gZer-mig, the *'Dus-pa rin-po-che'i-rgyud gzer-mig*, rediscovered by Drang-rje bTsun-pa gSer-mig (a contemporary of rMe'u lHa-ri gNyen-po *STNN*

1024–91), 2 vols. ka, kha (Delhi, 1966). Chapters i–vii ed. and trans. by A. H. Francke, *gZer-mig*, *A Book of the Tibetan Bonpos*, Asia Major, i (1924), iii (1926), iv (1927), v (1928), vi (1930), N.S. i, part ii (1949).

gYung-drung bon-gyi bstan-pa byung-ba brjod-pa of dPal-ldan Tshul-khrims, composed in 1964–6. Manuscript in the possession of the Bon-po settlement in India.

Legs-bshad-mdzod, the *Legs-bshad rin-po-che'i-mdzod dpyod-ldan dga'-ba'i char* of bKra-shis rGyal-mtshan, composed in 1922. Xyl. 274 folios, ed. Shar-rdza.

Shar-ba rnal-'byor-gyi 'gur-'bum (Section ka) by Shar-ba rNal-'byor, a disciple of Dam-pa Rang-grol (b. *STNN* 1149), manuscript in Snellgrove Collection, 13 folios.

Srid-rgyud, the *Srid-pa rgyud-kyi rnam-thar kha-byang chen-mo*, attributed to Dran-pa Nam-mkha', rediscovered by Gyer Thogs-med in 1310, manuscript in Richardson Collection, 111 folios.

A-khrid, the *A-khrid thun-mtshams bco-lnga-pa* by Bru rGyal-ba gYung-drung (*STNN* 1242–90). Published by the Bon-po Foundation, Delhi, 1967.

C. BUDDHIST SOURCES

Grub-mtha' chen-mo, the *Grub-mtha'i rnam-bshad rang-gzhan grub-mtha' kun dang zab-don mchog-tu gsal-ba kun-bzang zhing-gi nyi-ma lung-rig rgya-mtsho skye-dgu'i re-ba kun-skongs* by 'Jam-dbyangs bZhed-pa (1648–1722), ed. Ma-su-ri, 1962.

rGyal-po bka'-yi thang-yig, one of the *bKa'-thang sde-lnga*, rediscovered by O-rgyan Gling-pa in 1347 (*TPS*, p. 114). Xyl. ed. lHa-sa.

rGyal-sras padma 'byung-gnas-kyi rnam-par thar-ba mdor-dril-ba bsgrags-pa bon-lugs ltar bstan-pa by 'Jam-dbyangs mKhyen-brtse (1820–92), *Rin-chen gter-mdzod*, vol. ti, Xyl.

Chos-'byung mkhas-pa'i dga'-ston, also known as *lHo-brag chos-'byung*, by dPa'-bo gTsug-lag 'Phreng-ba (1504–66 *Re'u-mig*), completed in 1564. Published by Lokesh Chandra, Delhi, 1959.

mChod-rten chen-po bya-rung kha-shor-gyi lo-rgyus thos-pas grol-ba, Xyl.

gTer-mdzod gter-brgya'i rnam-thar, the *Zab-mo gter-dang gter-ston grub-thob ji-ltar byon-pa'i lo-rgyus mdor-bsdus bkod-pa rin-chen vaiḍūrya'i phreng-ba* of Kong-sprul Yon-tan rGya-mtsho, vol. ka of the *Rin-chen gter-mdzod*, Xyl.

Ti-se gnas-bshad, the *Gangs-ri chen-po ti-se dang mtsho-chen ma-dros-pa bcas-kyi sngon-byung-gi lo-rgyus mdor-bsdus-su brjod-pa'i rab-byed shel-dkar me-long* of dKon-mchog bsTan-'dzin Chos-kyi Blo-gros, the 34th abbot of 'Bri-gung, composed in 1896. Xyl. ed. Thub-bstan yang-ri-sgar.

Dad-ldan pad-tshal bzhed-pa'i nyin-byed snang-ba, the biography of the 5th Pan-chen Bla-ma Blo-bzang dPal-ldan chos-kyi grags-pa bstan-pa'i dbang-phyug (1855–81), composed in 1889 by Blo-bzang bsTan-'dzin dBang-rgyal. Xyl, ed. bKra-shis lhun-po.

Deb-ther sngon-po, the *dPal-ldan skal-bzang yongs-kyi mgrin-pa'i rgyan* of 'Gos Lo-tsā-ba gZhon-nu-dpal (1392–1481), composed in 1476–8. Xyl. ed. Kun-bde-gling. Translated by G. N. Roerich, the *Blue Annals* (2 vols.), Calcutta, 1949 and 1953.

Th'u-bkvan grub-mtha', the *Grub-mtha' thams-cad-kyi khungs dang 'dod-tshul ston-pa legs-bshad shel-gyi me-long* of Th'u-bkvan Chos-kyi Nyi-ma (1737–1802), composed in 1802. Varanasi, 1963. Section ta was rendered into English by S. C. Das, 'Contributions on Tibet', *JASB* 50 (1881), part i, pp. 187–205.

dPag-bsam ljon-bzang by Sum-pa mKhan-po Ye-shes dPal-'byor (b. 1704, *Re'u-mig*), completed in 1748. (Professor L. Petech says in the preface to Part III of the *dPag-bsam ljon-bzang*, New Delhi, 1959, that Sum-pa mKhan-po died in 1776 at the age of seventy-three, but according to the colophon of the *mTsho-sngon-gyi lo-rgyus-sogs bkod-pa'i tshangs-glu gsar-snyan* contained in Part 2 of the *Vaiḍūrya ser-po*, New Delhi, 1960, he composed the work in 1786 at the age of eighty-three.) Published by Lokesh Chandra, New Delhi, 1959.

Bu-ston chos-'byung, the *bDe-bar gshegs-pa'i bstan-pa rigs-'byed chos-kyi 'byung-gnas gsung-rab* of Bu-ston Rin-chen-grub (1290–1364), composed in 1322 (*Re'u-mig*), Xyl. Translated in part by E. Obermiller, *History of Buddhism by Bu-ston*, Parts I and II (Materialen zur Kunde des Buddhismus 18–19), Heidelberg, 1931–2.

Bod-kyi deb-ther dpyid-kyi rgyal-mo glu-dbyangs of the 5th Dalai Lama (1617–82), composed in 1643, Varanasi, 1967.

sBa-bzhed. Published with a résumé by R. A. Stein, *Une chronique ancienne de bSam-yas: sBa-bzed*, Paris, 1961.

Mahāvyutpatti, ed. R. Sakaki.

mTsho-sngon-gyi lo-rgyus sogs bkod-pa'i tshangs-glu gsar-snyan of Sum-pa mKhan-po Ye-shes dPal-'byor, composed in 1786. Published by Lokesh Chandra in Part 2 of the *Vaiḍūrya ser-po*, New Delhi, 1960.

Vaiḍūrya ser-po, the *dPal mnyam-med ri-bo dga'-ldan-pa'i bstan-pa cod-pan 'chang-ba'i ring-lugs chos thams-cad-kyi rtsa-ba gsal-bar byed-pa vaiḍūrya ser-po'i me-long* of sDe-srid Sangs-rgyas rGya-mtsho (1653–1705), composed in 1698. Published by Lokesh Chandra, Parts I and II, New Delhi, 1960.

Re'u-mig contained in the *dPag-bsam ljon-bzang* (New Delhi, 1959).

Lam-rim chen-mo, the *Byang-chub lam-rim chen-mo* of Tsong-kha-pa Blo-bzang Grags-pa (1357–1419), Xyl. ed. Kalimpong.

Abhidharmakoṣakārikā by Vasubandhu, Otani vol. 115, no. 5590.

THE TREASURY OF GOOD SAYINGS

Tibetan text (Romanized version)

IV

(115b3) gnyis pa bstan bdag gshen gyi gdung[1] rabs la gnyis /

dngos dang /
spyi don no /

dang po la drug /

dmu rigs gshen /
rgyal rigs bru /
dbang ldan zhu /
grub thob spa /
mkhas pa rme'u[2] /
dam pa khyung gi gdung rabs byung tshul lo /

dang po la gnyis /

stag gzig 'ol mo'i gling gi dmu gshen dang /
bod yul gtsang gi dmu gshen gyi gdung[3] rabs so /

dang po ni / sngar bshad pa'i dmu rgyal rgyal bon thod dkar gyi sras ston pa gshen rab kyi sku'i sras brgyad kyi nang tshan kong bza' khri lcam las 'khrungs pa'i rgyal sras g·yung drung dbang ldan gyi gdung brgyud ni / phyi rabs ston pa ma (116a) byon bar du brgyud pa mi 'chad par lung bstan pa ni / bstan pa gnyer gtad kyi mdo las /

rgyal sras kong tsha dbang ldan khyod || zhes pa nas /
phyi rabs ston pa ma byon bar ||
mi rje srid pa'i gdung brgyud spel ||
rgyal rigs dmu yi rgyal sa zungs ||

zhes so / de'i rgyal brgyud 'dzin pa ni da ltar yang yod de / rdzu 'phrul can dngos su phyin cing las can gyi mjal[4] snang las byung ba'i lo rgyus bsam gyis mi khyab pa bla ma grub thob rnams kyi rnam thar las 'byung ba bzhin no /

[1] gdungs [2] rmi'u [3] gdungs [4] 'jal

gnyis pa bod yul gtsang gi dmu gshen gyi gdung brgyud ni / rgyal sras g·yung drung dbang ldan la sras bzhi / 'od kyi rgyal po / thog gi rgyal po / 'brug gi rgyal po / 'gar bu chung dang bzhi'o / che ba 'od kyi rgyal po la dmu bon a ba ru ring dang / dmu rje thum thum rnal med dang / dmu rje rgyal dang gsum las dmu gshen snang ba'i mdog can sogs che brgyud rnams rim par byon / bar na thog gi rgyal po las dmu gshen dran pa nam mkha' yab sras kyi bar du 'bring brgyud rnams rim par byon / chung gong 'brug gi rgyal po las bod yul (116b) gtsang gi dmu rigs gshen gyi gdung rnams rim par byon te / de'ang 'brug gi rgyal po'i sras dmu bon yo'u brtan / de'i sras dmu bon thong ltol / de'i sras dmu bon skyes lo tshal / de'i sras gshen grol ba dang / dmu kha spo mi spo dang / dmu kha ye mu ye dang / dmu le yol ba dang / dmu long ste 'brum bu rnams so / de'i tshe bod rgyal gnya' khri'i sras mu khri btsan po bya ba bon la dad de spyi spungs gsang ba'i skor rnams thugs nyams su bzhes nas mchog thun gyi dngos grub brnyes / khyad par zhang zhung gi yul nas dmu kha spo mi spo dang dmu rje yang rgyal gnyis kyi gtsos zhang zhung gi mkhas pa brgya dang rtsa brgyad gdan drangs nas mchod gnas mdzad / de nas khri srong lde[1] btsan[2] yan rgyal rabs so bdun la bon gshen rnams mchod gnas su bkur ba las / bar der sngon gyi smon lam gyi rgyus rgyal blon gdug pa can du mas bsam sbyor ngan pas bstan pa bsnubs skabs gshen po rnams kyang bod du ma bzhugs par bon sde rnams gter du sbas nas / la la mkha' spyod du gshegs / la la dben par bsam gtan la bzhugs / la la sog po sprel slags (117a) can gyi yul du gshegs so / dmu gshen de gnyis ni gco btsun dang mu zi la sogs pa bzhin du[3] tshe'i rig 'dzin grub pas gdung rabs de tsam la bod du bzhugs nas bstan pa spel / de nas shar tsong kha'i[4] yul du gshegs so / dmu gshen de gnyis kyi gdung las dmu bkra gsal klu yi rgyal po bya ba'i ring la'ang ma yul du yar byon nas 'bri mtshams su chags te yul sde kun la mnga' dbang bsgyur / der yum lha rgyan bya ba khab tu bzhes pa'i sras mi g·yo mgon po / rdo rje mgon po / dbang phyug mgon po dang gsum bltams / mi g·yo mgon po'i sras dpal mgon gsas / 'brug gsas / rgod gsas gsum mo / 'brug gsas la sras med nas srid sgrub byas pas sras gsum bltams te / gcen gnyis klu 'bum la brten nas gsos pas klu dga' dang klu bstegs / gcung ge khod lha bdar byas pas ge khod du btags te dpal mgon gsas la bon gyi srid g·yang babs zhes

[1] lde'u [2] btsun [3] tu [4] ka

kyang grags so / klu dga' man kyi gdung rabs ni 'og tu 'byung ngo /

gnyis pa rgyal rigs bru yi gdung rabs la / (117b) spyir sa bru gnam bru gnyis / sa bru ni dpal ldan sa skya ba ste gdung[1] rabs gzhan las shes so / gnam bru ni / sangs rgyas thams cad kyis sems can gyi don du thugs dgongs gcig tu dril ba'i lha'i bu 'od zer mdangs ldan bya ba 'og min stug po bkod pa'i zhing khams nas bar lha 'od gsal gyi gnas su byon / de nas mi yul du 'byon par dgongs te rtsa gsum lha gnas su babs te lha la bon 'khor bskor / ri rab kyi rtse nas gzigs pas / 'dzam bu'i gling na o rgyan dang bru sha dang tho gar gyi yul rnams su bdud ngam len nag po bya ba sprul ba du ma dang bcas te / mi phyugs la ye 'drog dang / lo tog la btsa' sad sogs gnod pa du mas gtse bar gzigs te / de dag 'dul ba'i phyir rdzu 'phrul gyi rtsal gyis rnga la bcibs te / ya ngal gshen gyis sna[2] drangs / mtsho[3] cog gshen gyis sku brten te rol mo'i sgra dang bcas / o rgyan dang bru sha dang tho gar gyi yul rnams su rim gyis byon / de'i tshe[4] na tho gar rgyal po sad ver gsal 'bar bya ba shin tu dad nas sku mkhar du gdan drangs te / bram ze gsal 'bar bya ba la lha sras 'di'i mtshan brtags nas don dang 'brel ba'i (118a) mtshan zhig gsol byas pas / bram zes /

phyi nang mtshungs pa'i rten 'brel las ||
gnam nas sa la brul bas bru ||
lha phrug gsha' mar 'dug pas sha ||
tshangs bug dbyings su dod pas na ||
bru sha gnam gsas spyi brtol bya ||

zhes gsol lo / der bru sha gnam gsas spyi brtol gyis bdud ngam len nag po bsgral / 'khor thams cad dam la btags nas mi phyugs bde la bkod / yul gyi mi rnams la theg pa chen po'i bon bstan pas grub pa thob pa du ma byung / khyad par tho gar gyi rgyal po sad ver gsal 'bar zhes bya bas rgyal srid bru sha gnam gsas la phul bas yul sde kun gyi rje bo mdzad / de'i sras lha bu gsas chung[5] / de'i sras lo tsā ba chen po ste mtsho btsan skyes zhes grags / de la sras dgu 'khrungs pa'i gcen po lnga bru sha'i yul du bzhugs / gcung bzhi btsad po rtsod sde bya ba dang sngar 'khon pa phyis dad nas mnga' ris su spyan drangs nas mchod gnas su bkur / mnga' ris skor gsum man chad nas bod yul ru bzhi yan chad kyi yul sde thams cad bru sha'i mnga' ris su 'dus /

[1] gdungs [2] sne [3] mcho [4] che [5] khyung

de'ang gcung bzhi'i (118b) ya gyal g·yung drung rgyal mtshan zhes bya ba gtsang du byon te / de la sras gnyis 'khrungs pa'i gcen khyung nag 'dzin / de'i sras g·yung drung seng ge / de la sras gsum yod pa'i gcen nam mkha' g·yung drung / de'i sras rin chen rgyal mtshan dang shes rab rgyal mtshan gnyis te / de ni 'chi med rgyal ba gnyis pa sprul sku gshen chen po byon pa dang dus mnyam pa ste / bla ma gshen chen klu dga'i zhabs la bru chen yab sras gnyis gtugs[1] nas 'du gnas chen po g·yas ru dben sar mtshan nyid srid pa'i mdzod phug la sogs pa'i bshad pa'i sde chen po btsugs nas 'chad rtsod rtsom gsum gyi sgo nas bstan pa la bya ba ches cher mdzad do / de man gyi gdung rabs ni 'og nas 'byung ngo /

gsum pa dbang ldan zhu yi gdung rabs ni / gdung rus ni smug po ldang las chad cing / de'ang stod na ba tshab dang 'bri g·yas gnyis las / 'bri g·yas gdung las byon pa ni sngon tshe 'dur gsas la snga ba ste / bar gyi lding gnyis las gri gum[2] gyi ring la bon bsnubs pa'i bka' chad kyis lo ngam rta rdzis rgyal po gri ru bkum pa la de'i sras spu lde[3] gung rgyal (119a) gyis bon gshen mang po gdan drangs nas yab kyi don du gri 'dur dang 'dren chog mang po byed skabs kun gyi gtso bo g·yas kyi bon po gshen lcags kyi bya ru can bya ba 'dur phug sum brgya drug cu mkhyen pa zhig byung ba de nyid zhu g·yas bka' brgyud[4] kyi khungs su snang ngo / de nas dbal bon dri rgod kyi sras srid gshen skal[5] pa bzang po nas thar ba byang chub kyi bar gdung rabs shel dkar gyi phreng ba ltar byon pa thams cad gtsang gi yul zhu yi ba mo zer bar stan chags pas zhu tshang zhes bla dvags su grags so / thar ba byang chub la sras gsum / lha legs dang / lha rung dang / legs po'o / legs pos gshen chen gyis bon gter thon pa thos nas 'bri mtshams su phyin pas bla mas slob ma snod ldan du dgongs te bon sde du ma gnang khyad par gsang ba sems phyogs skor gyi bdag por dbang bskur te sgom gshen chen po zhu g·yas legs po zhes grags so / de nas da lta'i bar du byon pa'i gdung rabs rags bsdus tsam 'og nas 'byung ngo /

bzhi pa grub thob spa yi gdung rabs ni / 'od gsal lha gnas nas sangs po (119b) 'bum khri dang chu lcam rgyal mo gnyis kyi gdung las grol ba'i skyes bu spa la mdzes pa zhig rtsa gsum lha'i gnas su babs te lha rnams la bon gyi 'khor lo bskor / de nas lho gling zhang zhung gi yul du bon gyi bstan pa spel bar dgongs

[1] gtug [2] rum [3] lde'u [4] rgyud [5] bskal

te zhang zhung rnam rgyal lha rtse bya bar babs / sprul ba mi 'dra ba du ma bstan / de nas ti se gangs kyi shel phug tu byon nas lo gsum la sgrub pa mdzad pas yi dam mgon po rnam gsum dang dbyer med du gyur te khri mon lcags kyi bya ru can zhes grags so / der sa la zhang zhung rgyal po che / gnam la lha bu spa ba[1] mdzes / zhes gleng ba byung ste grub thob spa tshang du grags / de'i gdung rabs rin po che'i phreng ba ltar byon pa mtha' dag bod kyi rgyal po rim byon gyi mchod gnas su bkur zhing bon gyi bstan pa phyogs kun tu dar bar mdzad / de'i gdung las spa ston spa mchog byon pa dang gshen chen klu dga' byon pa dus mnyam ste / spa ston nyid gshen chen gyis gter bton pa thos nas 'bri mtshams su mjal du byon pas gsang sngags kyi bdag po zhig 'dug gi gsungs nas khro bo dbang chen sogs gsang sngags kyi bka' babs so / de'i lo rgyus dang gdung rabs rim byon ni 'chad par 'gyur ro /

(120a) lnga pa mkhas pa rme'u tshang gi gdung rabs ni / srid pa yab yum las grol ba'i lha sras 'od kyi khye'u dkar po zhig 'od gsal lha las babs[2] / yig tshang can gyi gdung las chad de / sras rma dang rme'u[3] gnyis / rme'u[4] las ngam len skyol po bya bas dbal phur sgrubs pas lha zhal gzigs te grub pa thob / g·yu 'brug la chibs te phyag phreng rag shas lcags byas nas ti se gangs nas lha ri gyang tho'i rtser byon pas mi rje gnya' khri btsan po'i mchod gnas su bkur / de nas dung gi bya rgod gnyis su sprul te g·yas ru shang gi[5] sa char byon te 'phur 'phur lding lding du bskor mthar shun gyi sman mo g·yu mkhar gyi rtser babs te shel sgong 'od 'bar ba gnyis su gyur pa las gcen rme'u 'dul ba brtson bya ba dang / gcung g·yu gshen thod dkar bya ba gnyis 'khrungs pa las / zhog la stod smad gnyis su chad de / stod pa las smin grol rgya cher 'phel / smad pa la g·yu gshen / de'i sras rme'u[6] rgyal gyi lhun po / de'i sras skyid gsum 'dzom / de'i sras stong chab dang pad stong gnyis / stong chab kyi sras gsum gyi 'bring ba rme'u[7] rog dbal bon bya ba yin no / de'i sras lha ri gnyen[8] po ste smra ba'i (120b) seng ge gnyis par grags so / lha ri gnyen po'i sras gsas mkhar bla ma / de'i sras bzhi'i tha ltag shā kya brtan / de la sras bzhi'i gcen po rme'u[9] dgongs mdzod ri khrod pa chen po zhes grags pa de nyid do / lha ri gnyen po dang dam pa ri khrod pa gnyis la rme'u[10] ston sgom gnyis su grags pa ste / bla ma bru zhu spa gsum gyi zhabs la

[1] pha [2] bab [3] rmi'i [4] rmi'i [5] shangs kyi [6] rmi'i [7] rmi'u [8] gnyan [9] rmi'u [10] rmi'u

gtugs pa'i lo rgyus dang gdung rabs ni 'og tu 'chad 'gyur ltar ro /

drug pa dam pa khyung gi gdung rabs dngos la / kun tu bzang po'i sprul pa rig snang 'od kyi rgyal po zhes bya bas 'gro ba'i don la dgongs nas sku gsung thugs las sprul pa'i bya khyung gsum yas mar 'phur nas zhang zhung gi yul kha yug me tog mdzes pa'i tshal la babs / de la zhang zhung gi mi rnams ngo mtshar skyes nas mthong ma myong ba'i 'dab chags zer ba la / rgan po kha cig na re / rva co 'dug pas khyung pho yin 'dug zer / der khyung gsum dbyings su 'phur nas song ba'i shul du bltas pas / spar mo sa la reg pa'i drod rlangs las sgong nga dkar nag ser khra bzhir 'dril ba brdol ba'i nang nas mtshan dang ldan pa'i khye'u re re byung ba'i ming yang khyung po zhes btags te / che ba khyung dkar thog la 'bar / de 'og khyung (121a) ser lha khyung / de 'og khyung 'phags khra mo / chung ba mu khyung rgyan zhes grags so / de dag gis rin chen bla rdo'i pha bong re re / ma brtsigs pa'i rin chen sku mkhar re re / ma bskyil pa'i g·yu yi mtsho mo re re de rnams kyi mnga' bdag tu mdzad cing / khyung po skyid kyi mkhar re re bzhengs te / che ba khyung thog 'bar gyis 'od zer rab tu 'phro ba'i gsas khang brgya dang rtsa brgyad bzhengs / che 'og lha khyung rgyan gyis gsas khang zo bo khyung lag bzhengs / tha ltag khyung 'phags khra mos gsas khang lha rtse gung nam bzhengs / chung ba mu khyung rgyan gyis gsas khang brgyad bzhengs / tshe la rang dbang thob cing 'gro don yang dpag tu med par mdzad do / zhang zhung gi rgyal rabs gong ma rnams kyi ring nas dbu yi mchod gnas mdzad cing / bod kyi rgyal po gnya' khri btsan po nas seng khri btsan po yan chad kyis bla ru bkur / gri gum gyis bon bsnubs pa'i rjes su sras spu lde gung rgyal gyis mu khyung dang lha khyung gnyis sogs bon gshen mang po gdan drangs te bla ru bkur nas slar yang bstan pa rgya cher spel / mu khyung rgyan la sras gnyis 'khrungs pa ni / stag sgra don gtsug dang / dpal gyi gir ti'o / stag sgra don gtsug stag gzig[1] gi yul du (121b) phyin nas bon sde mang po zhang zhung dang bod du drangs te sgra bsgyur lo tsā mdzad nas bstan pa spel lo / khri srong lde[2] btsan gyis g·yo thabs kyis zhang zhung rgyal po bgrong pa'i shul du rgyal sa khyung po stag sgra don gtsug gis bzung nas rgyal khrims dang bon khrims gnyis ka mnyam du bskyangs / khyung po dpal gyi gir ti'i sras mchog gi sgron ma dpung sgra

[1] gzigs [2] lde'u

zur / de'i sras bkra rgyal / de'i sras legs mgon / de'i sras khyung po gyer chen zla med / de'i sras ra sangs khri ne dang ra sangs khod ram gnyis / de'i sras ra sangs klu rgyal lo / khyung po stag sgra don gtsug gi sras btsan sgra don[1] gstug / de'i sras gyer nam zur rtse / de'i sras stong rgyung ring[2] mo dang / khyung rgyal stag la skyes gnyis so / de'ang zhang zhung lig[3] mi rgya[4] bgrong[5] ba'i shul du stag sgra don gtsug gis rgyal sa bzung ba de'i gdan sa stong rgyung ring mos bzung pa la / zhang zhung yul stod nas sdong rgyal dang smad nas sdong dmigs gnyis kyis / tsha zhang gis rgyal sa 'dzin[6] mi rigs[7] zer nas dmag khyer nas byung bas / stong rgyung ring mos gdan sa dor nas phyis bros pa'i lam du grub rtags su / zhabs gnyis dang spa ber dang gsum sa la gar reg sar (122a) me tog gsum re lam lam skyes / rdo brag la gar reg sar rjes lam lam byung ba'i rting nas zhang zhung gi dmag mi sogs gyis ded pas khong gis de mkhyen nas / mdo khams nas rma'i bkra ring lha mtshor slebs pa'i tshe chur brdzus pas rjes bor te thar / der rnal 'byor la rtags mi 'dod kyang / rtags kyis rnal 'byor 'dod zer pa'i gtan tshigs kyang byung ngo / stag la skyes kyi sras khyung po rnal 'byor / de'i sras mi[8] la grub pa ste[9] shes rab rgyal mtshan yang zer / de'i sras mi[10] la thos pa dga' ba ste phyis mi[11] la ras par grags pa de'o / tha ltag khyung 'phags khra mo ni tshe'i rig 'dzin brnyes pas / zhang bod kyi rgyal rabs rim byon bla yi mchod gnas byas pa'i mthar / g·yu 'brug[12] sngon mo chibs su zhon te mdo smad rgya mo rong du byon nas lha mo mdangs ldan ma khab tu bzhes / de las bu 'bor g·yung drung bu bzhi sogs grol te / bon srid dang rgyal srid kun 'phel nas bstan pa rgyas so / 'di'i dus na be ro rgya mo rong du phebs pa dang dus mnyam mam snyam mo /

gnyis pa spyi don bsdus pa ni / de ltar stod na bru zhu spa rme'u[13] bzhi / (122b) bla na mtho ba'i dmu rigs gshen dang ldan / g·yas ru'i ston pa bco brgyad sogs dang / bar na khyung po dkar nag ser gsum dang / mdo khams zhig po bco brgyad sogs dang / smad na bu 'bor g·yung drung bu bzhi la sogs pa'i grub rigs de dang de dag las grol ba'i gdung rgyud bsam gyis mi khyab pa / gtsang dbus mdo khams su bzhugs pa de dag gi mi'i rgyud lha las grol bas rigs bzang / rig 'dzin pho mo'i gdung

[1] dun [2] rim [3] li [4] rgyal [5] grong
[6] bzung [7] rig [8] mid [9] te [10] mid
[11] mid [12] 'bug [13] rmi'u

las chad pa'i khungs btsun / phyogs bcu'i sangs rgyas rnams kyis byin gyis brlabs pas na 'gro don la thogs pa med de / bla ma rig 'dzin gyi skong ba las /

gdung rgyud byin gyis brlabs pa'i skyes bu de ||
'gro don thogs med yin par ma shes par ||
gshe skur ya ga rdzin tshig smod par byas ||
gdung rgyud bla ma rnams la mtho lo bshags ||

zhes pa lta bu yin / des na de dag gi gdung rgyud 'jig rten du ji srid gnas kyi bar de srid du sa steng gi rgyal rabs khyad par can dag gi rgyud pa yang mi 'chad cing sangs rgyas kyi bstan pa spyi dang bye brag kun kyang de bzhin 'gro don du dar zhing rgyas par gnas te / rgyal gshen bstan pa gsum dang po chab srid mnyam chags / bar du mchod yon zung 'brel / (123a) thar mar dbyings su tshom bu gcig tu grol ba'i gtan tshigs kyang yod do / g·yung drung bon gyi bstan pa'i 'byung khungs legs bshad rin po che'i mdzod las / rgyal gshen bstan pa gsum mnyam[1] chags su byung tshul bshad pa ste rab byed bzhi pa'o ||

[1] rgyal dang gshen gyi bstan pa mnyam /

V

de ltar bstan pa'i gzhi ma[1] rgyal gshen gyi brgyud[2] pa byung tshul bstan nas / 'ol mo'i gling nas yul spyi dang bod yul du bstan pa dar tshul bshad pa la gnyis /

spyi don dang /
bye brag gi don no /

dang po ni / mdo 'dus las / 'ol mo'i gling gi bka' dang rjes su bstan pa'i bon / lo tsā drug gis g·yung drung lha'i skad las / rang rang yul du skad rigs so sor bsgyur / zhes pa ltar / 'ol mo'i gling du ston pas gsungs pa'i bka' rnams dang / bsgrags pa gsum gyi bon sde zab mo rnams ston pa 'das rjes su 'ol mo'i gling du dar ba de dag kun lo tsā ba chen po drug gis mu cho'i mdun du shes rab gsum la rtsal sbyangs te bon rnams rang rang gi yul du drangs nas so sor skad du bsgyur nas dar bar mdzad do / de yang lo tsā ba drug ni / mdo 'dus dang rtsa rgyud nyi sgron mthun par / gdung sob (123b) mu chos shes pa'i rgyud sbyangs shing / mkhas pa'i phul du phyin pa'i lo tsā ba / rdzu 'phrul gyi zhabs dang ldan pa / stag gzig gi lo tsā ba dmu tsha[3] tra he[4] / zhang zhung la khri thog spa tsha[5] / sum pa la hu lu spa[6] legs / rgya gar la lha bdag sngags dro / rgya nag la legs tang rmang po / phrom la gser thog lce 'byams dang drug go / zhes so / sgra skad ji ltar bsgyur ba ni / g·yung drung lha'i skad ni / dmu gshen lha'i gsung las chad pa ste rgyal sa pho brang gling brgyad kyi mi rnams kyi skad do / de las skad rigs sum brgya dang drug cur bsgyur te / brgya dang drug cu rtsa bzhi ni 'ol mo'i gling na yod la / brgya dang dgu bcu rtsa drug ni 'ol mo'i gling gi gangs dbal so'i ra ba'i phyi rol du yod do / de dag la bon bsgyur du btub pa ste / bsgrags byang las / 'dzam bu'i gling 'di na skad rigs mi gcig pa stong yod pa las / bon thos pa sum brgya drug cu yod / ces so / de yang stag gzig gi lo tsā ba dmu tsha[7] tra he[8] / khri thog spa[9] tsha[10] / hu lu spa legs dang gsum gyis stag gzig sad spungs dun / gyer sangs[11] gtsug

[1] mar [2] rgyud [3] tsa [4] her pe [5] tsa
[6] gu hu li spar [7] tsa [8] her [9] spar [10] tsa [11] sang

phud / dmu tsha[1] ting rim / dmu bon[2] brtan / dmu mkha' lding nam / dmu rje spal pa dgu 'byung dang (124a) drug la sgra bsgyur nas bshad / de drug gis zhang zhung gi bon po mu khod / rgya gar gyi gshen po li sha / kha che'i gshen po bra ba me ru can / tho gar gyi gshen po pa va shang shang / bru sha ge lte ne lo rgya rnams la bstan te bsgyur ro / legs tang rmang pos rgya nag gi gshen po gtsug lag dpal ge / be ro tsa na gnyis la bshad de rgya nag tu dar ro / gser thog lce 'byams gyis ge sar rngam pa lce ring / sum pa mu spungs gsal tang / bod sha ri dbu chen / me nyag lce tsha mkhar bu rnams la brgyud de rang rang gi skad du bsgyur nas dar ro / gzhan yang gyer mi'i rnam thar las /

bka' gnang slob dpon mu cho'i dus su yang ||
dkar nag bkra gsal gsas khang 'bar ba ru ||
phyi nang sde snod rgyar phye bshad pa'i dus ||
bdag sogs rig 'dzin nyi shu rtsa gcig gis ||
mkhas pa'i bon rgyud gsan zhing phyogs bcur spel ||
gsang ba'i bon rnams phyogs bzhi dbus lnga ru ||
rdzu 'phrul stobs bsgyur yongs la khyab par spel ||

zhes sogs gsungs so /

gnyis pa bye brag gi don la bzhi /

dus nam tsam dar ba /
(124b) sa gang du dar ba /
bon gang zhig dar ba /
tshul ji ltar dar ba'o /

dang po ni / bon dar snga ba ni rgyu'i bon te / bsgrags byang las / bon dar snga ba ni rgyu'i bon rnams te tshe lo brgya ba'i dus nas byung / zhes so / de nas 'bras bu'i bon rnams dar te / snga ma las / 'bras bu'i bon rnams tshe lo dgu bcu'i dus nas byung ngo / zhes so / zhi khro rtsa 'grel las / rgyu 'bras kyi bon gnyis rim pa ltar tshe lo dgu bcu dang brgyad cu'i dus su byung bar bshad pa ni lo tsā ba rnams kyis rang rang gi yul du spel ba'i rjes nas lhag par dar bar gyur pa la dgongs so /

gnyis pa sa gang du dar ba ni / srid pa rgyud kyi kha byang las / 'phrul ngag bden pa'i bon dar te / shar smyug ma bu khur tshun chad du bon dang gshen dar / byang 'jag ma glu len

[1] tsa [2] ban

tshun chad du bon dang gshen dar / nub gnam mtsho gling dgu tshun chad du bon dang gshen dar / lho dom sgro nag po tshun chad du bon dang gshen dar ro / mtho khyung lung dngul mkhar man chad dang dma' sum pa glang[1] gi gyim shod dang brag shel le rgya skar yan chad du bon dang gshen dar ro / zhes so /

gsum pa bon gang zhig dar snyam na / sgra 'grel las / bshos (125a) kyi lha bon dang / grong gi 'dur bon dang / yang dag pa'i sems bon gsum dar ro / zhes pas yar lha la gsol mchod 'bul ba / mar 'dre la glud bsngo ba / bar gshin po la 'dur dang 'dren chog byed cing / gson po la sems don bstan nas thar par 'dren pa'o /

bzhi pa tshul ji ltar dar ba la gnyis /

spyir bshad pa dang /
bye brag tu bshad pa'o /

dang po ni / stag gzig 'ol mo'i gling nas rgya gar dang rgya nag dang zhang zhung du dar la / de gsum nas bod yul du dar ba ste / bdal 'bum las / ston pa mya ngan 'das rjes na gsung rab 'di rnams kyang lho phyogs su 'byung bar 'gyur ro / de nas shar du 'byung ngo / de nas byung du 'byung ngo / zhes pa'i byang phyogs ni bod kha ba can no / de ltar yang theg rim gsal sgron las / stag gzig nas rgya dkar nag dang zhang zhung du 'gyur / de gsum nas bod du 'gyur bas sum 'gyur ro / zhes so / 'on kyang sum 'gyur kho nar ma nges te / khri bdun gyi sku ring la stag gzig nas bod du 'gyur ba'ang yod de / nyi sgron las / lha sras khri btsan lde'i[2] sku ring la / khyung po stag (125b) sgra don gtsug / snya[3] li shu stag ring / bhe shod kram / gco bon khri gtsug dang bzhis rin chen gser phye khyer nas skad rigs mi mthun pa'i yul mang por bgrod de g·yung drung dgu brtsegs la sogs stag gzig gi yul du phyin / stag gzig gi mkhas pa sad spungs dun / gyer sangs la sogs lo tsā ba dgu dang / mkhas pa mi dgu dang / dpon gsas mang po'i zhal snga 'grims[4] / stag gzig gi gshen po rnams la nor gyis phongs pa med kyang bon gyi che ba 'byin pa'i phyir gser gyi maṇ ḍal phul nas gsang sngags spyi spungs bsgrags pa gsum gyi bon rnams zhus bzhin gnang ba la / rgyud chen brgyad cu rtsa drug / yan lag gi rgyud sum brgya / le'u khri drug stong / bon skyong srog sgrub skor le'u lnga brgya rnams stag gzig gi sgro bar bstsal[5] nas bse yi sgrom

[1] gling [2] sde [3] gnyan [4] 'grim [5] stsal

bur bcug / ku hrang / shang shang / kang ka / bya rgod kyi khal bzhi / phyi dbal phur nag po dang / nang lta ba sems nyid gtan la phabs[1] pa le'u sum brgya drug cu bya rgod kyi khal gsum / dbal ram rol ba 'bum pa ge khod srung ma dang bcas pa'i rgyud dang / sgrub skor ku hrang khal gnyis sogs / spyir bon gyi gsang sde chen po (126a) nyi shu rtsa brgyad stag gzig bon gyi yul / 'ol mo lung ring gi dbus / g·yung drung dgu brtsegs kyi ri bo nas 'ongs te / li bal zhang zhung gang gi yul du'ang ma bsdad par bod yul mnga' ris skor gsum du[2] phebs so / de nas gtsang dbus mdo khams kun tu dar zhing rgyas te / li shu stag ring la sogs mkhas pa mi bzhi la bod kyi lo tsā ba chen po bzhir grags so /

gnyis pa bye brag tu bshad pa la bzhi /
zhang zhung /
rgya gar /
rgya nag /
bod yul du bstan pa snga dar byung tshul lo /

dang po ni / gyer mi rnam thar las / stang[3] gi dmu tsha dbag dang / lde bon gyim tsha dang / snya bon li shu stag ring gsum gyis stag gzig gi yul nas phyi nang gsang ba'i bon rgyud dang sgrub skor rnams bya rgod khrung khrung la sogs 'dab chags brgya dang nyi shu la bkal nas / zhang zhung gi yul du 'ongs te / phyogs bcur rig 'dzin grangs med mkhas pa rnams kyis yongs la khyab par byas shing bon gyi bstan pa spel / phyi nang kun la bon gyi blo sbyangs[4] nas so so'i gnas su sgrub pa'i rkang tshugs te / grub pa thob pa bsam gyis mi khyab pa byung / zhes dang / rgyud nyi sgron las kyang / 'bum dang gsung rab gsas khang mchod rten rnams gtsang dbus (126b) su ma dar gong du zhang zhung gi yul du dar bar bshad do / 'dul ba'i lung dang sde snod kha cig ni rdzu 'phrul ye shes kyis stag gzig nas zhang zhung du bsgyur bar 'dul ba gling grags las bshad do / mdor na bod dang rgya dkar nag gang du bon dar ba phal cher zhang zhung nas so so'i yul du dar ba mang ste / dbu na yang zhang skad kyis khung mtshon pa mang ba'i phyir ro / 'ga' zhig ni rgya dkar nag sum pa me nyag sogs nas bsgyur te / dbu na de dag gi skad 'byung bas shes so / gzhan sdes sher phyin 'bum pa klu'i yul nas spyan drangs par bṣhaḍ pa de yang bdag cag gi

[1] phab [2] na [3] stongs [4] sbyongs

ston pas gsungs pa yin te / thub pa klu'i yul du byon nas 'gro don ma mdzad pa'i phyir ro /

gnyis pa rgya gar du bon dar tshul ni / rgya gar gyi bon skor rnams dang po stag gzig gi yul 'ol mo'i gling nas zhang zhung gi yul du byung zhing / de nas rgya gar du dar ba ste / mdzod kun las btus pa'i 'grel ba las / rgya gar ma rnams kyang dang por zhang zhung gi gshen po ga khyung spungs pa la dngos grub tu babs[1] pa la / rgya gar ba gsas 'od g·yung drung gi ring la rgya gar du 'gyur ba gsungs so / zhes pas so / theg rim la sogs pa'ang zhang zhung nas rgya gar yul dang / de nas bru sha'i yul du 'gyur zhing / de nas bod yul du 'gyur ba ste / (127a) dbu la dang po zhang zhung gi skad / de nas rgya gar skad / de nas bru sha'i skad / de nas bod skad byung ba'i go rim bzhin du 'gyur bar sems so / de'ang be ro tsa nas bod du bsgyur ba ste / theg rim las / bdag 'dra be ro tsa na yis / dka' ba srog dang bsdos nas g·yung drung bon chen bsgyur / mnga' bdag rje la gtad do / zhes so / gzhan sdes dus 'khor la sogs gsang sngags kyi rgyud sde mang po sham bha la nas bsgyur bar bshad pa sogs kyang 'ol mo'i gling nas gzhan du bsgyur ba yin te / rgya gar gyi mi rnams kyis zhing khams de la sham bha lar ming btags par mdo las bshad pas so / des na rgya gar gyi bon skor shin tu grangs mang ste / 'og tu cung zad 'chad par 'gyur ro /

gsum pa rgya nag tu g·yung drung gi bon dar tshul ni / rgya nag gi yul du dang por gtsug lag rtsis la sogs pa dar te / ston pa sangs rgyas gshen rab rab mi bos kong tse 'phrul rgyal gyi tsha bo 'phrul bu chung la gab tse sum brgya drug cu[2] bstan pa rnams ma 'ong[3] par rgya nag gi yul du dar bar 'gyur ba lung bstan pa ni / dri med las /

khrus bdag spang la gnam gshen khyod ||
'di nas dzam gling shar phogs kyi ||
ga cu rgya yi rgyal sa ru ||
cu tse 'phrul gyi rgyal por 'khrungs ||
bdud rgyal 'khor bas bsgyur ba yi ||
mi mthun log (127b) pa'i rtsis sbyor la ||
gtsug lag 'phrul gyi gab tser bsgyur ||

zhes so / gzhan yang rgyu'i bon bzhi'i nang tshan du gyur pa sman gyi rgyud bzhi sogs kyang bdag cag gi ston pas gsungs pa yin te / bdud rgyal ram pa dug 'gyed kyis sems can rnams

[1] bab [2] cur [3] 'ongs

la nad kyi bskal pa dar bar byas pa la / ston pas dpyad bu khri shes la bdud rtsi dpyad kyi mdo dgu sogs bstan nas sems can bde la bkod / ma 'ong[1] par drang srong yid las sprul ba 'dul ba'i gnyen por lung bstan te / mdo dri med las /

drang srong yid las sprul ba khyod ||
de dus de dang dus mnyam du ||
o rgyan pad ma spungs pa ru ||
'tsho mdzad ye shes bya bar sprul ||
bdud rgyal ram pas bsgyur ba yi ||
dug la bdud rtsi sman du bsgyur ||
nyi khri dpyad kyi 'khor lo bskor ||

zhes gsungs so / phyis su rgya nag nas gzhan lugs ltar bsgyur ba yin no / gzhan dag kha cig gis rgya nag gi yul du thub pa'i chos ma byung gi sngon du sangs rgyas dang de'i bstan pa sgra tsam du'ang ma grags so / zhes bshad pa ni rang bzor zad de / de'i sngon du bon gyi ston pa sangs rgyas kyi bstan pa yang dag gi bon rnams dar nas yod de / sangs rgyas gshen rab mi bo mya ngan las 'das pa'i 'og tu gdung sob mu cho'i (128a) mdun nas dzam gling mkhas pa'i rgyan drug gis shes rab sbyangs nas so so'i yul du bon sde rnams spel ba'i dus su / rgya nag gi mkhas pa chen po legs tang rmang[2] pos bon sde rnams rgya nag gi yul du sgra bsgyur nas spel bar mdzad pa gong du bshad zin par ma zad rdzogs chen gyi bon sde zhang zhung dang bod nas rgya nag tu 'gyur ba'ang yod de / rnam thar chen mo las / drod skyes 'chi med gtsug phud nas dpon chen hor ti chen po la brgyud / de nas brgyud pa bcu tsam 'das pa'i rjes ma ra sangs khri ne khod nas sum pa dang rgya nag gi yul du brgyud par bshad cing / brgyud pa'i gsol 'debs las /

sum pa'i yul du rdzogs chen bstan pa spel ||
sum bon a ba ldong[3] la gsol ba 'debs ||
rgya yi yul du rdzogs ldan[4] brgyud pa 'dzin ||
rgya bon gsal ba 'od ldan la gsol ba 'debs ||

zhes pas kyang shes so / gsang sngags kyi bon kyang rgya nag gi yul du dar te / g·yung drung skabs phrin las / rgya bon zing ba mthu chen gyis rgya yi gong bu dmar rur gsang sngags spyi spungs bsgrubs nas grub pa thob pa bshad pa dang / ma rgyud phyag mchod las kyang /

[1] 'ongs [2] rma [3] ltong [4] chen

rgya nag yul gyi ri bo la ||
mtshal phug nyi dbar mdangs len na ||
zing ba mthu chen dmar (128b) mdangs gsal ||

zhes dang /

rgya nag yul gyi ri bo'i mchog ||
rtse mang mtsho yi tshal gseb na ||
dod de rgya lcam zhes bya ba ||

zhes pas so / gzhan yang lo rgyus kha cig nas / rgya yi gong bu dmar ru la mon bon dgu dus gcig la sangs rgyas so / zhes so / bon sde'i nang du'ang rnam rgyal rgya nag ma zhes pa sogs yod do / rgya nag la bon gyi bstan pa med na grub pa thob pa dang sangs rgyas pa'ang yod mi srid do / de bas na blo tshad mar gnas pa zhig gis mi'i tshe gcig la srid pa'i thog mtha'i bar gyi 'gyur ldog la brtags kyang rtogs mi srid pa bzhin tu gang zag ma rig pa'i dbang du gyur pa dag gis de dag ji ltar brtag kyang don dang mthun par shes dka'o / de ltar phyi nang gsang ba'i bon sde rnams zhang zhung dang rgya dkar nag la sogs su dar nas so sos[1] nyams su blangs bas grub pa thob tshul la sogs pa bod du dar tshul bshad pa'i khongs su 'du bas 'di dag tu rgyas par ma spros so /

bzhi pa bod yul du dar tshul la mdor rgyas gnyis / dang po mdor bstan ni / snya chen li shu stag ring 'ol mo'i gling du byon nas stag gzig gi mkhas pa gsum la sogs bla ma mang po la gtugs nas bon (129a) sde mang po bod du bsgyur te / yang rtse klong chen las / snya chen li shu stag ring dgung lo stong dang nyis brgya bzhes dus su / stag gzig nas bon gyi yang bcud khri phrag bcu gcig khrung khrung kang ka dur bya la sogs la bkal nas / dro theb gcig gis ti se ru phebs / de nas dro theb gcig gis bsam yas su phebs / rgyal po'i bla mchod mdzad / ces so / zhang[2] zhung nas bod du bsgyur ba yang mang po yod de / rgyud nyi sgron las / bod kyi bon po rig pa gsal ba khyung po stag sgra don[3] gtsug / snya li shu stag ring / bhe shod kram / gco khri gtsug bzhi la gser phye 'brong ru gang bskur nas zhang zhung la bon tshol btang bas / gshen po de bzhis zhang zhung gi mkhas pa bzhi la gtugs te gser phye phul nas bon zhus pas / bon gyi gsang sde chen po bzhi / 'bum sde chen po lnga / phyi nang rgyas bsdus kyi bon sde mang po gnang ba bsnams nas zhang zhung yul nas bod yul dbus su phyin / bon rnams rje la

[1] so'i [2] zhung [3] dun

gzigs phul bas rje yang dgyes so / zhes so / mdo sngags phal cher zhang zhung stong rgyung mthu chen la bod se lde me gsum gyis zhus pas zhang zhung gi sgra las bod (129b) skad du bsgyur ba mang ste / bdal 'bum las / yul bye ma g·yung drung du zhang zhung stong rgyung mthu chen gyis / bod sha ri dbu chen la bon khri sde bshad cing bsgyur / zhes dang / mdzod las / zhang zhung stong rgyung mthu chen dang bod sha ri dbu chen gnyis kyis[1] yul bod dang zhang zhung gi ru mtshams / bye ma g·yung drung chu mig brgyad cu rtsa gnyis kyi mgo bor / gshen rab mi bo'i bka' gzhung las bod dang zhang zhung gi tshig gi tshom bsdebs nas snang srid gtan la phabs[2] / zhes so / de'ang zhang zhung la skad rigs mang yang bsdu na / phug pa'i skad bar ba'i skad sgo pa'i skad phal pa'i skad bzhi las / phal cher zhang zhung smar[3] gyi skad de sgo pa'i skad do /

gnyis pa rgyas bshad la /
spyi don dang /
sgos don no /

dang po ni / spyir bod khams zhes pa ni bon khams zhes pa'i sgra zur chags te bod khams zhes grags par snga rabs pas bzhed la / lung gis kyang nges te / g·yung drung las rnam par dag pa'i rgyud las / mkhas pa mi bzhi dang sku srung sde bzhi / ger mi spun gsum gyi ring la mnga' ris bon gyi sa skor du gyur[4] pa lags / zhes pas so / de[5] yang g·yung drung gi bon byung snga ba dang / rgyal ma byung ba'i gong du bon byung ba dang / (130a) rgyal khrims med pa'i gong du bon khrims yod pa'i don gyis[6] bon khams zhes grags so / bod kyi yi ge ni / dang po sangs rgyas kyis mdzad de / mdo las /

yi ge sum cus bon gyi khog yang phub ||
mgo yis lam drangs[7] shad kyis mdor yang bcad ||
tsheg[8] gis bar phye mi 'khrugs gsal bar snyoms ||
gug 'greng na ro zhabs kyu ya btags[9] kyis ||
skabs sbyor don du yan lag rgyas par btags ||

zhes pas / dang po dag pa lha'i yi ge stag gzig spungs yig tu bsgyur / de zhang zhung gi yig rgan du bsgyur / de smar sbrag tu bsgyur / de smar che chung du bsgyur / smar chen dbu can[10] nam gzab tu bsgyur / smar chung 'bru mar bsgyur / yig sna

[1] kyi [2] phab [3] smrar [4] 'gyur [5] der [6] gyi
[7] drang [8] tshig [9] sta [10] chen

'bru ma las brtsams zhes grags so / gzhan sde kha cig gis / bod yig ni srong btsan gyi ring la lo tsā ba thu mis mdzad pa ste / rgya gar gyi yi ge la ca cha ja gsum / zha za 'a gsum dang drug med pas za hor nas btsal zer / yang kha cig gis / o rgyan gyi yi ge la yod pas de nas byung zer ba'ang bab col smras pa ste / 'dra 'dra gcig rnyed na gnyis btsal mi dgos pa'i phyir ro / de dag gi[1] 'dod don gnam ri srong btsan yan chad rgyal rabs sum cu rtsa gnyis la bod na yi ge med (130b) pas / chos rgyal srong btsan ring nas yi ge'i srol btod zhes / rang bstan dang chos kyi rgyal blon la bstod cing / bon la smod pa'i thabs tsam ste / chos rgyal la bstod pa'i shugs las yab myes gong ma rnams sma phab par ma shes pa'o / des na rgyal po 'di yan la bod na sangs rgyas kyi bstan pa rgyu 'bras kyi bon rnams yod pas / bstan pa yod na yi ge med pa'i thabs mi srid do / der ma zad rgyal po chen po'i chab srid 'dzin pa la'ang yi ge med na 'jig rten gyi rnam bzhag legs nyes spang blang rgyal po'i dpya khral las kyi bskos bzhag sogs kyang bya thabs med pas dud 'gro dang mtshungs par ha cang thal lo / yang srong btsan gyi bka' chems las / rgya gar gyi skad[2] du e ka bod skad du bsgyur[3] ma btub nas bod yig gi ca bcug / dhar ma la chos ma btub nas cha bcug / lo ka'i sgra las 'jig rten ma btub nas ja bcug / na ma la zhes ma btub nas zha bcug / rū pa la gzugs ma btub nas za bcug / rgya'i yi ge ring po la bod kyi ring po ma btub nas 'a bcug zhes pa de rnams ma gtogs par rgya gar gyi yi ge yin par 'dod na'ang mngon sum gyis 'gal te / da lta rgya gar gyi yi ge dang bod yig rnams sgra gzugs brnyan dang bcas (131a) pa mi mthun par 'dug pa'i phyir dang / ma rgyud las / rgya bod yi ge gtan nas mi 'dra'o / zhes gsungs so / des na slob dpon pad ma'i zhal nas /

rgya gar chos rnams bod la bsgyur ba'i tshe ||
rgya gar yi ge bod du bsgyur ma btub ||
ka kha sum cu bod la dpe ru blangs ||
lha yi mtshan rnams 'byung ba'i sgra las drangs ||
sngags rnams ma bsgyur rgya gar rang sor bzhag ||

zhes gsungs pa la yid rton par bya'o /

gnyis pa sgos don la gnyis /

ston pa zhal bzhugs dus dang /
mya ngan 'das rje su dar tshul lo /

[1] gis [2] gyi skad absent [3] ci

dang po ni / ston pa bod du byon dus bod kyi bon po rnams la lha[1] gsol ba 'dre bkar ba yug phud pa'i lung phog pa gong du bshad zin pa rnams yin te / da lta bod kyi lha 'dre rnams bon gyi bka' la nyon cing ci bcol bsgrub pa ste / bon pos lha[2] mchod na mgon byed / 'dre brdung na thub / bkar na 'gro ba ni ston pa'i bka' gnyan po'i dam 'og tu ring nas tshud pa'i phyir te / bon po 'dre srin gyi kha gnon zhes grags pa'i rgyu mtshan yang yin no / de'i tshe ston pas kyang yas stags su rtsi shing ban bun dang / zhugs shangs gser skyems kyis mchod / 'dre la glud bsngo ba tsam phog / bon gshen gyi bka' la nyan pa'i chad[3] bsgos / dus der (131b) nges don zab mo rnams ma bstan te / nam zhig dar ba'i smon lam mdzad pa gong du bshad pa bzhin no /

gnyis pa ston pa mya ngan las 'das pa'i rjes nas dar tshul la gsum /

> gnya' khri'i dus na thog mar gang zhig dar tshul /
> de nas bzung khri bdun gyi ring nas bod du bon dar tshul /
> tha mar nub tshul lo /

dang po ni / byams ma las / rgyal po gnya' khri'i ring la rgyu'i bon shes pa can bcu gnyis dar te / mgon shes lha bon / g·yang shes phyva[4] bon / 'gro shes glud gtong / 'dur shes srid gshen / gtsang shes sel 'debs / sgrol shes lta bon / phan shes sman dpyad / skos shes rtsis mkhan / smra shes gto dgu / lding shes sha ba / 'phur shes ju thig / 'gro shes 'phrul bon / de rnams la shes pa bcu gnyis zhes bya'o / zhes pa'i rim pa ltar lha yar gsol bas mgon byed pa / g·yang tshur blangs bas nor phyug 'phel ba / glud phar btang bas 'dre tshims pa / shi ba 'dur bas bde ba thob pa / gtsang sme[5] phye has lha srung bskangs ba / dgra bgegs sgrol bas 'tshe ba med pa / nad gso bas tshe'i bar chad med pa / rtsis 'debs pas snga phyi'i ltas bzung ba / kham[6] sa'i glud bsngos pa 'dre la shag 'debs shes pa / bag phye'i sha ba gtong bas[7] (132a) btsan gyi yul du 'phur shes pa / mo lha bdar bas legs nyes mngon shes gsal ba / rtsi shing ban bun bsngos pas lha 'dre'i yul du rang 'gros byed cing lha 'dre'i gnod pa zhi ba la sogs so / rgyal po de'i sku srung gi gshen po mtshe gco'u gnyis la dbal chen ram pa'i bstan pa rang babs su byung ba zhus nas spyod / rgyal gyi sku sgra la mtha' bzhi'i dmag ldang skabs / dbal ram gyi lha tshogs la gsol ba btab pas lha zhal

[1] lta [2] lta [3] chod [4] phya [5] smre [6] khams [7] ba

gzigs te grub pa thob / de'i tshe dmu gshen snang ba'i mdog can des / dri med las /

nam mkha' snang ba'i mdog can khyod ||
de dus de dang dus mnyam du ||
kha ba can gyi bod yul du ||
lha ri gyang tho bya ba ru ||
khri bdun pa la bdun tshigs dang ||
rgyal gshen bstan pa mnyam chags mdzod ||
gsang ba sngags kyi bstan pa spel ||

zhes rgyal bas lung bstan pa'i dus la babs[1] par gzigs nas / bod yul du bstan pa spel ba'i phyir rdzu 'phrul sman bzhis zhabs nas btegs / 'brug khyung seng ges mthar mnan te nam mkha' las[2] rdzu 'phrul gyis byon nas dog la babs te / rgyal po gnya' khri btsan po'i mchod gnas (132b) su mdzad cing / rgyal gshen bstan pa[3] gsum[4] mnyam chags su byung ste / bsgrags byang las / des gshen nam mkha' snang ba'i mdog can la / gsang sngags spyi spungs kyi bon skor zhus nas spyod[5] / ces so / rje de lha ri gyang tho'i kha nas yar lung sog khar[6] babs[7] pa mi rnams kyis gnya' bar btegs pas / ri lha ri gyang tho / rje gnya' khri btsan po / gshen snang ba'i mdog can / bon gsang sngags spyi spungs / mkhar byi ba stag rtse zhes gtam du grags so / rgyal gshen bstan pa gsum sa la mnyam chags kyi gtan tshigs de tsugs so /

gnyis pa khri bdun ring nas dar tshul la gnyis /
gzhan gyi 'dod lugs dgag pa /
rang lugs yang dag pa bzhag pa'o /

dang po ni / gzhan sde kha cig gis / gnam ri srong btsan yan rgyal rabs sum cu rtsa cig la chab srid bon dang sgrungs dang lde'u sogs kyis bskyangs / phyva snang 'phrul srid bzhi sogs 'jig rten pa'i theg pa rnams dar bas bod yul du grub mtha' la snga ba bon po yin pa'i gtan tshigs de nas byung / zhes bod yul du rgyal rabs de tsam gyi ring la 'bras bu'i bon rnams ches cher (133a) dar ba'i khungs 'gebs nas / bab col du smra ba'i gtam gyis bod du bon po'i grub mtha'i byung tshul bshad par mthong ste / de dag de'i grub mthar zhen ches pa'i rang gzhan bstod smad la dga' ba rnams kyi blo ngor bltas nas re zhig

[1] bab [2] la [3] rgyal gshen gnyis kyi bstan pa
[4] gsum absent [5] spyad [6] dkar [7] bab

byas pa yin nam snyam ste / don du bzung bar mi rigs so / gal te de ltar yin par bzung na / mdo dri med las /

nam mkha' snang ba'i mdog can khyod ||

zhes pa nas /

khri bdun pa la bdun tshigs dang ||
rgyal gshen bstan pa mnyam chags mdzod ||
gsang ba sngags kyi bstan pa spel ||

zhes gong du drangs ba dang / dbal ram las / gnya' khri rgyal blon gyis dbal ram bsgrubs nas mkha' spyod du gshegs / zhes dang / nyi sgron las / mu khri btsan pos snang mdog la khro bo dbang chen rgyud gzhung ma bu 'tshams par zhus / zhes dang / skabs phrin las / mu khri btsan pos lha ri gyang ma gyang tho la spyi spungs[1] bsgrubs / zhes so / ma zad rgyal po rim bzhin byon pa dag gis rgyu 'bras kyi bon rnams la spyod tshul byams ma las gsungs pa ltar 'chad par 'gyur ro / des na gang zag la[2] blo tshad mar brtsi ba gang gis kyang sangs rgyas kyi lung bzlog tu mi nus te / sangs rgyas kyi lung tshad ma las gang zag tshur (133b) mthong gi blo bzor tshad mar brtsi ba ni rmongs pa dag gi rnam thar ro /

gnyis pa la gsum /
'dul ba /
gsang sngags /
rdzogs chen dar tshul lo /

dang po ni / ston pas kyang sangs rgyas la rab[3] byung gi bsnyen pa ye nas rdzogs kyang gzhan ngor drang srong legs ldan rgyal ba'i drung du khrims bzhes tshul dang / 'khor rnams rab tu byung bar mdzad cing / gsungs pa'i bon rnams bshad srol btod / mkhas pa'i rgyan drug gis sgra bsgyur nas dzam gling so sor spel / khyad par 'dul ba ni / mkhas pa'i rgyan drug gi nang tshan stag gzig dmu tsha[4] tra hes mtshan ldan khye'u bzhi dang mjal nas drang srong chig rdzogs su mdzad de / brag dgon dka' thub kyi sde bzung / de'i slob ma khri lde 'od pos bka' gzhung nyan bshad kyi sde bzung / de'i slob ma lhang lhang gtsug phud kyis 'dul ba[5] rgyud drug gi 'grel ba rnam 'byed lde mig mdzad / de'i slob ma dvangs[6] ba yid ring gis mngon pa sde bzhi'i 'grel ring dri med gsal ba'i lde mig mdzad /

[1] spung [2] las [3] rang [4] tsa [5] ba'i [6] dvang

de'i slob ma thugs dkar ye shes kyis las khrigs bzhi bcu pa'i phyag len gsal sgron mdzad / de'i slob ma gung rum ye shes kyis bstan pa rgya cher spel / de'i slob ma 'od lha gsal 'bar gyis dus chen gyi sde (134a) bzung / de'i slob ma rdzu 'phrul ye shes kyis zhang bod gnyis su 'dul bstan spel ba'i dus la bab par dgongs nas rang byung gi mchod rten bzhi'i nang nas ston pa'i gdung sha rī ram lnga brgya gdan drangs te / rdzu 'phrul gyis zhang bod du byon nas bstan pa rgya cher spel lo / de yan chad stag gzig gi mkhan brgyud do / de'i dus na zhang zhung ge khod dpal bya ba'i nyams snang la na bza' 'od zer sna drug gon pa'i btsun pa zhig yang yang byung bar gsol ba btab pas rdzu 'phrul ye shes dang dngos su mjal nas drang srong chig rdzogs su mdzad de mtshan du ye shes tshul khrims btags / de'i slob ma g·yung drung tshul khrims kyis shel gyi brag dkar rtse rdzong la g·yung drung lha rtse'i gsas khang bzhengs / de'i slob ma gtsug phud tshul khrims kyis dgra bcom pa dpal gyi ri la g·yung drung brtsegs pa'i gsas khang bzhengs / ston pa'i 'khor sde bzhi[1] ya bzhi zung brgyad du phyes / zhang zhung gi yul du bstan pa dar zhing rgyas par mdzad do / de'i slob ma ga cu gtsug phud rgyal bas 'dam shod snar mar g·yung drung khri 'dus kyi lha khang dang / brag nag rta mgo gsum par (134b) khri 'dul gsang ba'i lha khang bzhengs / de'i slob ma ya gong ye shes rgyal ba dang / pham shi dpal gyi dbang phyug gnyis so / de gnyis la bod kyi mi gnyis zhes kyang grags so / 'dul rgyud bsgrags pa gling grags las / gtsug phud tshul khrims kyi mkhan bu bzhi ste / ga cu gtsug phud rgyal ba / ya gong ye shes rgyal ba / pham shi dpal gyi dbang phyug / lde btsun rab gsal lo / de'i tshe gshen gyi 'dul brgyud[2] ma 'cham par sde rigs gnyis su chad / ga cu pham shi gnyis sde gcig / ya gong lde btsun gnyis kyis sde gcig bzung / zhes so / de'ang sde ba gnyis su chad pa'i ya gong gis so thar gyi sde bzung / sgom pa ni bzod pa'i don bsgom / spyod pa tshul dang khrims la spyod / 'bras bu sgo thar du 'dod / lha sa'i yer ba'i klung du bdud 'dul g·yung drung khrims gnas kyi lha khang bzhengs / bdud nag po ser gdong tshar bcad / zang zang lha rtse la sogs 'du gnas nyi shu rtsa dgur 'phel lo / pham shis dus chen gyi sde bzung / sgom pa ni 'gog pa la snyoms par 'jug / spyod pa tshul khrims la spyod / 'bras bu bskal chen gcig (135a) rdzogs te bstan pa rdzogs nas sangs rgya bar 'dod / ra za g·yung rol la sogs dgon sde sum

[1] bzhin [2] rgyud

cu rtsa brgyad 'phel lo / de'ang bod 'dir 'dul ba ni khri bdun gyi ring nas byung ste / nyi sgron las / gnam gyi khri bdun zhes bya ste / rgyal po re la sku srung bon gshen res mdzad pas bon gshen mnga' thang che'o / de dus ga cu ya gong pham shi lde btsun bzhis[1] lha khang mchod rten dgon sde chen po rnams 'phel lo / zhes pas so / de yang ya gong brgyud pa nyer lnga / pham shi'i brgyud pa sum cu 'das pa'i bar du 'dul bstan dar zhing rgyas so / de nas ya gong rgyal ba'i mkhan bu lde btsun rab gsal / de'i mkhan bu mu zi gsal bzang ngo / pham shi'i mkhan bu gco btsun ye shes so / lung 'ga' zhig nas mu zis lde gco gnyis ka'i drung du tshul khrims mnos par yang bshad / gco btsun ye shes ni tshe la dbang thob pas gdung rabs[2] de tsam gyi yun la bstan pa'i gnyer 'dzin mdzad do / de nas rdzu 'phrul ye shes kyi drung du ma 'ong ba na rgyu 'bras kyi bstan pa dar ba'i[3] lung bstan thob nas dga' brod dang bcas te mya ngan las 'das so / mu zi ni ma 'ong ba na bstan pa'i sa bon mdzad par (135b) dgongs nas mdo smad rma ri del gsum gyi ri rtse'i brag dkar rtse 'dus kyi phug tu 'gog par bzhugs so / de yan chad mnga' ris stod kyi mkhan brgyud do / de nas bzung dbus gtsang kun tu 'dul ba'i bstan pa shin tu rgyas te / nyi sgron las / de'i dus na bsam spyod bon la byed / las spyod tshul khrims la gnas / rnam dag 'bum gyi skor bris klog 'don gsum byed / bar chad tsha tsha[4] dang mchod gtor gyis sel / dge spyod pha rol du phyin pa bcu la spyod / zhes gsungs so /

gnyis pa gsang sngags dar tshul la gnyis /

bskyed rim gyi skor dang /
rdzogs rim gyi skor dar tshul lo /

dang po la gnyis /

gsang sngags spyi spungs dar tshul dang /
mchog gzhan rnams dar tshul lo /

dang po la /

spyi'i don dang /
so so'i sgrub pa mdzad tshul lo /

dang po ni / mu khri btsan po nas gnam gyi khri drug gi bar du gsang sngags kyi bon rnams dang / khyad par spyi spungs kyi bon rnams dar te / nyi sgron las / mu khris snang ba'i mdog

[1] bzhi [2] rab [3] bstan pa dar ba'i rgyu 'bras dang [4] sva tsā

can la khro bo dbang chen gyi rgyud gzhung ma bu 'tshams[1] par zhus / lha ri gyang tho la bsgrubs pas grub rtags bsam gyis mi khyab / ces dang / byams ma las / de'i sras mu khri btsan pos bslabs[2] pas[3] (136a) don go / bsgrubs pas[4] don grub / bsgoms pas don rtogs nas / stag gzig la sogs dzam bu gling gi lo tsā bsgyur / zhang zhung nas mkhas pa chen po brgya dang rtsa brgyad gdan drangs / bod du bon gyi 'du gnas chen po sum cu rtsa bdun btsugs[5] / zhes so / 'du gnas so bdun ni / sgra 'grel las / dbu ru na 'du gnas bcu gsum / g·yon ru na bdun / g·yas ru na brgyad / ru lag na dgu ste so bdun no / zhes so / dbu ru'i bcu gsum ni / ngan lam ral gsum / 'dam shod snar mo / 'phan yul brag[6] dkar / mal dro ba rab / mchims[7] gyi grag dmar / has po ri thang / lha sa yer ba / gnam gyi re gong[8] / gnam mtsho do ring / stod ros[9] lung gsum / skyi shod lung nag / re rkyang sha mtha' / mchog gon rgyal mo khang dang bcu gsum mo / g·yon ru'i bdun ni / 'ol kha[10] shug gcig / nyang yul shing nag / kong yul bre sna / g.ye[11] lung gangs bar[12] / yar lung sog kha[13] / klum shod thang dmar[14] / ma[15] dro mtsho shod dang bdun no / g·yas ru'i brgyad ni / 'u yug sa nag / shangs[16] kyi zhong zhong[17] / brud[18] kyi mkhar gdong / rta nag rkyang[19] phu / (136b) 'jad kyi rgyang[20] mkhar / sta phu dros[21] lhas / gtsang gi gyer phug / zang zang lha brag dang brgyad do / ru lag gi dgu ni / nyang stod stag tshal / chu mgo rdo ring / mkhar chen brag dkar / mtsho rnga'i[22] dril chung / gnyan rtse thang shod / gram pa kha'u / rag za thang zlum[23] / mang mkhar[24] mdo phug[25] / lha yul gung[26] thang dang dgu'o / de rnams su 'chad nyan sgom sgrub ches cher dar ba ni / de nyid las / ngan lam ral gsum bon gyi 'du 'tshogs gnas / 'dam shod snar mo bon gyi 'du 'tshogs gnas / zhes pa nas / lha yul gung thang bon gyi 'du 'tshogs gnas / zhes pa'i bar du'o / gzhan yang bsgrags byang las / khyung lung dngul mkhar / gangs ti se / spos ri ngad ldan / mtsho ma phang[27] / brag phug rong chen / mtshal ri zur gsum / rgyal mkhar ba chod / gangs kyi byi ba mkhar / chu mig brgyad cu rtsa gnyis / gangs gnyan rta sgo / mtsho mu le khyud / dang ra'i mtsho / khri 'od khyung rtse / khri 'od ri thang / mang mkhar lcags 'phrang / ra za g·yung drung rol ba / lcim lung brag phug mtha' ka ru / zar

[1] mtshams [2] bslab [3] pa [4] pa [5] btsug [6] srab [7] shun
[8] gad [9] ris [10] ka [11] g·ya' [12] sar [13] ka [14] dkar [15] mal
[16] shad [17] zhang tshal [18] grud [19] rgyang [20] rkyang [21] dron
[22] lnga [23] zla [24] dkar [25] phub [26] gra [27] pang

gyi stag sna / rta nag rkyang phu[1] / gtsang brag zang zang (137a) mo / dgon pa bya rgod tshang / nyang ro rta shal / nyang ro sham po rtse dgu / nyang ro srubs kyi stag tshal / yar gyi thang lha / yar lung gi lha ri gyang tho[2] / yar lung gi mkhar btang ka med / bsam yas brag dmar / 'gran gyi ri bo / 'phan yul 'gro mar phug mo / gnam mtsho phyug mo / zlum shod sgang[3] tshal / kong yul se mo bon thang / kong yul bre sna / rgya'i gong bu dmar ru / sum pa glang gi gyim shod / shel le rgya skar dang so bdun no / zhes so / de dag skyong ba'i gshen po ni / bsgrags byang las / de rnams su bzhugs pa'i gshen po drug cu rtsa bdun byung / zhes so / de yang grub pa thob pa'i gshen dgu / mkhas pa mi dgu / mthu bo che mi dgu / bon chen bzhi bcu rnams so / nyi sgron las / 'du gnas sum cu rtsa bdun du / sgrub pa po zhe brgyad / bon chen nyi shu rtsa bzhi / g·yu rnga can bcu gsum / mkhas pa dgu / mthu chen dgu rnams so / zhes so / 'a zha blo gros kyis grub pa'i gshen bcur yang bzhed de / mu khri btsan po / ha ra ci par / stag ver li ver / a nu 'phrag thag / sad ne ga'u / zing[4] ba mthu chen / shad (137b) bu ra khug / spe bon thog 'phrul / spe bon thog rtse / thad mi thad ke dang bcu'o / gleng[5] gzhi bstan pa'i 'byung khungs las / mnga' bdag sgrub pa'i gshen bcu las shad bu ra khug ma gtogs dgur bshad do / mkhas pa dgu ni / zhang zhung gi mkhas pa stong rgyung mthu chen / stag gzig gi mkhas pa za rang me 'bar / rgya gar gyi mkhas pa lha bdag sngags dro / rgya nag gi mkhas pa legs tang rmang po / phrom gyi mkhas pa gser thog lce 'byams / ge sar gyi mkhas pa rngam pa lce ring / bod kyi mkhas pa sha ri dbu chen / me nyag gi mkhas pa lce tsha mkhar bu / sum pa'i mkhas pa mu spungs gsal tang dang dgu'o / lho gter ltar na / rgyud lung man ngag la mkhas pa se sha ri / sngags gyi gab gsang la mkhas pa lde gyim tsha / tshigs su bcad pa'i mdo sde la mkhas pa me nyag mkhar bu / 'bum gyi 'gres rkang la mkhas pa mtha' bzhi bum chung / rigs bgre la mkhas pa spe bon gto rgyal / dkyil 'khor phyi nang gsang gsum la mkhas pa rgya bon 'bri thang sna ba / sgra skad bye brag la mkhas pa dmu gshen ting ver / spro bsdu'i (138a) don la mkhas pa 'gro mgon lha dpal klu ring / lta sgon spyod pa la mkhas pa khyung po gyer zla med rnams so / de dag ni rig[6] pa'i gnas spyi dang[7] bye brag kun la mkhas pa'i rtser gshegs pa kho na'o / lo pan

[1] phub [2] to [3] sgad [4] zings [5] gling [6] rigs
[7] dang/

gshen brgyad ni / rngam pa lce ring / dmu tsha gyer med / za rang me 'bar / mu spungs gsal tang / dran pa nam mkha' / rgyung bon mu khod / rje rgyal lha sgom / blon chen mu thur dang brgyad do / mkhas pa nyi shu ni / gnub bon dran pa nam mkha' / khyung[1] po stag sgra don[2] gtsug / snya[3] chen li shu stag ring / gu rub btsan dor mi sar / phu lu gru 'dzin / bhe bon shod kram[4] / gyim thang rma bo / sum pa mu phya / has po dug 'dul / phyva[5] bon stag ra gyer shag / ba gor dod de rgyal ba / ljang tsha 'phel snang / gnub mar gshen gzhi btsan / khyim gi ra mon par / mgar lha gshen 'phyis pa / sku gyim thang rma bo / 'gur dpon blon gsas chen / mchims khri zur stong lod / mkha' 'gro co za bon mo / 'gos khri stong rgyal po ste nyi shu'o / mthu bo che mi dgu ni / gangs ri sor mos 'degs pa'i li bon mu cho / (138b) rtsi shing rang sdud byed pa'i gco gyim bu lan tsha / gnam sa go zlog[6] nus pa'i rgya bon mu cho / rgya mtsho bal 'dab[7] la spur ba'i sum pa mu phya / has po ri me'i zhags[8] pas bcing ba'i khu bon mthong grags / bdud srin dngos su 'gug[9] pa'i zhang zhung mu cho / yar chab gyen du zlog[10] pa'i ljang tsha 'phel[11] snang / ri rab 'dzub rtses gsor ba'i 'jang bon 'phen snang / skyi gtsang gom[12] pas 'jal ba'i rma bon thugs dkar dang dgu'o / bon chen bzhi bcu rtsa gnyis ni / rgyal gyi sku 'tsho ba'i gshen bcu / blon gyi gros 'tsho ba'i gshen bcu / rgya bod kyi mtha' srung ba'i gshen bcu / sum pa stong sde'i smad na srung ba'i gshen bcu / bkra shis g·yang len ngo sprod gnyis te bzhi bcu rtsa gnyis so / de dag phrin las phyogs gcig gi cha nas bskos thob kyi ming btags pa las don du rig 'dzin rnam bzhi'i go 'phang brnyes pa sha stag go / de'i dus na rgyal khams ni bon gyi rgyal khams / mnga' ris ni bon gyi mnga' ris te / bla na rgyal che / gong na gshen gnyan / bar na khrims dam / 'og na 'bangs skyid / de'i tshe bod dang zhang zhung na mi rje lhas mdzad pas (139a) mgon skyob[13] che / sku srog gshen gyis bskyabs[14] pas sku tshe brtan / las spyod dge la spyad pas 'di phyir bde / dmu thag gnam nas drangs bas 'dzegs skas bzang / lha ru gtsang rigs bsten pas sdong grogs che / blon po gros la mkhas pas rgyal srid brtan te lugs gnyis zung 'jug gi phrin las dar zhing rgyas so / de'i tshe grub pa thob pa'i gshen dgu la sogs pas sems can thar bar drangs[15] / mkhas pa nyi shu la sogs

[1] khyud [2] dun [3] snyan [4] dram [5] phya [6] bzlog [7] 'dabs
[8] zhag [9] bkug [10] bzlog [11] 'phen [12] goms [13] skyabs
[14] skyob [15] 'dren

pas 'chad rtsod rtsom pa'i 'khor lo bskor / mthu chen mi dgu la sogs pas log lta'i rgol ba 'joms / bon chen zhe gnyis la sogs pas gson gshin bde la bkod / rab byung rnams kyis[1] tshul khrims bsrungs[2] / sgom pa po rnams kyis[3] ting 'dzin bsgoms[4] / sgrub pa po rnams kyis[5] bsnyen sgrub las sbyor sogs bshad sgrub las gsum gyi bstan pa ches cher dar bar mdzad / de'i dus na rgya gar na chos / rgya nag tu rtsis / phrom na sman dpyad / bod dang zhang zhung gi yul na g·yung drung gi bon rkyang pa dar zhing / yan lag tu rig pa'i gnas gzhan rnams kyang shin tu dar ro / de'i dus na / (139b) spyir rab tu byung ba rnams bla'i mchod gnas su bkur zhing / khyad par sku gshen mthu rtsal can sogs rig 'dzin rnams kyi grub rtags la rgyal po'ang dgyes te / rgyal po'i gong na gshen btsun pa'i rtags su gtsigs gsum phul te / sku la gtsigs su dbu skra sil ma rtse rgyal la 'breg tu med pa / dar dkar po'i 'gying thod[6] la bya rgyal rgod kyi ldem phod btsugs[7] pa / dbyi dkar gyi slag pa la stag gzig gung gsum gyi gong lag byas pa / za 'og gi 'bol[8] lham la dngul gyi chag sgrogs btags pa gnang / gsung la gtsigs su gshen ngag tshig gsum ma smras bar du gong nas rgyal pos[9] bka' mi stsal zhing / 'og nas blon pos gros mi 'cha' / thugs la gtsigs su dpya khral rgyal po dang mnyam par mdzad do / de'i tshe mdo sngags kyi bstan pa gnyis mnyam du dar do / de yang gnam gyi khri bdun gyi ring la bon sde gang zhig dar ba'i nges pa ni / bla ma che drug gi bon rnams dar ba ste / byams ma las / phal chen bla na med pa'i bon / theg pa bla na med pa'i bon / spyod pa bla na med pa'i bon / 'bras bu bla na med pa'i bon / (140a) don dam bla na med pa'i bon rnams dar ro / lta ba dang sgom pa dang 'gog par snyoms par 'jug go / zhes so / da lta'i 'gog pa rnams de dus nas byung bar bshad do /

gnyis pa ni / de yang gnya' khri'i sras mu khri btsan po'i ring nas gsang sngags spyi spungs kyi bon rnams dar so che ste / 'di ltar dmu gshen snang ba'i mdog can gyis rgyal gshen dang klu grub gnyis la zhus nas / ri rgyal lhun po'i pho brang du lha mo 'od ldan zer 'phro ma grogs su btsal nas bsgrubs pas / lha bran rnams dbang du 'dus pa / lha srin dregs pa can dam la thogs pa / lha rnams 'dud cing gsol zas 'dren pa / nam mkha' las me tog gi char 'bab pa sogs thun mong gi grub rtags dpag med mnga' zhing mchog ye shes kyi lha dang gnyis med du gyur to / snang mdog gis rgyal gshen mu khri btsan po la brgyud de /

[1] kyi [2] bsrung [3] kyi [4] bsgom [5] kyi [6] dar la seng dkar po'i 'gying thod [7] btsug [8] 'bo [9] po'i

mu khris lha ri gyang ma gyang tho'i gnas su rdzu 'phrul sman bżhis grogs mdzad nas bsgrubs pas grub rtags thun mong du nam mkha' la bya bzhin du 'phur ba / chu la mi bying ba / bar snang la 'brug khyung seng ger spurl nas byon pa / mya ngam snam bu la me tog 'khrungs nus pa / lung (140b) skam la chu bo 'bab pa / ljags mchil la me 'bar ba / gnam lcags phab ste bdud rigs 'joms pa / nyi zla maṇḍal du bkod pa / lha srin bran du 'khol ba / sman bzhi 'khor du 'dus pa / ting nge 'dzin gyi zas kyis 'tsho ba sogs ngo mtshar ba du ma bstan / mchog dbal gsas rngam pa'i sku dang gnyis med du gyur / der rgyal pos bon zab pa'i gnad kyis spel ba la phongs nas gzhan la ma bstan pas mi rabs gsum du gsang ba rtsa 'gags su song bas / rgyal po'ang de'i skyon gyis thun mong gi grub rtags sum cha bri'o / de'i tshe gsang sngags[1] kyi bon nub par dgongs nas rdzu 'phrul gyi sman mo ne slas sa'i lha mo / li mun rlung gi lha mo / tshangs stang me'i lha mo / ting nam chu'i lha mo dang bzhis rgyal po'i gsang mdzod nas bsve'i sgrom bu phyungs te / mon yul du mon bon ha ra ci par la dngos grub tu stsal te mon bon gyis ma bslab par mkhyen nas / lho ri mon ri rgya ri gsum gyi gnas su bon mo stag ver[2] li ver grogs su bsten nas bsgrubs pas mchog gi dngos grub brnyes te sku 'od du gyur /[3] thun mong gi grub rtags ni brag gi phug nas 'ja' 'od kyi zhags pa 'dren nas[4] mi rgod dang srin po (141a) bcing ba / the'u rang[5] bran du bkol ba / chu bo gyen la ldog pa / ri dvags rta ltar zhon pa / ri bo zor du 'phen pa / gran la gzigs pa tsam gyis 'gre ba sogs ngo mtshar ba du ma bstan / bon mo stag ver li ver gyis mtsho mu le'i 'gram du bsgrubs pas grub pa thob ste / gcan gzan rnams be'u lug ltar 'khol / klu gnyan sa bdag dbang du 'dus / lus cir yang brdzu ba sogs grub rtags dpag med mnga' / mi yul du lo sum brgya dang drug cur bzhugs nas sku lus ma bor bar mkha' spyod du gshegs so / de gnyis kyis zhang zhung a nu 'phrag thag la brgyud de / des gangs ti se la g·yung drung rgyal mo grogs su bsten[6] nas bsgrubs pas lha lnga'i zhal dngos su gzigs / gser dzvas srin yul bsregs pa dang / pra mo ha'i dzva 'phangs[7] bas bstan dgra bsgral ba dang / dug dzvas gran lus gzhigs[8] pa dang / dug zas ltar gsol ba dang / mi min bran du bkol ba sogs grub rtags dpag med mnga'[9] / dgung lo nyis brgya lnga bcu rtsa lnga bzhugs nas 'od kyi skur sangs rgyas so / des

[1] sngag [2] za [3] (/ absent) [4] 'dren pa/ [5] brang [6] brtan
[7] 'phang [8] gzhig [9] mda'

zhang zhung sad ne ga'u la brgyud de / des dang ra (141b) g·yu bun gyi gnas su klu lcam 'bar ma grogs su bsten nas bsgrubs pas / mdze nad gso ba / dmag sna shva sna chu sna bzlog pa / gcan gzan[1] la khal 'gal ba / sku la me 'bar ba sogs rdzu 'phrul du ma bstan / sku nam mkha' dvangs[2] ba ltar sangs rgyas so / des thad mi thad ke la brgyud de / des dang ra khyung rdzong gi gnas su sman gcig g·yu lo ma las gyi phyag rgyar bzung nas bsgrubs pas mchog gi dngos grub thob / zhang zhung se lde dang / tal dang / ta mi dang / shud dang / kye mang sde dang / gu ge la sogs pa dmag khri drug stong dus gcig tu byung ste thad mi la do bsdo[3] ba'i tshe / ting 'dzin gyi mthus dmag mi rnams stabs gcig tu brgyal thabs su 'gyel bar mdzad / dbu zhva nam mkhar 'phangs pa bya klag tu gyur te bstan dgra 'ded pa / chag lham bong bur sprul nas the'u rang[4] bsgral ba / yul mkhar la me mched pa mchil mas bsad pa sogs rdzu 'phrul gyi bkod pa bsam las 'das / lo nyis brgya bdun cu rtsa bdun bzhugs nas g·yu 'brug la zhon te nam mkhar mi snang bar gshegs so / des shad bu ra khug la brgyud / des drung gi stag (142a) tshal phug tu rang gsal don ldan ma sgrub pa'i phyag rgyar bzung nas bsgrubs pas mchog gi dngos grub brnyes / thun mong du stag gzig tu brdzus nas gcan 'phrang bsgral ba dang / bya rgod du sprul nas nam mkha' la lding ba dang / gran gyi sha khrag la dbal mo dngos su dbab pa dang / pha rol gyi sems shes pa dang / mya ngan gyis non pa'i sems la bde ba skyed pa sogs ngo mtshar ba'i grub rtags du ma bstan / lo nyis brgyar bzhugs nas 'ja' 'od du gshegs so / des rgya nag gi yul du rgya bon zing[5] ba mthu chen la gdams ngag bstan / des rgya yul gong bu dmar rur rgya lcam dkar mo grogs su bsten nas sgrub pa mdzad pas mchog gi grub pa brnyes te / grub rtags su sku lus spyang kur sprul nas gran dngos su bkug pa dang / rgya mkhar gyi dbus su chu bton pa dang / tshe zad pa'i tshe bsring ba dang / nyi zer la na bza' bkal ba dang / rgya rje'i sku glud rang 'gros su btang ba sogs bsam las 'das / des spe bon la gdams pa phog nas mkha' spyod du gshegs so / spe bon gyis yar lha sham por dkar mo spyan gcig (142b) mas grogs mdzad nas bsgrubs pas grub pa'i go 'phang brnyes / zhang zhung kha yug gi mtsho g·yu ri bya ba smra zhi hrangs kyis zhag gsum gyis 'khor ba zhig yod pa g·yu gar[6] ljang du byas nas ltag par bzhes pa dang / bdud dang mtsho sman bran du bkol ba dang / nyi zer la zhon nas

[1] zan [2] dangs [3] bsngo [4] brang [5] zings [6] gal

'dzam gling bskor ba dang / me tog gi char 'bebs pa dang / sku du mar sprul nas 'gro don mdzad pa sogs mchog gi rnam thar mnga' / lo nyis brgya drug cu rtsa gcig bzhugs nas spe bon thog rtse la brgyud de phung po gzhi la ma lus par sangs rgyas so / spe bon thog rtses 'phan yul brag dkar gyi gnas su spa za kun dga' ma grogs su btsal nas bsgrubs pas mchog thun gyi grub pa'i go 'phang rnyes te / g·yag rgod dang chu srin la zhon nas ma[1] bdud btsan gsum bran du bkol ba dang / dus gcig la sprul ba du ma ston pa sogs ngo mtshar ba'i rnam thar bsam las 'das / lo brgya dang sum cu rtsa lnga lon nas phung po lhag med du sangs rgyas so / des zhang zhung stong rgyung mthu chen la brgyud pas / stong rgyung gis gnam mtsho do ring gi gnas su mtsho sman rgyal mos grogs byas te (143a) bsgrubs pas grub pa thob / gser dang nyung dkar 'thor bas dgra bgegs bsgral ba dang / gnam mtsho dar dkar gyi mthu bar dril te khyer ba dang / ri brag zor du 'phen pa dang / ting 'dzin gyi zas kyis 'tsho ba dang / rigs lnga'i lha byang khog nas lam mer ston pa sogs grub rtags bsam las 'das / mi dang mi min gyi 'gro don rgya cher mdzad nas mkha' spyod du gshegs so / des se dmu tsha sha ri dbu chen dang / me nyag lce tsha mkhar bu chung dang / lde bon gyim tsha rma chung gsum la brgyud de / de gsum gyis mang mkhar lcags 'phrang phug tu lha lcam 'od 'phro / klu za mthing btsun / rma btsun phyug mo gsum grogs su btsal nas bsgrubs pas / grub pa'i rtags su sha ris chu rta sngon po la zhon nas mtsho g·yu bun gyi nang du gshegs bzhud mdzad pa dang / mtsho sman gyis dro 'dren pa dang / lce tshas sku gser gyi mi rtar sprul nas skyin chu dang rma chu bsgyur ba dang / gyim tshas pha bong la zhon nas rgyug pa dang / gcan gzan la khal 'gel ba sogs ngo mtshar bsam las 'das / gsum ka nam mkha' la 'phur te phung (143b) po lhag ma med par gshegs so /

gnyis pa mchog gzhan rnams dar tshul la gnyis /
phur pa dang /
ge khod dar tshul lo /

dang po ni / stag la me 'bar nas dbal bon kha yal me 'bar la brgyud tshul yan gong bshad ltar la / kha yal me 'bar gyis stag tshal rgod kha'i yul du dbal bon gnod sbyin 'dul la bshad / des dbal 'bar lha'i yul du dbal bon 'od spungs la bshad / des stag rtse lha'i mkhar du dbal bon khyung lag can la bshad /

[1] dmu

des dbal yul 'od ma'i tshal du dbal bon stag slag can la bshad / des grug yul grug stod du gru gu'i bon po kha yal me 'bar la bshad / des 'ol yul 'ol mkhar du 'ol bon mig gcig la bshad / des mu stegs[1] kha 'bar gyi yul du ti ti me slag can la bshad / des bram ze 'thib gnon gy yul du bram ze'i bon po kha yal me lce can la bshad / des rgya gar dur khrod kyi gnas su rgya gar gyi bon po a ga ru nag po la bshad / des bal yul thang shod du bal po'i bon po tsan tsan lce ring la bshad / des kha che'i yul du kha che'i bon po gyang ti gsas la bshad / (144a) des li yul ljang ra smug por li bon spungs[2] rgyung mthu chen la bshad / des zhang zhung gi yul du ge ti gsas rnga chung can la bshad / des bod yul du smra'i bon po ko[3] long lha gsas la bshad / des 'phan yul stod du 'phan[4] bon kha 'byams lcags kyi bya ru can la bshad / des rgya yul 'grim thang du rgya bon dbal 'bar lha gsas la bshad / des yar yul lha'i thang la gsas mkhar me 'bar la bshad / des bod yul du bla chen dran pa nam mkha' la bshad pas thugs kyi brnag par mdzad do /

gnyis pa la gnyis / me ri ni / ston pa gshen rab nas khri lde lcags kyi bya ru can la brgyud tshul yan gong bshad ltar la / de nas tshe spungs zla ba rgyal mtshan yan chad sems phyogs dang brgyud kha mthun te 'og tu 'chad do / ge khod ni / lcags kyi bya ru can gyis zhang zhung stag sna rgyal po la brgyud / des khri 'od gsas la brgyud / des gsang ba gting rum la brgyud / des sad ne ga'u la brgyud / des rgyung ne khod spungs la brgyud / de bzhin du hris pa gyer med / tso mi[5] gyer chen / this dmar spungs (144b) rgyung / dran pa nam mkha' rnams rim par brgyud do /

gnyis pa rdzogs rim la gnyis /
ma rgyud dang /
rdzogs chen snyan brgyud dar tshul lo /

dang po ni / snang mdog yan bshad zin ltar la / snang mdog la zhang zhung bar ba'i paṇ ḍi ta a nu 'phrag thag gis zhus te / dka' ba chen po sum brgya drug cu rtsa drug gis nyams su blangs[6] pas mchog thun mong gi dngos grub brnyes / de la zhang zhung sgo pa'i paṇ ḍi ta[7] sad ne ga'us zhus te / rtogs pa chen po nyi shu rtsa gsum gyis sa tshigs bgrod cing nyams su blangs[8] pas grub pa'i go 'phang brnyes so / spyir ma rgyud la /

[1] steg [2] stong [3] kro [4] 'phen [5] min [6] blang
[7] tas [8] blang

bon sku mchog gi brgyud pa / mnga' bdag mkha' 'gro'i brgyud pa / bsdus pa bka'i brgyud pa / sems dpa' brda'i brgyud pa / grub chen snyan khungs brgyud pa / mkhas pa lo paṇ brgyud pa dang drug yod la / de'ang zhang zhung sgo phug bar gsum nas 'gyur ba ste / phug pa'i snang ba'i mdog can / bar ba'i a nu 'phrag thag / sgo pa'i sad ne ga'u sogs kyis bsgyur ba'o / spyir na dus de tsam na zhang zhung kha yug gi yul nas bod yul yan chad grub chen brgyad cur tshang (145a) par byon pa ste / de'ang stod kyi bla ma che drug / bar gyi gdung brgyud bcu gsum / smad kyi mkhas pa mi bzhi / lo paṇ mkhas pa sde dgu / byin rlab brgyud pa'i gshen dgu / mthu bo che mi dgu / grub thob rdzu 'phrul ma dgu / mtha' 'dul zil non gshen dgu / bka' khrims bka' 'dzin che dgu / brgyud 'dzin sems dpa' rnam gsum bcas brgyad cu'o / de dag mchog dang thun mong gi dngos grub gang la'ang mnga' brnyes shing tshe'i grub pa brnyes pa sha stag ste / che ba'i yon tan gyi lo rgyus rgyas pa ni ma spros so /

gnyis pa rdzogs chen ni / spyir rdzogs chen bon sgo la bsam gyis mi khyab kyang / bsdus na bka' brgyud[1] skor bzhi dang / bsgrags pa skor gsum dang / sems smad sde dgu sogs la 'dus pas / de dag las / dang po[2] bka' brgyud skor bzhi ni / phyi lta ba spyi gcod / nang man ngag dmar khrid / gsang ba rig pa cer mthong / yang gsang gnas lugs phugs chod dang bzhi/[3] de la'ang ring brgyud (145b) dang / nye brgyud dang / brgyud pa rkang 'dril gsum / ring brgyud la'ang 'khrug can dang / 'khrug min gnyis las / 'khrug can ni 'khrug min la ltos nas 'khrug pa ltar snang bas 'khrug can zhes bya la / de'ang 'chi med dang brgyud khungs kyi ston pa gsang ba 'dus pa gnyis nas brgyud pa kha yar ba gsum gyi mdor gyer spungs la thug pa de'o / 'khrug[4] min ni / dgongs brgyud dgu'i ma tha gsang ba 'dus pa nas / lha klu mi gsum gyi gshen po gsum nas bar gyi gshen po nyer bzhi la rim gyis brgyud pa'o / nye brgyud ni / ta pi hri tsas gyer spungs la brgyud pa de'o / brgyud pa rkang 'dril ni / 'khrug can 'khrug min nye brgyud dang lnga'i 'dus so gyer spungs nas da lta yan gyi brgyud pa de'o / de bas na dgongs brgyud dgu dang gsang 'dus nas lha klu mi'i gshen gsum la brgyud tshul yan bstan zin la / 'dir 'khrug[5] can ltar gyer spungs yan gyi bla ma rnams kyi grub pa brnyes tshul cung zad gleng na / 'chi med gtsug phud nas dpon chen hor ti la brgyud / des kun.

[1] rgyud [2] dang po ni/ [3] (/ absent) [4] 'khrugs [5] 'khrugs

mkhyen don grub la brgyud / de gnyis kas snang lus sems gsum (146a) dbyings su bskyal nas gdod ma'i gzhi thog tu grol / kun mkhyen gyi slob ma tshe spungs zla ba rgyal mtshan gyis brag dmar shad kyi gnas su lo dgur bsgoms pas phyi nang gi snyigs ma dvangs te 'ja' 'od du yal / de'i slob ma ra sangs klu rgyal gyis gnas spo dmar du bsgoms pas snang bzhi tshad du phyin / de'i slob ma dpon chen ta pi hri tsas stag thabs seng ge'i brag la lo dgur bsgoms pas ye shes rdzogs pa'i sku brnyes / de'i slob ma ra sangs ku ma ra dzas gnas ne ring du lo dgur bsgoms pas sku gsum lam snang du chod / de'i slob ma ra sangs bsod rtses dben par lo bcu gsum bsgoms pas bon nyid zad sar bskyal / de'i slob la zhang zhung sad ne ga'us brag phug tu lo bcu drug tu bsgoms pas 'byung ba rang sar dengs / de'i slob ma gu rub lha sbyin gyis grong yul ma mthong bar bya tshang gi gnas su lo bcu gcig bsgoms pas 'od lus su grol / de'i slob ma gu rub dpal bzang gis rir 'grims nas nyams su blangs pas zag bcas kyi phung po zag med du grol / de'i slob ma ra sangs khri ne khod kyis lho gcan rong du nyams (146b) su blangs pas mchog thun mong gi dngos grub brnyes / de'i slob ma sum pa'i bon po a ba ldong dang / de'i slob ma rgya bon gsal ba 'od chen gnyis kyis sum pa dang rgya nag gi yul du brgyud / rgya bon gyi slob ma 'jag[1] rong gsas mkhar bya ba byung / gsum ka'ang rdos bcas kyi snang ba zad nas dvangs ma'i sku ru gyur / 'jag gsas[2] kyi sras gsum las bar ba grub pa rgyal mtshan la gdams pa bstan pas des brag dmar stag tshang du lo brgyad bsgoms pas phyi nang gi rdos pa kun las grol / de'i slob ma khyung po bkra rgyal gyis zhang zhung sa ti'i phug tu lo nyer gcig bsgoms pas zag pa med pa'i sku brnyes / de'i slob ma sras legs mgon gyis mtsho ri ti'i do[3] la lo brgyad bsgoms pas dngos snang 'od du yal / de'i slob ma ma hor stag gzig gis gangs ti se la lo bcu gnyis bsgoms kyang da dung yid ma ches nas slar log te / bla ma la lo de tsam du nyams su blangs kyang yid ches ma rnyed pas gdams ngag cig zhu zhus te gser srang bcu phul bas / bla mas gser mi 'dod gsungs / gdams ngag gnang bas / khos lo (147a) drug bsgoms pas gzod grub pa thob po /

gzhan yang gsang 'dus nas brgyud pa kha yar ba gnyis dang / 'khrug min ltar brgyud khungs nas gyer spungs yan bla ma nyer bzhir byon pa rnams kyang 'ja' lus pa sha stag yin no / gyer spungs kyi bla ma[4] ta pi hri tsa yang 'ja'[5] lus pa ste / khong gis

[1] jag [2] jag sras [3] dol [4] slob ma [5] 'dza'

stag thabs seng ge'i brag la lo dgur bsgoms / gyer spungs nyid dgung grangs lnga brgya dang don gsum par le'u brgyad pa'i gdams[1] pa gnang ba'i mod nas 'pho chen gyi sku bzung ste 'gro don mtha' yas par mdzad nas gzhi dbyings su snyoms par zhugs so / de'i slob ma rgya tig gsas chung gis gnas me la rgyung du bsgoms pas bon sku'i dgongs pa brnyes / lo sum brgya dang bcu bdun bzhugs nas dbyings su gshegs so / de'i slob ma dmu tso ges yun ring por nyams su blangs pas phung po'i snyigs ma dag ste lo brgya dang don gsum bzhugs te bya nam mkha' la 'phur ba ltar gshegs so / de'i slob ma dmu tso stong gis shang shel rong bya ba'i sgrub gnas su bsgoms pas 'byung ba rang sar dag ste (147b) lo brgya dang bcu gsum nas khyung nam mkha' la lding ba ltar gshegs so / de'i slob ma dmu shod kram[2] chen pos gangs gnyan rta sgo ru bsgoms pas ye shes rdzogs pa'i sku brnyes te lo brgya dang bcu bdun nas seng ge gnam la mchongs pa ltar gshegs so / de'i slob ma dmu rgyal ba blo gros gyis zang zang lha brag gi gnas su bsgoms pas snang bzhi tshad du phyin nas lo nyis brgya dang bdun cur bzhugs nas sems can mtha' yas pa'i don rgya cher mdzad nas bar snang gi rlung zhi ba ltar sangs rgyas so / de'i slob ma dpon rgyal[3] btsan po bya bas / g·yas ru shang brag gi ri la bsgoms pas rgyal ba'i dgongs pa brnyes / 'gro don du lo stong dang drug brgyar bzhugs nas slar lho nub srin po'i kha gnon du g·yu bya khu byug tu sprul nas gshegs so / mdor na bon zab pa'i kha pho tsam la ltos ma dgos par 'ja' lus su gshegs par byung ba mngon sum tshad mar rung ba de lta bu ni grub mtha' kun la ngo mtshar ba'i gleng[4] gzhir snang bas rgyas par spros 'os kyang re zhig yi ges 'jigs so / de 'phros kyi brgyud pa'i rkang grangs tsam 'og tu 'byung ngo /

(148a) gnyis pa bsgrags pa skor gsum ni / sku gsum nas lha klu mi gsum la brgyud tshul bshad zin la / klu grub kyis stag gzig gi slob dpon 'od zer dpag med la brgyud / des mun pa kun gsal / des 'phrul gshen snang ldan / des gsang ba 'dus pa bzhi la rim gyis brgyud de g·yung drung sems dpa'i brgyud pa'o / gsang 'dus nas stong rgyung mthu chen la brgyud / des se bon sha ri dbu chen / des lde gyim tsha rma chung / des me nyag lce tsha mkhar bu bzhi la rim par brgyud de mkhas pa lo paṇ gyi brgyud pa zhes bya'o / khyad par bsgrags gsum bon gyi mnga' bdag chen po ni snya[5] chen li shu stag ring yin te / de nyid rgyal po gnyan stag spungs bya ba stang dbyal gnyis yod

[1] gdam [2] dram [3] chen [4] gling [5] snyan

pas sprul ba'i bu mo mtshan dang ldan pa zhig me tog gi gling nas sras kyi skal par rnyed pa de la ming stag bza' li ver du btags / des mchog lnga'i sgrub pa mdzad pas mo lus pho ru gyur te gnyan gyi gdung 'dzin pas gnyan li shu stag ring ngo / der mi lo brgyad cu rtsa gnyis su rgyal srid bzung nas bstan pa spel / de nas stag gzig tu phebs nas bon sgo mang po (148b) zhus te / nyams su blangs pas mchog thun mong gi dngos grub brnyes / dgong lo bdun brgya bzhes pa'i dus dbal bon rum po la drag sngags skor rnams zhus / rgya dkar nag la sogs pa'i lo tsā ba rnams las bon sgo mang po bsgyur / dur khrod gnas brgyad du mkha' 'gro ma rnams dbang du bsdus / lo stong dang nyis brgya'i dus su stag gzig tu byon nas bon gyi yang bcud mang po bod du bsgyur / bod yul du grub rtags bsam gyis mi khyab pa bstan / lde gyim tsha rma chung gi sras mo co za bon mo gsang ba'i phyag rgyar bsten / rtsa rlung thig le la rang dbang thob / phyi nang gsang ba'i lha thams cad zhal gzigs / dzam gling gi yul gyi snying po drug la sogs su rang rang gi skad du bon bsgyur zhing bstan pa spel / lo nyis stong lnga brgya'i bar du 'gro don mdzad / zag med kyi sku brnyes pas skye 'chi dang bral zhing grub rtags dang rdzu 'phrul bsam gyis mi khyab ste rgyas pa rnam thar las gsal lo / de ltar li shu yab yum gnyis nas mkhas pa grub chen bco brgyad la sogs la brgyud nas dar ba ste de rnams kyang mchog thun gyi dngos grub (149a) brnyes pa sha stag[1] go /

gsum pa sems smad sde dgu ni / khu byug las gsungs pa ltar na / ye nyid ston pa'i dgongs pa zab mo de nyid ston pa gshen lha 'od dkar gyis dgongs pa'i ngang nas g·yu bya khu byug tu sprul te ston pa 'chi med gtsug phud la brgyud par bshad la / de'ang g·yu bya khu byug ni rig pa'i ston pa tshad med 'od ldan nyid yin te / thugs rje'i ston pa'i sprul ba yin pa'i phyir ro / 'chi med gtsug phud kyis gshen gsang ba 'dus pa dang / yum bzang bza' ring btsun gnyis la brgyud pa ste / mang 'grel dang nyung 'dus gnyis su gyes par bshad pas so / de yan chad la dgongs brgyud drug ces bya'o / yang khu byug las / gsang 'dus nas rma lo dar dpyangs / des lha gshen yongs su dag pa / des mi lus bsam legs / des ye shes snying po / des snang ba'i mdog can la brgyud / ces pas gsang 'dus bcas la bla ma che drug ces bya la / gsang sngags ltar na rma lo mi brtsi bar stag la bcas drug go / de nas mu khri btsan po / des ha ra ci par / des stag ver li ver / des a

[1] stags

nu 'phrag thag / (149b) des sad ne ga'u / des thad mi thad ke / des shad bu ra khug / des zing[1] ba mthu chen / des spe bon thog rtse / des spe bon thog 'phrul / de dag gi steng du khu byug las gsungs pa'i hring ni mu ting / sum pa dbu dkar / glang chen mu ver dang gsum bsnan pas bcu gsum ni gdung brgyud bcu gsum mo / rdzu 'phrul sman bzhi 'dir mi brtsi ba ni mu khri btsan pos gsang sngags zab 'dzin byas pa de nyid rgya bkrol nas mon bon ha ra ci par dang stag ver li ver gnyis la ston pa'i sngags kyi bdag mo yin pas de bzhi de dag gi grangs su brtsi ba las 'dir sems phyogs la brtsi mi dgos pa yin nam snyam pa kho bo'i blos rtog go / de[2] nas stong rgyung mthu chen / des se lde me gsum la brgyud de mkhas pa mi bzhi zhes zer ro /

gsum pa tha mar nub tshul la bzhi /
yul gang du nub pa /
bon gang zhig nub pa /
rgyal gshen gang gi ring la nub pa /
tshul ji ltar nub pa'o /

dang po yul ni / kha cig gis gtsang du nub la dbus su ma nub par bshad / kha cig gis bod kho nar nub par bshad de / de yang lung gtan tshigs che bas lung las gsungs pa (150a) ltar na / bsgrags byang las / de gtsang du nub pa las dbus man chad du ma nub / ces dang / sgra 'grel las / dbus kyi sa skor du bon ma nub par spyod / ces dang / dbang chen las / bod kyi sa skor du srid pa'i bon thang cig nub / ces pa'i lung dang po gnyis kyis gtsang du nub par bshad pa ltar 'dod la / phyi mas ni bod kyi sa skor du 'bras bu'i bon nub pa la dgongs sam snyam / rgyu'i bon ni ma nub te / dbang chen las / rgyal po'i zhal nas / yul 'dir nga yi rgyal srid dang / khyod kyi bon srid gnyis mi shong bas / lha'i bon sgo bzhi dang / de bton pa'i ge khod this 'phen dang / gco gyim bu lan tsha gnyis bdag gi sku srung du bzhag 'tshal / phyi ma rnams bod ru bzhi las 'das par gshegs shig / ces[3] dang / gyim bu lan tsha'i zhal nas / lha'i bon sgo bzhi dar na gsas mkhar gyi srog zin pas bdag kyang bsdad pa legs lha'i bon yang ma nub na dga' zer nas 'gro ma 'dod pa la bon sgo phyed dang gnyis byin pa ni / rgyu bon zang ma'o / zhes pas gtsang du rgyu 'bras kyi bon rnams nub la bod dbus skor du 'bras bon nub cing rgyu bon 'ga' (150b) zhig dar ram snyam /

[1] zings [2] des [3] zhes

'o na rgyal pos phyi ma rnams bod ru bzhi las 'das par gshegs shig ces gsungs pa ci zhe na / de ni bon gshen gzhan rnams gshegs shig ces pa'o /

gnyis pa bon gang zhig nub pa ni / dbang chen gyi lung las / gco gyim bu lan tsha'i mchid gnang ba la / bon sgo phyed dang gnyis byin te rgyu bon zang ma'o / zhes pa snang gshen bon rang mal dang / srid gshen gyi bon phyed ma nub par bstan la / rdzogs pa gsas mkhar las / bon bshos kyi lha bon ni ma nub / grong gi 'dur bon phyed nub / yang dag pa'i sems bon ni yo nub / ces dang / rnam dag las / 'bum sde chen po dang / gsas mkhar sems phyogs thams cad gter du sbas / zhes pa rnams kyis shes so /

gsum pa rgyal gshen gang gi ring la nub na / dbang chen las / rgyal gri gum[1] btsan po glen pa'i ring la / gshen po dang rgyal po'i bar du snyan phra zhugs te / zhes dang / phyi rgyud las / lde gyim tsha rma chung gis bstan srung mthu chen bsgrubs te / mthu'i dregs pa skyes pas / rgyal po dang gshen po'i[2] bar du snyan phra zhugs te / zhes pas / rgyal po ni gri gum[3] (151a) btsan po'i ring dang gshen ni rtsa rgyud nyi zer sgron ma las / mkhas pa mi bzhi'i sku tshe'i stod la nub / ces bshad do / yun ni rgyal pos / nyi sgron las / lo nyi shu rtsa bdun yan du bon la spyad / ces dang /[4] ju thig rgyud 'bum las / de nas lo bcu gsum lon pa'i rjes su rgyal po lo ngam rta rdzis[5] bsad / spu lde gung rgyal gdan sa thob po / zhes pas lo bcu gsum du lo ngam gyis rgyal sa bzung / de nas spu ldes rgyal sa thob ste / bon bsnubs nas bon bstan spel ba'i bar du lo bcu bdun song bar bshad do /

bzhi pa ji ltar nub tshul la gsum /

nub pa'i rgyu mtshan /
nub tshul dngos /
dbu yog byung tshul lo /

dang po ni / mkhas bzhi'i gab 'grel las / bon gyi sgo mo brgyad khri bzhi stong dang / mtshan ma can du btags pa'i bon thams cad ni / 'ga' zhig ni dus kyis nub la / 'ga' zhig las kyis nub / 'ga' zhig rkyen gyis nub po / zhes pa ltar / dus dang / las dang / rkyen dbang gis nub pa'o / dang po dus ni /[6] spyir sems can gyi las spyod dman pas tshe lo mar phri nas snyigs ma la thug pa'i dbang gis bstan pa'i snying po (151b) sa'i steng na

[1] rum [2] gshen po absent [3] rum [4] (/ absent) [5] rdzi [6] (/ absent)

bzhugs dka' ba ste / 'grel ba las / sems can spyi'i bsod nams phri[1] bas g·yung drung gi bon zab mo 'di yang thang cig nub tu tho / zhes so / gnyis pa las ni / sgos bod rnams bsod nams chung zhing dug lnga rags pa dang / yang sgos rgyal po bsod nams zad cing nyon mongs che ba'i sdig bcu kha tshang du spyad pas bstan pa'i snod du mi rung ba'i phyir te / sems can mi gtso las nyid gtso / zhes pa bzhin no / gsum pa rkyen ni /[2] bsgrags byang las / che gsum dbang gi me 'bar ba / chung gsum phra ma'i shing bsnan nas / zhes pa ltar / rgyal po ni kun gyi gtso bor gyur pas / mnga 'thang gi dregs che ste zhe sdang gi me 'bar / gshen po rnams yon tan gyi[3] dregs che ste nga rgyal gyi me 'bar / blon po ni blo'i dregs che ste phrag dog gi me 'bar zhing / chung gsum ni blon po la sogs pas phra ma bskyal[4] ba dang / rgyal po'i thugs la gdon zhugs pa dang / bod 'bangs kyi kha smras ngan pa mched pa ste gsum po me'i thog tu shing bsnan pa lta bur gyur nas g·yung drung gi bon nub bo / de yang phra ma ji ltar bcug pa ni / blon po li btsan bzher na re / (152a) rje rgyal lags / bon po mgo mtho na rje yi mnga' thang khyer / zhes pa la sogs dang / blon po zing pa rad na bya ba na re / rje lags / gshen po rnams mtha' ru spyug[5] pa'i bka' mchid gsung[6] par zhu / zhes sogs dang / rgya gar gyi sprang po rgyal khams su 'khyam pa rad na sid dhi bya ba zhig gis kyang da lta rgyal gshen do mnyam tsam gda' ste / sras dbon[7] rnams kyi sku ring la / rgyal srid bon pos khyer ba mchi'o / zhes sogs kyi phra ma rgyal gshen gyi bar du bcug go /

gnyis pa nub lugs dngos ni / de ltar dus dang / las dang / rkyen gsum ka dus gcig tu 'dzoms[8] pas rgyal po'i thugs la dogs pa med par g·yung drung gi bon bsnub par dran pa la / bru sha gnam gsas[9] na re / rgyal po lags / gros 'di bshol bar zhu / cis kyang mdzad na / bon bshos kyi lha bon sgo bzhi dang / de bton pa'i sku gshen gcig bzhag 'tshal / de ltar ma mdzad na / lha rgod lcam dral ru 'thur bas rgyal po rang sku mi rtag nyen mchi'o / zhes mchid glengs[10] pas / der rgyal pos gshen po rnams bsogs ste gsungs pa / sku gshen rnams gson dang / nga yi rgyal srid dang / khyod kyi bon srid (152b) gnyis tsam mnga' ris 'di ru mi shong ba 'dra bas / lha bon sgo bzhi dang / ge khod this 'phen dang / gco gyim bu lan tsha rnams dbag gi sku srung du bzhag 'tshal / phyi ma rnams bod ru bzhi las 'das par gshegs

[1] bri [2] (/ absent) [3] gyis [4] skyal [5] sgyug [6] gsungs
[7] dben [8] 'dzom [9] sras [10] gleng

shig / ces gsungs pas / blon chen ra sangs khod ram gyis zhus pa / kye rje rgyal btsad po lags /

sdig pa sgos khur yin pas ngan song gnas su ltung ||
dge ba spyi mthun yin pas mtho ris skas la 'dzegs ||
lta ba la chen zlos na nyid du mngon sangs rgya ||
g·yung drung bon la spyod na 'di dang phyi mar bde ||
rje rgyal btsan pos bka' de mi gsung[1] bar zhu ||

zhes zhus kyang / rgyal pos nga yi rgyal srid dang bon gyi[2] bon srid gnyis mi shong gsungs te ma bzhed do / der rgyung ya bla chen khod spungs kyis gsungs pa / kye gshen po kun /

rgyal pos[3] smra ba thang cig[4] yin ||
gcam bus smra ba yang yang yin ||
yus bos brdung ba khus kyis brdung ||
bon gshen rnams kyang mtha' ru gshegs ||
gyim bu lan tsha yang ma bzhugs gshegs par zhu ||

zhes gsungs pas / gyim bu lan tsha na re / dgung gnam la sprin thag ma chad na sos kar char pa sprin las 'bab / dgun chu (153a) sa la ma skam na drod gsher dpyid na ldang / dge ba tshe 'dir spyod[5] na dge rtags phyi mar 'byung / lha bon sgo bzhi dar na gsas mkhar srog 'dzin[6] pas / bdag kyang sdod[7] pa legs lha bon yang ma nub na dga' zhes zer nas / 'gro ma 'dod pa la bon sgo phyed dang gnyis byin pa ni rgyu bon zang ma'o / bon sgo phyed dang gnyis byang phyogs gsang ba'i brag rgya'o la sbas so / ge khod this 'phen na re / gshen po kun mi bzhag na / bdag kyang mi 'dug zer nas bzhugs su ma 'dod do / de'i tshe gshen po rnams kyis rgyu 'bras kyi bon sgo chen po drug ku hrang ma he la sogs la bkal nas gshegs te / zhang zhung kha yug gi ri mtshams byi ba mkhar du 'tshogs[8] nas / bka' bsgros pa'i dus su / skye chen mu thur gyis gsungs pa /[9] skyur 'thung mtshon thogs gdon gyis brlabs / za ma mo dang rgyal 'khor la / bag dang ldan par ma byas na / gshen po rnams kyang sku bkrong srid / bstan pa yang me chu la 'chor yang srid / de bas na bon sde cha gcig khye'u dran pa dang / khod nan yo phyas bsnams la yar lung sog khar gshegs / bon sde cha gcig mkhas pa mi bzhis bsnams la (153b) lho dom sgro nag po la bstan pa 'dzug tu gshegs / bon sde cha gcig dmu tsha gyer med dang / blon ra sangs khod ram gyis bsnams la byang 'brog gnam

[1] gsungs [2] gyis [3] po'i [4] gcig [5] spyad [6] zin [7] bsdad
[8] tshogs [9] (/ absent)

du gshegs shig / nam mkha' stong pa la rlung gi[1] 'khor los bsgyur ba'i[2] nyi zla gza' skar yang 'char zhing nub pa bzhin / da dung yang mtha'i rgyal po dbus su skyes pa gcig gi ring la'ang nub par 'gyur kyang / nyi zla nub kyang 'char ba bzhin du bon yang slad nas khad kyis dar bar 'gyur ro / zhes gsungs / gshen po phyi ma rnams ni / la la g·ya' ri dang gangs brag la gshegs / la la nags khrod dang mtsho do la gshegs / la la byang gi mya ngam la dmu yad rang babs su bsgrubs nas bzhugs so / dbang chen las / gshen po rnams lho bal mon gyi yul du bstan pa 'dzug par dgongs nas gtsang stod byi ba mkhar nas chas te gshegs so / bstan pa mi tshugs pa'i rtags byung ste / nam mkha' la sgra mi snyan pa dang / kha ba bu yug rlung dmar la sogs byung nas / rnil mtsho rde'u mgul nas slar log te / bon thams cad gter du sbas te / sa rtags mtshan dang ldan pa 'bri mtshams mtha' (154a) dkar la sbas / dran pa dang yo phyas yar lung ram po dpal ri la sbas / dmu tsha[3] dang ra sangs khod ram gnyis kyis byang 'brog tu byon te / zang zang lha brag / dang ra khyung rdzong[4] / rgyung[5] srub gsang ba'i brag la sbas / de ltar bon rnams rin po che'i gter du sbas nas gshen po rnams sum pa glang gi gyim shod nas mar chas te / sog po spre'u slag gon pa dang / 'jang mi mig dgu dang / hor dang rtsa mi shing mi la sogs la 'gro ba'i bar ma chad par phyin par gyur cig / g·yung drung bon gyi bstan pa gnyan par gyur cig / bstan pa gter du sbas pa rnams kyang me tog spang la rdol ba ltar dus la bab tsa na las dang skal pa ldan pa'i gzhon nu dal 'byor can kha cig gis rnyed par gyur cig / rnyed nas kyang bstan pa tshugs shing bkra shis par gyur cig / ces gsungs te smon lam bcas gter du sbas so / ces so / rnam dag las / rgyal po bdud mo la bstab pa'i brnag pa mdzad nas sum pa glang gi gyim shod la gshegs so / zhes so /

'dul bstan yang kha cig gis gri gum[6] dang / kha cig gis khri srong gi ring la nub par bshad la / khyung po blo gros (154b) dang mkhan nyi bstan gnyis kyis 'dul ba'i sde pa gnyis nang 'khrugs pa'i dus na / rgya gar dar ma ghir ti bya bas snyan phra[7] gsol ba la brten nas / zhang zhung rgyal po'i gdung rgyud ma yin pa'i rgyal po mu la mu sangs bya bas bkyon phab nas nub par bshad do / gang ltar yang 'dul bstan nub nas mu[8] zi 'gog par zhugs pa'i mi lo stong dang brgyad brgya'i

[1] gis [2] bas [3] tsa [4] rdzongs [5] rgyu [6] rum [7] phran
[8] mi

dus na sog ston gyis ting 'dzin las slong bar 'dul ba gling grags las gsungs pa bzhin rje bla mas kyang bzhed / khri srong gi dus su yang 'dul ba yod par sems te / srid rgyud las / bon gyi rab byung lnga brgya dus gcig la chos btsun du bsgyur bar bshad pa dang / de dus 'tsho bon don grub dang / rno bon khye'u cho snang ldan dang / gshen bon lha gnyan gsum gyis / gshen gyi 'dul ba mdzad khrims la sogs pa'i / shog dril bam po gsum stag gzig yul du khyer bas gter du ma tshud[1] par bshad la / de ni 'dul ba stod lugs su grags pa de nyid yin par mkhan nyi bstan[2] gyis[3] bzhed la / sga ston kyis slar yang de gsum lo so lnga nas 'khor te / la stod du 'dul ba spel bar gsungs shing / byams ma las kyang bon (155a) rgyal bzhi'i ring la / 'dul ba rgyud drug la mkhas pa'i bon gshen yod par gsungs pa'i phyir ro / gri gum[4] gyi ring la rgyu bon 'ga' zhig las rgyu 'bras kyi bon yo nub kyang / 'dul brgyud 'dzin pa'i bla ma tshe'i grub pa brnyes pa dag yul mtha' dbus gang rung la bzhugs pa rnams kyis 'dul ba'i brgyud pa 'dzin nas yod pa de dag khri srong gi dus na nub par mngon no /

gsum pa dbu yog byung tshul ni / rtsa rgyud nyi sgron las / gri gum[5] btsan po bon gyi dgra ru skyes / zhes pa nas / bon snyad med pa bsnubs / bon gshen mtha' ru spyugs / bon bsnubs pa'i dbu yog rgyal la bab / rgyal po the'u rang mang snya u ver gyi skye ba yin / 'bangs[6] lo ngam rta rdzi yis ltag pa gcus nas bsad / ces 'byung ba bzhin / bon bsnubs pa'i rjes su rgyal blon rnams sku dal gyis bro glu byed cing yod pa la / bar snang du mi dkar po 'jigs su rung ba zhig 'ongs[7] nas / khyod rgyal blon rnams kyi srog rtsa myur du bcad kyis zer nas mi snang ngo / der bon gyi bka' chad kyis rgyal po'i thugs su gdon zhugs nas / 'bangs[8] lo ngam la phrin brdzangs te / nga (155b) dang mnyan pa'i bon po ni spyugs / da nga la 'thab zla med pas / khyod kyis 'thab zla byed dgos gsungs pas / lho brag gi lo ngam[9] na re / khyod spyi phud kyi rgyal po chen po yin / bdag rgyal phran bcu gnyis kyi yab yin / rgyal 'bangs 'khrug pa ga la 'os / rje'i 'thab zla bdag gis mi 'ong bas bka' de mi gsung[10] bar zhu byas kyang ma gsan te / khyod rang dmag gyis la shog / mi 'ong na bdag gis dmag bya la khyod 'khor bcas myur du brlag par bya gsungs / der lo ngam blo sems ma bde bar yod tsa na / do nub rmi lam du bon gyi bka' srung skyes phran

[1] chud [2] ston [3] gyis / absent [4] rum [5] rum [6] 'bang [7] 'ong [8] 'bang [9] ngam gyis [10] gsungs

chas bzang zhig tu sprul ba zhig na re / lo ngam khyod skrag mi dgos kyi rgyal po ni bon gyi dbu yog gis / ma bdud kyis snying dkrugs[1] nas yod kyi / khyod kyi stobs kyis mi thub kyang lha dbye'i rdzas 'di rnams byas shing 'thab na thub pas / rgyal po la 'di skad smros shig / da ci nas kyang thugs dgyes na rje'i 'thab zla bdag gis mi 'ong mod / ku re'i tshul du rol mo zhig 'bul ba lags pas / zla ba phyi ma'i nya la rgyal rta phum dmar la chibs la byon / sprel dang byi la snga shad dang phyi shad (156a) la thogs / dpral bar dngul dkar me long gis brgyan / ral gri dmu tsha klad la bskor zhing / ba dmar glang dmar brgya la thal sgro mdung rtse srin mo rkang bcug[2] pa re khol la byon / de rnams phyogs thub kyi rdzas lags so / de ltar ma byas na bdag cag yod pa'i sa phyogs kyi lha 'dre rnams kyang[3] ru 'thur bas / rje'i sku tshe la gnod pa gang nas 'ong ma nges lags pas / de ltar mdzad par zhu zer ba zhes[4] smros shig zer ro / der lo ngam gyis kyang de ltar smras pas / rgyal po dgyes te / lo ngam snying bzang thos pa che bas de ltar bya'o gsungs / lo ngam gyis[5] dmag dang bcas nas 'ong bar 'thab dus bgos so / der lo ngam gyis dmag dang go mtshon bstar / sgra dang rol mo'i chas mang du bsags te / dus tshigs ma nor bar 'ongs so / rgyal pos kyang chad la brtson te lo ngam gyis ji ltar bsgo ba bzhin chas te byon / de'i tshe lo ngam gyis rgyal po la gser yig btang ste / 'o skol gnyis la rje 'bangs kyi khyad 'dug pas / sngon du ngas khyod la bsu ba zhig bgyi / de'i rjes gang gsungs kyi skyo sangs bgyi'o / zhes springs[6] pas / (156b) rgyal pos kyang khos zer ba bden gsungs nas / 'o skol gnyis mi mnyam pas khyod kyis dang por nga la bsu ba gyis shig dang de nas 'khrug pa yang bya dgos zer ro / der lo ngam nas sgra dang rol mos bsu ba byas pas / ba dmar dang glang dmar rnams 'grogs / thal sgro thams cad mdung rtses[7] phug / las rlung gis g·yos te thal 'tshubs su ring gis song bas / sa de la da lta[8] nyang ro thal ba tshal bya ba yod skad / de'i tshe rje'i sku nyen na dmu thag dang dmu skas sum cu rtsa gsum du 'gro ba yod pa ni ral gris bcad / pho lha dang mo lhas skyob pa yang spre'u dang byi las gnam du 'phangs / thal gseb la me long gsal ba la gtad nas mda' brgyab ste bsad do / de ltar yang gri bshad las /

dus dang bskal pa de tsam na ||
rgyal po gri gum[9] btsan po la ||

[1] dkrug [2] btsug [3] yang [4] ces [5] gyi [6] sprengs [7] tses [8] ltar [9] rum

log chos rgyal 'dre snying la zhugs ||
rgyal pos 'thab pa'i do ma brnyes ||
gri bdud ha la'i sprul ba ni ||
gri rgyal lo ngam rta rdzi de ||
rgyal pos 'thab pa'i do ru btsal ||
'thab mo kha dang lag pas phyungs[1] ||
mtshon cha las dang shugs las byung ||
rgyal po gri gum[2] btsan po de ||
rgyal rta phum dmar chibs (157a) su bcibs ||
sprel dang byi la 'phang la bskyon ||
ral gri dmu tsha klad la bskor ||
ba dmar glang dmar khal du ded ||
sprel dang byi la bskyon pa yis ||
rje yi mgur lha gnam du yar ||
ral gri dmu tsha bskor ba yis ||
dmu thag dmu skas rked nas bcad ||
ba dmar glang dmar ded pa yis ||
snang ba'i nyi ma mun par song ||
gri rgyal lo ngam rta rdzi des ||
gdug[3] pa'i gri mda' lto nag de ||
dpral ba'i dbyings su brgyab ste bsad ||
rgyal po gri gum[4] btsan po des ||
zhal nas dmod pa ngan pa bor ||
nga yi lus la gri rtags yod pa des ||
gri byed gnam du dar bar shog ||
dpral ba'i khrag gi sme ba des ||
gri yul gri mtshon rgyas par shog ||
dkor du mtshon cha yod pas kyang ||
mi srog mtshon gyis gcod par shog ||
drag rtsal log chos spyad pa yis ||
log chos mtha' nas dar bar shog ||
'jig rten khams su mtshon dar nas ||
rgyal khams 'khrug pas khengs par shog ||
lha ru tshangs pa bsten pas kyang ||
rgyal 'dre mgo lo rgod par shog ||
gdon 'dre yas dad che bar shog ||
de ltar dmod pa bor nas ni ||
rgyal po dmangs gyis gri ru bkrongs ||
gri gum zhes kyang de (157b) la bya ||

[1] phyung [2] rum [3] gdub [4] rum

zhes so / der lo ngam gyis de'u zhig gi steng du kha ltag par bstan nas bsad pas da lta yang nyang ro ltag zhal bya ba yod do / dmu thag bzang yag dang dmu skas them dgu chad pas / spur sa la lus pa de lo ngam gyis zangs kha sprod du bcug ste / 'da' le zang kha nas nyang chu la bskyur ro / sras spu lde[1] dang nya khri gnyis dvags kong gnyis su spyugs / blon po drag pa rnams bsad / zhan pa rnams spyugs / btsun mo la lug rdzir byed du bcug / sras mo lha lcam khab tu blangs nas rgyal sa lo bcu gsum khos bzung ngo / dus de tsa[2] na rje'i btsun mo dbal[3] za khri btsun bya ba nyin gcig phu na yar lug 'tsho ru phyin pas gnyid du song ba'i rmi lam du / skyes phran yid du 'ong ba zhig dang 'tshos par rmis sad nas bltas tsa na sngas na g·yag dkar po zhig nyal nas snang / de nas nam zhig na mo la pha med pa'i bu khrag sha lag mgo tsam zhig skyes so / mos gzhan la ngo tsha ste g·yag ru'i nang du bcug nas / ma sgyed kyi rtsa ru gsos pas bu tsha gzhan pas skye che ba sgo drag pa zhig byung ste / ming yang khrag gi bu ru las skyes su btags / bu de cher skyes nas ma (158a) la nga'i pha gang yin dris pas / mas khyod g·yag ru'i nang nas rnyed pa yin / pha su yin cha med zer ro / yang yid ma ches te nan bskyed nas dris pas / khyod la pha yod na da lta ma bu 'di e 'dra zer te bshad du ma 'dod do / de nas bus[4] phu na yar rta 'tshor phyin pas nyin gcig mi dkar rta dkar can zhig byung nas / nga ni yar lha sham po yin / khyod nga'i bu yin / pha gri gum[5] btsan po bya ba yod pa ni / lo ngam gyis bsad nas rgyal sa khos thob pa yin zer ro / der bus ma la de skad smras pas / mas kyang de dag de ltar yin te / rgyal sa 'di kun khyod kyi pha mes kyi pho brang yin / gcen po spu lde gung[6] rgyal bya ba da lta kong yul du bros nas yod / ces zhib tu bzlas so / der ru las skyes kyis spu lde[7] spyan drangs rgyal mkhar byi ba stag rtser rgyal sar bton / dbus kyi 'bangs rnams kyis ru las skyes kyang[8] rgyal sar bton te rgyal phran byas / ming rgyal po khri smon bzung du btags / de nas gtsang du dmag drangs bas gtsang 'bangs rnams kyis kyang / nged kyi rje byon zer nas dmag sna nang du drangs te / sham po rtse (158b) nas phabs / lo ngam pha bu dmag stong dang bcas pa gri ru bsad do / yang kha cig tu ru las skyes kyis / lo ngam gyi khyi dkar po dung gi rna ba can zhig yod pa la / reg pa'i dug bskus te btang ba la lo ngam gyis de la reg pas gum zhes

[1] lde'u [2] tsam [3] bal [4] pus [5] rum [6] lde'u gong
[7] lde'u [8] yang

kyang bshad do / dus der yul de ru mi nor la nad rim sna tshogs dang / lo thog la btsa' sad ser ba la sogs pa'i mi dge ba 'ba' zhig byung ba la / mo rmi ltas brtag pa kun na re / rgyal po'i spur chu la bskyur[1] bas lan da spur btsal 'tshal zer bas / gtsang po'i rgyud kun btsal bas ma rnyed / nam zhig na nyang stod stag tshal du / rtsis mkhan mkhas pa zhig la rtsis byas pas / rgyal po'i spur ni kong yul gyi klu lcam khod de ring mos bzung 'dug pas / de la bslu ba'i thabs klu lcam mnyes pa'i mchod pa mang po byas na rnyed pa 'gyur ro / zhes zer ro / der klu lcam mnyes pa'i mchod pa dang spyan gzigs yas glud sna tshogs chu bo'i gzhung la btang bas / klu dgyes te rgyal po'i spur chu khar thon to / de nas yar lung gi drang mo drang chung g·yag la bang so btab / rgyal dur la de (159a) snga bas da lta rje'i dur sa bang so khrod bya ba yod do / srid pa'i bang so sa la zug pa yang de lags so / g·yung drung bon gyi bstan pa'i 'byung khungs legs bshad rin po che'i mdzod las / rgya dkar nag zhang zhung dang / khyad par kha ba can gyi bod yul du sangs rgyas kyi bstan pa g·yung drung gi bon rin po che thog mar byung zhing bshad sgrub kyi bstan pa rgyas tshul dang nub tshul cung zad bshad pa ste rab byed lnga pa'o ||

[1] bskur

VI

nang pa'i grub mtha' yongs rdzogs kyi gzhi dang rtsa ba / dmu rigs gshen gyi bstan pa rgyu 'bras kyi bon rnams 'ol mo'i gling nas yul gyi snying po drug dang khyad par bod yul du bon bstan sngar dar nub byung tshul bshad nas / slar yang bod kyi rje 'bangs[1] rnams bon gyis bskyab lugs bshad pa ni / de ltar lo ngam kha cig nas dug gis grong ba dang / kha cig nas gri ru gum par bshad la / gang ltar yang lo ngam 'das nas spu lde gung rgyal gyis rgyal sa thob nas bon gyi bstan pa dar tshul dang / slar yang nub lugs gnyis su yod pa las /

dang po bon bstan dar tshul (159b) ni / dran pa'i lung bstan chung ba las / slob dpon stong rgyung gnam mtsho'i do la byin rlabs bcu gnyis kyi sgrub pa mdzad cing bzhugs pa'i tshe na / btsan po spu ldes gdan drangs nas zhus pa /

mkhas rtogs don dang ldan pa'i paṇ ḍi ta ||
bdag ni sngon nas lha sras gnyan gyi[2] sras ||
g·yung drung bon gyi brgyud pa zam[3] ma chad ||
bdag gi yab kyi thugs su gdon gsol te ||
bon bsnubs gshen po rnams kyang mtha' ru spyugs ||
bka' chad bdag cag rgyal blon kun la byung ||
rgyal po'i sku bkrongs rgyal srid 'bangs[4] kyis khyer ||
yab mes gong mas bzhengs pa'i[5] gsas khang bshig ||
nyang ro sham po'i pho brang thog gis bsgyel ||
la la mthar spyugs la la bran du bkol ||
khyod kyi thugs rjes bzung zhing bka' la 'dogs par zhu ||

zhes zhus pas / stong rgyung gis bon gyi bstan pa dar bar bya ba'i phyir / rig 'dzin brgya rtsa spyan drangs te / bstan pa gter nas bton te spel bar dgongs / zhes gsungs pa ltar gshen po brgya dus gcig la spyan drangs / kong yul bre snar rgyal gyi gri 'dur mdzad pas / gson po bkra shis te spu ldes (160a) rgyal sa zin / gshin po gnas spar te gri gum[6] thar pa thob po / da lta yang rgyal gri gum[7] gyi gri 'dur yog bar pa sum brgya drug cu bya ba'i bon bzhugs so / gshen po la gtsigs sngar bzhin du byin

[1] 'bang [2] gyis [3] zom [4] 'bang [5] pas [6] rum [7] rum

no / yab kyis bon la sdang yang ngas bon dar du 'jug / bon khrims srid pa'i tho chen 'dzug dgos zhes gsungs te / dus der bon bstan dar rgyas su spel bar dgongs pa la / gter bdag dang lha srin gyis ma sgrib[1] pa'i bon kha yar las gter nas ma thon pas zhang zhung gi yul nas khyung po[2] mu khyung rgyan dang / lha khyung rgyan sku mched gnyis gdan drangs nas / bod yul du 'bum sde lnga dang / bon sgo bcu gnyis dang / bon gyi mdzod sgo mang po dang / phra mo bcu dang / theg pa tha dad pa'i bon sgo mang po spel nas slar yang bstan pa dar bar gling grags la sogs nas bshad do / rgyal po des bstan pa dang 'gro ba gang la'ang legs par byas pas tho legs btsan po zhes kyang grags so / spu lde'i gdung rgyud la rgyal po sa la legs drug dang / chu la sde brgyad ste / spu lde[3] man chad nas rgyal rabs bcu gsum la bon sde gang dar zhe na / byams (160b) ma las / bar gyi gdung rgyud bcu gsum gyi bon dar te / pha rgyud lung chen / lta ba rdzogs chen / byang sems theg chen / gsas mkhar rgyud chen / kun gsal byams chen / 'bum khog dbang chen / rṭse 'dus khog chen / sde lnga mdo chen / gsang lung dbang chen / rgyas lnga 'bum chen / sde bzhi gzungs[4] chen / rig pa'i gnas chen / bon theg pa rim dgu la spyod / ces pa'i go rim ltar / pha rgyud kyi bon sde / sras rgyud rdzogs chen gyi bon sde / byang chub sems dpa'i bon sde / gsang sngags la gsas mkhar che lnga dang rgyud chen sde lnga'i bon sde / byams ma rgyas pa'i bon sde / g·yung drung yongs rdzogs dbang 'bum la sogs pa'i bon sde / gsas mkhar mtho thog la sogs pa'i bon sde / mdo mang rin chen lnga la sogs pa'i bon sde / rgyud sde chen po lnga la sogs pa'i bon sde / bye ma nyi khri la sogs 'bum gyi bon sde / gzungs sde bzhi la sogs pa'i gzungs[6] kyi[7] bon sde / rig pa'i gnas lnga la sogs pa'i bon sde[8] / theg pa rim pa dgu ste bon sde de dag rnams dar ro / de'ang byams ma las / byi ba stag rtse la sogs pa'i rgyal[9] mkhar dang gsas (161a) mkhar lha khang bcu gsum bzhengs nas / bon khrims srid pa'i tho chen btsug / ces so / 'dren pa'i dpon gsas kyang gdung rgyud bcu gsum po de dag phal cher bzhugs so / rkang grangs[10] ni / rgyal gshen mu khri btsan po / ha[11] ra ci par / stag ver li ver / a nu 'phrag thag / sad ne[12] ga'u / dạd mi thad ke / shad bu ra khug / zing[13] ba mthu chen / spe bon thog 'phrul / spe bon thog rtse dang bcu ni / mnga' bdag grub pa'i gshen bcu zhes bshad do /

[1] bsgribs [2] pho [3] lde'u [4] gzung [5] thog [6] gzung [7] gi [8] ste [9] rgya [10] drangs [11] ta [12] ni [13] zings

de'i steng du gsang sngags spyi spungs ltar na / sdong po dgu 'dus kyi blo brdeg las / mu khri btsan po nas khri ma stong 'phyo / 'phyo ma ye sangs / gnam sman dkar mo / gnam phyi gung rgyal la bshad / gsang ba rtsa 'gags su song ba'i sna la de bzhis mon bon ha ra ci par la bshad / ces so / rdzu 'phrul sman bzhi rtsis[1] pa de dag la bzhed do / sems phyogs ltar na khu byug las gsungs pa'i / hring ni mu ting / sum pa dbu dkar / glang[2] chen mu[3] ver dang gsum bsnan pas bcu gsum du bshad pa yin no / de nas rgyal tho ri lung btsan yan chad bar gyi btsan lnga'i ring la / g·yung drung bon gyi bstan pa'i nyi ma shar / mkhas pa'i lo (161b) paṇ gyi 'od zer bkyes / gdul bya 'gro ba'i blo mun sel ba'i[4] 'dzam bu gling gi rgyan chen po drug zhes bya ba / stag gzig gi mkhas pa dmu tsha[5] tra[6] he[7] ni rig gnas lnga ka la mkhas / rgya gar gyi mkhas pa lha bdag sngags dro ni nang rig pa la mkhas / rgya nag gi mkhas pa legs tang rmang po ni phyi rig pa la mkhas / phrom[8] gyi mkhas pa gser thog lce 'byams ni gso ba rig pa la mkhas / zhang zhung gi mkhas pa tso mi[9] gyer rgyung ni sgra rig pa la mkhas / bod dang me nyag gi mkhas pa nam ra tse sku ni srid pa'i rgyud la mkhas / zhes byams ma las gsungs so / de dag ni[10] rig pa'i gnas gang la'ang mkhas shing theg pa mtha' dag thugs su chud pa / skad rigs sum brgya drug cu bsgyur shes pa / rdzu 'phrul gyi zhabs dang ldan pa sha stag go / drug po de dag kun bod du byon pa mi gsal kyang de drug la gtugs pa'i mkhas pa mang du bzhugs so / btsan drug gi tham ma tho ri lung btsan nam lha tho tho ri snyan shal yan chad du bod na chos kyi sgra ma grags pa la / gzhan sdes lha tho tho ri snyan shal ring la dam pa chos kyi dbu brnyes zhes pa'i don yang / rgya gar nas bod du gser gyi (162a) mchod rten mu dras btab pa gcig 'di chos kyi mchod rten yin zer nas ston pa zhig byung bas / rgyal pos mchod rten pa ma bkag ste / chos zhes bya ba yang yod par 'dug zer ba byung ngo / zhes bsgrags byang las gsungs / byams ma las / de yan chad du bod na chos kyi sgra med pa la tho tho ri snyan shal la bstan pa phran bu gnam babs su byung ste / tsin da ma ṇi'i sku / pang skong phyag rgya pa rnams byung / zhes dang / srid rgyud las /

lha tho tho[11] ri snyan shal la ||

[1] brtsis [2] glangs [3] ma [4] bas/ [5] tsa [6] dra [7] he pe
[8] phram [9] min [10] gi [11] tho absent

zhes pa nas /

dus la bod na chos 'byung rtags ||
gser gyi mchod rten khru gang bcas ||
chos bzang lha yi 'dun sa nas ||
rigs gsum mgon pos chos kyi skyes ||
bar snang khams nas 'phangs te btang ||
rgyal po'i phyag tu bab nas bltas ||
phyag rgya snying po mu dra dang ||
byang chub ltung bshags bya ba byung ||
ji snyam thugs ni ma ches nas ||
chos ni rgya cher ma spyod de ||
thugs rje chen po cung tsam dar ||

zhes sogs gsungs pa'i chos de dag bod du byung na'ang rgyal blon gang gis kyang ma spyad par sbas pa la / thugs rje chen po'i snying po kha thon byed pa 'ga' zhig byung ba la bshad (162b) pa yin no / gzhan sde'i don lnga las / rgyal po khri thog btsan yan chad la gangs ri'i khrod 'dir ni dkon mchog gsum gyi sgra ma grags pa na / de'i sras tho tho ri snyan shal gyi ring la / gser gyi mchod rten / dge ba bcu'i mdo / pang skong phyag rgya pa gsum pho brang yum bu bla mkhar gyi steng du / nam mkha' nas byon pa ni dam pa chos kyi dbu brnyes pa yin zhes pa'i / dkon mchog gsum gyi sgra ma grags zer ba de rgyal po de yan chad la chos la skyabs 'gro byed pa med pas chos kyi dkon mchog gsum gyi sgra ma grags zhes pa'i don yin na yin du'ang rung / spyir dkon mchog gsum gyi sgra ma grags pa la byed na bzhad gad kyi rgyu yin ste / khri bdun gyi ring nas rgyal po 'di yan chad kyis g·yung drung bon kyi dkon mchog rnam pa bzhi la skyabs su zhus te 'di dang phyi ma'i 'jigs pa dang 'jigs pa chen po gang la'ang bskyabs nas mthar thug gi bde 'bras thob pa yin pa'i phyir ro / de nas gnam ru srong btsan yan chad bon rgyal bzhi'i ring la / byams ma las / ngo mtshar bka' bzhi'i bon rnams dar te / rgyas pa 'bum / 'dul ba rgyud drug / mngon pa sde bzhi / mtshan nyid (163a) sde lnga ste de dag la mkhas pa'i gshen po yang grangs med pa byung ngo / zhes pas / sngar gyi bon sde bcu gnyis dang / khyad par ngo mtshar gyi bon sde bzhi la sogs pa dar / de dag la[1] mkhas pa'i lo paṇ grub pa brnyes pa grangs med pa byung ngo / bon sde bzhi'i ngos bzung ni 'og tu 'chad do / rgyal po 'di dag gi ring

[1] las

la khyung po stag sgra don[1] gtsug / li shu stag ring / bhe shod kram chen po / sum pa mu phya dang bzhis stag gzig dang zhung zhung nas bon sde mang po bod du bsgyur bar gling grags la sogs las gsungs so / 'di dag gi dus na stong rgyung dang se lde me gsum ste mkhas bzhi'i grags pas bod chen po'i zhing khams thams cad du khyab pa byung ngo / de nas chos kyi srol 'byed[2] kyi rgyal po lnga'i dang po srong btsan sgam[3] po des / thugs dam ni zhi ba rgyas pa dang / khro bo rgyas pa dang / gser lung dri med dang / nyi khri chig 'bum dang / dri med shel mdog rnams la mdzad / sku tshe'i dkyil man chad la / rgya gar nas chos me stag tsam zhig byung ste / srid rgyud las /

> lha sras srong btsan sgam[4] po la ||

zhes pa nas /

> de dus dam chos za ma tog ||
> dkon mchog gsum gyi mdo sde dang ||
> rdor gcod (163b) pad ma dkar po byung ||
> rgyal po'i thugs dam byas pa las ||

zhes pa ltar rgyal pos bon la spyod pa'i zhor du zur nas chos la'ang cung zad nyams su blangs pa la / gzhan sdes srong btsan sgam[5] pos chos kyi srol btod ces zer ro / byams ma las / zhang zhung nas zhang zhung bza' lig tig sman blangs / stag gzig 'ol mo'i gling gi gsas khang dkar nag bkra gsal nas byon pa'i zhang[6] zhung gi lha gshen rab ston pa'i gtso bo dgung lo gcig pa'i sku tshad spyan drangs nas them chen lha khang bzhengs / bal yul nas bal bza' khri btsun blangs / bal po'i lha dngul gyi byams pa 'khor lo spyan drangs nas ra sa lha khang bzhengs / rgya yul nas rgya bza' kong co blangs / rgya nag gi lha gshen rab dgung lo brgyad pa'i sku tshad spyan drangs nas ra mo che'i lha khang bzhengs / rgya gar nas dge slong a kar[7] shī la ma ti bya ba mchod gnas su gteg cing / rgya gar gyi lha tsan dan gyi sku rang byung spyan drangs nas lha sa'i bcu gcig zhal khyad du 'phags[8] pa bzhengs / zhes so / 'on kyang rgyal pos chos spyad pas rje'i mgur lha rnams dang / 'jig rten gyi lha klu rnams ko long che bas lha sa'i mkhar chung thog (164a) gis bshig / mi mang po yang thog gis[9] bsad / nad mug dang lo nyes byung / rgyal po yang dgung lo sum cu rtsa drug pa la gshegs so / de'i

[1] dun [2] byed [3] sgom [4] sgom [5] sgom [6] zhung [7] dkar
[8] 'phag [9] gi

tshe blon po dar ma bya bas / chos 'di bkra mi shis pa zhig byung zer nas bsnubs so / zhes bshad la / srid rgyud las kyang /

rgyal po'i thugs dam chos spyad pas ||
rje yi mgur lha bcu gsum dang ||
bod kyi lha gsas gnam du 'phangs ||
mnga' ris mi bde 'khrug pa byung ||
de chos dang du blangs pa'i skyon ||
de'i tshe chos kyang lan cig[1] nub ||

ces so / khri rje gtsug brtan yan lnga la chos kyi srol 'byed ces zer yang / bon kho na las chos spyod pa cher med pa bsgrags byang las bshad do / srid rgyud las kyang /

khri rje gtsug brtan yan chad du ||
rgyal srid g·yung drung bon gyis bskyangs ||

zhes dang /

de yan gdung rabs sum cu drug ||
rgyal srid g·yung drung bon gyis bskyangs ||
rje yi gdung brgyud mnga' thang ldan ||

zhes pas / khri srong lde[2] btsan yan la rgyal rabs sum cu rtsa brgyad song 'dug pas / srong btsan dang khri srong gnyis kyis chos la spyad pas de gnyis mi brtsi la / de gnyis kyi yab mes gong ma sum cu rtsa drug gi (164b) ring la bon la bskyabs pas 'dir[3] bde phyi mar thar pa thob po / 'o na gri gum[4] gyis kyang bon bsnubs pas so zhe na / de'i tshe stod yan la bon spyod pa tsam la brtsi'o / des na khri srong lde[5] btsan sku tshe'i stod yan rgyal po lnga'i ring la 'dren pa'i dpon gsas kyang / mthu chen mi dgu dang / gshen dran pa nam mkha' la sogs pa bzhugs / mthu chen mi dgu'i rkang grangs ni gong du bshad pa de dag go / gzhan yang srid rgyud las / spe ne gu / phrom[6] bon mthu chen / bhe shod kram / rgya bon legs tang rmang po la sogs pa'i rdzu 'phrul dang mthu rtsal gyi nus pas / 'jang dang ga gon dang phrom dang rgya nag dang mon la sogs pa'i rgyal khams mang po'ang bod kyi mnga' zhabs su bsdus / phyogs kyi dgra thams cad kyi kha gnon / lha sa klu'i gling du sangs rgyas mchod cing gsang sngags sgrub pa dang / gsung rab[7] klog bshad dang / sems don sgom[8] pa dang / gsas khang dang / mchod rten bzhengs pa la sogs pas lha sa bkang / de dus na gzhan yang

[1] gcig [2] lde'u [3] 'di [4] rum [5] lde'u [6] phram [7] rabs
[8] bsgom

snya li shu stag ring / khyung po spu dang gzu tse dang / gu rub btsan po / khyung po ra sangs rje rgyal / phu lu gru 'dzin / 'gas po he (165a) dug 'dul / stag sgra gyim shad / gnub mang gnyer gzhu btsan / 'gar lha bzher tshe gsar / bon blon gsas chen / vas khri zung stong slod de dag la sogs mkhas grub bsnyems[1] pa grangs med pa bzhugs / bon mo grub pa bsnyems[2] pa'ang mang du bzhugs so / gtsigs dang yig tshang sngar ltar gnang ngo / de dus kyi bon po rnams la mtshan gyi yig tshang ni / rgyal po'i sku 'tsho bas sku gshen / blon gyi gros 'tsho bas gshen blon / rgyal gyis[3] bla na bkur[4] bas bla bon / srid pa'i grol phug shes pas kun shes / sangs rgyas bon bstan spel bas bon gshen / dge sdig rgyu 'bras ston pas ston pa / rgyal gyis che rtags byin pas bon chen / dman la pha ltar mgon pas pha ba / gshen khrims tshad mar bsrungs bas gshen btsun / shi ba 'dur gyis bskyabs[5] pas 'dur gshen / thar pa'i lam mchog bstan pas 'dren pa'i dpon gsas / de ltar ming gi yig tshang gnang ngo / de yan chad bod kha ba can 'dir g·yung drung bon gyi bstan pa rin po che bar du dar tshul zur tsam mo /

gnyis pa nub lugs la gsum /
(165b) yul gang du nub pa /
rgyal gshen gang gi ring la nub pa /
tshul ci ltar nub pa'o /

dang po yul ni / zhang zhung dang / bod dbus gtsang rnams su nub pa'o /

gnyis pa la rgyal po ni / rnam 'byed las / khri srong lde[6] btsan gyi ring la nub / ces dang / zhang zhung snyan brgyd las / rgyal po ni / zhang zhung na lig mi rgya / mon gyi rgyal po paṇ ṭa li kha / bod na rgyal po khri srong lde[7] btsan bzhugs pa'i dus / zhes so / gshen po ni / yang rtse klong chen las / bla chen dran pa nam mkha' dang / snya li shu stag ring bzhugs pa'i dus / mnga' bdag khri srong lde[8] btsan gyi sku tshe'i smad la nub / ces dang / zhang zhung snyan brgyud las / mkhas btsun grub pa thob pa rnams kyis bstan pa bskyangs / sgrub pa po rgyal theb rnams kyis bstan pa 'dzin / mthu che la rdzu 'phrul dang ldan pa rnams kyis bstan pa bsrungs[9] / bod dang zhang zhung gnyis ka na bon ma gtogs chos med / dus de tsam na / zhang zhung na grub pa thob pa mang yang / grub thob tso mi[10] gyer

[1] brnyems [2] brnyems [3] gyi [4] bskur [5] skyob [6] lde'u
[7] lde'u [8] lde'u [9] srung [10] min

chen bzhugs pa'i dus / bod na grub pa thob pa mang yang / spa ji phrom dkar po / stong rgyung mthu chen sogs[1] mkhas pa mi bzhi / bla chen dran (166a) pa nam mkha' bzhugs pa'i dus / zhes so /

gsum pa tshul ci ltar nub pa la gsum /
rgyu rkyen /
nub lugs dngos /
dbu yog byung tshul lo /

dang po la rgyu rkyen gnyis las /

dang po rgyu la'ang gangs can bod du dam chos 'byung ba'i smon lam btabs pa'i tshul dang /

phyis nas gri gum[2] gyi[3] smon lam log pa'i dbang gnyis so /

dang po ni srid rgyud las / sngon tshe rgya gar rgyal po'i yul shod du / sprang po mi gsum gyis slong nor bsogs nas / phyis su nor bsogs[4] te bsam pa bzang po dran / mchod rten chen po bya rung kha shor bya ba brtsigs / grub ma thub pa la gsum ka rgas te shi / 'chi khar smon lam bzang po btabs[5] te / bsam pa bzang pos phyi ma'i dge brgyags su brtsigs pa'i mchod rten 'di'i 'phro lus / bdag cag sprang po gsum mi tshe ma skyol bas slar dge ba 'di'i 'phro mthud nas dag pa'i lus thob par smon te / de yang gcig gis mchod rten 'di brtsig[6] pa'i skos mkhan zhig[7] tu skye bar shog cig zer / gcig gis mchod rten 'di brtsig[8] pa'i yon bdag cig tu skye bar shog cig zer / gcig gis mchod rten 'di brtsig[9] pa'i (166b) bzo mkhan zhig tu skye bar shog cig zer / der sprang po mi gsum yang smon lam gyi mthus rgya gar du skyes pas / mchod rten de'i 'phro mthud nas brtsigs pas grub ste / de gsum gyis 'chi khar yang smon lam btabs[10] ste / sngar gyi mchod rten brtsigs pa'i yon bdag tu skyes pa des nam zhig mnga' ris rgyal khams su / bdag ni dbang bsgyur rgyal po zhig tu skye bar shog cig zer / mchod rten skos mkhan des bdag ni bod yul du chos bshad pa'i ban de zhig tu skye bar shog cig zer / mchod rten gyi bzo bo des bdag ni bod yul du bon bsnub[11] pa'i lo tsā ba zhig tu skye bar shog cig gi smon lam btabs so / phyis su de ltar du skyes te sngar gyi mchod rten brtsigs pa'i yon bdag ni khri srong lde[12] btsan du skyes / sngar gyi mchod rten skos mkhan ni pad ma 'byung gnas su rdzus te skyes / sngar

[1] sogs absent [2] rum [3] gyis [4] sogs [5] btab [6] brtsigs
[7] cig [8] brtsigs [9] brtsigs [10] btab [11] bsnubs [12] lde'u

gyi mchod rten bzo bo ni bo dhi sa tvar skyes / khri srong lde[1] btsan ni rgyal po'i bu / pad ma 'byung gnas ni rdzu 'phrul sras / bo dhi sa tva ni bran phrug ste / 'chi khar bon bsnub[2] pa'i smon lam btabs pas / de'i nyes skyon gyis dman pa'i rigs su skyes so / zhes so /

gnyis pa gri gum[3] (167a) gyis log pa'i smon lam btabs[4] pa'i dbang gis byas te / gri bshad las /

> dus dang bskal pa da lta la ||
> rgyal po blo log skyes pa dang ||
> gdon 'dre yas dad che ba dang ||
> las ngan 'khrug pa dar ba rnams ||
> dus dang bskal pa snga ma la ||
> gri gum[5] btsan po dmod pa las ||

zhes rgyu dmod pa ngan pa de dag 'dzom pa las byung ngo /

gnyis pa rkyen la yang gnyis /
gzhan rkyen dang /[6]
rang rkyen no /

dang po gzhan rkyen ni / srid rgyud las / rgyal pos sngon gyi smon lam gyi dbang gis bon las chos lhag par[7] dgongs nas bon la gsang nas chos spyad pas / mi yis ma tshor yang lhas tshor te / srid pa'i lha rgod gnyan[8] po rnams kyis de ma bzhed nas / rje btsan po lha'i sras la skyon yang babs / 'dre dang bdud kyis[9] bla g·yu brkus / lha sa ru nad yams dang 'khrug pa dang thog dang ser ba byung / mi nad lang dgu dang phyug nad dal rim byung / der yul khams su mo ba btsal du btang ba la spe ne gu bya ba'i mo ba zhig btsal nas byung ba la / btsan po rgyal blon 'bangs[10] gsum 'dus nas mo btabs[11] pa la / rgyal po na re / da 'u bu'i rgyal khams 'di ru nad (167b) yams dang / 'khrugs pa dang / thog ser dang / phyug yams chen po dar ba 'di'i nyes skyon ci yin / gto cis phan dris pas / spe ne gu'i zhal nas / rgyal po lags / yul khams 'di ru nad yams dang / 'khrul pa dang mi bde ba sna tshogs byung ba de rnams / pha med pa'i nal phrug cig gi[12] nal sna phog zin pas de nal mi zan snying dmar gyi cho 'phrul yin pas de lta bu'i nal phrug des gdon zin pas gtsang ma'i lha rigs dang mgur lha bcu gsum gyis de ma bzhed pas yul du mi bde ba sna tshogs byung ba yin no / zhes rmed pas / de la

[1] lde'u [2] bsnubs [3] rum [4] btab [5] rum [6] (/ absent) [7] pa
[8] gnyen [9] kyi [10] 'bang [11] btab [12] gis

rgyal blon kun gyis rtog pa skyes te / mo ba la gser g·yu la sogs pa'i yon phul nas blon po rnams kyis nal phrug ngos bzung bar dang / phyis gto cis phan dris pas / mo bas mi thams cad 'tshogs pa'i nang nas nal phrug[1] de ngos bzung nas 'dzin na[2] bon po rus mi gcig pa du mas sel byas te glang khams pa la bskyon nas yas stags[3] sna tshogs dang bcas pa / nyi ma lho nub mtshams su btang na phan no zer / der kun 'tshogs nas btsal bas bu tsha lo bco lnga pa zhig la ngos bzung nas (168a) 'di yin zer / der yas glud bcas bu glang[4] la bskyon te nyi ma lho nub mtshams su btang bas / de rgya gar gyi yul du phyin pa la / ban[5] de rnams na re / mdangs mnal ba'i rmi lam du byang chub shing la nyi ma shar ba rmis / khye'u 'di las can zhig yin par 'dug zer / khye'us chos bslabs[6] pas sngar gyi las 'phro sad nas mkhas shing rdzu 'phrul mnga' ba'i paṇ ḍi ta zhig tu byung ba la / ming yang an ḍa bo dhi sa tva[7] ru btags so / de sngar bon bsnubs pa'i smon lam btabs[8] pa'i mtha' btsan / 'phral du bon gyis glud du btang bas bon po la sems brnag nas rgyal blon gnyis kyi snyan du bon bsnubs nas chos spyod pa de lhag pa'i phrin yig brdzangs pa dang / rgyal po chos la dad pa gnyis 'dzoms[9] pas byas so / zhes gab 'grel sogs las kyang de bzhin gsungs so / gzhan yang bsgrags byang las / blon po g·yu sgra ne ra bya bas rje lags / yab myes las lhag pa'i las stobs[10] shig dgos pas na / yab kyi gtsug lag khang thog gis bshig pa 'di gso 'tshal / de'i cha rkyen du rgya gar du (168b) chos bya ba / bon dang mi 'dra ba'i bya sla la khur yang ba zhig yod par 'dug pas de bod du gdan 'dren[11] 'tshal zer ro / blon po mchims bzheṛ na re / bon 'di bkur na yang lci / bslab tu yang rgya che / bsgrub tu yang gting zab / lha srung yang ru 'thur bas bsnub 'tshal zer ro / rje yang sngon gyi smon lam shugs dang / yab mes las lhag par bzhed nas 'phrig pa zos so / zhes pas so / gab pa'i 'grel las / dus de tsam na nyi ma'i 'od kyang 'grib pa zhig byung ngo / zla ba'i 'od kyang shi ba zhig byung ngo / mon gyi rgyal po paṇ ṭa li kha'i[12] rmang lam du / gser gyi nyi ma stong gsum dros pa zhig yod pa sa'i gting du nub nas de'i rje su dung gi zla ba zhig tshe pa rmis so / rgyal pos[13] rgyal bu hang yag la rmi lam de bshad / des mon gyi blon po re ba de sho la bzlas / des gcig nas gcig tu bsdebs te bod kyi rgyal po'i snyaṇ du gsan no / zhes 'byung ngo /

[1] phrul [2] zin na [3] stag [4] glang bu [5] bon [6] bslab [7] ta [8] btab [9] dzom [10] stabs [11] drangs [12] ling ga [13] po'i

gnyis pa rang rkyen ni / lde btsun rab gsal gyis ya gong gi brgyud pa bzung zhing / gco btsun ye (169a) shes kyis pham shi'i brgyud pa 'dzin no / lde gco gnyis ka la tshul khrims nos pa mu[1] zi gsal bzang gis / sad ne[2] ga'u las tshe'i dngos grub thob / de dus stong rgyung mthu chen dang / spa ji phrom[3] dkar po dang / snang bzher lod po dang / dran pa nam mkha' dang / li shu stag ring rnams kyi ring la bstan pa drag tu dar yang / dus mar 'grib pa'i dbang gis log par spyod pa mang bas / bon gyi 'dul sde[4] rnams kyang tshul khrims nyams nas 'chal bar spyod pa mang du byung ba dang / bon gshen gsang sngags sgrub pa po rnams kyang mthu'i dregs pas nga rgyal ba sogs kyis g·yung drung rol ba la sogs pa gnas sde chen po bzhi dang / gnas phran bcu gnyis bshig[5] / gshen rab kyi sku gdung rnams kyang nam mkha' la 'od du 'phros te yal / tshul khrims srung[6] ba je nyung la song / der rgyal pos kyang bo dhi sa tvas 'phrin rdzong lugs sam / bon gyi 'dul sde rnams kyis kyang[7] sdig spyod byed lugs sam / nyi zla'i 'od[8] (169b) 'grib[9] lugs sam / mon gyi rgyal po'i rmi lam sogs la brtag na / g·yung drung gi bon 'di yang nub pa'i dus la bab pa 'dra gsungs nas bsnubs so /

gnyis pa nub lugs la gnyis /
nub lugs dngos dang /
gter du sbas tshul lo /

dang po la /[10]
zhang zhung du nub lugs dang /
bod du nub lugs so /

dang po ni / zhang zhung snyan brgyud las / khri srong lde[11] btsan gyi ring la phyi blon bcu / nang blon bcu / 'phrin blon bcu dang sum cu yod cing / rgyal po mnga' thang che ste / stag gzig nor gyi rgyal po btul / tshong lam mtha' bar chu chen pos chod pa la shing ring gi zam pa btsug par khas blangs / phrom ge sar rgyal po btul / mnyan lam mtha' bzhir khas blangs / rgya gar chos kyi rgyal po btul / yon mchod byed par khas blangs / zhes pa ltar stobs kyis ma yin kyang las kyis rgyal khams mang po mnga' 'og tu bsdus te dbang bsgyur bas nga rgyal te / zhang zhung gi rgyal po gdul bar dran / zhes dang / yang zhang zhung gi rgyal po lig[12] mi rgya bzhugs pa'i dus te / zhang zhung

[1] mi [2] ni [3] kram [4] Here there is a note: de dus 'dul ba smad lugs med kyang stod lugs yod pas/ [5] zhig [6] bsrung [7] yang [8] 'od kyi [9] 'gribs [10] (/ absent) [11] lte'u [12] li

la dmag stong sde dgu khri dgu 'bum yod pa'i steng du / sum (170a) pa stong bu chung yan chad mnga' ris yin la / bod la stong sde bzhi bcu rtsa gnyis stong bu chung gcig dang rtsa gsum las med pas / zhang zhung gi rgyal po bod rgyal gyis dngos su btul mi thub mod / bod rgyal thugs la brnag pa ngan pas g·yo sgyus btul bar dran te / de'i dus na zhang zhung gi rgyal po la btsun mo chung shos[1] snang bza' sgron legs bya ba lo bco brgyad pa zhig yod pa de la / bod kyi rgyal po'i 'phrin blon zhe ngan la g·yo che ba snam nam legs grub bya ba zhig gis gser phye 'brong ru gang khyer / snang bza' sgron legs la byin nas smras pa / snang bza' sgron legs khyed lta bu / zhang zhung gi rgyal po'i khab yang[2] chun byed pa / bod rang dag a cang yang che ste / bod kyi rgyal pos kyang mi bzod pa 'dug na / 'di smad pa'i thabs yod dam / yod na bod kyi rgyal pos yang khab chen mo bya la / bod kyi mnga' ris sum gnyis ster bar 'dug go / zhes smras pas / sgron legs na re / zhang zhung gi rgyal po la dmag sa gzhir khebs pa yod / bod kyi rgyal po la dmag ba bre mo'i gzhung tsam las med (170b) pas dngos su btul mi thub / ngan g·yo dang thabs kyis 'dul na zhang zhung rgyal po ni / zla ba phyi ma la zhang zhung gi yul nas sum pa glang gi gyim shod du / sku rkyen dang bcas 'dun ma la bzhud kyi[3] der sgug la bsgrong mdzod / de'i thabs bdag gis gdod bya'o / zhes bud med kyi blo la ltos pa bcar mi 'dod pas de skad smras so / de yang tshes 'di la 'ong gi brda la khar 'jog par chad do / der bod rgyal blon dmag stong sde mang po dang chas nas 'ong ste / sna nam legs grub dang rgyal po gnyis sngon du la khar byon nas bltas pas chu sla[4] nga gang gi nang du gser chung dang dung chung gcig / dug mdel gcig dang gsum bzhag gda'o / bod rgyal na re / chu sla nga gang ni zla ba phyi ma'i nya la 'ong ba yin / gser chung dang dung chung ni dang ra'i gser phug dang / dung phug gnyis su dmag gis chod la sgug cig zer ba yin / dug mda' ni brnag pa skyed la sod cig bya ba yin zer te de ltar bsgugs so / der rgyal po gnyis mjal nas bod dmag gis zhang zhung rgyal po bkrongs so / der (171a) zhang zhung 'bum sde ni pham / bod khri sde ni rgyal lo / zhes 'byung ngo /

gnyis pa bod du nub lugs ni / rnam 'byed 'phrul lde las / rgyal po khri srong lde[5] btsan gyis blon po rnams bsags nas nga'i bla mchod du / rgya gar nas chos pa gdan 'dren dgos gsungs pas / 'gos khri bzang yab lhag na re / rje lha sras sku gzhon pa

[1] shes [2] yung [3] kyis [4] slang [5] lde'u

lags / mes gri gum[1] btsan pos kyang bon thang cig bsnubs pas sku tshe thung ste / sum cu rtsa drug pa la 'bangs[2] lo ngam gyis bkrongs / yab mes srong btsan sgam[3] pos kyang snub grabs mdzad pas sku tshe thung ste sum cu rtsa drug pa la gshegs / gtsug lag khang thog gis bshig pas da yab myes kyi sri kha lang bar mchi'o / zhes zhus pas / nga'i las 'phro chos yin cis kyang gdan 'dren dgos gsungs / 'gos khri bzang yab lhag na re / de sngon gdung rabs sum cu rtsa brgyad yan chad la / dam pa'i chos kyi bka' drin yod ma myong / da shes dang mi shes / slob dang mi slob / lha sras mnga' che rang gang dgyes mdzod cig zer skad / zhes so / srid rgyud las / der rgyal pos lo tsā btang nas / rgya gar nas slob dpon pad ma sam (171b) bha ba dang / an ḍa bo dhi chos dang bcas pa gdan drangs te / bon gyi rab byung lnga brgya dus gcig tu ban der bsgyur / mtsho rnga'i gnas kyang chos su phyungs / dus der ma zhang[4] phrom pa na re / dus kyi mtha' 'di lta bu shar / sngon gyi le'u bon po ni spangs / log spyod spyad pas rgyal khams 'khrugs / rje 'bangs[5] phung ba 'ong ngo zer / zhes dang / yang khri srong lde[6] btsan na re / bon ban gnyis bden rdzun rdzu 'phrul dang mthu rtsal che chung / gang bden gtug gshar bya dgos zer te / der bon ban mang po bsogs nas ras kyi 'on shang sbrel gur te / khra ther[7] te la kha yang phub te / brag dmar mgrin bzang bya bar / bon ban gnyis 'gran du bcug te / 'jig rten gsum gyi lugs dper bzhag nas / bon chos gnyis kyi kha 'dzin so sor bskos pa'i / bon po kun gyi kha 'dzin ni / ngam stag ra klu gong dang / sna nam phrom pa skyes gnyis bzhag / ban dhe kun gyi kha 'dzin ni / shākya rung gi bra ba dang / snyar stag btsan ldong gzig de gnyis bzhag / mgo pa kun gyi drang mkhan ni / 'gos khri bzang yab lhag la bcol / bon gyi shag mkhan dran pa nam mkhas byas / chos kyi shag mkhan bo dhi sa tvas byas te / gang (172a) bden so sor 'gran par chas so / der khri srong lde[8] btsan na re / bden rdzun rdzu 'phrul gang che ltos / bon ban gnyis lan gcig rtsal 'gran dgos zer / de nas rdzu 'phrul gyi rtsal 'gran pa la / stong rgyung mthu chen bya ba des / rnga gram po gzhung rgyal la bcibs nas bar snang mkha' la 'phur te gshegs / slob dpon pad mas nang par nyi rtse shar dus nyi ma'i zer la chos gos bkal / dran pa nam mkhas gnam la nyi zlas cha lang brdeb / bo dhi sa tvas rdo rje bar snang la 'phang te nyi ma dro skabs gcig gi bar nam mkha'

[1] rum [2] 'bang [3] sgom [4] zhi [5] 'bang [6] lde'u [7] the [8] lde'u

la rdo rje 'dzug / se sha ri dbu chen gyis mtsho ma phang[1] du gshegs nas chu rta bcibs nas mkha' la gshegs / gnubs nam mkha'i snying pos bar snang la phreng ba dpyangs te bzhag / me nyag lce tsha mkhar bus sog chu gyen du bsgyur / rlang dpal gyi snying pos ba snang la gzha' tshon ri mo bris / lde gyim tsha rma chung gis gcan gzan la khal bkal nas 'ded / 'bre dpal[2] gyi blo gros kyis ri dvags bzung nas 'o ma bzhos / sku gyim thang rma bos rnga dang shang la me spar / rlang[3] gtsug tor rin chen gyis sha rkyang gtso dgo g·yung par btul / khyung po (172b) stag sgra don gtsug gis stag gzig dom dred sgo khyir bkol / rma a tsa ra rin chen gyis bar snang la skyil mo krung gis bzhugs / snya li shu stag ring gis bya rgod du sprul nas nam[4] mkha' la lding / ka ba dpal brtsegs kyis dbu bcad nas sngar bzhin sbrel / spe ne gus lha bdar bas lha gsas mngon du phebs / ba gor be ro tsa na rkang mgyogs bya dang mnyam / rma bon thugs dkar bya bas rma chu gom pa gsum gyis bcad / gnyan pa dpal sbyin gyis bar snang la bum pa bzhag / co za bon mo bya bas ral gri la mdud pa lan gsum byas / lang gro dkon mchog 'byung gnas me chen po'i nang du bzhugs kyang ma tshig go / der rgyal blon kun kyang yid rangs so / de bzhin du bon ban rnams[5] rtsal che chung 'gran pa / bsad pa slong ba / 'dur slong ba / shag 'dren pa la sogs rgyal po'i bka' bzhin du byas pa la / bon po rnams khyad par 'phags tshul sogs bka' lung kun nas mang du bshad kyang yi ges ma drangs so / de ltar bon bsnub[6] pa'i snyad du rgyal pos de lta bu rnams bon ban gnyis la byed du bcug kyang / bon po rnams pham du ma nyan te gong du dpag pas ci (173a) byar ma btub pa la / rgyal po yang sngon gyi smon lam dbang gis chos spyad pa la dga' ba dang / ban de rnams dang blon po chos la dga' ba rnams kyis rgyal po dang bon po'i bar du bsam sbyor ngan pas ma nyes pa'i phra ma mang po yang yang bcug pas dang / mar 'grib kyi sems can rnams bsod nams dman zhing sdig spyod mang bas dang / bod kyi 'gro ba rnams bstan pa'i snying po g·yung drung gi bon rin po ches gdul ba'i zhing du ma gyur pa la sogs pas bstan pa lan gcig nub pa'i dus la bab ste / de dus dbus kyi bsam yas lhun po rtse dang / mtha' 'dul dang ru gnon gyi gtsug lag[7] khang rnams bzhengs su gsol / spyir chos kyi lha khang brgya rtsa brgyad bzhengs par khas blangs kyang sum cu las ma grub par grags so / de'i tshe rgyal pos sku

[1] pang [2] dpas [3] rlangs [4] nam absent [5] rnam [6] bsnubs
[7] lags

gshen rnams mdun du bsogs nas smras pa / sku gshen rnams tshe 'di dang phyi mar gnyis kar dam pa'i chos 'di bzang bar gda' bas / bon bsnub[1] la chos spyad 'tshal lags pas / khyod bon po rnams chos la zhugs nas ban de byed pa dang / chang dkar chab gsol ba dang / bod ru bzhi las (173b) 'das pa'i sa mtha' ru spyugs par 'gro ba rnams gang dga' ba zhig 'dom dgos zhes rgyal po'i mchid tshig de skad gsungs so / der gshen dran pa nam mkhas ras kyi shva gzhi bting ba'i steng du bden rdzun gyi shva rdel bzhag / rin chen chags shing klad[2] la bskor / gser gyi btsag[3] bu zhig snam phrag tu bcug te / 'di skad smras so /

kye gson dang khyod cag dpon g·yog gis ||
nged gyi yig tshang 'phrog pa 'dra ||
spyir mi lus thob pa shin tu dka' ||
gtsang ma mi lus thob dus 'dir ||
skyes nas chab gsol rngo mi thogs ||

de skad gsungs nas gser gyi btsag bus dbu skra bcad de snam phrag tu bcug ste gsungs pa /

bod yul spu rgyal btsan po dang ||
ma rtogs sems can nyon mongs dang ||
bla ban grangs su bzhugs pa kun ||
med pa'i chos la thugs ches pas ||
rgyal khams dkar po byed 'dod dang ||
sangs rgyas sa la gshegs 'dod na ||
nga dang khyod du ci ste dbye ||
bon dang chos su ci ste dbye ||
shes rab thabs kyi rgyal po la ||
stobs dang rig pa shar ba yin ||
thub dang ma thub bya ba'i tshul ||
gnyis su byed pa snying re rje ||
lhun grub yon tan rdzogs (174a) pa la ||
grub min dbye ba snying re rje ||
ye 'byung gdod nas dag pa la ||
yod med 'byed pa snying re rje ||
sems can rig pa'i klong shar ba ||
dge sdig dbye ba'i ban de 'khrul ||
de ltar ma rtogs lung gis bcings ||
sangs rgyas btsal bas mi rnyed snying re rje ||
bdag 'dra nam mkha'i nyi zla'i tshul |

[1] bsnubs [2] glad [3] gtsag

sems can kun la byams sdang med ||
ku lang rin chen sa le sbram ||
mnyam nyid rtogs pa'i skyes bu la ||
bon chos gnyis la bye brag med ||
dgra dang bu ru dbye ba med ||
gcig tu rgyal po gnyan[1] pa dang ||
gnyis su ban btsun phrag dog rkyen ||
gsum du bdag la dbyer med mnyam ||
de phyir rab byung nga yang byung ||

zhes gsungs te / dbu'i gtsug phud chan gris breg nas nan ban byas so / de'i tshe bon gshen kun gyi thugs la'ang bon lan gcig nub pa'i dus la bab par mkhyen nas / brnag pa'i las sbyor drag pos rgyal blon rnams skad cig la brlag par sla yang / thugs zhi ba mdzad nas drag shul gyi las ma mdzad par snyoms par bzhugs par dgongs so / rgyal pos kyang de shes nas rgyal blon rnams kyis bon bsnub[2] pa'i thabs sham pa dran pa la sogs pas kyang (174b) thugs la sa ler mkhyen / de'i tshe na mtha' bzhi khro gsas 'od gzungs bya bas yon bdag byas nas bon gshen rnams kyis bon rnams la las dar dkar gyi byang bu la mtshal gyis bris / la las rgya shog dang bod shog la tshos khas bsgyur nas snag tshas bris / 'bri ma khom pa rnams phal cher rgyal po la gsang ste gter du sbas so / bris zin pa'i dpe 'ga' zhig rgyal 'bangs btsun mo rnams la gtad / shin tu zab pa rnams khro chus rgyas btab ste / pho brang bsve sgo can du sbas so / de dus ban de rnams kyis bon sde mang po chos su bsgyur te / de'ang bon gyi sems phyogs kyi sde rnams chos kyi sems lung phyogs su bsgyur / bon g·yung drung khams brgyad ni / chos stong phrag brgya bar bsgyur / bon g·yung drung gser gyi yang zhun ni chos lta ba gcer mthong bya bar bsgyur / bon byang sems gab pa ni chos sems smad phyogs su bsgyur zhing bcos / bon bsgrags pa rin po che[3] ni chos mdzod gong mar bya bar bsgyur ro / de bzhin du bon sde mang po chos su bsgyur te mtshan spos / bon gyi gsas khang dang mchod rten la la bshig / la la nying zhal byas nas chos (175a) kyi gtsug lag khang du ming bsgyur ro / de dus ma bdud srid pa'i rgyal mo'i thugs su bsnyung nas rgyal po gnyid pa'i rmi lam du bud med nag mo lcags kyi ral ba phya le ba / spyan gsum mche ba gtsigs pa / sku la rma bya'i thul ba gon pa zhig gis / rgyal po la 'di skad du / nga'i bon sgo bzhi

[1] gnyen [2] bsnubs [3] che absent

mdzod dang lnga / gzhung cha lag 'grel ba rnams nga la gtod cig / gal te mi gtad par bsgyur zhing bsnub na / log chos khe drag la spyad kyang mi khom par / khyod kyi tshe nyi ma thal ba dang snyoms pa'i rting du ti'i dmyal khams su sbyong ngo / gsungs nas med de song ngo / rgyal po yang thugs skrag nas de phyin chad bon rnams chos su bsgyur zhing snub pa'i phod pa chung ngo / de'i tshe na spe ne gu / bhe shod kram / lha[1] ru gser yag / khu lha 'dzin bzhis rje la bzlog pa'i ko long la / bsve'i 'dan dkar dang / rnga gshang phrug gcig brdzangs te gru nang du bcug ste / yar chab gtsang po'i gzhung la bskyon te btang bas / 'ben gang tsam du sleb pa dang / spe ne gus bsve'i 'dan dkar gtsug ste lha la bos pas yar chab gtsang po gyen du log nas / rgyal khams su chus gang bar (175b) byas pas da dung yang lha sa dang bsam yas phan chad du sa gzhi bye mas gang ba'i gtan tshigs de tsug yin / der bon po bzhis rnga gshang thogs te nam mkha' la 'phur te yul g·ya' gang khyim zhur bya bar babs so / zhang zhung ver stag / khu stod bya zhu can / stag lo bya ru can / sum pa dbal rgod bzhi sogs bon gshen mang po zhig gis rdzu 'phrul dang pra rtags kyi bon rnams spyang sngon dang stag gzig la bkal nas shar phyogs hor dang 'jang dang rgya yul du byon / sum pa kha khyer la sogs 'ga'[2] zhig ni bon rnams zangs kyi ga'ur bcug nas ku hrang la bkal te sog po sprel slag can gyi yul du byon / zhang zhung ral ba can / mtha' bzhi bum bu chung sogs kha cig ni bon sde 'ga' zhig bsnams te shar rgya mo rong du byon / tshe bon don grub / snang bon stag thul can / se bon khyab tse / gshen tshad la mi gsum la sogs pa 'ga' zhig gis ni mdzad khrims dang 'dul ba'i shog dril bam re khyer nas stag gzig tu byon / dbal lha khri / me nyag stag gsas / khyung po ne khrom la sogs pa bon gshen 'ga' zhig ni byang mya ngam la byon nas dmu (176a) yad rang babs su bzhugs so / stong gyer rgyung / nyang dpal mthong sogs ni lho brag gi gting du byon no / snyan gyer rgyung / zhang zhung stag thul can la sogs ni bal po bse ris la byon no / rdzu 'phrul dang ldan pa la la nam mkha' la 'phur te gshegs / la la me chu rlung gsum du brdzus te gshegs / la la khyung dang bya rgod dang ngang par sprul te gshegs / la las nyi ma mtshan du bsgyur te gshegs so / de dus na bod yul na mkhas pa mi bzhi / mthu chen mi dgu / li shu stag ring / gshen dran pa nam mkha' ma gtogs pa bon gshen rnams bon dum re khyer te so sor gshegs nas song ngo / de dag

[1] lta [2] 'gag

ni srid pa rgyud kyi kha byang dang bsgrags byang sogs mang po las btus so /

gnyis pa gter du sbas tshul ni / srid rgyud las / dran pa nam mkhas rgyal po la / bdag rab tu byung nas chos par byas lags na / srid pa'i dvangs ma g·yung drung gi bon 'di lags pas mi bsnub par gter du gzhug par zhu 'tshal gsungs pas / rje'i zhal nas / dran pa nam mkha' khyod rab tu byung ba legs / bon 'di rnams shog ser la bris te mi brlag par (176b) sa la gter du sbos shig / khyod rang yang smon lam legs par thob cig gsungs / zhes so / bsgrags byang las / der mthu bo che mi dgu dang dran pa la sogs kyis glang lo dpyid zla ra ba'i gdugs la bon rnams sde tshan so sor phyes nas / gter gyi rgyal po gcig / blon po bzhi / yang blon gcig dang drug / khyad par du gsang gter che ba lnga / gter phran stong dang bdun brgya sbas / rje'i gtsug lag khang thams cad du bon sde re re sbas / de bzhin du ri brag mchod rten la sogs su gter kha shin tu mang ba sbas / zhes pa ltar / bye brag tu gnas gang la bon sde gang zhig sbas pa ni / spyir ston pa'i bka' la 'bum bla med sde bzhi dang / 'bum phran brgya dang rtsa brgyad yod pa'i / 'bum sde bzhi las gzungs kyi 'bum ni sum pa glang gi gyim shod la sbas / de la gzungs sna 'bum yod pa ni pha rol phyin pa bcu phyogs bcur grags pa'i rgyud khri ste 'bum mo / mdo 'bum ni byang sgro rtsar sbas / de la mdo sde chen po bzhi / mdo phran 'bum mo / mdo sde bzhi ni / khams gsum sems can skye 'chi'i mdo / snod bcud bskal pa chags 'jig mdo / dus gsum bde (177a) gshegs byung khungs mdo / bla med go 'phang sgrub thabs kyi mdo dang bzhi'o / mdo phran ni mdo sde chen po bzhi la rgyud sum khri sum stong / de la mdo phran 'bum yod / gsang sngags kyi 'bum ni zhang zhung khri sde khyung lung du sbas / de la rgyud 'bum yod pa ni / phyi rig[1] sngags la rgyud khri / nang gsang sngags la rgyud bzhi khri / gnyis ka ma yin pa'i sde la rgyud khri / drag po'i sngags la rgyud khri / thugs rje rgyun sngags la rgyud khri / zhang zhung this sngags la rgyud khri / bdud rtsi sman gyi gong khal la rgyud khri ste 'bum mo / shes rab 'bum la zab mi zab bzhi / srid pa snang ldan dkar po'i 'bum sde rnams lho brag khom[2] mthing la sbas / khams brgyad gtan la phab pa'i 'bum ni cog ro mtha' dkar la sbas / thugs rje nyi ma stong khyab kyi 'bum ni spa gro stag tshal seng ge phug tu sbas / bon nyid snying po bdal ba'i 'bum ni lha sa'i yang dben yer

[1] rigs [2] kham

ba'i rdzong la sbas so / de yang gter bod du sbas pa'i sa ni / nub phyogs o rgyan dang bod kyi mtshams zhang zhung khyung lung dang / shar phyogs rgya dang bod kyi mtshams sum pa glang gi gyim shod dang / (177b) lho phyogs bal po dang bod kyi mtshams brag smyug ma bu khur can dang / byang phyogs hor dang bod kyi mtshams li ving sgong ring sogs gter gnas chen po bzhi[1] ru gter kha sum brgya drug cu sbas so / gter gyi rgyal po bzhi ni / bsam yas mchod rten nag po / mchims kyi gad pa stag 'bring / ra sa'i 'phrul snang / gtsang stod bye ma g·yung drung dang bzhi la sbas so / gter gyi blon po sum cu rtsa bdun ni / glo yul gang 'bar / gangs ti se'i mgul / spos ri ngad ldan gyi shar / mang nam brag phug / mang yul byams sprin / khyung lung dngul mkhar / za dum dgu rtse / spa gro stag tshal seng ge phug / sku lha thang lha'i mgul / dbu ru[2] ka tshal / sku lha skyog khrom gyi rtse / spa sha gangs kyi rtse mo / byang sgro rtsa / cog[3] ro mtha' dkar / lho brag khom[4] mthing / g·yas ru gtsang 'phrang / g·yas ru khra 'brug / brag rgya bo / rta sgo gangs mdun / mang mkhar lcags 'phrang / zang zang lha brag / yar lha sham po / rma pom ra'i g·yas zur / mtshal gyi phug mo che / lho brag mkhar chu / lho nub kha byang / gong gi dbu rtse / gser thang sha ba can / tsha ba rong gi snyog / lcum (178a) nag po'i brag / rta nag rkyang phu / skya ra'i phu / brung gi g·ya' sil / mang yul byang nam / spa gro skyer chu / brag phu[5] gsang dmar / nyan gyi se[6] bo ri rnams la sbas so / gter gyi yang blon chen po gcig ni / bod yul dbus kyi lha sa'i yang dben yer ba'i rdzong[7] la sbas so / gzhan yang gnam mtsho phyug mo'i gong / pha bong ru rtse'i shar / seng ge kha yel la yang gter mang du sbas / rgyal po dang bka' bgros nas / bsam yas dbus kyi ka ba dang / zur bzhi'i ka ba la gter sgrom lnga lnga sbas / rnam par snang mdzad kyi thugs kar sgrom gcig / rgyal ba byams pa'i byin pa gnyis la sgrom re re / gshin rje gshed kyi thugs ka dang / rta mgrin gyi thugs ka na ngan sngags thog dang 'dra ba sum brgya / sgo'i phyi na khra spyang dang ma them gyi 'og na 'dre srin bu dgu'i sgrub pa rnams sbas / kha non dang ru non gyi lha khang rnams la'ang gter kha lnga lnga sbas / lha dgu / rgyung dgu / bon gyi 'du gnas dang brag ri rnams la yang gter kha brgya rtsa sbas / mchod rten dmar po / pho brang bsve sgo can / khrom pa gyang / gas kyi byi ba mkhar / long 'gro rtag rdzong / khri 'od stag rtse (178b) la sogs su sbas so /

[1] brgyad [2] g·yon ru [3] co [4] kham [5] gu [6] bre [7] rdzongs

sbas khar gshen po rnams kyis g·yung drung gi bon gnyan[1] po 'di yang spyad dbang med par sbas pas mi 'gyur gser ltar shog / 'dul ba'i dus la bab tsa na / las 'phro can dang 'phrad nas sems can kha lo bsgyur bar shog / ces smon lam bcas sbas so / mkhas pa mi bzhi dang khyung po gyer zla med / dran pa nam mkha' la sogs pa'i gshen chen rdzu 'phrul dang ldan pa dang / gshen phran rkang mgyogs grub pa rnams kyis / mdo khams stod smad du sba bar chas te / ti se shel phug man chad dang / rgya yul dar rtse yan chad du / gter kha sum brgya drug cu / gter phran grangs med pa rnams gter du sbas te smon lam dkar nag btab / bon gshen rnams kyang la la rdzu 'phrul rtsal gyis so sor gshegs / la la mkha' spyod kyi zhing khmas rnams su gshegs / la la srid pa'i lugs dang bstun nas sngar gyi bon gshen gyi chas rnams bskyur te / dbu la dam zhu dom ra re re gon / sku la dugs po rtsi ber re re mnabs / phyag na kha ṭām spa ber re re bzung / rgyab tu be bum pa tra can re re khur nas sum pa glang gi gyim shod du gshegs (179a) par chos so /

gsum pa dbu yog byung tshul la gnyis /
zhang zhung snyan brgyud las bshad pa /
byang gter las bshad pa'o /

dang po ni / khri srong lde[2] btsan gyis zhang zhung gi rgyal po bkrongs pas / zhang zhung khri sde ni yar chad / sum pa'i stong sde ni mar bud / bod sil bur song ba'i dus na / zhang zhung rgyal po'i khab chen ma khyung bza' mtsho rgyal ma bya bas / bod rgyal la sems kyi brnag pa skyes te gyer spungs snang bzher lod[3] po spyan drangs nas zhus pa / sku gshen chen po lags / bod rgyal khri srong lde[4] btsan gyis rje lig mi[5] rgya[6] ni bkrongs / bon khrims dar gyi mdud pa ni bshig[7] / rgyal khrims gser gyi gnya' shing ni chag / g·yung drung bon gyi bstan pa ni bsnubs te / 'di lta bu'i dus byung bas na / 'di la thugs kyi brnag pa zhig cis kyang zhu 'tshal zhus pas / gyer spungs kyi zhal nas / nga la spu zhes bya ba gser srang gang la lo gsum du bsgrub na bod ru bzhi brlag nus pa dang / khyung zhes bya ba srang phyed zla ba gsum du bsgrub na / yar lung gi sar khri srong 'khor dang bcas pa brlag (179b) nus pa dang / rngub bya ba gser zho gang la zhag bdun du bsgrubs nas 'phangs na rgyal po nyid sod pa rnams yod na gang bya gsungs / khyung bza' mtsho rgyal ma byang sems dang ldan pas / bod khams pa rnams kyis ma lan te / rgyal

[1] gnyen [2] lde'u [3] lad [4] lde'u [5] min [6] rgyal [7] zhig

po nyid lan pa lags pas / rngub mdzad pa zhu zhus pas / gyer spungs chen pos da rog gi mtsho gling la dar dkar sha ba ri'i gur phub / za 'og gi gdan la bzhugs nas gser zho gang la zhag bdun du bsgrubs te gser nam gcig gsum du bcad de sum nam gcig srod la 'phangs pa sog kha'i[1] spun po ri la sha ba yu mo bdun nyal ba la phog pas gnyis bsad / lnga rengs[2] pas da lta yar lung sha ba rengs[3] zhes bya ba'i ri yod do / sum nam gcig nam gung du 'phangs pa yar lung sham po mgul gyi mtsho la phog pas / mtsho skam klu bros pas da lta yar lung mtsho skam bya ba yod do / sum nam gcig tho rangs su 'phangs[4] pa mkhar byi ba stag rtse la phog pas me 'bar zhing / rgyal po snyung gis zin to / de'i tshe rgyal po rig pa can de'i zhal nas / bon skyong rgyal po bkrongs / g·yung drung bon gyi bstan pa bsnubs pas / da nang tho (180a) rangs dzva 'ong lugs kyis gyer spungs chen po thugs khros pa yin pas slar btegs 'tshal zhes gsungs nas / gyer spungs snang bzher lod po gdan 'dren du rta pa brgya la gser phye mang du brdzangs te mngag pa dra phye'i lung par phyin te / zhang zhung gi mi gcig la gser phye byin nas gu rub snang bzher lod po gar bzhugs sogs dris pas mi de na re / gyer spungs chen po nyid da rog gi do la bzhugs mod / sku ma nges cir yang sprul bas gang snang la gsol ba thob cig dang zhal bstan par 'gyur ro / zhes zer ro / der mtsho la gru gzings bcos te do la phyin pas za 'og gi gdan la shel gyi gna' ru 'od 'phro ba zhig snang ngo / de gyer spungs yin par shes nas de la phyag 'tshal gser phye phul te lo rgyus bsnyad nas gsol ba btabs pas / shel gyi gna' ru de nyid gyer spungs kyi skur bzhengs[5] te zhal bstan te gsungs pas / bon skyong[6] rgyal po bkrongs / g·yung drung gi bon bsnubs / sems la brnag pa skyes kyang bod kyi rgyal po sku bgrong na bod khams phung du 'gro bas ran tsam byas pa yin gsungs / der bod mi rnams gyis bod kyi rgyal po snyung la (180b) 'bangs sdug / bon dang gshen gyi bka' chad de ltar byung ba lags / da[7] rje'i bla mchod du gdan 'dren pa lags pas gshegs 'tshal zhes zhus pas / 'o na nga la chad gsum dgos te / zhang zhung rgyal po'i sku tshab tu gser gyi mchod rten zhig bzhengs pa dang / gu rub kyi mi sde la yar lung sog kha byin nas bla dang blon gyi khral med pa dang / ngas spyod pa'i zhang zhung gi bon sde sum brgya drug cu de mi bsnub par bzhag pa'i chad gsum dgos gsungs pas / de dbang blon gsum gyis khas blangs nas gdan drangs so / bod kyi rje blon 'bangs rnams

[1] ka [2] rings [3] ring [4] 'phang [5] bzhings [6] skyongs [7] de

kyis phyag byas te ci gsungs nyan no zhus pas / der gyer spungs kyis gsang this kyi sngags mdzad pas / rgyal po'i sku las gser rta rnga lta bu mang po thon nas rgyal po'i bsnyung pa dvangs so / 'bangs rnams kyang sdug bsngal las grol bar mdzad do / zhes so /

gnyis pa byang gter las bshad pa ni / de ltar bon bsnubs nas chos spyod pa'i ban btsun rnams kyang re zhig nas spyod pa 'chal nas sgrub pa'i phyag rgya mar snyad btags nas 'bangs kyi chung ma dang bu sring bslad / tshogs la snyad btags nas (181a) mi ro zas su zos / dam rdzas la snyad btags nas mi gtsang ba sna tshogs la 'byol nyog tu spyad pas / rje'i mgur lha rnams thugs 'khrugs te yar lha sham po'i zhal nub tu gzigs / thang lha yar bzhugs[1] byang du gzigs / rma pom ras shar du gzigs / ldong lha dgung grags lho ru gzigs / gtsang rigs kyi lha rnams dgung du yar / yul lha dang yul sman rnams gzhan du bros / lha rnams mnol te / shul du rgya gar gyi dam 'gong zhugs / bar der chos pa rnams kyis 'dur lung med du byas pas mi shi tshad 'dre ru song ba dang bsdong nas bod du mi la nad rims / phyugs[2] la god kha sna tshogs byung / gnam la char pa ma bab / sdong gi bon po sngags pa gter bcug bya bas thog smad bco brgyad phab pas / dkar chung gi gtsug lag khang thog gis bshig / rgyal po yang snyung gis zin / ban de rnams kyis tshe chog byas pas kyang ma phan no / dus der mo btab phyva[3] blan pas / bon po spyugs nas bon bsnubs pas lan / da slar spyan drangs nas rje'i mgur lha gsol / dran pa nam mkha' nan ban nas bton na phan zer ro / (181b) de'i tshe brag mkhar ba can na co za bon mo gtsigs 'og na chud nas yod pa la zhus pas / bdag gis spyan 'drong gsungs pas / la la na re bon gshen rnams byang mya ngams su shi nas med zer / co za na re / gshen po rnams byang spang shong gi khyim na brag srin mig dmar 'khol po byas / ri dvags spu sdug gi 'o ma 'jo yin yod zer ro / 'o na co lcam bzhud la bon gshen rnams nyid kyis spyan drangs 'tshal zhus te gser dngul bya bo gang phul bas / bon mos dre'u 'phar ma dgu rkang zhig bcibs nas ldong lha gsol gyin byon pas gshen po rnams dang mjal te / bod du mi bde ba sna tshogs byung nas gshen po rnams spyan 'dren du mchis pas gshegs 'tshal zhus pas me nyag lce tsha mkhar bu na re / bon la 'gro don las med / sems can la snying rje bas 'gro dgos gsungs nas gshen po rnams byon no / de'i tshe bsam yas kyi phyi mthar phebs te mchod rten bzhi

[1] bzhur [2] phyug [3] phya

gzigs nas gco gshen phyag dkar gyis 'di nyid ci lags gsungs pa la / 'di me btsa'i mchod rten chen po bzhi lags / bskor ba byas na sgrib pa dag zer / (182a) 'dus byas kyi mchod rten la ya mtshan mi brtsi gsungs nas phyag rgya bar snang la bsgyur bas bdud 'dul sgra sgrogs g·yung drung brtsegs pa'i mchod rten zhig bar snang la kun gyi mthong yul du bkra lam mer byung ste / de las 'od 'phros pa lha sa'i brag la babs pas da lta rang byung shel gyi mchod rten du grags pa de'o / de nas sgo nang du byon pas lder so chen po zhig gda' ba 'di ci lags gsungs pas / 'di sgo srung khro bo chen po ma hā ka la bya ba yin 'di la phyag byas na bar chod sel zer / khu bon mthong grags na re / snang srid sku dang zhing khams la / sgo sung khro bos ci zhig bsrungs / gsungs nas se gol btabs pas lder so rdul du zhig go / des na da lta yang sgo srung med pa'i don de yin no / de nas dbu rtser byon nas 'dag sku rnams la rnam snang gtso 'khor la gzigs nas 'di dag ci lags gsungs pas dbus kyi rnam snang dang byang chub sems dpa'[1] brgyad lags / 'di dag la phyag mchod byas na mchog thun mong gi dngos grub thob par 'gyur zer ba la / sum pa mu cho[2] na re / 'dus byas kyi gzugs brnyan la mchog thun mi re (182b) gsungs nas brang shag gis slog nas bstan pas thugs ka na yi dam yab yum 'khril sbyor du bzhugs pa lam mer gda'o / ban blon kun kyang ngo mtshar ro / de nas pho brang du byon te rgyal po dang zhe sa rtse sprod du mdzad do / de nas bon pos dang por rgyal 'gong gi kha gnon du gsas khang zhig bzhengs dgos gsungs nas be dkar gling du gsas khang zhig bzhengs / mchod rten nag po bon lugs su bzhengs so / des nad kyi bskal pa chad nas sdug bsngal bde ba la bkod do / da lta yang mchod rten des gdon thub pa de tsug yin no / dran pa nam mkha' nan ban nas bton te / rje la tshe dbang bskur bas bsnyung ba dvangs so / der bon po rnams la yul gsum phul ba ni / stod du 'o mo lung / smad du kong yul bre sna / bar du yar 'brog thun gsum mo / stod nas 'bangs[3] gsum phul ba ni / so dang so ngan klo bo[4] gsum mo / dbus nas 'bangs gsum phul ba ni / dre[5] dang slong dang kong dang gsum mo / lha sa'i thang gsum ni lha gsol sar phul / yar lung sog[6] kha[7] ni bzhugs pa'i gnas su phul la / de'i tshe rje'i zhal nas / bon[8] chos gnyis snga mar thang re bsnubs te / (183a) da lta spyan drangs pas sngar gyi bon gter thon la bon chos lhan mar spyad 'tshal gsungs te / bon chos

[1] dpa' absent [2] co [3] 'bang [4] 'o [5] ze [6] so [7] ka
[8] ban

gnyis mnyam du spyod pa'i tha tshig bgos pas lo gsum du de ka ltar gnas so / de nas yang ban blon gyis phra ma byas pas rgyal pos chad gsol te chos la spyad cing bon la ma spyad kyang bon gtan med du ma bsnubs pas da lta bod gangs can 'dir bon gyi bstan pa bzhugs pa'i gtan tshigs kyang de'o / khri srong lde[1] btsan la khab gsum yod do / rgya bza' kong cu / tshe spungs bza' dmar rgyan / chun ma 'bro[2] bza' dkar mo dang gsum / 'bro[3] bza' dang rgya bza' gnyis la sras med kyang chos la dkar bas mnga' thang che / rgya bza' la pho yangs bza' dang gyim sham bza' sogs ming tha dad snang / tshe spungs bza' ni sras gsum gyi ma yin kyang bon la dkar bas rgyal pos thabs kyis spangs te mnga' thang chung / ban de rnams kyis kyang tshe spungs bza' la smod pa'i thabs mang po bshad pa snang ngo / de la sras gsum ni che ba mu tig btsan po / 'bring mu ne bstan po / chung ba mu thug btsan po'o / mu ne btsan po yab kyi rgyal sar bton nas / bsam yas su mchod pa (183b) chen po'i gzhi btsug / bod 'bangs kyi phyug dbul lo gsum snyoms / chab srid lo gcig dang zla ba bdun du mdzad de bcu bdun pa la yum gyis dug btang te 'das so / de ban des 'dur bas bla ma khug ste / mi rnams kyi khong du zhugs nas glo brdol gyi gtam smra bar byed la / ban de la 'dur phug med pas bon la dpe blangs pa bod 'bangs rnams kyis shes nas gzod yid ma ches so / der dran pa nam mkhas rnam shes bkug thugs phab pas / rje khri srong yang bon la thugs ches nas gshin 'dur gyi bon med na gshin po gnas nas mi 'drong bar 'dug gsungs / bon mgo g·yo ba la 'dur bon snga'o / da lta yang rgyal po mu ne'i lhe 'dur bya ba'i bon yod do / de'ang bsgrags[4] byang las / bon la dgyes pa'i lha sras gtsang du spyugs / zhes pas / sras mu tig dang mu ne gnyis bkrongs pas rgyud chad nas / yab khri srong dgung du gshegs nas sras mu thug spa gro gnas spyan drangs te rgyal sar bton / de dus lha sras bod 'bangs la thugs chad nas yab kyi dkor mdzod nas bon sde mang po dang sman dpyad dang bzo khyad par can rnams bsnams nas khyung po gyer zla med dang gnyis kyis (184a) spa gro phug gcal du gter du sbas / dbal phur gyi rgyud cha lag kun kyang rje mu thug dang khyung po gyer zla med gnyis kyis gter srung drug la gtad nas spa gro phug gcal du sbas par bshad do / der rgyal po yang sku tshe thung ste lnga bcu rtsa dgu pa la gshegs so / zhes byang gter dang rnam 'byed gnyis mthun par bshad do / kha cig gis 'bro[5] bza' dkar

[1] de'u [2] 'brom [3] 'brom [4] sgrags [5] 'brom

mo rje'i thugs la btags pas btsun mo un chung dang dmar rgyan gnyis ma dga' nas dug btang bas mnga' bdag sum cu rtsa drug pa la bkrongs[1] so / zhes bshad pa'ang snang ngo / mu thug la sras gsum las dar ma ral ba can sku bsod che ste 'dzam gling sum gnyis mnga' 'og tu bcug zhes pa'i grags pa thob / dgung lo bco brgyad lon pa la 'on 'jang rdo'i pho brang dgu thog brtsigs / kha che dzi na mi tra spyan drangs nas / sngar bsgyur ba'i chos rnams skad gsar bcad kyis gtan la phab cing / dka' spyad rnam pa gsum mdzad de / sde ba bye brag tu gzhi thams cad yod par smra ba'i 'dul ba las / gzhan dang gsang sngags rnams ma bsgyur zhig gi bkas bcad / tha na bre dang srang dang zhva la sogs kyang rgya gar dang mthun par bcos / (184b) rab tu byung ba re re la 'bangs mi khyim bdun bdun phul zhing dbu'i thod gdan du gting nas zhabs spyi bor len no / de'i sku ring la chos shin tu dar so che / sku srung ni bon po khyung po stag sgra don[2] gtsug dang / zhang zhung bon po dun tang rgyal ba gnyis kyis mdzad / mthu rtags su 'gran gyi chu mig gyen du drangs ba dang / 'gran gyi ri bo la rnga bsgril ba'i rnga'i mchongs pa re re'i shul du shing shug pa re re ldem ldem skyes / gshang brag la brdab pas chu mig gtsang ma bdun brdol bas / lha sras kyi zhal nas / nga'i mnga' 'og 'dus tshad kyis bon po'i sku la mi bsdo ba dang / rnga thogs kyi dkor la ma 'bags pa shig par bka' stsal / chal dang gtsigs ni yab myes gong mas gnang ba la brten no / lha sras dar ma'i sku srung ni / me nyag gi bon po rgyal sum dpal legs dang / se bon ye shes dpal gyis bsrungs / mthu rtags su kham sa'i mi mos smra ba / mi min dngos su bkug pa sogs bsam las 'das par grub / khri dar ma 'od srung dang / khri lde yum brtan gnyis kyi sku ring la / so khri thog rgyal ba / nyang bon rdo rje mkhar / g·yag rgod me btsan / bhe shod kram bzhis sku bsrungs / (185a) so khri thog rgyal bas ri rab g·yo zhing 'gul ba dang mtsho chen po skam pa dang / nyang bon gyis nam mkha' la 'phur ba dang / g·yag rgod me btsan gyis stag dang spyang kur sprul nas dro bar gcig gis zhang zhung gi yul nas dzva sngags blangs pa dang / bhe shod kram gyis spa khug gnam du bskyur bas / gnam thel nag pos skad ngan tse re re bton pa sogs grub rtags ya mtshan pa du ma mnga' / lha sras dpal 'khor btsan gyi sku ring la / pha ba bstan legs kyis sku gshen dang blon po gnyis ka byas / bkra shis brtsegs pa dpal gyi sku ring la zas dkar chos nyid kyis sku srung mdzad do / de

[1] bgrongs [2] dun

dag ni bka' 'bum la sogs nas btus te bkod pa'o / 'di man chad nas rgyal sa 'bangs la shor bas / rje'i gdung rgyud mtha' la 'khyar te / bod khams sil bu song ngo / 'on kyang 'di man chad du yang rgyal po'i gdung rgyud gar yod du yang / sku srung gi bon po srol kha mi chad tsam re yod par bshad pa'i lo rgyus mang du snag yang gtsigs su mi che bas ma drangs so / ding sang kong po rong la sogs su bod kyi rgyal brgyud[1] kha cig grong sprang (185b) du byed pa yod par bshad pa'ang 'dug go / g·yung drung bon gyi bstan pa'i 'byung khungs legs bshad rin po che'i mdzod las / bod kha ba can du sangs rgyas g·yung drung bon gyi bstan pa rin po che bar du dar nub byung tshul mdo tsam bshad pa'i skabs te rab byed drug pa'o ||

[1] rgyud

VII

de ltar bod gangs can gyi zhing du g·yung drung bon gyi bstan pa rin po che bar du dar nub dang gter du sbas tshul bshad nas / slar yang rdzogs pa'i sangs rgyas dang rig 'dzin rnams kyi smon lam gyi mthus bod kyi gdul bya rnams 'dul ba'i dus la bab nas / bka' gter snyan brgyud kyi bon rnams rig 'dzin rnams kyi sprul pa mang pos bstan pa spel zhing g·yung drung gi bon gter du bzhugs pa rnams stod smad kyi gter gnas so so nas gdan drangs te bstan pa phyis su dar tshul bshad pa la gnyis /

bka' ma dang /
gter ma'i lo rgyus so /

dang po la gnyis /

mtshan nyid pa dang /
der gtogs pa'o /

dang po la gnyis /

'dul ba dang /
sngags sems so /

dang po ni / rgyal po lag ngan gyi sras lha thu khra thang bya ba la rgya spun (186a) mang gis[1] chad pa phog te / sog po'i yul du spyugs nas sog po stong dpon dpal 'bar bya ba'i rta 'tshos te yod pa / de me nyag gi rgyal po rab rtse 'dus kyis bslus nas rta rdzir bcug / sog po'i yul nas spre'u slag pa zhig gon nas 'ong pas ming sog po spre'u slag can tu btags / des rma ri del gsum du rta 'tshor phyin pas / brag dkar rtse 'dus kyi phug pa sgo nag la phug dkar ba zhig tu phyin pas nang du na bza' rab byung gi cha byad la / dbu skra sa la 'khyil ba zhig 'dug / de mjal[2] ba tsam gyis las sad nas dga' spro skyes te phyag 'tshal nas / skyes bu chen po[3] dgongs pa glod par zhu zhus pas / ci yang mi gsungs / sang nangs par yang phyin nas de skad zhus pas spyan gyi rdzi ma 'gul tsam / yang de'i phyi nyin na zhus pas zhal gyi dkyil 'khor 'gul tsam / de'i phyi nyin zhus pas dgongs pa las bzhengs te zhal nas / kye ma dus la

[1] gi [2] 'jal [3] Here there is a note: mu zi gsal bzang

bar chod khyod / mi'am mi min ci'i rkyen gsungs / rta rdzi na re / bdag dman pa'i lus can / sdug pa'i blo can / gzhan gyis bdag byas pa zhig lags zhus pas / 'o na khyod kyis bstan pa'i sa bon nus sam gsungs / (186b) bdag kyang khyed kyi rjes su zhu byas pas / sa bon nus gegs mi brtsi gsungs nas / rta rdzis drang srong chig rdzogs su mdzad de / tshul ming khri 'bar tshul khrims su btags so / de yang mu zi gsal bzang ni gdung sob mu cho'i sprul pa yin te / srid rgyud las /

mu cho'i thugs kyi sprul pa ni ||
mu[1] zi gsal bzang bya ba 'byung ||
mi rtag sgyu mar rtogs nas kyang ||
'dan ma'i brag la 'gog par 'jug ||

zhes so / rta rdzi ni / g·yung drung gtsug gshen rgyal ba'i sprul pa ste / de nyid las /

gtsug gshen rgyal ba'i sprul pa ni ||
'khor ba'i 'du 'dzi spangs pa yi ||
sog po khri[2] 'bar tshul khrims mtshan ||

zhes so / de'i slob bu 'dan ma mu 'bar gyi sras / 'dan ma rin bzang[3] ngam g·yag slag can du grags pa / tshul ming rgyal ba gtsug phud de / snga ma las /

drang srong rgyal ba'i sprul pa ni ||
'dan ma rgyal ba gtsug phud do ||

zhes so / de'i slob bu grum bon dbal 'bar gyi sras grum bu shing slag can / tshul ming tshul khrims gtsug phud de gtsug sras rma bo'i sprul par gsungs so / de'i slob bu ni zi[4] khrom 'bar gyi bu ya zi bon ston / tshul ming shes (187a) rab tshul khrims te / bla mu thur dgongs pa rab gsal zhes kyang zer /

dmu tsha[5] tra he'i sprul pa ni ||
drang srong lus la mkhyen pa can ||
ya zi bon ston zhes kyang bya ||
bar du mu thur dgongs par gsal ||
tshul ming shes rab tshul khrims mtshan /
sum snang rma yi brag la 'byung ||

zhes srid rgyud las so / de'i slob bu gnyos a rin bya bas dka' ba spyad nas gtsang nas mdo smad du phyin pa / mu thur dgongs pa rab gsal dang mjal[6] nas rab byung mdzad pa'i tshul

[1] mi [2] khrims [3] bzung [4] gzi [5] tsa [6] 'jal

ming rin chen rgyal mtshan te khri lde[1] 'od po'i sprul pa yin / bla chen dgongs pa rab gsal la chos pa'i slob bu mang po byung ste / de yang rgyal po glang dar gyis chos bsnubs nas ban de'i rab byung la la bsad / la la khyi ra ba'am rngon par bcol / la la spyugs te chos sgra mi grags pa lo brgyad cu byung / kha cig gis lo bdun cu don gnyis sam don drug yang zer / de'i tshe brag dkar phug mo che na lha lung dpal gyi rdo rje gsang spyod la zhugs nas yod pa des / sa thel nag por brdzus te 'ong nas rgyal po la dug mda' brgyab nas dkrongs / de nas bar thel (187b) khra bo dang / gnam thel dkar por brdzus nas bros so / phyis chos kyi bstan pa spel du bod na chos btsun med pa'i tshe / gnyos btsun la lha lung dpal rdos dris nas / khyod kyi mkhan po su yin byas pas / gnyos btsun na re / nga'i mkhan po rma ri del gsum gyi brag la bla mu thur dgongs pa rab gsal bya ba yod gsungs / der bod pa rnams gros byas te gtsang nas mi bzhi / dbus nas mi gsum ste bdun phyin te / drug mkhan po dang mjal sdom khrims rnams rdzogs par blangs so / bla chen gyi zhal nas / nga'i 'dul brgyud[2] 'di bon la thug cing / so thar gyi sde yin pas de'i rjes su zungs / spyod pa tshul khrims la spyod / mkhan po mi brjed pa'i rtags bzhi blang dgos / khyod rnams kyi[3] bstan pa rgya chen po yong bar 'dug ste / sangs rgyas kyi bstan pa gang dar kyang legs pa yin gsungs nas 'dul khrims phog / mkhan po'i rtags bzhi ni / sham thabs kyi ka ba sngon po / thang pa'i snas tsha sngon po / pad zhu'i dbu rtse sngon po / gding[4] ba g·yu mdangs sngon po dang bzhi dgos / de dag ma grub na skud pa sngon pos lhan tshugs su tsems dgos gsungs so / bka' (188a) rtags de bzhin byas pa'i sngon gyi snam sbyar la sogs pa chos lugs kyi dgon rnying 'ga' la'ang snang ngo / chos pa mi bdun gyi gtsang gi mi bzhi ni / lo ston rdo rje dbang phyug / tshang ge shes rab seng ge / 'a zha rgyal ba blo gros / 'bri ye shes snying po dang bzhi / dbus kyi mi gsum ni / klu[5] mes tshul khrims shes rab / rag shi tshul khrims 'byung gnas / rba ye shes blo gros dang gsum mo / des na gzhan sde'i smad 'dul gyi brgyud pa dang / rang lugs kyi 'dul brgyud gcig pa yin te / srid rgyud las /

dar ma sprel mgos chos bsnubs pas ||
de yi dbu yog rgyal po yang ||
lha lung dpal gyi rdo rje yis ||

[1] sde [2] rgyud [3] kyis [4] gdeng [5] snub

thabs dang sprul pas mtshon gyis bsad /
chos kyi bsnyen chos sdom pa nyams ||
dam chos 'dul khrims brgyud pa'ang chad ||
de rjes chos kyi sdom pa'i brgyud ||
sog 'dan grum gsum nas brgyud pa'i ||
mu thur dgongs pa rab gsal zhes ||
gnyos btsun a rin bya bas zhus ||
ban de rnams la 'ang de ltar 'bogs ||

zhes so / de dang mthun par gzhan sde'i chos 'byung kun gsal[1] las kyang / bon dgongs pa rab gsal la dbus nas (188b) klu mes tshul khrims shes rab sogs mang pos gtug ste bsnyen pa rdzogs par mdzad / der klu mes mkhan po bon la bdag dbus su 'gro ba la mchod pa'i rten zhig zhu byas pas / bon pos 'obs[2] zhu phog nas zhva la sa ser zhig btabs nas 'di gyon pa nga dran pa gyis gsungs / zhva ser gyon pa de nas dar / dbus gtsang bod du 'dul grva bsam gyis mi khyab pa 'byung zhes lung bstan to / rang lugs gtsang gi 'dul brgyud gnyos btsun rin chen rgyal mtshan gyi mkḥan bu / lhang lhang gtsug phud kyi sprul pa / gnyos kun dga' tshul khrims / de'i mkhan bu dvangs[3] ba yid ring gi sprul pa mgar rin chen gtsug phud / de'i mkhan bu thugs dkar[4] ye shes kyi[5] sprul pa pra phud tshul khrims / de'i mkhan bu gang rum gtsug phud kyi sprul pa gnyos lag drug pa tshul khrims ye shes / de'i mkhan bu dran pa nam mkha'i sprul pa khro tshang 'brug lha dang / 'od lha gsal 'bar gyi sprul pa sher btsun g·yung drung pra phud gnyis / sher btsun gyi mkhan bu ye shes tshul khrims kyi sprul pa gur btsun g·yung drung rgyal mtshan / de'i mkhan bu g·yung drung (189a) tshul khrims kyi sprul pa 'tsho btsun nam mkha' rgyal mtshan dang / pra phud tshul khrims kyi sprul pa g·yung btsun jo gdung gnyis so / de gnyis kyis[6] mkhan slob mdzad pa'i mkhan bu dam pa ri khrod pa dang / sum ston tshul blo gnyis te / srid rgyud las /

gser thog lce 'byams sprul pa ni ||
rme'u[7] 'dul 'dzin dam pa'i mtshan ||
ting 'dzin rtogs pa'i shes rab can ||
bstan pa dar rgyas 'dzin cing ston ||
legs tang rmang po'i sprul pa ni ||
sum pa'i gdung 'dzin tshul blo'i mtshan ||

[1] Here there is a note: gnam lcags rdo rjes mdzad pa/ [2] 'bo [3] dang
[4] kar [5] kyis [6] kyi [7] rmi'u

zhes so / de rnams ni 'dul ba gling grags dang / srid rgyud gnyis mthun par ma 'ong par 'byon 'gyur du lung bstan pa bzhin du byon nas dbus gtsang kun tu 'dul ba'i bstan pa 'dzin nas 'gro don mdzad pa sha stag go / de nas 'dul brgyud bru zhu spa gsum dang gshen dang bzhi gyes pa'o / de dag rnams kyi 'dul brgyud 'dzin pa'i mkhan bu byon tshul ni bstan pa'i rnam bshad dar rgyas gsal sgron sogs gzhan du gsal la / 'dir sa gsum na 'gran zla bral ba'i rje mnyam med chen po'i 'dul ba'i brgyud pa byung tshul ni dam pa'i mkhan bu (189b) yar 'brog me ston shes rab 'od zer te / lung bstan las /

khar bo gang bzang shar mgul du ||
shes rab 'od zer bya ba 'byung ||
de yang nga yis byin gyis brlabs ||

zhes so / de'i mkhan bu dran pa nam mkha'i sprul pa gshen nam mkha' rgyal mtshan / de'i mkhan bu dran pa'i sprul pa bru yi rgyal thebs / g·yor me ston grags pa'i dpal / de'i mkhan bu zhang zhung lha khri'i sprul pa 'a zha bdud rtsi rgyal mtshan / de'i mkhan bu hris pa gyer med kyi sprul pa 'a zha blo gros rgyal mtshan dang / bru'i rgyal sras dam pa dar ma rin chen rgyal mtshan gnyis / gong gi dam pa'i mched grogs sum ston tshul blo'i mkhan bu / bru rje btsun dang mar ston rgyal legs te sman gong ba gnyis / sman gong ba'i mkhan bu ba thang zhang ston bsod nams dpal / de'i mkhan bu sum ston lha 'bum / bru ston dar ma dang / sum ston lha 'bum gnyis kyis mkhan slob mdzad pa'i mkhan bu gshen ston blo gros rgyal mtshan / de'i mkhan bu gshen ston ye shes blo gros / de'i mkhan bu sman gong ba 'dul ba blo gros / de'i mkhan bu sman gong ba shes rab blo gros / de'i mkhan bu rgya (190a) rong ba mkhar snar bzhugs pa g·yung drung ye shes / de'i mkhan bu rje mnyam med chen po'i mkhan po bru ston tshul khrims ye shes so / de rnams kyang rig 'dzin gong ma'i rnam sprul ma 'ong[1] lung gis zin pa sha stag byon pa ste / yi ge mang bas ma bris so / rje mnyam med chen po man chad kyi brgyud 'dzin mkhan rabs ni 'og tu 'chad par 'gyur ro /

gnyis pa sngags sems la gsum /

zhang zhung /
rgya gar /
yong lugs kyi bon skor ro /

1 'ongs

dang po zhang zhung gi bon skor ni / zhang zhung snang bzher[1] lod pos gser dzvas bod rgyal dbang du bsdus nas zhang zhung gi bon skor sum brgya drug cu mi bsnub[2] par khas blangs pa'i gtso bo zhang zhung snyan brgyud[3] ces grags pa'i sngags sems gnyis po gyer spungs nas dpon rgyal btsan po yan chad brgyud tshul gong du bshad pa ltar la / dpon rgyal btsan po nas stod smad gnyis su gyes pa'i / stod brgyud ni / dpon rgyal[4] btsan po gu ge blo ldan la / bka' brgyud skor bzhi bstan nas / rtogs ldan 'khrul zhig drug nas stod du dar ba la / snyan brgyud stod lugs su grags / smad brgyud (190b) ni / shang gi khyung byid mu thur la nyams brgyud rgyas 'bring bsdus gsum dang / sngags snyan brgyud me ri'i phrin las che chung gnyis la sogs bstan nas rnam sprul grub chen lnga nas smad du dar ba la snyan brgyud smad lugs su grags so / de nas stod lugs kyi rtog med zhig po dang / smad lugs kyi 'ol sgom kun 'dul gnyis nas / yang ston chen po la man ngag kun rdzogs par bstan / yang ston chen po nas brgyud pa mang yang lho brgyud byang brgyud gnyis la 'dus te / lho brgyud ni / dam pa 'bum rje nas cig chod dad shes yan yin / byang brgyud ni / lung sgom rtog med nas rnam grol mu lto ba chen po yan no / stod smad gnyis lho byang gnyis dang bzhi po de yang bla ma rnams kyi sa gnas kyi mtho dman dang / bzhugs yul gyi khyad par la ltos nas de ltar bshad pa'o / brgyud bla'i rkang grangs tsam ni / rtogs ldan 'khrul zhig drug / rnam sprul grub chen lnga / khungs ldan bla ma dgu / sngags sems bla ma lnga / bka' brgyud rig 'dzin dgu / zab lam mnga' bdag brgyad / 'gro ba'i mgon po gnyis / brgyud ldan (191a) bla ma gsum / mnyam med gdengs ldan brgyad la sogs pa nas da lta'i bar du gong mas 'og ma la tshig brgyud dang nyams brgyud gnyis ka zung 'brel du brgyud pas / de dag rnams las kyang 'od lus dang / lhag med grub pa dang / bar do dang rang bzhin sprul pa'i zhing tshun chad du mngon par sangs rgyas pa'i rtags su sgra dang 'od dang sa g·yo ba sku dang yig 'bru byon pa la sogs pa ni rnam thar chen mo las gsal lo / yang me ri'i bon skor kha cig ni tshe spungs zla ba rgyal mtshan yan spyir gcig cing de la zhang zhung bon po kha yal me phung kyis zhus / des gdung rus dbang las yab btsan sgra byin rlab dpal bya ba'i sras gsum gyi bar pa mes this pa lha legs la brgyud / this pa lha legs kyi sras kho ne rog / de'i sras yang ne rog / de'i sras gtsug phud

[1] bzhed [2] bsnubs [3] rgyud [4] rgyal absent

rnam rgyal / de la sras bzhi yod pa'i bar pa dbang gi rgyal mtshan ral ba can / de'i sras ring ne / de'i sras khro mo / de'i sras zang nge / de'i sras dpal rtse / de'i sras btsan rgyal / de'i sras btsan grags / de'i sras smra lo / de'i sras drang srong 'od rgyal te / de rnams sras rgyud yin te gcig (191b) nas gcig la brgyud / 'od rgyal la gco ston smon lam blo gros kyis zhus / de la dre ston rgyal mtshan gyis zhus / de la spa nyi dpal bzang pos zhus / de la spa bstan rgyal bzang pos zhus / de la ba ye ye shes rgyal mtshan gyis zhus te dar ro /

gnyis pa rgya gar bon skor ni / zag med thugs rje'i brgyud tshul gong du bshad la / de nas gong ltar dran pa nam mkha' nas tshe dbang rig 'dzin la brgyud cing / tshe dbang gis lung bon lha gnyan la brgyud tshul ni / srid rgyud las /

> tshe dbang rig 'dzin sprul pa ni ||
> lung bon lha gnyan bya ba 'byung ||
> snang ba ma bsgribs dag snang can ||
> rig 'dzin nyid dang mi bzhin gtam ||

zhes pa'i lung gis bsngags pa'i lung bon lha gnyan[1] nyid 'khor ba la skyo ba skyes te / sngar gong du ser ba phab pa'i bshags pa la / lo gsum 'bru spangs / lo gsum skyid spangs te nyams len mdzad pas dgung lo so gcig lon tshe tshe dbang ri khrod pa dang mjal nas gdams ngag zhus pas / khyod dang nga las 'phro mthun pas phrad pa yin / da 'di ru ma 'dug yul du rgyug / lam du mkha' 'gro ma la dbang zhus dang tshe la phan / khyod kyi (192a) yul na yon bdag jo rje bya ba / bon min[2] chos min[3] gyi spyod pa byed pa de / 'jam dpal phyi nang la grub pa bsnyems pa yin / de khyod kyi slob mar 'dug ste / slob dpon du bzung la mos gus phar gyis / tshe dbang ri khrod pa dang zhal mjal na tshe 'dir[4] sangs rgya ba'i gdams ngag 'byung bas / nyang stod kyi ri 'grim zhing tshol cig gsungs / de nas grub thob des gsungs pa nyan nas / mkha' 'gro ma tshol tu phyin pas ngam ring du btsun ma bongs chung ba rgyud ngan pa / kha ral ba / mir sdang ba / za rgyu med pa zhig 'dug pa de mkha' 'gro mar 'dug pas / phyag 'tshal te gang yod phul nas dbang dang byin rlabs zhur byas pas / de skad sus zer ngas ci shes zer nas dang por rgol du byung / yang yang zhus pas byin rlabs gnang / de nas yul du byon pas kun dga' / yon bdag jo rje tshur phyag 'bul ba la / phar la phyag rten phul / de nas dgung lo so gnyis lon

[1] gnyen [2] men [3] men [4] 'di

nas nyang stod kyi ri la 'grim[1] par 'dod kyang kun gyis bzung nas lo gsum du 'gror ma ster / so lnga lon nas lhod byung bas nyang stod smad ri lung kun la / rje tshe (192b) dbang ri khrod pa btsal bas ma rnyed / da btsal bas mi rnyed par 'dug ste / phyi la mi ldog par dbus khams thag ring ba zhig tu 'gro snyam nas / nyang stod nying ro nas pho ma byang ngos su phyin pas / tshe dbang ri khrod pa dang mjal te / rnal 'byor pa ras phyam dmar po dang stag sham mnab pa / 'khrung bzang ba / gzi mdangs che ba / spyan rtsa mtho ba / dbu skra ser ba / sku sha bu chung ltar gzhon pa zhig dang gtugs kyis phrad pas / khong gi zhal nas khyod nga btsal nas ci byed gsungs / de ka la skyi sha bun gyis song nas dad pa skyes / sngar mang po btsal bas yus che bas ngus pas / rje'i zhal nas / 'khor ba'i sdug bsngal bsam nas ngus shig / mi khom pa'i gnas brgyad la bsam nas ngus shig / skye rga na 'chi'i sdug bsngal la bsam nas ngus shig / ngan song gi sdug bsngal la bsam nas ngus shig gsungs / ngu 'phro bcad nas phyag 'tshal te gdams ngag zhu zhus pas / nor btsal lugs mang du gsungs byung / bdag nor mi btsal / lta sgom spyod 'bras kyi gdams ngag zhu lags zhus pas / lta rgyu yang med / bsgom (193a) rgyu yang med / spyod rgyu yang med / grub rgyu yang med pas / rang yul du rgyug gsungs / gdams ngag mi gnang na rje gar gshegs gar bzhugs kyi drung du bdag kyang 'dug lags / zhus pas / za rgyu mi 'dug pas rgyug gsungs / za rgyu yang bdog mi 'gro lags zhus pas / ma 'dug gis phye tshum de 'gam / nangs par nga yis gcig sbyin gsungs / nub mo brag phyam zhig gi rgyab tu rje gzims song / ma rgyob tu bla ma lha gnyan[2] gzims / nangs par rje bzhugs sam bltas pas bzhugs 'dug da gdams ngag zhu zhus pas / sngar ngus shig pa'i tshig rnams la brten nas drang don gsungs / lta rgyu yang med ces pa'i tshig rnams la brten nas nges don gsungs so / zhag nyi shu rtsa gcig drung du bzhugs nas gdams ngag zhus so / de ltar bkra shis phyug mo / pho ma snying ring / rin chen spungs pa la sogs su mjal nas gdams ngag gsungs pa'i bon la / dran pas mdzad pa'i drang don mun sel sgron ma / nges don nam mkha' 'phrul mdzod / rgyud kyi skor la ye khri mtha' sel / mchong lung nyi shu rtsa lnga / rdzogs chen nyi ma'i snying po / rgya gar (193b) grub chen bco lnga'i zhal gdams la sogs bon sde mang po rnams lung bon lha gnyan gyis lung bon 'khor lo rgyal po la brgyud de dar ro /

[1] mgrims [2] gnyen

gsum pa yong[1] lugs kyi bon skor ni / dbal chen ram pa la sogs yong[2] lugs kyi bon sde rnams ni me nyag khyung gsas kyis zhang zhung rgod kyi yul nas spyang ku sngon po la bkal te 'ong / mdo khams smad du dar te mon tri ston pa shes rab grags pa dang / shar rtsa drung mu /[3] skya rtse va pa la sogs grub thob zam ma chad par brgyud do / bstan pa mtha' nas rgya cher 'phel ba'i gzhi ru gyur to /

gnyis pa der gtogs pa ni / rig 'dzin rnams kyi sprul pa'i bla ma rnams la / lha dang rig 'dzin mkha' 'gro rnams kyis lung bstan nas snyan du brgyud pa'i bon sde rnams te / gter ma'i lo rgyus bshad pa'i shugs las bstan pas shes par 'gyur ro / 'dir 'phros su bon bstan khad dang rim gyis dar tshul cung zad bshad na / khri srong lde[4] btsan gyi ring la'ang bon gtan med du ma nub pa'i gtan tshigs gong du bshad pa bzhin dang / de nas bod rgyal glang dar dang dus mtshungs su rgya bod (194a) hor gsum gyi sa mtshams na / me nyag gha'i rgyal po byung ba'i ring[5] la / bon kyang mdo smad nas 'dul ba'i dbu brnyes te so thar gyi brgyud pa cung zad 'phel / de nas bka' gter gnyis kyang rim par dar zhing 'phel ba ste / zhang zhung bon skor gyi brgyud 'dzin dpon rgyal btsan po yang / gshen klu dga'i sku tshe'i stod yan chad la bod du bzhugs nas / khyung byid mu thur[6] dang grom pa lha rtse gnyis la gdams pa gtad de / khong nyid g·yu bya khu byug tu sprul nas nub phyogs srin po'i kha gnon du gshegs par khyung po blo gros kyis gsungs so / me nyag gi rgyal po byung ba'i rjes su ji 'ghin hor gyi rgyal rabs bcu gsum tsam byung nas / rgya bod hor gsum 'jang sog po me nyag rgya gar zang gling tshun chad du yul khams mang po la rgyal khrims zug pa'i dus su / bod kyi bon po la yang / do yon las 'dzin nyi shu rtsa gcig tsam byung nas bru zhu spa rme'u la sogs mdo dbus gtsang gsum du bon gyi bstan pa je rgyas su byung ngo / de nas hor gyi rgyal sa shor te shar phyogs rgya nag la tad min thas slod rgyal po chu mo (194b) glang gi lo la rgyal sar bton nas bzung rgya nag gi rgyal rabs lnga tsam byung ba'i ring la / bod du bon gyi bstan pa mtho dman snyoms par gnas shing / ser gyon dang phreng thogs ni mang ba byung / this tsong yab sras kyi rtsa ba'i bla mchod dngos ni / rgya nag gi bon po cang thang thas sri bya ba ste / bod skad du gnam gyi bon po zer ba'o /

[1] yang [2] yang [3] (/ absent) [4] lde'u [5] rim
[6] tur

gnyis pa gter ma la gsum /
bon gter brdol ba'i dus ngos bzung ba /
gter ston rnams kyis gter ji ltar drangs[1] tshul /
de dag lho byang dbus dang khams gter gter gsar gyi khongs su bsdu ba'o /

dang po ni / dran pa nam mkha'i zhal nas / bon 'di sbas kyang phyis su mi nub rang shugs rdol / zhes dang / mtha'i dmag rnams ston kha'i lo tog bzhin du rdol / bod 'bangs mi rnams 'dul zhing bkol / bod rnams nyams shing dma' dus na / bon rnams dar zhing spyod par mchi / zhes so / gzhan yang rgyal rgyud nyams shing dmangs khas drag pas rgyal por byed cing rgyal khams sdig spyod rnams kyis gang ba'i dus rnams su spang la sha mong rdol ba bzhin du bon rnams mthar nas dar te 'ong bar lung kun nas (195a) bshad do / gzhan nas kyang / dus kyi mtha' mar gyur tsam na / mi rnams kyis zas srog la byed pa 'byung / gos lcags la byed pa 'byung / las sdig la byed pa 'byung / lam yob chen la byed pa 'byung / nyal sa sga gong na byed pa 'byung / lcags mgo bas g·yul sna 'dzin / de dus rigs ngan mi la bon gyi sa bon 'debs / bon po'i tshogs rnams rig pa'i khyung chen 'phyo / gu ru bdag kyang bon gyi bstan pa 'dzin / de nas shar phyogs nas can bzhi'i rgyal po bya ba rgyal po chen po bzhi 'byung ste / bon po'i blon po can dang / bong bu'i rna mchog can dang / mi sha'i za ma can dang / rdzing bu'i pho brang can dang bzhi 'byung nas bon gyi bstan pa dar zhing rgyas par byed do / ces pa rnams pad 'byung gis lung bstan to /

gnyis pa gter ston rnams kyis gter ji ltar drangs[2] tshul la gnyis /

spyi dang /
bye brag tu bshad pa'o /

dang po ni / rgyal po khri srong gis lo sum cu so gnyis dus bon bsnubs pa nas / bla ma gshen chen klu dgas gter thon pa'i bar du lo nyis brgya dang drug cu re brgyad song (195b) zhing / 'di nyid kyi gong du bon gyi gter ston bco lnga tsam byon pa rnams las snga ba ni lho bal gyi a tsa ra mi gsum yin par bshad do / skabs 'dir mkhan po nyi ma bstan 'dzin gyis / 'ga' zhig gis gshen gter 'di sogs bar dar du byas te / phyi dar ni gter gsar

[1] drang [2] drang

rnams byon pa nas yin no zhes bshad pa ni / bstan pa bar dar dang phyi dar gyi tha snyad mi shes pa'i skyon yin te / dang po bstan pa'i dbu brnyes pa nas snga dar dang / de nyid log pa'i rkyen gyis bsnubs te nyams par gyur ba'i tshe / slar yang nyams pa gsos te dar ba la phyi dar du tha snyad byed cing / de la'ang bsnubs te dar ba lan gnyis byung ba'i sngon ma la snga dar dang / rjes ma la phyi dar du ming btags pa ni mkhas grub gong ma rnams kyi[1] bzhed srol yin pa'i phyir / des na gter gsar dang 'di gnyis kyi bar du bstan pa la 'pho 'gyur ma byung bas / dar nub kyi tha snyad la dgos pa med pas / a tsa ra gsum gyis gter gyi dbu brnyes pa nas bzung bon phyi dar du 'dod dgos so zhes bzhed pa ltar 'dir 'dod do /

gnyis pa bye brag tu bshad (196a) pa la / thog mar bsam yas nas a tsa ra mi gsum gyis gter thon tshul la gnyis /

lo rgyus dang /
dbye ba'o /

dang po ni / dran pa nam mkha' la sogs rig 'dzin rnams kyi smon lam gyi mthu btsan[2] pas / lho bal gyi a tsa ra mi gsum gyi snyan lam du bod na gser ci 'dod pa blang du yod zer ba thos pas rkyen byas / a tsa ra dkon mchog grags pa / nya mo mgon po / sad ku[3] rad na gsum bod du 'ong bas la stod du sleb kyang gser ma rnyed / der dris pas bsam yas na gser mang po yod zer / bsam yas su phyin nas bskor ba 'dra byas pas dkor[4] gnyer ba na re / khyod lho bal gyi mi dad pa can 'dug pas mos gus gyis zer nas a tsa ra gsum lha khang nang du bcug nas sgo bcad de song ngo / der sgrom gcig la khro chus rgyas btab pa zhig 'dug pa btegs pas ljid che ste gser yin snyam nas khyer te / nyin par nags gseb tu bsdad / nub mo bros te phyin / de nas ngan lam gyi lung pa sri bya bar sleb te khro chu'i rgya bcag nas bltas pas / stag sgro / gzig sgro / dom sgro gsum byung ngo / kha phyes pas thams (196b) cad bon du 'dug go / de nas skyi shod nas stod lung du 'ong bas der sleb pa dang rgyags chad pas / sgro ba dang mi gcig gnyer la bzhag go /

gnyis pa dbye ba la smad dang stod gnyis so / dang po smad la gsum /

lo rgyus /
dbye ba /
brgyud rim mo /

[1] kyis [2] brtson [3] kun [4] bkor

dang po ni / mi gnyis rgyags tshol du phyin pas grong zhig na rnga ding ding 'dug / ci byed pa yin dris pas mtha' bzhi 'phrul gsas bya bas bon byed pa yin zer / de mtha' bzhi la mjal 'dod byas pas sgor byon pa la / nged la bon yod de nyid la ster / rgyags 'dra ba slong byas pas / zas chang dang rtsam khal gcig sha gzugs gcig rnams byin te mtha' bzhi dang 'grogs nas phyin pas / a tsa ra na re 'dam du mi 'jug gang 'dod pa'i po ti gcig khyer cig zer ro /

gnyis pa dbye ba ni / mtha' bzhi na re / che ba stag sgro che / snying du gzig sgro sdug / 'on kyang bon dom sgro nas 'dod zer te / po ti gcig bton nas bltas pas nag po rgyud gsum gyi bon sgrub thabs rtsa 'grel dang bcas pa / ma mo nyi shu khra spyang sa bdag gi sgrub chung rnams byung ngo / dkyil 'khor dpe chung yang glegs shing (197a) gi ngos la 'dug skad / gzhan yang rdzu 'phrul gyi bon mang po snang ngo /

gsum pa brgyud rim ni / de yang srid rgyud las /

> 'phrul gsas sgom pa'i sprul pa ni ||
> mtha' bzhi 'phrul gsas bya ba 'byung ||
> sbas pa'i gter sgo phyed pa 'ong ||

zhes pa'i mtha' bzhi la 'u[1] yug gi rgya ston khro 'phen gyis zhus / de la yar 'brog gi zug 'phan dang / shang gi ra ston klu btsan gnyis kyis zhus / ra ston la lha rje ba sgom gyis zhus / de la bru nam mkha' g·yung drung gis zhus te dar ro / de ni mtha' bzhi'i brgyud pa ste smad brgyud do /

gnyis pa stod brgyud la gsum /

lo rgyus /
dbye ba /
brgyud rim mo /

dang po lo rgyus ni / de nas a tsa ra gsum stod lung nas yar thon te / byang nam ra bya bar sleb pas / la stod kyi mdog sras rong nas / 'dar ban shākya mu ne / mchims shākya bra ba / 'o ma byang chub seng ge dang gsum gyi rta khal dang chas nas 'ong ste byang 'brog[2] ru'i thog tu 'phrad pas / a tsa ra na re gar 'gro byas pas bsam yas su chos gter 'don du 'gro / rta khal 'di lde mig pa'i rngan pa la ster zer / der a tsa ras chos (197b) gter nged kyis thon nas yod / rta khal nged la byin cig dang gter sgro khyod la sbyin byas pas khong rnams 'khrig nas sgro ba blangs

[1] 'o [2] 'phrog

kyang gang 'then pa la 'od dang me stag 'phro yin 'dug pas chos zab mo 'dug snyam ste nor a tsa ra la byin gter sgro ban de gsum gyis khyer nas song / lam du kha phye 'dod kyang cho 'phrul mang du byung bas phye ma nus / de nas phyin te la stod mdog gi sman gong du / gze[1] ban shes rab rgyal mtshan gyi khyim du bsdad pas / tsha bo gze sgur bya ba'i bon po zhig kyang 'dug / der nas dkar mo 'bru bdun gyis mchod / lha phyag yang 'tshal gsol ba btabs nas sgro ba kha phyes te bltas pas thams cad bon du 'dug / ban de gnyis na re me la bsreg zer bas cho 'phrul sna tshogs byung / 'dar ban gyis nya ra byas pas shes rab rgyal mtshan na re / 'di rnams la bka' srung btsan po yod nges pas yu bu ban de red pas bzung mi nyan / tsha bo gze sgur la byin dang bon pos nor 'bul srid ces zer bas gze sgur la byin no /

gnyis pa dbye ba ni / der gze sgur gyis sgro ba kha phyes te bltas pas / stag sgro nang nas 'dul ba (198a) rgyud drug / gsas mkhar sa le sgron ma la sogs sa le lung bcu / man ngag lha khrid / mdo par ti ka / tshes phyag sum cu pa / za phyag nar ma rnams dang / nang rten 'brel gyi bon sde la / ye sangs rang 'dul gyi rgyud la sogs rgyud bdun / dug lnga lam khyer / gsang ba bsgrags[2] pa rgyud kyi dpe'u rtse stong gsum rgyun 'chad chen po / bsgrags pa bar ma snod bcud bstan pa'i rgyud / bsgrags pa tha ma sdong po dgu 'dus kyi rgyud rnams byung ngo /

gzig sgro'i nang nas 'bum phyi nang gsang gsum byung ste / phyi khams brgyad gtan la phab pa'i 'bum pod brgyad / rtsa 'grel chen po dang dgu / nang 'bum sde bzhi / gsas 'bum sde bzhi / 'dul 'grel pod dang bcu / gsang ba'i 'bum dgu gsas dang bcu ni / lha mo'i dbyings 'bum / rma 'bum gar chad / gtsug 'bum 'bar ba / theg pa gser 'bum / nyi ma 'od 'bum / rin chen spungs 'bum / nyi khri chig 'bum / thugs rje'i rgyun 'bum / g·yung drung ye 'bum / rdzogs pa lha 'bum dkar po dang bcu / de dag gi 'grel ba gto sgrom 'bum tig dang bcu gcig / klu 'bum dkar nag pod bzhi ste (198b) 'bum sde po ti sum cu rtsa bzhi byon no /

dom sgro'i nang nas gsang sngags phyi nang gsang gsum dang / khyad par 'phags pa'i rdzogs chen rnams byung ste / spyi khog bzhed mang gi sde la phyi 'dur nang 'dur gnyis te / phyi gri 'dur / btsun 'dur / bkra 'dur / lhe'u 'dur / sman 'dur ro / nang gson bon la / lha snyegs 'khon 'don / gsas bzhi / legs brgyad / thar glud / sel bon dang / gtsug ri gling grags che

[1] gzer [2] bsgrag

chung / na rag gting sbyongs / kun rig lha srin sde brgyad kyi dkyil 'khor / lcug le'i sgros pa'i spur sbyong / lcug le'i sātsha / snang gshen gyi me mchod / klong rgyas sbyin sreg / cha gsum che chung bzhi / gto bu lag ngan gyi pang skong / phyi nang gsang ba'i dbang mi 'dra ba dgu / dbang khrid chen mo dang bcu /

nang rdzogs chen gyi sde la / bdud rtsi sman rdzogs / lha rtse dbang rdzogs / rdzu 'phrul gting rdzogs / g·yung drung khro rdzogs / ma mo'i klong rdzogs / sku gsung thugs rdzogs / de re re la'ang rgyud gsum gsum / re nag / phyar nag / lteng nag ste nag po rgyud gsum / gze phur dmar nag / ge khod dkar nag / zhang zhung this 'phen / gser gyi tso sgrub / (199a) phur pa la yang rgyud bzhi / lung thabs bzhi / rtsa 'grel chen chung / phyag rgya 'phrul gyi lde mig / phung po ti ka'i rtsa 'grel / khug ma lnga la khug sde bcu / de la rgyud chen po gsum / srid pa das chad kyi rgyud la das chad dgu / srid pa ye 'grol gyi rgyud la gnas 'grel bdun / bse khog chen mo'i rgyud la phyi nang gsang ba'i gse khog bco lnga / kun 'dus rin chen rtsa rgyud la 'grel ba che chung gsum / gzhan yang mang ngo /

gsang ba yang rtse'i bon sde la / sems phyogs rgyud gsum ste / sems kyi mtha' rim chen mo gab pa dgu skor gyi rgyud la nam mkha' byang mdzod la sogs dgu / sems kyi khog lung g·yung drung mtha' skor gyi rgyud la gsas mkhar dbyings kyi rtse mo la sogs mtha'[1] skor bcu gsum /[2] sems kyi ye rtogs chen mo g·yung drung ye khyab la sems smad bcu bzhi rnams byung ngo /

dom sgro'i mthil na nas dkar mo bre gang byung ste / sa bon shag smug ma'i gtan tshigs kyang de nas byung ngo / khyon bsdoms bon sde mi 'dra ba sum brgya dang bzhi bcu byung bar bshad do /

gsum pa brgyud rim ni / gze bon[3] la slob ma ka ba chen po bzhi / gsang ba po gcig dang lnga (199b) byung ste / bka' bab bzhi ni / sa ston 'brug lha / stong 'byams sgra[4] bla skyabs / dbang dang sna ro gnyis te bzhi'o / gsang ba po gcig ni / gshen rnel byid gur te gsang nas phag tu phur pa la sogs mang du zhus / der rnel byid kyis bsam pa la nga'i slob dpon 'di chos pa yin pas bon mi dgos las che bsam ste gze sgur[5] gdan drangs te chang drang nas bzi ba dang / 'khar ba dang phreng ba khyer nas jo mo la bstan te / bdag la dpe sgrom rnams bskur byas pas

[1] mthar [2] (/ absent) [3] ban [4] dgra [5] sgu

jo mos bskur ro / der rnel byid kyis bla ma la nor mang po phul nas / bon rnams bdag la gnang bar zhu byas pas / slob dpon na re / khyod rang bris la zhu dag legs par gyis / ma dpe mi ster gsungs / de skad gsungs kyang dpe ma gtad pas slob dpon ma dgyes skad / des lan nam yang na phur pa'i sa bdag mo bsgrubs pas gtor ma sbrul rigs lngar song ste / ltas ngan du bzung[1] ste ske breg pas lan nam rnel byid la mdze byung ngo / khong ma na ba'i gong du slob ma zhang blon sgom ring mo bya bas zhus / de'i slob ma rme'u rog dbal pos zhus te / de ni phur nag la grub pa thob pa ste / gur zhog na bkra'i brag la phur pa thebs pa (200a) la sogs rtags mang po thon / des lha ri gnyen po la brgyud de dar ro / sa ston[2] 'brug lha'i slob ma byang gi zhu grang ra bon pos zhus / de'i slob ma zhu g·yas legs pos zhus / de nas skyid po dang skye se nas brgyud de dar ro / gzhan yang legs po la zug ra 'phan gyis zhus te de ni stod kyi brgyud pa'o / stod smad gnyis ka la thub pa zug 'phan te zug phur pa la mkhas pa zhes grags so / stod smad gnyis ka mthun par byung ba de la nyams len ding sang yang mang ngo / phur pa'i gter srung rang chas yin pas 'jig rten pa'i gter srung med do / byang gter 'di sus spyod pa de bkra shis la mthu che bar grags so / bsam yas skor khang nas a tsa ra gsum gyis bton nas byang brgyud 'grim nas la stod byang du bka' babs pas byang gter zhes grags so ||

stag la me 'bar gyi sprul pa sa ston 'brug lhas yar lung brag dmar nas thon pa'i bon sde la / srid pa ka ba nag po'i rgyud / gsas mkhar ri rong nag po'i rgyud / sha 'bal zo bo sum sgril gyi rgyud / sa le rnam drug sgron ma'i rgyud / snang grol bco bgryad kyi rgyud / das chad bcu gnyis kyi rgyud / (200b) khug ma'i bon skor / lha mo'i snying khung gi bon skor / gsang sngags rtsa 'grel ti ka dang bcas pa / mchod rten rin chen zur mang gi rgyud / lcags kyi spyang mo chig rgyug gi rgyud / srid pa spyi grel chen po'i rgyud / chags shing khro bo'i rgyud / chab dkar spyi gcod kyi rgyud / chab nag don ston gyi rgyud / gsang ba sdong po dgu 'dus kyi rgyud / nam mkha' sems mdzod 'phrul gyi rgyud / gsas mkhar rtse mo ye srid kyi rgyud / g·yung drung ye khyab chen mo'i rgyud / skye shi 'bros 'ded kyi rgyud rnams so ||

bsam yas ka khol ma'i lo rgyus la bzhi / dang po sbas tshul ni / rgya gar gyi gshen po dran pa ye shes kyis khri srong lde[3] btsan dang bka' bgros nas gter sgrom smug por bcug ste / bsam yas

[1] gzung [2] stong [3] lde'u

dbus kyi ka ba khra mo'i dkyil brkos te nang du sbas nas phyi na srubs med par byas so / nam zhig dus la bab tsa na / skal ldan bong che ba dbyibs sgur[1] ba sha rtsa dkar ba zhig gis thon nas khams kyi mtha' nas rgyas zhes lung bstan no /

gnyis pa gter thon tshul ni / dus nam zhig na chu pho khyi'i lo la rko bo yon sgom thar mo bya ba bsam yas su phyin pas ka ba (201a) la ser ga chen po zhig snang ba la gzigs pas sgrom bu smug po srubs med pa zhig 'dug pa bton nas bltas pas bon du 'dug ste khams su byon no /

gsum pa them byang ni / de'i nang nas phur pa dmar po dbu dgu phyag bco brgyad pa'i sgrub skor / kun bzang dmar po zhal gcig phyag bzhi ba'i sgrub skor / mkha' 'gro'i sgrub skor / gdams ngag skor tshom bdun pa / khog 'grel las kyi byang bu / gas btsan gsang sgrub la sogs mang po byung ngo /

bzhi pa slob ma'i gyes tshul ni / rko bos shar bu 'bor sgong du spel bas phyis su shar pa gter ston du grags shing rko bo la bla ma ye shes la sogs kyis zhus te dar ro ||

gzhan yang bsam yas dbu rtse nas mtha' bzhi ye shes blo gros kyis[2] gter thon tshul la gsum las / dang po gter thon tshul ni / mtha' bzhi nyid khams nas sprang po'i chas byas te bsam yas su phyin pa'i / nub gcig rmi lam du mi ser po be con thogs pa zhig gis / sprang po khyod nangs par bsam yas dbu rtse'i yang thog gi / bya rgyal khu byug gi tshang gi thad kar nor sna gcig yod kyi de longs shig / khyod li shus[3] (201b) byin gyis brlabs pa yin zer ba zhig byung / snga mor langs nas bltas pas bya khu byug tshang nas 'phur[4] thal / tshang nang na khung bu 'dug pa nas bltas pas / dar ser po srid du mda' gang zhing du 'dom[5] gang yod pa zhig la yi ge bris pa dang / yang de bas 'dug gam snyam nas bltas pas / dar ser ldem pa zhig la ri mo bris pa dang / rdo sngon po phyi nang gsal ba sgo nga tsam zhig 'dug pa rnams blangs nas gzhi la byon no /

gnyis pa them byang ni / de'i nang nas thon pa'i bon la bsgrags[6] byang rin chen bon sde / zo bo dbu dgu'i phur rgyud / dbal gsas kyi skong zlog bsad gsum gyi mdos la sogs bon sde bcu gnyis byung bar bshad do /

gsum pa gang la brgyud pa ni / de nas dbus kyi 'phan brag[7] dkar du byon pas ston pa ye shes rgyal mtshan bya ba dang sa pho byi ba'i khyi zla'i tshes bcu gsum la mjal[8] nas lo rgyus dang

[1] rgur [2] kyi [3] shu'i [4] 'phul [5] 'doms [6] sgrags [7] drab
[8] 'jal

bla bo byas pas / khong gis ther thang dmar po zhig phul nas gdams ngag yang zhus / dpe bris zhib thug byas te dar ro ||

yang nga 'phrang lha'i dbang phyug gis gangs ti se nas thon pa'i bon sde la / gsung rab srid pa'i 'bum dgu rdzogs pa dang bcu / (202a) 'grel ba 'bum ti ka dang bcas pa / ye dbang lhun rdzogs / dbang chen bco brgyad / sha chen gzhung bzhi / ti ka dmar po / lha mo gnas dkar / chu bo rab 'byams / phrin las zo bo dgu pa / mde'u thung drug cu rtsa gcig / spos mar me me tog rnga gshang ste mchod pa gzhung bzhi'i stong mchod / ma rgyud dur khrod ba mo che ste[1] ma mo bdun cu rtsa gsum bya ba dang / gyad mo thang mo / bdud rtsi shug gu rang 'gyur / lta ba dbyings gcod / sdong po dgu 'dus / pad ma dbyings 'khyil / yang gsang thugs kyi dpe'u rtse / gsas mkhar sa le sgron ma / snang srid gtan 'bebs / chags shing khro bo / dpon gsas gzhed sgom / mar me'i bshad 'grel cho ga dang bcas pa / ro sreg bon sde sogs mang du byung ngo ||

yang spu rangs shel mtsho mu le had kyi 'gram nas mar pa 'phen bzang la sogs khyi ra ba gsum gyis / shing sdong zhig gi rtsar rdo rko byas pas sol ba thar thor byung ba slog pas shing sgrom gsum byung ba'i nang nas / shog dril mang po byung ba yul du 'ong nas shu bon dge bsnyen la btsong de las byung ba'i bon sde la / klu 'bum (202b) dkar nag khra gsum pod gsum / klu gnyan sa bdag gtod[2] kyi 'bum pod bzhi cha lag dang bcas pa rnams byung ngo ||

gzhan yang byang gser thang sha ba can[3] nas / khrom bzlog la sogs rgyu'i bon mang du byon no / yang shel gyi pha bong g·yu ris can nas gnyan rje'i sgrub thabs la sogs mang du byung bar yang bshad do ||

yang[4] srid rgyud las /

li shu stag ring sprul pa ni ||
khro tshang 'brug lha bya ba 'byung ||

zhes pa de nyid kyis bon gter drang tshul la gsum / dang po gter ji ltar drang tshul ni / yab khro tshang gsas gnyan / yum dar za sgron gnyis kyi sras su 'khrungs sku bltams pa dang 'brug grags pa 'dzoms[5] pas 'brug lhar grags / de yang chung nas bon la thos bsam sbyangs te don dam pa nyams len mdzad cing bzhugs pa'i dus nam zhig na phyva keng tses lung bstan te byang gi gsang brag rgya bo la gter yod par dgongs nas phyin

[1] ni [2] gtad [3] can absent [4] yang/ [5] 'dzom

pas / khyung lding brag gi ngos la yi ge a'i mtshan ma 'dug pa nas brkos pas phyi nang gsang ba'i bon sde mang du byon no /

gnyis pa them byang ni / phyi sgrub gnyan rje gong sngon / nang sgrub a ma dred (203a) de / gsang sgrub a dkar 'od chen / gnyan[1] gyi snying bcos dkar nag / srog gi seg bdar che chung / dbal khyung dmar po'i[2] las thig / snyan brgyud 'jam dbyangs dkar po'i rgyud / keng tse'i sgrub skor cha lag bcas / rkang mgyogs kyi man ngag rnams byung /

yang zar gyi stag sna nas thon pa'i gsang ba ma rgyud skor la / shes rab byams ma la mdo 'bum gzungs gsum rgyud dang bzhi / kun gsal rgyas pa'i sgrub skor / rtsa sgrub / dbang sgron / dgra byad gza' gsum gyi 'grel ba skyob phran brgyad dang bcas pa / sbyin pa byams ma'i nor sgrub la sogs byon no /

gsum pa gang la brgyud pa ni / rje btsun nyid dgung lo brgya dang nyi shu rtsa gnyis kyi thog tu shang gi[3] sa char sku 'gyur ba'i dus na / rang gi dbon brgyud a da lha gsas la gsungs pa gzhon nu ma 'di bar do la las 'phro len nas lha ru 'gyur zhing / de las 'phos nas gzhon nu'i ming can bon spyod pa zhig 'byung bas / khyod kyis byams ma'i bon skor 'di rnams de la gtod gsungs nas tshigs su bcad de gsungs pa /

lha las 'phos nas mi lus len ||
(203b) gzhon nu'i ming can dal 'byor ldan ||
bla ma dam pas byin brlabs shing ||
ma rgyud snying po'i bon skal len ||
tshe dang ldan pa mthar phyin nas ||
sangs rgyas 'bras bu 'thob par 'gyur ||

zhes lung bstan nas rje btsun nyid zhi bar gshegs / de dus hor dmag byung bas a da'i bon dang / khro tshang gi bon rnams shang[4] phug brag la sbas so / phyis brag ral bas btsal kyang ma rnyed / lha btsan gyis bu lha rgyal la rang re'i yang myes bsgres pa'i dus su zhal gleng la / rje btsun gyi bon dang rang gi bon rnams ya gi brag la lus pa yin bya ba thos zhes yang yang gsungs[5] / lha rgyal gyi bu lha mgon bya ba rabs chad rgan por gyur pa de sngar gyi brag rtsa der shing thur phyin pas / nga'i yab mes kun gyis brag la bon bskungs zer ba de brag 'di'i logs la yin nam snyam nas bltas tsa na / yi ge thar re 'dug pa kun bsdus nas bltas pas / la la rul nas zur zad / la la byams

[1] gnyen [2] mo'i [3] shangs kyi [4] shangs [5] gsung

ma rtsa ba'i mdo yin zer ro / de thams cad bzung nas 'ong ste byams ma'i bon skor rnams byung ba'i nga'i yab myes kyis[1] gzhon nu'i ming can la gtod zer ba 'di yin (204a) las che snyams nas bla ma gzhon la phul lo / bla mas kyang rta dang gos shig gnang skad / de nas bla ma gzhon kong po nas lho mthar brgyud de kong po sgom pa g·yung drung skyob la brgyud / des sgom pa rin chen dpal la brgyud / des mtha' bzhi'i yul du ka gdams ye shes rgyal mtshan la brgyud / de la kho rang gi dbon po ye shes blo gros kyis zhus so / yang lo rgyus kha cig nas ka gdams pa dbus gtsang du 'ong snga ba la zhang ston bsod rgyal gyis zhus kyang rgyud la sogs pa'i zab skor rnams ma gnang zhes zer /[2] phyis mkhan chen grags rgyal mtha' bzhir byon nas rtsad bcad pas gzhon gyi phyag dpe dngos la thug cing dpe cha tshang ma dag po dang 'phrad kyang lung byed nus pa dang ma thug pas dpe de nyid la smon lam btab cing / phyis dar lding nas zhang ston gdan drangs lung zhus skad / zhang ston dang mkhan chen grags rgyal gnyis ka la bsod nams seng ge / de la skyabs ston rin chen 'od zer gyis zhus te dar ro ||

bstan pa'i gsal byed chen po gshen klu dgas bod rgyal gri gum[3] gyi ring la nub pa'i bon 'bri mtshams mtha' dkar du sbas pa (204b) thon tshul la bzhi /

gter ston gyi lo rgyus /
gter gyi thon lugs /
bon gyi them byang /
slob ma'i gyes tshul lo /

dang po ni / srid rgyud las /

stong rgyung mthu chen sprul pa ni ||
'chi med gtsug phud dngos mtshungs pa'i ||
dmu rigs sga tsha gshen gyi rgyud ||
gshen sgur klu dga' bya ba 'byung ||
mtsho rnga brag gi gter sgo 'byed ||

ces[4] pa'i gter chen 'di'i gdung ni sga tsha dmu rigs / yab dpal mgon gsas la sras gsum yod pa'i gcen po klu dga' / 'bring klu brtsegs / chung ba ge khod do / de'ang dmu gshen gyi rgyud las grol tshul yab mes kyi gdung[5] rabs ni gong du bshad zin to /

gnyis pa gter thon lugs ni / 'dra min mang yang nyid kyi zhal

[1] kyi [2] (/ absent) [3] rum [4] zhes [5] gdungs

gsung las byung ba ni / bdag lo bcu gsum lon dus pha jo na re / khyed dang ge khod gnyis song la spang rgyan dkar po dang spra ba thus la shog zer bas ge khod kyis spang rgyan thus / bdag mtha' lung gi brag la spra ba tshol du phyin pas nam mkha' nas gzugs med pa'i sgra / gshen klu dga' bon gyi dngos grub ster zer ba zhig grags byung / bltas pas pha bong zhig gi steng mar khus (205a) gang nas 'dug / de dngos grub tu bsam nas pha ma la gsang ngo / brag der 'dug rtsis byas kyang lo 'ga' la bsdad ma grub / de dus dbus gtsang dang zhu g·yas gnyis 'thab pas de'i bar la phyin pa la mda' yo bas phog nas klu brtsegs[1] grong / stong du spu ra spu lug mgo g·yag bsdus pa la lo gcig 'gyangs so / spur ya gyad pas mgo g·yag ster du ma 'dod pas / khong rta thog nas bsdad pa dang sa ling byas nas brgyug pas pho shed can du grags so / de skabs sne nag ye mkhyen dang rtsal 'gran pas rked tshigs bud de bcos kyang ma phan par lo bco brgyad nas bdag sgur por song bas gshen sgur du grags / sngar gong dmu yad byung tsam nas bsdad mno ba la ma grub pa'i de'i chad pa yin nam snyam / lo bcu dgu'i steng nas dbon ra shag la g·yung drung zhi rgyan khro rgyan gnyis / a nu'i chab gtor shog gcig ma zhus nas brag dkar[2] ru la stag lor sgrub pa mdzad pas /[3] sgrub lo nas rtags dang mtshan ma dmu yad 'khyil ba sogs rtags bzang po byung / de nas yab grong ste mtsham las thon[4] nas dge rtsa ma zin par bsdad pas 'brug lo bar (205b) 'gyangs[5] / de lo gar za dpal sgron blangs bas de lo 'gyangs[6] / sbrul lo'i srod zhig na bud med nag mo ral ba phrag gong non pa zhig mche[7] ba gtsigs shing za tshul ston pa zhig byung bas / 'jigs pa ma skyes par dgongs pa la bsdad pas de nub rdza skya seng nge ri'i thad la bskyal nas snang / nangs par dgon par 'ong ste brag dkar gyi mdor sleb tsam na / khye'u g·yu'i zur phud can dang / bud med dar gyi la'u can mang pos bsu zhing phyag mchod me tog 'thor ba byung / de la'ang dga' spro med par bsdad pas gar song cha med du thal / yang srod la rgya 'bag chen po zhig byung nas khyed za'o zer ba byung / 'jigs skrag ma byas par bsdad pas de nub mdun ri chen po'i rtse la bskyal nas snang / nangs par gnas su 'ong bas bon po stag slag can rnga gshang dkrol[8] ba mang pos mdun bsu zhing gar song cha med do / srod la sbal pa chen po zhig gis sprul pa sna tshogs ston pa zhig byung / de nub gnas kyi byang

[1] rtsegs [2] kar [3] (/ absent) [4] don [5] 'gyang [6] 'gyang
[7] mchve [8] bkrol

rgyab ru bskyal nas snang / nangs par tshur 'ong ba'i lam na brag mi ngo 'dra ba zhig gi nang / chu dkar po la ser po'i zar bu chags pa zhig thig thig 'dug / (206a) zangs gzhong bzed[1] pas na ra ra byung nas khengs so / srin mdzub kyis blangs te lce la bzhag[2] pas ro mchog brgya dang ldan / bdud rtsi red bsam nas theng gcig btung / nyin par chab gtor btang bas zangs theb gnam la 'phur zhing sa la bab / bar snang la shel 'od 'dra ba mang po 'phro zhing bdag la 'du ba byung / de nas sgra chen po gsum grags pa'i rting la nam mkha' nas bud med dkar mo dar dkar gyi la'u gyon pa bzhis 'brug khyung seng stag bzhir chibs nas bdag gi mdun du babs te / klu dga' bon gyi dngos grub ster bas bslab na sgrogs shes sam / bstan na bsgom[3] nus sam zer ba byung / bdag gis bslab na sgrogs shes bstan na bsgom[4] nus pas bon gyi dngos grub gnang bar zhu byas nas / phug nas zho blangs te mchod pa phul bas / khong rnams na re / 'o na khyod sprul pa'i sku yin pas shel gyi phur pa sor brgyad pa 'di khyer la lo bskor gcig tu gsang zhig gsungs nas nam mkha' la gshegs nas thal / phur pa la bltas pas bon theg pa rim dgu yod / shel gyi skas them dgu la babs na sdong po la ca gcus pa 'dra (206b) ba yod / de'i 'og pha bong gru bzhi'i mnya' na mtshal gyi g·yung drung zhig yod / gsham na shel gyi g·yung drung zhig yod zer ba snang / de btsal bas rnyed pa la de ltar 'dug / pha bong bzlog btub bam bltas pas btub par 'dug ste / jo mo dpal sgron btang ste ge khod la tog tse[5] khyer la shog byas pas ge khod byung ste / der pha bong bzlog pas ma btub ste kha ba rlung dmar byung bas bshol / de nub rmi lam du ge khod bya ba gza' mig dmar gyi sprul pa yin pas bstan pa bzhag pa'i gnas med pas khyod rang tshol zer ba byung / nangs par ngas khyod la ku re byas pa yin / 'di 'dra'i brag las gter 'ong ba ga la yod / tog tse zhog la khyod rang song byas pas ge khod na re / khyod la bon gter bas zan gter zhig mkho ba snang zer nas thal / der me mo'i sbrul lo'i dgun zla 'bring po'i nyi shu bzhi skar ma khra'i nyin par pha bong bzlog pas 'og nas kham[6] sa sngon po zhig byung ba'i rting la / pha bong gru bzhi la mtshal dang shel gyis g·yung drung bris pa zhig 'dug / de'i 'og nas sgam che chung gnyis byung / der bltas pas che shos kyi nang nas rgyu 'bras (207a) kyi bon mang du byung / chung shos kyi nang nas 'bras bu'i bon mang du byung ngo / shog ser rnams khyer nas 'ong bas dar cig na gar song cha med du song /

[1] bzod [2] bzhig [3] sgom [4] sgom [5] rtse [6] khom

slar gter khung du phyin nas bltas pas shog ser rnams 'dug pa khyer nas 'ong ba yang 'phur nas song / nub mo bud med nag mo zhig dang mi nag po zhig mdun du byung nas nged kyi de tsho ma khyer zhig / 'dod na lug dkar mo mtshal mig dang / g·yag dkar gta' ru tshugs / 'brang rgyas mtshal gyi thig phran can dang bshos bu byin cig / mig sngar sdod la zhal shus shig ces zer ba de bzhin byas te zhal bshus so / zhes[1] gsungs so /

gsum pa them byang la gsum /

sngar thon pa'i bon sde /
da yod pa'i bon sde /
'phros su smra ngan tshar gcod pa'o /

dang po ni / sgam che shos g·yam pa la bris / chung ngu nas khams brgyad dang / mdzod dang gsang sngags phyi nang / sems phyogs la sogs mang ba byung / zhes pas /

phyi khams brgyad la pod bcu drug / gud du bkol ba'i 'bum pod bzhi / srid pa'i mdzod phug chen mo / 'grel chung dang bcas pa / thang ma 'od rgyal gyi mchod gtor (207b) ti ka rtsa 'grel dang bcas pa / mu tra lha'i phyag rgya / rab gnas skor gsum / sātsha shog gcig ma / lder so'i spyan dbye / kun snang khyab pa'i dkyil 'khor / kun rig lha ma srin sde brgyad kyi sbyin sreg mde'u thung dang bcas pa /

sngags nang ma la zhi ba g·yung drung yongs rdzogs stod khog thig le dbyings bshags yan / man ngag thig le dbyings 'chad rtsa 'grel dang bcas pa / rtsa rgyud gsang ba bsen thub / khro bo dbang chen rgyud drug dang bcas pa / dbang chu bo rab 'byams che chung / dus drug ma mo'i sgrub skor / srid rgyal dre'u dmar mo'i skor la ma mo'i 'dus pa'i yang snying gi rgyud dang bcas pa /

sems phyogs gab pa la sogs sems phran sde dgu /

ngan ngag la mu stegs a mu kha phung gi rgyud / shan pa ma bzhi'i gsang sgrub / stong rgyung gi ser ba dbab bcad rnams byung /

gnyis pa da yod pa'i bon sde la / kha cig gis sgam so bdun yod pa la gnyis ma thon zer ba lus pa dang thon pa nor bar zad do / yang kha cig gis sgam gnyis las med zer ba ma yin te / gshen nyid kyi zhal nas / sgam sum cu rtsa bdun yod pa las kho bos (208a) gnyis bas ma thon gsungs pas shes so / so lnga da dung gter khung[2] du yod pa'i them byang ni /[3] khos yo'i

[1] ces [2] khang [3] (/ absent)

kha byang las / bye ma nyi khri chu rgyun gyi 'bum / 'phyong[1] chen po bzhi / zhal chem dkar nag gi rgyud / gtsang ma klu 'bum gyi rgyud / ti ka rin po che'i rgyud / thugs rje yum chen gyi rgyud / ba ga klong dar gyi rgyud / phyi mchod pa dkar po'i rgyud / nang rak ta dmar po'i rgyud / pad ma klongs yangs kyi rgyud / skyin 'dang kha gnon gyi rgyud / sku gdung 'bar ba'i rgyud / bon spyi gzhung bshad pa'i rgyud / 'phan yul bye brag gi rgyud / khu byug rig pa'i mdo rgyud / gangs ri brtsegs pa'i rgyud / man ngag klong bshad kyi rgyud / bdud rtsi 'khyil ba'i rgyud / ngan sdigs gze ma tan tra'i rgyud / srog gi seg bdar che chung gi rgyud / dus drug bsad pa'i rgyud / dbal phur nag po'i bon skor la sogs shin tu mang ngo /

gsum pa smra ngan tshar gcod pa ni / gzhan sde kha cig gis / gshen sgur klu dga' zer ba zhig gis sangs rgyas kyi chos mang po bon du bsgyur te / yum rgyas pa la khams chen / nyi shu rtsa lnga pa la khams chung / gtan la dbab pa la bon (208b) mdo / gzungs[2] sde la klu 'bum dkar nag ces btags / brda chad dang brjod bya chos dang mi 'dra ba sna tshogs byas te / mtsho rnga 'dre'u chung gi brag la gter du sbas / phyis kho rang gis thon pa ltar byas nas bton / zhes bshad pa 'dug go / de la 'o na / yum rgyas pa khams chen du bsgyur ba yin na khams brgyad gtan la phab pa la glegs bam bcu drug / de la le'u brgya rtsa gcig / bam po sum brgya drug cu / phyag rgya'i[3] yan lag stong dang rtsa brgyad du yod pas 'khor 'das kyi bon thams cad bon gyi dbyings spros bral du gtan la phab pa la 'phro lus med pas / khyed kyi yum rgyas pa la glegs bam bcu gnyis las med pas bzhi lhag pa ci'i phyir / bon gyi yum rgyas pa chos lugs su bsgyur ba'i 'phro glegs bam bzhi bsgyur 'phro lus pa ma yin nam / des na grub mtha' gang dang gang zhig yin kyang de dag gi byung tshul mi shes na rmongs pa'i rang bzos rmongs pa rnams tshims kyang mkhas pa dag gi thugs khrel ba'i rgyu'o / der ma zad gshen klu dga'i gter kha la sngags phyi nang zhi rgyas dbang drag gi bon zab pa mtha' yas pa dag / las can (209a) gyi slob ma rnams la brgyud de de dag gis bsgrubs pas grub rtags bsam gyis mi khyab pa byung zhing grub par brnyes[4] pa sha stag yin na / bsgyur bon 'dra chos la de 'dra'i rtags mtshan dang grub thob 'byung ba yod dam / klu[5] 'bum sogs kyang gshen sgur[6] gyi gter ma ma yin pas 'khyal gtam du zad do /

[1] phyong [2] gzung [3] brgya [4] bsnyes [5] klu'i [6] rgur

bzhi pa slob ma'i gyes tshul la gnyis /

spyi don dang /
sgos don no /

dang po ni / lo bskor[1] gcig gi gsang rgya yod kyang lo bcu gcig las ma thub ste / sbrag sto ku ras byang chub mchod rten bzhengs par lha rje zhang gis rab gnas byed pa la chos sku dang sbyar ba'i mchod rten gang lags dris pa'i lan ma byung ba la / der bon bsgrags pas lo bcu gcig na gsang ba shor ro / de nas bon zhu ba la snga ba me nyag na gus rta gcig dang ja sig gcig phul nas gtor ma dmar po'i bon zhig zhu zer ba la / snod ldan du dgongs nas khro bo dbang chen gnang ngo / de nas zhu yi legs pos sgor nyal byas nas bon mang po zhus / de nas lcog[2] la g·yu skyid byung nas gsung rab la sogs pa zhus / de nas mtshe mi shag 'bar gyis kyang zhus so / de bzhi (209b) la nyang stod kyi dpon bzhir grags so / de nas nyang smad kyi ka ba brgyad ni / rong khu a tsa ra / rong khu g·yung drung gtsug phud / phug pa rgod gsas skyob / stag sgom tsang po 'bar / ra shag 'phan pa skyob / ra shag syid dpal / bru sha lha mgon gsas dang brgyad kyis kyang zhus so / de rjes rgyal mtshan thob pa bzhi ni / ja sgom g·yung drung rgyal mtshan / bru sha khyung gi rgyal mtshan / mar pa shes rab rgyal mtshan / 'dzi ston dbang gi rgyal mtshan dang bzhis zhus so / de rjes ra shag mu mkhar / dre ston ye shes zla ba / 'dzi bon 'phan 'bar / com pa'i zi[3] lha rtse / shud kyi[4] skyid 'brug dang lngas zhus ste cog ro srid pa'i mi lngar grags so / de nas gzu ye shes bla ma / gzu mgon chen / shu[5] bon dge bsnyen gtsug phud dang gsum gyis zhus te nyang stod pa yin no / de rnams ni gshen sgur dngos la gtugs pa'i slob ma'o /

gnyis pa sgos don la gnyis /

sras brgyud dang /
slob brgyud do /

dang po ni / gshen sgur gyi sras rin chen rgyal mtshan dang byang chub rgyal mtshan gnyis yin / rin chen rgyal mtshan gyi sras tha ru dang sman rgod gnyis / tha ru sras khyung (210a) rgod / de'i sras jo 'khor / de'i sras jo bo bla ma 'od / sman rgod kyi sras dam pa rgyal tshab / de'i sras bzhi'i che ba jo bkra / jo bkra'i sras bzhi yod pa'i gcen nam mkha' rgyal mtshan rab tu byung / de 'og jo rtse'i sras gnyis kyi che ba gshen ston yon

[1] skor [2] cog [3] zi 'di [4] kye [5] rgya

rgyal rab tu byung / chung ba jo rgyal la sras gnyis kyi che ba shes rab rgyal mtshan / de la yum gnyis las sras drug 'khrungs pa'i bram ze me tog rgyan la 'od 'bum / 'bum dar / rin chen 'bum gsum / zhu za la che ba khro 'bum / bar pa khri skyong dar po / chung ba khri rje 'bum dang gsum / bar pa khri skyong dar po rab tu byung ba'i mtshan gshen ston ye shes blo gros / de nyid kyis gdan sa dar lding bkod pa mdzad nas dge 'dun pa stong phrag du ma'i dbus na mkhas pa'i bya ba gsum gyis bstan pa phyogs bcur rgyas par mdzad / gcen po khro 'bum kyi sras seng ge grags / de'i sras bsod rgyal dpal dang dpal 'od dar gnyis / bsod rgyal dpal gyi sras dpal ldan bsod nams dang / rnam dag dri med gnyis rab tu byung / dpal 'od dar gyi sras bdag po dpal ldan rnam rgyal / kun dga' dpal ldan gnyis / dpal ldan rnam (210b) rgyal rgya nag tu phebs nas yig tshang tham ka blangs shing / dge lding gi pho brang lcags ri dang bcas pa gsar bskrun mdzad / kun dga' dpal ldan sras a skyid dpal / gong gi gshen dam pa rgyal tshab kyi sras bzhi'i chung gong 'bum me nag po'i sras byang chub blo gros / de'i sras legs pa byang chub / de'i sras mgon po rin chen dpal bzang / de'i sras bzang po dpal / yang gshen dam pa rgyal tshab kyi sras bzhi'i che 'og lha rje jo 'brug / de'i sras don 'grub[1] 'bum / de'i sras 'bum dar / de'i sras g·yung drung khro rgyal / de la sras gnyis 'khrungs te / rgyal mtshan grags pa / gzi brjid do / che ba rgyal mtshan grags kyi sras grags pa seng ge / de'i sras dbang grub rgyal mtshan stod mnga' ris su bzhugs pa'i gdan sa chen por gdan drangs / de'i sras dmu gshen mchog legs rgyal mtshan / de'i sras gshen nyi ma rgyal mtshan te / de nyid kyis khri bstan nor bu'i rtse'i gtsug lag khang chen po bkod pa mdzad do / de'i sras khri 'od rgyal mtshan nas bzung ste / da lta'i stod rta zam gyi gshen nyi zla tshe dbang gi sras gdan sa chen por gdan (211a) drangs pa gshen 'dzam gling dbang 'dus kyi bar du gdung brgyud shel dkar gyi phreng ba lta bu byon pa ni / srid pa rgyud kyi lung bstan las /

gshen la klu dga'i ming can 'byung ||

zhes pa nas /

de'i brgyud[2] 'dzin grangs med 'byung ||
byin chen re ni rtag par gnas ||
brgyud pa dus mtha'i bar du gnas ||

[1] 'brug [2] rgyud

zhes pas 'dzam gling 'di na khyad par 'phags pa'i gdung brgyud yin te rig 'dzin gyis[1] byin gyis brlabs pa re re rtag par rgyun mi chad par 'byung bas 'brel ba cung zad yod pas kyang ngan 'gro las skyob par lung las gsungs shing / gdan sa ni khyad par bcu gsum gyis 'khags pa'i dar lding ri rgyal dgon no /

gnyis pa slob brgyud[2] ni / bka' bab bzhi / rgyal mtshan thob pa bzhi / stod kyi mi bzhi / smad kyi mi brgyad / cog ro'i mi lnga / dad can gsum / mos pa can nyer lnga la sogs pa'i nang nas kyang bka' bab chen po bzhi byung ste / gsung rab lcog la / sngags 'dzi ston dang me nyag / sems phyogs zhu sgom /[3] bru zhu spa gsum la gtugs pa'i rme'u ston sgom gnyis / mtshan nyid mdzod bru la bka' bab pa'o / de'i dang po (211b) lcog la g·yu skyid ni / dran pa'i zhal nas /

'jag rong[4] gsas mkhar sprul pa ni ||
lcog la g·yu skyid bya ba 'byung ||

zhes pa de nyid kyis gshen sgur gyis[5] gter thon pa zer ba'i skad thos nas byung ste / bdag la bstan 'tshal zer / bstan pa'i mnga' bdag tu go nas khams brgyad 'di 'bri bar zhu zer / de nga rang gis ma bzhengs par btang na mi 'ong byas pas / slob dpon la'ang bdag gis bzhengs pa 'bul / de nas bdag rang la 'bri ba lags zer / de tsam 'grub bam gsungs pas / tshegs med zer nas kho rang 'bum bas lhag pa zhig bzhengs nas bla 'bum de bla ma la phul / de nas kho rang la bris par bshad do / ding sang mdo smad phyogs sogs la lcog la'i khams brgyad bya ba'i 'gres rkang rgyas par phyes pa'ang yod pa snang ngo / lcog las g·yu sgro legs pa la brgyud / des rme'u lha ri gnyen po la brgyud / des rme'u mkhas pa dpal chen la brgyud / de nas bzung kho bo'i bla ma dran pa nam mkha' dngos dang mtshungs pa dus gsum kun mkhyen dbra sprul bstan 'dzin dbang rgyal gyi bar du brgyud de / de'i bar gyi bla ma rnams ni brgyud rim gyi yi ge ltar ro /

(212a) gnyis pa sngags kyi bka' bab tshul ni / 'dzi bon 'phan rgyal gyis khro bo dbang chen zhus pas dpe yang gnang / bdud rtsi'i ga'u dang ru ma yang gnang / mtshan dbang rgyal du spos so / 'dir kha cig gis spa ston dpal mchog gshen sgur gyi zhal ma sleb nas 'dzi bon dang me nyag la gtugs zhes zer te / 'on kyang gshen sgur sku bsnyungs bzhes skabs mjal[6] ba la / khro bo'i dbang zhig bskur nas las can gsang sngags kyi bdag

[1] gyi [2] rgyud [3] (/ absent) [4] rung [5] gyi [6] 'jal

po cig 'dug gis / byin rlabs kyi rdzas rnams dang / dpe dang cha lag bkrol byang rnams zhib par 'dzi bon dbang rgyal la mnos shig gsungs nas lung bstan / de nas 'dzi ston la gtugs nas zhus te / dpe rnams dang 'chi med gtsug phud man chad nas mkhas pa mi bzhi yan chad kyi phud gta' sman phab / gar mdung dang bsve'i ga'u bcas gnang nas gsang sngags kyi bdag tu bskos so / de nas yang dben dgon par khro bo bsgrubs pas srid rgyal gzhung bzhin du zhal gzigs / lan cig srid rgyal spyan nas glog 'khyug pa / shangs nas rlung 'tshubs pa / snyan nas 'brug ldir ba / ral pa sprin ltar 'thibs pa / (212b) dur khrod chas kyis brgyan zhing / spyan bzlog shangs[1] gnyer zhal gdangs[2] zhal mdzad nas / phyag gis brang shag gis gshags pa'i khog po'i nang gi rtsa gsum 'khor lo drug / thugs ka'i 'khor lo'i[3] dbus na gtso mchog gi sku gsal la dvangs[4] pa ma bsgribs par gzigs / phur bu dgu'i sman sgrub la bdud rtsi'i zil thigs babs / dbal mo rnams kyis dkyil 'khor la bskor ba byed / lung bstan pa'i dbyangs byed cing 'khrab shon byed pa dang / be dkar dang sde brgyad mi ma yin rnams gus nas / na mo dbang chen gzhal yas 'bar ba na / zhes pa sogs dbyangs su gyer nas gus pas phyag 'tshal ba byung / mchog thun mong gi dngos grub brnyes nas grub pa mngon sum du thob kyang tshangs spyod la gces spras mdzad de / sku tshe'i smad rab tu byung bar dgongs nas khro tshang gi mdun du byon pas / rje 'brug gis dbu skra bzhar bar brtsams pas / dbu skra nyag ma re la khro bo yab yum 'khril sbyor re 'dug pa gzigs nas / dar dkar po kha gang la spu gri dril nas spa ston la phul te / khyod rab tu byung na dbal mo rnams ko long byed par gda' bas / (213a) skya sgom mdzod la bstan pa spel cig gsungs so / sras brgyud[5] ni kho rang gi dbon po spa ston dar ma ste / dpon gsas khyung rgod kyi slob ma spa rgyal ba shes rab / de'i sras spa don 'grub 'bum nas bzung / da lta'i spa nyi ma 'bum gsal zhes pa rim gnyis kyi rtogs pa mngon du gyur pa kho bos zhal mjal[6] zhing gsung gi byin rlabs kyang thob pa de nyid kyi bar du byon pa rnams ni rig 'dzin gyi rnam sprul du lung gis zin pa sha stag ste[7] / de dag gi gdan sa ni spa la bug ces de nyid do / slob brbgyud ni / spa ston la slob ma mang yang khyad par du 'phags pa gshen dam pa rgyal tshab / rme'u lha ri gnyen po / rme'u dam pa ri khrod pa / kho rang gi dbon po spa ston dar ma dang bzhi'o / spa ston dar ma'i slob ma spa

[1] shang [2] gdong [3] lor [4] dangs [5] rgyud [6] 'jal
[7] stags te

ston khyung 'bar / de'i slob ma khro chung 'bar sogs grub thob rim par brgyud pa ste / spa dpal ldan bzang pos gza' bdud dam la btags te tha tshig bzhag pas ding sang grub thob spa'i brgyud pa'i bla ma rnams kyi dbu skra na bza' sogs kyis kyang gza' grib la sogs bsrung[1] nus par grags so /

gsum pa sems phyogs zhu (213b) la bka' bab tshul ni / zhu g·yas legs pos bla ma gshen chen po'i gter gyi snyan pa thos nas drung du phyin pas / bla mas slob ma'i tshad nyul ba'i phyir lo brgyad kyi bar rtsva shing breg pa / zhing la lud skyel ba / tsher ma skyel 'dren byed pa sogs la dka' tshegs dpag tu med pa byed bcug pas / legs po'i dad pa la 'gyur ldog med par gser lta bu / yid ches pa dgun gyi gzhu rgyud lta bu thang lhod med par gzigs nas / byang sems gab pa la sogs sems smad sde dgu'i lung zhal khrid nyams myong dang bcas pa bum pa gang byo'i tshul du gnang ngo / de'i sras brgyud[2] ni legs po'i sras lha rje skyid po / de nas bzung sras brgyud ma chad par byon pa'i da lta rig 'dzin g·yung drung mthong grol gyi bar du byon pa rnams yin la / gdung brgyud gser gyi phreng ba la log pa'i g·ya' dris ma gos pa'i mchog sprul chen po sha stag ste / zhu tshang gi gdan sa da lta dpal ldan ri zhing zhes pa de nyid do / slob brgyud[3] ni / legs pos zhu skyid po / des skye se / des rme'u ston sgom gnyis sogs nas rim gyis brgyud tshul brgyud rim ltar ro /

(214a) bzhi pa rme'u ston sgom gnyis kyis bru zhu spa gsum la gtugs pa'i tshul ni / spyir bshad srol la snga ba bru zhu spa gsum ste / bru sha khyung gi rgyal mtshan gyis mdzod la ṭi ka byas te mtshan nyid kyi bshad srol btod / zhu g·yas legs po'i sras skyid pos gab pa la 'grel ba btab te sems phyogs kyi bshad srol btod / spa ston dpal mchog gis thig le dbyings 'chad la 'grel ba mdzad nas bshad srol btod[4] do / bla ma de gsum ka la gtugs pa rme'u lha ri gnyen po'o / rme'u sgom dam pa ri khrod pa ni zhu skye se dang sgrol ba gnyis ka la gtugs shing de gnyis gyis[5] 'chad nyan dang 'dul ba dang sgom nyams len gyi srol bzung / bstan pa dar rgyas su mdzad pa ste / srid rgyud las / dran pa'i zhal nas /

kho bos byin gyis brlabs pa'i bu ||
rme'u'i gdung 'dzin lha ri'i mtshan ||
phyi nang gsang gsum bon sgo la ||
sbyangs rtogs bstan pa dar bar byed ||

[1] bsrungs [2] rgyud [3] rgyud [4] btad [5] gyi

ces dang / skyang[1] 'phags kyi gnad byang las /

> tshad med 'od ldan sprul pa la ||
> rme'u sgom[2] dam pa ri khrod ces[3] ||
> kun tu bzang po'i thugs dgongs ldan ||
> rjes 'breng[4] brgya rtsa mngon sangs rgya ||
> (214b) brgyud 'dzin bcu yis 'gro don byed ||
> 'bum phrag lnga bcu'i thar lam phyed ||
> brgyud pa dus mtha'i bar du gnas ||

zhes 'byung ngo / de'ang rme'u'i sras brgyud ni / lha ri gnyen po'i sras gsum yod pas / gcen gsas mkhar bla ma / de'i sras bzhi'i tha ltag de shākya brtan[5] / de'i sras bzhi'i che ba rme'u dam pa ri khrod pa ste / de nas bzung da lta'i rme'u sku zhabs rin po che 'di nyid kyi bar du byon pa dag go / gdan sa ni shang gi[6] gur zhog da lta dpal ldan bzang po ri bya ba de nyid do / slob brgyud[7] ni / rme'u lha ri gnyen po la sngags sems mtshan nyid kyi srol 'dzin pa'i slob ma mang du byung ba'i nang nas mchog tu gyur pa / stod na mi gsum / smad na mi gsum / bar na dbus pa mi bzhi la sogs pa mkhas grub ka pā 'dzin pa brgya stong khri las brgal ba byung ngo / rme'u ri khrod pa'i slob brgyud 'dzin pa ni / kha byang lung bstan las /

> stag la me 'bar sprul pa ni ||
> sgom chen 'bar ba'i mtshan can 'byung ||

zhes pa sogs bka' bab kyi thugs sras bzhi / lcam gnyis / gcung brgyad / tha chung gnyis / grub pa thob pa lnga bcu rtsa brgyad / ri 'grim sgom chen brgya stong (215a) las 'das pa / bka' 'brel thob pa 'bum las brgal ba tsam byung ngo /

lnga pa mtshan nyid bru la bka' bab tshul ni / gshen klu dga' la bru sha nam mkha' g·yung drung dang / sras khyung gi rgyal mtshan te / bru chen yab sras gnyis kas snang srid mdzod phug la sogs mtshan nyid kyi bon mang po gsan te / g·yas ru dben sa'i dgon chen du bshad pa'i srol chen po btsug go / grva sa'i 'dus grva stong dang khri ru 'phel ba byung ste / rtsod bral gyi mkhas pa mang po byon no / bru tshang gi sras brgyud[8] ni / bru sha nam mkha' g·yung drung gi sras bzhi'i tha chung shes rab rgyal mtshan / de'i sras bzhi'i tha chung ye shes grub pa / de'i sras bzhi'i che ba nyi ma rgyal mtshan / gcung zla ba rgyal

[1] skyong [2] ston [3] zhes [4] 'bring [5] brten [6] shangs kyi [7] rgyud [8] rgyud

mtshan / zla rgyal sras ye shes rgyal mtshan / gcen nyi rgyal ni rma ston srol 'dzin gyi bon la sogs pa'i lho byang gi gter kha kun gyi bdag por gyur te dbang lung khrid gsum mtha' yas pa spel / de'i sras nam mkha' rgyal mtshan te / de nas bzung ste da lta gtsang bkra shis lhun po'i paṇ chen rin po che sku mched gnyis kyi bar du (215b) byon pa'o / kha byang las /

rtsa gsum lha la bon 'khor bskor ||

zhes pa'i lung bstan dang mthun par bar mi'i yul gyi 'gro don re zhig rdzogs te / da ltar rtsa gsum gyi lha gnas su bon 'khor bskor nas 'gro don mdzad pa'i dus la babs so / gdan sa ni g·yas ru'i dben sa'i dgon chen te da ltar zhing gi bkod pa bsdus nas smon lam gyis 'gro don du bkra shis sman ri'i dgon pa phyis su chags nas da ltar bshad sgrub kyi 'du gnas chen por gyur pa 'di nyid do / slob brgyud la zhi rgyas dbang drag sems bon kun gyi bdag nyid du gyur pas brgyud pa'ang so sor 'dren du yod mod / bru tshang la bka' bab pa'i mtshan nyid kyi bon mdzod ni / bru sha nam mkha' g·yung drung nas bru sha khyung gi rgyal mtshan la brgyud / des bru bdag nyid rje btsun la brgyud / des bru ston nyi ma rgyal mtshan / des me gnyos rnam gnyis nas / 'a zha bdud rtsi rgyal mtshan / 'a zha blo gros rgyal mtshan / bru 'dul ba rgyal mtshan / bru rgyal ba g·yung drung / nam mkha' 'od zer / bsod nams[1] rgyal mtshan / bsod nams[2] blo gros / nam mkha' bsod nams / tshe dbang rgyal mtshan / nam mkha' (216a) rin chen / bru rnam rgyal ka ra / mkhas grub rin chen blo gros kyi bar du brgyud cing spel nas des mnyam med shes rab rgyal mtshan la brgyud pa ste /

de'ang blo ldan gyi kha byang gsal byed nyi ma'i dkyil 'khor[3] las /

stong rgyung sprul pa shes rab rgyal mtshan gyis ||
dbu[4] ru'i dkyil du bslab gsum bstan pa 'dzug[5] ||

ces lung gis bsngags pa'i rje rin po che 'di nyid ni / yul shar phyogs rgya mo rong / sa gnas gab tog sha ba ri'i 'gram stegs skyog ces[6] par yab dbra rigs klu rgyal dang / yum rin chen sman gnyis kyi sras su 'khrungs / bltams pa'i tshe nam mkha' la nyi zla skar gsum bkra zhing 'ga' zhig gis lha dang lha mo mang pos gar bsgyur ba mngon sum du mthong / yig 'bru sum cu ma bslab par mkhyen / de nas yab kyi drung du rgyu'i bon

[1] nam [2] nam [3] 'khor lo [4] dbus [5] gtsug [6] zhes

rnams sbyangs tshul mdzad cing / dgung lo bcu bzhes tshe phyva rla g·yung drung rgyal mtshan gyi drung du gtsang gtsug gi sdom pa bzhes te mtshan kyang shes rab rgyal mtshan du gsol / de sogs bla ma mang po la bon sde 'ga' zhig gi dbang lung gsan / de nas ma mchog srid rgyal gyis lung bstan byung ste / grva sar phebs khar yab yum la lan gcig (216b) mjal bar zhal gyis bzhes nas byon / mdo smad 'bri chu gser ldan khar rje btsun blo bzang grags pa dang mjal nas bstod tshig[1] shva lo ka re phan tshun phul / de nas tsha ba sgang stod du mkhas grub rin chen blo gros dang mjal nas bon phyi nang gsang ba yang gsang gi dbang lung mang po nos / de nas dbus kyi na lan trar[2] rong[3] ston shes bya kun rig gi mdun du phar tshad 'dul mngon dbu sdom gyi gzhung lugs kun la thos bsam sbyangs shing dbus gtsang gi rtsod grva[4] kun la dam bca' mdzad / mkhas pa'i bya ba gsum gyis pha rol gyi rgol ba'i tshogs las rnam par rgyal te / rab 'byams chen po'i mtshan snyan gyi grags pas khyab / dgung lo so gcig steng g·yas ru dben sa kha'i sgrigs lam la zhugs / na ring me ston kun bzang rgyal mtshan mdun du / dbal phur sde skor don gsum gyi dbang lung zhus pa'i tshe / me ston nyid stag la me 'bar[5] dang / sras rnams lha dang lha mor dngos su mjal / khu tsha zla 'od kyi gter phur dang bon yongs rdzogs gnang nas bstan pa'i bdag por lung bstan / yi dam lha dang rig 'dzin mkha' 'gro mang po'i zhal mthong zhing dbang bskur lung gnang ba la (217a) sogs ngo mtshar ba'i yon tan mang po bshad du yod kyang gzhan du shes so / de nas bru'i gdung 'dzin rnam gnyis kyis dbu rtse dkar dmar gyi gdan sa phul te 'chad rtsod rtsom gsum la sogs pa'i sgo nas bstan pa la bya ba rgya cher mdzad do / skabs der sngar gyi tha tshig la dgongs nas yab yum dang mjal du phebs / yab yum dang 'phrad nas slar dar mdor sleb skabs dun tse'i phrag dog la brten nas dgon chen dben sa kha 'byung bas 'jig[6] pa'i rtags shar / de'i tshe thugs chad nas bzhugs tsa na bstan pa'i bdag por 'gyur[7] ba'i rtags nyi zla khong du mid pa sogs ltas bzang po byung / srid rgyal gyis lung bstan pas bstan pa slar tshugs par dgongs te gtsang du phebs / de'i tshe dben sa kha'i shul nas bru yi thugs dam gyi khams chen dang gser mchod la sogs pa'i rten skal mang po'i dngos grub brnyes / de nas dben gnas g·yas ru mkhar snar byon nas sgrub pa mang po mdzad / der dbu skra gtor ba las sku shug 'khrungs / phyag gis rdo la yi ge ka bris pa dang /

[1] tshigs [2] tra [3] rang [4] gra [5] 'bad [6] 'jigs [7] gyur

'khar gsil[1] dang zhabs kyi rjes sogs mi 'gyur ba'i bka' rtags du ma bzhag / mtshan nyid (217b) sngags sems kyi bon la dgongs 'grel bka' brten mang po mdzad / de nas dgung lo lnga bcu'i thog tu bkra shis sman ri'i dgon sde btab[2] ste / gnas der rnal 'byor pa gnyis bzhugs pa 'gro grab byed pa la rjes bzhugs shig dang ja bskol gsungs / khong gnyis na re chu thag ring ngo zhes zhus pas / rjes 'khar gsil[3] btsug pa'i shul nas chu mig brdol te khong rnams ngo mtshar skyes te der ja bskol / de nas sa ga'i dus bzang la slob ma rin chen rgyal mtshan la / gzan zur du rdo dkar gang khyer la mig btsum la gom[4] pa dgu re'i sar rde'u re zhog cig gsungs[5] bzhin mdzad pas 'ur sgra chen po byung bas gzigs pas grva shags[6] drug cu'i rten 'brel du gyur / der rje'i zhal nas / mig btsums nas rdo dkar thams cad bkod grub na sngar dben sa'i 'dus grva[7] las lhag par chags rgyu la cung ma 'grig pas / da rgya cher mi 'grub kyang rgyun ring ba 'ong zhes lung bstan / dgon pa bzhengs grub nas sgrigs lam dang phyi nang gsang ba'i bshad sgrub kyi bstan pa rgyas par mdzad / gzhan yang dmu gshen nyi ma rgyal mtshan dang bstan pa'i che ba 'don phyir nam mkhar snga (218a) phyi lan gnyis su 'phur ba'i dbu zhva nyi ma'i zer gyis tshig pa ding sang dbu zhva me dug ma zhes pa mjal du yod pa dang / bka' skyong[8] ma bdud btsan gsum bran bzhin du 'khol nas las thams cad thogs med du sgrub pa dang / stong rgyung dang dran pa dngos su zhal mjal nas phyi nang gsang ba'i bon gyi dbang bskur zhing lung bstan mang po mdzad pa dang / bon sde zab mo 'ga' zhig snyan du brgyud pa dang / gzhan yang rdzu 'phrul dang grub rtags bsam gyis mi khyab / de nas dgung lo drug cu shing lug lor slob ma rin chen rgyal mtshan rgyal tshab tu mnga' gsol te / bstan pa la bya ba mdzod cig gi bka' dang ma 'ong gi lung bstan mang po gnang nas / gter chu'i khar khra ther phub ste nyin mo rjes 'dzin grva[9] slob dang / nub mo mi ma yin du ma la bon gyi 'khor lo bskor nas dbyar zla tha chung gi tshes brgyad kyi tho rangs skya reng shar tsam na dgongs pa dbyings su gshegs so / de nas zhag gsum song ba'i dus na sku gdung gdan la ma reg par khru gang tsam gyis bar snang la 'phags pa la / thugs sras rnam gnyis sogs rjes 'jug rnams kyis gdung rten du[10] (218b) bzhugs pa'i gsol ba btab pas mar sa la babs te bzhugs / de nas sku gdung zhugs la bzhen pas phyogs kun nas

[1] mkhar sil [2] bstab [3] mkhar bsil [4] goms [5] gsung [6] gra gshags [7] gra [8] skyongs [9] gra [10] du absent

'ja' tshon gyi gur phub / nub phyogs nas 'ja' 'od kyi lam nas sprul pa'i bya rgod gcig byung ste mkha' la lan gsum du lding zhing bskor nas slar nub phyogs su phebs / de'i tshe rgyal tshab nyid kyis zhal dngos su mjal nas cho 'phrul zla ba'i tshes lnga la slar yang 'byon par zhal gyis bzhes so / rjes su dad pa'i gdung rten du sku rten kun tu bzang po'i sku / gsung rten shes rab smra seng sku dang yig 'bru a om hūm gsum / thugs rten sha rī ram che ba lcog ga'i sgong nga tsam gsum / 'bring sran 'bru tsam bdun / chung ba nyungs 'bru tsam pa mang du byung / che ba gcig de lha'i yul / gcig klu'i yul du sgra 'od zer bcas gshegs / gcig da lta'i gser gdung nang du bzhugs so / de'i slob ma la thugs sras gnyis ni / rgyal tshab rin chen rgyal mtshan / mnga' ris bsod nams rgyal mtshan no / gzhan yang bru shes rab seng[1] ge / bru nam mkha' rgyal po / bru kun dga' dbang ldan sogs mchog chen bcu / 'dul bstan sngags sems kyi rjes 'jug smin grol nus pa brgya phrag (219a) las lhag pa / sdom pa sna re dang dbang lung gdams ngag thob pa stong phrag / mdor na da lta gangs can bon kyi 'dul sngags sems gsum gyi sgor zhugs nas nyams su len pa kun rje'i slob brgyud[2] du gtogs so / gdan sa'i khri 'dzin ni rgyal tshab[3] nas bzung bstan 'dzin skyes bu lnga / mtshungs med ud 'bar gsum / bstan pa'i srol 'dzin bzhi / bsgrun med skyes chen gsum / yongs 'dzin dam pa bzhi / bslab gsum phul phyin dgu sogs da lta'i sku mdun phun tshogs blo gros dbang gi rgyal po'i bar du byon pa rnams te / de dag rnams kyang drang srong rig pa 'dzin pa sha stag ste / srid rgyud las /

> de rnams sprul pa'i sku ru ston ||
> las can skyes bu de rnams kyis ||
> sems bskyed smon lam thob pa dang ||
> bka' dbang 'brel ba gang yod dang ||
> dbang gi chu la gang 'thung ba ||
> ngan song gsum las rab thar nas ||
> phyi mar g·yung drung sa la 'khod ||

ces so / mdor na rim byon gyi[4] mkhan rabs bgrang ba tsam ma yin par sar gnas kyi sems dpa' kho nar nges pa ni mnyam med chen po'i bka' gtsigs dang ma 'ong[5] lung gis zin pa so so'i rnam thar las shes shing drang srong rig pa 'dzin pa sha stag go ||

(219b) spa gro ma'i lo rgyus la lnga las / dang po gter sbas

[1] sing [2] rgyud [3] tshabs [4] rang bzhin gyis [5] 'ongs

tshul ni / khri srong gis[1] bon bsnubs pa'i dus su / bla chen dran pa nam mkhas rtsis sman sogs man ngag gi skor dang / dbal phur nag po la bon sde gsum du phyes te / lung don rgyas pa'i sde ni lcags kyi sgrom bur bcug ste pho brang bsve sgo can du sbas / las thig gi skor ni seng ldeng gi sgrom bur bcug ste pho brang dbus kyi yang rtser sbas / man ngag gi skor ni rin po che'i sgrom bur bcug ste lha khang gi khro bo bdud rtsi 'khyil ba'i[2] thugs kar sbas so / der lha sras mu thug btsan po rgyal sar bton pas lha sras de bod la thugs chad nas / man ngag zab mo'i bon skor rtsis sman rnams dang / phur pa sde skor don gsum gyi sgrom bu rnams pho brang bsve sgo can nas khyung po gyer zla med dang lha sras gnyis kyis bton te / spa gro phug gcal gyi g·yon ngos / brag sog po dmag la chas pa 'dra ba'i rked / seng ge dkar mo kha gdangs pa 'dra ba'i 'og / rus sbal nag po chu 'thung ba 'dra ba'i 'gab / pha bong sdig ru can gyi rtsar / brag dmar nag me ri mched pa 'dra ba'i dbus / brag phug nyi ma ris su yar lha sham po sogs gter srung drug la gnyer gtad (220a) nas sbas so /

gnyis pa gter ston gyi lo rgyus ni / 'jad rta nag gi btsad po zhig bsam yas su phyag bskor[3] la 'ong ba'i lam na nyang rong stag tshal du khu ye bya ba'i khyim du tshugs mal byas nas / bsdad pas khu ye'i bu mo zhig yod pa dang 'tshos so / de nas btsad pos bsam yas su song / mar me btang bas[4] gter gyi kha byang rnyed pa khyer nas yul du log der khu ye'i bu mo la bu zhig skyes pa / ma khu mo yin pa dang tshes bco lnga'i zla ba shar ba dang mnyam du skyes pas ming khu tsha zla 'od du grags / sad ne ga'u'i sprul pa yin no / de cher skyes nas ma la pha gar yod dris pas rta nag gi btsad po zhig yin zer bas der byon nas yab sras mjal te nga khyod kyi bu yin byas pas / brtag dgos gsungs nas lha bdar bas dgun zla tha chung la 'brug glog[5] khu 'phang la sogs byung skad / btsad po na re / nga yi bu yin te 'on kyang bur mi btub / nor skal 'di khyer la song byas nas spa gro'i kha byang byin to / bu ma'i gam du byon te lo bco brgyad lon pa dang / ban de zhig byung ba la mas chang drangs bas ban de na re / 'u bu gnyis gter 'don du 'gro la bon byung (220b) na khyod / chos byung na bdag / nor byung na phyed phyed bya zer ro /

gsum pa gter thon lugs ni / de nas khu tsha dang ban de gnyis spa gror phyin te btsal kyang gter ma rnyed / zla ba phyed tsam

[1] gi [2] bas [3] skor [4] ba'i [5] klog

bzhugs kyang yod bsam pa ma byung bas ban de song skad / khu tshas slar btsal bas pha bong sdig ru la na bza' 'thog pas der yod snyam te kha byang gi chag tshad gzhal nas brkos pas brag phug la sgo chung bzhi yod pa zhig rnyed de / sgo gong ma la gshang / de 'og dril bu / de 'og gab tse / de 'og btsag bu byung ngo /

bzhi pa them byang ni / gshang las bon / dril bu las chos / gab tse las rtsis / btsag bu las sman dpyad rnams byung ba la / bon sde ni /

bdag nyid rol ba sngags kyi sde bzhi ni / gsang ba zhi khro'i sde la / rgyud drug / phrin las rgyas 'bring drug / sgrub pa'i yan lag bco brgyad do /

drag po phur pa'i sde la don skor gsum ste / lung don rgyas pa'i skor la rgyud dgu 'grel dang bcu / thabs gsum / gnad bzhi / mchong lnga / don drug / sgrub chung nyi shu rtsa gcig / man ngag rno dang bcas pa'o /

las thig 'grel chung skor la / rtsa 'grel gnyis / phrin las gsum / 'khor lo gsum / dbab (221a) bcad bzlog gsum / mdos gsum / bcud[1] la bor ba'i gdams ngag drug / gab gsang bcu gnyis rtsa 'grel dang bcas pa'o /

dbal phur yang gsang don gyi skor la / rgyan gyi 'od lnga / lung bzhi / man ngag bzhi / thabs bzhi / rtsa ba bzhi / 'grel chung bcu gnyis / sa bcad[2] bcu gnyis / cha rkyen drug go /

bdud rtsi sman gyi sde la / thabs kyi rgyud lnga / shes rab kyi rgyud drug / khog dbub bzhi / las byang zung gsum ya drug / yan lag bcu drug dang bcas pa'o /

drag[3] sngags gzer[4] phur gyi skor la / rgyud gsum / sgrub gzhung gnyis /[5] don lnga / las kha drug / sgrub chung bco brgyad don 'grel dang bcas pa'o /

mthu stobs bstan pa srung ba'i bon sde bzhi yod pa'i / dang po gtsang ma zhang zhung gi sde la / gyad phur sku'i sgrub pa / de la pho skor la me ri rtsa ba'i rgyud gsum / sgrub thabs gsum / phrin las kyi sgrub pa la rgyud gnyis so /

srid pa gnyan gyi sde la /[6] pho rgyud lnga / mo rgyud lnga / mdo rgyud lnga / sgrub thabs dang bcas pa'o /

dregs[7] pa lha rgyud kyi sde la gsum / skong bzlog mdos la sogs pa'o / de gsum[8] ka ma yin pa gsang sngags kun 'dus la / bon skor (221b) sum cu rtsa gsum yod /

[1] gcud [2] gcod [3] drags [4] gze [5] (/ absent) [6] (/ absent) [7] dreg [8] gnyis

gnas lugs nyams len khyad par can gyi bon sde lnga / lta ba gtan la 'beb pa g·yung drung ye khyab dum bu lnga[1] ma dang drug / sems don gtan la 'beb[2] pa byang sems gab pa rtsa 'grel dang bcas pa / nyams su len pa kun bzang gshen lha phyi nang gsang gsum gyi rgyud dgu / rang rang gi cha lag dang bcas pa'o / bka' shes rab kyi pha rol du phyin pa khams brgyad rtsa tshig rnam par dag par bkod pa'o / sngags phyi rgyud gtan la 'beb[3] pa g·yung drung las rnam par dag pa'i rgyud / sgrub thabs rgyas 'bring bsdus gsum la sogs pa'o /

lnga pa gang la brgyud pa ni / de'i tshe sngar gyi ban de de byung nas khyod kyis gter bton pas / nga la yang slong zer ba la chos rnams byin no / khu tsha la sbas yul rong gi bar sgom ye shes rgyal mtshan gyis kun bzang gi skor zhus so / der khu tshas gnub yul rong gi mgar nag 'bum chung bya ba la / ngas gter thon pas gter shog yod pa khyod rang 'bri na sbyin byas pas / mgar na re / bdag lho gter la slob sbyangs lo gcig la byas pas bag tsam shes / da yang bon zhig zhu zer nas na bza' dang rta zhig (222a) phul nas gzer phur gyi skor rnams zhus te bris / de nas gter sgrom rnams mgar la bcol te / khu tsha nyid sman la mkhas pas dmu'i brang ti sman pas phrag dog byas te / khong nyang stod du bzhud pa'i lam kar mi lngas bsgug pas khu tsha rta lcags kyis brab nas byon te shor / der khu tsha'i sman chung gcig mdas phog te rgyu ma bton[4] pa la khu tshas rgyu ma 'o mas bkrus te nang du phul nas rma kha rta dkar po'i rgyus pa'i btsem pas sos / bu khyod kyis nga'i srog bton pa yin gsungs nas gdams ngag kun gnang / phyis su khu tsha sman pa'am mkhas pa g·yu thog tu grags so / mgar nag gis khams brgyad gcig / re phrug dang zhing khal gnyis phul nas bon cha[5] tshang zhu byas pas / 'dir sman pa brang ti mi dgyes pas mi 'dug / nor dang gsung rab mi dgos / bon rnams 'bri bas chog pas da lan nga lho brag tu 'gro ba'i shul du khyod rang 'bri mkhan dang shog bu tshol zhig gsungs / bon sgro rnams la cas rgyas btab ste / nga ma byung gi bar kha ma phye / gal te nga shi na spyod chog gsungs / sman gyi gter shog rnams bsnams nas lho brag tu gshegs (222b) so / der mgar gyis khu tsha grong zer ba thos pas mgar nag gi sras khro rgyal gsal bya ba g·yog tu khrid nas bltar phyin pas bla ma grong zin te sras khro rgyal slar log te der gter srung mchod nas sgro ba drug 'dug pa kha phyes nas yi ger bshus te dngos grub mgar la babs so / mgar yab sras la

[1] lnga absent [2] 'bebs [3] phab [4] don [5] tsha

slob ma mang yang / bu chen bzhi yod de / mdo khams kyi jo ston skal ldan shes rab / la stod kyi slan ston ti se ba / rngod kyi yang la thugs rje / stag sde'i gnyan ston thugs rje'i 'od dang bzhi'o / rtsis kyi gter shog rnams shang gi spug ston la byin pas gsas mkhar mar grags so / yang mgar ston khro rgyal 'bum gyis spa gro'i[1] skyer chu nas rdzogs chen lta ba klong rdol dang / phur pa'i sgrub phran bco brgyad sogs zab pa'i gdams ngag mang du thon par bshad do ||

de nas zhang zhung this kyi bon skor thon tshul la bzhi / dang po gter du sbas tshul ni / thog mar zhang zhung gi bon po khyung la dgra 'dul la sogs gdung rabs dgu bcu rtsa gnyis kyi bar du rim par brgyud nas bstan pa dar nub dus su zangs sgrom du bcug ste gangs ti se'i rtse mor sbas / (223a) phyis zhang zhung gi bon po u gu dgra 'dul gyis rnyed / de nas brgyud de zhang zhung gi bon po lha tho dkar pos lha srin bran du bkol te la stod gtsang por sbas so /

gnyis pa gter thon tshul ni / chos pa'i gze ston spu gu rgyal mtshan gyi rmi lam du bon po'i chas can gsum na re / slob dpon bzhengs dang dngos grub yod zer / ci yod byas pas / gnas kyi shar phyogs pha bong g·yag 'dra'i rtsa ba nas shar lhor 'dom bzhi bcal ba'i sa na / bsad gso dbab bzlog mang du yod pa snoms shig zer / der gze ston gyis yon bdag rngog byang chub rdo rje la tog tse[2] g·yar nas brkos pas / ser ba 'bab cing nub ngos kyi brag la thog brgyab / de nub bud med ro stod g·yu la ro smad zangs su 'dug pa zhig dang / mi bsve yi ral ba can zhig dang mi nag rta nag sbrul thod can zhig byung nas khyod za'o zer bas / der nga la phyi ma'i dge sbyor zhig gal che bas bskyur snyam tsa na / sngar gyi bon po gsum byung nas dngos grub la 'gyod pa ma skye / ser ba byung ba ni gsol ba ma btab pas lan / gter bdag gsum la 'brang rgyas dang klu bshos dmar gtor (223b) byin cig zer / de ltar mdzad nas slog pas mi thod zhig byung / yang slog pas zangs kyi sgrom bu zhig byung ngo /

gsum pa them byang ni / sgrom de'i nang nas zhang zhung this kyi bon skor rnams byung ste / this dkar gso ba'i rgyud la sde bzhi / this dmar bzlog[3] pa'i rgyud la gsum / this nag bsad pa'i rgyud la gnyis / 'dzab this dang bcu byung ngo /

bzhi pa brgyud rim ni / der rngog byang chub rdo rje na re / bdag la ser ba byung / sang phod kyang 'ong nyan snang bas / slob dpon la ser ba bsrung thabs shig zhu zer ba la / 'dzab[4]

[1] dro'i [2] rtse [3] zlog [4] dzab

this gnang zhing tog tse yang bskur skad / de nas gze ston gyis ba gor dben sa[1] khar byon nas bon rnams bru sha rje btsun la bstan te phul lo / de la dod ci rgya bon gyis zhus so / yang gze ston la zhang grags bon pos zhus te dar ro ||

de nas ra ljags kyis zab gter thon tshul la gsum / gter bab tshul / them byang / brgyud rim mo / dang po gter bab lugs ni / ra shag gi bon po ra ston dngos grub 'bar dang ra sgom g·yu bo gnyis kyis / yar 'brog gi yul du zug ra 'phan[2] bya ba'i mdun du bon zhus nas yod pa la / zug gi[3] jo mo na re / (224a) ra ljags kyi bon po gnyis la btsun pa gnyis kyis sgor ltos shig zer ro smras pas / der phyin pas btsun pa gnyis kyis nged la bon sgro ba gang yod pa de 'dod dam zer / 'dod byas pas tshur tshes pa'i nya la rta zhig ster dgos len du 'ong zer nas sgro ba gtad nas song / der bon po gnyis dga' ches te bon nyan 'phro bzhag nas khyim du 'ong bas slob dpon ma dgyes skad / bon ster ba'i btsun pa ni sprul pa'i rnal 'byor ram phyis rta len pa la su ma byung zhing gar song gi cha yang med do / yang kha cig gis drang nga ba nas byung ba'i lo rgyus dag pa snang ngo / zhes bshad do / ra ljags kyi bon po ni[4] / khod spungs kyi lung bstan las /

ra sangs khod ram sprul pa ni ||
ra ljags g·yu bo bya ba 'byung ||

zhes so /

gnyis pa them byang ni / sgro ba kha phyes te bltas pas sems phyogs sde bcu byung ste / man ngag sde bzhi don dang lnga / mdo bzhi rgyud dang lnga'o /

man ngag sde bzhi don dang lnga ni / rig pa dkar po rgyud lung gi sde / de la lung don sde bcu byung ste / rig pa dkar po rgyud kyi lung la sogs pa bu dgu ma dang bcas pa'o /

mu med nam (224b) mkha' yongs khyab kyi sde / de la nam mkha' sems kyi rtsa lung la sogs ma bu bdun /

sems smad bco brgyad byang sems gab pa'i sde / de la rgyud smad drug ni spyi lung yongs su rdzogs pa'i rgyud la sogs drug / lung smad drug ni / gab pa sems kyi lung la sogs drug / man ngag smad drug ni / man ngag don gyi thig le dgu skor la sogs drug / byang sems gab pa rtsa 'grel sa bcad dang bcas pa'o / kha[5] tshar ni sems lung bzhi pa'o /

[1] sa'i [2] 'phen [3] zugs kyi [4] gnyis ni / [5] khar

rgyud[1] smad bcu bdun man ngag rtsa ba'i sde / de yang rgyud la ma lnga ni / rgyal po'i yang gter la sogs lnga / bu ni spros bral thig le yi ge med pa'i rgyud la sogs bcu / ma tshang ba kha bskang ba ni / rgyud kyi rgyal po gser gyi rus sbal g·yung drung theg pa rgyud kyi mdo / rgyud bu bcu gnyis ni byang sems theg pa rtsa ba'i rgyud la sogs bcu gnyis so / sa bcad bcu bdun / 'grel ba bcu bdun / mdo rtsa bcu dbun la sogs pa'o /

lta sgom spyod pa'i lung dgu gsum nyi shu rtsa bdun / kun tu bzang po'i nges tshig rnams so /

mdo bzhi rgyud dang lnga ni / gsal ba ye shes sgron ma'i mdo la sogs bzhi dang / mu med (225a) nam mkha' klong gi rgyud dang lnga'o /

rgyu bon la /[2] gson mdo / gshin mdo mi mthun pa sum brgya drug cu / bgegs rigs stong phrag brgyad cu'i dbye bshad / skos byang lnga / gson gshin la shan gyi ti ka / dbang dang phur bu'i dkyil 'khor gyi ti ka / gtam rgyud rnams byung ngo /

der ra shag ston sgom gnyis kyis shog ser rnams bgos te / rig pa dkar po'i skor dang / sems smad bco brgyad / gab pa'i skor rnams ra ston dang / gsang ba yang gter gyi rgyud ma bu'i skor dang / gser gyi rus sbal rgyud smad bcu bdun / lta sgom spyod pa'i lung / gson gshin gyi yig sna /[3] dbang dang phur pa'i ti ka'i skor rnams ra sgom gyis thob skad / ra sgom mtshams bcad nas bris / ra ston gyi jo mo ngan pas yul du ma bzhugs par byes su phyin nas bris pas dpe ra shag ston pa bzang skad / bar du ra ston gyi sras jo sras kha bo dang / ra sgom gyi sras snying po gnyis ma dum ste sel zhugs par grags / bru ston nyi rgyal gyis ra shag gi yig cha gab pa rtsa 'grel gyis lho gter gyi gab pa yang bkral nas bshad do / de gong lho gter gyi gab pa ma khrol bas ra shag gi gter ma 'di zab (225b) par brtsi'o / sngags nang ma dang gson gshin gyi shog ser rnams drang nga mdo las khyer nas nyang stod nas yul du byon pa'i lam du gnyan ston khye'u grags dang 'phrad pas / drang nga la sngo thul zhig yod pas bon po e yin zer / yin byas pas / bon yod dam zer / bon yod de mos na ster byas pas / khrab dang / g·yu / phrug zhig phul nas dpe zhus te bris / sngags nang ma dang gson gshin gyi bon zhu ba la gnyan ston snga ba'o / de nas drang nga la lam chas phul te yul du byon no / drang nga mdo la'i sras seng ge rgyal la sras med pas chun mar dre mo g·yung lcam bya ba blangs pas / chen mas sdod du ma ster bas dre mos shog ser brkus te

[1] sems [2] (/ absent) [3] (/ absent)

'brong bu rtse mthon bya ba'i dgon par dbyil he ru ka bya ba la btsong ste /

de las byon pa'i them byang ni / gson bon bcu gsum / gto mig che chung / gson gshin la chings brgyad / 'dur lung che chung gi rgyud gsum / sel lung dgu la sogs mang du byung ngo /

sngags ni /[1] rin chen spyi spungs la / spyi spungs rtsa ba'i rgyud / lung rgyun thag phyi ma'i rgyud / yang snying mdo rsta ma tshang kha bskang gi rgyud dang gsum mo / phrin las gsang ba lha rgyan / khro bo 'bar ba (226a) gnyis/ 'dzab kyi 'khor lo / phrin las rnam bzhi sbyin sreg sogs / g·yung drung khyab pa spyi rgyud rtsa rgyud phyi ma'i rgyud dang gsum / zhi ba lung non / khro bo yang gsang 'dus pa / yang gsang la che mchog mkha' 'gying lha'i rgyud la sogs gsum / bdud rtsi la rgyud gsum / sgrub thabs gsum / dbang rin chen sgron ma / dbang gi lag khrid / dbal phur rtsa ba'i rgyud sgrub thabs / gsang ba'i phur gcig ma / srung ma rnam gsum gyi sgrub pa / bdud phur nag po / dbang chen myur byed kyi skor rnams byung ngo /

gsum pa brgyud rim ni / dbyil he ru ka'i sras shes rab seng ge / de la yar 'brog gi rgya bla ma khri mkhar gyis zhus / de la yar 'brog gi me gnyan dga' / de la sman thang gi zhang ston grags / de la mgar ston shes rab bla mas zhus te dar ro ||

gnyan gyi se bo ri nas bon thon pa' i lo rgyus la gsum / dang po sbas tshul ni / ba gor be ro tsa na tsha ba rong du gshegs khar sems phyogs dang bstan srung zab mo gnyan gyi se bo ri la sbas te gter bdag lha btsan la bcol lo /

gnyis pa gter thon tshul ni / yul gnyan (226b) gyi ra ston 'bum rje bya bas / sngags pa zhig gi lag nas byung ba'i kha byang zhig rnyed pa la / der se bo ri la gter yod par bshad pa btsal bas rnyed do /

gsum pa them byang ni / sems phyogs la[2] / man ngag bco brgyad de / nyams myong drod rtags kyi man ngag 'pho ba nyams nga med pa'i man ngag la sogs pa'o ||

bstan srung la srog ser gtad gsum te / srog la brag srin sha zan gyi skor / mu stegs tsa kra gzer mgo can gyi skor / spu gri srog gi mtshon cha'i skor / ma mo seg bdar ma'i skor / kha la me 'bar gyi sngags rgod sogs sngags rgod bzhi /

ser ba la skyin 'dangs lo 'joms / chu 'khyag 'khor lo / ljang ser lo rgyug / lo zan nag mo'i skor dang bzhi /

gtad la klu bdud nag po srog len /[3] mdze nag srog gi shan pa /

[1] (/ absent) [2] la/ absent [3] (/ absent)

klu bdud nag po mthong rgol / dug ri kha'i gtad khram[1] dang bzhi'o / srung zlog sogs gzhan yang mang ngo / lo bzhi'i gsang rgya yol nas rim par dar ro ||

yer rdzong ma'i lo rgyus la bzhi las / dang po sbas tshul ni / khri srong gi dus su / dran pa dang / be ro gnyis kyis rgya gar gyi bon skor rnams lha sa'i yer ba'i[2] rdzong la sbas te gter bdag (227a) has po ri'i dur bdud nag po / bsam yas brag btsan dmar po /[3] lha sa'i klu mo dkar mo gsum la bcol lo /

gnyis pa gter thon tshul ni / lung bstan las /

> dge slong be ro tsa na'i sprul pa ni ||
> gtsang gi ban de ras pa dpon g·yog gis ||
> gling gi chu bar gter nyid thon te 'ong ||

zhes pa ltar gtsang gi ban de sum pa dbang tshul / 'bre tshul seng / gcer bu dbang phyug dang gsum bsam yas su chos gter tshol du song bas ma rnyed de lo 'ga' 'gor / de nas yar log te rang re drag shos gsum gyis gter ma thon pa ngo tsha zer nas yer bar btsal bas / gter rnyed kyang bon du 'dug pas ma 'dod de mdo stod kyi lung ston 'od 'bar ram gnyen ston gzi brjid kyi phyag tu phul lo /

gsum pa them byang ni / de la gsung rab ni / bon nyid snying po bdal ba'i 'bum pod brgyad / 'bum rtsa gcig dang dgu / mngon rtogs rig pa rtse mo'i 'bum pod bcu / theg pa'i rim pa mngon du bshad pa'i mdo rgyud / 'grel ba me long dgu skor dang bcas pa / tshad ma smra seng / mu stegs tshar gcod gtan tshigs thigs pa'i mdo rgyud / phyi ma gzungs[4] 'dus rgyab (127b) chog re dang bcas pa / mchod gtor gyi rgya cher 'grel / thugs rje byams ma'i mdo rtsa / shes rab snying po la sogs mdo dgu yan lag bsdus pa dang bcu /

sngags nang ma la /[5] khro bo mngon rol / yang gsang mchog gi rtsa rgyud la sogs rgyud[6] bcu gsum / don 'grel khog dbub chen mo dang bcu bzhi / khug ma gsum / nges[7] tshig gsum / mtha' rgyas gsum / zhi ba'i phrin las / khro bo'i phrin las / mchong dang cha lag mang ngo /

spyi spungs skor la / zhi khro yang gab / phyag rgya gsang this / thog ser srog gsum gyi sgrub pa /

'chi bdag bdud phur gyi skor la / bdud phur nag po la rgyud

[1] khrom [2] po'i [3] (/ absent) [4] gzung [5] (/ absent)
[6] brgyud [7] das

gsum zhal gdams dang bcas pa / phur pa sha 'bal[1] ma'i skor sogs dang / li shu'i phyi nang gsang sgrub /

rdzogs chen gyi skor la / byang sems nam mkha' dbyings rgyud don 'grel dang bcas pas sems nyid gting rdzogs 'khor ba dong sprugs kyi rgyud / bla med kyi mdo gsum / thad ke'i tshad ma / kun gzhi 'phrul gyi me long / thig le nyi ma'i snying po sa bcad dang bcas pa rnams byung /

ngan sngags la /[2] dregs pa sngags rgod kyi sgrub pa thog smad dgu 'grol dang bcas pa / gter bdag (228a) gsum gyi sgrub pa la sogs byung ngo /

bzhi pa brgyud rim ni / gnyen ston la gyer ston khro gsas kyis zhus / de la lung bon lha gnyan[3] dang mi la ras pa gnyis cig car du zhus te gnyis kas ser ba phabs so / mi las mar pa la sgom zhus nas ban der byas so / yang gnyen ston la gyer dbang grub kyis zhus / de la gyer ston[4] nam g·yung / de la lung bon lha gnyan[5] gyis zhus te dar ro ||

shel brag ma'i lo rgyus la bzhi'i / dang po sbas tshul ni / lde gyim tsha rma chung gis gtsang po nu ma'i brag la smon lam bcas sbas te gter srung ldong btsan dkar po la bcol lo /

gnyis pa gter thon tshul ni / yul nyang stod gnya' lung brag ra na / spe ne gu'i sprul pa gnyan[6] ston shes rab rdo rje bya ba / rkang pa 'theng[7] bas gnyan 'theng[8] re ngan yang zer / khong ra lug 'tshor phyin pas nyin gcig la 'od dkar po zhig rtsar byung / de'i rjes su phyin pas brag dkar po zhig gi rtsar 'od yal nas song / der brtags pas brag de la sgo srub ded de 'dug / de phyes te bltas pas brag phug gi logs thams cad yi ge po tis gang nas 'dug / de la dpe blangs nas bris (228b) pas phyis gnyan ston shes rab seng ger grags so /

gsum pa them byang ni / de la bon sde chen po dgu bzhugs te / gson gshin don byed rkang pa lta bu'i sde la / gson gyi gyer sgo la stod kyi gsas bzhi legs drug / bar gyi g·yen dgu smrang khungs /[9] smad kyi glud kha ngos len / sel dkar nag khra gsum / 'gro ba las kyi khog dbub / rgyud bzhi rtsa 'grel / tshangs pa lha'i gto dgu / yul sa dang pho lha'i gto dgu / lha dang btsan[10] gyi snyegs / lha'i lam sel / srung ma dgu sel / mkhan bya khrus tshan dang gsum gyi sel rabs / klu'i bang ra dgu skor / mtsho sman che chung gnyis / dung sha dkar mo'i yo bcos sogs yo bcos gsum / sa bdag lto 'phye'i bsdum sogs bsdum[11] gnyis /

[1] 'bar [2] (/ absent) [3] gnyen [4] bstan [5] gnyen [6] gnyen
[7] 'thing [8] 'thing [9] (/ absent) [10] btsun [11] bsdum absent

bsdum chung sgo bzhi / snying bsdum byad bkrol / sa bdag dbyen sob sogs sob pa gsum / srid pa'i spyi mdos sogs mdos gnyis / yang khol mdos bzhi / rin po che'i zhal bsgyur / shva ru rang 'gros / shva ba ru rgyas / bla bslu zor las / g·yang 'gugs sogs gson bon mang du byung ngo /

gshin bon la /[1] sel 'dur sbyang[2] gsum ste / gshin sel la (229a) 'brug gi kha sel la sogs sel gsum /

'dur la[3] / lha 'dur la khams gsum spyi 'dul / gshen rab bla ma'i 'dur / mched grogs kyi 'dur / gshen phran slad ma'i 'dur / mi 'dur la sangs po yab yum dang / sras pho mo'i dang / rabs chad gsum / gri dang / mtshun dang / pra dang / le'u'o / 'dur gyi ti ka dgu / yang dag don gyi gshed 'dur /

sbyang ba la phyi sbyang nang sbyang gnyis / pho sbyang mo sbyang gnyis / sgyu ma gzugs brnyan gyi gshed bsad / gtad yar / bde ba'i lam bstan / 'khor ba med pa'i lam bstan pa rnams byung ngo /

mtshan nyid shes bya byang khog lta bu'i sde la / mtshan nyid sde lnga la[4] / ting 'dzin dag pa'i mdo sde ni[5] / sngags kyi mdo lnga /

tshul khrims dag pa'i 'dul sde ni / 'dul ba rgyud drug / mdo drug / tshes phyag che chung /

shes rab dag pa'i 'bum sde ni / srid pa rtser chib lta ba'i 'bum / yod med dkar nag shan 'byed 'bum / srid pa'i gling bzhi khams kyi 'bum / rgyas pa nyi khri chu rgyun 'bum / 'dus pa rtsa ba don gyi 'bum / khams chung po ti brgyad pa / sdud (229b) pa tshigs su bcad pa 'grel bcas dang /

srid pa mdzod kyi sde la / mdzod gnas bcu bdun / mdor bsdus 'jig rten gtan phab / lha sras don 'grel / drang srong rgyal ba'i 'bru 'grel /

gzhal bya dag pa rig[6] pa'i sde ni / dbu ma bden gnyis rtsa 'grel bcas /

mdo kun 'jug lag pa lta bu'i sde la / mdo phran brgya rtsa gcig thon pa la / 'thor nas nyi shu rtsa gcig tu song ste deng sang mdo phran nyer gcig par grags pa / theg pa'i rtsa ba bka' mdo che chung mdzad pa drug cu rtsa gcig pa'i mdo / zhal chems kyi mdo / theg dgu 'chad pa'i spyi 'grel / gzungs sde lnga / gzungs[7] mchog bzhi dang bcas pa /

phyi nang sngags don snying lta bu'i sde la / phyi rnam dag

[1] (/ absent) [2] sbyangs [3] lha [4] la absent [5] ni absent [6] rigs [7] gzung

yum gyi sgrub pa che chung gsum / kun rig la gsum / glegs bam gyi mchod pa 'grel bcas / mchod rten gleng gzhi'i gzhung chen / sku gdung las rim gsum / chab gtor che 'bring chung gsum / dzam bha la ser nag gnyis kyi phyi nang gsang ba'i sgrub pa drug / klu mchod bzhi / klu gtor che chung /

nang gsang sngags la zhi ba rin chen dra ba rgyud 'grel dang bcas pa / khro bo (230a) dbal gsas rngam pa / lha sgrub / gsang sgrub / gtad khram bcu gnyis / sbyin sreg che chung / srid pa bde 'gro'i 'phyong sogs 'phyong bzhi / phur pa ye shes bla ma sde drug cha rkyen dang bcas pa / bdu rtsi'i ga'u klong dgu / rgyud gsum / sgrub pa gsum / sgrub pa nyi shu rtsa gcig /

lta dgongs dbang po lta bu'i sde la / gab pa dgu skor rtsa 'grel dang bcas pa / thig le yongs rdzogs / phra mo bcu gnyis / rdzogs chen gzer bu rtsa 'grel dang bcas pa / dug lnga lam khyer / phyag rgya chen po / nam mkha' mtha' bral / man ngag ngo sprod /

dge spyod nar ma kha zas lta bu'i sde la / skyabs 'gro che chung gsum / maṇḍal che chung gsum / yi ge brgya pa / phyag mchod / a gcig ma'i bgrang lugs phan yon dang bcas pa /

ngan sngags mtshon cha lta bu'i sde la / pho sgrub dgu / mo sgrub dgu / ma ning sgrub pa /

rang gzhan srung ba go cha lta bu'i sde la / rang srung / gdon srung / nad srung / mdze srung / dkor nor srung ba / 'dre srung / sri'u srung ba / tshe srung ba / mig rno ba / rkang mgyogs sgrub pa /

dbang po mgo lta (230b) bu'i sde la / dbang rgyud chen mo / man ngag gser phreng / ngo sprod / phrin las khog dbub / dbang don bshad pa rnams byung ngo /

gnya' ston rdo rje na re /[1] da ji tsam yod dris pas / da dung po tis brag[2] phug gang nas 'dug gsungs pas / 'o na de tsam bri tshod mi gda' lags pas gang dgos 'ga' longs zer bar / der phyin pas gter sgo rub nas ma thon skad / gnya' ston rdo rjes bon 'ga' zhig chos su bsgyur bas mdzes grongs so /

bzhi pa brgyud rim ni / bla ma gnyan 'theng[3] gis gter bton pa la gza' mig dmar gyis bar chad byas pas ma dar te lkugs pa'i bon zhes grags mod / gter shog 'thor ba tsam gyis mdo dbus gtsang gsum du phal cher dar nas skal ldan rnams kyis spyod do ||

lho brag khom mthing ma'i lo rgyus la lnga'i dang po gter sbas tshul ni / bstan pa dar nub skabs li shus khom mthing lha khang du sbas te bya ra ma gsum la gtad do /

[1] (/ absent) [2] phrag [3] mthing

gnyis pa gter ston gyi lo rgyus ni / li shu nyid kyi sprul pa bzhod[1] ston dngos grub grags pa ni / yul lho brag gi lung pa sman thang du / yab bzhod[2] ston lha tho dang (231a) yum shākya lcam gnyis kyi sras su 'khrungs / chung ngu nas dpal ldan ri zhing du rab tu byung ste slob gnyer byas pas zhu'i dngos slob kun las mkhas par grags / mkhar chu'i brag la dgon pa chung ngu zhig brtsigs nas der bzhugs te byang sems gab pa la slob bshad mdzad pas mkhas pa mang du 'phel lo /

gsum pa gter thon tshul ni / skabs shig na gter bdag gi lung gis / khyod la rdzogs chen 'dod na khom mthing lha khang gi dkor mdzod dbus ma na yod pas de thon cig zer / der khong khom mthing du phyin nas mdzod dbus ma'i sgo phyes pas de'i nang na khri srong gi seng ldeng gi rga / gser gyi yab chen / gser srab g·yu mthur / dngul gyi chag sgrogs / sba lcags sogs nor mang po 'dug pa bzhag / gter shog sngags pa'i phod kha gang 'dug pa khyer nas bltas pas thams cad chos su 'dug / phyir log ste mkha' 'gro ma la gsol ba btab / gter bdag mchod nas bltas pas / der mdzod sgo bco lnga yod pa'i gong ma gsum gyi dbus ma'i sgo phyes pas srid pa gsum yang sa ler gzigs (231b) so / der shog dril 'dug pa rnams la gzigs pas thams cad bon du 'dug pa bton te / yul du byon nas lo gsum du mtshams bcad cing tshogs kyi 'khor lo bskor nas gzigs rtog mdzad pas mkhyen no /

bzhi pa them byang la /[3] gzhung dang / man ngag gnyis kyi thog ma bsgrags pa skor gsum la / steng lha'i yul du bsgrags pa lung drug ni /[4] rtsol bral nyag gcig dgongs pa'i lung la sogs drug / byang sems sgrub[5] thabs kyi man ngag la sogs man ngag brgyad / gsang ba dbang gi yig chung sogs yig chung bzhi / 'khrul gzhi lta ba la sogs don gsum ste nyi shu rtsa gcig / cha rkyen lung drug gi sa bcad drug / 'grel chung drug /[6] bshad thabs lnga / 'khrul gzhi rtsad gcod / ye gshen gtsug phud kyi stong thun la dpe drug don drug / gol sa bcad pa /[7] co za'i mgur[8] 'bum la sogs so /

bar mi'i yul du bsgrags pa la /[9] rdzogs chen sde bcu / 'grel chung bcu / gal dmigs dgu / 'da' kha'i zhal chems / lta sgom zung 'grel gyi gdams ngag / ngo bo'i 'dug tshul rnams so /

'og klu'i yul du bsgrags pa la / lung seng (232a) ge'i sgra bsgrags / man ngag 'khor ba dong sprugs /

[1] bzhed [2] bzhed [3] (/ absent) [4] (/ absent) [5] sgrubs
[6] (/ absent) [7] (/ absent) [8] 'gur [9] (/ absent)

sngags la rgyud gsum / bskyed rdzogs gsum / zhi khro phur gsum gyi yang zhun / rgyal mo gsum gyi sgrub pa / man ngag lung gi tshad ma rtsa 'grel / sa bcad dang bcas pa / gzhan gzhung 'geg pa'i rigs 'gros bzhi / rang gzhung sgrub pa'i rigs 'gros bdun / gtar kha gags sel gyi rigs 'gros / gting skyen rtsa gcig gnad du rdeg pa'i rigs 'gros / gsang ba dbang gi rgyud la sogs rgyud lnga / de la sa bcad lnga / klong lnga / brnag pa gsum /[1] thig le drug la sogs mang ngo /

gnyis pa man ngag yang rtse klong chen la / thun mong gi gdams pa drang don skor / thun min nges don skor / dgongs brgyud drug gi glad don / nyi shu rtsa bzhi rnams kyi man ngag / rgyal thebs dbang khrid skor / 'od gsal zhal shes yig chung dang bcas pa / mtshon pa gtam brgyud sgron ma la sogs sgron ma lnga / li shu'i skor / dmar byang che chung la sogs pa'o /

lnga pa slob ma'i gyes tshul ni / thugs sras bzhi / mkhas btsun bzhi'o / yar 'brog gi 'or ston spun gnyis (232b) kyis nor mang po phul bas thugs zin / gtam shul gyi bla ma mye ston lo bco brgyad la nyer gnas byas pas thugs zin / la stod 'bum khri 'od kyis thag ring ba nas 'ong bas thugs zin no / mkhas btsun bzhi ni / gtam shul gyi snyi ston / la stod kyi bkra shis 'od / zhang ston nam mkha' / dbu ri'i bla ma jo lde dang bzhi'o / de dag gis lha rje'i[2] gsung sgros ci bzhin du mkhyen pas mkhas par grags so / de dag gi nang nas kyang mkha' 'gro'i[3] lung thob pa ni rgya jo lde yin te / de la ye shes dbal mos bzhod[4] ston dngos grub grags pa la tshe gcig gis 'tshang rgya ba'i bon yod pas khyod la gdams pa'i las 'phro yod pas de zhus shig ces lung bstan / khong bzhod[5] ston dang mjal nas de ltar zhus pas / nga la yod de su la'ang ma bstan khyod las can zhig yin gsungs nas shog dril bcu gcig byung ba la / bstan pas nges shes de ga la skyes te / gser srang phyed dang gsum / rta gcig tsha khal gnyis bcas / dbus phrug gi na bza' zhig phul bas shog ser gnang ba gnyan drag nas bcang du ma nyan par (233a) zhal bshus[6] te bdud 'dul lha khang du sbas so / bla ma jo lde la bla ma gnam lcags kyis zhus / de nas g·yo ston lhun grub dpal gyi bar du brgyud de dar ro / snyan brgyud che ba ni bla ma jo lde / des zhig po snang seng / des skyo ston sngags pa / des g·yo ston la brgyud de dar ro / snyan brgyud chung ba ni / rgya ston gnyag chung la bstan pas / des a po sngon po / des chos ston zhig po / des lce ston

[1] (/ absent) [2] rjes [3] 'gros [4] bzhed [5] bzhed [6] bshul

gzung grags / des zur bo che shākya 'byung gnas la bstan pas / des chos su bsgyur dbur rgya skad bzhag chos kyi brda chad du bcos / gter ston rdo rje bzhed par bsgyur te ming snyan brgyud thugs kyi me lung du btags nas ding sang chos pa kun gyis[1] spyod pa yin no ||

gyer mi nyi 'od la bka' gter bab tshul la gsum / dang po gyer mi'i lo rgyus ni / se ka ston pa bya ba yul phug chung ra mor bzhugs pa'i gam du / mi g·yu thul can mgo la bya zhu gon pa zhig byung bar / gang nas byon byas pas / 'di nas 'ong gi gtad pa mi gda' gsungs / yul ga na bdog byas pas /

stong gsum 'jig rten bon dbyings (233b) la ||
gud pa'i yul 'dod sems can blo ||
skyes pa zhang zhung yul du skyes ||

gsungs / rus ci lags byas pas /

kun gyi dngos gzhi sangs rgyas la ||
rus dang rigs rtog sems can blo ||
pha yi rus ni gyer mi lags ||

gsungs / ming ji skad bgyi lags byas pas /

don la nges pa med pas na ||
bdag gi ming la nges pa med ||
la las nyi ma 'od zer zer ||
la las bon zhig nag po zer ||
la las g·yu lus bya mgo zer ||

gsungs / lo du tsam lon[2] byas pas /

dus la snga phyi med pas na ||
lo dus 'dzin pa sems can blo ||
lo yang mang ba lon te mchi ||

gsungs / ber ga 'di la 'di tsam cal col btags pa ci bgyi byas pas /

'dod spyod sna tshogs rin chen gter ||
'dod na btsal yang[3] mi rnyed la ||
mi 'dod spangs kyang mi spang ste ||
sna tshogs snang la mngon zhen med ||
'dzin med 'bral med 'di ka yin ||

[1] gyi [2] len [3] kyang

gsungs / bon po yin nam chos pa yin byas pas /

gser gyi ri la nyi shar na ||
gser yang[1] ri la ri yang gser ||
gnyis su bzung na mtha' ru ltung ||

gsungs / snga mar gang du phyin da gar 'gro byas pas /

'ong ba zhang zhung (234a) stod nas 'ongs ||
'grim pa byang lam dbus mar 'grims[2] ||
phyin pa slob[3] dpon can du phyin ||

gsungs / gdams ngag cig zhu byas pas / 'o na skyes pas mi 'chi mi srid / shi bas mi skye mi srid / skyes pas mi 'khor mi srid / 'khor ba la bde ba mi srid pa shes sam gsungs / zhag 'ga' 'di gar bzhugs byas pas /

ri mtho sa gtsang bde nyams skye ||
des na grong yul spangs pa yin ||

gsungs / sngo thul 'di gon byas pas /

gos su sprin dang lhag rlung gon ||
gon pa dro la zad pa med ||

gsungs / rgyags ci tsam 'tshal ba sbyar gyis ri brag cig la bzhugs[4] byas pas /

a byis 'jigs la chags zhen skye ||
kha zas mi ma yin gyis ster ||

gsungs / zhag 'ga' bdag phyi na 'bring byas pas ||

bdag nyin mor 'thing gin ri rtser 'grim[5] ||
nub mor 'phur gyin mkha' klong nyul ||
khyod rang dge ba lugs bzhin sdod ||
nga nyi 'od nam mkhar sdud las che ||

gsungs nas gshegs so / de nas yar byon pas la stod tshab sde[6] bya bar[7] rta zhon ber gyon nas 'ong ba dang phrad pas / mu lto ba 'di gar phyin (234b) zer ba la / mu lto ba khyod rang yin byas pas / nga la zas nor gos gsum 'dod tshad yod nga las phyug pa ga na yod zer ba la lan byas pa gda' / mi kun gyis mdog chu dang gtsang po la ko ba med par thal zer ba ngo mtshar che byas pas /

'khor ba'i chu las ma brgal na ||
gtsang chu las brgal bas mi phan ||

[1] kyang [2] 'grim [3] slon [4] bzhug [5] mgrim [6] sder
[7] ba

gsungs / la stod mchod rten zhig gi rtsar yod tsam na / chos pa grub thob cig byung nas phyogs gcig na grub rtags byung ba zhig[1] 'dug 'ang zer nas / mchod rten de phyag mthil du blangs te spyi bor 'jog gin 'dug pa la kun gyis ngo mtshar che zer / der phyag 'khar la btags pa'i byang bu gcig byis pa zhig gis bcad nas khyer bas / nga'i de ga re zer gyin sher ba la / mi kun gyis de 'dra zhig la de tsam bsher nas ci bgyi byas pas /

> nga nyi 'od chags med bsgom pa la ||
> byang bu gcig gis mi dmar te ||
> de la bdag po gud na yod ||
> kho dag rang la bar chad 'ong ||

gsungs pas / der byis pa yang gum skad / re 'gar 'jar re nyal nas mi dang phrad tsam na / bdud khyab pa lag ring dang gshen rab (235a) kyi 'thab mo de 'cham nas 'dug ge gsungs / cha med byas tsa na / mnyam pa nyid la ma bzhag na 'cham po rang mi yong gsung skad / yang mi'i sngun na byon nas / bla ma skye med kyis skye med rtogs nas 'dug ge gsungs nas / a sa med na skye med kyis skye med rtogs pa dka' gsungs / re 'ga' byis pa kun las mar skogs dang thud skogs rus pa snum can blangs te me la bsregs gsur mchod pa byas nas / gzhob gsol nas am khyil gyis ma btang na zhen pa ma ldog yin gsungs skad / zas byin pa mi 'dod / ma byin pa 'dod zer gyin gtad tsam na gtor nas btang skad do / bla ma de ni khod[2] spungs dran pa'i sprul pa ste / dgung lo sum brgya mi'i yul na bzhugs / lo rgyus kha cig nas khyung po gyer zla med kyi sras yin par yang bshad do / gter ni de nyid kyi rnam thar las /

> gsang ba'i gter kha gang 'byed thogs pa med ||
> dgung lo nyi shu rtsa gnyis lon pa'i dus ||
> bya rgod gsang ba gter gyi zhal yang phyes ||

zhes sogs lo rgyus mang ngo /

gnyis pa la bka' gter gnyis su byung ste / nyams len lnga skor[3] / man ngag (235b) tshig bzhi / lde mig dgu skor / a gsal phrin las dang bcas pa rnams dran pa nam mkhas snyan du brgyud pa'i bka' dang / yang dang ra khyung rdzong nas sa pho byi ba'i lo la gter zhal phyes nas bton pa'i rtsa rgyud gsang ba bsen thub sogs zhi khro'i rgyud cha lag dang bcas shin tu mang ba

[1] cig [2] gyer [3] bskor

dang / gzhan yang g·yung drung las rnam par dag pa'i rgyud la sogs pa'i gter dang gnyis so /

gsum pa gang la brgyud pa ni / sngar se ka[1] khri thung ngam se ka[2] ston pa dang 'phrad skabs / se ston gyis 'khor ba la mi ltung ba'i snying po zhig zhu byas pas / sngar snying po ci bslabs gsungs / ba sgom g·yung drung gis bslabs pa'i a dkar sa le 'od bzlas lags byas pas / snyan brgyud a gsal sgron ma 'di la nyams kyi man ngag tshig bzhi gdab tu yod gsungs nas a gsal gyi gdams ngag gnang ste / 'di kun tu bzang po man chad nas da lta yan chad du snyan nas snyan du brgyud pa zhig gda' bas / bka' byang mi la ma ston cig gsungs so / de se ka[3] ston pas bla ma rma ston la gnang nas yi ger (236a) bkod pa'o / rtsa rgyud gsang ba bsen thub ni rma ston srol 'dzin la gnang nas 'di'i zla bo dgos na dang ra khyung rdzong gi brag la 'dug pa thon cig ces lung bstan no ||

bsam yas ca ti ma'i lo rgyus la bzhi'i / dang po sbas tshul ni / li shu dang be ro tsa na gnyis kyis bsam yas gling gi lho nub khri dang dur khrod du srin po'i kha gnon ca ti sgo mang mchod rten dmar por sbas te gter srung pom ra la bcol lo /

gnyis pa gter thon tshul ni / mchod rten dmar po'i so phag gog nas shog dril 'ga' zhig byung bar bltas pas bon du 'dug ste me la bsregs pas mi rung ba sna tshogs byung skad / yang lcags mo bya yi lo la so phag gog nas byung ba la / zhig gsos byas pas sgrom gcig byung ba la bltas pas shog dril mang du byung ba yang bon du 'dug / der na ning yang ma rung bas gnyan por 'dug zer nas me la ma sreg par bsam yas lha khang gi lder so'i[4] rgyab tu sbas so / de sad gu rin chen grsags pa dang / dre'u rgya ra dza gnyis kyis dkor gnyer byas pas bton te / nub mo rta la bkal nas kong po'i yul du lam phyung ste (236b) khams kyi lhor phyin no /

gsum pa bon gyi them byang ni / bon sde brgyad byung ba'i gsung rab kyi sde la / bye ma nyi khri chu rgyun gyi 'bum glegs bam sum cu rtsa gnyis 'khor zhu ba po bcu drug gis zhus pa bzhugs so /

mdo sde la bzhi / dus gsum bde gshegs byung khungs kyi mdo / khams[5] gsum sems can skye 'chi'i mdo / snod bcud 'byung ba chags 'jig gi mdo / bla med go 'phang sgrub thabs kyi mdo dang[6] bzhi'o / de'i cha lag la mang du byung ngo /

[1] gar [2] kar [3] kar [4] 'ded se [5] kham [6] dang absent

mdo phran la spyir nyi shu rtsa gcig byung ba'i / sgos gtso bzhi la bstod pa'i mdo sde gnyis gnyis te brgyad do / gzhan yang thig le'i mdo / yi ge brgya pa'i mdo / ltung bshags kyi mdo / sa dang lam gyi mdo la sogs nyer gnyis so /

sngags nang ma la / khro bo la rgyud lnga ste / khro gsas mkha' 'gying ri rab g·yo 'gul gyi rgyud / rngam gsas mkha' 'gying rlung nag 'tshubs ma'i rgyud / dbal gsas mkha' 'gying me dpung 'bar ba'i rgyud / gtum gsas mkha' 'gying chu bo rba klong gi rgyud / gtso mchog mkha' 'gying nam mkha' gsal byed kyi rgyud / de rnams la sgrub thabs (237a) re re dang bcas pa'o / khro bo u dum 'bar ba'i rgyud gsum cha lag dang bcas pa /

phur pa la rgyud dgu sgrub thabs re re dang bcas pa /

ge khod la rgyud gsum las / gnam lcags thog mda'i rgyud la ye shes dang 'jig rten gnyis / ye shes la khro bo bdun / 'jig rten la gsum ste bcu'o / mu mar gser dzva[1] zhun ma'i rgyud la me ri dang ge khod gnyis so / mnga' bdag me lce phreng ba'i rgyud la a ti mu ver rtsa 'grel gzhung gsum khyung dang bzhi'o /

gso dpyad la rtsa 'grel gnyis / lag len dang bcas pa /[2] shing sbyor rdo sbyor ldum bcas gsum /[3] dpyad bu khri shes kyi sman mdo sogs byung ngo /

sgrub pa ngan sngags kyi sde la / sgra bla ma du ba sngon mo'i rgyud la sogs bzhi / sgrub thabs brgyad cu rtsa gnyis / dmag dpon gas btsan la sbas pa gser gyi nyi ma sogs rtsa rgyud che 'bring chung gsum la gsum gsum dgu / spyi sgrub lha ma srin sde brgyad kyi sgrub thabs mang du byung ngo /

ngan thabs[4] bca' sbyor la / rdo sgyogs gsum / chu sgyogs gnyis dang lnga / chu rba gyen drangs dang drug /

gson bon gyi sde la / rgyal phung das chad /[5] (237b) shva ru thod pa /[6] mdos sku glud rang 'gros la sogs dang /

ltas ngan gyi sde la / khang pa mes tshig / chu bo gal bsgyur[7] / mkhar khang sgyel ba / mkhar steng du dur bya nag po dbab par byed pa sogs mang du byung ngo /

gzhi pa slob ma'i gyes tshul ni / dus de tsam na khams pa dbus gtsang du slob gnyer byed pa'i snga shos dir gyi dbu ston bya ba zhu g·yas kyi slob ma cig yod pa'i sar phyin te / nged la bon gyi gter shog yod pa 'dod dam byas pas / kho na re / ngas dbus gtsang du phyin te bla ma gshen gyis thon pa'i shog

[1] dza [2] (/ absent) [3] (/ absent) [4] thab [5] (/ absent)
[6] (/ absent) [7] sgyur

ser dum zhig 'dod kyang ma byung / de min khyod la sog ser med las che zer / de dus rje gur zhog pa dang rgya khri rje'i slob ma khams kyi grva sa ba snga shos sum pa gto ston bya ba la bon bstan te 'dod dam byas pas / 'dod de mi gzhan la ma ston cig / nga'i yul du 'gro la bon spel / khyod rang gnyis kyang che sar bzhag gsungs / sum pa gto ston la gtad de de la sgrom drug yod skad / gto ston gyis yon bdag gcig la bcol lo / dre'u rgya dang sad gu gnyis mo 'debs shing gzhan du byon pa dang / yul der tshong pa byung ba dang (238a) 'thab mo byung ste gto ston dbu chag nas 'das pas / gter ston gnyis byon nas dpe rtsad bcad pas ma chod skad / nam zhig na sngar gyi gter sgrom[1] bcol ba'i yon bdag mo skas nas lhung nas mgo chag pas / dbu mchod phur pa 'bar bya ba'i bon po sman shes pa zhig yod pa bos nas khrab cig phul te 'di bcos pa zhus pas / khong gis gter sgrom[1] mthong nas / yon bdag mo ngas sos par byed / khrab 'di khyod rang zungs la slob dpon gyis gter sgrom[1] bcol ba nga la slong zer ro / yon bdag mo dga' ste / khrab bzung nas gter sgrom[1] khong la phul lo / de ltar dbu mchod phur pa 'bar la dngos grub tu babs so / de nas cung zhig na / dir gyi dbu ston chen po 'das kyang de'i dbon po dir gyi ston btsun bya ba des ja skol te / mi mang po bsags nas / rta bzang po zhig la dar yug gcig btags te dbu mchod la phul nas / 'di nyid gter ston yin pas bon po rnams kyis slob dpon du khur zhig gsungs te kho rang gis bon zhus skad do / dbu mchod dir ston gnyis la khungs su byed do / dbu mchod la snya li shu stag ring gi sgrib shing yod pas dpe cha la sogs (238b) gar bzhugs kyang mi mthong skad / rje dir ston chen po la slob dpon sum bham la sogs kyis zhus te dar ro ||

yang khrag 'thung rol ba'i skor ni li shu stag ring gis bsam yas ca ti dmar po la sbas te / phyis dus la bab tsa na dre'u rgya dang sad gu gnyis kyis bton pas bon sde rgyud skor sgrub gzhung cha lag man ngag dang bcas pa rnams 'dru yon sgom thar mo la brgyud / des slob dpon dbu rol la brgyud de dar ro ||

bka' drang nga ma'i lo rgyus la gsum / dang po gter sbas tshul la /

spyi dang /
bye brag gnyis kyi /

dang po ni / kun tu bzang po nas rim par brgyud nas rgyal

[1] sgro

po rā dza spungs pa la dngos grub tu bab / de nas zhang zhung gi bon po li mur gtsug phud la / ba gor be ro tsa nas zhus te bod du bsgyur nas / mnga'[1] bdag khri srong lde[2] btsan gyi phyag la gtad pas / rgyal po'i bla 'tsho ba'i bon zhes grags so / der rje la btsun mo dang bon blon rnams gyis phra ma gsol nas bstan pa bsnubs te / be ro tsha ba rong du sphyugs skabs / bon sde 'di rnams gsang nas spyad / mnga' bdag (239a) 'das khar sras mu tig btsan po la gtad / des mnga' bdag ral ba can la gtad / des dar ma la gtad / dar ma'i sras 'od srung dang / btsun mo chen ma'i sras yum brtan gnyis ma 'dum pa'i dus su sku srung sngags mkhan drang nga dpal gyi yon tan la gtad / des dpal gyi grags pa la gtad / des sras rin chen dpal la gtad / de la sras med pas sku tshe'i smad la chun ma zhig blangs pa la bu drang nga mdo la bya ba skyes te / lo bzhi lon dus na yab grong khar bu la zhal chems su bzhag ste / tsha bo drang rje btsun pa dad pa tshul khrims dang / bu'i zhang po ra shag 'dre chung gnyis bos nas nga'i bu 'di lo bcu gsum ma lon par bon 'di rnams gter du sbos la de'i gong du ma bstan cig zer ba'i mna' bsgag / de nas thon la khyod rang gnyis kyang spyod / nga'i bu la yang byin gsungs so / der khong gnyis kyis drang nga'i zhal chems bzhin nyang smad du sbas so /

gnyis pa bye brag tu mdo gzer mig gi[3] lo rgyus ni / mdo de nyid las gling gi lho[4] phyogs kyi khri dang dur khrod kyi nang nas rnyed nas 'phel ba'o / zhes pas / (239b) 'di la g·yung drung ye shes kyis / bsam yas gter 'byung[5] las lho nub khri dang dur khrod kyi gling du srin po'i kha gnon ca ti dmar po bzhengs / zhes pa la brten nas ca ti nas bton zer la / kha cig gis bsam yas has po ri'i zhol gyi dur khrod du drang rje nyid kyis sa la ri mo bris pas sol ba zhig byung bas brkos pas g·ya' ma'i khang bu zhig nas rnyed zer ba sogs 'dod pa mang yang khri zer ba'i ngos 'dzin med pas mi 'thad ces gsungs / des na bsam yas lha khang gi nang ngos / lho phyogs lder[6] so dmar po'i gdan khri'i rgyab / nang gi logs ris kyi gsham du bya gcan la sogs dur khrod kyi gling bris pa'i bar du lo brgyad sbas te bton par mkhas pa rnams mgrin gcig tu bshad do /

gnyis pa gter ston gyi lo rgyus ni / mar pa stag la dbang gis yul 'u yug 'dzin pa'i dus su / mu ge byung ste sprang mo ma bu gnyis yod pa'i gam[7] du phyin pa'i bu de la snying rje skyes nas

[1] mngag [2] lde'u [3] dmigs kyi [4] lto [5] byung [6] 'der
[7] gang

gsos shing / rus gang yin dris pas drang rje yin zer / bza' ba ma rnyed pas mu ges gdungs nas mig ser por song 'dug zer nas ming gser mig tu (240a) btags so / phyis su bsam yas su 'khyams nas der btsun pa byas pas dkor gnyer du tshud de drang[1] nga btsun par grags / de nas drang nga mdo la skyes lo bcu gsum lon pa dang / de gnyis kas nyang smad sogs nas gter drangs te nyang ro chu bar du bgos pas / drang nga btsun pa na re / nga dang po nas lo rgyus mkhan yin zer nas mdo gzer mig[2] le'u bco brgyad pa'i shog ser rnams khyer ro / nga la drin che ba mar pa stag la yin pas 'bul dgongs nas 'ong ba dang / mar pa stag la 'u yug nas 'ong ba dang lam du 'phrad pas / drang rje na re / nga la bsam yas nas bon gter nas thon ma thag pa zhig yod pa de bdag la jo bo drin che bas 'bul byas pas / mar pas gzigs pas shin tu mos nas bshus[3] so / shog ser ni drang ston rang gis khyer nas bsam yas su log zer / ra shag 'dre chung gis rgyud smad bcu bdun[4] pa'i sems phyogs rnams khyer nas yar 'brog tu[5] ra ston dngos grub 'bar dang / ra sgom g·yu bo gnyis la bka' babs pa de dag yin te / lo rgyus gong du bstan zin to /

gsum pa brgyud rim ni / (240b) mar pa stag las mi btang nas bya 'ong rin chen bya ba la / bon mdo gter nas thon ma thag pa zhig yod pas khyod rang bris shig gsungs pas / bya 'ong rin chen dpal gyis bris so / de la rme'u lha ri gnyen[6] pos zhus te phyogs bcur dus gcig la dar ro / yang mar pa la g·yung btsun jo gdung dang / bru bdag nyid rje btsun gnyis kyis cig[7] char du zhus / g·yung la dam pa ri khrod pas zhus / de la yar me ba / de la sangs rgyas zhu chen nas bzung da lta kho bo'i bar du brgyud pa'i phreng ba ma chad pa'o ||

yang sprul sku nyang ston gyis kong 'phrang gi brag nas thon pa'i bon sde la / ma ge spungs dkar gyi bon sde lnga / ma ge nag po'i bon sde lnga / sel gto yar bon gyi sde lnga la sogs bon sde mang du byung ste lo rgyus rgyas pa ni ma mthong ngo ||

yang khod spungs kyi lung bstan las /

ba gor dod[8] de'i sprul pa ni ||
slob dpon gang zhug thog rgyal gyis ||
mang mkhar lcags 'phrang gter sgo phye ||

zhes pa'i lung gis bsngags pa'i gter ston des / mang mkhar lcags 'phrang nas bton pa'i bon sde la. / phyi rgyud mchod pa'i

[1] grang [2] dmigs [3] zhus [4] bco brgyad [5] 'grogs su
[6] gnyan [7] gcig [8] ded

(241a) bon sde 'ga' zhig dang / bya gdong thugs dkar dang / rin po che gling grags dang / kun snang gi lha ngo bstan pa sogs rgyud sde lnga bcu tham pa byung ngo ||

dung phor ma'i lo rgyus la bzhi'i / dang po gter sbas tshul ni / bstan pa dar nub kyi dus su dung phor bkra shis gnas su sbas te / lam gyi bya ra ma drug la gnyer gtad do /

gnyis pa gter ston ni / lung las / don rtags bco brgyad dang ldan pas 'byin nas skal ldan zhig la gtad par 'gyur ro / zhes dang / srid rgyud las /

> thad[1] mi thad ke'i sprul pa ni /
> gu ru rnon rtse bya[2] ba 'byung ||
> rta nag dung phor[3] dngos grub len ||
> 'gro don 'bum phrag mang po 'dren ||

zhes lung bstan pa bzhin du sprul sku gu ru rnon rtse zhes grags pa de la lo gsum gyi gong nas mkha' 'gro mas lung yang yang bstan nas rta nag dung phor gter rnyed do /

gsum pa them byang ni / mu cho'i shel sku / rnga stong ri chem pa / 'dul ba rgyud drug / zhi khro rtsa 'grel chen mo / mtho thog[4] mdzod / gtso mchog gshog pa can gyi sgrub pa / gsang sngags rdzong 'phrang / du tri su'i sgrub skor / gyad byin gyi rtags sgrub yan chad byung / khro bo'i gzhung 'grel (241b) chen po / ge khod mu mar glog phreng gi rgyud / this drug rno dang bdun / tso sgrub skor / gyad phur dkar po'i rgyud la sogs me ri'i skor / me ri 'od gsal phrin las rgyud kyi 'grel ba / sad ne ga'u'i khrid rim / ma rgyud thugs rje nyi ma'i skor la gzhi lam 'bras bu'i rgyud gsum 'grel ba dang bcas pa / ma rgyud thugs kyi yang gab / brgya bzhi chen mo / nad glud sha brgya zan brgya la sogs mang du byon no /

bzhi pa gang gis zhus pa ni / bla ma gzhon gyi zhal nas / bdag btsun pa gzhon nu khams su yod tsa na / mkha' 'gro'i lung bstan gyis gu ru can du khyod rang gis bon skal long zer ba byung nas phyin te / dbang dang khrid sogs gdams pa mang du zhus / nyin gcig tshogs mchod cig bshams pa'i dus su / bla ma rnon rtses dar dkar yug gcig bzung nas / ngas ma rgyud dpe mang po bris pas dmus / dar yug 'di khyod kyi bris skal du gnang / khyod lha las 'phos pas blo gtsang zhing zhi dal che bas / sus ma mthong bar khyod rang gis bris shig gsungs nas ma rgyud kyi skor rnams gnang ngo / zhes so / de la sgom pa

[1] dad [2] byung [3] pho'i [4] mtho

rnam gnyis kyis[1] zhus / (242a) de la ka gdams ye rgyal gyis zhus / des zhang ston khu dbon nas da lta'i bar du brgyud cing dar ro ||

yang rma ston srol 'dzin gyis gter thon tshul la / dang po gter gyi lung bstan thob tshul ni / yul 'jad chu'i 'og gi sad ne ga'u'i sprul pa rma ston srol 'dzin bya ba longs spyod 'byor ba chung ba zhig yod pa de byang du rnyed pa tshol du phyin pas / sa phug cig na rnal 'byor pa g·yu thul dang bya zhu mnab pa zhig gzim nas 'dug pa la / khyod 'dir ci byed pa yin zhus / nga dum cig na bas khyod la gtsag cha 'dug gi gtar kha zhig gi rogs[2] dgos gsungs / der phyag rtsar gtar bas 'o ma byung skad / grub thob yin par shes nas phyag 'tshal te / skyes bu khyed kyi mtshan ci lags zhus pas / la las bon zhig nag po zer / las las bla ma bsam chil zer / la las g·yu lus bya mgo zer / zhang zhung yul du gyer mi nyi 'od zer gsungs / sman dpe yin tsug[3] byas nas rtsa rgyud gsang ba bsen thub gnang / 'di'i zla bo dgos na dang ra khyung rdzong gi brag la 'dug pa thon cig / nga ni slob dpon can du (242b) 'gro gsungs / slob dpon gang lags zhus pas / dran pa nam mkha' yin gsungs nas gshegs so /

gnyis pa gter thon tshul ni / de nas rma ston gyis bla mas[4] lung bstan pa bzhin du btsal bas / sa pho byi ba'i lo la gter sgo phyes[5] te / de yang sngon gshen po rnams byang rgyab tu byon pa'i dus su / sgrom chung ngu gcig byang dang rar lus pa de gyer mi nyi 'od kyis gter du sbas te dang ra'i mtsho sman dang / rta[6] sgo'i lha btsan gnyis la bcol lo /

gsum pa de nas thon pa'i them byang la mdzod rtsa 'grel gnyis / mde'u thung rnam 'byed 'phrul gyi lde mig / zhi ba sgron ma dgu skor[7] don drug / yang gab dgu skor[8] / snyan brgyud lde mig dgu skor[9] / kun snang khyab pa'i dkyil 'khor /

khro bo la rtsa rgyud gsang ba bsen thub / yan lag rgyud bu chung drug / gzhung skabs rgyas pa / zhi khro yang khol / zhi khro yongs 'dus / dbal mo las thig phrin las kyi rgyud stod 'grel smad 'grel dang bcas / gsal byed me long pra rtags kyi 'phyong la sogs 'phyong dgu'i rgyud dgu / khro bo gsang thus 'grel ba dang bcas pa / dbal gsas (243a) las rim sngags sgrub sku rdzogs dang bcas pa / bstan srung bdud btsan drva ba dmar nag gi skor / phyva tshe g·yang sgrub cha lag / gsang 'dur 'khor ba rgyun gcod / mkhas pa mi bzhi'i zhal gdams / gnyan gyi snying

[1] kyi [2] rog [3] gtsug [4] ma'i [5] phyed [6] sta
[7] bskor [8] bskor [9] bskor

bcos dkar nag / srog gi seg bdar che chung / yum sras lnga'i sgrub pa / dang ra dpon g·yog gi sgrub pa / gzhan yang tshe bdag nor bdag sgo bdag khyung sngon la sogs byung ngo /

bzhi pa brgyud rim ni / rma ston gyis zhu chen ye shes rin chen dang bru nyi ma rgyal mtshan gnyis la brgyud / bru ston gyis g·yor po me dpal sogs nas da lta'i bar du brgyud de dar ro ||

yang srid rgyud las / dran pa'i zhal nas /

nga yi mchog gi sprul pa la ||
zhig po khyung nag bya ba 'byung ||

zhes pa'i lung zin gyi skyes bu bon zhig khyung nag la srid pa rgyal mos snyan du brgyud pa'i dri med lhan skyes kyi skor cha lag dang bcas pa dang / gtso mchog gi sgrub pa rnams 'khrul zhig ldong bu nas brgyud de dar ro ||

yang rma ston srol 'dzin gyi sras rma lcam me ni dran pa'i sprul pa ste / de nyid las /

nga yi byin gyis brlabs pa'i bu ||
(243b) rma ston lcam me bya ba 'byung ||

zhes so / de nyid kyis byang gi gsang brag rgya bo nas sku gshen pra phud kyis gter sbas pa rnyed pa'i rtsis byang la / gtan tshigs nges pa'i gal mdo / rtsod zlog rag sha spyi chings / zhi gzungs khro gzungs gsang gzungs chog drug dang bcas pa / kun bzang a dkar lha[1] sgrub / rnam dag sgron ma / rnam dag rgyun mchod rnams so / mu tra'i las rim ni yab rma ston gyi shog ser yin par yang bshad do / de rnams rma ston drang srong la brgyud / des khu ston lhun grub 'od zer la brgyud de dar ro ||

yang ba rong ston pa bya ba la sras shig yod pa de cher ma song bar yab grong / sras de la yum gyis ri la shing bag re thur bcug pas / nyin gcig yum gyis thag pa dang zan mar rdog po gcig bskur nas zla bo 'ga' zhig dang 'grogs nas shing bsgrub pa la btang bas / lam du zla bo rnams song / kho 'gro ma 'dod nas sa gcig tu gnyid log pa'i rmi lam du mi zhig gis[2] / khyod ma smad sdug ma sems shig / da ste lo gcig gnyis na dngos grub cig 'ong gi zer ro / gnyid sad nas bltas pas mi de mig snga na (244a) va ler 'dug / yang gnyid log nas bsdad pas zag med kyi bde ba rgyud la skyes so / yang re zhig kho'i rmi lam du bya chen po nam mkha' khebs pa tsam gyi spyi gtsug tu shel gyi khye'u tshon gang ba zhig gi ngag tu / a dkar sa le 'od brjod

[1] lta [2] gi

pa zhig rmis / gnyid sad pa dang khos kyang 'ga' re bzlas pas rig pa gzhi thog tu gnas pa byung / de nas rgyun du bzlas pas lta ba nam mkha' lta bu rgyud la skyes te phyis dus su ba rong[1] sgom chen g·yung drung grags bya ba byung ngo / de nyid kyis rta[2] sgo gangs nas nang dmar tshogs kyi bon / drang mkhan lha[3] dkar gyi bon la sogs phyi nang gsang ba'i rgyud sde mang po dang / snyan brgyud kun bzang a skor sogs byung ba rnams lha[4] rje ba sgom gyis bka' gter gnyis ka gur sgom la brgyud de dar ro ||

yang sham po'i g·ya' ma dmar po nas bal zho sgom chen gyis thon pa'i bon sde la / rin chen gangs ri brtsegs pa'i rgyud / mdo spyi rgyud chen mo lnga / thugs rje rtse mo'i rgyud / mdzes pa me tog gi rgyud la sogs man ngag gi rgyud bcu gcig / khyung chen lding ba la sogs gsang rgyud drug / zhi ba (244b) sku'i sgrub pa la g·yung drung yongs rdzogs / thig le dbyings 'chad / khro bo gsung gi sgrub pa la zla gam gcig pa khro bo mkha' 'gying gi sgrub pa / zla gam dgu pa bde gshegs rigs lnga'i sgrub pa / zla gam drug cu rtsa gcig pa dbang chen pho nya bco brgyad / zla gam brgyad pa gsang phur nag po'i sgrub pa / dbang chen thugs sgrub / dag pa sems kyi sgrub pa gsum / tshe sgrub gsum / bdud rtsi chu bo'i sgrub pa gsum / dbal mo sde bzhi'i sgrub pa / ma bdud stong bdud la sogs mang ngo ||

yang 'gog po seng rdzong gi gter ni / 'jing ston lha dga' bya ba 'bri mtshams yen rang gi dgon pa seng grags bya bar brag phug cig yod pa la nyal bas der lung bstan byung nas gter sgo phyes[5] pa'i bon la / bdud rtsi ba ga thigs pa'i rgyud la bdud rtsi'i sgrub pa chen mo chu sbyin che chung / shel ne tshe'i bdar gzhung / ge khod rnol ba'i this dgu dang bcas pa / ge khod chu bo glog dmar gyi rgyud dzvo[6] sgrub dang bcas pa / sgra bla thugs dkar thugs dmar gyi skor / snang gshen rtsa ba'i mdo dgu / gson gyi srog phyva[7] / gsas mkhar me ru 'khyil ba / glud khog chen mo (245a) bdud kyi zhal bsgyur sogs bon mang po yod do /

der 'jing ston mu lto ba la / stag lo tshes pas zhus / de la glog skya ba zhang grags kyis zhus te dar ro ||

yang bu mtsho srid pa'i rgyal pos gtsang stod rdo rje gsang phug nas sman sgrub bdud rtsi phum phum dgu dang / bdud rtsi sman gyi rgyud dgu thon pa gshen dam pa rgyal tshab[8] la brgyud de dar ro ||

[1] rang [2] sta [3] lta [4] lta [5] phyed [6] dzo [7] phya
[8] tshabs

yang[1] rma lcam me'i sras rma lha rgod thog pa'am rma ston shes rab seng ges yar lha sham po nas rnyed pa'i rtsis byang la / 'dul ba gsang lung / mdo mun sel sgron ma / lha gshen gyi mchod skor lnga pa / rab gnas mun sel sgron ma / du tri su mun sel sgron ma / khod spungs kyi sgrub skor / zhi khro sbrag sgrub / maṇḍal gsang skor / bon spyod bcu dgu'i rim pa / zhi ba g·yung drung yongs rdzogs / zhi khro spyi bskul[2] / rig 'dzin 'dus pa / gsang ba don 'grel / this dmar gsang ba'i rgyud / gsang this kyi skor de rnams rma ston drang srong dang de nas zhu lhun grub 'od zer la brgyud nas dar ro ||

yang 'jad dol gyi 'or sgom phug pa bya ba la / rma ston gyis[3] lung bstan nas / rgyung (245b) srub gsang ba'i brag nas / kun bzang a dkar thig le'i sgrub skor / zhi khro yang snying cha lag dang bcas pa / gnam lcags srog 'khor / mkha' klong mdos chen mde'u kha dang bcas pa / mdos bu chung bzhi / sde brgyad zlog pa'i gzungs[4] ring / seng ge'i mdos dang bcas pa / na rak pang kong / yum sras gtor bskang / brag btsan gtor bskang la sogs 'or sgom la spa ston rin chen lhun grub kyis zhus te dar ro ||

yang zhang zhung glang mu ne ver gyi sprul pa chu sa skyo ston dang / khyung po legs blo gnyis kyis ge khod gnyan lung nas thon pa la / ge khod lha sum brgya drug cu'i rgyud sde lnga / khro bo[5] gser tso dbal thog gsum gyi rgyud sde / mda' phur nyungs kar bon gyi skor tshoms / sku bla phyi sgrub bon gyi rgyud sde / bdud rtsi sman sgrub kyi rgyud sde / gser dzva sgrub pa'i rgyud sde / sngags thun che chung 'bring la sogs byung ngo ||

yang mar ston rgyal legs la mkha' 'gro dkar mo spyan gcig mas snyan du brgyud pa la / du tri su'i zhi gcod cha lag dang bcas pa / gzhan yang phan byed kyi gdams pa mang du yod pa rnams rnal 'byor rtogs pa'i seng ge la brgyud de dar ro ||

yang sum pa mu cho'i[6] (246a) sprul pa mtsho bon khyung gsas kyis skyid mkhar sngo phug[7] nas bdud rtsi g·yu 'brang phyug mo'i skor / sman a ma ra'i sgrub skor / bdud rtsi ne'u le'i rgyud bcu gnyis / gsang sngags nang ma'i rgyud sde bzhi / sngags phyi rgyud kyi rgyud sde gnyis la sogs pa rnyed pa de zhu sgrol ba gshen rgyal la brgyud de dar ro ||

yang gyer mi nyi 'od kyi sprul pa skyang[8] 'phags mu la drung mus theb chu brag dkar bya rgod nas thon pa la / g·yung drung

[1] dbang [2] skul [3] gyi [4] gzung [5] bo absent [6] phyo
[7] phum [8] spyang

chu 'bum gnyan 'bum lha 'bum ba ga yum 'bum sogs 'bum sde bzhi la glegs bam sum cu'am bzhi bcu yod kyang zer te / ding sang mdo khams smad phyogs sogs su bzhugs so ||

de nas lung bstan las /

tshe dbang rig 'dzin sprul pa ni ||
dam pa rang grol bya ba 'byung ||

zhes pa'i lung zin gyi skyes bu de la tshe dbang rig 'dzin gyis snyan du brgyud pa'i bon sde la / phun sum tshogs pa'i mdo sde / rin chen nor bdun skor sogs kyi mdo / khro rgyal sme brtsegs rtog[1] 'joms kyi skor / bskang mdos / 'ban zlog / drang chung / zhi khro thos grol skor / klu chen rigs lnga'i char 'beb[2] / klu chog 'o ma'i rgya mtsho / snang (246b) srid zhi ba / lha rgod drag bdar / tshan bsang / smra seng 'jam dbyangs dmar po'i skor / gtso mchog yab yum dgra brub / ltung bshags la sogs yod pa rnams shar chung rin chen rgyal mtshan la brgyud de dar ro ||

yang grub thob shar ba rnal 'byor la snyan du brgyud pa'i bon la / shar ba'i don dril zab mo dang / phyi nang dge spyod kyi yan lag la sogs mang du bzhugs so ||

yang rig 'dzin thugs sprul gter ston g·yu lo dkar po yis rma rgyal gyal ga'i gter gnas nas rigs drug thar lam gyi mdo la sogs pa'i gdams pa zab mo 'ga' zhig thon pa'o ||

yang lha bzher g·yung drung bla ma dang / bra bo rgyal ba grags pa gnyis kyis / mtho la rmog mgo'i gter gnas nas dpon gsas rig 'dzin gyi skor tshom sogs skor tshom mi 'dra ba bcu gcig dang / yang tsong kha'i[3] skabs gnyen mtsho nag nas rdzogs chen nyi ma'i snying po / dbal phur rag sha bdud 'dul / khro bo dbang chen rol ba / rigs drug thar lam mdo / dran pa'i sgrub skor / rgyud nyi zer sgron ma / khro bo gting zlog la sogs thon no /

bra bo sgom nyag (247a) gis do khong phyogs med la gnang / des nag dpe khro rgyal rin chen la brgyud / des khong gi sras shes rab 'bum la brgyud de dar ro ||

yang dpon gsas ma'i lo rgyus bzhi'i dang po gter ston gyi lo rgyus ni / lung bstan las / dran pa'i zhal nas /

nga yi mchog gi sprul pa la ||
dbyil ston he ru ka zhes 'byung ||

[1] rtogs [2] 'bebs [3] btsang ka'i

phyis su khyung rgod rtsal zhes grags ||
bon du gsang gter kha 'byed 'gyur ||

zhes 'byung ba de nyid yab dbyil ston rdo rje seng ge'i sras su 'khrungs / chung nas dad pa shes rab dang ldan / dgung lo nyi shu rtsa gsum na bsnyung gzhi cig byung nas de'i tshe rigs drug gi sbyong tshad zhag bdun la mthong ba byung / de dngangs[1] rjes ti se shel phug na dran pa la sogs rig 'dzin dgus phyi nang gsang ba'i dbang bskur nas gsang mtshan du khyung rgod rtsal du btags so /

gnyis pa gter thon tshul ni / zhal bzang brag la phyin pas brag gi rked pa na maṇḍal 'dra ba'i rdo gru bzhi zhig la shel gyi g·yung drung zhig lam mer 'dug / der thag pa la phyin nas gzong rgyab pas sgo byung / de'i nang na rdo nag gi maṇḍal gru bzhi zhig gi steng na (247b) phyogs bzhi dbus lngar rdza bum la kha dog ti tshas sngo ljang du bsgyur ba lnga'i khar phur pa lnga la rang rang gi rigs rtags bris pa 'dug pa'i bum pa'i kha phyes nas shog dril rnams blangs pa'i shul 'bru sman gyis bkang / sgo sngar bzhin du bsgrigs te bzhag cing lo gcig la gsang nas spyod do /

gsum pa so so'i them byang la / de nas byung ba'i bon sde la /[2] rdzogs chen g·yung drung klong yangs / rdzogs chen nyi ma rab gsal / rdzogs chen thig le 'dus pa / sgron ma dgu skor / dri med shel gyi snying po / thig le dgu skor[3] / g·yung drung lung bcu / drang don mdo dgu / nges don mdo dgu / phur pa sha 'bal ma'i skor / kun bzang rgyal 'dus kyi skor / dran pa phyi nang gsang gsum / tshe dbang phyi nang gsang gsum / skal[4] bzang phyi nang gsang gsum / rigs lnga mkha' 'gro'i sgrub pa / ge khod kyi skor / bstan srung yum sras lnga'i rkyang sgrub dang dril sgrub / sman rtsis la sogs byung /

rgyang lha khang gi rta mgrin[5] thugs ka nas bon la /[6] phur pa drag sgrub skor / sgrub chung nyer lnga / dran pa'i lung bstan che 'bring chung gsum /

chos la /[7] rdo rje (248a) sems dpa'i mngon rtogs / phyag rdor gyi sgrub pa / bro nad gso thabs / gu ru drag sgrub rnams byung /

rgyang yon po lung nas thog ser ma bu la sogs[8] drag sngags mang du byon /

[1] dangs [2] (/ absent) [3] bskor [4] bskal [5] 'grin [6] (/ absent) [7] (/ absent) [8] sogs/

zang zang lha brag nas snyan brgyud chog drug / yang gsang rtsod zlog / tshe gzungs[1] / dran pa rdzus skyes / tshe dbang zhang zhung ma / ye dbang chen mo / gter bdag lha btsan mchod thabs rnams byon /

mang mkhar lcags 'phrang nas kun rig[2] rgyas bsdus mde'u thung dang bcas pa / khro bo sgron ma zhi ba dang bcas pa / sde brgyad gzungs ring cha lag dang bcas pa / rgyud ting mur g·yu rtse / dbal gsas srung zlog gzir gsum / stag la spu gri dmar nag gi skor / drag po skor gsum gyi sbyin sreg / stong rgyung sgrub skor / mi bdud khrag mgo mdos dang bcas pa / gter bdag bdud btsan mched bdun gyi mchod thabs rnams byon /

pra dum rta mgrin lto ba nas rta mgrin sgrub skor / rgyal po dbyug them che chung / gso dpyad bdud rtsi bum pa che chung / pad mas mdzad pa'i gza' bcos / chung dpyad rnams byung ba gu ru chos dbang la gnang skad /

yang bu la'i gangs nas g·yu (248b) dang shel sgang bon sde rnams thon skad /

ti se gangs nas nye lam sde bzhi / gtsug gtor gdugs dkar dang gdugs nag mo / gshen rab chag shing rnams byon no /

gzhan yang tshe dbang gis snyan du brgyud pa'i rtog 'joms ye shes me dpung la phyi nang gsang ba'i sgrub pa gsum / zhi rgyas dbang drag gi sgrub ba bzhi / man ngag zhal shes la sogs pa mdor na bon sde bcu gsum la dbang bar bshad /

bzhi pa slob ma'i gyes tshul la / bka' bab kyi slob ma bzhi ni / smad du dar bar byed pa 'a zha blo gros rgyal mtshan dang bru 'dul ba rgyal mtshan gnyis / stod du dar bar byed pa spa mkhan chen g·yung drung seng ge dang spa ston rgyal ba shes rab gnyis te bzhi'o / de bzhi la gtug pa'i slob ma ni shin tu mang ngo ||

mtshan ldan drung mu ha ra la rig 'dzin stong rgyung mthu chen gyis snyan du brgyud pa'i bon sde la / gsang sngags yid bzhin nor bu la rgyud dang gzhung cha lag man ngag dang bcas pa / bskal bzang pod gnyis / chu sbyin / mna' bshags[3] sbrul mdo / stong rgyung brngan bsang / sa tsha rigs[4] lnga /[5] a bsve'i skor / skong ba sogs dang /

(249a) gzhan yang gtso mchog thugs 'bum la sogs 'bum sde chen po nyi shu rtsa gcig / 'khor ba sgrol mdo / rgyu 'bras mdo sogs mdo sde chen po nyi shu rtsa gcig / dpon gsas bla ma'i rgyud gzungs sogs gzungs sde chen po nyi shu rtsa gcig / bla

[1] gzung [2] rigs [3] bshags/ [4] rig [5] (/ absent)

ma rig 'dzin yi dam mkha' 'gro'i sgrub pa cha lag man ngag dang bcas pa / drang don / nges don gyi bon sde / lta sgom spyod pa'i man ngag / rig 'dzin mkha' 'gro'i zhal gdams / gab sbas gsang ba'i yig chung / rtsa rlung thig le'i nyams len / 'grel dang ti ka las tshogs[1] la sogs shin tu rgya che ste / de dag drung mus rtsi ra 'od zer rgyal mtshan la brgyud de dar ro ||

yang rnam rgyal rgya nag ma dang zhang zhung ma'i lo rgyus la bzh'i / dang po sbas tshul ni bstan pa 'phel 'grib dus su / rnam rgyal zhang zhung ma ni gyim tsha rma chung gis rag phrom na gter du sbas / rgya nag ma ni (249b) rgya nag legs tang rmang pos rgya'i mchod rten ka ru sogs su sbas so /

gnyis pa gter drangs tshul ni / dran pa'i zhal nas /

> nga yi mchog gi sprul pa ni ||
> dbang ldan gshen gsas[2] bya ba 'byung ||
> spyod pa chags med rgyan shar ba ||
> gsang gter bon gyis[3] 'gro ba 'dren ||

zhes lung bstan pa'i gter ston go lde 'phags pa'am dbang ldan gshen gsas[4] lha rje'am gnyos nyi ma shes rab kyis gter gnas gnyis nas gdan drangs te / rke bu na ro'i gsang phug tu dag pa lha'i yi ge bod yig tu bsgyur nas phab pa'o / gzhan yang gshang khri lo gnam grags sogs mang du thon no /

gsum pa bon gyi them byang ni / rgya'i mchod rten ka ru nas thon pa la /[5] gzungs sde le'u lnga bcu rtsa lnga pa / mdo thung dang bcas pa rnams byung /

khams yul rdo di gangs dkar dang rag phrom nas rnam rgyal rtsa sgrub / bkra shis yon tan / nad yam bzlog pa / phyva[6] g·yang gi sgrub pa / gza' 'dul gtso mchog rnam 'jom / rgyud mi 'dra ba'i skor bcu byung ngo /

gzhan yang gtsang gi byang phyogs g·yung drung seng mchong[7] gi brag nas / bla med go 'phang sgrub thabs (250a) kyi mdo rgyud / g·yung drung klong rgyas le'u nyi shu rtsa brgyad pa / kun rig[8] / gshen gyi dka' thub la sogs thon no / snyan brgyud kyi bka' la /[9] rdzogs chen[10] dran pa gser gdams skor sogs mang du yod do /

bzhi pa brgyud[11] rim ni / go lde 'phags pas khyung po nang chen grags pa dang / kho rang gi dbon po dpon dge gnyis la gnang / de gnyis ka la khyung po bsod rgyal pas zhus te dar ro ||

[1] tshog [2] sras [3] gyi [4] sras [5] (/ absent) [6] phya
[7] mtshong [8] rigs [9] (/ absent) [10] chen/ [11] rgyud

gzhan yang pom ra ma'i lo rgyus la gsum gyi / dang po gter thon tshul ni / rma pom ra'i g·yas zur bka' rtags can gyi brag nas sprul sku kyu ra gter ston gyis thon pa'o /

gnyis pa them byang la /[1] rag sha spyi 'dul gyi skor la phyi rgyud 'od zer drva[2] ba / nang rgyud sgyu 'phrul drva ba / gsang rgyud me dpung drva ba / de la sku gsung thugs yon tan phrin las lnga'i rgyud du phyes pa / zhi khro yongs rdzogs sku'i rgyud / rag sha dmar po gsung gi rgyud / bdud rtsi 'khyil ba thugs kyi rgyud / me ri 'khyil ba yon tan rgyud / me dpung 'bar ba phrin las rgyud dang lnga byung ngo / zhi rgyas dbang drag bzhi re phyes pa'i snang srid zhi byed sku'i rgyud / srid pa skyed byed rgyas pa'i (250b) rgyud / khams gsum zil gnon dbang gi rgyud / dug lnga mngon sgrol drag po'i rgyud dang bzhi'o / gzhan yang sgrub gzhung cha lag kha tshar dang bcas pa / chig sgrub rta dbu dmar chung gi skor / stag la spu gri dmar nag gi gzhung cha lag sogs mang du byon no /

gsum pa slob brgyud[3] ni / sprul sku kyu ra la bka' bab kyi bu chen bzhi yod do / zhi khro yongs rdzogs kyi bka' tsong kha'i dge bshes la bab / thugs sgrub kyi bka' 'dan ma ri ba la bab / go cha che chung gi bka' rko ston g·yung drung la bab / sgrol byed spu gri sum cu'i bka' khrom a dpal la bab cing de dag so sor nas dar ro / khyad par du gter ston gyi dbon po shes rab 'od zer la rgya ru khro bo rgyal mtshan gyis zhus te dar ro ||

yang bon zhig g·yung drung gling pa'am rdo rje gling pa'ang zer ba de nyid kyis[4] dgung lo nyer gsum par be ros sbas pa'i spa gro stag tshang nas rdzogs chen gser thur / dran pa yab sras kyi sgrub pa cha lag bcas / pom ra'i skor / nyang stod phyug mo dpal ri nas tshe dbang bod yul ma zhes pa'i gzhung cha lag khrid yig skor / byang gi sha ba ri (251a) nas bon sku kun bzang gi khrid yig / srung ma srid rgyal drel dkar ma / longs sku rigs lnga'i khrid yig / srung ma drel dmar ma / sprul sku gshen rab kyi khrid yig / srung ma drel nag ma / be ro tsa na'i rnam thar / ma 'ong[5] lung bstan / re kyang shang mtha' nas lha klu'i nor bu / ne'u chung gi rna g·yu dkar chag dang bcas pa / btsan sgrub skor / gtsang 'phrang lha khang gi them 'og tu bo dhi sa tvas mnan pa'i gshen rab kyi sku gzugs g·yu gar ljang las grub pa ngo mtshar che ba thon pa da lta rgyal rigs bru'i phyag na bzhugs so /

slob brgyud la tshe dbang gi skor rnams gter ston gyis mtha'

[1] (/ absent) [2] dra [3] rgyud [4] kyi [5] 'ongs

bzhi ye shes rang shar la brgyud de lung zin bu dgu sogs nas dar ro / dran pa'i skor la sogs bru mtshungs med bsod nams blo gros la brgyud / des rdza bo g·yung drung rgyal mtshan la brgyud de dar ro ||

tshe dbang bod yul ma'i lung bstan las /

> khye'u chung thugs kyi sprul pa la ||
> bru la bsod nams mtshan can 'byung ||
> de dang gang 'brel thar pa 'thob ||

ces pa'i lung zin gyi bru mtshungs[1] med bsod nams blo gros[2] (251b) la mdzod kyi gzhal bya bsdus pa / gsang sngags ngag don / spyi spungs sdom tshig nang bskyed kyi rtsa 'khor gnas lugs sogs bka' brten dang / dpon gsas bla ma'i sgrub thabs / pom ra shel khrab kyi skor sogs dag snang gi las tshogs dang / rnam sras zhal gzigs kyi bstod bskul sogs khyad par 'phags pa'i bon skor mang du yod do ||

gzhan yang gang ston klu ston rnam gnyis kyis kyang yang dben yer ba'i brag rdzong nas snang ba 'od ldan gyi rgyud dang sgrub skor / gnam phyi'i bdud rtsi bum sgrub / zhang zhung bon skor lha rgod drag bdar[3] la sogs mang du thon par bshad do ||

yang khams kyi drang srong sgom[4] pa rin chen gyis rma rgyal pom ra'i g·yas zur nas rdzogs chen nyi ma'i snying po / dbal phur nag po bdud 'dul kyi skor / khro bo dbang chen rol ba sogs sgrub chen mang po gter las thon par bshad pa snang ngo ||

yang kong po gter ston gung grags bya bas sku bla gangs brag nas drangs pa'i mdo sde bskal pa bzang po pod gnyis dang / bon spyod la sogs mang du thon no ||

yang khyung po lha (252a) bzher / nyang dpal mthong / zhang zhung lha sgra gsum gyis khom mthing lha khang gi dkor mdzod dang por sbas pa / phyis su la stod spa bon khyung thog dang rgyud ston ra dza gnyis kyis bton pa la / snang gshen gyi rgyud g·yung drung gsal byed / rtsa ba rin chen rgya mdud / bon khog srid pa rnam grol / lag len rin chen sgron ma la sogs rgyu'i bon mang po'i dngos grub brnyes te / de dag gis[5] lha 'od dkar dang / des g·yor po gnyer ston la brgyud de dar ro ||

yang sprul sku bu kyi bu nam gyis bsam yas ca ti dmar po nas gter nas thon pa'i shog ser glang 'od la thung gi phyag tu babs te / brda yig bkrol ba las a bsve btsan sgrub skor than srog

[1] mtshung [2] gros / [3] gdar [4] sgam [5] d'i sras

dril sgrub la sogs pa byung ba rnams / khyung po nang chen grags pa la brgyud / des bsod rgyal pa la brgyud de dar ro ||

yang rdzong brag bla ma dbu rnal bya bas gtsang gi rin chen brag rdzong nas / dmag dpon gsang sgrub la sogs thon par bshad do ||

yang sbas kyi dang la 'byams pa dang khyung po klu mgon gnyis kyis lha sa'i phur sgo'i shar phyogs nas drangs[1] pa'i bon sde la / (252b) mgon lha dkar po'i sgrub tshogs / dbal dang ma tshogs kyi sgrub pa / gsang sgrub che chung rgyud sde / gsang ba 'phrul gyi lde mig / drang don gyi rgyud sde / mtho thog spyi rgyug gi bon sde 'ga' zhig byon no ||

yang gnam gshen mthong grags kyi sprul pa gter ston khu 'dzin 'jing nag gis lho ri nag po nas thon pa'i bon sde la / bdud kyi gzhung sgrub / btsan sgrub che chung / klu'i mnan gtad snying gzer / gsas mkhar dbang gi ti ka / gsas mkhar rgyud mo che / lha bran bon sde rnams yod do ||

yang sprul sku la byi rda rma la brag btsan gyis lung bstan nas a bsve'i thugs sgrub las tshogs drug pa la sogs man ngag gi skor mang po byon pa rnams / a khol do skya bsod nams rgyal mtshan la brgyud de dar ro ||

yang ma hor stag gzig gi sprul pa lo pa'i rngon pa ma ngor gyis brag dmar rtse gsum nas thon pa la / gshen rab lha mdzod chen po'i rgyud / 'khor lo rgyud sbyang gi rgyud sde / gshin 'dur phra mo'i rgyud sde / 'dus byas bon gyi rgyud sde / rgyud dang sgrub phran mi 'dra ba dgu byung bar (253a) bshad do ||

yang rgya rong se gnyan zhig pos dmu rdo g·yung drung spungs rtse'i g·yas zur nas bsve sgrom gsum thon pa'i bon sde la / sgrom bu gcig las 'dul ba rgyud 'bum la glegs bam drug / rtsa 'dus kyi 'bum la sogs 'bum gyi sde dang /

bdud rtsi bcud 'bebs thig le / 'byung ba gting rdzogs khu byug mdo / bdud rtsi dpyad mdo / mtha' sel mdo / g·yung drung spyi phud nam mkha'i mdo / zhi byed mdo sogs mdo yi sde dang /

rdzogs chen mu med bdal ba'i rgyud / yang gsang bla med lde mig rgyud / tan tra gsang ba sems kyi rgyud / thig le grub pa'i me long rgyud / rin chen spyi spungs rtsa ba'i rgyud / gting zlog gi rgyud / ma mo'i rgyud / ge shan sgrol byed dbal mo'i rgyud / myur mgyogs drag po thog 'bebs rgyud / 'byung 'khrug phyag cha sum cu'i rgyud / gsang ba dgu 'dus pra shan rgyud / bzlas chog rgyud la sogs rgyud sum cu byung /

[1] drang

bsve sgrom gcig las[1] brda tshom skor / gsas mkhar sum brgya'i byung khungs / gsang 'dus rtsa 'grel / gab pa'i skor / sangs rgyas mdo / snang (253b) gsal mdo / khams 'grel man ngag bcu drug / sbas yig / dus kyi rtsis byang / lung dang man ngag kha byang sogs bon sde lnga gsum bco lnga byung /

bsve sgrom gcig las gyim bu'i snang rabs gto / srid rabs 'dur / rdzu 'phrul skor gsum / 'byung sel / ye ngam rgyud sde / mu cho'i khrom 'dur / nad sel skor / sbyang rgyud bdun skor / zhi bcos dregs pa dgu'i skor / gnyan[2] chen sde drug / sa bdag 'khrug sbyor / kong[3] tse'i gto / rno mthong / drag sngags / rgyud dgu / mi mgo skad 'don me dpung rgyud / gar gsas rgyud / rdzas byor / 'phrul cho'i ya stag rgyud la sogs bon sde nyi shu rtsa gsum byung bar bshad do ||

yang gling gshen[4] mu la thogs[5] med la stong rgyung gis snyan du brgyud pa'i gser 'od nor bu 'od 'bar dang / gzhan yang char 'beb[6] klu sgrub kyi skor / sgra bla rgyal mo'i skor sogs yod do ||

yang gter ston gu ru ban chung gis zangs 'brug 'khyil ba nas ku be ra'i sgrub skor / char 'beb yang dag ma'i skor dang / rgya rong 'brug ri khyung mgo nas / yongs su dag pa'i bon skor / (254a) gsas mkhar me ri 'khyil ba dang / khams kyi gnyan tshungs nas / mdo dung lo ljon pa / g·yu lo ljon pa / gser lo ljon pa / zangs lo ljon pa ste mdo bzhi /[7] rma pom ra nas rab gnas spur chog la sogs rnyed do ||

yang gter ston lhun grub thogs[8] med kyis / rdo di[9] gangs dkar la dran pa sogs grub pa'i gshen dgus sbas pa'i skye sgo gcod pa'i mdo la sogs zab pa'i bon sde 'ga' zhig dngos grub tu rnyed do ||

yang rgya rong mu rdo'i nub phyogs kyi rdza bo rig pa rang shar la tshe dbang rig 'dzin gyis snyan du brgyud pa'i bon sde la rdzogs chen lta ba thog 'beb[10] kyi klad gzhung mjug la sa bcad[11] bco lnga 'grel ba dang bcas pa dang / gzhan yang gsang 'dus khyung sprul sad srung gi skor / gsang sngags phyi nang gsang gsum / drang mkhan la sogs mang du yod do ||

sbar zhabs brag nas gter thon tshul la / dang po sbas tshul ni bon dar nub kyi dus su legs tang rmang pos bon sde du ma mdo smad sbar zhabs brag dkar gyi phrag pa g·yas gong brag seng ge'i kha gdangs pa 'dra ba'i gong du gtad rgya kha byang (254b) smon lam dang bcas sbas so /

[1] la [2] gnyen [3] kang [4] zhig [5] thog [6] 'bebs [7] (/ absent)
[8] thog [9] thi [10] 'bebs [11] gcod

gnyis pa gter ston ni / srid pa rgyud kyi kha byang las / zla ba rgyal mtshan gyi rnam 'phrul dbra rigs gyer thogs med bya bas / sbar zhabs brag dkar kyi gter sgo phye / zhes pa de nyid do /

gsum pa gter thon tshul la / rtsa ba dang yan lag gnyis kyi / dang po sbar zhabs brag gi gter thon tshul ni / dgung lo nyi shu rtsa gnyis bzhes tshe rig 'dzin gyi lung bstan byung ste / nyams snang du rnal 'byor pa mang du byung ba'i nang nas a tsa ra'i cha byad can zhig na re / nged rnams ni rgya gar dang zhang zhung yul nas 'ong / smad du sbar zhabs brag dkar du bon gyi gsang gter yod pa thon cig zer / der phyin nas bzhugs pas gter srung gi cho 'phrul sna tshogs byung skad / de nas srid pa rgyal mos zhal bstan te brag dkar gyi gong la btsas kyi dkyil du rdo ring la gter gyi kha byang bris nas yod gsungs pa bzhin btsal bas / rdo ring gi ngos su 'di nas 'og tu khru gang na gter yod / 'di drang ba'i mis gter srung la lug nag spyi dkar zhig phul la gter khung du rin po che sna lnga'i bum gter zhog / zla ba dgu'i bar du gsang rgya sbas rgya u ya aga tham zer ba rnyed do / de nas brkos pas (255a) shog ser rnams byung ste /[1]

bod yig tu phab pa'i them byang ni / shes rab rdzogs pa gsang ba'i 'bum / 'khor ba dong sprug gi mdo / yid bzhin nor bu gser 'od kyi gzungs / rdzogs chen mngon rtogs lta ba'i rgyal po / srid pa rgyud kyi bsgrags byang chen mo / rig 'dzin brgyad cu'i mtshan phyag / zhi khro bcud dril / gsang sngags skor tshom / dbal khyung dmar po'i sgrub skor / lha rgod sku rdzogs kyi sgrub pa / gsang sngags gzer bu bcu pa / phur pa'i srung zlog stong thun dang bcas pa / srid pa rgyal mo las kyi tan tra / dran pa thugs sgrub / tshe dbang gsang sgrub / skal[2] bzang sogs mkha' 'gro rigs lnga'i sgrub pa / thugs rje kun sgrol skor / spu gri nag po'i bsad pa / dmod mo bsad pa dgu sgril / sgra bla ma dang yum sras kyi skor / dbal bon rum[3] po'i dri khams gnyen po / mi bdud sum sgril bsad pa'i tan tra / mkha' 'gro'i srog yig / bsad pa'i mde'u thung / yum gcod / ye snying char 'beb / bdud rtsi ra sa ya na'i rgyud / phan byed nyer gcig / gnod (255b) byed nyer gcig / a ma dred de khyung nag gi sgrub pa / yas stags[4] rtsi shing rang 'gros / mar bon bco brgyad / gyer bon skor / lha srin gtad pa rdzong 'debs bcas klu gnyan[5] sa bdag gtad sprug skor / klu bdud snying gzer sogs byung ngo /

gter khung nas 'jal ba'i mda' do'i sa na phug pa gnyis kyi

[1] (/absent) [2] bskal [3] ram [4] stag [5] gnyen

bar du mtsho nag zangs kha tsam gyi dkyil na sbrul nag po mdung tsam zhig 'dug / mtsho'i 'gram du yas stags[1] rang 'gros kyi skor rnams 'dug ste ma drangs so / phug pa'i nang na rin po che'i zhal bu sna tshogs 'dug pas 'gro bsam kyang / sbrul des[2] 'jigs tshul bstan pas 'gro ma nus / phug pa phyi ma na gshen rab kyi ring srel cha lnga / bram ze skye bdun gyi thod pa dang bcas pa gdan drangs so /

gnyis pa yan lag gi gter la gsum gyi / dang po sbas tshul ni / lo chen be ro tsa nas rta gnyan pha bong bon mdzod du sbas te smon lam gyis rgyas btab po /

gnyis pa gter drangs tshul ni / nyin gcig nyams snang la rnal 'byor pa kha ṭam bsnams pa zhig gis skal[3] pa bzang mo'i bsnyen pa la 'bad na dngos (256a) grub 'byung gis zhes zer ba byung / de'i phyi lor khye'i dar dkar gyon pa zhig byung nas / khyod la las 'phro yod pas rta[4] gnyan pha bong[5] bon mo'i gter rnams[6] lcags pho khyi la drongs la / lcags mo phag la sgrogs shig zer ba byung / ston zla ra ba'i tshes bcu gnyis kyi tho rangs su / mi dmar dar dmar gyi na bza' can bsve rmog gyon pa / lag na sbrul zhags bzung zhing rta dmar zhon pa zhig gis / nga ni btsan rgod dmar po yin / nga'i rjes su shog dang pha bong bon mo la dngos grub yod pa sbyin zer nas rlung 'tshub[7] cig tu brdzus te song / nangs par der phyin pas srod thun la srid pa rgyal mos 'di nas mar mtho bdun 'jal ba'i sa na kha byang yod ces lung bstan pa bzhin btsal bas kha byang byung ste 'di nas mar 'dom gsum gcal ba'i sar brag la sgo rang dod kyi nang du rgyud sde sum cu rtsa bzhi dang / de bzhin gshegs pa'i ring srel dang gser sku gser 'bum yod ces pa byung / der brag la sgo rang dod la rdo'i kha leb sprad pa zhig 'dug pa kha phyes nas sangs rgyas gser sku gser 'bum shog dril (256b) mang po yod pa rnams dngos grub tu blangs so /

gsum pa them byang ni / srid pa rgyud kyi kha byang chen mo / rig 'dzin pho byang / mkha' 'gro mo byang / be ro'i rdzogs chen yang tig bsdus pa / bzhi brgya rtsa bzhi nad kyi gnyen po bdud rtsi ha sa ra'i 'grel ba / mu bdud kham pa'i srog sgrub / btsan bdud he ru ka'i[8] drag sgrub / btsan rgod dmar po'i tan tra / gzhan yang tshe sgrub nyi shu rtsa gcig / srung ba nyer gcig / zlog pa nyer gcig / bsad pa nyer gcig / rdzas sbyor nyer gcig / rten 'brel sbyor ba nyer gcig / nor sgrub

[1] stag [2] de'i [3] bskal [4] lta [5] vang [6] rnams/ [7] tshub [8] kha'i

nyer gcig / dbang sdud nyer gcig / dgra brub nyer gcig / mnan pa nyer gcig rnams byung ngo /

snyan brgyud la bskal bzang pod gnyis / tshe dbang bya ri ma / char 'beb[1] skor / pom ra'i skor rnams yod do /

bzhi pa slob ma'i gyes tshul ni / dung dkar thogs pa bdun la sogs mang du byung zhing / khyad par du bka' bab chen po bzhis kun tu spel te ches cher dar ro ||

yang sprul sku blo ldan snying po la stang chen dmu tsha gyer med sogs rig 'dzin mkha' 'gros snyan (257a) du brgyud pa'i bon skor la bzhi'i / dang po phyi mdo la dri med gzi brjid bstan pa'i mdo la glegs bam bcu gnyis / dri med rtsa ba'i mdo dang bcu gsum /[2] sangs rgyas khri dang bdun stong gi mtshan brjod mdo / lhun po brtsegs pa rgyud kyi mdo / bkra shis dpal 'bar khab kyi mdo dang bzhi /

gnyis pa nang sngags la rol ba gzungs sngags / phur pa rig[3] sngags/ brtsod zlog drag sngags / zhi khro rab 'byams yang gsang gi sngags dang bzhi /

gsum pa gsang ba la rig pa khu byug yab kyi rgyud / rig 'dzin 'dus pa thabs kyi rgyud / mkha' 'gro yang snying shes rab kyi rgyud gsum /

bzhi pa yang gsang bla med la nam mkhar spyi gcod lta ba'i rgyud la sogs pa mang du yod do /

sprul sku blo ldan nas / bhe tsha grags pa rgyal mtshan sogs la brgyud nas dar ro ||

yang gsang mchog mthar thug gis byin gyis brlabs pas dgongs gter nam mkha'i mdzod la mnga' bsnyems shing / dkyil 'khor stong dang drug brgya la nges pa'i snang ba rgyas pa'i dmu rgyal sprul sku nyi ma rgyal (257b) mtshan gyi dgongs gter dkyil 'khor bcu drug la sogs glegs bam bcu gnyis yod do ||

yang sprul sku khro gnyen gyi snyan brgyud[4] bskal bzang mdo pod gnyis / gsang gcod yid bzhin nor bu'i skor sogs mang du yod do ||

gzhan yang gter ston 'tsho sprul bya bas lci'i ra sa rdzong[5] mgo nas dran pa yab sras kyi dbang bum dngul bum cha gcig / bon sde la kun bzang thugs sgrub rin chen sgron ma / ge khod me ri gyad phur gyi gzhung mchod skor dang bcas pa byung ba la / kun bzang sgrub skor rnams dar zhing / ge khod skor rnams bu dpe la ma phab cing / shog ser dngos dang dngul

[1] 'bebs [2] (/ absent) [3] rigs [4] rgyud [5] rdzang

bum gcig ding sang dbon rgyud kyi phyag na yod la / dngul bum gcig dbang ldan zhu tshang gi phyag na yod do ||

yang u go g·yung drung 'bum bya bas kha shu ra 'dra nas khro bo dbang drag / gsang gcod / gsang ba 'bum chen sogs thon no ||

yang pho chen[1] nam mkha' 'od zer dang / gar tsha bsod nams rgyal mtshan gnyis kyis 'jing gi pha bong gru bzhi nas / khro klong rnams gsum / pom ra'i sgrub skor dang / gshen rab ljags mchil (258a) las grub pa'i sha ri ram cha gnyis / kha byang shog ser rnams drangs te / sha ri ram dang shog ser ni ding sang dbon rgyud kyi phyag na bzhugs so ||

yang srid rgyud las /

> tshe dbang rig 'dzin rnam 'phrul ni ||
> mtha' bzhi mi nub g·yung drung rgyal po 'byung ||

zhes pa'i lung gis zin pa'i dam pa gang des brag dmar ke ru nas bya ra ma dgu la sogs bon sde mi 'dra ba bco brgyad thon no ||

yang srid rgyud las /

> gyer mi nyi 'od byin gis brlabs pa'i bu ||
> ngu za nyi ma'i mtshan can 'byung ||

zhes pa de nyid kyis brag dkar yang dben[2] nas bskal pa bzang po mdo sde dang / lde mig skor tshom gsum gsum ste drug thon par bshad do ||

yang srid rgyud las / dran pa'i zhal nas /

> kho bo'i byin gyis brlabs pa'i bu ||
> a thang yon rin bya ba yis[3] ||
> 'dzing kha rag ldong phrom gyi dngos grub len ||

zhes pas / zhang zhung sgra bla ma'i sgrub skor gsum thon no ||

yang rong bon g·yung drung 'od zer la 'od kyi yi ger babs pa'i stag la spu gri dkar dmar nag gsum /[4] dbal chen gsang ba thugs rgyud kyi skor dang / btsan bdud keng (258b) gsum gyi skor rnams yod do ||

yang stag za rin chen mtsho mo'i snyan brgyud ma rgyud kyi rgyud gsum / bla ma yi dam mkha' 'gro'i skor / ma rgyud las tshogs gter phreng / tshe dbang skor / bka' srung yum sras sde lnga / 'pho ba'i man ngag / dug bsal la sogs yod do ||

yang dbu za rin chen gsal la snyan du brgyud pa'i gcod kyi gdams pa sogs mang du yod do ||

[1] che [2] dbon [3] bas [4] (/ absent)

yang gu ru yon tan seng ges rgya rong gab tog brag ri nas drangs pa'i char 'beb g·yu mtsho mer ba'i skor / tso mi[1] char 'beb dngul g·yu ma'i skor /[2] ma 'ong lung bstan sde drug / gter srung srid rgyal skor rnams yod do ||

gling gshen bsod nams blo gros la snyan du brgyud pa'i ma gsum gcod dang sgrub phran 'ga' zhig yod do ||

khyung po bkra shis rgyal mtshan gyis tsha rong kha ba dkar po nas drangs pa'i dran pa a dkar dgongs 'dus sogs be ro'i bka' 'ga' yod do ||

g·yung drung tshe dbang rgyal pos tshe spungs gsang ba'i gnas nas drangs pa'i rdzogs chen gser gyi yang zhun gyi skor dang srid rgyal gyi skor la sogs yod do ||

yang shel zhig (259a) g·yung drung rgyal po la snyan du brgyud pa'i bon sde la zhi khro dgongs 'dus / smra seng gi skor / khro bo dzva dmar 'khyil ba / yab sras dril sgrub / rkyang sgrub / dran pa gsang sgrub / tshe dbang yang zhun skor / drag gcod gnam lcags thog mda' / tshe dbang thugs sgrub / rol ba bam chen rgyud gzhung skor / rdzogs chen gser zhun / bla ma zhi drag gi sgrub skor / ge khod gsang this / nyams yig che chung / sngags 'bum / a dkar dgongs 'dus sogs mang du yod do ||

yang sprul sku sangs rgyas gling pa la bka' gter gnyis las / dang po snyan brgyud bka' ma'i skor la / gnas rten bcu drug gi cho ga / gsang mchog rol ba / dran pa bdud dpung 'dul / tshe dbang g·yung drung gur khang / thugs rje kun sgrol[3] / stag la'i skor / rdzong 'phrang le'u gsum pa rnams yod /

gnyis pa gter la / tshe sgrub rdo rje go khrab / bla ma dgongs 'dus / bka' thang kun snang gsal sgron glegs bam bzhi / che mchog dran pa drag po / tshe dbang ga'u dmar nag / don zhags skor / 'od dpag med la sogs mang ngo /

rdzas gter la (259b) mthing sku pad ma 'od 'bar / bram ze'i thod pa / mkha' 'gro kun sgrol sku tshab[4] / tshe dbang phyag sil / be ro'i phyag tsha sogs gter nas thon no ||

rig 'dzin kun grol grags pa la gter ni / ma mo rbod gtong snang srid zil gnon gyi sgrub skor dang / rtsa rlung mkha' 'gro gsang mdzod la sogs pa dang / dgongs gter gyi phyogs su gtogs pa zhi khro dgongs 'dus / mkha' 'gro dgongs 'dus / bla ma dgongs 'dus / dmar khrid dgongs 'dus sogs dang / gzhan yang dag snang gi skor dang khrid la sogs shin tu mang ngo ||

[1] min [2] (/ absent) [3] grol [4] thsabs

skabs 'dir gzhan sde kha cig gis / blo ldan snying po / mi shig[1] rdo rje / sangs rgyas gling pa / kun grol grags pa rnam bzhi la phyis byon sprul sku rnam bzhi'i lugs zhes gter gsar gyi grangs su brtsi ste / 'di rnams o rgyan chen po dang rje 'bangs rnams kyis sems can 'dul thabs bsam gyis mi khyab pa'i rnam rol chos la bon ming btags pas / lta spyod bka' rtags kyi phyag rgya bzhi po dang mi 'gal bar thar lam yod nges can du snang / zhes bshad pa ni ma brtags pa'i tshig tu 'dug pas na (260a) mi 'thad do / de'ang bon dang bon nyid kyi ngo bo stong pa nyid spros pa'i mtha' thams cad dang bral bar gnas te / mdzod las /

> bon dang bon nyid thams cad ni ||
> stong pa dam pa'i mchog ldan pas ||
> bla med 'bras bu 'thob pa ni ||
> skye dang skye med gdod nas dag ||
> kun kyang stong pa'i mtshan nyid 'dzin ||

zhes pas so / de lta bu'i bon nyid kyi gnas lugs la bon dang chos zhes pa ris su chad pa med nges pa la / tshig bla dvags su bon nyid dang chos nyid ces zer ba ni btags ming ste don dam par smra bsam brjod 'das so / kun rdzob tu rang bzhin tshig dang yi ge'i tshogs su gnas pa ste / de'i byed las sems can thams cad gnas skabs dang mthar thug gi 'jigs[2] pa dang 'jigs pa chen po las skyob par byed de / mdo las /

> bon ni mi g·yo skyob pa'i sgra ||

ces so / des na chos kyi ming bon ma yin te / bon dang chos gnyis ka la brjod bya'i don dang rjod byed kyi tshig gnyis su 'byung ba las / bon zhes pa ni ming dang tshig gi bla dvags tsam ste / mdzod las /

> ming gi 'du byed khams gsum 'khor ||
> nyid la bla dvags mtshan nyid (260b) 'dzin ||

zhes dang /

> tshig gi 'du byed khams gsum 'khor ||
> khyad kyi bla dvags mtshan nyid 'dzin ||

zhes pas / ming tshig ni rjod byed kyi ngag tsam ste / de'i brjod bya ni bon rang lugs la bslab pa gsum dang / bden pa gnyis sogs yin te / chos btags ming de ni ma yin no / gal te chos btags

[1] shigs [2] 'jig

ming de'i ming bon yin na / rjod byed tshig tsam de / brjod bya'i don du 'gyur la / de ltar na rjod byed tshig tsam gyi ngor / brjod bya'i don yang dag pa mi gnas te / dper na lhas[1] sbyin zhes pa'i ming tsam gyi ngor / lhas[2] sbyin yang dag pa med pa bzhin no / der ma zad sprul sku rnam bzhi'i bka' rnams bka' rtags kyi phyag rgya bzhi dang mi 'gal zhing thar lam yod nges can yin zhes pa ltar na / gter snying bon rnying ma thams cad de ltar ma yin pa 'gyur te / de ni bon gyi sgo tsam yang mthong ma myong ba'i phug rgyus bshad stang byed pa dang mtshungs te / phyogs zhen che ba'i gtam du zad do / sprul sku bzhi'i bon gsar ma rnams o rgyan rje 'bangs[3] rnams kyi bka' kho nar 'dod pa'ang 'gal te / o rgyan chen po yan gyi bon gyi sku gsum rdzogs pa'i sangs rgyas (261a) nas rim gyis brgyud pa'i bka' yin pa'i phyir / bon gsar rnying gnyis la zab zhan cung zad kyang med pa'o / de'i phyir bon zhes pa dang chos zhes pa ni ming gi tha snyad tsam ste ngo bo nyid la 'gyur ba med do / de lta na'ang sangs rgyas rnams kyis sems can gyi don mdzad pa la thabs thugs ma 'gags pa'i rnam rol bon dang chos gnyis su snang ba yang gnas skabs tsam gyi thabs mkhas kyi mdzad pa de ltar snang ba'o / des na bon dang chos gnyis kyang kun rdzob tsam du bon gyi sku gsum nas rim gyis brgyud pa'i tshig dang yi ge la bon zhes dang / chos kyi sku gsum nas rim gyis brgyud pa'i tshig dang / yi ge la chos zhes pa'i ming btags nas rang rang gi grub mtha' bzung ste don gnyis lhun gyis grub par byed pa yin no / des na bon gsar ma zhes pa yang bon gyi sku gsum nas rim gyis brgyud pa'i phyir bon yin la chos ma yin no / gal te dkyil 'khor yang gzhan la de nyid chos kyi sku gsum nas chos lugs ltar rim gyis brgyud par 'dug na chos zhes pa'i tha snyad kyang rung zhing bkag kyang mi bkag (261b) go / de dag zhar byung du smos pa'o ||

gzhan yang khro bo lha rgod thog pa snang srid zil gnon gyi sgrub pa cha lag dang bcas pa dran pa nam mkhas bstan pa dar nub dus su dang ra khyung rdzong du gter du sbas te gter srung la bcol ba phyis su sku mdun bsod nams blo gros la mkha' 'gros lung bstan nas gter zhal phyes te / slar lcags mo yos lo zla ba dang po'i tshes la mkha' 'gro'i bka' rgya yol nas shog ser yig phreng sum cu tham pa slar bod shog la phab ste / bka' bab thugs kyi slob ma skam[4] rigs g·yung drung nyi rgyal la brgyud de dar ro / gzhan yang dam pa de'i snyan brgyud du

[1] lha'i [2] lha'i [3] 'bang [4] rkam

tri su mun sel sgron ma'i gzhung la sogs yod pa rnams snang ston zla ba rgyal mtshan la brgyud de dar ro ||

yang dbal 'bar stag slag can gyis gter nas thon pa'i dbal phur gyi rgyud dang sgrub pa cha lag dang / bka' skyong[1] drel[2] nag gi skor la sogs mang du yod par grags so ||

yang kho bo'i bla ma bde chen gling pa'am phyi nang gsang ba'i mtshan gyi snyan pas mdo khams stod smad kun tu khyab pa (262a) de nyid ma 'ong[3] lung gis[4] zin tshul dang gter gyi dngos grub brnyes pa lung gis bstan pa ni / gshin rje gshed nag gi rgyud las /

> de nas mi rabs bdun tsam song ba'i mtshams ||
> slob dpon chen pos byin gyis brlabs[5] pa'i bu ||
> gshed bzhi lo pa mi 'gyur mtshan can 'byung ||
> mkha' spyod o rgyan yul du dngos grub len ||
> gsang ba'i bon sgo bcu gsum dag la dbang ||
> khyad par sngon gyi rtsa 'gags[6] song ba rnams ||
> o rgyan me tog spungs mdzes dgon pa ru ||
> rig 'dzin rnams dang mjal te dngos grub len ||
> chad pa'i bon rnams ma lus spel nas kyang ||
> bstan pa mtha' ru rgyas par byed par 'gyur ||

zhes pa'i lung mthun gyi gter ston dam pa de nyid dgung lo bcu gsum lor o rgyan gsang chen mkha' spyod dur khrod du phebs te bka' gter chen po bcu gsum gyi bka' bab par phyi nang gsang ba yang gsang bzhi / de re re la yang rgyud lung man ngag ste bcu gnyis / gnyis ka ma yin pa dang bcu gsum du yod pas / dang po phyi mdo la / kun bzang nam mkha'i rgyal po rgyud (262b) kyi mdo / mthar phyin dga' ba dge ldan lung gi mdo / dus kyi 'khor lo 'byung ba man ngag gi mdo dang gsum / de dag gi cha lag dang bcas pa dang /

gsnyis pa nang sngags la / bde gshegs bka' brgyad gsang 'dus rgyud kyi sngags / dbal phur thugs kyi gzer bu lung gi sngags / bde gshegs dgongs 'dus thugs sgrub man ngag gi sngags dang gsum / de dag la yang cha lag dang bcas pa dang /

gsum pa gsang ba la / dbyings chen zab mo bstan pa rgyud kyi sde / mkha' 'gro shes rab gsang ba ba ga'i rgyud / mkha' gsang gab pa sgron me lung gi sde / rig 'dzin thabs kyi skor la sde tshan gsum dang / srid pa klong gi man ngag rgyud kyi skor / ma mo yang snying 'dus pa rbod gtong gi skor dang /

[1] skyongs [2] dril [3] 'ongs [4] gi [5] brlab [6] 'gag

dug mtsho khol ma 'jigs[1] byed gshin rje'i skor dang / gser 'od nor bu mchog rgyal thabs kyi skor dang gsum / de dag gi cha lag zhib rgyas rnams dang / bon gyi yang snying bla med rdzogs pa chen po phyi nang gnyis su bstan pa dang / gnyis ka ma yin pa la rdzong 'phrang gsum bcas yod do / (263a) gzhan yang snyan brgyud kyi skor yang mang ngo / bka' gsang zab mo de rnams bka' bab bzhi la sogs las can rnams la brgyud de dar ro ||

yang gter ston gsang sngags gling pa'i bka' gter skor ni / kha byang las /

> 'gro don gnas chen bzhi la gter sgo 'byed ||
> nyi shu rtsa lnga'i zab gter dngos grub 'byung ||

zhes pas / de dag phyi nang gsang ba gsum thun mong ma yin pa'i sde dang bzhi'i / dang po phyi la / char 'beb bdud rtsi rgya mtsho / klu chog sogs dang /

nang la/[2] gsang sngags la me ri'i dzva sgrub this 'dur bcas / stag la'i sgrub pa srid 'dur dang bcas pa / yang stag la gri 'dur can / gshin rje gshed nag zhi drag gnyis / drel dmar sgrub skor / drel nag sgrub skor / gtad sprug man ngag bcas / spyi spungs gsang ba 'dus pa'i rgyud / lung rgyud sogs dang / tshe sgrub skor la / tshe sgrub yang snying 'dus pa/ rtsa gsum tshe sgrub / gu[3] ru la brten pa'i tshe sgrub dang /

gsang ba la gu ru zhi drag seng gsum rdzogs rim gyi khrid skor dang bcas pa / sku gsum phur sgrub rim gnyis (263b) kyi nyams len rdzogs chen dang bcas pa / thugs rje kun sgrol gyi gcod gdams skor / smra seng sgrub pa rnams dang /

thun min 'chi med tshe dbang rig 'dzin chen po'i rnam thar glegs bam bzhi / yang gyer chen dran pa nam mkha'i rnam thar glegs bam brgyad sogs mang ngo ||

yang mkha' 'gro bde chen dbang gi sgron ma'i bon gter la / mkha' 'gro'i bka' thang glegs bam gcig / snying thig bcu gsum sogs yod do ||

gzhan yang 'dir ma zin pa du ma zhig da lta'i yul mtha' dbus rnams su yod mod kyi re zhig dkar chag ma 'dzom pas 'bri bar ma nus la / 'dir smos pa rnams ni skyes bu dam pa thun mong dang thun mong ma yin pa'i shes rab kyi spyan ras yangs pa rnams kyis bstan 'byung du bkod pa dang tshad mar grags pa rnams las thos thos dang du blangs pa ni med de / ji skad du /

[1] 'jig [2] (/ absent) [3] pu

gter min gter 'dra gter rdzun lung pa gang ||
shes med grub mtha' brtsod cing bud med dad ||

ces gsungs pa bzhin bdud kyis bstan pa la tho brtsam pa'i phyir gter ston du brdzu ba dang / sems can gyi las (264a) dbang bsam gyis[1] mi khyab pas zog po gter rdzus lo 'dod sgrub pa'ang rang gzhan gyi sde kun la shin tu mang bas bstan pa'i gshed du che ba'i phyir ro /

gzhan yang bru zhu spa rme'u me gnyos 'gro mgon sga ston skyabs ston mnyam med chen po sogs mkhas grub gnyis ldan gyi lung zin dam pa rnams kyi mdzad[2] byang bka' brten du bsdu bar 'os pa ches mang yang re zhig yi[3] ges 'jigs so /

gsum pa la gsum /
de dag lho byang dbus gter sogs lngar bsdu ba /
bka' dang bka' brten gnyis su bsdu ba /
zhar byung phyis rgyal bstan ji tsam gnas pa bstan pa'o /

dang po la lnga /
byang gter /
lho gter /
dbus gter /
khams gter /
gter gsar ro /

dang po byang gter dngos ni lho bal gyi a tsa ra gsum gyi bka' gter rnams yin la / der gtogs[4] pa ni nga 'phrang lha'i dbang phyug / mar pa 'phan bzang / khro 'brug / chos kyi gze ston spu gu'i bon skor dang / go lde 'phags pas g·yung drung seng mchong brag nas bton pa sogs so /

gnyis pa lho gter gyi gtso bo ni gshen klu dgas (264b) bton pa'i bon sde rnams yin la / der gtogs[5] pa ni spa gro ma / shel brag ma / lho brag khom mthing ma sogs dang / gzhan yang sa ston[6] 'brug lha / ra ljags kyi bon skor / bal zho[7] sgom chen / 'jing ston mu lto ba / bu mtsho srid pa'i rgyal po / mtshe mi gsas khyung / khu 'dzin 'jing nag sogs kyis bton pa'i bon sde rnams so /

gsum pa dbus gter la yer rdzong ma dang / bsam yas skor khang ma ni a tsa ra gsum gyis bton pa rnams te gong du byang gter du bshad la / bsam yas ca ti ma / drang nga ma'i skor / bsam yas ka khol ma / ra ston 'bum rjes thon pa rnams so /

[1] gyis absent [2] mdzod [3] ye [4] gtog [5] gtog [6] stong [7] ba co

bzhi pa khams gter la snga ba gu ru ban chung / khod po blo gros / sprul sku skyang[1] 'phags / dbang ldan gshen gsas / bra bo sgom nyag[2] / kyu ra rnal 'byor / rko bo gter ston / se gnyan zhig po / tshil po gter ston / 'tsho sprul / u go g·yung drung 'bum / pho chen nam mkha' 'od zer sogs kyis bton pa sogs mang ngo /

lnga pa gter gsar la / rma ston srol 'dzin / rma lcam me[3] / rma sher seng / spa bon khyung thog / gu ru rnon rtse / dpon gsas (265a) khyung rgod / g·yung drung gling pa sogs kyi bka' gter sogs la snga rabs pa dag gis gter gsar du bzhag pa ding sang ni de dag gter gsar du mi btub kyang sa bcad 'di'i khongs su bsdus te / ding sang ni shel zhig g·yung drung rgyal po man chad gter gsar du grags so /

gnyis pa bka' dang bka' brten du bsdu tshul la gsum /

bka' dang /
bka' brten[4] /
gnyis ka'i don no /

dang po ni / bka'i dbye sgo bcu gsum la sogs mang yang re zhig sde tshan dbye 'byed sla zhing thams cad 'thus pa'i dbang du byas na / bka' phun sum tshogs pa mdo yi sde / rnam dag rgyas pa 'bum gyi sde / zab lam gsang sngags kyi sde / bla med sems phyogs kyi sde dang bzhir phyes na legs par mngon to / mdo 'dus las kyang /

nga ni mya ngan 'das 'og tu ||
mdo 'bum rgyud mdzod bzhir phyes la ||
'khor rnams bka' yi bsdu ba gyis ||

zhes so /

gnyis pa bka' brten la mdor bsdu na bka' rgyud so so'i dgongs pa 'grel ba'i bka' brten dang / bka' spyi yi dgongs pa 'grel ba'i bka' brten dang (265b) gnyis yod do /

gsum pa gnyis ka'i don ni / bka' dang bka' brten[5] gyi 'gyur ji ltar sgrig[6] tshul yin te mkhan chen nyi ma bstan 'dzin gyis bka' dang bka' brten[7] gyi rnam bshad nyi 'od rab gsal dang / sde tshan sgrig tshul gyi dkar chag gshen bstan pad mo'i nyi 'od ces pa'i le'u tshan gnyis yod pa la / lung rig[8] tshad ma'i gnod pa med cing mkhas pa'i legs bshad du snang bas de la yid rton par rigs so ||

[1] spyang [2] nag [3] med [4] rten [5] rten [6] sgrigs
[7] rten [8] rigs

GLOSSARY

ABBREVIATIONS

Ch	*Tibetan–Chinese Dictionary* of dGe-bshes Chos-gyi Grags-pa, Peking, 1957
D	*Dag-yig*, the *Gangs-can bod-kyi brda-sprod dpag-bsam ljon-pa'i snye-ma* by Hor-btsun bsTan-'dzin Blo-gros rGya-mtsho. Published by S. T. Jongdong and S. G. Karmay, Kalimpong, 1961
Das	*Tibetan–English Dictionary* by Sarat Chandra Das, Calcutta, 1960
J	Jaschke's *Tibetan–English Dictionary*, Kegan Paul, London, 1958
Lit.	Literally
LShDz	*Legs-bshad-mdzod* by Shar-rdza bKra-shis rGyal-mtshan
Ny	*sGra-yi don-sdeb snang-gsal sgron-me* by Zhu Nyi-ma Grags-pa, Delhi, 1965
Skr.	Sanskrit

ku-hrang (Ny: = rkyang) = 'wild ass', 238[27]

bka'-chad = 'disfavour', 'punishment', 240[28], 245[19], 265[31]

bkrol-byang = 'treatise', 'note', 297[2]

rkang-grangs = 'list', 246[33], 250[27], 276[23]

rkang-'dril = 'combination', 231[25]

rkang-tshugs-pa = 'established', 212[25-6]

skya-sgom (mdzad-pa) = 'to meditate as a layman', 297[27]

skyur-'thung (= chang) = 'beer', 238[28]

bskos-thob = 'assignment', 225[26]

kha-byang = 'guide', 304[23, 33], 305[3], 310[27], 337[37]

kha-tshar (D: = rim-bzhin gdags-pa) = 'additional', 308[37], 334[14]

kha-'dzin = 'overseer', 257[24, 26]

kha-yar (-ba) = 'few', 231[29], 246[3]

kham-sa = 'clay', 218[30], 269[26], 291[33]

khus = 'repeating', 'persistence', 238[13]

khyung-(po), *name of a clan*, 201[11], 206[3], *passim*

khra-ther (D: = gur) = 'tent', 257[21], 302[30]

'khrab-shon (byed-pa) (D: shon-'khrabs) = 'to dance', 297[17]

gab-tse = 'astrology', 213[35]; 'horoscope chart', 305[8]

gar-mdung, *a spear used in a particular dance*, 297[5]

gung = 'caracal', 226[16]

gong-lag = 'collar', 226[16]

gran (Ny: = dgra) = 'enemy', 'opponent', 'antagonist', 227[25], 228[22, 30]

gri-'dur (byed-pa) = 'to perform the posthumous evocation ritual of the killed', 204[19], 245[29, 31], 313[11] (*see also* 'dur)

grol-phug = 'original', 251[10-11]

'gog-pa = 'cessation of the senses', 221[37], 222[18], 226[27], 239[38], 272[12-8]

'gying-thod = 'turban', 226[15]

'gres-rkang (= rigs-bgre q.v.), 224[31], 296[24-5]

rgyan-shar(-ba) = 'display', 333[15]

sgo-thar-du = 'individually', 221[32-3]

sgos-khur (Das: = yi-dvags zhig-gi-ming) = 'individual burden', 238[3]

snga-shad = 'pommel', 241[8]

ca-ti (?Skr. caitya) = 'tomb', 'temple', 320[16], 322[30], 323[26], 335[36]

cha-rkyen (D: = cha-lag mthun-rkyen) = 'ancillary', 314[10], 315[29-30]

cha-lag (= cha-rkyen q.v.) = 'ancillary', 'supplementary', 261[1], 319[36], 320[38], 321[11], 326[37], 329[28], 332[32], 333[1], 334[27], 345[29, 33], 346[2-3]

cha-lang = 'cymbals', 257[37]

chag-(chab)sgrogs = 'chain', 'belt', 226[17], 315[14]

chab (*also* dkar-chab) -gsol-ba = 'to commit suicide by drinking water', 259[5, 15] chig-rdzogs-su (mdzad-pa) = 'to confer at one and the same time the four degrees of ordination' (viz. bsnyen-gnas, dge-bsnyen, gtsang-gtsug, and drang-srong), 220[31], 221[12–13], 272[6]

ja-sig (D: ja-sigs = ja-bag dang ja-sgam) = 'a block of tea', 294[9]

'ja'-lus = Lit. 'rainbow-body' (*see* p. 53 n. 1), 232[38], 233[25]

gnyan-pa = 'exalted', 'dignified', 'solemn', 239[24], 253[21], 260[6]

ting-nam (Ny & LShDz: = chu) = 'water', 227[16]

te-la-kha, *name of a tent*, 257[21]

gtug-gshar (Ch: gtug-bsher) = 'contest', 257[20]

dam-rdzas = 'sacred items', 266[10]

dam-zhu dom-ra, *a hat made of bear skin*, 264[14]

dar-so (che-ba) = 'popular', 226[30], 269[15]

dun-tse (Ny: = ban-log = a lapsed Buddhist) = Buddhist, 301[30]

do (*in* mtsho-do) 'island in a lake', 239[8], 245[11], 265[20]

do bsdo-ba = 'to attack', 'to measure oneself against someone', 228[11]

drang-mkhan (D: = gzu-bo) = 'referee', 'arbitrator', 257[28]

drang-srong (D: rang-rgyud drang-bas drang gzhan-rgyud srong-bas srong), *the highest ordination of a Bon-po monk corresponding to Buddhist* dge-slong, *see* chig-rdzogs-su, 221[12], 272[5]

dro-theb gcig (J: dro 2) = 'the space of a meal time', 215[28]

'dan-dkar = 'cane', 'sceptre', 261[9]

'du-gnas = 'religious centre', 223[7, 8], 224[13]

'dur(-ba) (D: 'dur-sbyong = gshed-ma 'dur gnas-ngan sbyong) = 'to evoke the spirits of the dead', viz. 'to perform the posthumous evocation rituals', 218[21, 27], 268[19]

'dur-phug = 'rituals involving the evocation of the spirits of the dead', 204[21], 268[21]

'dur-bon = 'rituals involving the evocation of the spirits of the dead', 211[8], 236[9]

'dur-lung = 'authorization to transmit the posthumous evocation rituals', 266[17]

'dur-slong-ba = 'to restore the spirits of the dead to their bodies by means of evocation rituals', 258[21]

'dur-gsas = 'a holy person who performs the posthumous evocation rituals', 204[15]

'dur-gshen = 'priests who perform the posthumous evocation rituals', 251[15]

'dus-so = 'confluence', 231[34]

'dren-chog = Lit. 'ritual of guidance', *a particular kind of* 'dur-phug q.v., 204[19–20]

ldem-phod(-phru) = 'feather', 226[15]

nan-ban = 'forced abjuration of one's religion', 260[10], 266[25], 267[28–9]

nam (*in* gser-nam Ch: = gser-zho'i skar-ma) = 'a drachm of gold', 265[4, 7, 10]

ne-slas (Ny: slas = sa; LShDz: sa) = 'earth', 227[15]

mnol = 'impurity', 266[16]

brnag-pa = 'aggressiveness', 'ferocity', 'revenge', 'evil disposition', 230[17], 254[17], 256[5, 32], 260[12], 264[25, 30], 265[28]

pra (-rtags) = 'prognostication', 261[19]

dpon-gsas = 'preacher', 'master', 211[32] 246[32], 250[25], 251[16]

spa (i) (D: = byin chags-pa) = 'gracious', 204[37], 205[6]; (ii) (-tshang), *name of a clan*, 201[9], 204[35], 205[11], 275[4], 279[29], 298[24], 347[8], *passim*

spyi-mthun = 'common', 238[4]

spyi-spungs (= spyi-'dus) = Lit. 'the heap of universality' (*name of a certain group of Bon-po tantras, see* p. 45 n. 2), 211[35], 219[17], 220[13], 222[35], 226[30], 247[1]

spyi-phud = 'sublimity', 240[32]

sprin-thag chad-pa='cloudless', 238[15–16]

phod-kha (D: phod-kha-can = sngags-pa'i gos) = 'tantric cloak', 315[15]

phya blan-pa = 'to consult a soothsayer', 266[23]

phyi-shad = 'the back of a saddle', cf. snga-shad q.v., 241[8]

ban-bun = 'to rise', 'to spread' (of smoke or incense), 218[8–9, 33]

bon = (i) 'text', 209[27], 215[38], 239[14], 246[3], 260[19, 25], 261[19], 262[11], 282[4], 288[29], 308[11], 309[33], 311[17], 314[31], *passim*; (ii) 'doctrine', 'teaching', 209[28], 210[24],

26, 28, 211[8-9], 212[32], 213[23], 215[11], 216[23], 217[10], 218[17], 226[8], 233[24, 37], 235[16], 237[2, 16, 28], 238[6], 244[15, 18], 245[16], 248[27], 250[16], 251[17], 258[33], 262[5], 264[1, 29], 265[28], 270[9, 11], 273[18], 343[6, 34], 344[8, 11, 12], *passim*; (iii) 'phenonmenal elements', 'absolute truth', 343[9, 11, 17-18]

bon-skor = 'texts', 275[38], 276[34], 288[20], 289[2], 307[9], 311[6]; 'doctrines', 279[19]

bon-sde = 'texts', 202[24], 215[24], 238[33-6], 246[20-9], 260[25, 32], 261[24], 262[15, 17], 268[32], 278[38]; 'doctrines', 204[30], 214[20], 215[17], 226[22], 265[37], 301[4]

bon-po = 'a follower of Bon', 'a Bon-po', 218[1], 254[17], 258[29], 259[3-4], *passim* 'priest', 237[18, 24], 240[30], 261[15], *passim*

bon-mo = 'priestess', 266[26-7, 33]

bon-gshen = 'priest of Bon', 202[21], 204[18], 218[10], 222[3], 236[2], 238[14], 240[13], 251[11-12], 255[10], 260[11, 18], 261[38], 264[11], 266[28, 32]

bya-zhu = 'feathered hat', 317[8], 326[8]

bru(-tshang), *name of a clan*, 201[7], 203[3], 275[4], 279[29], 298[24], 299[27], 300[16], 347[8], *passim*

bre-mo (J: = unfit, useless, worthless) = 'a cow of inferior kind', 256[17]

bla-dvags (D: = ming-lhag-gam ming-tshig) = 'appellation', 204[27], 343[26, 32]

bla-bo (byed-pa) (D: = go-brda 'phrad-pa) = 'to talk', 'to converse', 'to explain', 287[1]

dbal-mo, *a class of goddesses*, 228[23], 297[15, 26]

dbu-yog = 'retribution', 236[31], 240[19, 22], 241[2], 252[8], 264[18], 273[37] (*see* p. 61 n. 1)

'byol-nyog = 'indulgence', 266[11]

'brang-rgyas, *a kind of sacrificial cake*, 292[5], 307[30]

ma-tha = 'last', 231[30]

me-btsa' (Ch: me-tsa = sa-gnad che-ba) = 'an appropriate site for erecting *stūpas or temples*', 267[2]. (*This term was originally used in medicine where vegetable tinder is burned on the part where the pain is in the belief that it will relieve it.*)

dmu, *name of a royal lineage*, 201[6, 14, 24], 289[29, 32]

dmu-skas = 'the ladder of dMu', 241[32], 242[16], 243[3]

dmu-thag = 'the cord of dMu', 241[32], 242[16], 243[3]

dmu-tsha = ?'sword', 241[10], 242[11]. (*This is usually the name of a person belonging to* dMu (q.v.). *Hence* Lit. 'the nephew of dMu'.)

dmu-yad (D: = dngos-grub). (*But usually occurring with* 'khyil-ba *corresponding to* Skr. amṛitakuṇḍalī = bdud-rtsi 'khyil-ba.) *Hence* = 'nectar', 'ambrosia', 290[17, 22].

dmu-gshen, *abbreviation of* dmu-rigs gshen, i.e. the gshen (q.v.) *belonging to the lineage of* dMu, 201[6, 13, 14], 202[1, 6, 7, 9-10, 27, 30], 289[34]

rme'u(-tshang), *name of a clan*, 201[10], 205[16], 279[29], 298[24], 347[8]

gtsag/btsag-bu (D & Ch: = khrag 'thon-par byed-pa'i lag-cha) = 'razor', 259[10, 16], 305[8], 326[10]

gtsigs (D: gtsigs byin-pa = che-rtags byin-pa) = 'edict', 'decree', 'honour', 'privilege', 226[13-14, 18, 20], 245[32], 251[7], 266[27], 269[23], 303[35]

rtsa-'gags = 'disappearance', 227[12], 247[4], 345[16]

rtsi-shing (D: = rtsva-ljon spyi) = 'aromatic shrubs', 218[8, 33]

rtse-rgyal = 'the end of the hair of a holy person', 226[14]

tshangs-stang (D & LShDz: me) = 'fire', 227[16]

tshangs-bug = 'cranium', 203[25]

tshigs (*in* bdun-tshigs) = 'joint', 'middle', 219[7], 220[5]

tshe-chog = 'rituals for procuring long life', 266[22]

'tshos-pa = 'to have intercourse', 243[12], 304[22]

dzva (*also* btso) = 'bomb', 227[34], 265[14], 269[34], 276[2]

zhu(-tshang), *name of a clan*, 201[8], 204[13, 22], 275[4], 279[29], 298[6, 24], 341[2], 347[8]

zhugs-shangs (D: = shel-tshigs) = 'roasted barley grains', 218[9]

za-ma-mo (Ch: za ma = 1 bud-med) = 'woman', 238[29]

zang-ma (D: = kho-na'am rkyang-pa) = 'exclusive', 235[36], 236[6], 238[22]

zor = 'an offering hurled towards the enemy', 227[25], 229[16]

bzang-yag (D: zangs-yag = byu-ru dang rtse-rnon—coral and sharply pointed; Ny: *also* byi-ru). *Usually*

bzang-yag (*cont.*):
occurs with dmu-thag (q.v.) = ? 'the red cord of dMu', 243^{3}

'on-shang-sbrel, *name of a kind of cloth*, 257^{21}

'obs-zhu, *a kind of hat*, 274^{13}

yas-glud = 'ransom', 254^{9}

yas-stags = 'ritual objects', 218^{8}, 254^{6}

yas-dad = 'rise up', 'emerge', 242^{36}, 253^{10}

yug (*often preceded by* byur) = 'a demon who brings misfortune', 218^{2}

yus-bo (D: yu-bo = rva-med) = 'a cow without horns', 238^{13}

ye-'byung = 'spontaneous', 259^{32}

ye-'drog (D: ye-'brog = 'go-ba'i nad-yams) = 'infectious diseases', 203^{12}

g·yung-drung (D: = 'gyur-ba med-pa'i brda) = 'eternal', 'everlasting', 207^{26}, 209^{21}, 213$^{16, 23}$, 216^{23}, 226^{8}, 237$^{2, 16, 28}$, 238^{6}, 244$^{15, 18}$, 245^{16}, 246^{23}, 248^{27}, 250^{16}, 251^{18}, 258^{33}, 262^{5}, 264$^{1, 29}$, 265^{27}, 270$^{9, 10-11}$, 303^{32}; *also* = swastika, 291^{21}, 331^{12}

rang-mal = 'whole' *in the sense* 'every part of' *or* 'all that there is', 236^{8}

rabs-chad (D: = shul-chad) = 'barren', 'without offspring', 288^{34}

rigs-'gre (D: rigs-'grel = 'dra-ba'i 'gres-rkang) = 'parallel or identical enumerations', 224^{32}

ru 'thur-ba (D: 'thur-ba = 'khrugs-pa) = 'to be offended', 237^{32}, 241$^{13-14}$, 254^{28}

ru-ma = 'lees', 296^{34}

ru-mtshams = 'military frontier', 216^{8}

rlung-dmar = 'storm', 'gale', 239^{13}, 291^{26}

la-chen zlos-pa (D: la bzla-ba = pha-rol-tu phyin-pa'i ming; J: zla-ba = to pass, to get beyond) = 'to accomplish', 238^{5}

lam-snang-du chod-pa = 'to penetrate', 'to comprehend', 232^{10}

li-mun (LShDz & Ny: li = rlung) = 'air', 227^{15}

le'u/lhe'u (D: = dpon-gsas q.v.) = 'preacher', 'priest', 257^{16}, 313^{11}

shva-rdel = 'dice', 259^{9}

shva-gzhi = 'dice-board', 259^{8}

shag-mkhan = 'advocate', 257^{29}

shag 'dren-pa = 'to debate', 'to dispute', 258$^{21-2}$

shog-dril = 'writings', 'manuscript', 240$^{7-8}$, 261^{27}, 316$^{29-30}$, 320$^{21, 24}$, 339^{29}

shog-ser = 'manuscripts found as gter, i.e. hidden texts', 291^{38}, 309$^{17, 30}$, 316^{32}, 322^{1}, 324$^{9, 14}$, 327^{23}, 338^{19}, 340^{38}, 341^{10}, 344$^{36-7}$

gshin-'dur = 'rituals involving the evocation of the spirits of the dead', 268^{24}

gshen(-po) = 'a priest', 202^{24}, 210$^{4, 5, 36}$, 211$^{1-3, 5, 33}$, 218^{35}, 219$^{14, 20}$, 224$^{9-10, 16}$, 225$^{22, 29, 31}$, 231$^{12, 31, 36}$, 236$^{13, 14, 17, 19}$, 237$^{11, 20, 23, 25}$, 245^{27}, 285^{38}, *passim*

gshen(-tshang), *name of a clan*, 201^{14}, 202^{1}, 289^{34} (cf. dmu-gshen q.v.)

bshos = 'edible tributes', 211^{7}, 236^{8}

sa-ling (byed-pa) = 'to run on foot with one who rides on horse', 290^{13}

sel (byed-pa) = 'to perform the rituals of exorcism', 254^{5}, 313^{6}

sri-kha (lang-ba) = 'to meet one's fate', 257^{5}

srid-sgrub (byed-pa) = 'to perform the rites of child-procuring', 202^{36}

gsas-khang = 'temple', 212$^{27-8}$, 249^{22}, 250^{35}, 260^{33}, 267^{24}

gsas-mkhar = 'temple', 'citadel', 235^{34}, 236^{8}, 238^{19}, 246$^{15-16, 21-2, 24, 30}$

gser-skyems (D: = chang) = 'libation', 218^{9}

NOTE ON THE INDEXES

The Tibetan family names, personal names, and titles have always been a cause of confusion for the Tibetologists. It is hoped that the following analysis will help to clarify the Tibetan use of titles and their interchangeable nature. The family names are usually combined (often in shortened forms) with the titles according to the status of the person. For example, in the family gShen(-tshang) we may find: gShen-sgom—the ascetic of gShen; gShen-chen—the Great One or gShen the Great; gShen-rje—the Lord of gShen; gShen-ston, a shortened form of gShen-gyi ston-pa—the scholar or master of gShen; gShen-sprul short for gShen-gyi sprul-sku—an incarnation born in the family of gShen; gShen-bon short for gShen-gyi Bon-po—the priest of gShen; gShen-bla short for gShen-gyi bla-ma—the spiritual guide of gShen; gShen-mi—the man of gShen; gShen-btsun short for gShen-gyi btsun-pa—the monk of gShen; gShen-tsha—the nephew of gShen; gShen-za—the daughters of gShen; gShen-gsas—the preacher of gShen.

However, gShen(-po) and Bon(-po) often seem to mean 'priest'. They usually occur either with the name of a country or that of a family, e.g. Zhang-zhung-gi gShen-po or Bon-po—the priest from Zhang-zhung; Gling-gshen, a shortened form of Gling-gi gShen-po—the priest of Gling and sPa-bon, a shortened form of sPa-yi Bon-po—the priest of sPa.

There are also other titles which are inconsistently used in our text. I have put them in brackets after the names in the index to facilitate their identification. They are sKu-mdun, sKu-gshen, mKhan-po or mKhan-chen, mKha'-'gro, Grub-thob, Grub-dbang, 'Gro-mgon, rGyal-tshab, sGom-chen, rJe-rgyal, gTer-ston, sTon-pa, mTshan-ldan, Drang-srong, rNal-'byor, dPon-gsas, sPrul-sku, Bla-ma or Bla-chen, and lHa-rje.

The most common family names are gShen, Bru or Bru-zha, Zhu, rMe'u and Khyung-po. As there are numerous people belonging to these families our author seems reluctant to use their family names and many are mentioned without any family name. In these cases I have also put their family names in brackets after their personal names whenever it was possible to trace their lineage.

DIVINITIES

EARTHLY BEINGS